THE BEST OF
MODERN
HUMOR

THE BEST OF
MODERN
HU*MOR

EDITED BY
Mordecai Richler

ALFRED A. KNOPF   NEW YORK   1983

THIS IS A BORZOI BOOK PUBLISHED BY ALFRED A. KNOPF, INC.

Copyright © 1983 by Mordecai Richler
All rights reserved under International and Pan-American Copyright Conventions.
Published in the United States by Alfred A. Knopf, Inc., New York.
Distributed by Random House, Inc., New York.
Published in Canada by McClelland & Stewart, Ltd., Toronto.

Owing to limitations of space,
all acknowledgments of permission to reprint material
will be found at the end of the book.

LIBRARY OF CONGRESS CATALOGING IN PUBLICATION DATA
Main entry under title:

The best of modern humor.

1. American wit and humor.   2. English wit and humor.
3. American literature—20th century.
4. English literature—20th century.
I. Richler, Mordecai.
PN6162.B5   1983   817'.5'08   83-48102
ISBN 0-394-51531-5

Manufactured in the United States of America
FIRST AMERICAN EDITION

For my family—
Florence, Daniel, Noah, Emma, Martha and Jacob

Contents

*

Foreword

*

by Mordecai Richler

Years ago a young lady out of Oklahoma City was sufficiently intrepid to write James Thurber asking him if there were any standard rules for writing humor. The best Thurber could come up with was a list of proscriptions. Avoid comic stories, he warned, "about plumbers who are mistaken for surgeons, sheriffs who are terrified by gunfire, psychiatrists who are driven crazy by women patients, doctors who faint at the sight of blood, adolescent girls who know more about sex than their fathers do, and midgets who turn out to be the parents of a two-hundred-pound wrestler." Thurber, after twenty years of sifting through unsolicited manuscripts, also recommended to neophyte humorists that the word "I'll" should not be divided so that the "I' " is on one line and the "ll" on the next, because the reader's attention can never be recaptured. "It also never recovers," he wrote, "from such names as Ann S. Thetic, Maud Lynn, Sally Forth, Bertha Twins, and the like."

In principle, I share Thurber's aversion to knee-slapper names. However, that rule has been successfully broken not only by Ben Jonson and Sheridan, but also by one of the funniest of recent British humorists, Beachcomber (J. B. Morton), who for forty years wrote the "By the Way" column in the *Daily Express*. Beachcomber gave us the immortal Captain Foulenough, Dr. Smart-Allick of Narkover, Mr. Justice Cocklecarrot and Dr. Strabismus (Whom God Preserve) of Utrecht. Even so fastidious a prose stylist as Evelyn Waugh was not above dealing in funny names (Lord Pastmaster, Lady Metroland), and neither is Joseph Heller, who has already given us Major Major Major and Milo Minderbinder.

Incidentally, a rule not mentioned by Thurber is that it is usually unwise to ask one comic novelist to pronounce on another. In 1961,

Nina Bourne, then with Simon & Schuster, sent Waugh a copy of *Catch-22*, soliciting a jacket quote. Waugh replied:

> Thank you for sending *Catch-22*. I am sorry that the book fascinates you so much. It has many passages quite unsuitable to a lady's reading. It suffers not only from indelicacy but from prolixity. . . . You may quote me as saying: "This exposure of corruption, cowardice and incivility of American officers will outrage all friends of your country (such as myself) and greatly comfort your enemies."

It is a strange force, Dorothy Parker once wrote, that compels a writer to be a humorist. The world is stacked against him. *Go ahead, make me laugh, you twit.* You can play percentage baseball, paint by numbers, even raise your own children according to Dr. Spock, but there are no guidelines for writing good humor. "Dying is easy," said actor Edmund Gwenn on his deathbed. "Comedy is difficult."

Surprisingly, comedy, or—if you must—"light writing," is also sometimes regarded as necessarily second-rate. An occupation not quite respectable for the mature writer. According to P. G. Wodehouse, the trouble in his day began at their public schools: If a boy merely talked amusingly, he was a silly ass. If his conversation took a mordant or satirical turn, he was a funny swine. "You think you're a funny swine, don't you?" Whichever, wrote Wodehouse, the wits were scorned and despised, and lucky not to get kicked.

"When you do comedy," Woody Allen once said, "you are not sitting at the grownups' table."

The same critics who will give the benefit of the doubt to a solemn novel, the more intractable the better, tend to patronize comedy. Such a fine writer as Ring Lardner was underestimated in his day, seen by many—including himself—as no more than a mere entertainer. John Lardner has written that the enduring popularity of *You Know Me Al* startled his father, "but it totally failed to cause him to think of what he had written as literature." Virginia Woolf—who didn't know a squeeze play from a pitch-out, and would never have been called upon to umpire a ball game even in East Hampton—thought otherwise. In an essay published in 1925, she wrote: "Mr. Lardner has talents of a remarkable order. With extraordinary ease and aptitude, with the quickest of strokes, the surest touch, the sharpest insight, he lets Jack Keefe the baseball player cut out his own outline, fill in his own depths, until the figure of the foolish, boastful, innocent athlete lives before us."

If you don't count some of Jehovah's injunctions, there are no humorists I can recall in the Bible, although the Talmud has a kind word for them: ". . . And Elijah said to Berokah, 'These two will also share in the world to come.' Berokah then asked them, 'What is your occupation?' They replied, 'We are merrymakers. When we see a person who is down-hearted, we cheer him up.' "

Once, the humorist was a sort of comic dwarf. "In the Middle Ages," wrote P. G. Wodehouse in *Some Thoughts on Humorists*, "the well-bred and well-to-do thought nothing so funny as a man who was considerably shorter than they were, or at least cultivated a deceptive stoop. Anyone in those days who was fifty inches tall or less was *per se* a humorist. They gave him a comical cap and a stick with little bells at-tached to it and told him to caper about and amuse them. And as it was not a hard life and the pickings were pretty good, he fell in with their wishes."

Shakespeare, no slouch with one-liners himself, clearly appreciated the proper place of the humorist in the social order. No sooner does Prince Hal become Henry V than he puts Falstaff, the tutor and feeder of his riots, behind him:

> I know thee not, old man: fall to thy prayers;
> How ill white hairs become a fool and jester!

Actually, poor old white-haired Falstaff was probably not nearly so dissolute as he appeared. Surely he worked extremely hard at burnishing his quips, he didn't simply pluck them out of the air. Humor, after all, is a very serious business—as a rule, the easier it looks, the harder it came. So, in my experience, contemporary humorists, away from their punish-ing work, tend to be a most melancholy, even morose, lot. Unchained from their typewriters, they are often considerable drinkers. At parties, they are inclined to hide themselves away in corners, lest officious strangers sneak up on them and demand they say something funny *right now* or, even worse, dig in their heels and begin, "Hey, have you ever heard the one about . . . ?"

"Humor to me," Dorothy Parker once wrote, "takes in many things. There must be courage; there must be awe. There must be criticism, for humor, to my mind, is encapsulated in criticism. There must be a disci-plined eye and a wild mind. There must be a magnificent disregard for your reader, for if he cannot follow you, there is nothing you can do about it."

In the last pages of *Heartburn* (or, Portia's Complaint), a comic, thinly disguised autobiographical novel about the breakup of her marriage, Nora Ephron writes:

> Of course I'm writing this later, much much later, and it worries me that I've done what I usually do—hidden the anger, covered the pain, pretended it wasn't there for the sake of the story . . .
> Vera said: "Why do you feel you have to turn everything into a story?"
> So I told her why:
> Because if I tell a story, I control the version.
> Because if I tell a story, I can make you laugh, and I would rather have you laugh at me than feel sorry for me.

Obviously, humor can conceal or even heal pain. The best revenge on experience is writing well, recalling past humiliations not so much in tranquility as with laughter, biting back the anger, making it all seem wonderfully absurd in retrospect. But, make no mistake, there is a good deal of hurt at the core of *Portnoy's Complaint. Catch-22* is also a cry of anguish. Wodehouse, ostensibly so good-natured, obviously found pretentious people an abomination. I would not like to have been in the same room when S. J. Perelman was dealing with a bore. Waugh's magnificent and hilarious trilogy about the British in World War II (*Men at Arms, Officers and Gentlemen, The End of the Battle*) is also an exposure of corruption, cowardice and incivility among the British officer class during the battle for Crete.

Waugh, of course, was a notorious reactionary. As a rule, however, uncompromising political commitment seems to preclude a sense of humor. Come to think of it, I've never read a really funny piece by either a fascist or a communist, although lapsed communists—Jessica Mitford, say—have been highly amusing about their experiences. Another former communist informed by a sense of fun was Claude Cockburn. In his autobiography, Cockburn recalled that while he was working nights on the desk at the London *Times*, during the thirties—hard put to stay awake—he and his colleagues had devised a competition, the winner being the man who succeeded in slipping the dullest possible headline into the next morning's edition. Cockburn once won with a headline that read:

SMALL EARTHQUAKE IN CHILE
NOT MANY KILLED

This, of course, was in appalling bad taste. It poked cruel fun at a Third World country, possibly even suggesting that life was held cheap there.

Such a headline, considering the spirit of the *Times* competition, smacked of racism and imperialist condescension. It was also very witty.

The only humor that doesn't offend somebody out there is what Dorothy Parker has discounted as those little formula pieces that columnists milk until they moo with pain: "Over and over and on and on, they write these pieces, in the rears of magazines, in glossy Sunday supplements of newspapers, over and over and on and on, like a needle stuck in a phonograph record."

But truly good humor, charged with outlandish hooks and unexpected sharp jabs, is bound to offend, for, in the nature of things, it ridicules our prejudices and popular institutions. Alas, people have become so touchy that to be irreverent these days is to invite an outraged retort from some pompous organization or another. Even being funny about porcupines can be risky. "Just try it," wrote P. G. Wodehouse, "and see how quickly you find your letter-box full of communications beginning: 'Sir, With reference to your recent tasteless and uncalled-for comments on the porcupine . . .'"

A retired *New Yorker* editor recently told me that Woody Allen's delightful piece "Hassidic Tales, with a Guide to Their Interpretation by the Noted Scholar," which pokes fun at supposedly sage but actually simpleminded rabbinical fables, led to a batch of angry letters accusing Allen of being anti-Semitic. I know the feeling. Once, reviewing (for the now-defunct *Book Week*) an unintentionally hilarious book, *Encyclopedia of Jews in Sport,* I ventured to remark that—while I did not think it a good thing to hide our athletic accomplishments under a bushel—it was unnecessary, perhaps, to include:

> HERTZ, STEVE ALLAN. Infielder, b. Feb. 26, 1945, in Dayton, Ohio.
> Played for Houston in 1964. Total Games: 5. Batting Average: .000.

In the weeks that followed, I was overwhelmed by abusive mail, my favorite coming from a lady who signed herself A FELLOW JEWESS, thereby questioning my gender as well as my taste. I can only wonder, then, what sort of letters one of the most talented of the new American humorists, Roy Blount, Jr., earned when he wrote of the first Carter campaign: ". . . when Earl Butz was quoted as saying that all black folks want is 'a tight pussy, loose shoes, and a warm place to shit,' I wish Jimmy had responded by saying it sounded like a set of priorities that a lot of people could identify with."

For all I know, Blount is still in hiding.

• • •

How's it done?

That superb stylist A. J. Liebling, having been sent a batch of "how-to-write" books for review by an editor, bounced them right back with a note that read, "The only way to write is well and how you do it is your own damn business."

The truth is, there is no explaining how it's done; and only a foolish practitioner would dare to take his own machine apart—he might never be able to put it together again.

Instead of asking how it's done, we should, in these grim times, be grateful for what's available. And what's available is sometimes first-rate.

• • •

Collecting material for this anthology gave me both unanticipated pleasures and sharp disappointments. It was difficult, perhaps even unfair, to reread, in a cold editorial light, essays that broke me up thirty years ago. It was difficult, but necessary. Unfortunately, it also led me to find some of these pieces somehow wanting, dated. To go through the revered Benchley, for instance, was to discover a good many of his sketches astonishingly bland, so disarmingly gentle as to dissolve into the middle distance even before I got to the last line. I finally did come across something of Benchley's I liked, and have included it in these pages. But you will meet with no Dorothy Parker here. The legendary Miss Parker gave me endless trouble. I'm afraid I found her comic stories brittle, short on substance, and, to come clean, no longer very funny; and I can't help wondering how many of her devoted admirers have read her recently.

Put plainly, there was only one basic criterion (however imperfect) for the selection of the material that follows here. It had to make me laugh—sometimes at seven o'clock in the morning, before my first cup of coffee, which may have been playing dirty pool. Beyond that, I did impose certain limitations. There would be no cartoons or comic verse, not because I don't enjoy them, but because I have a natural predilection for comic prose and wanted to include as much of it as possible. I also decided, arbitrarily, to begin with Leacock, Baring, Mencken, Runyon and Wodehouse, and then to move on to the younger humorists, giving the most consideration to people who have been writing during the last twenty years. I have used the simplest possible chronology, laying out the selections in order of the writers' birthdates—from Leacock, born in 1869, to Ian Frazier, who came along as recently as 1951.

I had a good deal of help in compiling this anthology. I would especially like to thank Clifton Fadiman, Bob Gottlieb, Gordon Lish,

Roger Angell, and William Zinsser for their many suggestions. I am also grateful to Martha Kaplan at Knopf, Tina Angelico at the Book-of-the-Month Club, and Helen Stark of *The New Yorker* for the considerable help they gave me in tracking down out-of-print stories and books. Final responsibility for the selections is, of course, mine.

THE BEST OF
MODERN
HUM*OR

Stephen Leacock

*

GERTRUDE THE GOVERNESS
OR SIMPLE SEVENTEEN

Synopsis of Previous Chapters:
There are no Previous Chapters.

It was a wild and stormy night on the West Coast of Scotland. This, however, is immaterial to the present story, as the scene is not laid in the West of Scotland. For the matter of that the weather was just as bad on the East Coast of Ireland.

But the scene of this narrative is laid in the South of England and takes place in and around Knotacentinum Towers (pronounced as if written Nosham Taws), the seat of Lord Knotacent (pronounced as if written Nosh).

But it is not necessary to pronounce either of these names in reading them.

Nosham Taws was a typical English home. The main part of the house was an Elizabethan structure of warm red brick, while the elder portion, of which the Earl was inordinately proud, still showed the outlines of a Norman Keep, to which had been added a Lancastrian Jail and a Plantagenet Orphan Asylum. From the house in all directions stretched magnificent woodland and park with oaks and elms of immemorial antiquity, while nearer the house stood raspberry bushes and geranium plants which had been set out by the Crusaders.

About the grand old mansion the air was loud with the chirping of thrushes, the cawing of partridges and the clear sweet note of the rook, while deer, antelope, and other quadrupeds strutted about the lawn so tame as to eat off the sun-dial. In fact, the place was a regular menagerie.

From the house downwards through the park stretched a beautiful broad avenue laid out by Henry VII.

Lord Nosh stood upon the hearthrug of the library. Trained diplomat and statesman as he was, his stern aristocratic face was upside down with fury.

"Boy," he said, "you shall marry this girl or I disinherit you. You are no son of mine."

Young Lord Ronald, erect before him, flung back a glance as defiant as his own.

"I defy you," he said. "Henceforth you are no father of mine. I will get another. I will marry none but a woman I can love. This girl that we have never seen—"

"Fool," said the Earl, "would you throw aside our estate and name of a thousand years? The girl, I am told, is beautiful; her aunt is willing; they are French; pah! they understand such things in France."

"But your reason—"

"I give no reason," said the Earl. "Listen, Ronald, I give you one month. For that time you remain here. If at the end of it you refuse me, I cut you off with a shilling."

Lord Ronald said nothing; he flung himself from the room, flung himself upon his horse and rode madly off in all directions.

As the door of the library closed upon Ronald the Earl sank into a chair. His face changed. It was no longer that of the haughty nobleman, but of the hunted criminal. "He must marry the girl," he muttered. "Soon she will know all. Tutchemoff has escaped from Siberia. He knows and will tell. The whole of the mines pass to her, this property with it, and I—but enough." He rose, walked to the sideboard, drained a dipper full of gin and bitters, and became again a high-bred English gentleman.

It was at this moment that a high dogcart, driven by a groom in the livery of Earl Nosh, might have been seen entering the avenue of Nosham Taws. Beside him sat a young girl, scarce more than a child, in fact not nearly so big as the groom.

The apple-pie hat which she wore, surmounted with black willow plumes, concealed from view a face so face-like in its appearance as to be positively facial.

It was—need we say it—Gertrude the Governess, who was this day to enter upon her duties at Nosham Taws.

At the same time that the dogcart entered the avenue at one end there might have been seen riding down it from the other a tall young man, whose long, aristocratic face proclaimed his birth and who was mounted upon a horse with a face even longer than his own.

And who is this tall young man who draws nearer to Gertrude with every revolution of the horse? Ah, who, indeed? Ah, who, who? I wonder

if any of my readers could guess that this was none other than Lord
Ronald.

The two were destined to meet. Nearer and nearer they came. And
then still nearer. Then for one brief moment they met. As they passed,
Gertrude raised her head and directed towards the young nobleman two
eyes so eye-like in their expression as to be absolutely circular, while
Lord Ronald directed towards the occupant of the dogcart a gaze so gaze-
like that nothing but a gazelle, or a gas-pipe, could have emulated its
intensity.

Was this the dawn of love? Wait and see. Do not spoil the story.

Let us speak of Gertrude. Gertrude DeMongmorenci McFiggin
had known neither father nor mother. They had both died years before
she was born. Of her mother she knew nothing, save that she was
French, was extremely beautiful, and that all her ancestors and even her
business acquaintances had perished in the Revolution.

Yet Gertrude cherished the memory of her parents. On her breast
the girl wore a locket in which was enshrined a miniature of her mother,
while down her neck inside at the back hung a daguerreotype of her
father. She carried a portrait of her grandmother up her sleeve and had
pictures of her cousins tucked inside her boot, while beneath her—but
enough, quite enough.

Of her father Gertrude knew even less. That he was a high-born
English gentleman who had lived as a wanderer in many lands, this was
all she knew. His only legacy to Gertrude had been a Russian grammar,
a Roumanian phrase-book, a theodolite, and a work on mining engineering.

From her earliest infancy Gertrude had been brought up by her
aunt. Her aunt had carefully instructed her in Christian principles. She
had also taught her Mohammedanism to make sure.

When Gertrude was seventeen her aunt had died of hydrophobia.

The circumstances were mysterious. There had called upon her
that day a strange bearded man in the costume of the Russians. After he
had left, Gertrude had found her aunt in a syncope from which she
passed into an apostrophe and never recovered.

To avoid scandal it was called hydrophobia. Gertrude was thus
thrown upon the world. What to do? That was the problem that confronted her.

It was while musing one day upon her fate that Gertrude's eye was
struck with an advertisement.

"Wanted a governess; must possess a knowledge of French, Italian,
Russian, and Roumanian, Music, and Mining Engineering. Salary £1, 4

shillings and 4 pence halfpenny per annum. Apply between half-past eleven and twenty-five minutes to twelve at No. 41 A Decimal Six, Belgravia Terrace. The Countess of Nosh."

Gertrude was a girl of great natural quickness of apprehension, and she had not pondered over this announcement more than half an hour before she was struck with the extraordinary coincidence between the list of items desired and the things that she herself knew.

She duly presented herself at Belgravia Terrace before the Countess, who advanced to meet her with a charm which at once placed the girl at her ease.

"You are proficient in French?" she asked.

"*Oh, oui,*" said Gertrude modestly.

"And Italian?" continued the Countess.

"*Oh, si,*" said Gertrude.

"And German?" said the Countess in delight.

"*Ah, ja,*" said Gertrude.

"And Russian?"

"*Yaw.*"

"And Roumanian?"

"*Jep.*"

Amazed at the girl's extraordinary proficiency in modern languages, the Countess looked at her narrowly. Where had she seen those lineaments before? She passed her hand over her brow in thought, and spit upon the floor, but no, the face baffled her.

"Enough," she said, "I engage you on the spot; tomorrow you go down to Nosham Taws and begin teaching the children. I must add that in addition you will be expected to aid the Earl with his Russian correspondence. He has large mining interests at Tschminsk."

Tschminsk! why did the simple word reverberate upon Gertrude's ears? Why? Because it was the name written in her father's hand on the title page of his book on mining. What mystery was here?

It was on the following day that Gertrude had driven up the avenue.

She descended from the dogcart, passed through a phalanx of liveried servants drawn up seven-deep, to each of whom she gave a sovereign as she passed and entered Nosham Taws.

"Welcome," said the Countess, as she aided Gertrude to carry her trunk upstairs.

The girl presently descended and was ushered into the library, where she was presented to the Earl. As soon as the Earl's eye fell upon the face of the new governess he started visibly. Where had he seen those lineaments? Where was it? At the races? or the theatre? on a bus? No.

Some subtler thread of memory was stirring in his mind. He strode hastily to the sideboard, drained a dipper and a half of brandy, and became again the perfect English gentleman.

While Gertrude has gone to the nursery to make the acquaintance of the two tiny golden-haired children who are to be her charges, let us say something here of the Earl and his son.

Lord Nosh was the perfect type of the English nobleman and states-man. The years that he had spent in the diplomatic service at Constan-tinople, St. Petersburg, and Salt Lake City had given to him a peculiar finesse and noblesse, while his long residence at St. Helena, Pitcairn Island, and Hamilton, Ontario, had rendered him impervious to external impressions. As deputy paymaster of the militia of the county he had seen something of the sterner side of military life, while his hereditary office of Groom of the Sunday Breeches had brought him into direct contact with Royalty itself.

His passion for outdoor sports endeared him to his tenants. A keen sportsman, he excelled in fox-hunting, dog-hunting, pig-killing, bat-catching and the pastimes of his class.

In this latter respect Lord Ronald took after his father. From the start the lad had shown the greatest promise. At Eton he had made a splendid showing at battledore and shuttlecock, and at Cambridge had been first in his class at needlework. Already his name was whispered in connection with the All England ping-pong championship, a triumph which would undoubtedly carry with it a seat in Parliament.

Thus was Gertrude the Governess installed at Nosham Taws.

The days and the weeks sped past.

The simple charm of the beautiful orphan girl attracted all hearts. Her two little pupils became her slaves. "Me loves oo," the little Rase-hellfrida would say, leaning her golden head in Gertrude's lap. Even the servants loved her. The head gardener would bring a bouquet of beauti-ful roses to her room before she was up, the second gardener a bunch of early cauliflowers, the third a spray of late asparagus, and even the tenth and eleventh a sprig of mangel-wurzel or an armful of hay. Her room was full of gardeners all the time, while at evening the aged butler, touched at the friendless girl's loneliness, would tap softly at her door to bring her a rye whisky and seltzer or a box of Pittsburg Stogies. Even the dumb creatures seemed to admire her in their own dumb way. The dumb rooks settled on her shoulder and every dumb dog around the place followed her.

And Ronald! ah, Ronald! Yes, indeed! They had met. They had spoken.

"What a dull morning," Gertrude had said. *"Quel triste matin! Was für ein allerverdamnter Tag!"*

"Beastly," Ronald had answered.

"Beastly!!" The word rang in Gertrude's ears all day.

After that they were constantly together. They played tennis and ping-pong in the day, and in the evening, in accordance with the stiff routine of the place, they sat down with the Earl and Countess to twenty-five-cent poker, and later still they sat together on the verandah and watched the moon sweeping in great circles around the horizon.

It was not long before Gertrude realized that Lord Ronald felt to-wards her a warmer feeling than that of mere ping-pong. At times in her presence he would fall, especially after dinner, into a fit of profound subtraction.

Once at night, when Gertrude withdrew to her chamber and before seeking her pillow, prepared to retire as a preliminary to disrobing—in other words, before going to bed, she flung wide the casement (opened the window) and perceived (saw) the face of Lord Ronald. He was sitting on a thorn bush beneath her, and his upturned face wore an expression of agonized pallor.

Meantime the days passed. Life at the Taws moved in the ordinary routine of a great English household. At 7 a gong sounded for rising, at 8 a horn blew for breakfast, at 8:30 a whistle sounded for prayers, at 1 a flag was run up at half-mast for lunch, at 4 a gun was fired for afternoon tea, at 9 a first bell sounded for dressing, at 9:15 a second bell for going on dressing, while at 9:30 a rocket was sent up to indicate that dinner was ready. At midnight dinner was over and at 1 a.m. the tolling of a bell summoned the domestics to evening prayers.

Meanwhile the month allotted by the Earl to Lord Ronald was passing away. It was already July 15, then within a day or two it was July 17, and, almost immediately afterwards, July 18.

At times the Earl, in passing Ronald in the hall, would say sternly, "Remember, boy, your consent, or I disinherit you."

And what were the Earl's thoughts of Gertrude? Here was the one drop of bitterness in the girl's cup of happiness. For some reason that she could not divine, the Earl showed signs of marked antipathy.

Once as she passed the door of the library he threw a bootjack at her. On another occasion at lunch alone with her he struck her savagely across the face with a sausage.

It was her duty to translate to the Earl his Russian correspondence. She sought in it in vain for the mystery. One day a Russian telegram was handed to the Earl. Gertrude translated it to him aloud.

"Tutchemoff went to the woman. She is dead."

On hearing this the Earl became livid with fury, in fact this was the day that he struck her with the sausage.

Then one day while the Earl was absent on a bat hunt, Gertrude, who was turning over his correspondence, with that sweet feminine instinct of interest that rose superior to ill-treatment, suddenly found the key to the mystery.

Lord Nosh was not the rightful owner of the Taws. His distant cousin of the older line, the true heir, had died in a Russian prison to which the machinations of the Earl, while Ambassador at Tschminsk, had consigned him. The daughter of this cousin was the true owner of Nosham Taws.

The family story, save only that the documents before her withheld the name of the rightful heir, lay bare to Gertrude's eye.

Strange is the heart of woman. Did Gertrude turn from the Earl with spurning? No. Her own sad fate had taught her sympathy.

Yet still the mystery remained! Why did the Earl start perceptibly each time that he looked into her face? Sometimes he started as much as four centimetres, so that one could distinctly see him do it. On such occasions he would hastily drain a dipper of rum and Vichy water and become again the correct English gentleman.

The denouement came swiftly. Gertrude never forgot it.

It was the night of the great ball at Nosham Taws. The whole neighbourhood was invited. How Gertrude's heart had beat with anticipation, and with what trepidation she had overhauled her scant wardrobe in order to appear not unworthy in Lord Ronald's eyes. Her resources were poor indeed, yet the inborn genius for dress that she inherited from her French mother stood her in good stead. She twined a single rose in her hair and contrived herself a dress out of a few old newspapers and the inside of an umbrella that would have graced a court. Round her waist she bound a single braid of bagstring, while a piece of old lace that had been her mother's was suspended to her ear by a thread.

Gertrude was the cynosure of all eyes. Floating to the strains of the music she presented a picture of bright girlish innocence that no one could see undisenraptured.

The ball was at its height. It was away up!

Ronald stood with Gertrude in the shrubbery. They looked into one another's eyes.

"Gertrude," he said, "I love you."

Simple words, and yet they thrilled every fibre in the girl's costume.

"Ronald!" she said, and cast herself about his neck.

At this moment the Earl appeared standing beside them in the moonlight. His stern face was distorted with indignation.

"So!" he said, turning to Ronald, "it appears that you have chosen!"

"I have," said Ronald with hauteur.

"You prefer to marry this penniless girl rather than the heiress I have selected for you."

Gertrude looked from father to son in amazement.

"Yes," said Ronald.

"Be it so," said the Earl, draining a dipper of gin which he carried, and resuming his calm. "Then I disinherit you. Leave this place, and never return to it."

"Come, Gertrude," said Ronald tenderly, "let us flee together."

Gertrude stood before them. The rose had fallen from her head. The lace had fallen from her ear and the bagstring had come undone from her waist. Her newspapers were crumpled beyond recognition. But dishevelled and illegible as she was, she was still mistress of herself.

"Never," she said firmly. "Ronald, you shall never make this sacrifice for me." Then to the Earl, in tones of ice, "There is a pride, sir, as great even as yours. The daughter of Metschnikoff McFiggin need crave a boon from no one."

With that she hauled from her bosom the daguerreotype of her father and pressed it to her lips.

The Earl started as if shot. "That name!" he cried, "that face! that photograph! stop!"

There! There is no need to finish; my readers have long since divined it. Gertrude was the heiress.

The lovers fell into one another's arms. The Earl's proud face relaxed. "God bless you," he said. The Countess and the guests came pouring out upon the lawn. The breaking day illuminated a scene of gay congratulations.

Gertrude and Ronald were wed. Their happiness was complete. Need we say more? Yes, only this. The Earl was killed in the hunting-field a few days after. The Countess was struck by lightning. The two children fell down a well. Thus the happiness of Gertrude and Ronald was complete.

Maurice Baring

*

KING LEAR'S DAUGHTER

LETTER FROM GONERIL, DAUGHTER OF KING LEAR,
TO HER SISTER REGAN

I have writ my sister.
King Lear, Act I, Scene iv.

THE PALACE, *November.*

DEAREST REGAN,

I am sending you this letter by Oswald. We have been having the most trying time lately with Papa, and it ended today in one of those scenes which are so painful to people like you and me, who *hate* scenes. I am writing now to tell you all about it, so that you may be prepared. This is what has happened.

When Papa came here he brought a hundred knights with him, which is a great deal more than we could put up, and some of them had to live in the village. The first thing that happened was that they quarrelled with our people and refused to take orders from them, and whenever one told any one to do anything it was either—if it was one of Papa's men—"not his place to do it"; or if it was one of our men, they said that Papa's people made work impossible. For instance, only the day before yesterday I found that blue vase which you brought back from Dover for me on my last birthday broken to bits. Of course I made a fuss, and Oswald declared that one of Papa's knights had knocked it over in a drunken brawl. I complained to Papa, who flew into a passion and said that his knights, and in fact all his retainers, were the most peaceful and courteous people in the world, and that it was my fault, as I was not treating him or them with the respect which they deserved. He even said that I was lacking in filial duty. I was determined to keep my temper, so I said nothing.

The day after this the chief steward and the housekeeper and both my maids came to me and said that they wished to give notice. I asked them why. They said they couldn't possibly live in a house where there were such "goings-on." I asked them what they meant. They refused to say, but they hinted that Papa's men were behaving not only in an insolent but in a positively outrageous manner to them. The steward said that Papa's knights were never sober, that they had entirely demoralized the household, and that life was simply not worth living in the house; it was *impossible* to get anything done, and they couldn't sleep at night for the noise.

I went to Papa and talked to him about it quite quietly, but no sooner had I mentioned the subject than he lost all self-control, and began to abuse me. I kept my temper as long as I could, but of course one is only human, and after I had borne his revilings for some time, which were monstrously unfair and untrue, I at last turned and said something about people of his age being trying. Upon which he said that I was mocking him in his old age, that I was a monster of ingratitude— and he began to cry. I cannot tell you how painful all this was to me. I did everything I could to soothe him and quiet him, but the truth is, ever since Papa has been here he has lost control of his wits. He suffers from the oddest kind of delusions. He thinks that for some reason he is being treated like a beggar; and although he has a hundred knights—a hundred, mind you! (a great deal more than we have)—in the house, who do nothing but eat and drink all day long, he says he is not being treated like a King! I do hate unfairness.

When he gave up the crown he said he was tired of affairs, and meant to have a long rest; but from the very moment that he handed over the management of affairs to us he never stopped interfering, and was cross if he was not consulted about everything, and if his advice was not taken.

And what is still worse: ever since his last illness he has lost not only his memory but his control over language, so that often when he wants to say one thing he says just the opposite, and sometimes when he wishes to say some quite simple thing he uses *bad* language quite unconsciously. Of course we are used to this, and *we* don't mind, but I must say it is very awkward when strangers are here. For instance, the other day before quite a lot of people, quite unconsciously, he called me a dreadful name. Everybody was uncomfortable and tried not to laugh, but some people could not contain themselves. This sort of thing is constantly

happening. So you will understand that Papa needs perpetual looking
after and management. At the same time, the moment one suggests the
slightest thing to him he boils over with rage.

But perhaps the most annoying thing which happened lately, or, at
least, the thing which happens to annoy me most, is Papa's Fool. You
know, darling, that I have always hated that kind of humour. He comes
in just as one is sitting down to dinner, and beats one on the head with a
hard, empty bladder, and sings utterly idiotic songs, which make me feel
inclined to cry. The other day, when we had a lot of people here, just as
we were sitting down in the banqueting-hall, Papa's Fool pulled my chair
from behind me so that I fell sharply down on the floor. Papa shook with
laughter, and said: "Well done, little Fool," and all the courtiers who
were there, out of pure snobbishness, of course, laughed too. I call this
not only very humiliating for me, but undignified in an old man and a
king; of course Albany refused to interfere. Like all men and all husbands, he is an arrant coward.

However, the crisis came yesterday. I had got a bad headache, and
was lying down in my room, when Papa came in from the hunt and sent
Oswald to me, saying that he wished to speak to me. I said that I wasn't
well, and that I was lying down—which was perfectly true—but that I
would be down to dinner. When Oswald went to give my message Papa
beat him, and one of his men threw him about the room and really hurt
him, so that he has now got a large bruise on his forehead and a sprained
ankle.

This was the climax. All our knights came to Albany and myself,
and said that they would not stay with us a moment longer unless Papa
exercised some sort of control over his men. I did not know what to do,
but I knew the situation would have to be cleared up sooner or later. So
I went to Papa and told him frankly that the situation was intolerable;
that he must send away some of his people, and choose for the remainder
men fitting to his age. The words were scarcely out of my mouth than
he called me the most terrible names, ordered his horses to be saddled,
and said that he would shake the dust from his feet and not stay a
moment longer in this house. Albany tried to calm him, and begged him
to stay, but he would not listen to a word, and said he would go and live
with you.

So I am sending this by Oswald, that you may get it before Papa
arrives and know how the matter stands. All I did was to suggest he
should send away fifty of his men. Even fifty is a great deal, and puts us
to any amount of inconvenience, and is a source of waste and extrava-
gance—two things which I cannot bear. I am perfectly certain you will

not be able to put up with his hundred knights any more than I was. And I beg you, my dearest Regan, to do your best to make Papa listen to sense. No one is fonder of him than I am. I think it would have been difficult to find a more dutiful daughter than I have always been. But there is a limit to all things, and one cannot have one's whole household turned into a pandemonium, and one's whole life into a series of wrangles, complaints, and brawls, simply because Papa in his old age is losing the control of his faculties. At the same time, I own that although I kept my temper for a long time, when it finally gave way I was perhaps a little sharp. I am not a saint, nor an angel, nor a lamb, but I do hate unfairness and injustice. It makes my blood boil. But I hope that you, with your angelic nature and your tact and your gentleness, will put everything right and make poor Papa listen to reason.

Let me hear at once what happens.

Your loving
GONERIL.

P.S.—Another thing Papa does which is most exasperating is to quote Cordelia to one every moment. He keeps on saying: "If only Cordelia were here," or "How unlike Cordelia!" And you will remember, darling, that when Cordelia was here Papa could not endure the sight of her. Her irritating trick of mumbling and never speaking up used to get terribly on his nerves. Of course, I thought he was even rather unfair on her, trying as she is. We had a letter from the French Court yesterday, saying that she is driving the poor King of France almost mad.

P.P.S.—It is wretched weather. The poor little ponies on the heath will have to be brought in.

H. L. Mencken

*

RECOLLECTIONS OF NOTABLE COPS

Some time ago I read in a New York paper that fifty or sixty college graduates had been appointed to the metropolitan police force, and were being well spoken of by their superiors. The news astonished me, for in my reportorial days there was simply no such thing in America as a book-learned cop, though I knew a good many who were very smart. The force was then recruited, not from the groves of Academe, but from the ranks of workingmen. The best police captain I ever knew in Baltimore was a meat-cutter by trade, and had lost one of his thumbs by a slip of his cleaver, and the next best was a former bartender. All the mounted cops were ex-hostlers passing as ex-cavalrymen, and all the harbor police had come up through the tugboat and garbage-scow branches of the merchant marine. It took a young reporter a little while to learn how to read and interpret the reports that cops turned in, for they were couched in a special kind of English, with a spelling peculiar to itself. If a member of what was then called "the finest" had spelled *larceny* in any way save *larsensy*, or *arson* in any way save *arsony*, or *fracture* in any way save *fraxr*, there would have been a considerable lifting of eyebrows. I well recall the horror of the Baltimore cops when the first board to examine applicants for places on the force was set up. It was a harmless body headed by a political dentist, and the hardest question in its first examination paper was "What is the plural of *ox*?," but all the cops in town predicted that it would quickly contaminate their craft with a great horde of what they called "professors," and reduce it to the level of letter-carrying or school-teaching.

But, as I have noted, their innocence of *literae humaniores* was not necessarily a sign of stupidity, and from some of them, in fact, I learned the valuable lesson that sharp wits can lurk in unpolished skulls. I knew cops who were matches for the most learned and unscrupulous lawyers at the Baltimore bar, and others who had made monkeys of the oldest and crabbedest judges on the bench, and were generally respected for it. Moreover, I knew cops who were really first-rate policemen, and loved their trade as tenderly as so many art artists or movie actors. They were badly paid, but they carried on their dismal work with unflagging diligence, and loved a long, hard chase almost as much as they loved a quick, brisk clubbing. Their one salient failing, taking them as a class, was their belief that any person who had been arrested, even on mere suspicion, was unquestionably and *ipso facto* guilty. But that theory, though it occasionally colored their testimony in a garish manner, was grounded, after all, on nothing worse than professional pride and *esprit de corps*, and I am certainly not one to hoot at it, for my own belief in the mission of journalism has no better support than the same partiality, and all the logic I am aware of stands against it.

In those days that pestilence of Service which torments the American people today was just getting under way, and many of the multifarious duties now carried out by social workers, statisticians, truant officers, visiting nurses, psychologists, and the vast rabble of inspectors, smellers, spies and bogus experts of a hundred different faculties either fell to the police or were not discharged at all. An ordinary flatfoot in a quiet residential section had his hands full. In a single day he might have to put out a couple of kitchen fires, arrange for the removal of a dead mule, guard a poor epileptic having a fit on the sidewalk, catch a runaway horse, settle a combat with table knives between husband and wife, shoot a cat for killing pigeons, rescue a dog or a baby from a sewer, bawl out a white-wings for spilling garbage, keep order on the sidewalk at two or three funerals, and flog half a dozen bad boys for throwing horse-apples at a blind man. The cops downtown, especially along the wharves and in the red-light districts, had even more curious and complicated jobs, and some of them attained to a high degree of virtuosity.

As my memory gropes backward I think, for example, of a strange office that an old-time roundsman named Charlie had to undertake every Spring. It was to pick up enough skilled workmen to effect the annual redecoration and refurbishing of the Baltimore City Jail. Along about May 1 the warden would telephone to police headquarters that he needed, say, ten head of painters, five plumbers, two blacksmiths, a tile-setter, a roofer, a bricklayer, a carpenter and a locksmith, and it was Charlie's duty to go out and find them. So far as I can recall, he never failed, and usually he produced two or three times as many craftsmen of each category as were needed, so that the warden had some chance to pick out good ones. His plan was simply to make a tour of the saloons and stews in the Marsh Market section of Baltimore, and look over the drunks in congress assembled. He had a trained eye, and could detect a plumber or a painter through two weeks' accumulation of beard and dirt. As he gathered in his candidates, he searched them on the spot, rejecting those who had no union cards, for he was a firm believer in organized labor. Those who passed were put into storage at a police-station, and there kept (less the unfortunates who developed delirium tremens and had to be handed over to the resurrection-men) until the whole convoy was ready. The next morning Gene Grannan, the police magistrate, gave them two weeks each for vagrancy, loitering, trespass, committing a nuisance, or some other plausible misdemeanor, the warden had his staff of master-workmen, and the jail presently bloomed out in all its vernal finery.

Some of these toilers returned year after year, and in the end Charlie recognized so many that he could accumulate the better part of his convoy in half an hour. Once, I remember, he was stumped by a call for two electricians. In those remote days there were fewer men of that craft in practice than today, and only one could be found. When the warden put on the heat Charlie sent him a trolley-car motorman who had run away from his wife and was trying to be shanghaied for the Chesapeake oyster-fleet. This poor man, being grateful for his security in jail, made such eager use of his meagre electrical knowledge that the warden decided to keep him, and even requested that his sentence be extended. Unhappily, Gene Grannan was a pretty good amateur lawyer, and knew that such an extension would be illegal. When the warden of the House of Correction, which was on a farm twenty miles from Baltimore, heard how well this system was working, he put in a requisition for six experienced milkers and a choirleader, for he had a herd of cows and his colored prisoners loved to sing spirituals. Charlie found the choirleader in no time, but he bucked at hunting for milkers, and got rid of the nuisance by sending the warden a squad of sailors who almost pulled the poor cows to pieces.

Gene had been made a magistrate as one of the first fruits of the rising reform movement in Baltimore, and was a man of the chastest integrity, but he knew too much about reformers to admire them, and lost no chance to afflict them. When, in 1900, or thereabout, a gang of snoopers began to tour the red-light districts, seeking to harass and alarm the poor working women there denizened, he instructed the gals to empty slops on them, and acquitted all who were brought in for doing it, usually on the ground that the complaining witnesses were disreputable persons, and could not be believed on oath. One day, sitting in his frowsy courtroom, I saw him gloat in a positively indecent manner when a Methodist clergyman was led out from the cells by Mike Hogan, the turnkey. This holy man, believing that the Jews, unless they consented to be baptized, would all go to Hell, had opened a mission in what was then still called the Ghetto, and sought to save them. The adults, of course, refused to have anything to do with him, but he managed, after a while, to lure a number of *kosher* small boys into his den, chiefly by showing them magic-lantern pictures of the Buffalo Bill country and the Holy Land. When their fathers heard of this there was naturally an uproar, for it was a mortal sin in those days for an orthodox Jew to enter a *Goy Schul*. The ritual for delousing offenders was an arduous one, and cost both time and money. So the Jews came clamoring to Grannan, and he spent a couple of hours trying to figure out some charge to lay against the evangelist. Finally, he ordered him brought in, and entered him on the books for "annoying persons passing by and along a public highway, disorderly conduct, making loud and unseemly noises, and disturbing religious worship." He had to be acquitted, of course, but Gene scared him so badly with talk of the penitentiary that he shut down his mission forthwith, and left the Jews to their post-mortem sufferings.

As I have noted in Chapter II, Gene was a high favorite among us young reporters, for he was always good for copy, and did not hesitate to modify the course of justice in order to feed and edify us. One day an ancient German, obviously a highly respectable man, was brought in on the incredible charge of beating his wife. The testimony showed that they had been placidly married for more than 45 years, and seldom exchanged so much as a bitter word. But the night before, when the old man came home from the saloon where he played *Skat* every evening, the old woman accused him of having drunk more than his usual ration of eight beers, and in the course of the ensuing debate he gave her a gentle slap. Astounded, she let off an hysterical squawk, an officious neighbor rushed in, the cops came on his heels, and so the old man stood before the bar of justice, weeping copiously and with his wife weeping even more copiously beside him. Gene pondered the evidence with a frown on his face, and then announced his judgment. "The crime you are accused of committing," he said, "is a foul and desperate one, and the laws of all civilized countries prohibit it under heavy penalties. I could send you to prison for life, I could order you to the whipping-post [it still exists in Maryland, and for wife-beaters only], or I could sentence you to be hanged. [Here both parties screamed.] But inasmuch as this is your first offense I will be lenient. You will be taken hence to the House of Correction, and there confined for twenty years. In addition, you are fined $10,000." The old couple missed the fine, for at mention of the House of Correction both fainted. When the cops revived them, Gene told the prisoner that, on reflection, he had decided to strike out the sentence, and bade him go and sin no more. Husband and wife rushed out of the courtroom hand in hand, followed by a cop with the umbrella and market-basket that the old woman had forgotten. A week or two later news came in that she was ordering the old man about in a highly cavalier manner, and had cut down his evenings of *Skat* to four a week.

The cops liked and admired Gene, and when he was in good form he commonly had a gallery of them in his courtroom, guffawing at his whimsies. But despite his popularity among them he did not pal with them, for he was basically a very dignified, and even somewhat stiff fellow, and knew how to call them down sharply when their testimony before him went too far beyond the bounds of the probable. In those days, as in these, policemen led a social life almost as inbred as that of the justices of the Supreme Court of the United States, and outsiders were seldom admitted to their parties. But reporters were exceptions, and I attended a number of cop soirées of great elegance, with the tables piled mountain-high with all the delicacies of the season, and a keg of beer every few feet. The graft of these worthy men, at least in my time, was a great deal less than reformers alleged and the envious common people believed. Most of them, in my judgment, were very honest fellows, at least within the bounds of reason. Those who patrolled the fish-markets naturally had plenty of fish to eat, and those who manned the police-boats in the harbor took a certain toll from the pungy captains who brought up Baltimore's supplies of watermelons, cantaloupes, vegetables, crabs and oysters from the Eastern Shore of Maryland: indeed, this last impost amounted to a kind of *octroi*, and at one time the harbor force accumulated so much provender that they had to seize an empty warehouse on the waterfront to store it. But the pungy captains gave up uncomplainingly, for the pelagic cops protected them against the thieves and highjackers who swarmed in the harbor, and also against the land police. I never heard of cops getting anything that the donor was not quite willing and even eager to give. Every Italian who ran a peanut stand knew that making them free of it was good institutional promotion and the girls in the red-light districts liked to crochet neckties, socks and pulse-warmers for them. It was not unheard of for a cop to get mashed on such a girl, rescue her from her life of shame, and set her up as a more or less honest woman. I knew of several cases in which holy matrimony followed. But the more ambitious girls, of course, looked higher, and some of them, in my time, made very good marriages. One actually married a banker, and another died only a few years ago as the faithful and much respected wife of a prominent physician. The cops always laughed when reformers alleged that the wages of sin were death—specifically, that women who sold their persons always ended in the gutter, full of dope and despair. They knew that the overwhelming majority ended at the altar of God, and that nearly all of them married better men than they could have had any chance of meeting and roping if they had kept their virtue.

One dismal New Year's Day I saw a sergeant lose an excellent chance to pocket $138.66 in cash money: I remember it brilliantly because I lost the same chance at the same moment. There had been the usual epidemic of suicides in the waterfront flop-houses, for the dawn of a new year turns the thoughts of homeless men to peace beyond the dissecting-room, and I accompanied the sergeant and a coroner on a tour of the fatal scenes. One of the dead men was lying on the fifth floor of a decaying warehouse that had been turned into ten-cent sleeping quarters, and we climbed up the long stairs to inspect him. All the other bums had cleared out, and the hophead clerk did not offer to go with us. We found the deceased stretched out in a peaceful attitude, with the rope with which he had hanged himself still around his neck. He had been cut down, but then abandoned.

The sergeant loosed the rope, and began a search of the dead man's pockets, looking for means to identify him. He found nothing whatever of that sort, but from a pants pocket he drew out a fat wad of bills, and a hasty count showed that it contained $416. A situation worthy of Scribe, or even Victor Hugo! Evidently the poor fellow was one of the Russell Sages that are occasionally found among bums. His money, I suppose, had been diminishing, and he had bumped himself off in fear that it would soon be all gone. The sergeant looked at the coroner, the coroner looked at me, and I looked at the sergeant. Then the sergeant wrapped up the money in a piece of newspaper lying nearby, and handed it to the coroner. "It goes," he said sadly, "to the State of Maryland. The son-of-a-bitch died intestate, and with no heirs."

The next day I met the coroner, and found him in a low frame of mind. "It was a sin and a shame," he said, "to turn that money over to the State Treasury. What I could have done with $138.67! (I noticed he made a fair split, but collared one of the two odd cents.) Well, it's gone now—damn the luck! I never *did* trust that flatfoot."

Damon Runyon

*

BUTCH MINDS THE BABY

One evening along about seven o'clock I am sitting in Mindy's restaurant putting on the gefillte fish, which is a dish I am very fond of, when in comes three parties from Brooklyn wearing caps as follows: Harry the Horse, Little Isadore and Spanish John.

Now these parties are not such parties as I will care to have much truck with, because I often hear rumors about them that are very discreditable, even if the rumors are not true. In fact, I hear that many citizens of Brooklyn will be very glad indeed to see Harry the Horse, Little Isadore and Spanish John move away from there, as they are always doing something that is considered a knock to the community, such as robbing people, or maybe shooting or stabbing them, and throwing pineapples, and carrying on generally.

I am really much surprised to see these parties on Broadway, as it is well known that the Broadway coppers just naturally love to shove such parties around, but here they are in Mindy's, and there I am, so of course I give them a very large hello, as I never wish to seem inhospitable, even to Brooklyn parties. Right away they come over to my table and sit down, and Little Isadore reaches out and spears himself a big hunk of my gefillte fish with his fingers, but I overlook this, as I am using the only knife on the table.

Then they all sit there looking at me without saying anything, and the way they look at me makes me very nervous indeed. Finally I figure that maybe they are a little embarrassed being in a high-class spot such as Mindy's, with legitimate people around and about, so I say to them, very polite: "It is a nice night."

"What is nice about it?" asks Harry the Horse, who is a thin man with a sharp face and sharp eyes.

Well, now that it is put up to me in this way, I can see there is nothing so nice about the night, at that, so I try to think of something else jolly to say, while Little Isadore keeps spearing at my gefillte fish with his fingers, and Spanish John nabs one of my potatoes.

"Where does Big Butch live?" Harry the Horse asks.

"Big Butch?" I say, as if I never hear the name before in my life, because in this man's town it is never a good idea to answer any question without thinking it over, as some time you may give the right answer to the wrong guy, or the wrong answer to the right guy. "Where does Big Butch live?" I ask them again.

"Yes, where does he live?" Harry the Horse says, very impatient. "We wish you to take us to him."

"Now wait a minute, Harry," I say, and I am now more nervous than somewhat. "I am not sure I remember the exact house Big Butch lives in, and furthermore I am not sure Big Butch will care to have me bringing people to see him, especially three at a time, and especially from Brooklyn. You know Big Butch has a very bad disposition, and there is no telling what he may say to me if he does not like the idea of me taking you to him."

"Everything is very kosher," Harry the Horse says. "You need not be afraid of anything whatever. We have a business proposition for Big Butch. It means a nice score for him, so you take us to him at once, or the chances are I will have to put the arm on somebody around here."

Well, as the only one around there for him to put the arm on at this time seems to be me, I can see where it will be good policy for me to take these parties to Big Butch, especially as the last of my gefillte fish is just going down Little Isadore's gullet, and Spanish John is finishing up my potatoes, and is dunking a piece of rye bread in my coffee, so there is nothing more for me to eat.

So I lead them over into West Forty-ninth Street, near Tenth Avenue, where Big Butch lives on the ground floor of an old brownstone-front house, and who is sitting out on the stoop but Big Butch himself. In fact, everybody in the neighborhood is sitting out on the front stoops over there, including women and children, because sitting out on the front stoops is quite a custom in this section.

Big Butch is peeled down to his undershirt and pants, and he has no shoes on his feet, as Big Butch is a guy who likes his comfort. Furthermore, he is smoking a cigar, and laid out on the stoop beside him on a blanket is a little baby with not much clothes on. This baby seems to be asleep, and every now and then Big Butch fans it with a folded newspaper to shoo away the mosquitoes that wish to nibble on the baby.

These mosquitoes come across the river from the Jersey side on hot nights and they seem to be very fond of babies.

"Hello, Butch," I say, as we stop in front of the stoop.

"Sh-h-h-h!" Butch says, pointing at the baby, and making more noise with his shush than an engine blowing off steam. Then he gets up and tiptoes down to the sidewalk where we are standing, and I am hoping that Butch feels all right, because when Butch does not feel so good he is apt to be very short with one and all. He is a guy of maybe six foot two and a couple of feet wide, and he has big hairy hands and a mean look.

In fact, Big Butch is known all over this man's town as a guy you must not monkey with in any respect, so it takes plenty of weight off of me when I see that he seems to know the parties from Brooklyn, and nods at them very friendly, especially at Harry the Horse. And right away Harry states a most surprising proposition to Big Butch.

It seems that there is a big coal company which has an office in an old building down in West Eighteenth Street, and in this office is a safe, and in this safe is the company pay roll of twenty thousand dollars cash money. Harry the Horse knows the money is there because a personal friend of his who is the paymaster for the company puts it there late this very afternoon.

It seems that the paymaster enters into a dicker with Harry the Horse and Little Isadore and Spanish John for them to slug him while he is carrying the pay roll from the bank to the office in the afternoon, but something happens that they miss connections on the exact spot, so the paymaster has to carry the sugar on to the office without being slugged, and there it is now in two fat bundles.

Personally it seems to me as I listen to Harry's story that the paymaster must be a very dishonest character to be making deals to hold still while he is being slugged and the company's sugar taken away from him, but of course it is none of my business, so I take no part in the conversation.

Well, it seems that Harry the Horse and Little Isadore and Spanish John wish to get the money out of the safe, but none of them knows anything about opening safes, and while they are standing around over in Brooklyn talking over what is to be done in this emergency Harry suddenly remembers that Big Butch is once in the business of opening safes for a living.

In fact, I hear afterwards that Big Butch is considered the best safe opener east of the Mississippi River in his day, but the law finally takes to sending him to Sing Sing for opening these safes, and after he is in and out of Sing Sing three different times for opening safes Butch gets sick and tired of the place, especially as they pass what is called the Baumes Law in New York, which is a law that says if a guy is sent to Sing Sing four times hand running, he must stay there the rest of his life, without any argument about it.

So Big Butch gives up opening safes for a living, and goes into business in a small way, such as running beer, and handling a little Scotch now and then, and becomes an honest citizen. Furthermore, he marries one of the neighbor's children over on the West Side by the name of Mary Murphy, and I judge the baby on this stoop comes of this marriage between Big Butch and Mary because I can see that it is a very homely baby, indeed. Still, I never see many babies that I consider rose geraniums for looks, anyway.

Well, it finally comes out that the idea of Harry the Horse and Little Isadore and Spanish John is to get Big Butch to open the coal company's safe and take the payroll money out, and they are willing to give him fifty percent of the money for his bother, taking fifty percent for themselves for finding the plant, and paying all the overhead, such as the paymaster, out of their bit, which strikes me as a pretty fair sort of deal for Big Butch. But Butch only shakes his head.

"It is old-fashioned stuff," Butch says. "Nobody opens pete boxes for a living any more. They make the boxes too good, and they are all wired up with alarms and are a lot of trouble generally. I am in a legitimate business now and going along. You boys know I cannot stand another fall, what with being away three times already, and in addition to this I must mind the baby. My old lady goes to Mrs. Clancy's wake tonight up in the Bronx, and the chances are she will be there all night, as she is very fond of wakes, so I must mind little John Ignatius Junior."

"Listen, Butch," Harry the Horse says, "this is a very soft pete. It is old-fashioned, and you can open it with a toothpick. There are no wires on it, because they never put more than a dime in it before in years. It just happens they have to put the twenty G's in it tonight because my pal the paymaster makes it a point not to get back from the jug with the scratch in time to pay off today, especially after he sees we miss out on him. It is the softest touch you will ever know, and where can a guy pick up ten G's like this?"

I can see that Big Butch is thinking the ten G's over very seriously, at that, because in these times nobody can afford to pass up ten G's, especially a guy in the beer business, which is very, very tough just now. But finally he shakes his head again and says like this:

"No," he says, "I must let it go, because I must mind the baby. My old lady is very, very particular about this, and I dast not leave little John

Ignatius Junior for a minute. If Mary comes home and finds I am not minding the baby she will put the blast on me plenty. I like to turn a few honest bobs now and then as well as anybody, but," Butch says, "John Ignatius Junior comes first with me."

Then he turns away and goes back to the stoop as much as to say he is through arguing, and sits down beside John Ignatius Junior again just in time to keep a mosquito from carrying off one of John's legs. Anybody can see that Big Butch is very fond of this baby, though personally I will not give you a dime a dozen for babies, male and female.

Well, Harry the Horse and Little Isadore and Spanish John are very much disappointed, and stand around talking among themselves, and paying no attention to me, when all of a sudden Spanish John, who never has much to say up to this time, seems to have a bright idea. He talks to Harry and Isadore, and they get all pleasured up over what he has to say, and finally Harry goes to Big Butch.

"Sh-h-h-h!" Big Butch says, pointing to the baby as Harry opens his mouth.

"Listen, Butch," Harry says in a whisper, "we can take the baby with us, and you can mind it and work, too."

"Why," Big Butch whispers back, "this is quite an idea indeed. Let us go into the house and talk things over."

So he picks up the baby and leads us into his joint, and gets out some pretty fair beer, though it is needled a little, at that, and we sit around the kitchen chewing the fat in whispers. There is a crib in the kitchen, and Butch puts the baby in his crib, and it keeps on snoozing away first rate while we are talking. In fact, it is sleeping so sound that I am commencing to figure that Butch must give it some of the needled beer he is feeding us, because I am feeling a little dopey myself.

Finally Butch says that as long as he can take John Ignatius Junior with him he sees no reason why he shall not go and open the safe for them, only he says he must have five percent more to put in the baby's bank when he gets back, so as to round himself up with his ever-loving wife in case of a beef from her over keeping the baby out in the night air. Harry the Horse says he considers this extra five percent a little strong, but Spanish John, who seems to be a very square guy, says that after all it is only fair to cut the baby in if it is to be with them when they are making the score, and Little Isadore seems to think this is all right, too. So Harry the Horse gives in, and says five percent it is.

Well, as they do not wish to start out until after midnight, and as there is plenty of time, Big Butch gets out some more needled beer, and then he goes looking for the tools with which he opens safes, and which he says he does not see since the day John Ignatius Junior is born, and he gets them out to build the crib.

Now this is a good time for me to bid one and all farewell, and what keeps me there is something I cannot tell you to this day, because personally I never before have any idea of taking part in a safe opening, especially with a baby, as I consider such actions very dishonorable. When I come to think things over afterwards, the only thing I can figure is the needled beer, but I wish to say I am really very much surprised at myself when I find myself in a taxicab along about one o'clock in the morning with these Brooklyn parties and Big Butch and the baby.

Butch has John Ignatius Junior rolled up in a blanket, and John is still pounding his ear. Butch has a satchel of tools, and what looks to me like a big flat book, and just before we leave the house Butch hands me a package and tells me to be very careful with it. He gives Little Isadore a smaller package, which Isadore shoves into his pistol pocket, and when Isadore sits down in the taxi something goes wa-wa, like a sheep, and Big Butch becomes very indignant because it seems Isadore is sitting on John Ignatius Junior's doll, which says "Mamma" when you squeeze it.

It seems Big Butch figures that John Ignatius Junior may wish something to play with in case he wakes up, and it is a good thing for Little Isadore that the mamma doll is not squashed so it cannot say "Mamma" any more, or the chances are Little Isadore will get a good bust in the snoot.

We let the taxicab go a block away from the spot we are headed for in West Eighteenth Street, between Seventh and Eighth Avenues, and walk the rest of the way two by two. I walk with Big Butch, carrying my package, and Butch is lugging the baby and his satchel and the flat thing that looks like a book. It is so quiet down in West Eighteenth Street at such an hour that you can hear yourself think, and in fact I hear myself thinking very plain that I am a big sap to be on a job like this, especially with a baby, but I keep going just the same, which shows you what a very big sap I am, indeed.

There are very few people in West Eighteenth Street when we get there, and one of them is a fat guy who is leaning against a building almost in the center of the block, and who takes a walk for himself as soon as he sees us. It seems that this fat guy is the watchman at the coal company's office and is also a personal friend of Harry the Horse, which is why he takes the walk when he sees us coming.

It is agreed before we leave Big Butch's house that Harry the Horse and Spanish John are to stay outside the place as lookouts, while Big Butch is inside opening the safe, and that Little Isadore is to go with

Butch. Nothing whatever is said by anybody about where I am to be at
any time, and I can see that, no matter where I am, I will still be an
outsider, but, as Butch gives me the package to carry, I figure he wishes
me to remain with him.

It is no bother at all getting into the office of the coal company,
which is on the ground floor, because it seems the watchman leaves the
front door open, this watchman being a most obliging guy, indeed. In
fact he is so obliging that by and by he comes back and lets Harry the
Horse and Spanish John tie him up good and tight, and stick a handkerchief in his mouth and chuck him in an areaway next to the office, so
nobody will think he has anything to do with opening the safe in case
anybody comes around asking.

The office looks out on the street, and the safe that Harry the Horse
and Little Isadore and Spanish John wish Big Butch to open is standing
up against the rear wall of the office facing the street windows. There is
one little electric light burning very dim over the safe so that when
anybody walks past the place outside, such as a watchman, they can look
in through the window and see the safe at all times, unless they are blind.
It is not a tall safe, and it is not a big safe, and I can see Big Butch grin
when he sees it, so I figure this safe is not much of a safe, just as Harry
the Horse claims.

Well, as soon as Big Butch and the baby and Little Isadore and me
get into the office, Big Butch steps over to the safe and unfolds what I
think is the big flat book, and what is it but a sort of screen painted on
one side to look exactly like the front of a safe. Big Butch stands this
screen up on the floor in front of the real safe, leaving plenty of space in
between, the idea being that the screen will keep anyone passing in the
street outside from seeing Butch while he is opening the safe, because
when a man is opening a safe he needs all the privacy he can get.

Big Butch lays John Ignatius Junior down on the floor on the blanket behind the phony safe front and takes his tools out of the satchel and
starts to work opening the safe, while Little Isadore and me get back in a
corner where it is dark, because there is not room for all of us back of
the screen. However, we can see what Big Butch is doing, and I wish to
say while I never before see a professional safe opener at work, and never
wish to see another, this Butch handles himself like a real artist.

He starts drilling into the safe around the combination lock, working very fast and very quiet, when all of a sudden what happens but John
Ignatius Junior sits up on the blanket and lets out a squall. Naturally this
is most disquieting to me, and personally I am in favor of beaning John
Ignatius Junior with something to make him keep still, because I am

nervous enough as it is. But the squalling does not seem to bother Big Butch. He lays down his tools and picks up John Ignatius Junior and starts whispering, "There, there, there, my itty oddleums. Da-dad is here."

Well, this sounds very nonsensical to me in such a situation, and it makes no impression whatever on John Ignatius Junior. He keeps on squalling, and I judge he is squalling pretty loud because I see Harry the Horse and Spanish John both walk past the window and look in very anxious. Big Butch jiggles John Ignatius Junior up and down and keeps whispering baby talk to him, which sounds very undignified coming from a high-class safe opener, and finally Butch whispers to me to hand him the package I am carrying.

He opens the package, and what is in it but a baby's nursing bottle full of milk. Moreover, there is a little tin stew pan, and Butch hands the pan to me and whispers to me to find a water tap somewhere in the joint and fill the pan with water. So I go stumbling around in the dark in a room behind the office and bark my shins several times before I find a tap and fill the pan. I take it back to Big Butch, and he squats there with the baby on one arm, and gets a tin of what is called canned heat out of the package, and lights this canned heat with his cigar lighter, and starts heating the pan of water with the nursing bottle in it.

Big Butch keeps sticking his finger in the pan of water while it is heating, and by and by he puts the rubber nipple of the nursing bottle in his mouth and takes a pull at it to see if the milk is warm enough, just like I see dolls who have babies do. Apparently the milk is okay, as Butch hands the bottle to John Ignatius Junior, who grabs hold of it with both hands and starts sucking on the business end. Naturally he has to stop squalling, and Big Butch goes to work on the safe again, with John Ignatius Junior sitting on the blanket, pulling on the bottle and looking wiser than a treeful of owls.

It seems the safe is either a tougher job than anybody figures, or Big Butch's tools are not so good, what with being old and rusty and used for building baby cribs, because he breaks a couple of drills and works himself up into quite a sweat without getting anywhere. Butch afterwards explains to me that he is one of the first guys in this country to open safes without explosives, but he says to do this work properly you have to know the safes so as to drill to the tumblers of the lock just right, and it seems that this particular safe is a new type to him, even if it is old, and he is out of practice.

Well, in the meantime John Ignatius Junior finishes his bottle and starts mumbling again, and Big Butch gives him a tool to play with, and finally Butch needs this tool and tries to take it away from John Ignatius Junior, and the baby lets out such a squawk that Butch has to let him keep it until he can sneak it away from him, and this causes more delay.

Finally Big Butch gives up trying to drill the safe open, and he whispers to us that he will have to put a little shot in it to loosen up the lock, which is all right with us, because we are getting tired of hanging around and listening to John Ignatius Junior's glug-glugging. As far as I am personally concerned, I am wishing I am home in bed.

Well, Butch starts pawing through his satchel looking for something and it seems that what he is looking for is a little bottle of some kind of explosive with which to shake the lock on the safe up some, and at first he cannot find this bottle, but finally he discovers that John Ignatius Junior has it and is gnawing at the cork, and Butch has quite a battle making John Ignatius Junior give it up.

Anyway, he fixes the explosive in one of the holes he drills near the combination lock on the safe, and then he puts in a fuse, and just before he touches off the fuse Butch picks up John Ignatius Junior and hands him to Little Isadore, and tells us to go into the room behind the office. John Ignatius Junior does not seem to care for Little Isadore, and I do not blame him, at that, because he starts to squirm around quite some in Isadore's arms and lets out a squall, but all of a sudden he becomes very quiet indeed, and, while I am not able to prove it, something tells me that Little Isadore has his hand over John Ignatius Junior's mouth.

Well, Big Butch joins us right away in the back room, and sound comes out of John Ignatius Junior again as Butch takes him from Little Isadore, and I am thinking that it is a good thing for Isadore that the baby cannot tell Big Butch what Isadore does to him.

"I put in just a little bit of a shot," Big Butch says, "and it will not make any more noise than snapping your fingers."

But a second later there is a big whoom from the office, and the whole joint shakes, and John Ignatius Junior laughs right out loud. The chances are he thinks it is the Fourth of July.

"I guess maybe I put in too big a charge," Big Butch says, and then he rushes into the office with Little Isadore and me after him, and John Ignatius Junior still laughing very heartily for a small baby. The door of the safe is swinging loose, and the whole joint looks somewhat wrecked, but Big Butch loses no time in getting his dukes into the safe and grabbing out two big bundles of cash money, which he sticks inside his shirt.

As we go into the street Harry the Horse and Spanish John come running up much excited, and Harry says to Big Butch like this:

"What are you trying to do," he says, "wake up the whole town?"

"Well," Butch says, "I guess maybe the charge is too strong, at that, but nobody seems to be coming, so you and Spanish John walk over to Eighth Avenue, and the rest of us will walk to Seventh, and if you go along quiet, like people minding their own business, it will be all right."

But I judge Little Isadore is tired of John Ignatius Junior's company by this time, because he says he will go with Harry the Horse and Spanish John, and this leaves Big Butch and John Ignatius Junior and me to go the other way. So we start moving, and all of a sudden two cops come tearing around the corner toward which Harry and Isadore and Spanish John are going. The chances are the cops hear the earthquake Big Butch lets off and are coming to investigate.

But the chances are, too, that if Harry the Horse and the other two keep on walking along very quietly like Butch tells them to, the coppers will pass them up entirely, because it is not likely that coppers will figure anybody to be opening safes with explosives in this neighborhood. But the minute Harry the Horse sees the coppers he loses his nut, and he outs with the old equalizer and starts blasting away, and what does Spanish John do but get his out, too, and open up.

The next thing anybody knows, the two coppers are down on the ground with slugs in them, but other coppers are coming from every which direction, blowing whistles and doing a little blasting themselves, and there is plenty of excitement, especially when the coppers who are not chasing Harry the Horse and Little Isadore and Spanish John start poking around the neighborhood and find Harry's pal, the watchman, all tied up nice and tight where Harry leaves him, and the watchman explains that some scoundrels blow open the safe he is watching.

All this time Big Butch and me are walking in the other direction toward Seventh Avenue, and Big Butch has John Ignatius in his arms, and John Ignatius is now squalling very loud, indeed. The chances are he is still thinking of the big whoom back there which tickles him so and is wishing to hear some more whooms. Anyway, he is beating his own best record for squalling, and as we go walking along Big Butch says to me like this:

"I dast not run," he says, "because if any coppers see me running they will start popping at me and maybe hit John Ignatius Junior, and besides running will joggle the milk up in him and make him sick. My old lady always warns me never to joggle John Ignatius Junior when he is full of milk."

"Well, Butch," I say, "there is no milk in me, and I do not care if I am joggled up, so if you do not mind, I will start doing a piece of running at the next corner."

But just then around the corner of Seventh Avenue toward which we are headed comes two or three coppers with a big fat sergeant with them, and one of the coppers, who is half out of breath as if he has been doing plenty of sprinting, is explaining to the sergeant that somebody blows a safe down the street and shoots a couple of coppers in the get-away.

And there is Big Butch, with John Ignatius Junior in his arms and twenty G's in his shirt front and a tough record behind him, walking right up to them.

I am feeling very sorry, indeed, for Big Butch, and very sorry for myself, too, and I am saying to myself that if I get out of this I will never associate with anyone but ministers of the gospel as long as I live. I can remember thinking that I am getting a better break than Butch, at that, because I will not have to go to Sing Sing for the rest of my life, like him, and I also remember wondering what they will give John Ignatius Junior, who is still tearing off these squalls, with Big Butch saying: "There, there, there, Daddy's itty woogleums." Then I hear one of the coppers say to the fat sergeant: "We better nail these guys. They may be in on this."

Well, I can see it is good-by to Butch and John Ignatius Junior and me, as the fat sergeant steps up to Big Butch, but instead of putting the arm on Butch, the fat sergeant only points at John Ignatius Junior and asks very sympathetic: "Teeth?"

"No," Big Butch says. "Not teeth. Colic. I just get the doctor here out of bed to do something for him, and we are going to a drug store to get some medicine."

Well, naturally I am very much surprised at this statement, because of course I am not a doctor, and if John Ignatius Junior has colic it serves him right, but I am only hoping they do not ask for my degree, when the fat sergeant says: "Too bad. I know what it is. I got three of them at home. But," he says, "it acts more like it is teeth than colic."

Then as Big Butch and John Ignatius Junior and me go on about our business I hear the fat sergeant say to the copper, very sarcastic: "Yea, of course a guy is out blowing safes with a baby in his arms! You will make a great detective, you will!"

I do not see Big Butch for several days after I learn that Harry the Horse and Little Isadore and Spanish John get back to Brooklyn all right, except they are a little nicked up here and there from the slugs the coppers toss at them, while the coppers they clip are not damaged so very much. Furthermore, the chances are I will not see Big Butch for several years, if it is left to me, but he comes looking for me one night, and he seems to be all pleasured up about something.

"Say," Big Butch says to me, "you know I never give a copper credit for knowing any too much about anything, but I wish to say that this fat sergeant we run into the other night is a very, very smart duck. He is right about it being teeth that is ailing John Ignatius Junior, for what happens yesterday but John cuts in his first tooth."

P. G. Wodehouse

*

UKRIDGE'S ACCIDENT SYNDICATE

"Half a minute, laddie," said Ukridge. And, gripping my arm, he brought me to a halt on the outskirts of the little crowd which had collected about the church door.

It was a crowd such as may be seen any morning during the London mating-season outside any of the churches which nestle in the quiet squares between Hyde Park and the King's Road, Chelsea.

It consisted of five women of cooklike aspect, four nursemaids, half a dozen men of the non-producing class who had torn themselves away for the moment from their normal task of propping up the wall of the Bunch of Grapes public-house on the corner, a costermonger with a barrow of vegetables, divers small boys, eleven dogs, and two or three purposeful-looking young fellows with cameras slung over their shoulders. It was plain that a wedding was in progress—and, arguing from the presence of the cameramen and the line of smart motor-cars along the kerb, a fairly fashionable wedding. What was not plain—to me—was why Ukridge, sternest of bachelors, had desired to add himself to the spectators.

"What," I enquired, "is the thought behind this? Why are we interrupting our walk to attend the obsequies of some perfect stranger?"

Ukridge did not reply for a moment. He seemed plunged in thought. Then he uttered a hollow, mirthless laugh—a dreadful sound like the last gargle of a dying moose.

"Perfect stranger, my number eleven foot!" he responded, in a coarse way. "Do you know who it is who's getting hitched up in there?"

"Who?"

"Teddy Weeks."

"Teddy Weeks? Teddy Weeks? Good Lord!" I exclaimed. "Not really?"

And five years rolled away.

It was at Barolini's Italian restaurant in Beak Street that Ukridge evolved his great scheme. Barolini's was a favourite resort of our little group of earnest strugglers in the days when the philanthropic restaurateurs of Soho used to supply four courses and coffee for a shilling and sixpence; and there were present that night, besides Ukridge and myself, the following men-about-town: Teddy Weeks, the actor, fresh from a six-weeks' tour with the Number Three "Only a Shop-Girl" Company; Victor Beamish, the artist, the man who drew that picture of the O-So-Eesi Piano-Player in the advertisement pages of the *Piccadilly Magazine*; Bertram Fox, author of *Ashes of Remorse*, and other unproduced motion-picture scenarios; and Robert Dunhill, who, being employed at a salary of eighty pounds per annum by the New Asiatic Bank, represented the sober, hard-headed commercial element. As usual, Teddy Weeks had collared the conversation, and was telling us once again how good he was and how hardly treated by a malignant fate.

There is no need to describe Teddy Weeks. Under another and a more euphonious name he has long since made his personal appearance dreadfully familiar to all who read the illustrated weekly papers. He was then, as now, a sickeningly handsome young man, possessing precisely the same melting eyes, mobile mouth, and corrugated hair so esteemed by the theatre-going public today. And yet, at this period of his career he was wasting himself on minor touring companies of the kind which open at Barrow-in-Furness and jump to Bootle for the second half of the week. He attributed this, as Ukridge was so apt to attribute his own difficulties, to lack of capital.

"I have everything," he said, querulously, emphasizing his remarks with a coffee spoon. "Looks, talent, personality, a beautiful speaking voice—everything. All I need is a chance. And I can't get that because I have no clothes fit to wear. These managers are all the same, they never look below the surface, they never bother to find out if a man has genius. All they go by are his clothes. If I could afford to buy a couple of suits from a Cork Street tailor, if I could have my boots made to order by Moykoff instead of getting them ready-made and second-hand at Moses Brothers', if I could once contrive to own a decent hat, a really good pair of spats, and a gold cigarette-case, all at the same time, I could walk into any manager's office in London and sign up for a West End production tomorrow."

It was at this point that Freddie Lunt came in. Freddie, like Robert Dunhill, was a financial magnate in the making and an assiduous frequenter of Barolini's; and it suddenly occurred to us that a considerable time had passed since we had last seen him in the place. We enquired the reason for this aloofness.

"I've been in bed," said Freddie, "for over a fortnight."

The statement incurred Ukridge's stern disapproval. That great man made a practice of never rising before noon, and on one occasion, when a carelessly-thrown match had burned a hole in his only pair of trousers, had gone so far as to remain between the sheets for forty-eight hours, but sloth on so majestic a scale as this shocked him.

"Lazy young devil," he commented severely. "Letting the golden hours of youth slip by like that when you ought to have been bustling about and making a name for yourself."

Freddie protested himself wronged by the imputation.

"I had an accident," he explained. "Fell off my bicycle and sprained my ankle."

"Tough luck," was our verdict.

"Oh, I don't know," said Freddie. "It wasn't bad fun getting a rest. And of course there was the fiver."

"What fiver?"

"I got a fiver from the *Weekly Cyclist* for getting my ankle sprained."

"You—*what?*" cried Ukridge, profoundly stirred—as ever—by a tale of easy money. "Do you mean to sit there and tell me that some dashed paper paid you five quid simply because you sprained your ankle? Pull yourself together, old horse. Things like that don't happen."

"It's quite true."

"Can you show me the fiver?"

"No; because if I did you would try to borrow it."

Ukridge ignored this slur in dignified silence.

"Would they pay a fiver to *anyone* who sprained his ankle?" he asked, sticking to the main point.

"Yes. If he was a subscriber."

"I knew there was a catch in it," said Ukridge, moodily.

"Lots of weekly papers are starting this wheeze," proceeded Freddie. "You pay a year's subscription and that entitles you to accident insurance."

We were interested. This was in the days before every daily paper in London was competing madly against its rivals in the matter of insurance and offering princely bribes to the citizens to make a fortune by breaking their necks. Nowadays papers are paying as high as two thousand pounds for a genuine corpse and five pounds a week for a mere dislocated spine; but at that time the idea was new and it had an attractive appeal.

"How many of these rags are doing this?" asked Ukridge. You could tell from the gleam in his eyes that that great brain was whirring like a dynamo. "As many as ten?"

"Yes, I should think so. Quite ten."

"Then a fellow who subscribed to them all and then sprained his ankle would get fifty quid?" said Ukridge, reasoning acutely.

"More if the injury was more serious," said Freddie, the expert. "They have a regular tariff. So much for a broken arm, so much for a broken leg, and so forth."

Ukridge's collar leaped off its stud and his pince-nez wobbled drunkenly as he turned to us.

"How much money can you blokes raise?" he demanded.

"What do you want it for?" asked Robert Dunhill, with a banker's caution.

"My dear old horse, can't you see? Why, my gosh, I've got the idea of the century. Upon my Sam, this is the giltest-edged scheme that was ever hatched. We'll get together enough money and take out a year's subscription for every one of these dashed papers."

"What's the good of that?" said Dunhill, coldly unenthusiastic.

They train bank clerks to stifle emotions, so that they will be able to refuse overdrafts when they become managers. "The odds are we should none of us have an accident of any kind, and then the money would be chucked away."

"Good heavens, ass," snorted Ukridge, "you don't suppose I'm suggesting that we should leave it to chance, do you? Listen! Here's the scheme. We take out subscriptions for all these papers, then we draw lots, and the fellow who gets the fatal card or whatever it is goes out and breaks his leg and draws the loot, and we split up between us and live on it in luxury. It ought to run into hundreds of pounds."

A long silence followed. Then Dunhill spoke again. His was a solid rather than a nimble mind.

"Suppose he couldn't break his leg?"

"My gosh!" cried Ukridge, exasperated. "Here we are in the twentieth century, with every resource of modern civilization at our disposal, with opportunities for getting our legs broken opening about us on every side—and you ask a silly question like that! Of course he could break his leg. Any ass can break a leg. It's a little hard! We're all infernally broke —personally, unless Freddie can lend me a bit of that fiver till Saturday, I'm going to have a difficult job pulling through. We all need money like the dickens, and yet, when I point out this marvellous scheme for collecting a bit, instead of fawning on me for my ready intelligence you sit and make objections. It isn't the right spirit. It isn't the spirit that wins."

"If you're as hard up as that," objected Dunhill, "how are you going to put in your share of the pool?"

A pained, almost a stunned, look came into Ukridge's eyes. He gazed at Dunhill through a lopsided pince-nez as one who speculates as to whether his hearing has deceived him.

"Me?" he cried. "Me? I like that! Upon my Sam, that's rich! Why, damme, if there's any justice in the world, if there's a spark of decency and good feeling in your bally bosoms, I should think you would let me in free for suggesting the idea. It's a little hard! I supply the brains and you want me to cough up cash as well. My gosh, I didn't expect this. This hurts me, by George! If anybody had told me that an old pal would—"

"Oh, all right," said Robert Dunhill. "All right, all right, all right. But I'll tell you one thing. If you draw the lot it'll be the happiest day of my life."

"I shan't," said Ukridge. "Something tells me that I shan't."

Nor did he. When, in a solemn silence broken only by the sound of a distant waiter quarrelling with the cook down a speaking-tube, we had completed the drawing, the man of destiny was Teddy Weeks.

I suppose that even in the springtime of Youth, when broken limbs seem a lighter matter than they become later in life, it can never be an unmixedly agreeable thing to have to go out into the public highways and try to make an accident happen to one. In such circumstances the reflection that you are thereby benefiting your friends can bring but slight balm. To Teddy Weeks it appeared to bring no balm at all. That he was experiencing a certain disinclination to sacrifice himself for the public good became more and more evident as the days went by and found him still intact. Ukridge, when he called upon me to discuss the matter, was visibly perturbed. He sank into a chair beside the table at which I was beginning my modest morning meal, and, having drunk half my coffee, sighed deeply.

"Upon my Sam," he moaned, "it's a little disheartening. I strain my brain to think up schemes for getting us all a bit of money just at the moment when we are all needing it most, and when I hit on what is probably the simplest and yet ripest notion of our time, this blighter Weeks goes and lets me down by shirking his plain duty. It's just my luck that a fellow like that should have drawn the lot. And the worst of it is, laddie, that now we've started with him, we've got to keep on. We can't possibly raise enough money to pay yearly subscriptions for anybody else. It's Weeks or nobody."

"I suppose we must give him time."

"That's what he says," grunted Ukridge, morosely, helping himself to toast. "He says he doesn't know how to start about it. To listen to him, you'd think that going and having a trifling accident was the sort of delicate and intricate job that required years of study and special preparation. Why, a child of six could do it on his head at five minutes' notice. The man's so infernally particular. You make helpful suggestions, and instead of accepting them in a broad, reasonable spirit of cooperation he comes back at you every time with some frivolous objection. He's so dashed fastidious. When we were out last night, we came on a couple of navvies scrapping. Good hefty fellows, either of them capable of putting him in hospital for a month. I told him to jump in and start separating them, and he said no; it was a private dispute which was none of his business, and he didn't feel justified in interfering. Finicky, I call it. I tell you, laddie, this blighter is a broken reed. He has got cold feet. We did wrong to let him into the drawing at all. We might have known that a fellow like that would never give results. No conscience. No sense of esprit de corps. No notion of putting himself out to the most trifling extent for the benefit of the community. Haven't you any more marmalade, laddie?"

"I have not."

"Then I'll be going," said Ukridge, moodily. "I suppose," he added, pausing at the door, "you couldn't lend me five bob?"

"How did you guess?"

"Then I'll tell you what," said Ukridge, ever fair and reasonable; "you can stand me dinner tonight." He seemed cheered up for the moment by this happy compromise, but gloom descended on him again. His face clouded. "When I think," he said, "of all the money that's locked up in that poor faint-hearted fish, just waiting to be released, I could sob. Sob, laddie, like a little child. I never liked that man—he has a bad eye and waves his hair. Never trust a man who waves his hair, old horse."

Ukridge's pessimism was not confined to himself. By the end of a fortnight, nothing having happened to Teddy Weeks worse than a slight cold which he shook off in a couple of days, the general consensus of opinion among his apprehensive colleagues in the Syndicate was that the situation had become desperate. There were no signs whatever of any return on the vast capital which was laid out, and meanwhile meals had to be bought, landladies paid, and a reasonable supply of tobacco acquired. It was a melancholy task in these circumstances to read one's paper of a morning.

All over the inhabited globe, so the well-informed sheet gave one to understand, every kind of accident was happening every day to practically everybody in existence except Teddy Weeks. Farmers in Minnesota were getting mixed up with reaping-machines; peasants in India were being bisected by crocodiles; iron girders from skyscrapers were falling hourly on the heads of citizens in every town from Philadelphia to San Francisco; and the only people who were not down with ptomaine poisoning were those who had walked over cliffs, driven motors into walls, tripped over manholes, or assumed on too slight evidence that the gun was not loaded. In a crippled world, it seemed, Teddy Weeks walked alone, whole and glowing with health. It was one of those grim, ironical, hopeless, grey, despairful situations which the Russian novelists love to write about, and I could not find it in me to blame Ukridge for taking direct action in this crisis. My only regret was that bad luck caused so excellent a plan to miscarry.

My first intimation that he had been trying to hurry matters on came when he and I were walking along the King's Road one evening, and he drew me into Markham Square, a dismal backwater where he had once had rooms.

"What's the idea?" I asked, for I disliked the place.

"Teddy Weeks lives here," said Ukridge. "In my old rooms." I could not see that this lent any fascination to the place. Every day and in every way I was feeling sorrier and sorrier that I had been foolish enough to put money which I could ill spare into a venture which had all the earmarks of a wash-out, and my sentiments towards Teddy Weeks were cold and hostile.

"I want to enquire after him."

"Enquire after him? Why?"

"Well, the fact is, laddie, I have an idea that he has been bitten by a dog."

"What makes you think that?"

"Oh, I don't know," said Ukridge, dreamily. "I've just got the idea. You know how one gets ideas."

The mere contemplation of this beautiful event was so inspiring that for a while it held me silent. In each of the ten journals in which we had invested dog-bites were specifically recommended as things which every subscriber ought to have. They came about half-way up the list of lucrative accidents, inferior to a broken rib or a fractured fibula, but better value than an ingrowing toenail. I was gloating happily over the picture conjured up by Ukridge's words when an exclamation brought me back with a start to the realities of life. A revolting sight met my eyes. Down the street came ambling the familiar figure of Teddy Weeks, and one glance at his elegant person was enough to tell us that our hopes had been built on sand. Not even a toy Pomeranian had chewed this man.

"Hallo, you fellows!" said Teddy Weeks.

"Hallo!" we responded, dully.

"Can't stop," said Teddy Weeks. "I've got to fetch a doctor."

"A doctor?"

"Yes. Poor Victor Beamish. He's been bitten by a dog."

Ukridge and I exchanged weary glances. It seemed as if Fate was going out of its way to have sport with us. What was the good of a dog biting Victor Beamish? What was the good of a hundred dogs biting Victor Beamish? A dog-bitten Victor Beamish had no market value whatever.

"You know that fierce brute that belongs to my landlady," said Teddy Weeks. "The one that always dashes out into the area and barks at people who come to the front door." I remembered. A large mongrel with wild eyes and flashing fangs, badly in need of a haircut. I had encountered it once in the street, when visiting Ukridge, and only the presence of the latter, who knew it well and to whom all dogs were as brothers, had saved me from the doom of Victor Beamish. "Somehow or other he got into my bedroom this evening. He was waiting there when I came home. I had brought Beamish back with me, and the animal pinned him by the leg the moment I opened the door."

"Why didn't he pin you?" asked Ukridge, aggrieved.

"What I can't make out," said Teddy Weeks, "is how on earth the brute came to be in my room. Somebody must have put him there. The whole thing is very mysterious."

"Why didn't he pin you?" demanded Ukridge again.

"Oh, I managed to climb on to the top of the wardrobe while he was biting Beamish," said Teddy Weeks. "And then the landlady came and took him away. But I can't stop here talking. I must go and get that doctor."

We gazed after him in silence as he tripped down the street. We noted the careful manner in which he paused at the corner to eye the traffic before crossing the road, the wary way in which he drew back to allow a truck to rattle past.

"You heard that?" said Ukridge, tensely. "He climbed on to the top of the wardrobe!"

"Yes."

"And you saw the way he dodged that excellent truck?"

"Yes."

"Something's got to be done," said Ukridge, firmly. "The man has got to be awakened to a sense of his responsibilities."

Next day a deputation waited on Teddy Weeks.

Ukridge was our spokesman, and he came to the point with admirable directness.

"How about it?" asked Ukridge.

"How about what?" replied Teddy Weeks, nervously, avoiding his accusing eye.

"When do we get action?"

"Oh, you mean that accident business?"

"Yes."

"I've been thinking about that," said Teddy Weeks.

Ukridge drew the mackintosh which he wore indoors and out of doors and in all weathers more closely around him. There was in the action something suggestive of a member of the Roman Senate about to denounce an enemy of the State. In just such a manner must Cicero have swished his toga as he took a deep breath preparatory to assailing Clodius. He toyed for a moment with the ginger-beer wire which held his pince-nez in place, and endeavoured without success to button his collar at the back. In moments of emotion Ukridge's collar always took on a sort of temperamental jumpiness which no stud could restrain.

"And about time you *were* thinking about it," he boomed, sternly.

We shifted appreciatively in our seats, all except Victor Beamish, who had declined a chair and was standing by the mantelpiece. "Upon my Sam, it's about time you were thinking about it. Do you realize that we've invested an enormous sum of money in you on the distinct understanding that we could rely on you to do your duty and get immediate results? Are we to be forced to the conclusion that you are so yellow and few in the pod as to want to evade your honourable obligations? We thought better of you, Weeks. Upon my Sam, we thought better of you. We took you for a two-fisted, enterprising, big-souled, one hundred-per-cent he-man who would stand by his friends to the finish."

"Yes, but—"

"Any bloke with a sense of loyalty and an appreciation of what it meant to the rest of us would have rushed out and found some means of fulfilling his duty long ago. You don't even grasp at the opportunities that come your way. Only yesterday I saw you draw back when a single step into the road would have had a truck bumping into you."

"Well, it's not easy to let a truck bump into you."

"Nonsense. It only requires a little ordinary resolution. Use your imagination, man. Try to think that a child has fallen down in the street

—a little golden-haired child," said Ukridge, deeply affected. "And a dashed great cab or something comes rolling up. The kid's mother is standing on the pavement, helpless, her hands clasped in agony. 'Dammit,' she cries, 'will no one save my darling?' 'Yes, by George,' you shout, 'I will.' And out you jump and the thing's over in half a second. I don't know what you're making such a fuss about."

"Yes, but—" said Teddy Weeks.

"I'm told what's more, it isn't a bit painful. A sort of dull shock, that's all."

"Who told you that?"

"I forget. Someone."

"Well, you can tell him from me that he's an ass," said Teddy Weeks, with asperity.

"All right. If you object to being run over by a truck there are lots of other ways. But, upon my Sam, it's pretty hopeless suggesting them. You seem to have no enterprise at all. Yesterday, after I went to all the trouble to put a dog in your room, a dog which would have done all the work for him—all you had to do was stand still and let him use his own judgement—what happened? You climbed on to—"

Victor Beamish interrupted, speaking in a voice husky with emotion.

"Was it you who put that damned dog in the room?"

"Eh?" said Ukridge. "Why, yes. But we can have a good talk about all that later on," he proceeded, hastily. "The point at the moment is how the dickens we're going to persuade this poor worm to collect our insurance money for us. Why, damme, I should have thought you would have—"

"All I can say—" began Victor Beamish, heatedly.

"Yes, yes," said Ukridge; "some other time. Must stick to business now, laddie. I was saying," he resumed, "that I should have thought you would have been as keen as mustard to put the job through for your own sake. You're always beefing that you haven't any clothes to impress managers with. Think of all you can buy with your share of the swag once you have summoned up a little ordinary determination and seen the thing through. Think of the suits, the boots, the hats, the spats. You're always talking about your dashed career, and how all you need to land you in a West End production is good clothes. Well, here's your chance to get them."

His eloquence was not wasted. A wistful look came into Teddy Weeks's eye, such a look as must have come into the eye of Moses on the summit of Pisgah. He breathed heavily! You could see that the man was mentally walking along Cork Street, weighing the merits of one famous tailor against another.

"I'll tell you what I'll do," he said, suddenly. "It's no use asking me to put this thing through in cold blood. I simply can't do it. I haven't the nerve. But if you fellows will give me a dinner tonight with lots of champagne I think it will key me up to it."

A heavy silence fell upon the room. Champagne! The word was like a knell.

"How on earth are we going to afford champagne?" said Victor Beamish.

"Well, there it is," said Teddy Weeks. "Take it or leave it."

"Gentlemen," said Ukridge, "it would seem that the company requires more capital. How about it, old horses? Let's get together in a frank, businesslike cards-on-the-table spirit, and see what can be done. I can raise ten bob."

"What!" cried the entire assembled company, amazed. "How?"

"I'll pawn a banjo."

"You haven't got a banjo."

"No, but George Tupper has, and I know where he keeps it."

Started in this spirited way, the subscriptions came pouring in. I contributed a cigarette-case, Bertram Fox thought his landlady would let him owe for another week, Robert Dunhill had an uncle in Kensington who, he fancied, if tactfully approached, would be good for a quid, and Victor Beamish said that if the advertisement-manager of the O-So-Eesi Piano-Player was churlish enough to refuse an advance of five shillings against future work he misjudged him sadly. Within a few minutes, in short, the Lightning Drive had produced the impressive total of two pounds six shillings, and we asked Teddy Weeks if he thought that he could get adequately keyed up within the limits of that sum.

"I'll try," said Teddy Weeks.

So, not unmindful of the fact that the excellent hostelry supplied champagne at eight shillings the quart bottle, we fixed the meeting for seven o'clock at Barolini's.

Considered as a social affair, Teddy Weeks's keying-up dinner was not a success. Almost from the start I think we all found it trying. It was not so much the fact that he was drinking deeply of Barolini's eight shilling champagne while we, from lack of funds, were compelled to confine ourselves to meaner beverages; what really marred the pleasantness of the function was the extraordinary effect the stuff had on Teddy. What was actually in the champagne supplied to Barolini and purveyed by him to the public, such as were reckless enough to drink it, at eight shillings the bottle remains a secret between its maker and his Maker; but three glasses of it were enough to convert Teddy Weeks from a mild and rather oily young man into a truculent swashbuckler.

He quarrelled with us. With the soup he was tilting at Victor Beamish's theories of Art; the fish found him ridiculing Bertram Fox's views on the future of the motion-picture; and by the time the leg of chicken with dandelion salad arrived—or, as some held, string salad—opinions varied on this point—the hell-brew had so wrought on him that he had begun to lecture Ukridge on his mis-spent life and was urging him in accents audible across the street to go out and get a job and thus acquire sufficient self-respect to enable him to look himself in the face in a mirror without wincing. Not, added Teddy Weeks with what we all thought uncalled-for offensiveness, that any amount of self-respect was likely to do that. Having said which, he called imperiously for another eight bobs'-worth.

We gazed at one another wanly. However excellent the end towards which all this was tending, there was no denying that it was hard to bear. But policy kept us silent. We recognized that this was Teddy Weeks's evening and that he must be humoured. Victor Beamish said meekly that Teddy had cleared up a lot of points which had been troubling him for a long time. Bertram Fox agreed that there was much in what Teddy had said about the future of the closeup. And even Ukridge, though his haughty soul was seared to its foundations by the latter's personal remarks, promised to take his homily to heart and act upon it at the earliest possible moment.

"You'd better!" said Teddy Weeks, belligerently, biting off the end of one of Barolini's best cigars. "And there's another thing—don't let me hear of your coming and sneaking people's socks again."

"Very well, laddie," said Ukridge, humbly.

"If there is one person in the world that I despise," said Teddy, bending a red-eyed gaze on the offender, "it's a snock-seeker—a seek-snocker—a—well, you know what I mean."

We hastened to assure him that we knew what he meant and he relapsed into a lengthy stupor, from which he emerged three-quarters of an hour later to announce that he didn't know what we intended to do, but that he was going. We said that we were going too, and we paid the bill and did so.

Teddy Weeks's indignation on discovering us gathered about him upon the pavement outside the restaurant was intense, and he expressed it freely. Among other things, he said—which was not true—that he had a reputation to keep up in Soho.

"It's all right, Teddy, old horse," said Ukridge, soothingly. "We just thought you would like to have all your pals round you when you did it."

"Did it? Did what?"

"Why, had the accident."

Teddy Weeks glared at him truculently. Then his mood seemed to change abruptly, and he burst into a loud and hearty laugh.

"Well, of all the silly ideas!" he cried, amusedly. "I'm not going to have an accident. You don't suppose I ever seriously intended to have an accident, do you? It was just my fun." Then, with another sudden change of mood, he seemed to become a victim to an acute unhappiness. He stroked Ukridge's arm affectionately, and a tear rolled down his cheek. "Just my fun," he repeated. "You don't mind my fun, do you?" he asked, pleadingly. "You like my fun, don't you? All my fun. Never meant to have an accident at all. Just wanted dinner." The gay humour of it all overcame his sorrow once more. "Funniest thing ever heard," he said cordially. "Didn't want accident, wanted dinner. Dinner daxident, danner dixident," he added, driving home his point. "Well, good night all," he said, cheerily. And, stepping off the kerb on to a banana skin, was instantly knocked ten feet by a passing lorry.

"Two ribs and an arm," said the doctor five minutes later, superintending the removal proceedings. "Gently with that stretcher."

It was two weeks before we were informed by the authorities of Charing Cross Hospital that the patient was in a condition to receive visitors. A whip-round secured the price of a basket of fruit, and Ukridge and I were deputed by the shareholders to deliver it with their compliments and kind enquiries.

"Hallo!" we said in a hushed, bedside manner when finally admitted to his presence.

"Sit down, gentlemen," replied the invalid.

I must confess even in that first moment to having experienced a slight feeling of surprise. It was not like Teddy Weeks to call us gentlemen. Ukridge, however, seemed to notice nothing amiss.

"Well, well, well," he said buoyantly. "And how are you, laddie? We've brought you a few fragments of fruit."

"I'm getting along capitally," replied Teddy Weeks, still in that odd precise way which had made his opening words strike me as curious. "And I should like to say that in my opinion England has reason to be proud of the alertness and enterprise of her great journals. The excellence of their reading-matter, the ingenuity of their various competitions, and above all, the go-ahead spirit which has resulted in this

accident insurance scheme are beyond praise. Have you got that down?"
he enquired.

Ukridge and I looked at each other. We had been told that Teddy
was practically normal again, but this sounded like delirium.

"Have we got what down, old horse?" asked Ukridge, gently.

Teddy Weeks seemed surprised.

"Aren't you reporters?"

"How do you mean, reporters?"

"I thought you had come from one of these weekly papers that have
been paying me insurance money, to interview me," said Teddy Weeks.

Ukridge and I exchanged another glance. An uneasy glance this
time. I think that already a grim foreboding had begun to cast its shadow
over us.

"Surely you remember me, Teddy, old horse?" said Ukridge, anxiously.

Teddy Weeks knit his brow, concentrating painfully.

"Why, of course," he said at last. "You're Ukridge, aren't you?"

"That's right. Ukridge."

"Of course. Ukridge."

"Yes. Ukridge. Funny your forgetting me!"

"Yes," said Teddy Weeks. "It's the effect of the shock I got when
that thing bowled me over. I must have been struck on the head, I
suppose. It has had the effect of rendering my memory rather uncertain.
The doctors here are very interested. They say it is a most unusual case.
I can remember some things perfectly, but in some ways my memory is
a complete blank."

"Oh, but I say, old horse," quavered Ukridge. "I suppose you
haven't forgotten about that insurance, have you?"

"Oh, no, I remember that."

Ukridge breathed a relieved sigh.

"I was a subscriber to a number of weekly papers," went on Teddy
Weeks. "They are paying me insurance money now."

"Yes, yes, old horse," cried Ukridge. "But what I mean is, you
remember the Syndicate, don't you?"

Teddy Weeks raised his eyebrows.

"Syndicate? What Syndicate?"

"Why, when we all got together and put up the money to pay for
the subscriptions to these papers and drew lots, to choose which of us
should go out and have an accident and collect the money. And you
drew it, don't you remember?"

Utter astonishment, and a shocked astonishment at that, spread
itself over Teddy Weeks's countenance. The man seemed outraged.

"I certainly remember nothing of the kind," he said severely. "I cannot imagine myself for a moment consenting to become a party to what from your own account would appear to have been a criminal conspiracy to obtain money under false pretences from a number of weekly papers."

"But, laddie—"

"However," said Teddy Weeks, "if there is any truth in this story, no doubt you have documentary evidence to support it."

Ukridge looked at me. I looked at Ukridge. There was a long silence.

"Shift ho, old horse?" said Ukridge, sadly. "No use staying on here."

"No," I replied, with equal gloom. "May as well go."

"Glad to have seen you," said Teddy Weeks, "and thanks for the fruit."

The next time I saw the man he was coming out of a manager's office in the Haymarket. He had on a new Homburg hat of a delicate pearl grey, spats to match, and a new blue flannel suit, beautifully cut, with an invisible red twill. He was looking jubilant, and, as I passed him, he drew from his pocket a gold cigarette-case.

It was shortly after that, if you remember, that he made a big hit as the juvenile lead in that piece at the Apollo and started on his sensational career as a *matinée* idol.

Inside the church the organ had swelled into the familiar music of the Wedding March. A verger came out and opened the doors. The five cooks ceased their reminiscences of other and smarter weddings at which they had participated. The cameramen unshipped their cameras. The costermonger moved his barrow of vegetables a pace forward. A dishevelled and unshaven man at my side uttered a disapproving growl.

"Idle rich!" said the dishevelled man.

Out of the church came a beauteous being, leading attached to his arm another being, somewhat less beauteous.

There was no denying the spectacular effect of Teddy Weeks. He was handsomer than ever. His sleek hair, gorgeously waved, shone in the sun, his eyes were large and bright; his lissome frame, garbed in faultless morning-coat and trousers, was that of an Apollo. But his bride gave the impression that Teddy had married money. They paused in the doorway, and the cameramen became active and fussy.

"Have you got a shilling, laddie?" said Ukridge in a low, level voice.

"Why do you want a shilling?"

"Old horse," said Ukridge, tensely, "it is of the utmost vital importance that I have a shilling here and now."

I passed it over. Ukridge turned to the dishevelled man, and I perceived that he held in his hand a large rich tomato of juicy and over-ripe appearance.

"Would you like to earn a bob?" Ukridge said.

"Would I!" replied the dishevelled man.

Ukridge sank his voice to a hoarse whisper.

The cameramen had finished their preparations. Teddy Weeks, his head thrown back in that gallant way which has endeared him to so many female hearts, was exhibiting his celebrated teeth. The cooks, in undertones, were making adverse comments on the appearance of the bride.

"Now, please," said one of the cameramen.

Over the heads of the crowd, well and truly aimed, whizzed a large juicy tomato. It burst like a shell full between Teddy Weeks's expressive eyes, obliterating them in scarlet ruin. It spattered Teddy Weeks's collar, it dripped on Teddy Weeks's morning-coat. And the dishevelled man turned abruptly and raced off down the street.

Ukridge grasped my arm. There was a look of deep content in his eyes.

Arm in arm, we strolled off in the pleasant June sunshine.

Ring Lardner

*

THE BUSHER'S HONEYMOON
EXCERPT FROM *You Know Me Al*

[In an introduction to the 1959 edition of the book, the author's son, John Lardner, wrote: "The busher letters were not written with artistic prestige in mind. They were written because there was an urgent need around the home of the two hundred dollars that each of the first installments brought from *The Saturday Evening Post*. . . . Almost as soon as the *Post* began to publish them, the letters made their author as famous as the President of the United States. (They were to keep him famous in the same degree throughout the next two or three administrations.) This turn of events startled my father, but it totally failed to cause him to think of what he had written as literature."—ED.]

Chicago, Illinois, October 17.

FRIEND AL: Well Al it looks as if I would not be writeing so much to you now that I am a married man. Yes Al I and Florrie was married the day before yesterday just like I told you we was going to be and Al I am the happyest man in the world though I have spent $30 in the last 3 days incluseive. You was wise Al to get married in Bedford where not nothing is nearly half so dear. My expenses was as follows:

License	$2.00	Show tickets	3.00
Preist	3.50	Flowers	.50
Haircut and shave	.35	Candy	.30
Shine	.05	Hotel	4.50
Carfair	.45	Tobacco both kinds	.25
New suit	14.50		

You see Al it costs a hole lot of money to get married here. The sum of what I have wrote down is $29.40 but as I told you I have spent

$30 and I do not know what I have did with that other $0.60. My new brother-in-law Allen told me I should ought to give the preist $5 and I thought it should be about $2 the same as the license so I split the difference and give him $3.50. I never seen him before and probily won't never see him again so why should I give him anything at all when it is his business to marry couples? But I like to do the right thing. You know me Al.

I thought we would be in Bedford by this time but Florrie wants to say here a few more days because she says she wants to be with her sister. Allen and his wife is thinking about takeing a flat for the winter instead of going down to Waco Texas where they live. I don't see no sense in that when it costs so much to live here but it is none of my business if they want to throw their money away. But I am glad I got a wife with some sense though she kicked because I did not get no room with a bath which would cost me $2 a day instead of $1.50. I says I guess the club-house is still open yet and if I want a bath I can go over there and take the shower. She says Yes and I suppose I can go and jump in the lake. But she would not do that Al because the lake here is cold at this time of the year.

When I told you about my expenses I did not include in it the meals because we would be eating them if I was getting married or not getting married only I have to pay for six meals a day now instead of three and I didn't used to eat no lunch in the playing season except once in a while when I knowed I was not going to work that afternoon. I had a meal ticket which had not quite ran out over to a resturunt on Indiana Ave and we eat there for the first day except at night when I took Allen and his wife to the show with us and then he took us to a chop suye resturunt. I guess you have not never had no chop suye Al and I am here to tell you you have not missed nothing but when Allen was going to buy the supper what could I say? I could not say nothing.

Well yesterday and to-day we been eating at a resturunt on Cottage Grove Ave near the hotel and at the resturunt on Indiana that I had the meal ticket at only I do not like to buy no new meal ticket when I am not going to be round here no more than a few days. Well Al I guess the meals has cost me all together about $1.50 and I have eat very little myself. Florrie always wants desert ice cream or something and that runs up into money faster than regular stuff like stake and ham and eggs.

Well Al Florrie says it is time for me to keep my promise and take her to the moveing pictures which is $0.20 more because the one she likes round here costs a dime apeace. So I must close for this time and will see you soon.

Your pal, JACK

Chicago, Illinois, October 22.

AL: Just a note Al to tell you why I have not yet came to Bedford yet where I expected I would be long before this time. Allen and his wife have took a furnished flat for the winter and Allen's wife wants Florrie to stay here untill they get settled. Meentime it is costing me a hole lot of money at the hotel and for meals besides I am paying $10 a month rent for the house you got for me and what good am I getting out of it? But Florrie wants to help her sister and what can I say? Though I did make her promise she would not stay no longer than next Saturday at least. So I guess Al we will be home on the evening train Saturday and then may be I can save some money.

I know Al that you and Bertha will like Florrie when you get acquainted with her spesially Bertha though Florrie dresses pretty swell and spends a hole lot of time fusing with her face and her hair.

She says to me to-night Who are you writeing to and I told her Al Blanchard who I have told you about a good many times. She says I bet you are writeing to some girl and acted like as though she was kind of jealous. So I thought I would tease her a little and I says I don't know no girls except you and Violet and Hazel. Who is Violet and Hazel? she says. I kind of laughed and says Oh I guess I better not tell you and then she says I guess you will tell me. That made me kind of mad because no girl can't tell me what to do. She says Are you going to tell me? and I says No.

Then she says If you don't tell me I will go over to Marie's that is her sister Allen's wife and stay all night. I says Go on and she went downstairs but I guess she probily went to get a soda because she has some money of her own that I give her. This was about two hours ago and she is probily down in the hotel lobby now trying to scare me by makeing me believe she has went to her sister's. But she can't fool me Al and I am now going out to mail this letter and get a beer. I won't never tell her about Violet and Hazel if she is going to act like that.

Yours truly, JACK.

Chicago, Illinois, October 24.

FRIEND AL: I guess I told you Al that we would be home Saturday evening. I have changed my mind. Allen and his wife has a spair bedroom and wants us to come there and stay a week or two. It won't cost nothing except they will probily want to go out to the moving pictures nights and we will probily have to go along with them and I am a man Al that wants to pay his share and not be cheap.

I and Florrie had our first quarrle the other night. I guess I told you the start of it but I don't remember. I made some crack about Violet and

Hazel just to tease Florrie and she wanted to know who they was and I would not tell her. So she gets sore and goes over to Marie's to stay all night. I was just kidding Al and was willing to tell her about them two poor girls whatever she wanted to know except that I don't like to brag about girls being stuck on me. So I goes over to Marie's after her and tells her all about them except that I turned them down cold at the last minute to marry her because I did not want her to get all swelled up. She made me sware that I did not never care nothing about them and that was easy because it was the truth. So she come back to the hotel with me just like I knowed she would when I ordered her to.

They must not be no mistake about who is the boss in my house. Some men lets their wife run all over them but I am not that kind. You know me Al.

I must get busy and pack my suitcase if I am going to move over to Allen's. I sent three collars and a shirt to the laundrey this morning so even if we go over there to-night I will have to take another trip back this way in a day or two. I won't mind Al because they sell my kind of beer down to the corner and I never seen it sold nowheres else in Chi. You know the kind it is, eh Al? I wish I was lifting a few with you to-night.

Your pal, JACK.

Chicago, Illinois, October 28.

DEAR OLD AL: Florrie and Marie has went downtown shopping because Florrie thinks she has got to have a new dress though she has got two changes of cloths now and I don't know what she can do with another one. I hope she don't find none to suit her though it would not hurt none if she got something for next spring at a reduckshon. I guess she must think I am Charles A. Comiskey or somebody. Allen has went to a colledge football game. One of the reporters give him a pass. I don't see nothing in football except a lot of scrapping between little slobs that I could lick the whole bunch of them so I did not care to go. The reporter is one of the guys that travled round with our club all summer. He called up and said he hadn't only the one pass but he was not hurting my feelings none because I would not go to no rotten football game if they payed me.

The flat across the hall from this here one is for rent furnished. They want $40 a month for it and I guess they think they must be lots of suckers running round loose. Marie was talking about it and says Why don't you and Florrie take it and then we can be right together all winter long and have some big times? Florrie says It would be all right with me. What about it Jack? I says What do you think I am? I don't have to live in no high price flat when I got a home in Bedford where they ain't no people trying to hold everybody up all the time. So they did not say no more about it when they seen I was in ernest. Nobody cannot tell me where I am going to live sister-in-law or no sister-in-law. If I was to rent the rotten old flat I would be paying $50 a month rent includeing the house down in Bedford. Fine chance Al.

Well Al I am lonesome and thirsty so more later.

Your pal, JACK

Chicago, Illinois, November 2.

FRIEND AL: Well Al I got some big news for you. I am not comeing to Bedford this winter after all except to make a visit which I guess will be round Xmas. I changed my mind about that flat across the hall from the Allens and decided to take it after all. The people who was in it and owns the furniture says they would let us have it till the 1 of May if we would pay $42.50 a month which is only $2.50 a month more than they would of let us have it for for a short time. So you see we got a bargain because it is all furnished and everything and we won't have to blow no money on furniture besides the club goes to California the middle of Febuery so Florrie would not have no place to stay while I am away.

The Allens only subleased their flat from some other people till the 2 of Febuery and when I and Allen goes West Marie can come over and stay with Florrie so you see it is best all round. If we should of boughten furniture it would cost us in the neighborhod of $100 even without no piano and they is a piano in this here flat which makes it nice because Florrie plays pretty good with one hand and we can have lots of good times at home without it costing us nothing except just the bear liveing expenses. I consider myself lucky to of found out about this before it was too late and somebody else had of gotten the tip.

Now Al old pal I want to ask a great favor of you Al. I all ready have payed one month rent $10 on the house in Bedford and I want you to see the old man and see if he won't call off that lease. Why should I be paying $10 a month rent down there and $42.50 up here when the house down there is not no good to me because I am liveing up here all winter? See Al? Tell him I will gladly give him another month rent to call off the lease but don't tell him that if you don't have to. I want to be fare with him.

If you will do this favor for me, Al, I won't never forget it. Give my kindest to Bertha and tell her I am sorry I and Florrie won't see her right away but you see how it is Al.

Yours, JACK.

Chicago, Illinois, November 30.

FRIEND AL: I have not wrote for a long time have I Al but I have been very busy. They was not enough furniture in the flat and we have been buying some more. They was enough for some people maybe but I and Florrie is the kind that won't have nothing but the best. The furniture them people had in the liveing room was oak but they had a bookcase bilt in in the flat that was mohoggeny and Florrie would not stand for no joke combination like that so she moved the oak chairs and table in to the spair bedroom and we went downtown to buy some mohoggeny. But it costs to much Al and we was feeling pretty bad about it when we seen some Sir Cashion walnut that was prettier even than the mohoggeny and not near so expensive. It is not no real Sir Cashion walnut but it is just as good and we got it reasonable. Then we got some mission chairs for the dining room because the old ones was just straw and was no good and we got a big lether couch for $9 that somebody can sleep on if we get to much company.

I hope you and Bertha can come up for the holidays and see how comfertible we are fixed. That is all the new furniture we have boughten but Florrie set her heart on some old Rose drapes and a red table lamp that is the biggest you ever seen Al and I did not have the heart to say no. The hole thing cost me in the neighborhood of $110 which is very little for what we got and then it will always be ourn even when we move away from this flat though we will have to leave the furniture that belongs to the other people but their part of it is not no good anyway.

I guess I told you Al how much money I had when the season ended. It was $1400 all told includeing the city serious money. Well Al I got in the neighborhood of $800 left because I give $200 to Florrie to send down to Texas to her other sister who had a bad egg for a husband that managed a club in the Texas Oklahoma League and this was the money she had to pay to get the divorce. I am glad Al that I was lucky enough to marry happy and get a good girl for my wife that has got some sense and besides if I have got $800 left I should not worry as they say.

Your pal, JACK.

Chicago, Illinois, December 7.

DEAR OLD AL: No I was in ernest Al when I says that I wanted you and Bertha to come up here for the holidays. I know I told you that I might come to Bedford for the holidays but that is all off. I have gave up the idea of comeing to Bedford for the holidays and I want you to be sure and come up here for the holidays and I will show you a good time. I would love to have Bertha come to and she can come if she wants to only Florrie don't know if she would have a good time or not and thinks maybe she would rather stay in Bedford and you come alone. But be sure and have Bertha come if she wants to come but maybe she would not injoy it. You know best Al.

I don't think the old man give me no square deal on that lease but if he wants to stick me all right. I am grateful to you Al for trying to fix it up but maybe you could of did better if you had of went at it in a different way. I am not finding no fault with my old pal though. Don't think that. When I have a pal I am the man to stick to him threw thick and thin. If the old man is going to hold me to that lease I guess I will have to stand it and I guess I won't starv to death for no $10 a month because I am going to get $2800 next year besides the city serious money and maybe we will get into the World Serious too. I know we will if Callahan will pitch me every 3d day like I wanted him to last season. But if you had of approached the old man in a different way maybe you could of fixed it up. I wish you would try it again Al if it is not no trouble.

We had Allen and his wife here for thanksgiveing dinner and the dinner cost me better than $5. I thought we had enough to eat to last a week but about six o'clock at night Florrie and Marie said they was hungry and we went downtown and had dinner all over again and I payed for it and it cost me $5 more. Allen was all ready to pay for it when Florrie said No this day's treat is on us so I had to pay for it but I don't see why she did not wait and let me do the talking. I was going to pay for it any way.

Be sure and come and visit us for the holidays Al and of coarse if Bertha wants to come bring her along. We will be glad to see you both. I won't never go back on a friend and pal. You know me Al.

                                        Your old pal, JACK.

Chicago, Illinois, December 20.

FRIEND AL: I don't see what can be the matter with Bertha because you know Al we would not care how she dressed and would not make no kick if she come up here in a night gown. She did not have no license to say we was to swell for her because we did not never think of nothing like that. I wish you would talk to her again Al and tell her she need not get sore on me and that both her and you is welcome at my house any time I ask you to come. See if you can't make her change her mind Al because I feel like as if she must of took offense at something I may of wrote you. I am sorry you and her are not comeing but I suppose you know best. Only we was getting all ready for you and Florrie said only the other day that she wished the holidays was over but that was before she knowed you was not comeing. I hope you can come Al.

Well Al I guess there is not no use talking to the old man no more. You have did the best you could but I wish I could of came down there and talked to him. I will pay him his rotten old $10 a month and the next time I come to Bedford and meet him on the street I will bust his jaw. I know he is a old man Al but I don't like to see nobody get the best of me and I am sorry I ever asked him to let me off. Some of them old skinflints has no heart Al but why should I fight with a old man over chicken feed like $10? Florrie says a star pitcher like I should not ought never to scrap about little things and I guess she is right Al so I will pay the old man his $10 a month if I have to.

Florrie says she is jealous of me writeing to you so much and she says she would like to meet this great old pal of mine. I would like to have her meet you to Al and I would like to have you change your mind and come and visit us and I am sorry you can't come Al.

Yours truly, JACK.

Chicago, Illinois, December 27.

OLD PAL: I guess all these lefthanders is alike though I thought this Allen had some sense. I thought he was different from the most and was not no rummy but they are all alike Al and they are all lucky that somebody don't hit them over the head with a ax and kill them but I guess at that you could not hurt no lefthanders by hitting them over the head. We was all down on State St. the day before Xmas and the girls was all tired out and ready to go home but Allen says No I guess we better stick down a while because now the crowds is out and it will be fun to watch them. So we walked up and down State St. about a hour longer and finally we come in front of a big jewlry store window and in it was a swell dimond ring that was marked $100. It was a ladies' ring so Marie says to Allen Why don't you buy that for me? And Allen says Do you really want it? And she says she did.

So we tells the girls to wait and we goes over to a salloon where Allen has got a friend and gets a check cashed and we come back and he bought the ring. Then Florrie looks like as though she was getting all ready to cry and I asked her what was the matter and she says I had not boughten her no ring not even when we was engaged. So I and Allen goes back to the salloon and I gets a check cashed and we come back and bought another ring but I did not think the ring Allen had boughten was worth no $100 so I gets one for $75. Now Al you know I am not makeing no kick on spending a little money for a present for my own wife but I had allready boughten her a rist watch for $15 and a rist watch was just what she had wanted. I was willing to give her the ring if she had not of wanted the rist watch more than the ring but when I give her the ring I kept the rist watch and did not tell her nothing about it.

Well I come downtown alone the day after Xmas and they would not take the rist watch back in the store where I got it. So I am going to give it to her for a New Year's present and I guess that will make Allen feel like a dirty doose. But I guess you cannot hurt no lefthander's feelings at that. They are all alike. But Allen has not got nothing but a dinky curve ball and a fast ball that looks like my slow one. If Comiskey was not good hearted he would of sold him long ago.

I sent you and Bertha a cut glass dish Al which was the best I could get for the money and it was pretty high pricet at that. We was glad to get the pretty pincushions from you and Bertha and Florrie says to tell you that we are well supplied with pincushions now because the ones you sent makes a even half dozen. Thanks Al for remembering us and thank Bertha too though I guess you paid for them.

Your pal, JACK.

Chicago, Illinois, January 3.

OLD PAL: Al I been pretty sick ever since New Year's eve. We had a table at 1 of the swell resturunts downtown and I never seen so much wine drank in my life. I would rather of had beer but they would not sell us none so I found out that they was a certain kind that you can get for $1 a bottle and it is just as good as the kind that has got all them fancy names but this lefthander starts ordering some other kind about 11 oclock and it was $5 a bottle and the girls both says they liked it better. I could not see a hole lot of difference myself and I would of gave $0.20 for a big stine of my kind of beer. You know me Al. Well Al you know they is not nobody that can drink more than your old pal and I was all O. K. at one oclock but I seen the girls was getting kind of sleepy so I says we better go home.

Then Marie says Oh, shut up and don't be no quiter. I says You better shut up yourself and not be telling me to shut up, and she says What will you do if I don't shut up? And I says I would bust her in the jaw. But you know Al I would not think of busting no girl. Then Florrie says You better not start nothing because you had to much to drink or you would not be talking about busting girls in the jaw. Then I says I don't care if it is a girl I bust or a lefthander. I did not mean nothing at all Al but Marie says I had insulted Allen and he gets up and slaps my face. Well Al I am not going to stand that from nobody not even if he is my brother-in-law and a lefthander that has not got enough speed to brake a pain of glass.

So I give him a good beating and the waiters butts in and puts us all out for fighting and I and Florrie comes home in a taxi and Allen and his wife don't get in till about 5 oclock so I guess she must of had to of took him to a doctor to get fixed up. I been in bed ever since till just this morning kind of sick to my stumach. I guess I must of eat something that did not agree with me. Allen come over after breakfast this morning and asked me was I all right so I guess he is not sore over the beating I give him or else he wants to make friends because he has saw that I am a bad guy to monkey with.

Florrie tells me a little while ago that she paid the hole bill at the resturunt with my money because Allen was broke so you see what kind of a cheap skate he is Al and some day I am going to bust his jaw. She won't tell me how much the bill was and I won't ask her to no more because we had a good time outside of the fight and what do I care if we spent a little money?

Yours truly, JACK.

Chicago, Illinois, January 20.

FRIEND AL: Allen and his wife have gave up the flat across the hall from us and come over to live with us because we got a spair bedroom and why should they not have the bennifit of it? But it is pretty hard for the girls to have to cook and do the work when they is four of us so I have a hired girl who does it all for $7 a week. It is great stuff Al because now we can go round as we please and don't have to wait for no dishes to be washed or nothing. We generally almost always has dinner downtown in the evening so it is pretty soft for the girl too. She don't generally have no more than one meal to get because we generally run round downtown till late and don't get up till about noon.

That sounds funny don't it Al, when I used to get up at 5 every morning down home. Well Al I can tell you something else that may sound funny and that is that I lost my taste for beer. I don't seem to care for it no more and I found I can stand allmost as many drinks of other stuff as I could of beer. I guess Al they is not nobody ever lived can drink more and stand up better under it than me. I make the girls and Allen quit every night.

I only got just time to write you this short note because Florrie and Marie is giving a big party to-night and I and Allen have got to beat it out of the house and stay out of the way till they get things ready. It is Marie's berthday and she says she is 22 but say Al if she is 22 Kid Gleason is 30. Well Al the girls says we must blow so I will run out and mail this letter.

Yours truly, JACK.

Chicago, Illinois, Januery 31.

AL: Allen is going to take Marie with him on the training trip to California and of course Florrie has been at me to take her along. I told her postivly that she can't go. I can't afford no stunt like that but still I am up against it to know what to do with her while we are on the trip because Marie won't be here to stay with her. I don't like to leave her here all alone but they is nothing to it Al I can't afford to take her along. She says I don't see why you can't take me if Allen takes Marie. And I says That stuff is all O. K. for Allen because him and Marie has been grafting off of us all winter. And then she gets mad and tells me I should not ought to say her sister was no grafter. I did not mean nothing like that Al but you don't never know when a woman is going to take offense.

If our furniture was down in Bedford everything would be all O. K. because I could leave her there and I would feel all O. K. because I would know that you and Bertha would see that she was getting along O. K. But they would not be no sense in sending her down to a house that has not no furniture in it. I wish I knowed somewheres where she could visit Al. I would be willing to pay her bord even.

Well Al enough for this time.

Your old pal, JACK.

Chicago, Illinois, Febuery 4.

FRIEND AL: You are a real old pal Al and I certainly am greatful to you for the invatation. I have not told Florrie about it yet but I am sure she will be tickled to death and it is certainly kind of you old pal. I did not never dream of nothing like that. I note what you say Al about not excepting no bord but I think it would be better and I would feel better if you would take something say about $2 a week.

I know Bertha will like Florrie and that they will get along O. K. together because Florrie can learn her how to make her cloths look good and fix her hair and fix up her face. I feel like as if you had took a big load off of me Al and I won't never forget it.

If you don't think I should pay no bord for Florrie all right. Suit yourself about that old pal.

We are leaveing here the 20 of Febuery and if you don't mind I will bring Florrie down to you about the 18. I would like to see the old bunch again and spesially you and Bertha.

Yours, JACK.

P. S. We will only be away till April 14 and that is just a nice visit. I wish we did not have no flat on our hands.

Chicago, Illinois, Febuery 9.

OLD PAL: I want to thank you for asking Florrie to come down there and visit you Al but I find she can't get away. I did not know she had no engagements but she says she may go down to her folks in Texas and she don't want to say that she will come to visit you when it is so indefanate. So thank you just the same Al and thank Bertha too.

Florrie is still at me to take her along to California but honest Al I can't do it. I am right down to my last $50 and I have not payed no rent for this month. I owe the hired girl 2 weeks' salery and both I and Florrie needs some new cloths.

Florrie has just came in since I started writing this letter and we have been talking some more about California and she says maybe if I would ask Comiskey he would take her along as the club's guest. I had not never thought of that Al and maybe he would because he is a pretty good scout and I guess I will go and see him about it. The league has its skedule meeting here tomorrow and may be I can see him down to the hotel where they meet at. I am so worried Al that I can't write no more but I will tell you how I come out with Comiskey.

Your pal, JACK.

Chicago, Illinois, Febuery 11.

FRIEND AL: I am up against it right Al and I don't know where I am going to head in at. I went down to the hotel where the league was holding its skedule meeting at and I seen Comiskey and got some money off of the club but I owe all the money I got off of them and I am still wondering what to do about Florrie.

Comiskey was busy in the meeting when I went down there and they was not no chance to see him for a while so I and Allen and some of the boys hung round and had a few drinks and fanned. This here Joe Hill the busher that Detroit has got that Violet is hooked up to was round the hotel. I don't know what for but I felt like busting his jaw only the boys told me I had better not do nothing because I might kill him and any way he probily won't be in the league much longer. Well finally Comiskey got threw the meeting and I seen him and he says Hello young man what can I do for you? And I says I would like to get $100 advance money. He says Have you been takeing care of yourself down in Bedford? And I told him I had been liveing here all winter and it did not seem to make no hit with him though I don't see what business it is of hisn where I live.

So I says I had been takeing good care of myself. And I have Al. You know that. So he says I should come to the ball park the next day which is today and he would have the secretary take care of me but I says I could not wait and so he give me $100 out of his pocket and says he would have it charged against my salery. I was just going to brace him about the California trip when he got away and went back to the meeting.

Well Al I hung round with the bunch waiting for him to get threw again and we had some more drinks and finally Comiskey was threw again and I braced him in the lobby and asked him if it was all right to take my wife along to California. He says Sure they would be glad to have her along. And then I says Would the club pay her fair? He says I guess you must of spent that $100 buying some nerve: He says Have you not got no sisters that would like to go along to? He says Does your wife insist on the drawing room or will she take a lower birth? He says Is my special train good enough for her?

Then he turns away from me and I guess some of the boys must of heard the stuff he pulled because they was laughing when he went away but I did not see nothing to laugh at. But I guess he ment that I would have to pay her fair if she goes along and that is out of the question Al. I am up against it and I don't know where I am going to head in at.

Your pal, JACK.

Chicago, Illinois, Febuery 12.

DEAR OLD AL: I guess everthing will be all O. K. now at least I am hopeing it will. When I told Florrie about how I come out with Comiskey she bawled her head off and I thought for a while I was going to have to call a doctor or something but pretty soon she cut it out and we sat there a while without saying nothing. Then she says If you could get your salery razed a couple of hundred dollars a year would you borrow the money ahead somewheres and take me along to California? I says Yes I would if I could get a couple hundred dollars more salery but how could I do that when I had signed a contract for $2800 last fall allready? She says Don't you think you are worth more than $2800? And I says Yes of coarse I was worth more than $2800. She says Well if you will go and talk the right way to Comiskey I believe he will give you $3000 but you must be sure you go at it the right way and don't go and ball it all up.

Well we argude about it a while because I don't want to hold nobody up Al but finally I says I would. It would not be holding nobody up anyway because I am worth $3000 to the club if I am worth a nichol. The papers is all saying that the club has got a good chance to win the pennant this year and talking about the pitching staff and I guess they would not be no pitching staff much if it was not for I and one or two others—about one other I guess.

So it looks like as if everything will be all O. K. now Al. I am going to the office over to the park to see him the first thing in the morning and I am pretty sure that I will get what I am after because if I do not he will see that I am going to quit and then he will see what he is up against and not let me get away.

I will let you know how I come out.

Your pal, JACK.

Chicago, Illinois, Febuery 14.

FRIEND AL: Al old pal I have got a big supprise for you. I am going to the Federal League. I had a run in with Comiskey yesterday and I guess I told him a thing or 2. I guess he would of been glad to sign me at my own figure before I got threw but I was so mad I would not give him no chance to offer me another contract.

I got out to the park at 9 oclock yesterday morning and it was a hour before he showed up and then he kept me waiting another hour before he showed up and then he kept me waiting another hour so I was pretty sore when I finally went in to see him. He says Well young man what can I do for you? I says I come to see about my contract. He says Do you want to sign up for next year all ready? I says No I am talking about this year. He says I thought I and you talked business last fall. And I says Yes but now I think I am worth more money and I want to sign a contract for $3000. He says If you behave yourself and work good this year I will see that you are took care of. But I says That won't do because I have got to be sure I am going to get $3000.

Then he says I am not sure you are going to get anything. I says What do you mean? And he says I have gave you a very fare contract and if you don't want to live up to it that is your own business. So I give him a awful call Al and told him I would jump to the Federal League. He says Oh, I would not do that if I was you. They are having a hard enough time as it is. So I says something back to him and he did not say nothing to me and I beat it out of the office.

I have not told Florrie about the Federal League business yet as I am going to give her a big supprise. I bet they will take her along with me on the training trip and pay her fair but even if they don't I should not worry because I will make them give me a contract for $4000 a year and then I can afford to take her with me on all the trips.

I will go down and see Tinker to-morrow morning and I will write you to-morrow night Al how much salery they are going to give me. But I won't sign for no less than $4000. You know me Al.

Yours, JACK.

Chicago, Illinois, Febuery 15.

OLD PAL: It is pretty near midnight Al but I been to bed a couple of times and I can't get no sleep. I am worried to death Al and I don't know where I am going to head in at. Maybe I will go out and buy a gun Al and end it all and I guess it would be better for everybody. But I cannot do that Al because I have not got the money to buy a gun with.

I went down to see Tinker about signing up with the Federal League and he was busy in the office when I come in. Pretty soon Buck Perry the pitcher that was with Boston last year come out and seen me and as Tinker was still busy we went out and had a drink together. Buck shows me a contract for $5000 a year and Tinker had allso gave him a $500 bonus. So pretty soon I went up to the office and pretty soon Tinker seen me and called me into his private office and asked what did I want. I says I was ready to jump for $4000 and a bonus. He says I thought you was signed up with the White Sox. I says Yes I was but I was not satisfied. He says That does not make no difference to me if you are satisfied or not. You ought to of came to me before you signed a contract. I says I did not know enough but I know better now. He says Well it is to late now. We cannot have nothing to do with you because you have went and signed a contract with the White Sox. I argude with him a while and asked him to come out and have a drink so we could talk it over but he said he was busy so they was nothing for me to do but blow.

So I am not going to the Federal League Al and I will not go with the White Sox because I have got a raw deal. Comiskey will be sorry for what he done when his team starts the season and is up against it for good pitchers and then he will probily be willing to give me anything I ask for but that don't do me no good now Al. I am way in debt and no chance to get no money from nobody. I wish I had of stayed with Terre Haute Al and never saw this league.

Your pal, JACK.

Chicago, Illinois, Febuery 17.

FRIEND AL: Al don't never let nobody tell you that these here lefthanders is right. This Allen my own brother-in-law who married sisters has been grafting and spongeing on me all winter Al. Look what he done to me now Al. You know how hard I been up against it for money and I know he has got plenty of it because I seen it on him. Well Al I was scared to tell Florrie I was cleaned out and so I went to Allen yesterday and says I had to have $100 right away because I owed the rent and owed the hired girl's salery and could not even pay no grocery bill. And he says No he could not let me have none because he has got to save all his money to take his wife on the trip to California. And here he has been liveing on me all winter and maybe I could of took my wife to California if I had not of spent all my money takeing care of this no good lefthander and his wife. And Al honest he has not got a thing and ought not to be in the league. He gets by with a dinky curve ball and has not got no more smoke than a rabbit or something.

Well Al I felt like busting him in the jaw but then I thought No I might kill him and then I would have Marie and Florrie both to take care of and God knows one of them is enough besides paying his funeral expenses. So I walked away from him without takeing a crack at him and went into the other room where Florrie and Marie was at. I says to Marie I says Marie I wish you would go in the other room a minute because I want to talk to Florrie. So Marie beats it into the other room and then I tells Florrie all about what Comiskey and the Federal League done to me. She bawled something awful and then she says I was no good and she wished she had not never married me. I says I wisht it too and then she says Do you mean that and starts to cry.

I told her I was sorry I says that because they is not no use fusing with girls Al specially when they is your wife. She says No California trip for me and then she says What are you going to do? And I says I did not know. She says Well if I was a man I would do something. So then I got mad and I says I will do something. So I went down to the corner salloon and started in to get good and drunk but I could not do it Al because I did not have the money.

Well old pal I am going to ask you a big favor and it is this I want you to send me $100 Al for just a few days till I can get on my feet. I do not know when I can pay it back Al but I guess you know the money is good and I know you have got it. Who would not have it when they live in Bedford? And besides I let you take $20 in June 4 years ago Al and you give it back but I would not have said nothing to you if you had of kept it. Let me hear from you right away old pal.

Yours truly, JACK.

Chicago, Illinois, Febuery 19.
AL: I am certainly greatful to you Al for the $100 which come just a little while ago. I will pay the rent with it and part of the grocery bill

and I guess the hired girl will have to wait a while for hern but she is sure to get it because I don't never forget my debts. I have changed my mind about the White Sox and I am going to go on the trip and take Florrie along because I don't think it would not be right to leave her here alone in Chi when her sister and all of us is going.

I am going over to the ball park and up in the office pretty soon to see about it. I will tell Comiskey I changed my mind and he will be glad to get me back because the club has not got no chance to finish nowheres without me. But I won't go on no trip or give the club my services without them giveing me some more advance money so as I can take Florrie along with me because Al I would not go without her.

Maybe Comiskey will make my salery $3000 like I wanted him to when he sees I am willing to be a good fellow and go along with him and when he knows that the Federal League would of gladly gave me $4000 if I had not of signed no contract with the White Sox.

I think I will ask him for $200 advance money Al and if I get it may be I can send part of your $100 back to you but I know you cannot be in no hurry Al though you says you wanted it back as soon as possible. You could not be very hard up Al because it don't cost near so much to live in Bedford as it does up here.

Anyway I will let you know how I come out with Comiskey and I will write you as soon as I get out to Paso Robles if I don't get no time to write you before I leave.

Your pal, JACK.

P. S. I have took good care of myself all winter Al and I guess I ought to have a great season.

P. S. Florrie is tickled to death about going along and her and I will have some time together out there on the Coast if I can get some money somewheres.

Chicago, Illinois, Febuery 21.

FRIEND AL: I have not got the heart to write this letter to you Al. I am up here in my $42.50 a month flat and the club has went to California and Florrie has went too. I am flat broke Al and all I am asking you is to send me enough money to pay my fair to Bedford and they and all their leagues can go to hell Al.

I was out to the ball park early yesterday morning and some of the boys was there allready fanning and kidding each other. They tried to kid me to when I come in but I guess I give them as good as they give me. I was not in no mind for kidding Al because I was there on business and I wanted to see Comiskey and get it done with.

Well the secretary come in finally and I went up to him and says I wanted to see Comiskey right away. He says The boss was busy and what did I want to see him about and I says I wanted to get some advance money because I was going to take my wife on the trip. He says This would be a fine time to be telling us about it even if you was going on the trip.

And I says What do you mean? And he says You are not going on no trip with us because we have got wavers on you and you are sold to Milwaukee.

Honest Al I thought he was kidding at first and I was waiting for him to laugh but he did not laugh and finally I says What do you mean? And he says Cannot you understand no English? You are sold to Milwaukee. Then I says I want to see the boss. He says It won't do you no good to see the boss and he is to busy to see you. I says I want to get some money. And he says You cannot get no money from this club and all you get is your fair to Milwaukee. I says I am not going to no Milwaukee anyway and he says I should not worry about that. Suit yourself.

Well Al I told some of the boys about it and they was pretty sore and says I ought to bust the secretary in the jaw and I was going to do it when I thought No I better not because he is a little guy and I might kill him.

I looked all over for Kid Gleason but he was not nowheres round and they told me he would not get into town till late in the afternoon. If I could of saw him Al he would of fixed me all up. I asked 3 or 4 of the boys for some money but they says they was all broke.

But I have not told you the worst of it yet Al. When I come back to the flat Allen and Marie and Florrie was busy packing up and they asked me how I come out. I told them and Allen just stood there stareing like a big rummy but Marie and Florrie both begin to cry and I almost felt like as if I would like to cry to only I am not no baby Al.

Well Al I told Florrie she might just as well quit packing and make up her mind that she was not going nowheres till I got money enough to go to Bedford where I belong. She kept right on crying and it got so I could not stand it no more so I went out to get a drink because I still had just about a dollar left yet.

It was about 2 oclock when I left the flat and pretty near 5 when I come back because I had ran in to some fans that knowed who I was and would not let me get away and besides I did not want to see no more of Allen and Marie till they was out of the house and on their way.

But when I come in Al they was nobody there. They was not nothing there except the furniture and a few of my things scattered round. I sit down for a few minutes because I guess I must of had to much to drink but finally I seen a note on the table addressed to me and I seen it was Florrie's writeing.

I do not remember just what was there in the note Al because I tore it up the minute I read it but it was something about I could not support no wife and Allen had gave her enough money to go back to Texas and she was going on the 6 oclock train and it would not do me no good to try and stop her.

Well Al they was not no danger of me trying to stop her. She was not no good Al and I wisht I had not of never saw either she or her sister or my brother-in-law.

For a minute I thought I would follow Allen and his wife down to the deepo where the special train was to pull out of and wait till I see him and punch his jaw but I seen that would not get me nothing.

So here I am all alone Al and I will have to stay here till you send me the money to come home. You better send me $25 because I have got a few little debts I should ought to pay before I leave town. I am not going to Milwaukee Al because I did not get no decent deal and nobody cannot make no sucker out of me.

Please hurry up with the $25 Al old friend because I am sick and tired of Chi and want to get back there with my old pal.

Yours, JACK.

P. S. Al I wish I had of took poor little Violet when she was so stuck on me.

Marianne Moore

*

CORRESPONDENCE WITH DAVID WALLACE

The Ford letters were composed by Mr. David Wallace but, with one exception, were transmitted over the signature of his associate, Mr. Robert B. Young. Addresses have been omitted here after the first exchange of letters.

The Ford letters should correct an impression persisting among inquirers that I succeeded in finding for the special new products division of an eminent manufacturer a name for the car I had been recruited to name; whereas I did not give the car the name it now has.

—MARIANNE MOORE

THE FORD CORRESPONDENCE

FORD MOTOR COMPANY
DEARBORN, MICHIGAN

October 19, 1955

Dear Miss Moore:

This is a morning we find ourselves with a problem which, strangely enough, is more in the field of words and the fragile meaning of words than in car-making. And we just wonder whether you might be intrigued with it sufficiently to lend us a hand.

Our dilemma is a name for a rather important new series of cars.

We should like this name to be more than a label. Specifically, we should like it to have a compelling quality in itself and by itself. To convey, through association or other conjuration, some visceral feeling of elegance, fleetness, and advanced features and design. A name, in short, that flashes a dramatically desirable picture in people's minds.

Over the past few weeks this office has confected a list of three hundred-odd candidates which, it pains me to relate, are characterized by an embarrassing pedestrianism. We are miles short of our ambition. And so we are seeking the help of one who knows more about this sort of magic than we.

As to how we might go about this matter, I have no idea. One possibility is that you might care to visit with us and muse with the new Wonder which now is in clay in our Advance Styling Studios. But, in any event, all would depend on whether you find this overture of some challenge and interest.

Should we be so fortunate as to have piqued your fancy, we will be pleased to write more fully. In summary, all we want is a colossal name (another "Thunderbird" would be fine). And, of course, it is expected that our relations will be on a fee basis of an impeccably dignified kind.

> Respectfully,
> Robert B. Young
> Marketing Research Department

Miss Marianne Moore
260 Cumberland Street
Brooklyn 5, New York

> October 21, 1955

Let me take it under advisement, Mr. Young. I am complimented to be recruited in this high matter.

I have seen and admired "Thunderbird" as a Ford designation. It would be hard to match; but let me, the coming week, talk with my brother who would bring ardor and imagination to bear on the quest.

> Sincerely yours
> and your wife's*
> Marianne Moore

Mr. Robert B. Young
Marketing Research Division / Special Products Division
Ford Motor Company
P.O. Box 637 / 16400 Michigan Avenue
Dearborn, Michigan

> October 27, 1955

Dear Mr. Young:

My brother thought most of the names I had considered suggesting to you for your new series, too learned or too labored, but thinks I

---

* Mr. Young's wife had met Miss Moore at luncheon at Mount Holyoke College. His first letter was reinforced by one from Mrs. Young, written on the same date, recalling the incident.

might ask if any of the following approximate the requirements.

THE FORD SILVER SWORD

This plant, of which the flower is a silver sword, I believe grows only in Tibet, and on the Hawaiian Island, Maui, on Mount Háleákalá (House of the Sun); found at an altitude of from 9,500 to 10,000 feet. (The leaves —silver-white—surrounding the individual blossoms have a pebbled texture that feels like Italian-twist back-stitch all-over embroidery).

My first thought was of a bird series—the swallow species—Hirundo or phonetically, Aërundo. Malvina Hoffman is designing a device for the radiator of a made-to-order Cadillac, and said in her opinion the only term surpassing Thunder-bird would be hurricane; and I then thought Hurricane Hirundo might be the first of a series such as Hurricane aquila (eagle), Hurricane accipiter (hawk), and so on. "A species that takes its dinner on the wing" ("swifts").

If these suggestions are not in character with the car, perhaps you could give me a sketch of its general appearance, or hint as to some of its exciting possibilities—though my brother reminds me that such information is highly confidential.

Sincerely yours,
Marianne Moore

November 4, 1955

Dear Miss Moore:

I'm delighted that your note implies that you are interested in helping us in our naming problem.

This being so, in compliance with procedures in this rigorous business world, I think we should make some definite arrangement for payment of a suitable fee or honorarium before pursuing the problem further.

One way might be for you to suggest a figure which could be considered for mutual acceptance. Once this is squared away, we will look forward to having you join us in continuing our fascinating search.

Sincerely yours,
Robert B. Young
Marketing Research

November 7, 1955

Dear Mr. Young:

It is handsome of you to consider remuneration for service merely enlisted. My fancy would be inhibited, however, by acknowledgment in advance of performance. If I could be of specific assistance, we could no doubt agree on some kind of honorarium for the service rendered.

I seem to exact participation; but if you could tell me how the suggestions submitted strayed—if obviously—from the ideal, I could then perhaps proceed more nearly in keeping with the Company's objective.

Sincerely yours,
Marianne Moore

November 11, 1955

Dear Miss Moore:

The Youngs' philodendron has just benefited from an extra measure of water as, pacing about the room, I have sought words to respond to your generous note.

Let me state my quandary thus. It is unspeakably contrary to Procedures here to accept counsel—even needed counsel—without a firm prior arrangement of conditions (and, indeed, without a Purchase Notice in quadruplicate and three competitive bids). But then, seldom has the auto business had occasion to indulge in so ethereal a matter as this.

So, if you will risk a mutually satisfactory outcome with us, we should like to honor your wish for a fancy unencumbered.

As to wherein your earlier suggestions may have "strayed," as you put it—they did not at all. We merely proposed a recess in production for orderly bookkeeping. Shipment 1 was fine and we would like to luxuriate in more of same. Even those your brother regarded as overlearned or labored.

For us to impose an ideal on your efforts would, I fear, merely defeat our purpose. We have sought your help to get an approach quite different from our own. In short, we should like suggestions that we ourselves would not have arrived at. And, in sober fact, have not arrived at.

Now we on this end must help you by sending some tangible representation of what we are talking about. Your brother was right; advance designs in Dearborn are something approaching the Sacred. But perhaps the enclosed sketches will serve the purpose. They are not IT, but they convey the feeling.

At the very least, they may give you a sense of participation should your friend, Malvina Hoffman, break into brisk conversation on radiator caps.

Sincerely yours,
Robert B. Young
Marketing Research

November 13, 1955

Dear Mr. Young:

The sketches. They are indeed exciting; they have quality, and the toucan tones lend tremendous allure—confirmed by the wheels. Half the magic—sustaining effects of this kind. Looked at upside down, furthermore, there is a sense of fish buoyancy. Immediately your word impeccable sprang to mind. Might it be a possibility? The Impeccable. In any case, the baguette lapidary glamor you have achieved certainly spurs the imagination. Car-innovation is like launching a ship— "drama."

I am by no means sure that I can help you to the right thing, but performance with elegance casts a spell. Let me do some thinking in the direction of the impeccable, symmechromatic, thunderblender. . . . (The exotics if I can shape them a little.) Dearborn might come into one.

If the sketches should be returned at once, let me know. Otherwise, let me dwell on them for a time. I am, may I say, a trusty confidant.

I thank you for realizing that under contract esprit could not flower. You owe me nothing, specific or moral.

Sincerely yours,
Marianne Moore

Some other suggestions, Mr. Young, for the phenomenon:
THE RESILIENT BULLET
or intelligent bullet
or bullet cloisonné   or bullet lavolta
(I have always had a fancy for THE INTELLIGENT WHALE— the little first Navy submarine, shaped like a sweet-potato; on view in our Brooklyn Yard).

THE FORD FABERGÉ (that there is also a perfume FABERGÉ seems to me to do no harm here, allusion to the original silversmith).

THE ARC-en-CIEL (the rainbow)   ARCENCIEL?

Please do not feel that memoranda from me need acknowledgment. I am not working day and night for you; I feel that etymological hits are partially accidental.

Sincerely yours,
Marianne Moore

The bullet idea has possibilities, it seems to me, in connection with mercury (with Hermes and Hermes trismegistus) and magic (white magic).

I seem to admire variety in the sections of your address!

November 28, 1955

TO: Mr. Robert B. Young
From: Marianne Moore
  MONGOOSE CIVIQUE
  ANTICIPATOR
  REGNA RACER (couronne à couronne) sovereign to sovereign
  AEROTERRE
  fée rapide (acrofère, aero faire, fée aiglette, magifaire) comme il faire
  tonnere alifère (wingèd thunder)
  aliforme alifère (wing-slender a-wing)
  TURBOTORC (used as an adjective by Plymouth)
  THUNDERBIRD allié (Cousin Thunderbird)
  THUNDER CRESTER
  DEARBORN diamanté
  MAGIGRAVURE
  PASTELOGRAM
  I shall be returning the sketches very soon.
                                 M.M.

December 6, 1955

TO: Mr. Robert B. Young
From: Marianne Moore
  regina-rex   astranaut
  taper-racer   taper acer   chaparral
  Varsity Stroke   tir à l'arc (bull's eye)
  angelastro   cresta lark
  triskelion (three legs running)
  pluma piluma (hairfine, feather-foot)
  andante con moto (description of a good motor?)

    My findings thin, so I terminate them and am returning the sketches—two pastels, two photos: from Mr. M. H. Lieblich.

    Two principles I have not been able to capture: 1. The topknot of the peacock and topnotcher of speed. 2. The swivel-axis (emphasized elsewhere)—like the Captain's bed on the whale-ship Charles Morgan—balanced so that it leveled, whatever the slant of the ship.

    If I stumble on a hit, you shall have it. Anything so far has been pastime. Do not ponder appreciation, Mr. Young. That was embodied in the sketches.

                                   M.M.
                                  (over)

I can not resist the temptation to disobey my brother and submit

TURCOTINGO (turquoise cotinga—the cotinga being a solid in-
digo South American finch or sparrow)

I have a three-volume treatise on flowers that might produce something but the impression given should certainly be unlabored.

M.M.

December 8, 1955

Mr. Young:

May I submit UTOPIAN TURTLETOP?
Do not trouble to answer unless you like it.

Marianne Moore

*The Ford Motor Company's response to this final suggestion was a
floral tribute composed of twenty-four roses and white pine and spiral
eucalyptus. The accompanying florist's Christmas card bore the greeting:*
TO OUR FAVORITE TURTLETOPPER

December 26, 1955

Dear Mr. Young:

An aspiring turtle is certain to glory in spiral eucalyptus, white pine
straight from the forest, and innumerable scarlet roses almost too tall for
close inspection. Of a temperament susceptible to shock though one may
be, to be treated like royalty could not but induce sensations unprece-
dently august.

Please know that a carfancyer's allegiance to the Ford automotive
turtle—extending from the Model T Dynasty to the Young Utopian
Dynasty—can never waver; impersonal gratitude surely becoming infinite when made personal. Gratitude to unmiserly Mr. Young and his
idealistic associates.

Marianne Moore

January 17, 1956

Dear Miss Moore:

Please excuse my long delay in responding to your generous notes.
Our label is still in a state of indecision. Contributions have been entered
from many directions, and those from our "favorite turtletopper" rate
among the most interesting of all.

We can scarcely begin to thank you for your interest and munifi-
cent help in our dilemma. The art of precise word picking is rarely joined
with the mechanical genius of our automotive personnel. Your aid in
this respect has been invaluable.

I hope you are entering another happy and healthy new year. Wishing you the best of everything. I remain your faithful utopian.

Robert B. Young
Marketing Research

November 8, 1956

Dear Miss Moore:

Because you were so kind to us in our early and hopeful days of looking for a suitable name, I feel a deep obligation to report on events that have ensued.

And I feel I must do so before the public announcement of same come Monday, November 19.

We have chosen a name out of the more than six-thousand-odd candidates that we gathered. It has a certain ring to it. An air of gaiety and zest. At least, that's what we keep saying. Our name, dear Miss Moore, is—Edsel.

I know you will share your sympathies with us.

Cordially,
David Wallace, Manager
Marketing Research

P.S. Our Mr. Robert Young, who corresponded with you earlier, is now and temporarily, we hope, in the service of our glorious U.S. Coast Guard.

I know he would send his best.

DW

November 11, 1956

Dear Mr. Wallace:

I thank you for the letter just received from you, of November 8th.

You have the certainly ideal thing—with the Ford identity indigenously symbolized. (I am a little piqued that I concentrated on physical phenomena.) At all events, thank you for informing me of the Company's choice—a matter to me of keen interest. Am quite partisan. I do wish the Company designs to "lead."

Sincerely yours,
Marianne Moore

Mr. Young is possessed of esprit and I hope is thriving.

Robert Benchley

*

OPERA SYNOPSES

SOME SAMPLE OUTLINES OF
GRAND OPERA PLOTS FOR HOME STUDY

I

DIE MEISTER-GENOSSENSCHAFT

SCENE: *The Forests of Germany.*
TIME: *Antiquity.*

CAST

STRUDEL, *God of Rain* . . . . Basso
SCHMALZ, *God of Slight Drizzle* . . . . Tenor
IMMERGLÜCK, *Goddess of the Six Primary Colors* . . . . Soprano
LUDWIG DAS EIWEISS, *the Knight of the Iron Duck* . . . . Baritone
THE WOODPECKER . . . . Soprano

ARGUMENT

The basis of "Die Meister-Genossenschaft" is an old legend of Germany which tells how the Whale got his Stomach.

ACT 1

The Rhine at Low Tide Just Below Weldschnoffen.—Immerglück has grown weary of always sitting on the same rock with the same fishes swimming by every day, and sends for Schwül to suggest something to do. Schwül asks her how she would like to have pass before her all the wonders of the world fashioned by the hand of man. She says, rotten. He then suggests that Ringblattz, son of Pflucht, be made to appear before her and fight a mortal combat with the Iron Duck. This pleases Immerglück and she summons to her the four dwarfs: Hot Water, Cold

Water, Cool, and Cloudy. She bids them bring Ringblattz to her. They refuse, because Pflucht has at one time rescued them from being buried alive by acorns, and, in a rage, Immerglück strikes them all dead with a thunderbolt.

ACT 2

A Mountain Pass.—Repenting of her deed, Immerglück has sought advice of the giants, Offen and Besitz, and they tell her that she must procure the magic zither which confers upon its owner the power to go to sleep while apparently carrying on a conversation. This magic zither has been hidden for three hundred centuries in an old bureau drawer, guarded by the Iron Duck, and, although many have attempted to rescue it, all have died of a strange ailment just as success was within their grasp.

But Immerglück calls to her side Dampfboot, the tinsmith of the gods, and bids him make for her a tarnhelm or invisible cap which will enable her to talk to people without their understanding a word she says. For a dollar and a half extra Dampfboot throws in a magic ring which renders its wearer insensible. Thus armed, Immerglück starts out for Walhalla, humming to herself.

ACT 3

The Forest Before the Iron Duck's Bureau Drawer.—Merglitz, who has up till this time held his peace, now descends from a balloon and demands the release of Betty. It has been the will of Wotan that Merglitz and Betty should meet on earth and hate each other like poison, but Zweiback, the druggist of the gods, has disobeyed and concocted a love-potion which has rendered the young couple very unpleasant company. Wotan, enraged, destroys them with a protracted heat spell.

Encouraged by this sudden turn of affairs, Immerglück comes to earth in a boat drawn by four white Holsteins, and, seated alone on a rock, remembers aloud to herself the days when she was a girl. Pilgrims from Augenblick, on their way to worship at the shrine of Schmürr, hear the sound of reminiscence coming from the rock and stop in their march to sing a hymn of praise for the drying-up of the crops. They do not recognize Immerglück, as she has her hair done differently, and think that she is a beggar girl selling pencils.

In the meantime, Ragel, the papercutter of the gods, has fashioned himself a sword on the forge of Schmalz, and has called the weapon "Assistance-in-Emergency." Armed with "Assistance-in-Emergency" he comes to earth, determined to slay the Iron Duck and carry off the beautiful Irma.

But Frimsel overhears the plan and has a drink brewed which is given to Ragel in a golden goblet and which, when drunk, makes him forget his past and causes him to believe that he is Schnorr, the God of Fun. While laboring under this spell, Ragel has a funeral pyre built on the summit of a high mountain and, after lighting it, climbs on top of it with a mandolin which he plays until he is consumed.

Immerglück never marries.

II

IL MINNESTRONE
(PEASANT LOVE)

SCENE: *Venice and Old Point Comfort.*
TIME: *Early 16th Century.*

CAST

ALFONSO, *Duke of Minnestrone* .... Baritone
PARTOLA, *a Peasant Girl* .... Soprano

CLEANSO ⎫   ⎧ Tenor
TURINO ⎬ *Young Noblemen of Venice* ⎨ Tenor
BOMBO   ⎭   ⎩ Basso

LUDOVICO ⎫ *Assassins in the Service of* ⎰ Basso
ASTOLFO ⎭   *Cafeteria Rusticana*   ⎱ Methodist
         Townspeople, Cabbies and Sparrows

ARGUMENT

"Il Minnestrone" is an allegory of the two sides of a man's nature (good and bad), ending at last in an awfully comical mess with everyone dead.

ACT 1

A *Public Square, Ferrara.*—During a peasant festival held to celebrate the sixth consecutive day of rain, Rudolpho, a young nobleman, sees Lilliano, daughter of the village bell-ringer, dancing along throwing artificial roses at herself. He asks of his secretary who the young woman is, and his secretary, in order to confuse Rudolpho and thereby win the hand of his ward, tells him that it is his (Rudolpho's) own mother, disguised for the festival. Rudolpho is astounded. He orders her arrest.

ACT 2

Banquet Hall in Gorgio's Palace.—Lilliano has not forgotten Breda, her old nurse, in spite of her troubles, and determines to avenge herself for the many insults she received in her youth by poisoning her (Breda). She therefore invites the old nurse to a banquet and poisons her. Presently a knock is heard. It is Ugolfo. He has come to carry away the body of Michelo and to leave an extra quart of pasteurized. Lilliano tells him that she no longer loves him, at which he goes away, dragging his feet sulkily.

ACT 3

In Front of Emilo's House.—Still thinking of the old man's curse, Borsa has an interview with Cleanso, believing him to be the Duke's wife. He tells him things can't go on as they are, and Cleanso stabs him. Just at this moment Betty comes rushing in from school and falls in a faint. Her worst fears have been realized. She has been insulted by Sigmundo, and presently dies of old age. In a fury, Ugolfo rushes out to kill Sigmundo and, as he does so, the dying Rosenblatt rises on one elbow and curses his mother.

III
LUCY DE LIMA

SCENE: *Wales.*

TIME: 1700 *(Greenwich).*

CAST

WILLIAM WONT, *Lord of Glennnn* .... Basso
LUCY WAGSTAFF, *his daughter* .... Soprano
BERTRAM, *her lover* .... Tenor
LORD ROGER, *friend of Bertram* .... Soprano
IRMA, *attendant to Lucy* .... Basso
Friends, Retainers, and Members of the local Lodge of Elks.

ARGUMENT

"Lucy de Lima" is founded on the well-known story by Boccaccio of the same name and address.

George S. Kaufman

*

IF MEN PLAYED CARDS
AS WOMEN DO

The scene is JOHN'S *home—the living room. There are two doors, one leading to an outside hall, the other to the other rooms of the house. A card table has been set up in the middle of the room, with four chairs around it, and above it is another table on which are piled the necessary adjuncts for a poker game—a fancy cover for the table, cards, chips, a humidor. For the rest, you have only to imagine an average and good-looking room.*

As the curtain rises, JOHN *enters from another room, then turns and calls back through the open door, as though he had forgotten something.*

IMPERTINENCE FROM THE AUTHOR: *It is perhaps unnecessary to remark that the sketch derives its entire value from the fact that it is played in forthright and manly fashion. In other words, the actors must not imitate the voices of women.*

JOHN: And don't forget, I want things served very nicely. Use the best china and the filigree doilies. (*He starts to close the door—remembers another instruction.*) And at eleven o'clock just put the cigars and drinks right on the table and we'll stop playing. (*He closes the door and advances into the room. He looks the place over; rubs a suspecting finger along the table top in a quest for dust. He moves one chair a fraction of an inch and seems to think that that makes a difference in the appearance of the room. Then there comes a knock on the outer door.* JOHN *darts to the mirror and takes a quick look at himself; adjusts his tie.*) Come in! (BOB *enters.*) Hello, Bob!

BOB: Hello, John! I thought I'd run over early to see if I could help you with the lunch.

JOHN: Thanks—everything is ready. I baked a cake. Oh, say! That's a new hat, isn't it?

BOB: Why, no—don't you remember? It's the one I got at Knox's in the Spring. Then when they began wearing the bands higher, I said to myself, why should I buy a new hat when I can have a man in and get him to put on another band for me, just as easily as not? Do you like it?

JOHN: Very attractive. I wonder how it would look on me? (*Takes it; starts to try it on, then smooths his hair before he finally puts it on. He looks at himself in the mirror; turns.*) What do you think?

BOB: Lovely! Makes your face look thinner. (*Looks at the card table.*) Who's playing tonight?

JOHN: George and Marc.

BOB: Really? (*He takes his seat.*) Tell me—don't you think George is looking older these days? How are he and Ethel getting along? Any better?

JOHN: Not as good.

BOB: Funny what she saw in him. (*There is a knock on the door.*)

JOHN: Come in! (GEORGE *enters.*)

GEORGE: (*Greatly surprised, as though they were the last people he had expected to see*) Hello, boys!

JOHN: Hello, George! Well, well, well!

BOB: (*Rises*) Hello, George! Never saw you look so young!

GEORGE: (*In great excitement*) Say, I just met Ed Jennings down the street and what do you think? He says Jim Perkins told him that Will Harper's wife may leave him!

BOB: You don't say so! (*Sits again.*)

GEORGE: What do you think of that? (*His excitement dies a little; he looks around.*) The room looks lovely, John. You've changed things around, haven't you? Awfully nice. But if you don't mind just a little suggestion—I'm not sure that I like that table up there where you've got it. (*Another critical look.*) And if you had these chairs re-upholstered in blue—

JOHN: Well, what do you think of a plain chintz?

GEORGE: That would be nice. Oh, say! I've got a T.L. for you, Bob.

BOB: Oh, good! What is it?

GEORGE: Well, you owe me one first.

BOB: Oh, tell me mine! Don't be mean!

GEORGE: Well, all right. Frank Williams said you looked lovely in your dinner coat.

BOB: That *is* nice.

JOHN: How's the baby, George?

GEORGE: Awfully cranky lately. He's teething. I left him with the nurse tonight—first chance I've had to get out. (*Takes a seat at the table.*) Who else is coming?

JOHN: Just Marc.

GEORGE: (*With meaning*) Oh, is he? I want to speak to you boys about Marc. Don't you think he's been seeing a lot of that Fleming woman lately?

BOB: He certainly has. He was at the Biltmore, having tea with her yesterday—I know because a cousin of Tom Hennessey's saw him.

JOHN: Which cousin is that?

BOB: I don't know whether you know him—Ralph Wilson. He married that Akron girl—they have two children.

GEORGE: *You* remember—one of them is backward.

JOHN: Oh, yes! I heard that. (*Another knock on the door.*) Come in! (MARC *enters.*)

MARC: Hello, everybody!

GEORGE, JOHN *and* BOB: Hello, Marc!

MARC: I'm sorry to be the last, but we have a new maid, and you know what that means.

JOHN: That's all right. Say, I like the cut of that vest, Marc. Look, boys! Don't you like that vest?

MARC: It is nice, isn't it?

GEORGE: Oh, lovely! Turn around and let's see the back. (GEORGE *and* JOHN *both get up and examine his clothes, pull down his trousers, etc.*)

MARC: I had it made right in the house—I have a little tailor that comes in. Four dollars a day.

GEORGE: Excuse me—there's a little spot—(*He moistens a finger and rubs* MARC'S *lapel.*)

JOHN: Well, shall we play a little poker?

MARC: (*Sitting*) Yes, sure. Oh, John, may I trouble you for a glass of water?

JOHN: Why, of course, Marc. (GEORGE *and* BOB *sit again.*)

MARC: I'll get it myself if you'll tell me where—

JOHN: Oh, no—that's all right. (*He goes out. A pause. The men look at each other, meaningfully. Their heads come together.*)

MARC: John doesn't look well, does he?

BOB: No. Did you notice those lines? He can't hide them much longer.

MARC: He was very good-looking as a boy.

GEORGE: Isn't this room the most terrible thing you ever saw?

(MARC *goes to the table up stage; picks up a cigar and shows it to the others. They are scornful.*)

MARC: Huh! Ten cents. (*Pause.*) I really wanted to get that water myself. I'd like to see his kitchen. (JOHN *re-enters with the water.*) Oh, thanks, John. (MARC *drinks.*)

JOHN: Is it cold enough, Marc?

MARC: (*Indicating that it isn't*) Oh, yes. Of course, I generally put ice in, myself. (*Sits.*)

GEORGE: Say, we had the loveliest new dessert tonight!

BOB: Oh! What was it? It's awfully hard to find a new dessert.

MARC: (*With emphasis*) Is it?

GEORGE: Well, it was a sort of prune whip. You make it out of just nothing at all. And then, if company comes when you don't expect them—

BOB: I want the recipe.

MARC: How many eggs?

(JOHN *up at the rear table. Turns on this speech.*)

JOHN: Does it take much butter?

GEORGE: Oh, no—very little. I'll bring you the recipe Tuesday afternoon.

(MARC *feels a rough place on his chin. Rubs it, then takes a good-sized mirror out of his pocket and stands it on the table. Examines his chin. Then takes out a safety razor and starts to shave. After that he takes out two military brushes and combs his hair. The others pay no attention to this. JOHN is at the rear table, with his back to the audience; BOB is seated, fooling with the cards; GEORGE is seated, calmly smoking. After MARC has put everything away, BOB breaks the silence.*)

BOB: Are we ready?

JOHN: No! Wait just a minute. (*He brings down the fancy table cover, which he spreads on the table.*) There we are!

MARC: (*Feeling it*) That's nice, John. Where'd you get it?

JOHN: Why, I bought a yard of this plain sateen down at Macy's—

GEORGE: Really? How much was it?

JOHN: A dollar sixty-three. It was reduced. Then I had this edging in the house.

BOB: Awfully nice!

MARC: Oh, say! Walter Sharp just got back from Paris—

GEORGE: He did?

MARC: Yes. And *he* says they're wearing trousers longer over there.

GEORGE: Really? (*There is quite a fuss about it.*)

JOHN: (*Brings chips and takes his seat*) What'll we play for?

BOB: Oh, what's the difference? One cent limit?

GEORGE: Does it matter who deals? (*Takes the cards from* BOB.)

MARC: Say, did you hear about Eddie Parker?

JOHN: No.

MARC: Well, it seems he saw these advertisements about how to get thin, and he thought he'd try them. You know Eddie's taken on a lot of weight since his marriage.

GEORGE: Twenty pounds—absolutely.

MARC: Well, they sent him some powders and he began taking them, and what do you think?

GEORGE: Well? (MARC *whispers to him.*) You don't say so?

JOHN *and* BOB: (*Excited*) What was it? What was it? (GEORGE *whispers to* JOHN, *who whispers to* BOB. *Great excitement.*)

MARC: Who has the cards?

GEORGE: Here they are. (*Starts to deal—poker hands.*)

MARC: I don't want to play late. I've been shopping all day.

GEORGE: And I have an appointment at the barber's tomorrow. I'm going to try a new way of getting my hair cut. (*The deal is completed.*)

BOB: (*Picking up a few cards*) Which is higher—aces or kings?

GEORGE: Now, who bets first?

JOHN: Are these funny little things clubs?

MARC: What are the chips worth?

JOHN: Let's have them all worth the same thing.

BOB: A penny apiece. . . .

GEORGE: Say, Lord & Taylor are having a wonderful sale of nightgowns!

MARC: What do you pay your maid?

BOB: Sixty-five, but she isn't worth it. (*The three start talking at once about maids, and* JOHN *has a hard time being heard.*)

JOHN: (*Excited*) Boys! Boys! Listen to this! Boys!

ALL: Well?

JOHN: (*Excited*) I *knew* there was something I wanted to tell you!

ALL: (*They must not speak together*) What is it?

JOHN: Well, now in the first place you must promise not to breathe a word of it to anybody, because I got it in absolute confidence and I promised I wouldn't tell.

GEORGE: What is it?

MARC: Well?

BOB: Well?

JOHN: It's about Sid Heflin! Now, you won't tell anybody? At least, don't let on you got it from me!

ALL: No!

JOHN: Well, I'm told—and I got this pretty straight, mind you—I'm told that he's going to—ah—(*He puts the message across with his eyes.*)

MARC: I don't believe it!

BOB: What do you mean?

GEORGE: When?

JOHN: In April!

MARC: April! (*They count on their fingers, up to four.*)

GEORGE: What do you mean?

JOHN: Exactly! They were married late in January! (*They all throw down their hands and begin talking at once.*)

CURTAIN

Groucho Marx

*

LETTERS TO WARNER BROTHERS

*When the Marx Brothers were about to make a movie called "A Night
in Casablanca," there were threats of legal action from the Warner
Brothers, who, five years before, had made a picture called, simply,
"Casablanca" (with Humphrey Bogart and Ingrid Bergman as stars).
Whereupon Groucho, speaking for his brothers and himself, imme-
diately dispatched the following letters:*

DEAR WARNER BROTHERS:

Apparently there is more than one way of conquering a city and
holding it as your own. For example, up to the time that we contemplated making this picture, I had no idea that the city of Casablanca
belonged exclusively to Warner Brothers. However, it was only a few
days after our announcement appeared that we received your long, ominous legal document warning us not to use the name Casablanca.

It seems that in 1471, Ferdinand Balboa Warner, your great-great-
grandfather, while looking for a shortcut to the city of Burbank, had
stumbled on the shores of Africa and, raising his alpenstock (which he
later turned in for a hundred shares of the common), named it Casablanca.

I just don't understand your attitude. Even if you plan on re-releas-
ing your picture, I am sure that the average movie fan could learn in
time to distinguish between Ingrid Bergman and Harpo. I don't know
whether I could, but I certainly would like to try.

You claim you own Casablanca and that no one else can use that
name without your permission. What about "Warner Brothers"? Do you
own that, too? You probably have the right to use the name Warner, but
what about Brothers? Professionally, we were brothers long before you

were. We were touring the sticks as The Marx Brothers when Vitaphone was still a gleam in the inventor's eye, and even before us there had been other brothers—the Smith Brothers; the Brothers Karamazov; Dan Brothers, an outfielder with Detroit; and "Brother, Can You Spare a Dime?" (This was originally "Brothers, Can You Spare a Dime?" but this was spreading a dime pretty thin, so they threw out one brother, gave all the money to the other one and whittled it down to, "Brother, Can You Spare a Dime?")

Now Jack, how about you? Do you maintain that yours is an original name? Well, it's not. It was used long before you were born. Offhand, I can think of two Jacks—there was Jack of "Jack and the Beanstalk," and Jack the Ripper, who cut quite a figure in his day.

As for you, Harry, you probably sign your checks, sure in the belief that you are the first Harry of all time and that all other Harrys are imposters. I can think of two Harrys that preceded you. There was Lighthouse Harry of Revolutionary fame and a Harry Appelbaum who lived on the corner of 93rd Street and Lexington Avenue. Unfortunately, Appelbaum wasn't too well known. The last I heard of him, he was selling neckties at Weber and Heilbroner.

Now about the Burbank studio. I believe this is what you brothers call your place. Old man Burbank is gone. Perhaps you remember him. He was a great man in a garden. His wife often said Luther had ten green thumbs. What a witty woman she must have been! Burbank was the wizard who crossed all those fruits and vegetables until he had the poor plants in such a confused and jittery condition that they could never decide whether to enter the dining room on the meat platter or the dessert dish.

This is pure conjecture, of course, but who knows—perhaps Burbank's survivors aren't too happy with the fact that a plant that grinds out pictures on a quota settled in their town, appropriated Burbank's name and uses it as a front for their films. It is even possible that the Burbank family is prouder of the potato produced by the old man than they are of the fact that from your studio emerged "Casablanca" or even "Gold Diggers of 1931."

This all seems to add up to a pretty bitter tirade, but I assure you it's not meant to. I love Warners. Some of my best friends are Warner Brothers. It is even possible that I am doing you an injustice and that you, yourselves, know nothing at all about this dog-in-the-Wanger attitude. It wouldn't surprise me at all to discover that the heads of your legal department are unaware of this absurd dispute, for I am acquainted with many of them and they are fine fellows with curly black hair, double-breasted suits and a love of their fellow man that out-Saroyans Saroyan.

I have a hunch that this attempt to prevent us from using the title is the brainchild of some ferret-faced shyster, serving a brief apprenticeship in your legal department. I know the type well—hot out of law school, hungry for success and too ambitious to follow the natural laws of promotion. This bar sinister probably needled your attorneys, most of whom are fine fellows with curly black hair, double-breasted suits, etc., into attempting to enjoin us. Well, he won't get away with it! We'll fight him to the highest court! No pasty-faced legal adventurer is going to cause bad blood between the Warners and the Marxes. We are all brothers under the skin and we'll remain friends till the last reel of "A Night in Casablanca" goes tumbling over the spool.

Sincerely,
GROUCHO MARX

For some curious reason, this letter seemed to puzzle the Warner Brothers legal department. They wrote—in all seriousness—and asked if the Marxes could give them some idea of what their story was about. They felt that something might be worked out. So Groucho replied:

DEAR WARNERS:

There isn't much I can tell you about the story. In it I play a Doctor of Divinity who ministers to the natives and, as a sideline, hawks can openers and pea jackets to the savages along the Gold Coast of Africa.

When I first meet Chico, he is working in a saloon, selling sponges to barflies who are unable to carry their liquor. Harpo is an Arabian caddie who lives in a small Grecian urn on the outskirts of the city.

As the picture opens, Porridge, a mealy-mouthed native girl, is sharpening some arrows for the hunt. Paul Hangover, our hero, is constantly lighting two cigarettes simultaneously. He apparently is unaware of the cigarette shortage.

There are many scenes of splendor and fierce antagonisms, and Color, an Abyssinian messenger boy, runs Riot. Riot, in case you have never been there, is a small night club on the edge of town.

There's a lot more I could tell you, but I don't want to spoil it for you. All this has been okayed by the Hays Office, Good Housekeeping and the survivors of the Haymarket Riots; and if the times are ripe, this picture can be the opening gun in a new worldwide disaster.

Cordially,
GROUCHO MARX

Instead of mollifying them, this note seemed to puzzle the attorneys even more; they wrote back and said they still didn't understand the story line and they would appreciate it if Mr. Marx would explain the plot in more detail. So Groucho obliged with the following:

DEAR BROTHERS:

Since I last wrote you, I regret to say there have been some changes in the plot of our new picture, "A Night in Casablanca." In the new version I play Bordello, the sweetheart of Humphrey Bogart. Harpo and Chico are itinerant rug peddlers who are weary of laying rugs and enter a monastery just for a lark. This is a good joke on them, as there hasn't been a lark in the place for fifteen years.

Across from this monastery, hard by a jetty, is a waterfront hotel, chockfull of apple-cheeked damsels, most of whom have been barred by the Hays Office for soliciting. In the fifth reel, Gladstone makes a speech that sets the House of Commons in a uproar and the King promptly asks for his resignation. Harpo marries a hotel detective; Chico operates an ostrich farm. Humphrey Bogart's girl, Bordello, spends her last years in a Bacall house.

This, as you can see, is a very skimpy outline. The only thing that can save us from extinction is a continuation of the film shortage.

Fondly,

GROUCHO MARX

After that, the Marxes heard no more from the Warner Brothers' legal department.

TO GUMMO MARX

June, 1964

DEAR GUMMO:

Last night Eden and I had dinner with my celebrated pen pal, T.S. Eliot. It was a memorable evening.

The poet met us at the door with Mrs. Eliot, a good-looking, middle-aged blonde whose eyes seemed to fill up with adoration every time she looked at her husband. He, by the way, is tall, lean and rather stooped over; but whether this is from age, illness or both, I don't know.

At any rate, your correspondent arrived at the Eliots' fully prepared for a literary evening. During the week I had read "Murder in the Cathedral" twice; "The Waste Land" three times; and just in case of a conversational bottleneck, I brushed up on "King Lear."

Well, sir, as cocktails were served, there was a momentary lull—the kind that is more or less inevitable when strangers meet for the first time. So, apropos of practically nothing (and "not with a bang but a whimper") I tossed in a quotation from "The Waste Land." That, I thought, will show him I've read a thing or two besides my press notices from vaudeville.

Eliot smiled faintly—as though to say he was thoroughly familiar with his poems and didn't need me to recite them. So I took a whack at "King Lear." I said the king was an incredibly foolish old man, which God knows he *was*; and that if he'd been *my* father I would have run away from home at the age of eight—instead of waiting until I was ten.

That, too, failed to bowl over the poet. He seemed more interested in discussing "Animal Crackers" and "A Night at the Opera." He quoted a joke—one of mine—that I had long since forgotten. Now it was my turn to smile faintly. I was not going to let anyone—not even the British poet from St. Louis—spoil my Literary Evening. I pointed out that King Lear's opening speech was the height of idiocy. Imagine (I said) a father asking his three children: Which of you kids loves me the most? And then disowning the youngest—the sweet, honest Cordelia—because, unlike her wicked sister, she couldn't bring herself to gush out insincere flattery. And Cordelia, mind you, had been her father's favorite!

The Eliots listened politely. Mrs. Eliot then defended Shakespeare; and Eden, too, I regret to say, was on King Lear's side, even though I am the one who supports her. (In all fairness to my wife, I must say that, having played the Princess in a high school production of "The Swan," she has retained a rather warm feeling for all royalty.)

As for Eliot, he asked if I remembered the courtroom scene in "Duck Soup." Fortunately I'd forgotten every word. It was obviously the end of the Literary Evening, but very pleasant none the less. I discovered that Eliot and I had three things in common: (1) an affection for good cigars and (2) cats; and (3) a weakness for making puns—a weakness that for many years I have tried to overcome. T.S., on the other hand, is an unashamed—even proud—punster. For example, there's his Gus, the Theater Cat, whose "real name was Asparagus."

Speaking of asparagus, the dinner included good, solid English beef, very well prepared. And, although they had a semi-butler serving, Eliot insisted on pouring the wine himself. It was an excellent wine and no maitre d' could have served it more graciously. He is a dear man and a charming host.

When I told him that my daughter Melinda was studying his poetry at Beverly High, he said he regretted that, because he had no wish to become compulsory reading.

We didn't stay late, for we both felt that he wasn't up to a long evening of conversation—especially mine.

Did I tell you we called him Tom?—possibly because that's his name. I, of course, asked him to call me Tom too, but only because I loathe the name Julius.

Yours,
TOM MARX

Frank Sullivan

*

THE CLICHÉ EXPERT TESTIFIES
ON LOVE

Q—Mr. Arbuthnot, as an expert in the use of the cliché, are you prepared to testify here today regarding its application in topics of sex,
love, matrimony, and so on?

A—I am.

Q—Very good. Now, Mr. Arbuthnot, what is love?

A—Love is blind.

Q—Good. What does love do?

A—Love makes the world go round.

Q—Whom does a young man fall in love with?

A—With the Only Girl in the World.

Q—Whom does a young woman fall in love with?

A—With the Only Boy in the World.

Q—When do they fall in love?

A—At first sight.

Q—How?

A—Madly.

Q—They are then said to be?

A—Victims of Cupid's darts.

Q—And he?

A—Whispers sweet nothings in her ear.

Q—Who loves a lover?

A—All the world loves a lover.

Q—Describe the Only Girl in the World.

A—Her eyes are like stars. Her teeth are like pearls. Her lips are ruby.
Her cheek is damask, and her form divine.

Q—Haven't you forgotten something?

A—Eyes, teeth, lips, cheek, form—no, sir, I don't think so.

Q—Her hair?

A—Oh, certainly. How stupid of me. She has hair like spun gold.

Q—Very good, Mr. Arbuthnot. Now will you describe the Only Man?

A—He is a blond Viking, a he-man, and a square shooter who plays the game. There is something fine about him that rings true, and he has kept himself pure and clean so that when he meets the girl of his choice, the future mother of his children, he can look her in the eye.

Q—How?

A—Without flinching.

Q—Are all the Only Men blond Vikings?

A—Oh, no. Some of them are dark, handsome chaps who have sown their wild oats. This sort of Only Man has a way with a maid, and there is a devil in his eye. But he is not a cad; he would not play fast and loose with an Only Girl's affections. He has a heart of gold. He is a diamond in the rough. He tells the Only Girl frankly about his Past. She understands—and forgives.

Q—And marries him?

A—And marries him.

Q—Why?

A—To reform him.

Q—Does she reform him?

A—Seldom.

Q—Seldom what?

A—Seldom, if ever.

Q—Now, Mr. Arbuthnot, when the Only Man falls in love, madly, with the Only Girl, what does he do?

A—He walks on air.

Q—Yes, I know, but what does he do? I mean, what is it he pops?

A—Oh, excuse me. The question, of course.

Q—Then what do they plight?

A—Their troth.

Q—What happens after that?

A—They get married.

Q—What is marriage?

A—Marriage is a lottery.

Q—Where are marriages made?

A—Marriages are made in Heaven.

Q—What does the bride do at the wedding?

A—She blushes.

Q—What does the groom do?

A—Forgets the ring.

A—After the marriage, what?

A—The honeymoon.

Q—Then what?

A—She has a little secret.

Q—What is it?

A—She is knitting a tiny garment.

Q—What happens after that?

A—Oh, they settle down and raise a family and live happily ever afterward, unless—

Q—Unless what?

A—Unless he is a fool for a pretty face.

Q—And if he is?

A—Then they come to the parting of the ways.

Q—Mr. Arbuthnot, thank you very much.

A—But I'm not through yet, Mr. Untermyer.

Q—No?

A—Oh, no. There is another side to sex.

Q—There is? What side?

A—The seamy side. There are, you know, men who are wolves in sheep's clothing and there are, alas, lovely women who stoop to folly.

Q—My goodness! Describe these men you speak of, please.

A—They are snakes in the grass who do not place woman upon a pedestal. They are cads who kiss and tell, who trifle with a girl's affections and betray her innocent trust. They are cynics who think that a woman is only a woman, but a good cigar is a smoke. Their mottoes are "Love 'em and leave 'em" and "Catch 'em young, treat 'em rough, tell 'em nothing." These cads speak of "the light that lies in woman's eyes, and lies—and lies—and lies." In olden days they wore black, curling mustachios, which they twirled, and they invited innocent Gibson girls to midnight suppers, with champagne, at their bachelor apartments, and said, "Little girl, why do you fear me?" Nowadays they have black, patent-leather hair, and roadsters, and they drive up to the curb and say, "Girlie, can I give you a lift?" They are fiends in human form, who would rob a woman of her most priceless possession.

Q—What is that?

A—Her honor.

Q—How do they rob her?

A—By making improper advances.

Q—What does a woman do when a snake in the grass tries to rob her of her honor?

A—She defends her honor.

Q—How?

A—By repulsing his advances and scorning his embraces.

Q—How does she do that?

A—By saying, "Sir, I believe you forget yourself," or "Please take your arm away," or "I'll kindly thank you to remember I'm a lady," or "Let's not spoil it all."

Q—Suppose she doesn't say any of those things?

A—In that case, she takes the first false step.

Q—Where does the first false step take her?

A—Down the primrose path.

Q—What's the primrose path?

A—It's the easiest way.

Q—Where does it lead?

A—To a life of shame.

Q—What is a life of shame?

A—A life of shame is a fate worse than death.

Q—Now, after lovely woman has stooped to folly, what does she do to the gay Lothario who has robbed her of her most priceless possession?

A—She devotes the best years of her life to him.

Q—Then what does he do?

A—He casts her off.

Q—How?

A—Like an old shoe.

Q—Then what does she do?

A—She goes to their love nest, then everything goes black before her, her mind becomes a blank, she pulls a revolver, and gives the fiend in human form something to remember her by.

Q—That is called?

A—Avenging her honor.

Q—What is it no jury will do in such a case?

A—No jury will convict.

Q—Mr. Arbuthnot, your explanation of the correct application of the cliché in these matters has been most instructive, and I know that all of us cliché-users here will know exactly how to respond hereafter when, during a conversation, sex—when sex—when—ah—

A—I think what you want to say is "When sex rears its ugly head," isn't
    it?

Q—Thank you, Mr. Arbuthnot. Thank you very much.

A—Thank *you*, Mr. Untermyer.

J. B. Morton
(Beachcomber)

*

THE INTRUSIONS
OF CAPTAIN FOULENOUGH

AT DRAINWATER HOUSE

Captain Foulenough, who is causing so much disturbance in Scotland, made his appearance at lunchtime yesterday at Drainwater House, the residence of Colonel and Mrs. McGawke.

The McGawkes were entertaining a large house party, and luncheon was about to be served when the hostess heard voices in the entrance hall.

She heard her butler say, "What name did you say, sir?" and then a loud voice replied, "A Foulenough by any name would smell as sweet. He droppeth as the gentle dew from Heaven. Go hence, my man, and tell them that their old Uncle Fred waits without. Say their Aunt Emma has returned from sea. Say that I am the little waif you found abandoned in a linen basket on the doorstep. Say anything you please."

Mrs. McGawke then came to the great oaken door, and the captain flung his arms round her, crying, "My dear old godmother! Have you forgotten the old days? Is there anything to drink in this doss-house?"

The colonel joined his wife and endeavoured to rescue her from the embrace of the noisy intruder. He said, "If you do not go at once, I shall ring up the police. We have been warned about you."

"For the honour of your old regiment give me a meal," said the captain.

Then, picking up a bust of Joseph Chamberlain, he said, "What'll you give me on this? What am I bid?"

The colonel, edging the captain towards the doors, said, "Here's five shillings."

"The bust's yours," replied Foulenough, handing it to Mrs. McGawke with a bow.

They watched him go down the drive, and as he went he sang in a deep, thunderous voice, *"Flossie Is the Girl for Me."*

AT TINWHISTLE LODGE

Captain Foulenough turned up yesterday evening at Tinwhistle Lodge, near Cailzie, where Lord Lochstock and Barrel was entertaining heavily for the shooting. The captain, with that candour which disdains subterfuge, swung up the drive in full view of the guests gathered on the lawn, crying, "Any empties?"

Lady Lochstock and Barrel (before her marriage a Whussett) said haughtily:

"We have no empties, whatever they may be. You will find the tradesmen's entrance at the back."

"No empties?" replied Foulenough.

"Not one," said Lord Lochstock and Barrel.

"Any fulls, then?" asked the captain. "In other words—have you the wherewithal to wet my tyrannous whistle?"

At a sign from the master of the house Foulenough was taken to the servants' quarters and refreshed.

IMPASSE

The thud of hoofs is far from welcome on Clackwhidden Moor at this season of the year. The shoot was entirely ruined yesterday by a mysterious horseman who cantered up and down in front of the butts, waving a sword and crying, "Don't hold your fire! Charge!" One or two sportsmen recognized Captain Foulenough, who has made such a nuisance of himself in the district.

Colonel Grampound shouted to him, "I say! You are masking our fire. Can't you see you're in the way, there's a good fellow, I mean."

To which the irrepressible captain replied, "Fear nothing. Follow me. I will lead you against those birds. Don't cower in those trenches. Grouse don't bite. After them, boys!" And he raised himself in his stirrups and waved them on. "Take cover," he added, "when I blow two blasts on my bottle." So saying, he raised a pint bottle of stout to his lips and drank heartily.

Nobody knows quite what to do about it all.

• • •

London's Upper Thirty-seven, the cream of the *haut monde*, the life-above-stairs gang, are organizing a committee to concert measures for the ending, once and for all, of the Foulenough menace.

Several dowagers and other hostesses complain that the captain's name has crept into the accounts of their social activities which their secretaries have sent to the gossip writers. The general opinion is that the captain must be either a lunatic or a determined climber. The prospect of his attendance at dances and dinners and cocktail parties during the coming season is too much for most people to contemplate.

As an instance of what is happening, Lady Cabstanleigh read the following at the first committee meeting. It was taken from "Lobelia's" column of chatter in the *Evening Scream*:

> *Witty and intelligent Lady Cabstanleigh is giving a send-off cocktail party for the Trowser girls, who are off on one of their intrepid dashes to Scotland. The Bopples will be there, and Lady Urging and Mr. "Dirt" Cobblestone, and, of course, the handsome and popular Captain Foulenough.*

I append a few more extracts from various columns of social chatter, which have given great offence to Lady Cabstanleigh's committee, formed to combat Captain Foulenough's attempts to get into Society:

> *It is understood that the best man at the Garkington–Thwackhurst wedding will be Captain Foulenough, who describes himself as "an old friend of the groom, and of all other grooms." When informed of this news the groom, Mr. Ernest ("Stink") Garkington, said, "I've never even heard of the chap."*
>
> *. . . Among those who will bring parties to the dance given by Lady Vowpe for her daughter Celery is the popular Captain Foulenough. He will probably bring the Kempton Park gang.*
>
> *Captain Foulenough, whose address, according to him, is the Cavalry Club, calls every day for letters. He has been told that he is not a member, and has been asked not to call at the club. His invariable reply is, "I have to come here to get my letters. It's not my fault if everyone writes to me at this address. When I marry Babs, it will be different."*

This last remark has thrown many hostesses into a frenzy. Nobody knows whether the Babs in question is:

(a) Mrs. Simeon Grout's daughter;
(b) Lady Barger's niece;
(c) Sir Arthur Cutaway's widow;
(d) Lady Thistleburn's daughter;

(e) Lady "Connie" Clatter's daughter;
(f) The divorced Mrs. Rowdgett;
(g) The orphan Babs Watercress;
(h) A barmaid at the Horse and Hounds;
(i) One of the Farragut twins;
(j) Lady Nausea ("Babs") Bottledown.

Many hostesses have decided to employ detectives to scrutinize their guests on arrival. In this way it is hoped to keep Captain Foulenough away from houses where he is neither known nor wanted.

But this is a dangerous way of dealing with the menace, as is shown by the complaints of a Mr. Cowparsleigh, who has already been refused admission to two houses, owing to his resemblance to the captain. The fact of this resemblance is making people even more nervous, since none of them can afford to offend a banker's nephew of Mr. Cowparsleigh's status.

News has just come in of the appearance of Captain Foulenough at Lady Drain's cocktail party. He is said to have entered by the tradesmen's entrance. Suspicions were aroused when he seized the arm of Aurora Bagstone, and holding it to his lips, in the manner of a flute player, kissed it up and down the scale, from wrist to elbow. Aurora remarked afterwards, "One does like to know who is kissing one, after all."

Meanwhile, Mr. Cowparsleigh had been flung down the steps of Mrs. Woodle's house in Crabapple Mews, and has threatened to make his uncle call in her overdraft.

A COMEDY OF ERRORS

A ridiculous scene marred Lady Hounde's party the other night. "All one has to do," said the hostess, "to stop this man Foulenough from interfering with our social engagements is to search any suspect. The so-called captain always carries a bottle of strong drink in his pocket."

The arrival of the unfortunate Mr. Augustus Cowparsleigh, who is Foulenough's double, was the signal for an outbreak of suspicion that you could have cut with a knife. Cowparsleigh's recent misadventures have, of course, made him very timid, and he entered Lady Hounde's room blushing and looking guilty.

Lady Hounde pounced like a starving jaguar. "Have you a bottle on you?" she demanded sternly, while plunging her hand into his side pocket.

"I didn't know we were supposed to bring our own drink," retorted Cowparsleigh.

"Don't quibble," roared the hostess, "where's your bottle? I know you've got one."

"If you are as thirsty as all that," replied the victim testily, "why don't you get one of your own drinks?"

Taken aback, the hostess faltered. "I do believe it's really Augustus," she said. And everybody breathed freely.

The only other odd incident occurred half an hour later. Boubou Flaring crossed the room to speak to Cowparsleigh as he was leaving.

"I hear you were mistaken for Captain Foulenough," she said. The reply was a wicked wink, and Boubou was surprised to see him leave with a little box full of caviare sandwiches and a bottle in each pocket, and without saying goodbye to anybody.

Ten minutes later she was amazed to see him again. She said, "Where have you dumped the sandwiches and the booze?" Augustus Cowparsleigh flushed angrily. "I think you're all mad here," he said. Boubou pondered in silence.

At 7:15 the supply of drink failed—an unknown occurrence in that house. It was only then that Lady Hounde heard Boubou's story, and realized that the dreaded warrior had indeed slipped through her fingers.

• • •

Mr. Augustus Cowparsleigh, who has the misfortune to be Captain Foulenough's double, was refused admittance yesterday to the divorce reception given by Lady Doublecross to celebrate the divorce of her daughter Goatie from Sir Stanley Biskett. In vain did poor Augustus produce his card. In vain did he show the monogram on his shirt.

To make matters worse this mildest of men has been asked to resign from one of his clubs, because he came into the smoking room with his shirt outside his waistcoat, placed a funnel down the back of old General Dunderhead's neck, and poured Sir Raymond Funbelow's whisky down the funnel.

MR. COWPARSLEIGH AND FLORA SCREAMING

I learn that the timid but worthy Mr. Augustus Cowparsleigh is on the point of announcing his engagement to Flora, the lovely daughter of Mrs. Screaming.

Or should I say, "was on the point"?

Yesterday the fond suitor for the largest hand in Upper Beauclerque Mews had arranged to meet his lady in the cocktail bar at that most exclusive of pigsties, "Chez Nussbaum." She arrived punctually and seated herself on one of the red glass rockinghorses ranged round the bar. A moment later she was astounded to see her fiancé in animated conversation with a Creature. If ever there was a hussy this was one. Approaching cautiously, Flora saw the man who had always been so courtly and so reserved with her pinch the Creature's ear and smack her cheek playfully. He called her "Carrots." Feeling as though she had been slogged over the head with a steel hammer the poor girl called feebly for brandy.

When she came to, Augustus was bending over her tenderly, and saying repeatedly, "So sorry I was late."

Coldly she pushed him away and rose to her feet, then she left the premises in comparatively high dudgeon.

Mr. Cowparsleigh was dining quietly with Flora Screaming and her mother the other night, when their butler, Mason, uttered a loud cry in the kitchen. A moment or two later he brought in the fish, and Mrs. Screaming was about to ask him what had happened when he suddenly executed a dance step and whipped off a wig, revealing the red hair of Foulenough. Tongue-tied, they shrank from him. He said, "Cowparsleigh, old soak, I just wanted to thank you in person for settling that little matter for me. Flora, my love, I will not attempt to screen my identity. I am Foulenough, and proud of it. We came over with King Alfred. However, as I see violence in your lady mother's eye, I will do a scarper." And he left the room.

MR. COWPARSLEIGH DEVISES A SCHEME

"There is only one way out of this," said poor Mr. Cowparsleigh to Flora Screaming. "There is an infallible sign by which you can always distinguish me from Captain Foulenough. You see, fortunately, I have a birthmark about the size of a florin on my chest."

"Very nice," said Flora sarcastically. "And I am supposed to go about at parties asking to see people's chests?"

"Certainly not, my dear," said Mr. Cowparsleigh. "But when you are in doubt about me, I will—"

"Remove your shirt, I suppose?"

"Oh no. The birthmark is high up, near the throat. I need only take my collar and tie off, and unbutton the top button of my shirt."

"Splendid," sneered Flora. "Nobody would think it odd. And if I know the captain, he's quite capable of buying a sham birthmark and sticking it on. Then we should have the pair of you behaving like lunatics."

AND CARRIES IT OUT

Next day the Fauconbridge-Fauconbridge-Fauconbridges gave a little sherry-party, and asked Flora and her fiancé to look in. Flora arrived late, and when she saw Mr. Cowparsleigh beaming at her with more than his customary gaiety, thankful to have forestalled his double, she at once suspected that he was the dreaded captain, and turned her back on him. Whereupon the well-meaning Augustus shouldered his way towards her, but was intercepted by a voluble lady, who could not understand why he was fiddling with his tie and collar so nervously. When he whipped off his collar and undid his shirt at the neck she uttered a scream. People crowded round, and above the din the voice of the hostess was heard bawling, "Mason, show Captain Foulenough to the door!"

So Mr. Cowparsleigh's little scheme miscarried.

THE CAPTAIN AT LARGE

A paragraph in a local paper informs me that:

> *Captain de Courcy Foulenough, the well known clubman, has succeeded, by using the names of prominent London hostesses, in obtaining credit at some of the more shady whelk stalls at Brighton. It is difficult to imagine that the proprietors of the stalls can have had business dealings with any of these ladies, and it can only be assumed that they are sufficiently impressed by the captain's manner to believe that their bills will be settled by his rich friends.*

Lady Cabstanleigh commented on this paragraph yesterday. She said, "I, for one, have no intention of standing him whelks."

Mr. Cowparsleigh, who has received a bill for four dozen whelks, has sent the money, "Merely because I prefer to hush the matter up." Other well known people who have received bills are consulting their solicitors.

Mrs. Taswill-Fogstone has received this letter:

DEAR MADAM,

> *I enclose a bill for whelks inkurred by a gent what come ere with a lady and eat three doz. bitween them. I was give to understan you was his mother, so I enclose the bill for the whelks they eat. Any other custumiers you are cortious enough to send to my stall will be*

assuared the best intenteons of the house not counting credit and
the sky being the limmitt. A post order by return will oblige.

Your obedien servant,
TED RIGGER.

The unfortunate Mr. Cowparsleigh was dumbfounded yesterday
when he looked in at Dibbler's Club in Ryder Street for his letters, and
found this:

DEAR SIR,—*I enclose as requested the bill for the jamboree at my*
stall last Wednesday. The breakages come rather heavy, but you will
remember that Violet had words with Connie and threw a cup at
her. When the fun was over I found Aggie's hat under the counter,
and am forwarding it to you as I don't know her address. I've slipped
in Tom's outstanding account as you told me to, and am giving
Mabel and her friend tick. Hoping this is all right.

Yrs. respectfully,
ALFRED BIRAGO.

"What monstrous nonsense is this?" exclaimed poor Cowparsleigh
as he rang up his solicitors.

BEDSIDE READING

"So you dare to criticize the Captain of the School!"

The voice of the headmistress was ice-cold and as sharp as a
scimitar.

Joyce hung her head.

Then the Captain, a frank smile lighting up her young face,
advanced and held out her hand.

At this gesture of friendliness the whole school began to bawl
its eyes out. As for Joyce, she took the proffered hand and drenched
it with her tears.

The headmistress turned aside. She, too, was human.

(*From* The Beastliest Girl at St. Bede's.)

James Thurber

*

THE BREAKING UP OF THE WINSHIPS

The trouble that broke up the Gordon Winships seemed to me, at first, as minor a problem as frost on a windowpane. Another day, a touch of sun, and it would be gone. I was inclined to laugh it off, and, indeed, as a friend of both Gordon and Marcia, I spent a great deal of time with each of them, separately, trying to get them to laugh it off, too—with him at his club, where he sat drinking Scotch and smoking too much, and with her in their apartment, that seemed so large and lonely without Gordon and his restless moving around and his quick laughter. But it was no good; they were both adamant. Their separation has lasted now more than six months. I doubt very much that they will ever go back together again.

It all started one night at Leonardo's, after dinner, over their Bénédictine. It started innocently enough, amiably even, with laughter from both of them, laughter that froze finally as the clock ran on and their words came out sharp and flat and stinging. They had been to see *Camille*. Gordon hadn't liked it very much. Marcia had been crazy about it because she is crazy about Greta Garbo. She belongs to that considerable army of Garbo admirers whose enchantment borders almost on fanaticism and sometimes even touches the edges of frenzy. I think that, before everything happened, Gordon admired Garbo, too, but the depth of his wife's conviction that here was the greatest figure ever seen in our generation on sea or land, on screen or stage, exasperated him that night. Gordon hates (or used to) exaggeration, and he respects (or once did) detachment. It was his feeling that detachment is a necessary thread in the fabric of a woman's charm. He didn't like to see his wife get herself "into a sweat" over anything and, that night at Leonardo's, he unfortunately used that expression and made that accusation.

Marcia responded, as I get it, by saying, a little loudly (they had gone on to Scotch and soda), that a man who had no abandon of feeling and no passion for anything was not altogether a man, and that his so-called love of detachment simply covered up a lack of critical appreciation and understanding of the arts in general. Her sentences were becoming long and wavy, and her words formal. Gordon suddenly began to pooh-pooh her; he kept saying "Pooh!" (an annoying mannerism of his, I have always thought). He wouldn't answer her arguments or even listen to them. That, of course, infuriated her. "Oh, pooh to you, too!" she finally more or less shouted. He snapped at her, "Quiet, for God's sake! You're yelling like a prizefight manager!" Enraged at that, she had recourse to her eyes as weapons and looked steadily at him for a while with the expression of one who is viewing a small and horrible animal, such as a horned toad. They then sat in moody and brooding silence for a long time, without moving a muscle, at the end of which, getting a hold on herself, Marcia asked him, quietly enough, just exactly what actor on the screen or on the stage, living or dead, he considered greater than Garbo. Gordon thought a moment and then said, as quietly as she had put the question, "Donald Duck." I don't believe that he meant it at the time, or even thought that he meant it. However that may have been, she looked at him scornfully and said that that speech just about perfectly represented the shallowness of his intellect and the small range of his imagination. Gordon asked her not to make a spectacle of herself —she had raised her voice slightly—and went on to say that her failure to see the genius of Donald Duck proved conclusively to him that she was a woman without humor. That, he said, he had always suspected; now, he said, he knew it. She had a great desire to hit him, but instead she sat back and looked at him with her special Mona Lisa smile, a smile rather more of contempt than, as in the original, of mystery. Gordon hated that smile, so he said that Donald Duck happened to be exactly ten times as great as Garbo would ever be and that anybody with a brain in his head would admit it instantly. Thus the Winships went on and on, their resentment swelling, their sense of values blurring, until it ended up with her taking a taxi home alone (leaving her vanity bag and one glove behind her in the restaurant) and with him making the rounds of the late places and rolling up to his club around dawn. There, as he got out, he asked his taxi driver which he liked better, Greta Garbo or Donald Duck, and the driver said he liked Greta Garbo best. Gordon said to him, bitterly, "Pooh to you, too, my good friend!" and went to bed.

The next day, as is usual with married couples, they were both contrite, but behind their contrition lay sleeping the ugly words each had used and the cold glances and the bitter gestures. She phoned him, because she was worried. She didn't want to be, but she was. When he hadn't come home, she was convinced he had gone to his club, but visions of him lying in a gutter or under a table, somehow horribly mangled, haunted her, and so at eight o'clock she called him up. Her heart lightened when he said, "Hullo," gruffly: he was alive, thank God! His heart may have lightened a little, too, but not very much, because he felt terrible. He felt terrible and he felt that it was her fault that he felt terrible. She said that she was sorry and that they had both been very silly, and he growled something about he was glad she realized *she'd* been silly, anyway. That attitude put a slight edge on the rest of her words. She asked him shortly if he was coming home. He said sure he was coming home; it was his home, wasn't it? She told him to go back to bed and not be such an old bear, and hung up.

The next incident occurred at the Clarkes' party a few days later. The Winships had arrived in fairly good spirits to find themselves in a buzzing group of cocktail drinkers that more or less revolved around the tall and languid figure of the guest of honor, an eminent lady novelist. Gordon late in the evening won her attention and drew her apart for one drink together and, feeling a little high and happy at that time, as is the way with husbands, mentioned, lightly enough (he wanted to get it out of his subconscious), the argument that he and his wife had had about the relative merits of Garbo and Duck. The tall lady, lowering her cigarette holder, said, in the spirit of his own gaiety, that he could count her in on his side. Unfortunately, Marcia Winship, standing some ten feet away, talking to a man with a beard, caught not the spirit but only a few words of the conversation, and jumped to the conclusion that her husband was deliberately reopening the old wound, for the purpose of humiliating her in public. I think that in another moment Gordon might have brought her over, and put his arm around her, and admitted his "defeat"—he was feeling pretty fine. But when he caught her eye, she gazed through him, freezingly, and his heart went down. And then his anger rose.

Their fight, naturally enough, blazed out again in the taxi they took to go home from the party. Marcia wildly attacked the woman novelist (Marcia had had quite a few cocktails), defended Garbo, excoriated Gordon, and laid into Donald Duck. Gordon tried for a while to explain exactly what had happened, and then he met her resentment with a resentment that mounted even higher, the resentment of the misunderstood husband. In the midst of it all she slapped him. He looked at her for a second under lowered eyelids and then said, coldly, if a bit fuzzily,

"This is the end, but I want you to go to your grave knowing that Donald Duck is *twenty times* the artist Garbo will ever be, the longest day you, or she, ever live, if you *do*—and I can't understand, with so little to live for, why you should!" Then he asked the driver to stop the car, and he got out, in wavering dignity. "Caricature! Cartoon!" she screamed after him. "You and Donald Duck both, you—" The driver drove on.

The last time I saw Gordon—he moved his things to the club the next day, forgetting the trousers to his evening clothes and his razor— he had convinced himself that the point at issue between him and Marcia was one of extreme importance involving both his honor and his integrity. He said that now it could never be wiped out and forgotten. He said that he sincerely believed Donald Duck was as great a creation as any animal in all the works of Lewis Carroll, probably even greater, perhaps much greater. He was drinking and there was a wild light in his eye. I reminded him of his old love of detachment, and he said to the hell with detachment. I laughed at him, but he wouldn't laugh. "If," he said, grimly, "Marcia persists in her silly belief that that Swede is great and that Donald Duck is merely a caricature, I cannot conscientiously live with her again. I believe that he is great, that the man who created him is a genius, probably our only genius. I believe, further, that Greta Garbo is just another actress. As God is my judge, I believe that! What does she expect me to do, go whining back to her and pretend that I think Garbo is wonderful and that Donald Duck is simply a cartoon? Never!" He gulped down some Scotch straight. "Never!" I could not ridicule him out of his obsession. I left him and went over to see Marcia.

I found Marcia pale, but calm, and as firm in her stand as Gordon was in his. She insisted that he had deliberately tried to humiliate her before that gawky so-called novelist, whose clothes were the dowdiest she had ever seen and whose affectations obviously covered up a complete lack of individuality and intelligence. I tried to convince her that she was wrong about Gordon's attitude at the Clarkes' party, but she said she knew him like a book. Let him get a divorce and marry that creature if he wanted to. They can sit around all day, she said, and all night, too, for all I care, and talk about their precious Donald Duck, the damn comic strip! I told Marcia that she shouldn't allow herself to get so worked up about a trivial and nonsensical matter. She said it was not silly and nonsensical to her. It might have been once, yes, but it wasn't now. It had made her see Gordon clearly for what he was, a cheap, egotistical, resentful cad who would descend to ridicule his wife in front of a scrawny, horrible stranger who could not write and never would be able to write. Furthermore, her belief in Garbo's greatness was a thing she could not deny and would not deny, simply for the sake of living under the same roof with Gordon Winship. The whole thing was part and parcel of her integrity as a woman and as an—as an, well, as a woman. She could go to work again; he would find out.

There was nothing more that I could say or do. I went home. That night, however, I found that I had not really dismissed the whole ridiculous affair, as I hoped I had, for I dreamed about it. I had tried to ignore the thing, but it had tunneled deeply into my subconscious. I dreamed that I was out hunting with the Winships and that, as we crossed a snowy field, Marcia spotted a rabbit and, taking quick aim, fired and brought it down. We all ran across the snow toward the rabbit, but I reached it first. It was quite dead, but that was not what struck horror into me as I picked it up. What struck horror into me was that it was a white rabbit and was wearing a vest and carrying a watch. I woke up with a start. I don't know whether that dream means that I am on Gordon's side or on Marcia's. I don't want to analyze it. I am trying to forget the whole miserable business.

E. B. White

*

ACROSS THE STREET
AND INTO THE GRILL

(With respects to Ernest Hemingway)

This is my last and best and true and only meal, thought Mr. Perley as he descended at noon and swung east on the beat-up sidewalk of Forty-fifth Street. Just ahead of him was the girl from the reception desk. I am a little fleshed up around the crook of the elbow, thought Perley, but I commute good.

He quickened his step to overtake her and felt the pain again. What a stinking trade it is, he thought. But after what I've done to other assistant treasurers, I can't hate anybody. Sixteen deads, and I don't know how many possibles.

The girl was near enough now so he could smell her fresh receptiveness, and the lint in her hair. Her skin was light blue, like the sides of horses.

"I love you," he said, "and we are going to lunch together for the first and only time, and I love you very much."

"Hello, Mr. Perley," she said, overtaken. "Let's not think of anything."

A pair of fantails flew over from the sad old Guaranty Trust Company, their wings set for a landing. A lovely double, thought Perley, as he pulled. "Shall we go to the Hotel Biltmore, on Vanderbilt Avenue, which is merely a feeder land for the great streets, or shall we go to Schrafft's, where my old friend Botticelli is captain of girls and where they have the mayonnaise in fiascos?"

"Let's go to Schrafft's," said the girl, low. "But first I must phone Mummy." She stepped into a public booth and dialed true and well, using her finger. Then she telephoned.

As they walked on, she smelled good. She smells good, thought Perley. But that's all right, I add good. And when we get to Schrafft's, I'll order from the menu, which I like very much indeed.

They entered the restaurant. The wind was still west, ruffling the edges of the cookies. In the elevator, Perley took the controls. "I'll run it," he said to the operator. "I checked out long ago." He stopped true at the third floor, and they stepped off into the men's grill.

"Good morning, my Assistant Treasurer," said Botticelli, coming forward with a fiasco in each hand. He nodded at the girl, who he knew was from the West Seventies and whom he desired.

"Can you drink the water here?" asked Perley. He had the fur trapper's eye and took in the room at a glance, noting that there was one empty table and three pretty waitresses.

Botticelli led the way to the table in the corner, where Perley's flanks would be covered.

"Alexanders," said Perley. "Eighty-six to one. The way Chris mixes them. Is this table all right, Daughter?"

Botticelli disappeared and returned soon, carrying the old Indian blanket.

"That's the same blanket, isn't it?" asked Perley.

"Yes. To keep the wind off," said the Captain, smiling from the backs of his eyes. "It's still west. It should bring the ducks in tomorrow, the chef thinks."

Mr. Perley and the girl from the reception desk crawled down under the table and pulled the Indian blanket over them so it was solid and good and covered them right. The girl put her hand on his wallet. It was cracked and old and held his commutation book. "We are having fun, aren't we?" she asked.

"Yes, Sister," he said.

"I have here the soft-shelled crabs, my Assistant Treasurer," said Botticelli. "And another fiasco of the 1926. This one is cold."

"Dee the soft-shelled crabs," said Perley from under the blanket. He put his arm around the receptionist good.

"Do you think we should have a green pokeweed salad?" she asked. "Or shall we not think of anything for a while?"

"We shall not think of anything for a while, and Botticelli would bring the pokeweed if there was any," said Perley. "It isn't the season." Then he spoke to the Captain. "Botticelli, do you remember when we took all the mailing envelopes from the stockroom, spit on the flaps, and then drank rubber cement till the foot soldiers arrived?"

"I remember, my Assistant Treasurer," said the Captain. It was a little joke they had.

"He used to mimeograph pretty good," said Perley to the girl. "But that was another war. Do I bore you, Mother?"

"Please keep telling me about your business experiences, but not the rough parts." She touched his hand where the knuckles were scarred and stained by so many old mimeographings. "Are both your flanks covered, my dearest?" she asked, plucking at the blanket. They felt the Alexanders in their eyeballs. Eighty-six to one.

"Schrafft's is a good place and we're having fun and I love you," Perley said. He took another swallow of the 1926, and it was a good and careful swallow. "The stockroom men were very brave," he said, "but it is a position where it is extremely difficult to stay alive. Just outside that room there is a little bare-assed highboy and it is in the way of the stuff that is being brought up. The hell with it. When you make a break-through, Daughter, first you clean out the baskets and the half-wits, and all the time they have the fire escapes taped. They also shell you with old production orders, many of them approved by the general manager in charge of sales. I am boring you and I will not at this time discuss the general manager in charge of sales as we are unquestionably being listened to by that waitress over there who is setting out the decoys."

"I am going to give you my piano," the girl said, "so that when you look at it you can think of me. It will be something between us."

"Call up and have them bring the piano to the restaurant," said Perley. "Another fiasco, Botticelli!"

They drank the sauce. When the piano came, it wouldn't play. The keys were stuck good. "Never mind, we'll leave it here, Cousin," said Perley.

They came out from under the blanket and Perley tipped their waitress exactly fifteen per cent minus withholding. They left the piano in the restaurant, and when they went down the elevator and out and turned in to the old, hard, beat-up pavement of Fifth Avenue and headed south toward Forty-fifth Street, where the pigeons were, the air was as clean as your grandfather's howitzer. The wind was still west.

I commute good, thought Perley, looking at his watch. And he felt the old pain of going back to Scarsdale again.

Wolcott Gibbs

*

TIME . . . FORTUNE . . . LIFE . . . LUCE

Sad-eyed last month was nimble, middle-sized *Life*-President Clair Max-well as he told newshawks of the sale of the fifty-three-year-old gagmag to *Time*. For celebrated name alone, price: $85,000.

Said he: "*Life* . . . introduced to the world the drawings . . . of such men as Charles Dana Gibson, the verses of . . . James Whitcomb Riley and Oliver Herford, such writers as John Kendrick Bangs. . . . Beginning next month the magazine *Life* will embark on a new venture entirely unrelated to the old."

How unrelated to the world of the Gibson Girl is this new venture might have been gathered at the time from a prospectus issued by enor-mous, Apollo-faced C. D. Jackson, of Time, Inc.

"*Life*," wrote he, "will show us the Man-of-the-Week . . . his body clothed, and, if possible, nude." It will expose "the loves, scandals, and personal affairs of the plain and fancy citizen . . . and write around them a light, good-tempered 'colyumnist' review of these once-private lives."

29,000 die-hard subscribers to *Life*,* long accustomed to he-she jokes, many ignorant of King of England's once-private life (*Time*, July 25 *et seq.*), will be comforted for the balance of their subscription periods by familiar, innocent jocosities of *Judge*. First issue of new publication went out last week to 250,000 readers, carried advertisements suggesting an annual revenue of $1,500,000, pictured Russian peasants in the nude, the love life of the Black Widow spider, referred inevitably to Mrs. Ernest Simpson.

Behind this latest, most incomprehensible Timenterprise looms, as usual, ambitious, gimlet-eyed, Baby Tycoon Henry Robinson Luce, co-

***

* Peak of *Life* circulation (1921): 250,000.

founder of *Time*, promulgator of *Fortune*, potent in associated radio & cinema ventures.

"HIGH-BUTTONED . . . BRILLIANT"

Headman Luce was born in Tengchowfu, China, on April 3, 1898, the son of Henry Winters & Elizabeth Middleton Luce, Presbyterian missionaries. Very unlike the novels of Pearl Buck were his early days. Under brows too beetling for a baby, young Luce grew up inside the compound, played with his two sisters, lisped first Chinese, dreamed much of the Occident. At 14, weary of poverty, already respecting wealth & power, he sailed alone for England, entered school at St. Albans. Restless again, he came to the United States, enrolled at Hotchkiss, met up & coming young Brooklynite Briton Hadden. Both even then were troubled with an itch to harass the public. Intoned Luce years later: "We reached the conclusion that most people were not well informed & that something should be done. . . ."

First publication to inform fellowman was *Hotchkiss Weekly Record*; next *Yale Daily News*, which they turned into a tabloid; fought to double hours of military training, fought alumni who wished to change tune of Yale song from *Die Wacht am Rhein*. Traditionally unshaven, wearing high-buttoned Brooks jackets, soft white collars, cordovan shoes, no garters, Luce & Hadden were Big Men on a campus then depleted of other, older Big Men by the war. Luce, pale, intense, nervous, was Skull & Bones, Alpha Delta Phi, Phi Beta Kappa, member of the Student Council, editor of the *News*; wrote sad poems, read the *New Republic*, studied political philosophy. As successful, less earnest, more convivial, Hadden collected china dogs, made jokes.* In 1920 the senior class voted Hadden Most Likely to Succeed, Luce Most Brilliant. Most Brilliant he, Luce sloped off to Christ Church, Oxford, there to study European conditions, take field trips into the churning Balkans.

BEST ADVICE: DON'T

Twenty months after commencement, in the city room of Paperkiller Frank Munsey's *Baltimore News*, met again Luce, Hadden. Newshawks by day, at night they wrangled over policies of the magazine they had been planning since Hotchkiss. Boasted the final prospectus: "*Time* will be free from cheap sensationalism . . . windy bias."

In May, 1922, began the long struggle to raise money to start *Time*.

---

* Once, watching Luce going past, laden with cares & responsibilities, Hadden chuckled, upspoke: "Look out, Harry. You'll drop the college."

Skeptical at the outset proved Newton D. Baker, Nicholas Murray Butler, Herbert Bayard Swope, William Lyon Phelps. Pooh-poohed *Review of Reviews* Owner Charles Lanier: "My best advice . . . don't do it." From studious, pint-sized Henry Seidel Canby, later editor of Lamont-backed *Saturday Review of Literature*, came only encouraging voice in this threnody.

Undismayed Luce & Hadden took the first of many offices in an old brownstone house at 9 East 17th Street, furnished it with a filing cabinet, four second-hand desks, a big brass bowl for cigarette stubs, sought backers.*

JPMorganapoleon H. P. Davison, Yale classmate of Luce, Hadden, great & good friend of both, in June contributed $4,000. Next to succumb: Mrs. David S. Ingalls, sister of Classmate William Hale Harkness; amount, $10,000. From Brother Bill, $5,000. Biggest early angel, Mrs. William Hale Harkness, mother of Brother Bill & Mrs. Ingalls, invested $20,000. Other original stockholders: Robert A. Chambers, Ward Che-

---

* In return for $50 cash, original investors were given two shares 6% Preferred Stock with a par value of $25, one share Class A Common Stock without par value. 3,440 Preferred, 1,720 Class A Common were so sold.

170 shares of Class A Common, 8,000 shares of Class B Common, also without par value, not entitled to dividends until Preferred Shares had been retired, were issued to Briton Hadden, Henry R. Luce, who gave one-third to associates, divided remainder equally.

In 1925, authorized capital of Time, Inc., was increased to 19,000 shares; of which 8,000 were Preferred, 3,000 Class A; as before, 8,000 Class B.

In June, 1930 (if you are still following this), the Preferred Stock was retired in full & dividends were initiated for both Common Stocks. Corporation at this time had 2,400 shares Class A, 7,900 Class B outstanding.

By the spring of 1931 *Time* had begun to march, shares were nominally quoted at $1,000. Best financial minds advised splitting stock on basis of twenty shares for one. Outstanding after clever maneuver: 206,400 shares Common.

In 1933, outlook still gorgeous, each share of stock was reclassified into 1/10th share of $6.50 Dividend Cumulative Convertible Preferred Stock ($6.50 div. cum. con. pfd. stk.) and one share of New Common Stock. New div. cum. con. pfd. stk. was convertible into a share and a half of New Common Stock, then selling around $40 a share, now quoted at over $200.

Present number of shares outstanding, 238,000; paper value of shares, $47,000,000; conservative estimate of Luce holding, 102,300 shares; paper value, $20,460,000; conservative estimate of Luce income from *Time* stock (shares earned $9.74 in 1935, paid so far in 1936, $6.50; anticipated dividend for full year, $8), $818,400; reported Luce income from other investments, $100,000; reported Luce bagatelle as editor of Time, Inc., $45,000; reported total Lucemoluent, $963,400.

Boy!

ney, F. Trubee Davison, E. Roland Harriman, Dwight W. Morrow, Harvey S. Firestone, Jr., Seymour H. Knox, William V. Griffin. By November Luce & Hadden had raised $86,000, decided to go to work on fellowman.

"SNAGGLE-TOOTHED . . . PIG-FACED"

Puny in spite of these preparations, prosy in spite of the contributions of Yale poets Archibald MacLeish & John Farrar, was the first issue of *Time* on March 3, 1923. Magazine went to 9,000 subscribers; readers learned that Uncle Joe Cannon had retired at 86, that there was a famine in Russia, that Thornton Wilder friend Tunney had defeated Greb.

Yet to suggest itself as a rational method of communication, of infuriating readers into buying the magazine, was strange inverted Timestyle. It was months before Hadden's impish contempt for his readers,* his impatience with the English language, crystallized into gibberish. By the end of the first year, however, Timeditors were calling people able, potent, nimble; "Tycoon," most successful Timepithet, had been coined by Editor Laird Shields Goldsborough; so fascinated Hadden with "beady-eyed" that for months nobody was anything else. Timeworthy were deemed such designations as "Tom-tom" Heflin, "Body-lover" Macfadden.

"Great word! Great word!" would crow Hadden, coming upon "snaggle-toothed," "pig-faced." Appearing already were such maddening coagulations as "cinemaddict," "radiorator." Appearing also were first gratuitous invasions of privacy. Always mentioned as William Randolph Hearst's "great & good friend" was Cinemactress Marion Davies, stressed was the bastardy of Ramsay MacDonald, the "cozy hospitality" of Mae West. Backward ran sentences until reeled the mind.

By March, 1924, the circulation had doubled, has risen since then 40,000 a year, reaches now the gratifying peak of 640,000, is still growing. From four meagre pages in first issue, *Time* advertising has now come to eclipse that in *Satevepost*. Published *Time* in first six months of 1936, 1,590 pages; *Satevepost*, 1,480.

NO SLUGABED, HE . . .

Strongly contrasted from the outset of their venture were Hadden, Luce. Hadden, handsome, black-haired, eccentric, irritated his partner by playing baseball with the office boys, by making jokes, by lack of

---

* Still framed at *Time* is Hadden's scrawled dictum: "Let Subscriber Goodkind mend his ways!"

respect for autocratic business. Conformist Luce disapproved of heavy drinking, played hard, sensible games of tennis, said once: "I have no use for a man who lies in bed after nine o'clock in the morning," walked to work every morning, reproved a writer who asked for a desk for lack of "log-cabin spirit."

In 1925, when *Time* moved its offices to Cleveland, bored, rebellious was Editor Hadden; Luce, busy & social, lunched with local bigwigs, addressed Chamber of Commerce, subscribed to Symphony Orchestra, had neat house in the suburbs. Dismayed was Luce when Hadden met him on return from Europe with premature plans to move the magazine back to New York. In 1929, dying of a streptococcus infection, Hadden still opposed certain details of success-formula of *Fortune*, new beloved Lucenterprise.

OATS, HOGS, CHEESE . . .

In January, 1930, first issue of *Fortune* was mailed to 30,000 subscribers, cost as now $1 a copy, contained articles on branch banking, hogs, glassblowing, how to live in Chicago on $25,000 a year. Latest issue (Nov., 1936) went to 130,000 subscribers, contained articles on bacon, tires, the New Deal, weighed as much as a good-sized flounder.*

Although in 1935 *Fortune* made a net profit of $500,000, vaguely dissatisfied was Editor Luce. Anxious to find & express "the technological significance of industry," he has been handicapped by the fact that his writers are often hostile to Big Business, prone to insert sneers, slithering insults. In an article on Bernard Baruch, the banker was described as calling President Hoover "old cheese-face." Protested Tycoon Baruch that he had said no such thing. Shotup of this was that Luce, embarrassed, printed a retraction; now often removes too-vivid phrasing from writers' copy.

¶ Typical perhaps of Luce methods is *Fortune* system of getting material. Writers in first draft put down wild gossip, any figures that occur to them. This is sent to victim, who indignantly corrects the errors, inadvertently supplies facts he might otherwise have withheld.

¶ *March of Time* in approximately its present form was first broadcast on March 6, 1931, paid the Columbia System for privilege, dropped from the air in February, 1932, with Luce attacking radio's "blatant claim to be a medium of education." Said he: "Should *Time* or any other business feel obliged to be the philanthropist of the air; to continue to

---

* Two pounds, nine ounces.

pay for radio advertising it doesn't want in order to provide radio with something worthwhile?" So popular, so valuable to the studio was *March of Time* that it was restored in September of the same year, with Columbia donating its time & facilities. Since then *March of Time* has been sponsored by Remington Rand typewriter company, by Wrigley's gum, by its own cinema *March of Time*, has made 400 broadcasts.* Apparently reconciled to philanthropy is Luce, because time for latest version will be bought & paid for by his organization.

¶ No active connection now has Luce with the moving-picture edition of *March of Time*, which was first shown on February 1, 1935, appears thirteen times a year in over 6,000 theatres, has so far failed to make money, to repay $900,000 investment. Even less connection has he with *Time's* only other unprofitable venture. Fifty-year-old *Architectural Forum*, acquired in 1932, loses still between $30,000 and $50,000 a year, circulates to 31,000.

¶ *Letters*, five-cent fortnightly collection of *Time's* correspondence with its indefatigable readers, was started in 1931, goes to 30,000, makes a little money.

¶ For a time, Luce was on Board of Directors of Paramount Pictures. Hoped to learn something of cinema, heard nothing discussed but banking, resigned sadly.

FASCINATING FACTS . . . DREAMY FIGURES . . .

Net profits of Time, Inc., for the past nine years:

1927	3,860
1928	125,787
1929	325,412
1930	818,936
1931	847,447
1932	613,727†
1933	1,009,628
1934	1,773,094
1935	$2,249,823‡

* By some devious necromancy, statisticians have calculated that *March of Time* ranks just behind *Amos & Andy* as most popular of all radio programs; reaches between 8,000,000 and 9,000,000 newshungry addicts.

† Hmm.

‡ Exceeded only by Curtis Publishing Co. (*Satevepost*): $5,329,000; Crowell Publishing Co. (*Collier's*): $2,399,600.

In 1935 gross revenue of *Time-Fortune* was $8,621,170, of which the newsmagazine brought in approximately $6,000,000. Outside investments netted $562,295. For rent, salaries, production & distribution, other expenses went $6,594,076. Other deductions: $41,397. Allowance for federal income tax: $298,169.

¶ *Time's* books, according to Chicago Statisticians Gerwig & Gerwig, show total assets of $6,755,451. Liabilities, $3,101,584. These figures, conventionally allowing $1 for name, prestige of *Time*, come far from reflecting actual prosperity of Luce, his enterprises. Sitting pretty are the boys.

LUCE . . . MARCHES ON!

Transmogrified by this success are the offices, personnel of *Time-Fortune*. Last reliable report: *Time*, 308 employees; *Fortune*, 103; Cinemarch, 58; Radiomarch, 10; *Architectural Forum*, 40; *Life*, 47. In New York; total, 566. In Chicago, mailing, editorial, mechanical employees, 216. Grand total Timemployees on God's earth, 782. Average weekly recompense for informing fellowman, $45.67802.

From first single office, Timen have come to bulge to bursting six floors of spiked, shiny Chrysler Building, occupy 150 rooms, eat daily, many at famed Cloud Club, over 1,000 eggs, 500 cups of coffee, much bicarbonate of soda. Other offices: Cinemarch, 10th Avenue at 54th Street; Radiomarch, Columbia Broadcasting Building.

Ornamented with Yale, Harvard, Princeton diplomas, stuffed fish, terrestrial globes are offices of Luce & other headmen; bleak, uncarpeted the writer's dingy lair.

¶ Heir apparent to mantle of Luce is dapper, tennis-playing, $35,000-a-year Roy Larsen, nimble in Radio- & Cinemarch, vice-president & second largest stockholder in Time, Inc. Stock income: $120,000.

¶ Looming behind him is burly, able, tumbledown Yaleman Ralph McAllister Ingersoll, former Fortuneditor, now general manager of all Timenterprises, descendant of 400-famed Ward McAllister. Littered his desk with pills, unguents, Kleenex, Socialite Ingersoll is *Time's* No. 1 hypochondriac, introduced ant palaces for study & emulation of employees, writes copious memoranda about filing systems, other trivia, seldom misses a Yale football game. His salary: $30,000; income from stock: $40,000.

¶ Early in life Timeditor John Stuart Martin lost his left arm in an accident. Unhandicapped he, resentful of sympathy, Martin played par golf at Princeton, is a crack shot with a rifle or shotgun, holds a telephone with no hands, using shoulder & chin, chews paperclips. First cousin of Cofounder Hadden, joined in second marriage to daughter of Cunard Tycoon Sir Ashley Sparks, Timartin is managing editor of newsmagazine, has been nimble in Cinemarch, other Timenterprises, makes $25,000 a year salary, gets from stock $60,000.

¶ $20,000 salary, $20,000 from stock gets shyest, least-known of all Timeditors, Harvardman John S. Billings, Jr., now under Luce in charge of revamped *Life*, once Washington correspondent for the Brooklyn *Eagle*, once National Affairs Editor for *Time*. Yclept "most important man in shop" by Colleague Martin, Billings, brother of famed muralist Henry Billings, is naïve, solemn, absent-minded, once printed same story twice, wanted to print, as news, story of van Gogh's self-mutilation, drives to office in car with liveried chauffeur, likes Jones Beach.

¶ Fortuneditor Eric Hodgins is thin-haired, orbicular, no Big Three graduate. Formerly on *Redbook*, boy & girl informing *Youth's Companion*, Hodgins inherited Pill-Swallower Ingersoll's editorial job two years ago when latter was called to greater glory, higher usefulness, still writes much of content of magazine, is paid $15,000; from stock only $8,000.

¶ Doomed to strict anonymity are *Time-Fortune* staff writers, but generally known in spite of this are former *Times* Bookritic John Chamberlain, Meistersinger Archibald MacLeish. Both out of sympathy with domineering business, both irked by stylistic restrictions, thorns to Luce as well as jewels they. Reward for lack of fame: Chamberlain, $10,000; MacLeish, $15,000; each, two months' vacation.

Brisk beyond belief are carryings-on these days in Luce's chromium tower. *Time*, marching on more militantly than ever, is a shambles on Sundays & Mondays, when week's news is teletyped to Chicago printing plant; *Fortune*, energetic, dignified, its offices smelling comfortably of cookies, is ever astir with such stupefying projects as sending the entire staff to Japan; new whoopsheet *Life* so deep in organization that staff breakfasts are held to choose from 6,000 submitted photographs the Nude of the Week; so harried perpetually all editors that even interoffice memoranda are couched in familiar Timestyle,* that an appointment to lunch with Editor Luce must be made three weeks in advance.

---

* Sample Luce memorandum: "Let *Time's* editors next week put thought on the Japanese beetle. H.R.L."

Caught up also in the whirlwind of progress are *Time, Fortune's* 19 maiden checkers. Bryn Mawr, Wellesley, Vassar graduates they, each is assigned to a staff writer, checks every word he writes, works hard & late, is barred by magazine's anti-feminine policy from editorial advancement.

COLD, BAGGY, TEMPERATE . . .

At work today, Luce is efficient, humorless, revered by colleagues; arrives always at 9:15, leaves at 6, carrying armfuls of work, talks jerkily, carefully, avoiding visitor's eye; stutters in conversation, never in speech-making. In early days kept standing at Luce desk like butlers were writers while he praised or blamed; now most business is done by time-saving memoranda called "Luce's bulls." Prone he to wave aside pleasantries, social preliminaries, to get at once to the matter in hand. Once to interviewer who said, "I hope I'm not disturbing you," snapped Luce, "Well, you are." To ladies full of gentle misinformation he is brusque, contradictory, hostile; says that his only hobby is "conversing with somebody who knows something," argues still that "names make news," that he would not hesitate to print a scandal involving his best friend.

Because of his Chinese birth, constantly besieged is Luce by visiting Orientals; he is polite, forbearing, seethes secretly. Lunch, usually in a private room at the Cloud Club, is eaten quickly, little attention paid to the food, much to business. He drinks not at all at midday, sparingly at all times, takes sometimes champagne at dinner, an occasional cocktail at parties. Embarrassed perhaps by reputation for unusual abstemiousness, he confesses proudly that he smokes too much.

Serious, ambitious Yale standards are still reflected in much of his conduct; in indiscriminate admiration for bustling success, in strong regard for conventional morality; in honest passion for accuracy; physically, in conservative, baggy clothes, white shirts with buttoned-down collars, solid-color ties. A budding joiner, in New York, Luce belongs to the Yale, Coffee House, Racquet & Tennis, Union, & Cloud Clubs; owns a box at the Metropolitan; is listed in *Who's Who & Social Register*.

Colder, more certain, more dignified than in the early days of the magazine, his prose style has grown less ebullient, resembles pontifical *Fortune* rather than chattering *Time*. Before some important body he makes now at least one speech a year, partly as a form of self-discipline, partly because he feels that his position as head of a national institution demands it. His interests wider, he likes to travel, meet & observe the Great. Five or six times in Europe, he has observed many Great & Near Great. Of a twenty-minute conversation with King Edward, then Prince of Wales, says only "Very interesting." Returning from such trips, he always provides staff members with 10 & 12-page memoranda carefully explaining conditions.

Orated recently of conditions in this country: "Without the aristo-cratic principle no society can endure. . . . What slowly deadened our aristocratic sense was the expanding frontier, but more the expanding machine. . . . But the aristocratic principle persisted in the United States in our fetish of comparative success. . . . We got a plutocracy without any common sense of dignity and obligation. Money became more and more the only mark of success, but still we insisted that the rich man was no better than the poor man—and the rich man accepted the verdict. And so let me make it plain, the triumph of the mass mind is nowhere more apparent than in the frustration of the upper classes." Also remarked in conversation: "Trouble is—great anti-social develop-ment—is the automobile trailer. Greatest failure of this country is that it hasn't provided good homes for its people. Trailer shows that."

MILESTONES

Good-naturedly amused by Luce tycoon ambitions was Lila Hotz, of Chicago, whom he married there on Dec. 22, 1923. In 1935, the father of two boys, Luce was divorced by her in Reno on Oct. 5. Married in Old Greenwich, Conn., without attendants, on Nov. 23, 1935, were Luce, Novelist-Playwright Clare Booth Brokaw, described once by Anglo-aesthete Cecil Beaton as "most drenchingly beautiful," former wife of elderly Pantycoon George Tuttle Brokaw.

Two days before ceremony, "Abide with Me," by new, beautiful Mrs. Luce, was produced at the Ritz Theatre. Play dealt with young woman married to sadistic drunkard, was unfavorably reviewed by all newspaper critics.*

---

* Of it said Richard Watts, blue-shirted, moon-faced *Tribune* dramappraiser:

"One almost forgave 'Abide with Me' its faults when its lovely playwright, who must have been crouched in the wings for a sprinter's start as the final curtain mercifully de-scended, heard a cry of 'author,' which was not audible in my vicinity, and arrived onstage to accept the audience's applause just as the actors, who had a head-start on her, were properly lined up and smoothed out to receive their customary adulation."

In a quandary was Bridegroom Luce when *Time's* own critic submitted a review suggesting play had some merit. Said he: "Show isn't that good. . . . Go back. . . . Write what you thought." Seven times, however, struggled the writer before achieving an acceptable compromise between criticism, tact.

A MILLION ROOMS, A THOUSAND BATHS . . .

Long accustomed to being entertained, entertaining, is Mrs. Luce, intimate of Mr. & Mrs. A. Coster Schermerhorn, Bernard M. Baruch, Jock Whitney, glistening stage & literary stars. Many were invited last summer to 30-acre estate in Stamford to play tennis, croquet, swim; many more will be when Mrs. Luce has finished her new play, "The Women,"* when *Life's* problems, budding policies have been settled by Luce.

Many, too, will come to 7,000-acre, $100,000 Luce plantation, near Charleston, S.C.; will sleep there in four streamlined, prefabricated guest cottages. Given to first Mrs. Luce in divorce settlement, along with $500,000 in cash & securities, was French Manoir at Gladstone, N.J., where Luce once planned to raise Black Angus cows, to become gentleman farmer.

Described too modestly by him to Newyorkereporter as "smallest apartment in River House,"† Luce duplex at 435 East 52nd Street contains 15 rooms, 5 baths, a lavatory; was leased furnished from Mrs. Bodrero Macy for $7,300 annually, contains many valuable French, English, Italian antiques, looks north and east on the river. In décor, Mrs. Luce prefers the modern; evasive is Luce. Says he: "Just like things convenient & sensible." Says also: "Whatever furniture or houses we buy in the future will be my wife's buying, not mine."

WHITHER, WHITHER?

Accused by many of Fascist leanings, of soaring journalistic ambition, much & conflicting is the evidence on Luce political faith, future

---

* Among backers are sad, ramshackle George S. Kaufman, high-domed fur-bearing Moss Hart.
† Smallest apartment in River House has six rooms, one bath.

plans. By tradition a Tory, in 1928 he voted for Alfred E. Smith, in 1932 for Herbert Hoover, this year for Alfred M. Landon. Long at outs with William Randolph Hearst, it was rumored that a visit last spring to California included a truce with ruthless, shifting publisher. Close friend for years of Thomas Lamont, Henry P. Davison, the late Dwight Morrow, it has been hinted that an official connection with the House of Morgan in the future is not impossible. Vehemently denies this Luce, denies any personal political ambition, admits only that he would like eventually to own a daily newspaper in New York.

Most persistent, most fantastic rumor, however, declares that Yaleman Luce already has a wistful eye on the White House. Reported this recently Chicago's *Ringmaster*, added: "A legally-minded friend . . . told him that his Chinese birth made him ineligible. Luce dashed to another lawyer to check. Relief! He was born of American parents and properly registered at the Consulate."

Whatever the facts in that matter, indicative of Luce consciousness of budding greatness, of responsibility to whole nation, was his report to *Time's* Board of Directors on March 19, 1936. Declaimed he: "The expansion of your company has brought it to a point beyond which it will cease to be even a big Small Business and become a small Big Business. . . . The problem of public relations also arises. *Time*, the Weekly Newsmagazine, has been, and still is, its own adequate apologist. Ditto, *Fortune*. But with a motion-picture journal, a nightly radio broadcast, and with four magazines, the public interpretation of your company's alleged viewpoint or viewpoints must be taken with great seriousness." Certainly to be taken with seriousness is Luce at thirty-eight, his fellowman already informed up to his ears, the shadow of his enterprises long across the land, his future plans impossible to imagine, staggering to contemplate. Where it all will end, knows God!

Stella Gibbons

*

EXCERPT FROM
COLD COMFORT FARM

[In her introduction to *Cold Comfort Farm*, first published in 1932, the author wrote: "And it is only because I have in mind all those thousands of persons, not unlike myself, who work in the vulgar and meaningless bustle of offices, shops and homes, and who are not always sure whether a sentence is Literature or whether it is just sheer flapdoodle, that I have adopted the method perfected by the late Herr Baedeker, and firmly marked what I consider the finer passages with one, two or three stars. In such a manner did the good man deal with cathedrals, hotels and paintings by men of genius. There seems no reason why it should not be applied to passages in novels.

It ought to help the reviewers, too."—ED.]

Dawn crept over the Downs like a sinister white animal, followed by the snarling cries of a wind eating its way between the black boughs of the thorns. The wind was the furious voice of this sluggish animal light that was baring the dormers and mullions and scullions of Cold Comfort Farm.

The farm was crouched on a bleak hillside, whence its fields, fanged with flints, dropped steeply to the village of Howling a mile away. Its stables and outhouses were built in the shape of a rough octangle surrounding the farmhouse itself, which was built in the shape of a rough triangle. The left point of the triangle abutted on the farthest point of the octangle, which was formed by the cowsheds, which lay parallel with the big barn. The outhouses were built of roughcast stone, with thatched roofs, while the farm itself was partly built of local flint, set in cement, and partly of some stone brought at great trouble and enormous expense from Perthshire.

The farmhouse was a long, low building, two-storied in parts. Other parts of it were three-storied. Edward the Sixth had originally owned it in the form of a shed in which he housed his swineherds, but he had grown tired of it, and had it rebuilt in Sussex clay. Then he pulled it down. Elizabeth had rebuilt it, with a good many chimneys in one way and another. The Charleses had let it alone; but William and Mary had pulled it down again, and George the First had rebuilt it. George the Second, however, burned it down. George the Third added another wing. George the Fourth pulled it down again.

By the time England began to develop that magnificent blossoming of trade and imperial expansion which fell to her lot under Victoria, there was not much of the original building left, save the tradition that it had always been there. It crouched, like a beast about to spring, under the bulk of Mock-uncle Hill. Like ghosts embedded in brick and stone, the architectural variations of each period through which it had passed were mute history. It was known locally as "The King's Whim."

The front door of the farm faced a perfectly inaccessible ploughed field at the back of the house; it had been the whim of Red Raleigh Starkadder, in 1835, to have it so; and so the family always used to come in by the back door, which abutted on the general yard facing the cowsheds. A long corridor ran halfway through the house on the second story and then stopped. One could not get into the attics at all. It was all very awkward.

. . . Growing with the viscous light that was invading the sky, there came the solemn, tortured-snake voice of the sea, two miles away, falling in sharp folds upon the mirror-expanses of the beach.

Under the ominous bowl of the sky a man was ploughing the sloping field immediately below the farm, where the flints shone bone-sharp and white in the growing light. The ice-cascade of the wind leaped over him, as he guided the plough over the flinty runnels. Now and again he called roughly to his team:

"Upidee, Travail! Ho, there, Arsenic! Jug-jug!" But for the most part he worked in silence, and silent were his team. The light showed no more of his face than a grey expanse of flesh, expressionless as the land he ploughed, from which looked out two sluggish eyes.

Every now and again, when he came to the corner of the field and was forced to tilt the scranlet of his plough almost on to its axle to make the turn, he glanced up at the farm where it squatted on the gaunt shoulder of the hill, and something like a possessive gleam shone in his dull eyes. But he only turned his team again, watching the crooked passage of the scranlet through the yeasty earth, and muttered: "Hola, Arsenic! Belay there, Travail!" while the bitter light waned into full day.

Because of the peculiar formation of the outhouses surrounding the farm, the light was always longer in reaching the yard than the rest of the house. Long after the sunlight was shining through the cobwebs on the uppermost windows of the old house the yard was in damp blue shadow.

It was in shadow now, but sharp gleams sprang from the ranged milk-buckets along the ford-piece outside the cowshed.

Leaving the house by the back door, you came up sharply against a stone wall running right across the yard, and turning abruptly, at right angles, just before it reached the shed where the bull was housed, and running down to the gate leading out into the ragged garden where mallows, dog's-body, and wild turnip were running riot. The bull's shed abutted upon the right corner of the dairy, which faced the cowsheds. The cowsheds faced the house, but the back door faced the bull's shed. From here a long-roofed barn extended the whole length of the octangle until it reached the front door of the house. Here it took a quick turn, and ended. The dairy was awkwardly placed; it had been a thorn in the side of old Fig Starkadder, the last owner of the farm, who had died three years ago. The dairy overlooked the front door, in face of the extreme point of its triangle which formed the ancient buildings of the farm-house.

From the dairy a wall extended which formed the right-hand boundary of the octangle, joining the bull's shed and the pig-pens at the extreme end of the right point of the triangle. A staircase, put in to make it more difficult, ran parallel with the octangle, halfway round the yard, against the wall which led down to the garden gate.

The spurt and regular ping! of milk against metal came from the reeking interior of the sheds. The bucket was pressed between Adam Lambsbreath's knees, and his head was pressed deep into the flank of Feckless, the big Jersey. His gnarled hands mechanically stroked the teat, while a low crooning, mindless as the Down wind itself, came from his lips.

He was asleep. He had been awake all night, wandering in thought over the indifferent bare shoulders of the Downs after his wild bird, his little flower . . .

Elfine. The name, unspoken but sharply musical as a glittering bead shaken from a fountain's tossing necklace, hovered audibly in the rancid air of the shed.

The beasts stood with heads lowered dejectedly against the wooden hoot-pieces of their stalls. Graceless, Pointless, Feckless, and Aimless awaited their turn to be milked. Sometimes Aimless ran her dry tongue, with a rasping sound sharp as a file through silk, awkwardly across the bony flank of Feckless, which was still moist with the rain that had fallen upon it through the roof during the night, or Pointless turned her large dull eyes sideways as she swung her head upwards to tear down a mouthful of cobwebs from the wooden runnet above her head. A lowering, moist, steamy light, almost like that which gleams below the eyelids of a man in fever, filled the cowshed.

Suddenly a tortured bellow, a blaring welter of sound that shattered the quiescence of the morning, tore its way across the yard and died away in a croak that was almost a sob. It was Big Business, the bull, wakening to another day, in the clammy darkness of his cell.

The sound woke Adam. He lifted his head from the flank of Feckless and looked around him in bewilderment for a moment; then slowly his eyes, which looked small and wet and lifeless in his primitive face, lost their terror as he realized that he was in the cowshed, that it was half-past six on a winter morning, and that his gnarled fingers were about the task which they had performed at this hour and in this place for the past eighty years or more.

He stood up, sighing, and crossed over to Pointless, who was eating Graceless's tail. Adam, who was linked to all dumb brutes by a chain forged in soil and sweat, took it out of her mouth and put into it, instead, his neckerchief—the last he had. She mumbled it, while he milked her, but stealthily spat it out as soon as he passed on to Aimless, and concealed it under the reeking straw with her hoof. She did not want to hurt the old man's feelings by declining to eat his gift. There was a close bond: a slow, deep, primitive, silent down-dragging link between Adam and all living beasts; they knew each other's simple needs. They lay close to the earth, and something of earth's old fierce simplicities had seeped into their beings.

Suddenly a shadow fell athwart the wooden stanchions of the door. It was no more than a darkening of the pallid paws of the day which were now embracing the shed, but all the cows instinctively stiffened, and Adam's eyes, as he stood up to face the newcomer, were again piteously full of twisted fear.

"Adam," uttered the woman who stood in the doorway, "how many pails of milk will there be this morning?"

"I dunnamany," responded Adam, cringingly; " 'tes hard to tell. If so be as our Pointless has got over her indigestion, maybe 'twill be four. If so be as she hain't, maybe three."

Judith Starkadder made an impatient movement. Her large hands had a quality which made them seem to sketch vast horizons with their slightest gesture. She looked a woman without boundaries as she stood wrapped in a crimson shawl to protect her bitter, magnificent shoulders from the splintery cold of the early air. She seemed fitted for any stage, however enormous.

"Well, get as many buckets as you can," she said, lifelessly, half-turning away. "Mrs. Starkadder questioned me about the milk yesterday. She has been comparing our output with that from other farms in the district, and she says we are five-sixteenths of a bucket below what our rate should be, considering how many cows we have."

A strange film passed over Adam's eyes, giving him the lifeless primeval look that a lizard has, basking in the swooning Southern heat. But he said nothing.

"And another thing," continued Judith, "you will probably have to drive down into Beershorn tonight to meet a train. Robert Poste's child is coming to stay with us for a while. I expect to hear some time this morning what time she is arriving. I will tell you later about it."

Adam shrank back against the gangrened flank of Pointless.

"Mun I?" he asked piteously. "Mun I, Miss Judith? Oh, dunna send me. How can I look into her liddle flower-face, and me knowin' what I know? Oh, Miss Judith, I beg of 'ee not to send me. Besides," he added, more practically, " 'tes close on sixty-five years since I put hands to a pair of reins, and I might upset the maidy."

Judith, who had slowly turned from him while he was speaking, was now halfway across the yard. She turned her head to reply to him with a slow, graceful movement. Her deep voice clanged like a bell in the frosty air:

"No, you must go, Adam. You must forget what you know—as we all must, while she is here. As for the driving, you had best harness Viper to the trap, and drive down into Howling and back six times this afternoon, to get your hand in again."

"Could not Master Seth go instead o' me?"

Emotion shook the frozen grief of her face. She said low and sharp:

"You remember what happened when he went to meet the new kitchenmaid . . . No. You must go."

Adam's eyes, like blind pools of water in his primitive face, suddenly grew cunning. He turned back to Aimless and resumed his mechanical stroking of the teat, saying in a sing-song rhythm:

"Ay, then I'll go, Miss Judith. I dunnamany times I've thought as how this day might come . . . And now I mun go to bring Robert Poste's child back to Cold Comfort. Aye, 'tes strange. The seed to the flower, the flower to the fruit, the fruit to the belly. Aye, so 'twill go."

Judith had crossed the muck and rabble of the yard, and now entered the house by the back door.

In the large kitchen, which occupied most of the middle of the house, a sullen fire burned, the smoke of which wavered up the blackened walls and over the deal table, darkened by age and dirt, which was roughly set for a meal. A snood full of coarse porridge hung over the fire, and standing with one arm resting upon the high mantel, looking moodily down into the heaving contents of the snood, was a tall young man whose riding boots were splashed with mud to the thigh, and whose coarse linen shirt was open to his waist. The firelight lit up his diaphragm muscles as they heaved slowly in rough rhythm with the porridge.

He looked up as Judith entered, and gave a short, defiant laugh, but said nothing. Judith crossed slowly over until she stood by his side. She was as tall as he. They stood in silence, she staring at him, and he down into the secret crevasses of the porridge.

"Well, mother mine," he said at last, "here I am, you see. I said I would be in time for breakfast, and I have kept my word."

His voice had a low, throaty, animal quality, a sneering warmth that wound a velvet ribbon of sexuality over the outward coarseness of the man.

Judith's breath came in long shudders. She thrust her arms deeper into her shawl. The porridge gave an ominous leering heave; it might almost have been endowed with life, so uncannily did its movements keep pace with the human passions that throbbed above it.

"Cur," said Judith, levelly, at last. "Coward! Liar! Libertine! Who were you with last night? Moll at the mill or Violet at the vicarage? Or Ivy, perhaps, at the ironmongery? Seth—my son . . ." Her deep, dry voice quivered, but she whipped it back, and her next words flew out at him like a lash.

"Do you want to break my heart?"

"Yes," said Seth, with an elemental simplicity.

The porridge boiled over.

Judith knelt, and hastily and absently ladled it off the floor back into the snood, biting back her tears. While she was thus engaged, there was a confused blur of voices and boots in the yard outside. The men were coming in to breakfast.

The meal for the men was set on a long trestle at the farther end of the kitchen, as far away from the fire as possible. They came into the room in awkward little clumps, eleven of them. Five were distant cousins of the Starkadders, and two others were half-brothers of Amos, Judith's husband. This left only four men who were not in some way connected with the family; so it will readily be understood that the general feeling among the farm-hands was not exactly one of hilarity. Mark Dolour, one of the four, had been heard to remark: "Happen it had been another kind o' eleven, us might ha' had a cricket team, wi' me for umpire. As ut is, 'twould be more befittin' if we was to hire oursen out for carrying coffins at sixpence a mile."

The five half-cousins and the two half-brothers came over to the table, for they took their meals with the family. Amos liked to have his kith about him, though, of course, he never said so or cheered up when they were.

A strong family likeness wavered in and out of the fierce, earth-reddened faces of the seven, like a capricious light. Micah Starkadder, mightiest of the cousins, was a ruined giant of a man, paralysed in one knee and wrist. His nephew, Urk, was a little, red, hard-bitten man with foxy ears. Urk's brother, Ezra, was of the same physical type, but horsy where Urk was foxy. Caraway, a silent man, wind-shaven and lean, with long wandering fingers, had some of Seth's animal grace, and this had been passed on to his son, Harkaway, a young, silent, nervous man given to bursts of fury about very little, when you came to sift matters.

Amos's half-brothers, Luke and Mark, were thickly built and high-featured; gross, silent men with an eye to the bed and the board.

When all were seated two shadows darkened the sharp, cold light pouring in through the door. They were no more than a growing imminence of humanity, but the porridge boiled over again.

Amos Starkadder and his eldest son, Reuben, came into the kitchen.

Amos, who was even larger and more of a wreck than Micah, silently put his pruning-snoot and reaping-hook in a corner by the fender, while Reuben put the scranlet with which he had been ploughing down beside them.

The two men took their places in silence, and after Amos had muttered a long and fervent grace, the meal was eaten in silence. Seth sat moodily tying and untying a green scarf round the magnificent throat he had inherited from Judith; he did not touch his porridge, and Judith only made a pretence of eating hers, playing with her spoon, patting the porridge up and down and idly building castles with the burnt bits. Her eyes burned under their penthouses, sometimes straying towards Seth as he sat sprawling in the lusty pride of casual manhood, with a good many buttons and tapes undone. Then those same eyes, dark as prisoned king-cobras, would slide round until they rested upon the bitter white head and raddled red neck of Amos, her husband, and then, like praying mantises, they would retreat between their lids. Secrecy pouted her full mouth.

Suddenly Amos, looking up from his food, asked abruptly:

"Where's Elfine?"

"She is not up yet. I did not wake her. She hinders more than she helps o' mornings," replied Judith.

Amos grunted.

" 'Tes a godless habit to lie abed of a working day, and the reeking red pits of the Lord's eternal wrathy fires lie in wait for them as do so. Aye"—his blue blazing eyes swivelled round and rested upon Seth, who was stealthily looking at a packet of Parisian art pictures under the table —"aye, and for those who break the seventh commandment, too. And for those"—the eye rested on Reuben, who was hopefully studying his parent's apoplectic countenance—"for those as waits for dead men's shoes."

"Nay, Amos, lad—" remonstrated Micah, heavily.

"Hold your peace," thundered Amos; and Micah, though a fierce tremor rushed through his mighty form, held it.

When the meal was done the hands trooped out to get on with the day's work of harvesting the swedes. This harvest was now in full swing; it took a long time and was very difficult to do. The Starkadders, too, rose and went out into the thin rain which had begun to fall. They were engaged in digging a well beside the dairy; it had been started a year ago, but it was taking a long time to do because things kept on going wrong. Once—a terrible day, when Nature seemed to hold her breath, and release it again in a furious gale of wind—Harkaway had fallen into it. Once Urk had pushed Caraway down it. Still, it was nearly finished; and everybody felt that it would not be long now.

In the middle of the morning a wire came from London announcing that the expected visitor would arrive by the six o'clock train.

Judith received it alone. Long after she had read it she stood motionless, the rain driving through the open door against her crimson shawl. Then slowly, with dragging steps, she mounted the staircase which led to the upper part of the house. Over her shoulder she said to old Adam, who had come into the room to do the washing up:

"Robert Poste's child will be here by the six o'clock train at Beershorn. You must leave to meet it at five. I am going up to tell Mrs. Starkadder that she is coming today."

Adam did not reply, and Seth, sitting by the fire, was growing tired of looking at his postcards, which were a three-year-old gift from the vicar's son, with whom he occasionally went poaching. He knew them all by now. Meriam, the hired girl, would not be in until after dinner. When she came, she would avoid his eyes, and tremble and weep.

He laughed insolently, triumphantly. Undoing another button of his shirt, he lounged out across the yard to the shed where Big Business, the bull, was imprisoned in darkness.

Laughing softly, Seth struck the door of the shed.

And as though answering the deep call of male to male, the bull uttered a loud tortured bellow that rose undefeated through the dead sky that brooded over the farm.

Seth undid yet another button, and lounged away.

· · ·

Adam Lambsbreath, alone in the kitchen, stood looking down unseeingly at the dirtied plates, which it was his task to wash, for the hired girl, Meriam, would not be here until after dinner, and when she came she would be all but useless. Her hour was near at hand, as all Howling knew. Was it not February, and the earth a-teem with newing life? A grin twisted Adam's writhen lips. He gathered up the plates one by one and carried them to the pump, which stood in a corner of the kitchen, above a stone sink. Her hour was nigh. And when April like an over-lustful lover leaped upon the lush flanks of the Downs there would be yet another child in the wretched hut down at Nettle Flitch Field, where Meriam housed the fruits of her shame.

"Aye, dog's-fennel or beard's-crow, by their fruits they shall be betrayed," muttered Adam, shooting a stream of cold water over the coagulated plates. "Come cloud, come sun, 'tes ay so."

While he was listlessly dabbing at the crusted edges of the porridge-plates with a thorn twig, a soft step descended the stairs outside the door which closed off the staircase from the kitchen. Someone paused on the threshold.

The step was light as thistledown. If Adam had not had the rush of the running water in his ears too loudly for him to be able to hear any other noise, he might have thought this delicate, hesitant step was the beating of his own blood.

But, suddenly, something like a kingfisher streaked across the kitchen, in a glimmer of green skirts and flying gold hair and the chime of a laugh was followed a second later by the slam of the gate leading through the starveling garden out on to the Downs.

Adam flung round violently on hearing the sound, dropping his thorn twig and breaking two plates.

"Elfine . . . my little bird," he whispered, starting towards the open door.

A brittle silence mocked his whisper; through it wound the rank odours of rattan and barn.

"My pharisee . . . my cowdling . . ." he whispered piteously. His eyes had again that look as of waste grey pools, sightless primeval wastes reflecting the wan evening sky in some lonely marsh, as they wandered about the kitchen.

His hands fell slackly against his sides, and he dropped another plate. It broke.

He sighed, and began to move slowly towards the open door, his task forgotten. His eyes were fixed upon the cowshed.

"Aye, the beasts . . ." he muttered, dully; "the dumb beasts never fail a man. They know. Aye, I'd 'a' done better to cowdle our Feckless in my bosom than liddle Elfine. Aye, wild as a marsh-tigget in May, 'tes. And a will never listen to a word from anyone. Well, so 't must be. Sour or sweet, by barn or bye, so 'twill go. Ah, but if he"—the blind grey pools grew suddenly terrible, as though a storm were blowing in across the marsh from the Atlantic wastes—"if he but harms a hair o' her little goldy head I'll *kill* un."

So muttering, he crossed the yard and entered the cowshed, where he untied the beasts from their hoot-pieces and drove them across the yard, down the muddy rutted lane that led to Nettle Flitch Field. He was enmeshed in his grief. He did not notice that Graceless's leg had come off and that she was managing as best she could with three.

Left alone, the kitchen fire went out.

Evelyn Waugh

*

WINNER TAKES ALL

1

When Mrs. Kent-Cumberland's eldest son was born (in an expensive London nursing home) there was a bonfire on Tomb Beacon; it consumed three barrels of tar, an immense catafalque of timber, and, as things turned out—for the flames spread briskly in the dry gorse and loyal tenantry were too tipsy to extinguish them—the entire vegetation of Tomb Hill.

As soon as mother and child could be moved, they travelled in state to the country, where flags were hung out in the village street and a trellis arch of evergreen boughs obscured the handsome Palladian entrance gates of their home. There were farmers' dinners both at Tomb and on the Kent-Cumberlands' Norfolk estate, and funds for a silver-plated tray were ungrudgingly subscribed.

The christening was celebrated by a garden-party. A princess stood godmother by proxy, and the boy was called Gervase Peregrine Mountjoy St. Eustace—all of them names illustrious in the family's history.

Throughout the service and the subsequent presentations he maintained an attitude of phlegmatic dignity which confirmed everyone in the high estimate they had already formed of his capabilities.

After the garden-party there were fireworks and after the fireworks a very hard week for the gardeners, cleaning up the mess. The life of the Kent-Cumberlands then resumed its normal tranquillity until nearly two years later, when, much to her annoyance, Mrs. Kent-Cumberland discovered that she was to have another baby.

The second child was born in August in a shoddy modern house on the East Coast which had been taken for the summer so that Gervase might have the benefit of sea air. Mrs. Kent-Cumberland was attended by the local doctor, who antagonized her by his middle-class accent, and proved, when it came to the point, a great deal more deft than the London specialist.

Throughout the peevish months of waiting Mrs. Kent-Cumberland had fortified herself with the hope that she would have a daughter. It would be a softening influence for Gervase, who was growing up somewhat unresponsive, to have a pretty, gentle, sympathetic sister two years younger than himself. She would come out just when he was going up to Oxford and would save him from either of the dreadful extremes of evil company which threatened that stage of development—the bookworm and the hooligan. She would bring down delightful girls for Eights Week and Commem. Mrs. Kent-Cumberland had it all planned out. When she was delivered of another son she named him Thomas, and fretted through her convalescence with her mind on the coming hunting season.

2

The two brothers developed into sturdy, unremarkable little boys; there was little to choose between them except their two years' difference in age. They were both sandy-haired, courageous, and well-mannered on occasions. Neither was sensitive, artistic, highly strung, or conscious of being misunderstood. Both accepted the fact of Gervase's importance just as they accepted his superiority of knowledge and physique. Mrs. Kent-Cumberland was a fair-minded woman, and in the event of the two being involved in mischief, it was Gervase, as the elder, who was the more severely punished. Tom found that his obscurity was on the whole advantageous, for it excused him from the countless minor performances of ceremony which fell on Gervase.

3

At the age of seven Tom was consumed with desire for a model motorcar, an expensive toy of a size to sit in and pedal about the garden. He prayed for it steadfastly every evening and most mornings for several weeks. Christmas was approaching.

Gervase had a smart pony and was often taken hunting. Tom was alone most of the day and the motor-car occupied a great part of his thoughts. Finally he confided his ambition to an uncle. This uncle was not addicted to expensive present giving, least of all to children (for he was a man of limited means and self-indulgent habits), but something in his nephew's intensity of feeling impressed him.

"Poor little beggar," he reflected, "his brother seems to get all the fun," and when he returned to London he ordered the motor-car for Tom. It arrived some days before Christmas and was put away upstairs with other presents. On Christmas Eve Mrs. Kent-Cumberland came to inspect them. "How very kind," she said, looking at each label in turn, "how very kind."

The motor-car was by far the largest exhibit. It was pillar-box red, complete with electric lights, a hooter and a spare wheel.

"Really," she said. "How *very* kind of Ted."

Then she looked at the label more closely. "But how foolish of him. He's put *Tom's* name on it."

"There was this book for Master Gervase," said the nurse, producing a volume labelled "Gervase with best wishes from Uncle Ted."

"Of course the parcels have been confused at the shop," said Mrs. Kent-Cumberland. "This can't have been meant for Tom. Why, it must have cost six or seven pounds."

She changed the labels and went downstairs to supervise the decoration of the Christmas tree, glad to have rectified an obvious error of justice.

Next morning, the presents were revealed. "Oh, Ger. You *are* lucky," said Tom, inspecting the motor-car. "May I ride in it?"

"Yes, only be careful. Nanny says it was awfully expensive."

Tom rode it twice round the room. "May I take it in the garden sometimes?"

"Yes. You can have it when I'm hunting."

Later in the week they wrote to thank their uncle for his presents. Gervase wrote:

DEAR UNCLE TED,

Thank you for the lovely present. It's lovely. The pony is very well. I am going to hunt again before I go back to school.

Love from GERVASE.

DEAR UNCLE TED [*wrote Tom*],

Thank you ever so much for the lovely present. It is just what I wanted. Again thanking you very much.

With love from TOM.

"So that's all the thanks I get. Ungrateful little beggar," said Uncle Ted, resolving to be more economical in future.

But when Gervase went back to school he said, "You can have the motor-car, Tom, to keep."

"What, for *my own?*"

"Yes. It's a kid's toy, anyway."

And by this act of generosity he increased Tom's respect and love for him a hundredfold.

4

The war came and profoundly changed the lives of the two boys. It engendered none of the neuroses threatened by pacifists. Air raids remained among Tom's happiest memories, when the school used to be awakened in the middle of the night and hustled downstairs to the basement where, wrapped in eiderdowns, they were regaled with cocoa and cake by the matron, who looked supremely ridiculous in a flannel nightgown. Once a Zeppelin was hit in sight of the school; they all crowded to the dormitory windows to see it sinking slowly in a globe of pink flame. A very young master whose health rendered him unfit for military service danced on the headmaster's tennis court crying, "There go the baby killers." Tom made a collection of "War Relics," including a captured German helmet, shell-splinters, *The Times* for August 4th, 1914, buttons, cartridge cases, and cap badges, that was voted the best in the school.

The event which radically changed the relationship of the brothers was the death, early in 1915, of their father. Neither knew him well nor particularly liked him. He had represented the division in the House of Commons and spent much of his time in London while the children were at Tomb. They only saw him on three occasions after he joined the army. Gervase and Tom were called out of the classroom and told of his death by the headmaster's wife. They cried, since it was expected of them, and for some days were treated with marked deference by the masters and the rest of the school.

It was in the subsequent holidays that the importance of the change became apparent. Mrs. Kent-Cumberland had suddenly become more emotional and more parsimonious. She was liable to unprecedented outbursts of tears, when she would crush Gervase to her and say, "My poor fatherless boy." At other times she spoke gloomily of death duties.

5

For some years in fact "Death Duties" became the refrain of the household.

When Mrs. Kent-Cumberland let the house in London and closed down a wing at Tomb, when she reduced the servants to four and the gardeners to two, when she "let the flower gardens go," when she stopped asking her brother Ted to stay, when she emptied the stables, and became almost fanatical in her reluctance to use the car, when the bath water was cold and there were no new tennis-balls, when the chimneys were dirty and the lawns covered with sheep, when Gervase's cast-off clothes ceased to fit Tom, when she refused him the "extra" expense at school of carpentry lessons and mid-morning milk—"Death Duties" were responsible.

"It is all for Gervase," Mrs. Kent-Cumberland used to explain. "When he inherits, he must take over free of debt, as his father did."

6

Gervase went to Eton in the year of his father's death. Tom would normally have followed him two years later, but in her new mood of economy Mrs. Kent-Cumberland cancelled his entry and began canvassing her friends' opinions about the less famous, cheaper public schools. "The education is just as good," she said, "and far more suitable for a boy who has his own way to make in the world."

Tom was happy enough at the school to which he was sent. It was very bleak and very new, salubrious, progressive, prosperous in the boom that secondary education enjoyed in the years immediately following the war, and, when all was said and done, "thoroughly suitable for a boy with his own way to make in the world." He had several friends whom he was not allowed to invite to his home during the holidays. He got his House colours for swimming and fives, played once or twice in the second eleven for cricket, and was a platoon commander in the O.T.C.; he was in the sixth form and passed the Higher Certificate in his last year, became a prefect and enjoyed the confidence of his house master, who spoke of him as "a very decent stamp of boy." He left school at the age of eighteen without the smallest desire to re-visit it or see any of its members again.

Gervase was then at Christ Church. Tom went up to visit him, but the magnificent Etonians who romped in and out of his brother's rooms scared and depressed him. Gervase was in the Bullingdon, spending money freely and enjoying himself. He gave a dinner-party in his rooms, but Tom sat in silence, drinking heavily to hide his embarrassment, and was later sombrely sick in a corner of Peckwater quad. He returned to Tomb next day in the lowest spirits.

"It is not as though Tom were a scholarly boy," said Mrs. Kent-Cumberland to her friends. "I am glad he is not, of course. But if he had been, it might have been right to make the sacrifice and send him to the University. As it is, the sooner he Gets Started the better."

7

Getting Tom started, however, proved a matter of some difficulty. During the Death Duty Period, Mrs. Kent-Cumberland had cut herself off from many of her friends. Now she cast round vainly to find someone who would "put Tom into something." Chartered Accountancy, Chinese Customs, estate agencies, "the City," were suggested and abandoned. "The trouble is that he has no particular abilities," she explained. "He is the sort of boy who would be useful in anything—an all-round man—but, of course, he has no capital."

August, September, October passed; Gervase was back at Oxford, in fashionable lodgings in the High Street, but Tom remained at home without employment. Day by day he and his mother sat down together to luncheon and dinner, and his constant presence was a severe strain on Mrs. Kent-Cumberland's equability. She herself was always busy and, as she bustled about her duties, it shocked and distracted her to encounter the large figure of her younger son sprawling on the morning-room sofa or leaning against the stone parapet of the terrace and gazing out apathetically across the familiar landscape.

•　•　•

"Why can't you find something to *do?*" she would complain. "There are *always* things to do about a house. Heaven knows I never have a moment." And when, one afternoon, he was asked out by some neighbours and returned too late to dress for dinner, she said, "Really, Tom, I should have thought that *you* had time for that."

"It is a very serious thing," she remarked on another occasion, "for a young man of your age to get out of the habit of work. It saps his whole morale."

Accordingly she fell back upon the ancient country house expedient of Cataloguing the Library. This consisted of an extensive and dusty collection of books amassed by succeeding generations of a family at no time notable for their patronage of literature; it had been catalogued before, in the middle of the nineteenth century, in the spidery, spinsterish hand of a relative in reduced circumstances; since then the additions and disturbances had been negligible, but Mrs. Kent-Cumberland purchased a fumed oak cabinet and several boxes of cards and instructed Tom how she wanted the shelves re-numbered and the books twice entered under Subject and Author.

•　•　•

It was a system that should keep a boy employed for some time, and it was with vexation, therefore, that, a few days after the task was commenced, she paid a surprise visit to the scene of his labour and found

Tom sitting, almost lying, in an armchair, with his feet on a rung of the library steps, reading.

"I am glad you have found something interesting," she said in a voice that conveyed very little gladness.

"Well, to tell you the truth, I think I have," said Tom, and showed her the book.

It was the manuscript journal kept by a Colonel Jasper Cumberland during the Peninsular War. It had no startling literary merit, nor did its criticisms of the general staff throw any new light upon the strategy of the campaign, but it was a lively, direct, day-to-day narrative, redolent of its period; there was a sprinkling of droll anecdotes, some vigorous descriptions of fox-hunting behind the lines of Torres Vedras, of the Duke of Wellington dining in Mess, of a threatened mutiny that had not yet found its way into history, of the assault on Badajoz; there were some bawdy references to Portuguese women and some pious reflections about patriotism.

"I was wondering if it might be worth publishing," said Tom.

"I should hardly think so," replied his mother. "But I will certainly show it to Gervase when he comes home."

For the moment the discovery gave a new interest to Tom's life. He read up the history of the period and of his own family. Jasper Cumberland he established as a younger son of the period, who had later emigrated to Canada. There were letters from him among the archives, including the announcement of his marriage to a Papist, which had clearly severed the link with his elder brother. In a case of uncatalogued miniatures in the long drawing-room, he found the portrait of a handsome whiskered soldier, which by a study of contemporary uniforms he was able to identify as the diarist.

Presently, in his round, immature handwriting, Tom began working up his notes into an essay. His mother watched his efforts with unqualified approval. She was glad to see him busy, and glad to see him taking an interest in his family's history. She had begun to fear that by sending him to a school without "tradition" she might have made a socialist of the boy. When, shortly before the Christmas vacation, work was found for Tom, she took charge of his notes. "I am sure Gervase will be extremely interested," she said. "He may even think it worth showing to a publisher."

8

The work that had been found for Tom was not immediately lucrative, but, as his mother said, it was a beginning. It was to go to Wolverhampton and learn the motor business from the bottom. The first two years were to be spent at the works, from where, if he showed talent, he might graduate to the London showrooms. His wages, at first, were thirty-five shillings a week. This was augmented by the allowance of another pound. Lodgings were found for him over a fruit shop in the outskirts of the town, and Gervase gave him his old two-seater car, in which he could travel to and from his work, and for occasional weekends home.

It was during one of these visits that Gervase told him the good news that a London publisher had read the diary and seen possibilities in it. Six months later it appeared under the title *The Journal of an English Cavalry Officer during the Peninsular War. Edited with notes and a biographical introduction by Gervase Kent-Cumberland.* The miniature portrait was prettily reproduced as a frontispiece, there was a collotype copy of a page of the original manuscript, a contemporary print of Tomb Park, and a map of the campaign. It sold nearly two thousand copies at twelve and sixpence and received two or three respectful reviews in the Saturday and Sunday papers.

• • •

The appearance of the *Journal* coincided within a few days with Gervase's twenty-first birthday. The celebrations were extravagant and prolonged, culminating in a ball at which Tom's attendance was required.

He drove over, after the works had shut down, and arrived, just in time for dinner, to find a house-party of thirty and a house entirely transformed.

His own room had been taken for a guest ("as you will only be here for one night," his mother explained). He was sent down to the Cumberland Arms, where he dressed by candlelight in a breathless little bedroom over the bar, and arrived late and slightly dishevelled at dinner, where he sat between two lovely girls who neither knew who he was nor troubled to inquire. The dancing afterwards was in a marquee built on the terrace, which a London catering firm had converted into a fair replica of a Pont Street drawing-room. Tom danced once or twice with the daughters of neighbouring families whom he had known since childhood. They asked him about Wolverhampton and the works. He had to get up early next morning; at midnight he slipped away to his bed at the inn. The evening had bored him; because he was in love.

9

It had occurred to him to ask his mother whether he might bring his fiancée to the ball, but on reflexion, enchanted as he was, he had realized that it would not do. The girl was named Gladys Cruttwell. She was two years older than himself; she had fluffy yellow hair which she washed at home once a week and dried before the gas fire; on the day after the shampoo it was very light and silky; towards the end of the week, darker and slightly greasy. She was a virtuous, affectionate, self-reliant, even-tempered, unintelligent, high-spirited girl, but Tom could not disguise from himself the fact that she would not go down well at Tomb.

She worked for the firm on the clerical side. Tom had noticed her on his second day, as she tripped across the yard, exactly on time, bare-headed (the day after a shampoo) in a woollen coat and skirt which she had knitted herself. He had got into conversation with her in the can-teen, by making way for her at the counter with a chivalry that was not much practised at the works. His possession of a car gave him a clear advantage over the other young men about the place.

They discovered that they lived within a few streets of one another, and it presently became Tom's practice to call for her in the mornings and take her home in the evenings. He would sit in the two-seater outside her gate, sound the horn, and she would come running down the path to meet him. As summer approached they went for drives in the evening among leafy Warwickshire lanes. In June they were engaged. Tom was exhilarated, sometimes almost dizzy at the experience, but he hesitated to tell his mother. "After all," he reflected, "it is not as though I were Gervase," but in his own heart he knew that there would be trouble.

Gladys came of a class accustomed to long engagements; marriage seemed a remote prospect; an engagement to her signified the formal recognition that she and Tom spent their spare time in one another's company. Her mother, with whom she lived, accepted him on these terms. In years to come, when Tom had got his place in the London showrooms, it would be time enough to think about marrying. But Tom was born to a less patient tradition. He began to speak about a wedding in the autumn.

"It would be lovely," said Gladys in the tones she would have em-ployed about winning the Irish sweepstake.

He had spoken very little about his family. She understood, vaguely, that they lived in a big house, but it was a part of life that never had been real to her. She knew that there were duchesses and marchio-nesses in something called "Society"; they were encountered in the pa-pers and the films. She knew there were directors with large salaries; but the fact that there were people like Gervase or Mrs. Kent-Cumberland, and that they would think of themselves as radically different from her-self, had not entered her experience. When, eventually, they were brought together Mrs. Kent-Cumberland was extremely gracious and Gladys thought her a very nice old lady. But Tom knew that the meeting was proving disastrous.

"Of course," said Mrs. Kent-Cumberland, "the whole thing is quite impossible. Miss Whatever-her-name-was seemed a thoroughly nice girl, but you are not in a position to think of marriage. Besides," she added with absolute finality, "you must not forget that if anything were to happen to Gervase you would be his heir."

So Tom was removed from the motor business and an opening found for him on a sheep farm in South Australia.

10

It would not be fair to say that in the ensuing two years Mrs. Kent-Cumberland forgot her younger son. She wrote to him every month and sent him bandana handkerchiefs for Christmas. In the first lonely days he wrote to her frequently, but when, as he grew accustomed to the new life, his letters became less frequent she did not seriously miss them. When they did arrive they were lengthy; she put them aside from her correspondence to read at leisure and, more than once, mislaid them, unopened. But whenever her acquaintances asked after Tom she loyally answered, "Doing splendidly. And enjoying himself *very* much."

She had many other things to occupy and, in some cases, distress her. Gervase was now in authority at Tomb, and the careful régime of his minority wholly reversed. There were six expensive hunters in the stable. The lawns were mown, bedrooms thrown open, additional bathrooms installed; there was even talk of constructing a swimming pool. There was constant Saturday to Monday entertaining. There was the sale, at a poor price, of two Romneys and a Hoppner.

Mrs. Kent-Cumberland watched all this with mingled pride and anxiety. In particular she scrutinized the succession of girls who came to stay, in the irreconcilable, ever-present fears that Gervase would or would not marry. Either conclusion seemed perilous; a wife for Gervase must be well-born, well conducted, rich, of stainless reputation, and affectionately disposed to Mrs. Kent-Cumberland; such a mate seemed difficult to find. The estate was clear of the mortgages necessitated by death duties, but dividends were uncertain, and though, as she frequently pointed out, she "never interfered," simple arithmetic and her own close experience of domestic management convinced her that Gervase would not long be able to support the scale of living which he had introduced.

With so much on her mind, it was inevitable that Mrs. Kent-Cum-

berland should think a great deal about Tomb and very little about South
Australia, and should be rudely shocked to read in one of Tom's letters
that he was proposing to return to England on a visit, with a fiancée and
a future father-in-law; that in fact he had already started, was now on
the sea and due to arrive in London in a fortnight. Had she read his
earlier letters with attention she might have found hints of such an
attachment, but she had not done so, and the announcement came to
her as a wholly unpleasant surprise.

"Your brother is coming back."

"Oh good! When?"

"He is bringing a farmer's daughter to whom he is engaged—and
the farmer. They want to come here."

"I say, that's rather a bore. Let's tell them we're having the boilers
cleaned."

"You don't seem to realize that this is a serious matter, Gervase."

"Oh well, you fix things up. I dare say it would be all right if they
came next month. We've got to have the Anchorages some time. We
might get both over together."

In the end it was decided that Gervase would meet the immigrants
in London, vet them and report to his mother whether or no they were
suitable fellow-guests for the Anchorages. A week later, on his return to
Tomb, his mother greeted him anxiously.

"Well? You never wrote?"

"Wrote? Why should I? I never do. I say, I haven't forgotten a
birthday or anything, have I?"

"Don't be absurd, Gervase. I mean, about your brother Tom's unfortunate entanglement. Did you see the girl?"

"Oh, *that*. Yes, I went and had dinner with them. Tom's done
himself quite well. Fair, rather fat, saucer-eyes, good-tempered, I should
say, by her looks."

"Does she—does she speak with an Australian accent?"

"Didn't notice it."

"And the father?"

"Pompous old boy."

"Would he be all right with the Anchorages?"

"I should think he'd go down like a dinner. But they can't come.
They are staying with the Chasms."

"Indeed! What an extraordinary thing. But, of course, Archie
Chasm was Governor-General once. Still, it shows they must be fairly
respectable. Where are they staying?"

"Claridge's."

"Then they must be quite rich, too. How very interesting. I will write this evening."

11

Three weeks later they arrived. Mr. MacDougal, the father, was a tall, lean man, with pince-nez and an interest in statistics. He was a territorial magnate to whom the Tomb estates appeared a cosy small-holding. He did not emphasize this in any boastful fashion, but in his statistical zeal gave Mrs. Kent-Cumberland some staggering figures. "Is Bessie your only child?" asked Mrs. Kent-Cumberland.

"My only child and heir," he replied, coming down to brass tacks at once. "I dare say you have been wondering what sort of settlement I shall be able to make on her. Now that, I regret to say, is a question I cannot answer accurately. We have good years, Mrs. Kent-Cumberland, and we have bad years. It all depends."

"But I dare say that even in bad years the income is quite considerable?"

"In a bad year," said Mr. MacDougal, "in a *very* bad year such as the present, the net profits, after all deductions have been made for running expenses, insurance, taxation, and deterioration, amount to something between"—Mrs. Kent-Cumberland listened breathlessly— "fifty and fifty-two thousand pounds. I know that is a very vague statement, but it is impossible to be more accurate until the last returns are in."

Bessie was bland and creamy. She admired everything. "It's so *antique*," she would remark with relish, whether the object of her attention was the Norman Church of Tomb, the Victorian panelling in the billiard-room, or the central-heating system which Gervase had recently installed. Mrs. Kent-Cumberland took a great liking to the girl.

"Thoroughly Teachable," she pronounced. "But I wonder whether she is *really* suited to Tom . . . I *wonder* . . ."

• • •

The MacDougals stayed for four days and, when they left, Mrs. Kent-Cumberland pressed them to return for a longer visit. Bessie had been enchanted with everything she saw.

"I wish we could live here," she had said to Tom on her first evening, "in this dear, quaint old house."

"Yes, darling, so do I. Of course it all belongs to Gervase, but I always look on it as my home."

"Just as we Australians look on England."

"Exactly."

She had insisted on seeing everything; the old gabled manor, once the home of the family, relegated now to the function of dower house since the present mansion was built in the eighteenth century—the house of mean proportions and inconvenient offices where Mrs. Kent-Cumberland, in her moments of depression, pictured her own declining years; the mill and the quarries; the farm, which to the MacDougals seemed minute and formal as a Noah's Ark. On these expeditions it was Gervase who acted as guide. "He, of course, knows so much more about it than Tom," Mrs. Kent-Cumberland explained.

Tom, in fact, found himself very rarely alone with his fiancée. Once, when they were all together after dinner, the question of his marriage was mentioned. He asked Bessie whether, now that she had seen Tomb, she would sooner be married there, at the village church, than in London.

"Oh, there is no need to decide anything hastily," Mrs. Kent-Cumberland had said. "Let Bessie look about a little first."

· · ·

When the MacDougals left, it was to go to Scotland to see the castle of their ancestors. Mr. MacDougal had traced relationship with various branches of his family, had corresponded with them intermittently, and now wished to make their acquaintance.

Bessie wrote to them all at Tomb; she wrote daily to Tom, but in her thoughts, as she lay sleepless in the appalling bed provided for her by her distant kinsmen, she was conscious for the first time of a light feeling of disappointment and uncertainty. In Australia Tom had seemed so different from everyone else, so gentle and dignified and cultured. Here in England he seemed to recede into obscurity. Everyone in England seemed to be like Tom.

And then there was the house. It was exactly the kind of house which she had always imagined English people to live in, with the dear little park—less than a thousand acres—and the soft grass and the old stone. Tom had fitted into the house. He had fitted too well; had disappeared entirely in it and become part of the background. The central place belonged to Gervase—so like Tom but more handsome; with all Tom's charm but with more personality. Beset with these thoughts, she rolled on the hard and irregular bed until dawn began to show through the lancet window of the Victorian-baronial turret. She loved that turret for all its discomfort. It was so antique.

12

Mrs. Kent-Cumberland was an active woman. It was less than ten days after the MacDougals' visit that she returned triumphantly from a day in

London. After dinner, when she sat alone with Tom in the small draw-ing-room, she said:

"You'll be very much surprised to hear who I saw today. *Gladys.*"

"Gladys?"

"Gladys Cruttwell."

"Good heavens. Where on earth did you meet her?"

"It was quite by chance," said his mother vaguely. "She is working there now."

"How was she?"

"Very pretty. Prettier, if anything."

There was a pause. Mrs. Kent-Cumberland stitched away at a gros-point chair seat. "You know, dear boy, that I *never interfere*, but I have often wondered whether you treated Gladys very kindly. I know I was partly to blame, myself. But you were both very young and your pros-pects so uncertain. I thought a year or two of separation would be a good test of whether you really loved one another."

"Oh, I am sure she has forgotten about me long ago."

"Indeed, she has not, Tom. I thought she seemed a very unhappy girl."

"But how *can* you know, Mother, just seeing her casually like that?"

"We had luncheon together," said Mrs. Kent-Cumberland. "In an A.B.C. shop."

Another pause.

"But, look here, I've forgotten all about her. I only care about Bessie now."

"You know, dearest boy, I never interfere. I think Bessie is a de-lightful girl. But are you free? Are you free in your own conscience? You know, and I do not know, on what terms you parted from Gladys."

And there returned, after a long absence, the scene which for the first few months of his Australian venture had been constantly in Tom's memory, of a tearful parting and many intemperate promises. He said nothing. "I did not tell Gladys of your engagement. I thought you had the right to do that—as best you can, in your own way. But I did tell her you were back in England and that you wished to see her. She is coming here tomorrow for a night or two. She looked in need of a holiday, poor child."

• • •

When Tom went to meet Gladys at the station they stood for some minutes on the platform not certain of the other's identity. Then their tentative signs of recognition corresponded. Gladys had been engaged twice in the past two years, and was now walking out with a motor salesman. It had been a great surprise when Mrs. Kent-Cumberland sought her out and explained that Tom had returned to England. She had not forgotten him, for she was a loyal and good-hearted girl, but she was embarrassed and touched to learn that his devotion was unshaken.

They were married two weeks later and Mrs. Kent-Cumberland undertook the delicate mission of "explaining everything" to the Mac-Dougals.

They went to Australia, where Mr. MacDougal very magnanimously gave them a post managing one of his more remote estates. He was satisfied with Tom's work. Gladys has a large sunny bungalow and a landscape of grazing-land and wire fences. She does not see very much company nor does she particularly like what she does see. The neighbouring ranchers find her very English and aloof.

Bessie and Gervase were married after six weeks' engagement. They live at Tomb. Bessie has two children and Gervase has six race-horses. Mrs. Kent-Cumberland lives in the house with them. She and Bessie rarely disagree, and, when they do, it is Mrs. Kent-Cumberland who gets her way.

The dower house is let on a long lease to a sporting manufacturer. Gervase has taken over the Hounds and spends money profusely; everyone in the neighbourhood is content.

A. J. Liebling

*

"NOTHING BUT A LITTLE PISSANT"
EXCERPT FROM *The Earl of Louisiana*

[EARL LONG ADDRESSES HIS CONSTITUENTS AT ALEXANDRIA, LOUISIANA]

We had left New Orleans at four, and Earl was slated to speak at eight. The owner of the old station wagon had said he could make it to Alick in four hours easy. It began to look not at all that easy.

I tried to estimate the station wagon's speed by clocking it between signposts. From BUNKIE, 27 MI. to BUNKIE, 20 MI., I caught it in a consoling seven minutes, but the next post, a good bit farther on, said BUNKIE, 23 MI. Bunkie is the leading *bourgade* between Baton Rouge and Alick— it has a population of 4,666—but there were other one-street-of-storefronts towns that the road ran through. By now it was dusk and the stores were lighted, so that, coming out of the dark, we galloped episodically between plywood maple-finished bedroom suites in the windows on one side of the street and mannequins with $7.98 dresses on the other, scaring from our course gaunt hounds that looked like Kabyle dogs.

The entrance to Alick was little more impressive than these others, except for two electric signs. One was a straw-hatted spook flapping great wings over the Hocus-Pocus Liquor Store and the other a symbolic giraffe and dachshund over a used-car lot. They disappeared at every other flash in favor of a legend: "High Quality, Low Prices."

Hurrying through otherwise undistinguished streets, we passed between cars parked thick along the approaches to the courthouse square and heard the loudspeaker blaring long before we got there. Somebody was on the platform in front of the courthouse steps, standing too close to the microphone and blasting. The crowd, massed immediately around the speaker's stand, thinned out toward the sidewalks.

My companion let me out and drove on to find a parking space, and I ran onto the lawn for my first look at the Imam in the flesh. As I crossed over to the forum, a boy handed me a pink throwaway, which I examined when I got within range of the light diffused from the flood-lamps over the platform:

GOVERNOR LONG SPEAKS
Governor Long Opens Campaign for Re-Election

Come Out and Bring All your friends to hear the truth.
Come out and see Governor Long in person.
Nothing will be said to offend or hurt anyone.

The Governor, on the platform, was saying to somebody I could not see over in the other wing of the audience, "If you don't shut up your claptrap, I'm going to have you forcibly removed. You just nothing but a common hoodlum and a heckler."

"Amen," an old man in front of me yelled. "Give it to him, Earl."

Whoever it was that Earl was talking to in the crowd had no microphone, so we couldn't hear him, but he must have answered in tones audible to the Governor, because the latter shouted into the mike, "I knew your daddy, Camille Gravel, and he was a fine man. But you trying to make yourself a big man, and you nothing but a little pissant."

"Amen, Earl," the old man yelled. "Give it to him."

The fellow in the crowd, now identified for me as a lawyer from Alick who was the Democratic National Committeeman from Louisiana, must have spoken again, for the Governor thundered, "Mr. Gravel, I got nothing against you personally. Now you keep quiet and I won't mention your name. If you don't I'll have you removed as a common damn nuisance." He paused for the answer we couldn't hear and then bellowed, "If *you* so popular, why don't *you* run for Governor?"

It sounded like a dialogue between a man with the horrors and his hallucinations. But the National Committeeman, Earl's interlocutor, was there in the flesh. He had brought his ten children, and they were all mad at the Governor.

The night was like a heavy blanket pressed down on the lawn. Men stood in their sleeveless, collarless shirts, and sweat caked the talcum powder on the backs of the women's necks. Anti-Long newspapers the next day conceded the crowd was between three and four thousand so there may well have been more. Plenty of Negroes, always in little groups, were scattered among the whites—an example, I suppose, of Harry Golden's "vertical integration," because in public gatherings where there are seats, the two colors are always separated into blocs.

"That's the way I like to see it," the Governor said, from the stand. "Not all our colored friends in one spot and white friends in another. I'm the best friend the poor white man, and the middle-class white man, and the rich white man—so long as he behave himself—and the poor colored man, ever had in the State of Loosiana. And if the N.A.A.C.P. and that little pea-headed nut Willie Rainach will just leave us alone, then *sensible* people, not cranks, can get along in a *rea*sonable way. That Rainach wants to fight the Civil War all over again."

There were two colored couples, middle-aged, in front of me, next to the old white man who didn't like Gravel, and now one of the colored men shouted, "Amen!" The old white man gave him a reproving look, but he couldn't bawl him out for agreeing with a Long. Nobody can object to *rea*sonable and *sensible*, but Long hadn't said what he thought *rea*sonable and *sensible* were, and it occurred to me that he probably never would.

I had been looking at him with an amateur clinical eye since I got there, and his physical condition seemed to me to have improved several hundred per cent since his stump appearance with Joe Sims on the Fourth of July. Late hours and a diet of salted watermelon, buttermilk, and Vienna sausages cut up in chicken broth had put a dozen pounds back on his bones. Walking between grandstands and paddocks had legged him up, and he pranced under the floodlights that must have raised the temperature to 110 or so. I remembered when I had seen first the referee, Ruby Goldstein, and then the great Sugar Ray Robinson himself collapse under the heat of similar lights in a ring on a less oppressive night in New York.

Uncle Earl wore a jacket, shirt and tie, a pattern of statesmanlike conventionality, on a night when everybody off the platform was coatless and tieless. The tie itself was a quiet pattern of inkblots against an olive-and-pearl background, perhaps a souvenir Rorschach test from Galveston. The suit, a black job that dated from the days when he was fat and sassy, hung loosely about him as once it had upon a peg in the supermarket where the Governor liked to buy his clothes.

He left the dude role to Morrison. And in fact, before the evening was over, he said, "I see Dellasoups has been elected one of the ten best-dressed men in America. He has fifty-dollar neckties and four-hundred-dollar suits. A four-hundred-dollar suit on old Uncle Earl would look like socks on a rooster."

It is difficult to report a speech by Uncle Earl chronologically, listing the thoughts in order of appearance. They chased one another on and off the stage like characters in a Shakespearean battle scene, full of alarums and sorties. But Morrison, good roads, and old-age pensions popped in quite often.

Of Dodd, the state auditor, a quondam ally and now a declared rival for the Governorship, he said, "I hear Big Bad Bill Dodd has been talking about the inefficiency and waste in this administration. Ohyeah. Ohyeah. Well, let me tell you, Big Bad Bill has at least six streamlined deadheads on his payroll that couldn't even find Bill's office if they had to. But they can find that *post office* every month to get their salary check —Ohyeah."

It was after the "*rea*sonable and *sensible*" bit that he went into his general declaration of tolerance. "I'm not against anybody for reasons of race, creed, or any ism he might believe in except nuttism, skingameism or communism," he said.

"I'm glad to see so many of my fine Catholic friends here—they been so kind to me I sometimes say I consider myself forty per cent Catholic and sixty per cent Baptist." (This is a fairly accurate reflection of the composition of the electorate.) "But I'm in favor of *every* religion with the possible exception of snake-chunking. Anybody that so presumes on how he stands with providence that he will let a snake bite him, I say he deserves what he's got coming to him." The snake-chunkers, a small, fanatic cult, do not believe in voting.

"Amen, Earl," the old man said.

The expressions on the Governor's face changed with the poetry of his thought, now benign, now mischievous, now indignant. Only the moist hazel eyes remained the same, fixed on a spot above and to the rear of the audience as if expecting momentarily the arrival of a posse.

"I don't *need* this job," he said. "I don't *need* money." He stopped and winked. "I don't miss it except when I run out."

There were shouts of laughter, the effect he courted.

"Amen, Earl. You tell 'em, Earl."

His face turned serious, as if he had not expected to be so cruelly misunderstood.

"I'm serious about that," he said. "You know I'm no goody-goody. But if I have ever misappropriated one cent, by abuse of my office, and anyone can prove it, I'll resign.

"I know lots of ways to make a living. I know how to be a lawyer, and a danged good one. I know how to be a traveling salesman. I know how to pick cotton, and have many times, although I've seen the days when to get my hundred pounds I had to put a watermelon in the bag."

There were gales of tolerant laughter now, even from farmers who would shoot any of their own help they found cheating on weight.

"All I ask," he said, with the honesty throbbing in his voice like a musical saw, "is a chance once again to help the fine people of the Great State of Loosiana, and to continue to serve them as their Governor."

Even a group of great louts in T-shirts, perhaps high-school football players, were silent and by now impressed; earlier in the address they had made a few feeble attempts at heckling, like yelling, "Hey, Earl, what's in the glass?" when the Governor paused for a drink of water. These boys might be from well-to-do anti-Long families, but they had the endemic Southern (and Arabic) taste for oratory, and they knew a master when they heard him.

Mr. Gravel, down near the platform, must have again attracted the Governor's attention, but now Uncle Earl, the creature of his own voice, was in a benign mood from offering his own body to the Great State of Loosiana.

"Mr. Gravel," he said, "you got ten beautiful children there, I wish you would lend five of them to me to bring up." It was one of Earl's well-publicized sorrows that he, like the Shah of Iran then, had no legitimate heir, and he handed peppermint candies or small change to all children he saw, even in years when there was no election. "He bought those candies by grosses of dozens," an ex-associate told me.

Mr. Gravel, still inaudible except to Earl, must have declined this overture, because the Governor shouted to the crowd, "He used to be a nice fellow, but now he just a goddamn hoodlum!"

"Leave him alone, Earl, we come to hear *you* talk!" the old man near me shouted back.

"I was in Minneannapolis once, talking to the Governor of Minnesota, a great expert on insanity," Uncle Earl said, "and he told me an astonishing fact—there are ten times as many crazy people in Minnesota as Louisiana. I suppose that is on account of the cold climate. They cannot go around in their shirt-sleeves all year around, go huntin' and fishin' in all seasons, as we do. We got a wonderful climate," he said, and paused to wipe the sweat from his face with a handkerchief soaked in Coca-Cola, which he poured from a bottle out of a bucket of ice handed him by one of the lesser candidates on his ticket. The bugs soaring up at the edge of the lighted area and converging on the floodlights formed a haze as thick as a beaded curtain.

"On account we got so few crazy people, we can afford to let Camille Gravel run around."

"Leave him up, Earl," the old man yelled. "You got him licked."

"Some sapsuckers talk about cutting down taxes," the Governor said, apropos of nothing he had been talking about. "Where are they going to start cutting expenses? On the *spastic* school?" (When any opponent suggests a cut in welfare expenditures, Earl accuses him of wanting to take it out on the spastics. This is the equivalent of charging the fellow would sell his mother for glue.) "They want to cut down on the *spastics*? On the little children, enjoying the school lunches? Or on those fine old people, white-haired against the sunset of life"—and he bowed his own white head for a split second—"who enjoy the most generous state pensions in the United States?

"We got the finest roads, finest schools, finest hospitals in the country—yet there are rich men who complain. They are so tight you can hear 'em squeak when they walk. They wouldn't give a nickel to see a earthquake. They sit there swallowin' hundred-dollar bills like a bullfrog swallows minners—if you chunked them as many as they want, they'd bust."

"Amen, Earl," the old man said. "God have mercy on the poor people."

"Of course, I know many *fine* rich people," the Governor said, perhaps thinking of his campaign contributors. "But the most of them are like a rich old feller I knew down in Plaquemine Parish, who died one night and never done nobody no good in his life, and yet, when the Devil come to get him, he took an appeal to St. Peter.

" 'I done some good things on earth,' he said. 'Once, on a cold day in about 1913, I gave a blind man a nickel.' St. Peter looked all through the records, and at last, on page four hundred and seventy-one, he found the entry. 'That ain't enough to make up for a misspent life,' he said. 'But wait,' the rich man says. 'Now I remember, in 1922 I gave five cents to a poor widow woman that had no carfare.' St. Peter's clerk checked the book again, and on page thirteen hundred and seventy-one, after pages and pages of how this old stump-wormer loan-sharked the poor, he found the record of that nickel.

" 'That ain't neither enough,' St. Peter said. But the mean old thing yelled, '*Don't* sentence me yet. In about 1931 I give a nickel to the Red Cross.' The clerk found that entry, too. So he said to St. Peter, 'Your Honor, what are we going to do with him?' "

The crowd hung on Uncle Earl's lips the way the bugs hovered in the light.

"You know what St. Peter said?" the Governor, the only one in the courthouse square who knew the answer, asked. There was, naturally, no reply.

"He said, 'Give him back his fifteen cents and tell him to go to Hell.' "

He had the crowd with him now, and he dropped it.

"Folks," he said, "I know you didn't come here just to hear me talk. If this big mouth of mine ever shut up, I'd be in a devil of a fix. I want to introduce to you some of the fine *sin*cere candidates that are running with me on my ticket. My ticket and the independent candidates I have endorsed are trained, skilled, and have the wisdom and experience to make you honest, loyal and *sin*cere public servants."

He turned to the triple row of men and women who sat behind him on undertaker's chairs, the men swabbing, the women dabbing, at their faces with handkerchiefs, while the Governor talked like an intrepid trainer who turns his back on his troupe of performing animals.

A reporter who had his watch on the Governor said that his talk had lasted fifty-seven minutes, and he was not even blowing.

"And first," he said, "I want to introduce to you the man I have selected to serve under me as Lieutenant Governor during my next term of office—a fine Frenchmun, a fine Catholic, the father of twenty-three children, Mr. Oscar Guidry."

The number of children was politically significant, since it indicated that Mr. Guidry was a practicing, not a *soi-disant*, Catholic. The candidate for Lieutenant Governor had to be a Frenchman and a Catholic, because Uncle Earl was neither.

Mr. Guidry, a short, stocky man who reminded me of a muscular owl, arose from his chair like a Mr. Bones called to front center by Mr. Interlocutor. He appeared embarrassed, and he whispered rapidly to Uncle Earl.

"Oscar says he has only fourteen children," the Governor announced. "But that's a good beginnin'."

Mr. Guidry whispered again, agitated, and Earl said, "But he is a member of a family of twenty-three brothers and sisters." He turned away, as if washing his hands of the whole affair, and sat down.

Mr. Guidry, throwing back his head and clasping his hands in front of him, as if about to intone the "Marseillaise," began with a rush, sounding all his aitches: "I am *honored* to be associated with the Gret Governeur of the Gret Stet on his tiquette. Those who have conspired against him, fearing to shoot him with a pistol ball . . ." and he was off, but Earl, seated directly behind him, was mugging and catching flies, monopolizing attention like an old vaudeville star cast in a play with a gang of Method actors.

Pulling his chair slightly out of line, he crossed his legs and turned his profile to the audience, first plucking at his sleeves, which came down about as far as his thumbnails, then, when he had disengaged his hands, picking his nose while he looked over at Alick's leading hotel, the Bentley, across the street, described by the *Louisiana State Guide* as "a six-story building of brick and stone, with a columned façade and a richly decorated interior." He stared at it as if it contained some absorbing riddle.

When he had finished with his nose, he began to bathe his face, his temples and the back of his neck with Coca-Cola from the cold bottle, sloshing it on like iced cologne.

"Cool yourself off, Earl," a voice piped up from the crowd, and the Governor shouted back, "I'm a red-hot poppa."

When he had wet himself down sufficiently, he drank the heeltap and set the bottle down. Then he lit a cigarette and smoked, dramatically, with the butt held between his thumb and middle finger and the other fingers raised, in the manner of a ventriloquist. While he smoked right-handed, he pulled out his handkerchief and blotted his wet face with his left.

He sat unheeding of the rumpus raised by his adherents, like a player in a jazz band who has finished his solo, or a flashy halfback who poses on the bench while the defensive team is in. The candidates ranted and bellowed, putting across a few telling although familiar points.

"In the great state of Texas, biggest and richest in the United States, there is an old-age pension of thirty-one dollars a month. Here in Loosiana we got seventy-two."

But the bored crowd stood fast, knowing that a whistle would blow and the star would throw off his blanket and come onto the field again to run rings around the forces of Mammon. Sure enough, after what seemed to me an endless session of subordinate rant, the Governor threw away the last of a chain of cigarettes and shook his head like a man waking up on a park bench and remembering where he is. He got up and walked to the microphone so fast that the man using it had barely time to say, "I thank you" before the Governor took it away from him.

"You shall know the truth, and the truth shall set you free," the Governor said, "but you will never get to know the truth by reading the Alexandria *Town Talk*. You all read in that paper that I am crazy. Ohyeah. Do I look any crazier than I ever did? I been accused of saying the fella that owns that paper is a kept man. Maybe he ain't, but I'd like to be kep' as good as he is. He married a rich woman. That's about the best way I know to save yourself about ninety-eight years' hard work."

"Amen, Earl, it's the truth," the old man in front of me cried, and the Negroes laughed at what was apparently a well-established local joke.

"Maybe some of you are here because you've never seen a man out

of a nuthouse before," the Governor said tolerantly. "Maybe you want
to see a man who has been stuck thirty-eight times with needles. Oh, the
first man stuck me, stuck me right through the britches. He didn't get
me in the fat part, either, and oh, how it hurt! Maybe I lost a little weight,
but you would have, too. Occasionally I say hell or damn, but if it had
happened to you all, you'd say worse than that. Christ on the Cross
Himself never suffered worse than poor old Earl!

"Oh, not that I'm fit to walk in Christ's shoes!" he bellowed to
preclude any confusion. "I'm not good enough, when a fellow slugs me
on one cheek, to turn the other side of my scheming head. I'm going to
slug him back."

"Amen, Earl. You tell him, Earl. Who you goin' to hit first, Earl?"

"Down there in that court in Texas in Galveston before that Texas
judge, I felt like Christ between the two thieves. He reared back his head
and he said, 'Father, forgive them, for they know not what they do!' "

At this point he was interrupted by wild handclapping from a group
of elderly ladies wearing print dresses, white gloves, straw hats and space-
man eyeglasses, who had been seated quietly on the platform through
the earlier proceedings. They were under the impression that it was an
original line.

I next remember the Governor in his seat again, head down, exhausted, having given his all to the electorate, in a pose like Bannister
after running the first four-minute mile. It occurred to me that he was
like old blind Pete Herman fighting on heart alone, by a trained reflex.
Pete is a friend of the Governor's.

As Earl sat there, one of the assisting speakers, a fellow with a
strong voice, grabbed the microphone and declaimed the family battle
ode, "Invictus."

When the man came to the part where it says:

> *Under the bludgeonings of fate*
> *Ma haid is bloody, but* unbowed

Earl flung up his head like a wild horse and got up like a fighter about to
go into a dance to prove he hasn't been hurt. He called for a show of
hands by everybody who was going to vote for him, and I waved both of
mine.

I left him surrounded by children to whom he was passing out
coins, "a quarter to the white kids and a nickel to the niggers."

My companion had rejoined me after parking the car, and we
walked together through the breaking crowd.

"How could his wife have done him like she done?" a woman was asking another, and a man was saying, "Got to give da ol' dawg what's coming to him."

My friend saw Gravel, a handsome, tanned man in a white sports shirt and black slacks, standing where the lawn ended at the pavement, and walked over to him. Two or three reporters were already there, asking Gravel what he had said when Earl said what.

The National Committeeman said he had come to hear the speech because two or three men close to Earl had called him up and warned him that Earl was going to blacken his name.

"I wanted to be there to nail the lie," he said. He said Earl started the argument.

Six or eight of the ten Gravel children played hide-and-seek around their father's legs, and as he talked, another boy, about eleven years old, ran up and said to a slightly younger girl, his sister, "The Governor wanted to give me a quarter, but I wouldn't take it."

"Why not?" the girl asked, and I decided she had a bigger political future than her brother.

Gravel said he had to go home because there was a wedding reception there, and the rest of us walked back toward the Bentley, where all the rocking chairs on the porch were already occupied. The row of glowing cigar ends swaying in unison reminded me of the Tiller Girls in a glowworm number.

S. J. Perelman

*

FAREWELL, MY LOVELY APPETIZER

*Add Smorgasbits to your ought-to-know department, the newest of the three Betty Lee products. What in the world! Just small mouth-size pieces of herring and of pinkish tones. We crossed our heart and promised not to tell the secret of their tinting.—*CLEMENTINE PAD-DLEFORD'S *food column in the* Herald Tribune.

*The "Hush-Hush" blouse. We're very hush-hush about his name, but the celebrated shirtmaker who did it for us is famous on two continents for blouses with details like those deep yoke folds, the wonderful shoulder pads, the shirtband bow!—*Russeks adv. in the Times.

I came down the sixth-floor corridor of the Arbogast Building, past the World Wide Noodle Corporation, Zwinger & Rumsey, Accountants, and the Ace Secretarial Service, Mimeographing Our Specialty. The legend on the ground-glass panel next door said, "Atlas Detective Agency, Noonan & Driscoll," but Snapper Driscoll had retired two years before with a .38 slug between the shoulders, donated by a snowbird in Tacoma, and I owned what good will the firm had. I let myself into the crummy anteroom we kept to impress clients, growled good morning at Birdie Claflin.

"Well, you certainly look like something the cat dragged in," she said. She had a quick tongue. She also had eyes like dusty lapis lazuli, taffy hair, and a figure that did things to me. I kicked open the bottom drawer of her desk, let two inches of rye trickle down my craw, kissed Birdie square on her lush, red mouth, and set fire to a cigarette.

"I could go for you, sugar," I said slowly. Her face was veiled, watchful. I stared at her ears, liking the way they were joined to her head. There was something complete about them; you knew they were there for keeps. When you're a private eye, you want things to stay put.

"Any customers?"

"A woman by the name of Sigrid Bjornsterne said she'd be back. A looker."

"Swede?"

"She'd like you to think so."

I nodded toward the inner office to indicate that I was going in there, and went in there. I lay down on the davenport, took off my shoes, and bought myself a shot from the bottle I kept underneath. Four minutes later, an ash-blonde with eyes the color of unset opals, in a Nettie Rosenstein basic black dress and a baum-marten stole, burst in. Her bosom was heaving and it looked even better that way. With a gasp she circled the desk, hunting for some place to hide, and then, spotting the wardrobe where I keep a change of bourbon, ran into it. I got up and wandered out into the anteroom. Birdie was deep in a crossword puzzle.

"See anyone come in here?"

"Nope." There was a thoughtful line between her brows. "Say, what's a five-letter word meaning 'trouble'?"

"Swede," I told her, and went back inside. I waited the length of time it would take a small, not very bright, boy to recite *Ozymandias*, and, inching carefully along the wall, took a quick gander out the window. A thin galoot with stooping shoulders was being very busy reading a paper outside the Gristede store two blocks away. He hadn't been there an hour ago, but then, of course, neither had I. He wore a size seven dove-colored hat from Browning King, a tan Wilson Brothers shirt with pale-blue stripes, a J. Press foulard with a mixed red-and-white figure, dark-blue Interwoven socks, and an unshined pair of oxblood London Character shoes. I let a cigarette burn down between my fingers until it made a small red mark, and then I opened the wardrobe.

"Hi," the blonde said lazily. "You Mike Noonan?" I made a noise that could have been "Yes," and waited. She yawned. I thought things over, decided to play it safe. I yawned. She yawned back, then, settling into a corner of the wardrobe, went to sleep. I let another cigarette burn down until it made a second red mark beside the first one and then I woke her up. She sank into a chair, crossing a pair of gams that tightened my throat as I peered under the desk at them.

"Mr. Noonan," she said, "you—you've got to help me."

"My few friends call me Mike," I said pleasantly.

"Mike." She rolled the syllable on her tongue. "I don't believe I've ever heard that name before. Irish?"

"Enough to know the difference between a gossoon and a bassoon."

"What *is* the difference?" she asked. I dummied up; I figured I wasn't giving anything away for free. Her eyes narrowed. I shifted my two hundred pounds slightly, lazily set fire to a finger, and watched it burn down. I could see she was admiring the interplay of muscles in my shoulders. There wasn't any extra fat on Mike Noonan, but I wasn't telling *her* that. I was playing it safe until I knew where we stood.

When she spoke again, it came with a rush. "Mr. Noonan, he thinks I'm trying to poison him. But I swear the herring was pink—I took it out of the jar myself. If I could only find out how they tinted it. I offered them money, but they wouldn't tell."

"Suppose you take it from the beginning," I suggested.

She drew a deep breath. "You've heard of the golden spintria of Hadrian?" I shook my head. "It's a tremendously valuable coin believed to have been given by the Emperor Hadrian to one of his proconsuls, Caius Vitellius. It disappeared about 150 A.D., and eventually passed into the possession of Hucbald the Fat. After the sack of Adrianople by the Turks, it was loaned by a man named Shapiro to the court physician, or hakim, of Abdul Mahmoud. Then it dropped out of sight for nearly five hundred years, until last August, when a dealer in secondhand books named Lloyd Thursday sold it to my husband."

"And now it's gone again," I finished.

"No," she said. "At least, it was lying on the dresser when I left, an hour ago." I leaned back, pretending to fumble a carbon out of the desk, and studied her legs again. This was going to be a lot more intricate than I had thought. Her voice got huskier. "Last night I brought home a jar of Smorgasbits for Walter's dinner. You know them?"

"Small mouth-size pieces of herring and of pinkish tones, aren't they?"

Her eyes darkened, lightened, got darker again. "How did you know?"

"I haven't been a private op nine years for nothing, sister. Go on."

"I—I knew right away something was wrong when Walter screamed and upset his plate. I tried to tell him the herring was supposed to be pink, but he carried on like a madman. He's been suspicious of me since —well, ever since I made him take out that life insurance."

"What was the face amount of the policy?"

"A hundred thousand. But it carried a triple-indemnity clause in case he died by sea food. Mr. Noonan—Mike—" her tone caressed me

—"I've got to win back his confidence. You could find out how they tinted that herring."

"What's in it for me?"

"Anything you want." The words were a whisper. I leaned over, poked open her handbag, counted off five grand.

"This'll hold me for a while," I said. "If I need any more, I'll beat my spoon on the high chair." She got up. "Oh, while I think of it, how does this golden spintria of yours tie in with the herring?"

"It doesn't," she said calmly. "I just threw it in for glamour." She trailed past me in a cloud of scent that retailed at ninety rugs the ounce. I caught her wrist, pulled her up to me.

"I go for girls named Sigrid with opal eyes," I said.

"Where'd you learn my name?"

"I haven't been a private snoop twelve years for nothing, sister."

"It was nine last time."

"It seemed like twelve till you came along." I held the clinch until a faint wisp of smoke curled out of her ears, pushed her through the door. Then I slipped a pint of rye into my stomach and a heater into my kick and went looking for a bookdealer named Lloyd Thursday. I knew he had no connection with the herring caper, but in my business you don't overlook anything.

The thin galoot outside Gristede's had taken a powder when I got there; that meant we were no longer playing girls' rules. I hired a hack to Wanamaker's, cut over to Third, walked up toward Fourteenth. At Twelfth a mink-faced jasper made up as a street cleaner tailed me for a block, drifted into a dairy restaurant. At Thirteenth somebody dropped a sour tomato out of a third-story window, missing me by inches. I doubled back to Wanamaker's, hopped a bus up Fifth to Madison Square, and switched to a cab down Fourth, where the secondhand bookshops elbow each other like dirty urchins.

A flabby hombre in a Joe Carbondale rope-knit sweater, whose jowl could have used a shave, quit giggling over *The Heptameron* long enough to tell me he was Lloyd Thursday. His shoebutton eyes became opaque when I asked to see any first editions or incunabula relative to the *Clupea harengus*, or common herring.

"You got the wrong pitch, copper," he snarled. "That stuff is hotter than Pee Wee Russell's clarinet."

"Maybe a sawbuck'll smarten you up," I said. I folded one to the size of a postage stamp, scratched my chin with it. "There's five yards around for anyone who knows why those Smorgasbits of Sigrid Bjornsterne's happened to be pink." His eyes got crafty.

"I might talk for a grand."

"Start dealing." He motioned toward the back. I took a step forward. A second later a Roman candle exploded inside my head and I went away from there. When I came to, I was on the floor with a lump on my sconce the size of a lapwing's egg and big Terry Tremaine of Homicide was bending over me.

"Someone sapped me," I said thickly. "His name was—"

"Webster," grunted Terry. He held up a dog-eared copy of Merriam's Unabridged. "You tripped on a loose board and this fell off a shelf on your think tank."

"Yeah?" I said skeptically. "Then where's Thursday?" He pointed to the fat man lying across a pile of erotica. "He passed out cold when he saw you cave." I covered up, let Terry figure it any way he wanted. I wasn't telling him what cards I held. I was playing it safe until I knew all the angles.

In a seedy pharmacy off Astor Place, a stale Armenian whose name might have been Vulgarian but wasn't dressed my head and started asking questions. I put my knee in his groin and he lost interest. Jerking my head toward the coffee urn, I spent a nickel and the next forty minutes doing some heavy thinking. Then I holed up in a phone booth and dialed a clerk I knew called Little Farvel in a delicatessen store on Amsterdam Avenue. It took a while to get the dope I wanted because the connection was bad and Little Farvel had been dead two years, but we Noonans don't let go easily.

By the time I worked back to the Arbogast Building, via the Weehawken ferry and the George Washington Bridge to cover my tracks, all the pieces were in place. Or so I thought up to the point she came out of the wardrobe holding me between the sights of her ice-blue automatic.

"Reach for the stratosphere, gumshoe." Sigrid Bjornsterne's voice was colder than Horace Greeley and Little Farvel put together, but her clothes were plenty calorific. She wore a forest-green suit of Hockanum woolens, a Knox Wayfarer, and baby crocodile pumps. It was her blouse, though, that made tiny red hairs stand up on my knuckles. Its deep yoke folds, shoulder pads, and shirtband bow could only have been designed by some master craftsman, some Cézanne of the shears.

"Well, Nosy Parker," she sneered, "so you found out how they tinted the herring."

"Sure—grenadine," I said easily. "You knew it all along. And you planned to add a few grains of oxylbutane-cheriphosphate, which turns the same shade of pink in solution, to your husband's portion, knowing it wouldn't show in the post-mortem. Then you'd collect the three

hundred G's and join Harry Pestalozzi in Nogales till the heat died down.
But you didn't count on me."

"You?" Mockery nicked her full-throated laugh. "What are you
going to do about it?"

"This." I snaked the rug out from under her and she went down in
a swirl of silken ankles. The bullet whined by me into the ceiling as I
vaulted over the desk, pinioned her against the wardrobe.

"Mike." Suddenly all the hatred had drained away and her body
yielded to mine. "Don't turn me in. You cared for me—once."

"It's no good, Sigrid. You'd only double-time me again."

"Try me."

"O.K. The shirtmaker who designed your blouse—what's his
name?" A shudder of fear went over her; she averted her head. "He's
famous on two continents. Come on Sigrid, they're your dice."

"I won't tell you. I can't. It's a secret between this—this department
store and me."

"They wouldn't be loyal to you. They'd sell you out fast enough."

"Oh, Mike, you mustn't. You don't know what you're asking."

"For the last time."

"Oh, sweetheart, don't you see?" Her eyes were tragic pools, a
cenotaph to lost illusions. "I've got so little. Don't take that away from
me. I—I'd never be able to hold up my head in Russeks again."

"Well, if that's the way you want to play it . . ." There was silence
in the room, broken only by Sigrid's choked sob. Then, with a strangely
empty feeling, I uncradled the phone and dialed Spring 7-3100.

For an hour after they took her away, I sat alone in the taupe-
colored dusk, watching lights come on and a woman in the hotel opposite
adjusting a garter. Then I treated my tonsils to five fingers of firewater,
jammed on my hat, and made for the anteroom. Birdie was still scowling
over her crossword puzzle. She looked up crookedly at me.

"Need me any more tonight?"

"No." I dropped a grand or two in her lap. "Here, buy yourself
some stardust."

"Thanks, I've got my quota." For the first time I caught a shadow
of pain behind her eyes. "Mike, would—would you tell me something?"

"As long as it isn't clean," I flipped to conceal my bitterness.

"What's an eight-letter word meaning 'sentimental'?"

"Flatfoot, darling," I said, and went out into the rain.

Leo Rosten

*

MR. K★A★P★L★A★N,
THE COMPARATIVE,
AND THE SUPERLATIVE

EXCERPT FROM
The Education of Hyman Kaplan

For two weeks Mr. Parkhill had been delaying the inescapable: Mr. Kaplan, like the other students in the beginners' grade of the American Night Preparatory School for Adults, would have to present a composition for class analysis. All the students had had their turn writing the assignment on the board, a composition of one hundred words, entitled "My Job." Now only Mr. Kaplan's rendition remained.

It would be more accurate to say Mr. K★A★P★L★A★N's rendition of the assignment remained, for even in thinking of that distinguished student, Mr. Parkhill saw the image of his unmistakable signature, in all its red-blue-green glory. The multicolored characters were more than a trademark; they were an assertion of individuality, a symbol of singularity, a proud expression of Mr. Kaplan's Inner Self. To Mr. Parkhill, the signature took on added meaning because it was associated with the man who had said his youthful ambition had been to become "a physician and sergeant," the Titan who had declined the verb "to fail": "fail, failed, bankropt."

One night, after the two weeks' procrastination, Mr. Parkhill decided to face the worst. "Mr. Kaplan, I think it's your turn to—er—write your composition on the board."

Mr. Kaplan's great, buoyant smile grew more great and more buoyant. "My!" he exclaimed. He rose, looked around at the class proudly as if surveying the blessed who were to witness a linguistic *tour de force*, stumbled over Mrs. Moskowitz's feet with a polite "Vould you be so kindly?" and took his place at the blackboard. There he rejected several pieces of chalk critically, nodded to Mr. Parkhill—it was a nod of distinct reassurance—and then printed in firm letters:

My Job A Cotter In Dress Faktory
Comp. by
H★Y★

"You need not write your name on the board," interrupted Mr. Parkhill quickly. "Er—to save time . . ."

Mr. Kaplan's face expressed astonishment. "Podden me, Mr. Pockheel. But de name is by me *pot* of mine composition."

"Your name is *part* of the composition?" asked Mr. Parkhill in an anxious tone.

"Yas*sir!*" said Mr. Kaplan with dignity. He printed the rest of H★Y★M★A★N K★A★P★L★A★N for all to see and admire. You could tell it was a disappointment for him not to have colored chalk for this performance. In pale white the elegance of his work was dissipated. The name, indeed, seemed unreal, the letters stark, anemic, almost denuded.

His brow wrinkled and perspiring, Mr. Kaplan wrote the saga of A Cotter In Dress Faktory on the board, with much scratching of the chalk and an undertone of sound. Mr. Kaplan repeated each word to himself softly, as if trying to give to its spelling some of the flavor and originality of his pronunciation. The smile on the face of Mr. Kaplan had taken on something beatific and imperishable: it was his first experience at the blackboard; it was his moment of glory. He seemed to be writing more slowly than necessary as if to prolong the ecstasy of his Hour. When he had finished he said "Hau Kay" with distinct regret in his voice, and sat down. Mr. Parkhill observed the composition in all its strange beauty:

My Job A Cotter In Dress Faktory
Comp. by
H★Y★M★A★N K★A★P★I★★A★N

Shakspere is saying what fulls man is and I am feeling just the same way when I am thinking about mine job a cotter in Dress Faktory on 38 st. by 7 av. For why should we slafing in dark placc by laktric lights and all kinds hot for $30 or maybe $36 with overtime, for Boss who is fat and driving in fency automobil? I ask! Because we are the deprassed workers of world. And are being exployted. By Bosses. In mine shop is no difference. Oh how bad is laktric light, oh how is all kinds hot. And when I am telling Foreman should be better conditions he hollers, Kaplan you redical!!

At this point a glazed look came into Mr. Parkhill's eyes, but he read on.

So I keep still and work by bad light and always hot. But somday will the workers making Bosses to work! And then Kaplan will give to them bad laktric and positively no windows for the air should come in! So they can know what it means to slafe! Kaplan will make Foreman a cotter like he is. And give the most bad dezigns to cot out. Justice.
Mine job is cotting Dress dezigns.
T-H-E E-N-D

Mr. Parkhill read the amazing document over again. His eyes, glazed but a moment before, were haunted now. It was true: spelling, diction, sentence structure, punctuation, capitalization, the use of the present perfect for the present—all true.
"Is planty mistakes, I s'pose," suggested Mr. Kaplan modestly.
"Y-yes . . . yes, there are many mistakes."
"Dat's because I'm tryink to give *dip ideas*," said Mr. Kaplan with the sigh of those who storm heaven.
Mr. Parkhill girded his mental loins. "Mr. Kaplan—er—your composition doesn't really meet the assignment. You haven't described your *job*, what you *do*, what your work *is*."
"Vell, it's not soch a interastink job," said Mr. Kaplan.
"Your composition is not a simple exposition. It's more of a—well, an *essay* on your *attitude*."
"Oh, fine!" cried Mr. Kaplan with enthusiasm.
"No, no," said Mr. Parkhill hastily. "The assignment was *meant* to be a composition. You see, we must begin with simple exercises before we try—er—more philosophical essays."
Mr. Kaplan nodded with resignation. "So naxt time should be no ideas, like abot Shaksbeer? Should be only *fects*?"
"Y-yes. No ideas, only—er—facts."
You could see by Mr. Kaplan's martyred smile that his wings, like those of an eagle's, were being clipped.
"And Mr. Kaplan—er—why do you use 'Kaplan' in the body of your composition? Why don't you say 'I will make the foreman a cutter' instead of '*Kaplan* will make the foreman a cutter?' "
Mr. Kaplan's response was instantaneous. "I'm so glad you eskink

me dis! Ha! I'm usink 'Keplen' in de composition for plain and tsimple rizzon: becawss I didn't vant de reader should tink I am *prajudiced* against de foreman, so I said it more like abot a strenger: '*Keplen* vill make de foreman a cotter!' "

In the face of this subtle passion for objectivity, Mr. Parkhill was silent. He called for corrections. A forest of hands went up. Miss Mitnick pointed out errors in spelling, the use of capital letters, punctuation; Mr. Norman Bloom corrected several more words, rearranged sentences, and said, "Woikers is exployted with an '*i*,' not '*y*' as Kaplan makes"; Miss Caravello changed "fulls" to "fools," and declared herself uncertain as to the validity of the word "Justice" standing by itself in "da smalla da sentence"; Mr. Sam Pinsky said he was sure Mr. Kaplan meant "*opprassed* voikers of de voild, not *deprassed*, aldough dey are deprassed *too*," to which Mr. Kaplan replied, "So ve bote got right, no? Don' *chenge* 'deprassed,' only *add* 'opprassed.' "

Then Mr. Parkhill went ahead with his own corrections, changing tenses, substituting prepositions, adding the definite article. Through the whole barrage Mr. Kaplan kept shaking his head, murmuring "Mine gootness!" each time a correction was made. But he smiled all the while. He seemed to be proud of the very number of errors he had made; of the labor to which the class was being forced in his service; of the fact that his *ideas*, his creation, could survive so concerted an onslaught. And as the composition took more respectable form, Mr. Kaplan's smile grew more expansive.

"Now, class," said Mr. Parkhill, "I want to spend a few minutes explaining something about adjectives. Mr. Kaplan uses the phrase—er —'most bad.' That's wrong. There is a word for 'most bad.' It is what we call the superlative form of 'bad.' " Mr. Parkhill explained the use of the positive, comparative, and superlative forms of the adjective. " 'Tall, taller, tallest.' 'Rich, richer, richest.' Is that clear? Well then, let us try a few others."

The class took up the game with enthusiasm. Miss Mitnick submitted "dark, darker, darkest"; Mr. Scymzak, "fat, fatter, fattest."

"But there are certain exceptions to this general form," Mr. Parkhill went on. The class, which had long ago learned to respect that gamin, The Exception to the Rule, nodded solemnly. "For instance, we don't say 'good, gooder, goodest,' do we?"

"No, sir!" cried Mr. Kaplan impetuously. " 'Good, gooder, good-*est?*' Ha! It's to leff!"

"We say that X, for example, is good. Y, however, is—?" Mr. Parkhill arched an eyebrow interrogatively.

"Batter!" said Mr. Kaplan

"Right! And Z is—?"

"High-cless!"

Mr. Parkhill's eyebrow dropped. "No," he said sadly.

"*Not* high-cless?" asked Mr. Kaplan incredulously. For him there was no word more superlative.

"No, Mr. Kaplan, the word is 'best.' And the word 'bad,' of which you tried to use the superlative form . . . It isn't '*bad, badder, baddest.*' It's 'bad' . . . and what's the comparative? Anyone?"

"Worse," volunteered Mr. Bloom.

"Correct! And the superlative? Z is the—?"

" 'Worse' also?" asked Mr. Bloom hesitantly. It was evident he had never distinguished the fine difference in sound between the comparative and superlative forms of "bad."

"No, Mr. Bloom. It's not the *same* word, although it—er—sounds a good deal like it. Anyone? Come, come. It isn't hard. X is *bad*, Y is *worse*, and Z is the—?"

An embarrassed silence fell upon the class, which, apparently, had been using "worse" for both the comparative and superlative all along. Miss Mitnick blushed and played with her pencil. Mr. Bloom shrugged, conscious that he had given his all. Mr. Kaplan stared at the board, his mouth open, a desperate concentration in his eye.

"*Bad—worse.* What is the word you use when you mean 'most bad'?"

"Aha!" cried Mr. Kaplan suddenly. When Mr. Kaplan cried "Aha!" it signified that a great light had fallen on him. "I know! De exect void! So easy! *Ach!* I should know dat ven I vas wridink! *Bad—voise—*"

"Yes, Mr. Kaplan!" Mr. Parkhill was definitely excited.

"Rotten!"

Mr. Parkhill's eyes glazed once more, unmistakably. He shook his head dolorously, as if he had suffered a personal hurt. And as he wrote "W-O-R-S-T" on the blackboard there ran through his head, like a sad refrain, this latest manifestation of Mr. Kaplan's peculiar genius: "bad—worse—rotten; bad—worse . . ."

Eudora Welty

*

WHY I LIVE AT THE P.O.

I was getting along fine with Mama, Papa-Daddy and Uncle Rondo until my sister Stella-Rondo just separated from her husband and came back home again. Mr. Whitaker! Of course I went with Mr. Whitaker first, when he first appeared here in China Grove, taking "Pose Yourself" photos, and Stella-Rondo broke us up. Told him I was one-sided. Bigger on one side than the other, which is a deliberate, calculated falsehood: I'm the same. Stella-Rondo is exactly twelve months to the day younger than I am and for that reason she's spoiled.

She's always had anything in the world she wanted and then she'd throw it away. Papa-Daddy gave her this gorgeous Add-a-Pearl necklace when she was eight years old and she threw it away playing baseball when she was nine, with only two pearls.

So as soon as she got married and moved away from home the first thing she did was separate! From Mr. Whitaker! This photographer with the popeyes she said she trusted. Came home from one of those towns up in Illinois and to our complete surprise brought this child of two.

Mama said she like to made her drop dead for a second. "Here you had this marvelous blonde child and never so much as wrote your mother a word about it," says Mama. "I'm thoroughly ashamed of you." But of course she wasn't.

Stella-Rondo just calmly takes off this *hat*, I wish you could see it. She says, "Why, Mama, Shirley-T.'s adopted, I can prove it."

"How?" says Mama, but all I says was, "H'm!" There I was over the hot stove, trying to stretch two chickens over five people and a completely unexpected child into the bargain, without one moment's notice.

"What do you mean—'H'm!'?" says Stella-Rondo, and Mama says, "I heard that, Sister."

I said that oh, I didn't mean a thing, only that whoever Shirley-T. was, she was the spit-image of Papa-Daddy if he'd cut off his beard, which of course he'd never do in the world. Papa-Daddy's Mama's papa and sulks.

Stella-Rondo got furious! She said, "Sister, I don't need to tell you you got a lot of nerve and always did have and I'll thank you to make no future reference to my adopted child whatsoever."

"Very well," I said. "Very well, very well. Of course I noticed at once she looks like Mr. Whitaker's side too. That frown. She looks like a cross between Mr. Whitaker and Papa-Daddy."

"Well, all I can say is she isn't."

"She looks exactly like Shirley Temple to me," says Mama, but Shirley-T. just ran away from her.

So the first thing Stella-Rondo did at the table was turn Papa-Daddy against me.

"Papa-Daddy," she says. He was trying to cut up his meat. "Papa-Daddy!" I was taken completely by surprise. Papa-Daddy is about a million years old and's got this long-long beard. "Papa-Daddy, Sister says she fails to understand why you don't cut off your beard."

So Papa-Daddy l-a-y-s down his knife and fork! He's real rich. Mama says he is, he says he isn't. So he says, "Have I heard correctly? You don't understand why I don't cut off my beard?"

"Why," I says, "Papa-Daddy, of course I understand, I did not say any such of a thing, the idea!"

He says, "Hussy!"

I says, "Papa-Daddy, you know I wouldn't any more want you to cut off your beard than the man in the moon. It was the farthest thing from my mind! Stella-Rondo sat there and made that up while she was eating breast of chicken."

But he says, "So the postmistress fails to understand why I don't cut off my beard. Which job I got you through my influence with the government. 'Bird's nest'—is that what you call it?"

Not that it isn't the next to smallest P.O. in the entire state of Mississippi.

I says, "Oh, Papa-Daddy," I says, "I didn't say any such of a thing, I never dreamed it was a bird's nest, I have always been grateful though this is the next to smallest P.O. in the state of Mississippi, and I do not enjoy being referred to as a hussy by my own grandfather."

But Stella-Rondo says, "Yes, you did say it too. Anybody in the world could of heard you, that had ears."

"Stop right there," says Mama, looking at *me*.

So I pulled my napkin straight back through the napkin ring and left the table.

As soon as I was out of the room Mama says, "Call her back, or she'll starve to death," but Papa-Daddy says, "This is the beard I started growing on the Coast when I was fifteen years old." He would of gone on till nightfall if Shirley-T. hadn't lost the Milky Way she ate in Cairo.

So Papa-Daddy says, "I am going out and lie in the hammock, and you can all sit here and remember my words: I'll never cut off my beard as long as I live, even one inch, and I don't appreciate it in you at all." Passed right by me in the hall and went straight out and got in the hammock.

It would be a holiday. It wasn't five minutes before Uncle Rondo suddenly appeared in the hall in one of Stella-Rondo's flesh-colored kimonos, all cut on the bias, like something Mr. Whitaker probably thought was gorgeous.

"Uncle Rondo!" I says. "I didn't know who that was! Where are you going?"

"Sister," he says, "get out of my way, I'm poisoned."

"If you're poisoned stay away from Papa-Daddy," I says. "Keep out of the hammock. Papa-Daddy will certainly beat you on the head if you come within forty miles of him. He thinks I deliberately said he ought to cut off his beard after he got me the P.O., and I've told him and told him and told him, and he acts like he just don't hear me. Papa-Daddy must of gone stone deaf."

"He picked a fine day to do it then," says Uncle Rondo, and before you could say "Jack Robinson" flew out in the yard.

What he'd really done, he'd drunk another bottle of that prescription. He does it every single Fourth of July as sure as shooting, and it's horribly expensive. Then he falls over in the hammock and snores. So he insisted on zigzagging right on out to the hammock, looking like a half-wit.

Papa-Daddy woke up with this horrible yell and right there without moving an inch he tried to turn Uncle Rondo against me. I heard every word he said. Oh, he told Uncle Rondo I didn't learn to read till I was eight years old and he didn't see how in the world I ever got the mail put up at the P.O., much less read it all, and he said if Uncle Rondo could only fathom the lengths he had gone to to get me that job! And he said on the other hand he thought Stella-Rondo had a brilliant mind and deserved credit for getting out of town. All the time he was just lying there swinging as pretty as you please and looping out his beard, and poor Uncle Rondo was *pleading* with him to slow down the hammock, it was making him as dizzy as a witch to watch it. But that's what Papa-Daddy likes about a hammock. So Uncle Rondo was too dizzy to get turned against me for the time being. He's Mama's only brother and is a good case of a one-track mind. Ask anybody. A certified pharmacist.

Just then I heard Stella-Rondo raising the upstairs window. While she was married she got this peculiar idea that it's cooler with the windows shut and locked. So she has to raise the window before she can make a soul hear her outdoors.

So she raises the window and says, "*Oh!*" You would have thought she was mortally wounded.

Uncle Rondo and Papa-Daddy didn't even look up, but kept right on with what they were doing. I had to laugh.

I flew up the stairs and threw the door open! I says, "What in the wide world's the matter, Stella-Rondo? You mortally wounded?"

"No," she says, "I am not mortally wounded but I wish you would do me the favor of looking out that window there and telling me what you see."

So I shade my eyes and look out the window.

"I see the front yard," I says.

"Don't you see any human beings?" she says.

"I see Uncle Rondo trying to run Papa-Daddy out of the hammock," I says. "Nothing more. Naturally, it's so suffocating-hot in the house, with all the windows shut and locked, everybody who cares to stay in their right mind will have to go out and get in the hammock before the Fourth of July is over."

"Don't you notice anything different about Uncle Rondo?" asks Stella-Rondo.

"Why, no, except he's got on some terrible-looking flesh-colored contraption I wouldn't be found dead in, is all I can see," I says.

"Never mind, you won't be found dead in it, because it happens to be part of my trousseau, and Mr. Whitaker took several dozen photographs of me in it," says Stella-Rondo. "What on earth could Uncle Rondo *mean* by wearing part of my trousseau out in the broad open daylight without saying so much as 'Kiss my foot,' *knowing* I only got home this morning after my separation and hung my negligee up on the bathroom door, just as nervous as I could be?"

"I'm sure I don't know, and what do you expect me to do about it?" I says. "Jump out the window?"

"No, I expect nothing of the kind. I simply declare that Uncle Rondo looks like a fool in it, that's all," she says. "It makes me sick to my stomach."

"Well, he looks as good as he can," I says. "As good as anybody in reason could." I stood up for Uncle Rondo, please remember. And I said to Stella-Rondo, "I think I would do well not to criticize so freely if I were you and came home with a two-year-old child I had never said a word about, and no explanation whatever about my separation."

"I asked you the instant I entered this house not to refer one more time to my adopted child, and you gave me your word of honor you would not," was all Stella-Rondo would say, and started pulling out every one of her eyebrows with some cheap Kress tweezers.

So I merely slammed the door behind me and went down and made some green-tomato pickle. Somebody had to do it. Of course Mama had turned both the Negroes loose; she always said no earthly power could hold one anyway on the Fourth of July, so she wouldn't even try. It turned out that Jaypan fell in the lake and came within a very narrow limit of drowning.

So Mama trots in. Lifts up the lid and says, "H'm! Not very good for your Uncle Rondo in his precarious condition, I must say. Or poor little adopted Shirley-T. Shame on you!"

That made me tired. I says, "Well, Stella-Rondo had better thank her lucky stars it was her instead of me came trotting in with that very peculiar-looking child. Now if it had been me that trotted in from Illinois and brought a peculiar-looking child of two, I shudder to think of the reception I'd of got, much less controlled the diet of an entire family."

"But you must remember, Sister, that you were never married to Mr. Whitaker in the first place and didn't go up to Illinois to live," says Mama, shaking a spoon in my face. "If you had I would of been just as overjoyed to see you and your little adopted girl as I was to see Stella-Rondo, when you wound up with your separation and came on back home."

"You would not," I says.

"Don't contradict me, I would," says Mama.

But I said she couldn't convince me though she talked till she was blue in the face. Then I said, "Besides, you know as well as I do that that child is not adopted."

"She most certainly is adopted," says Mama, stiff as a poker.

I says, "Why, Mama, Stella-Rondo had her just as sure as anything in this world, and just too stuck up to admit it."

"Why, Sister," said Mama. "Here I thought we were going to have a pleasant Fourth of July, and you start right out not believing a word your own baby sister tells you!"

"Just like Cousin Annie Flo. Went to her grave denying the facts of life," I remind Mama.

"I told you if you ever mentioned Annie Flo's name I'd slap your face," says Mama, and slaps my face.

"All right, you wait and see," I says.

"I," says Mama, "I prefer to take my children's word for anything when it's humanly possible." You ought to see Mama, she weighs two hundred pounds and has real tiny feet.

Just then something perfectly horrible occurred to me.

"Mama," I says, "can that child talk?" I simply had to whisper! "Mama, I wonder if that child can be—you know—in any way? Do you realize," I says, "that she hasn't spoken one single, solitary word to a human being up to this minute? This is the way she looks," I says, and I looked like this.

Well, Mama and I just stood there and stared at each other. It was horrible.

"I remember well that Joe Whitaker frequently drank like a fish," says Mama. "I believed to my soul he drank *chemicals*." And without another word she marches to the foot of the stairs and calls Stella-Rondo.

"Stella-Rondo? O-o-o-o-o! Stella-Rondo!"

"What?" says Stella-Rondo from upstairs. Not even the grace to get up off the bed.

"Can that child of yours talk?" asks Mama.

Stella-Rondo says, "Can she what?"

"Talk! Talk!" says Mama. "Burdyburdyburdyburdy!"

So Stella-Rondo yells back, "Who says she can't talk?"

"Sister says so," says Mama.

"You didn't have to tell me, I know whose word of honor don't mean a thing in this house," says Stella-Rondo.

And in a minute the loudest Yankee voice I ever heard in my life yells out, "OE'm Pop-OE the Sailor-r-r Ma-a-an!" and then somebody jumps up and down in the upstairs hall. In another second the house would of fallen down.

"Not only talks, she can tap-dance!" calls Stella-Rondo. "Which is more than some people I won't name can do."

"Why, the little precious darling thing!" Mama says, so surprised. "Just as smart as she can be!" Starts talking baby talk right there. Then she turns on me. "Sister, you ought to be thoroughly ashamed! Run upstairs this instant and apologize to Stella-Rondo and Shirley-T."

"Apologize for what?" I says. "I merely wondered if the child was normal, that's all. Now that she's proved she is, why, I have nothing further to say."

But Mama just turned on her heel and flew out, furious. She ran right upstairs and hugged the baby. She believed it was adopted. Stella-Rondo hadn't done a thing but turn her against me from upstairs while I stood there helpless over the hot stove. So that made Mama, Papa-Daddy and the baby all on Stella-Rondo's side.

Next, Uncle Rondo.

I must say that Uncle Rondo has been marvelous to me at various times in the past and I was completely unprepared to be made to jump out of my skin, the way it turned out. Once Stella-Rondo did something perfectly horrible to him—broke a chain letter from Flanders Field—and he took the radio back he had given her and gave it to me. Stella-Rondo was furious! For six months we all had to call her Stella instead of Stella-Rondo, or she wouldn't answer. I always thought Uncle Rondo had all the brains of the entire family. Another time he sent me to Mammoth Cave, with all expenses paid.

But this would be the day he was drinking that prescription, the Fourth of July.

So at supper Stella-Rondo speaks up and says she thinks Uncle Rondo ought to try to eat a little something. So finally Uncle Rondo said he would try a little cold biscuits and ketchup, but that was all. So *she* brought it to him.

"Do you think it wise to disport with ketchup in Stella-Rondo's flesh-colored kimono?" I says. Trying to be considerate! If Stella-Rondo couldn't watch out for her trousseau, somebody had to.

"Any objections?" asks Uncle Rondo, just about to pour out all the ketchup.

"Don't mind what she says, Uncle Rondo," says Stella-Rondo. "Sister has been devoting this solid afternoon to sneering out my bedroom window at the way you look."

"What's that?" says Uncle Rondo. Uncle Rondo has got the most terrible temper in the world. Anything is liable to make him tear the house down if it comes at the wrong time.

So Stella-Rondo says, "Sister says, 'Uncle Rondo certainly does look like a fool in that pink kimono!' "

Do you remember who it was really said that?

Uncle Rondo spills out all the ketchup and jumps out of his chair and tears off the kimono and throws it down on the dirty floor and puts his foot on it. It had to be sent all the way to Jackson to the cleaners and re-pleated.

"So that's your opinion of your Uncle Rondo, is it?" he says. "I look like a fool, do I? Well, that's the last straw. A whole day in this house with nothing to do, and then to hear you come out with a remark like that behind my back!"

"I didn't say any such of a thing, Uncle Rondo," I says, "and I'm not saying who did, either. Why, I think you look all right. Just try to take care of yourself and not talk and eat at the same time," I says. "I think you better go lie down."

"Lie down my foot," says Uncle Rondo. I ought to of known by that he was fixing to do something perfectly horrible.

So he didn't do anything that night in the precarious state he was in—just played Casino with Mama and Stella-Rondo and Shirley-T. and gave Shirley-T. a nickel with a head on both sides. It tickled her nearly to death, and she called him "Papa." But at 6:30 A.M. the next morning, he threw a whole five-cent package of some unsold one-inch firecrackers from the store as hard as he could into my bedroom and they every one went off. Not one bad one in the string. Anybody else, there'd be one that wouldn't go off.

Well, I'm just terribly susceptible to noise of any kind, the doctor has always told me I was the most sensitive person he had ever seen in his whole life, and I was simply prostrated. I couldn't eat! People tell me they heard it as far as the cemetery, and old Aunt Jep Patterson, that had been holding her own so good, thought it was Judgment Day and she was going to meet her whole family. It's usually so quiet here.

And I'll tell you it didn't take me any longer than a minute to make up my mind what to do. There I was with the whole entire house on Stella-Rondo's side and turned against me. If I have anything at all I have pride.

So I just decided I'd go straight down to the P.O. There's plenty of room there in the back, I says to myself.

Well! I made no bones about letting the family catch on to what I was up to. I didn't try to conceal it.

The first thing they knew, I marched in where they were all playing Old Maid and pulled the electric oscillating fan out by the plug, and everything got real hot. Next I snatched the pillow I'd done the needle-point on right off the davenport from behind Papa-Daddy. He went "Ugh!" I beat Stella-Rondo up the stairs and finally found my charm bracelet in her bureau drawer under a picture of Nelson Eddy.

"So that's the way the land lies," says Uncle Rondo. There he was, piecing on the ham. "Well, Sister, I'll be glad to donate my army cot if you got any place to set it up, providing you'll leave right this minute and let me get some peace." Uncle Rondo was in France.

"Thank you kindly for the cot and 'peace' is hardly the word I would select if I had to resort to firecrackers at 6:30 A.M. in a young girl's bedroom," I says back to him. "And as to where I intend to go, you seem to forget my position as postmistress of China Grove, Mississippi," I says. "I've always got the P.O."

Well, that made them all sit up and take notice.

I went out front and started digging up some four-o'clocks to plant around the P.O.

"Ah-ah-ah!" says Mama, raising the window. "Those happen to be my four-o'clocks. Everything planted in that star is mine. I've never known you to make anything grow in your life."

"Very well," I says. "But I take the fern. Even you, Mama, can't stand there and deny that I'm the one watered that fern. And I happen to know where I can send in a box top and get a packet of one thousand mixed seeds, not two the same kind, free."

"Oh, where?" Mama wants to know.

But I says, "Too late. You 'tend to your house and I'll 'tend to mine. You hear things like that all the time if you know how to listen to the radio. Perfectly marvelous offers. Get anything you want free."

So I hope to tell you I marched in and got that radio, and they could of all bit a nail in two, especially Stella-Rondo, that it used to belong to, and she well knew she couldn't get it back, I'd sue for it like a shot. And I very politely took the sewing-machine motor I helped pay the most on to give Mama for Christmas back in 1929, and a good big calendar, with the first-aid remedies on it. The thermometer and the Hawaiian ukulele certainly were rightfully mine, and I stood on the step-ladder and got all my watermelon-rind preserves and every fruit and vegetable I'd put up, every jar. Then I began to pull the tacks out of the bluebird wall vases on the archway to the dining room.

"Who told you you could have those, Miss Priss?" says Mama, fanning as hard as she could.

"I bought 'em and I'll keep track of 'em," I says. "I'll tack 'em up one on each side the post-office window, and you can see 'em when you come to ask me for your mail, if you're so dead to see 'em."

"Not I! I'll never darken the door to that post office again if I live to be a hundred," Mama says. "Ungrateful child! After all the money we spent on you at the Normal."

"Me either," says Stella-Rondo. "You can just let my mail lie there and *rot*, for all I care. I'll never come and relieve you of a single, solitary piece."

"I should worry," I says. "And who you think's going to sit down and write you all those big fat letters and postcards, by the way? Mr.

Whitaker? Just because he was the only man ever dropped down in China Grove and you got him—unfairly—is he going to sit down and write you a lengthy correspondence after you come home giving no rhyme nor reason whatsoever for your separation and no explanation for the presence of that child? I may not have your brilliant mind, but I fail to see it."

So Mama says, "Sister, I've told you a thousand times that Stella-Rondo simply got homesick, and this child is far too big to be hers," and she says, "Now, why don't you all just sit down and play Casino?"

Then Shirley-T. sticks out her tongue at me in this perfectly horrible way. She has no more manners than the man in the moon. I told her she was going to cross her eyes like that some day and they'd stick.

"It's too late to stop me now," I says. "You should have tried that yesterday. I'm going to the P.O. and the only way you can possibly see me is to visit me there."

So Papa-Daddy says, "You'll never catch me setting foot in that post office, even if I should take a notion into my head to write a letter some place." He says, "I won't have you reachin' out of that little old window with a pair of shears and cuttin' off any beard of mine. I'm too smart for you!"

"We all are," says Stella-Rondo.

But I said, "If you're so smart, where's Mr. Whitaker?"

So then Uncle Rondo says, "I'll thank you from now on to stop reading all the orders I get on postcards and telling everybody in China Grove what you think is the matter with them," but I says, "I draw my own conclusions and will continue in the future to draw them." I says, "If people want to write their inmost secrets on penny postcards, there's nothing in the wide world you can do about it, Uncle Rondo."

"And if you think we'll ever *write* another postcard you're sadly mistaken," says Mama.

"Cutting off your nose to spite your face then," I says. "But if you're all determined to have no more to do with the U.S. mail, think of this: What will Stella-Rondo do now, if she wants to tell Mr. Whitaker to come after her?"

"Wah!" says Stella-Rondo. I knew she'd cry. She had a conniption fit right there in the kitchen.

"It will be interesting to see how long she holds out," I says. "And now—I am leaving."

"Good-bye," says Uncle Rondo.

"Oh, I declare," says Mama, "to think that a family of mine should quarrel on the Fourth of July, or the day after, over Stella-Rondo leaving old Mr. Whitaker and having the sweetest little adopted child! It looks like we'd all be glad!"

"Wah!" says Stella-Rondo, and has a fresh conniption fit.

"*He* left *her*—you mark my words," I says. "That's Mr. Whitaker. I know Mr. Whitaker. After all, I knew him first. I said from the beginning he'd up and leave her. I foretold every single thing that's happened."

"Where did he go?" asks Mama.

"Probably to the North Pole, if he knows what's good for him," I says.

But Stella-Rondo just bawled and wouldn't say another word. She flew to her room and slammed the door.

"Now look what you've gone and done, Sister," says Mama. "You go apologize."

"I haven't got time, I'm leaving," I says.

"Well, what are you waiting around for?" asks Uncle Rondo.

So I just picked up the kitchen clock and marched off, without saying "Kiss my foot" or anything, and never did tell Stella-Rondo good-bye.

There was a girl going along on a little wagon right in front.

"Girl," I says, "come help me haul these things down the hill, I'm going to live in the post office."

Took her nine trips in her express wagon. Uncle Rondo came out on the porch and threw her a nickel.

• • •

And that's the last I've laid eyes on any of my family or my family laid eyes on me for five solid days and nights. Stella-Rondo may be telling the most horrible tales in the world about Mr. Whitaker, but I haven't heard them. As I tell everybody, I draw my own conclusions.

But oh, I like it here. It's ideal, as I've been saying. You see, I've got everything cater-cornered, the way I like it. Hear the radio? All the war news. Radio, sewing machine, book ends, ironing board and that great big piano lamp—peace, that's what I like. Butter-bean vines planted all along the front where the strings are.

Of course, there's not much mail. My family are naturally the main people in China Grove, and if they prefer to vanish from the face of the earth, for all the mail they get or the mail they write, why, I'm not going to open my mouth. Some of the folks here in town are taking up for me and some turned against me. I know which is which. There are always people who will quit buying stamps just to get on the right side of Papa-Daddy.

But here I am, and here I'll stay. I want the world to know I'm happy.

And if Stella-Rondo should come to me this minute, on bended knees, and *attempt* to explain the incidents of her life with Mr. Whitaker, I'd simply put my fingers in both my ears and refuse to listen.

Peter de Vries

*

REQUIEM FOR A NOUN,
OR INTRUDER IN THE DUSK

(WHAT CAN COME OF TRYING TO READ WILLIAM FAULKNER
WHILE MINDING A CHILD, OR VICE VERSA)

The cold Brussels sprout rolled off the page of the book I was reading
and lay inert and defunctive in my lap. Turning my head with a leisure
at least three-fourths impotent rage, I saw him standing there holding
the toy with which he had catapulted the vegetable, or rather the reverse,
the toy first then the fat insolent fist clutching it and then above that the
bland defiant face beneath the shock of black hair like tangible gas. It,
the toy, was one of those cardboard funnels with a trigger near the point
for firing a small celluloid ball. Letting the cold Brussels sprout lie there
in my lap for him to absorb or anyhow apprehend rebuke from, I took a
pull at a Scotch highball I had had in my hand and then set it down on
the end table beside me.

"So instead of losing the shooter which would have been a mercy
you had to lose the ball," I said, fixing with a stern eye what I had
fathered out of all sentient and biding dust; remembering with that retroactive memory by which we count chimes seconds and even minutes
after they have struck (recapitulate, even, the very grinding of the bowels
of the clock before and during and after) the cunning furtive click, clicks
rather, which perception should have told me then already were not the
trigger plied but the icebox opened. "Even a boy of five going on six
should have more respect for his father if not for food," I said, now
picking the cold Brussels sprout out of my lap and setting it—not dropping it, setting it—in an ashtray; thinking how across the wax bland
treachery of the kitchen linoleum were now in all likelihood distributed

the remnants of string beans and cold potatoes and maybe even tapioca. "You're no son of mine."

I took up the thread of the book again or tried to: the weft of legitimate kinship that was intricate enough without the obbligato of that dark other: the sixteenths and thirty-seconds and even sixty-fourths of dishonoring cousinships brewed out of the violable blood by the ineffaceable errant lusts. Then I heard another click; a faint metallic rejoinder that this time was neither the trigger nor the icebox but the front door opened and then shut. Through the window I saw him picking his way over the season's soiled and sun-frayed vestiges of snow like shreds of rotted lace, the cheap upended toy cone in one hand and a child's cardboard suitcase in the other, toward the road.

I dropped the book and went out after him who had forgotten not only that I was in shirtsleeves but that my braces hung down over my flanks in twin festoons. "Where are you going?" I called, my voice expostulant and forlorn on the warm numb air. Then I caught it: caught it in the succinct outrage of the suitcase and the prim churning rear and marching heels as well: I had said he was no son of mine, and so he was leaving a house not only where he was not wanted but where he did not even belong.

"I see," I said in that shocked clarity with which we perceive the truth instantaneous and entire out of the very astonishment that refuses to acknowledge it. "Just as you now cannot be sure of any roof you belong more than half under, you figure there is no housetop from which you might not as well begin to shout it. Is that it?"

Something was trying to tell me something. Watching him turn off on the road—and that not only with the ostensible declaration of vagabondage but already its very assumption, attaining as though with a single footfall the very apotheosis of wandering just as with a single shutting of a door he had that of renunciation and farewell-watching him turn off on it, the road, in the direction of the Permisangs', our nearest neighbors, I thought *Wait; no; what I said was not enough for him to leave the house on; it must have been the blurted inscrutable chance confirmation of something he already knew, and was half able to assess, either out of the blown facts of boyhood or pure male divination or both.*

"What is it you know?" I said springing forward over the delicate squalor of the snow and falling in beside the boy. "Does any man come to the house to see your mother when I'm away, that you know of?" Thinking *We are mocked, first by the old mammalian snare, then, snared, by the final unilaterality of all flesh to which birth is given; not only not knowing when we may be cuckolded, but not even sure that in the veins of the very bantling we dandle does not flow the miscreant sniggering wayward blood.*

"I get it now," I said, catching in the undeviating face just as I had in the prim back and marching heels the steady articulation of disdain. "Cuckoldry is something of which the victim may be as guilty as the wrong-doers. That's what you're thinking? That by letting in this taint upon our heritage I am as accountable as she or they who have been its actual avatars. More. Though the foe may survive, the sleeping sentinel must be shot. Is that it?"

"You talk funny."

Mother-and-daughter blood conspires in the old mammalian office. Father-and-son blood vies in the ancient phallic enmity. I caught him by the arm and we scuffled in the snow. "I will be heard," I said, holding him now as though we might be dancing, my voice intimate and furious against the furious sibilance of our feet in the snow. Thinking how revelation had had to be inherent in the very vegetable scraps to which venery was probably that instant contriving to abandon me, the cold boiled despair of whatever already featureless suburban Wednesday Thursday or Saturday supper the shot green was the remainder. "I see another thing," I panted, cursing my helplessness to curse whoever it was had given him blood and wind. Thinking *He's glad; glad to credit what is always secretly fostered and fermented out of the vats of childhood fantasy anyway (for all childhood must conceive a substitute for the father that has conceived it (finding that other inconceivable?); thinking He is walking in a nursery fairy tale to find the king his sire.* "Just as I said to you 'You're no son of mine' so now you answer back 'Neither are you any father to me.'"

The scherzo of violence ended as abruptly as it had begun. He broke away and walked on, after retrieving the toy he had dropped and adjusting his grip on the suitcase which he had not, this time faster and more urgently.

• • •

The last light was seeping out of the shabby sky, after the hemorrhage of sunset. High in the west where the fierce constellations soon would wheel, the evening star in single bombast burned and burned. The boy passed the Permisangs' without going in, then passed the Kellers'. Maybe he's heading for the McCullums', I thought, but he passed their house too. Then he, we, neared the Jelliffs'. He's got to be going there, his search will end there, I thought. Because that was the last house this side of the tracks. And because *something was trying to tell me something.*

"Were you maybe thinking of what you heard said about Mrs. Jelliff and me having relations in Spuyten Duyvil?" I said in rapid frantic speculation. "But they were talking about mutual kin—nothing else." The boy said nothing. But I had sensed it instant and complete: the boy felt that, whatever of offense his mother may or may not have given, his father had given provocation; and out of the old embattled malehood, it was the hairy ineluctable Him whose guilt and shame he was going to hold preponderant. *Because now I remembered.*

"So it's Mrs. Jelliff—Sue Jelliff—and me you have got this all mixed up with," I said, figuring he must, in that fat sly nocturnal stealth that took him creeping up and down the stairs to listen when he should have been in bed, certainly have heard his mother exclaiming to his father behind that bedroom door it had been vain to close since it was not sound-proof: "I saw you. I saw that with Sue. There may not be anything between you but you'd like there to be! Maybe there is at that!"

Now like a dentist forced to ruin sound enamel to reach decayed I had to risk telling him what he did not know to keep what he assuredly did in relative control.

"This is what happened on the night in question," I said. "It was under the mistletoe, during the Holidays, at the Jelliffs'. Wait! I will be heard out! See your father as he is, but see him in no baser light. He has his arms around his neighbor's wife. It is evening, in the heat and huddled spiced felicity of the year's end, under the mistletoe (where as well as anywhere else the thirsting and exasperated flesh might be visited by the futile pangs and jets of later lust, the omnivorous aches of fifty and forty and even thirty-five to seize what may be the last of the allotted lips). Your father seems to prolong beyond its usual moment's span that custom's usufruct. Only for an instant, but in that instant letting trickle through the fissures of appearance what your mother and probably Rudy Jelliff too saw as an earnest of a flood that would have devoured that house and one four doors away."

A moon hung over the eastern roofs like a phantasmal bladder. Somewhere an icicle crashed and splintered, fruits of the day's thaw.

"So now I've got it straight," I said. "Just as through some nameless father your mother has cuckolded me (you think), so through one of Rudy Jelliff's five sons I have probably cuckolded him. Which would give you at least a half brother under that roof where under ours you have none at all. So you balance out one miscreance with another, and find your rightful kin in our poor weft of all the teeming random bonded sentient dust."

Shifting the grip, the boy walked on past the Jelliffs'. Before him—

the tracks; and beyond that—the other side of the tracks. And now out of whatever reserve capacity for astonished incredulity may yet have remained I prepared to face this last and ultimate outrage. But he didn't cross. Along our own side of the tracks ran a road which the boy turned left on. He paused before a lighted house near the corner, a white cottage with a shingle in the window which I knew from familiarity to read, "Viola Pruett, Piano Lessons," and which, like a violently unscrambled pattern on a screen, now came to focus.

Memory adumbrates just as expectation recalls. The name on the shingle made audible to listening recollection the last words of the boy's mother as she'd left, which had fallen short then of the threshold of hearing. ". . . Pruett," I remembered now. "He's going to have supper and stay with Buzzie Pruett overnight. . . . Can take a few things with him in that little suitcase of his. If Mrs. Pruett phones about it, just say I'll take him over when I get back," I recalled now in that chime-counting recapitulation of retroactive memory—better than which I could not have been expected to do. Because the eternal Who-instructs might have got through to the whiskey-drinking husband or might have got through to the reader immersed in that prose vertiginous intoxicant and unique, but not to both.

"So that's it," I said. "You couldn't wait till you were taken much less till it was time but had to sneak off by yourself, and that not cross-lots but up the road I've told you a hundred times to keep off even the shoulder of."

The boy had stopped and now appeared to hesitate before the house. He turned around at last, switched the toy and the suitcase in his hands, and started back in the direction he had come.

"What are you going back for now?" I asked.

"More stuff to take in this suitcase," he said. "I was going to just sleep at the Pruetts' overnight, but now I'm going to ask them to let me stay there for good."

Flann O'Brien
(Myles na Gopaleen)

*

KEATS AND CHAPMAN

[Brian O'Nolan wrote under the pen names Flann O'Brien and Myles na Gopaleen. He was, S. J. Perelman once wrote, "The best comic writer I can think of." Following, some excerpts from the column he wrote as Myles na Gopaleen. The column appeared in *The Irish Times* from 1939 until the author's death in Dublin on April 1, 1966.–ED.]

Chapman thought a lot of Keats's girl, Fanny Brawne, and often said so.
   "Do you know," he remarked one day, "that girl of yours is a sight for sore eyes."
   "She stupes to conquer, you mean," Keats said.

LITERARY CORNER
   Chapman was once complaining to Keats about the eccentric behaviour of a third party who had rented a desolate stretch of coast and engaged an architect to build a fantastic castle on it. Chapman said that no sane person could think of living in so forsaken a spot, but Keats was more inclined to criticise the rich man on the score of the architect he had chosen, a young man of "advanced" ideas and negligible experience. Chapman persisted that the site was impossible, and that this third party was a fool.
   "His B.Arch. is worse than his bight," Keats said.

A GLIMPSE OF KEATS
   Keats and Chapman were conversing one day on the street, and what they were conversing about I could not tell you. But anyway there passed a certain character who was renowned far and wide for his piety, and who was reputed to have already made his own coffin, erected it on trestles, and slept in it every night.

"Did you see our friend?" Keats said.

"Yes," said Chapman, wondering what was coming.

"A terrible man for his bier," the poet said.

* * *

Keats (in his day) had a friend named Byrne. Byrne was a rather decent Irish person, but he was frightfully temperamental, politically unstable and difficult to get on with, particularly if the running board of the tram was already crowded with fat women. He frightened (the life) out of his wife with his odd Marxist ideas.

"What shall I do?" she implored Keats. "Politics mean nothing to me; his love means much."

Keats said nothing, but wrote to her that night—"Please Byrne when Red."

* * *

Keats once bought a small pub in London and one day he was visited by Dr. Watson, confrère of the famous Baker Street sleuth. Watson came late in the evening accompanied by a friend and the pair of them took to hard drinking in the back snug. When closing time came, Keats shouted out the usual slogans of urgent valediction such as "Time now please!," "Time gents!," "The Licence gents!," "Fresh air now gents!" and "Come on now all together!" But Dr. Watson and his friend took no notice. Eventually Keats put his head into the snug and roared, "Come on now gents, have yez no Holmes to go to!"

The two topers then left in that lofty vehicle, high dudgeon.

* * *

A memoir of Keats. Number eighty-four. Copyright in all civilised countries, also in "Eire" and in the Sick Counties of Northern Ireland. Pat. Appd. For. The public is warned that copyright subsists in these epexegetic biographic addenda under warrant issued by the Ulster King of Farms (*nach maireann*) and persons assailing, invading or otherwise violating such rights of copy, which are in-alienable and indefeasible, will be liable to summary disintitulement *in feodo* without remembrances and petty sochemaunce pendent graund plaisaunce du roi.

A Memoir of Keats. No. 84. Copyright.

Keats once rented a trout-stream and managed to kill a sackful of fish every day. Transport was poor and he had no means of marketing the surplus, which, however, was not large. Chapman, hearing of this, presented his friend with a small mobile canning plant. (He managed to pick up, rather than buy, this machine for that odd mercantile cantata, a song.) Calling to see the poet some months later, he was astonished at his robust and girthy physique.

"You must be eating a lot," Chapman said. "I suppose you are making money out of the canned trout?"

"I eat what I can," Keats said.

• • •

Chapman had a small cousin whom he wished to put to a trade and he approached Keats for advice. The poet had an old relative who was a tailor and for a consideration this tailor agreed to accept the young man as an apprentice. For the first year, however, he declined to let him do any cutting, insisting that he should first master the art of making garments up.

One day Chapman accidentally spilled some boiling porridge over his only suit, ruining it completely. The same evening he had an appointment with a wealthy widow and was at his wits' end to know how he could get another suit in time. Keats suggested that the young apprentice should be called upon in the emergency. Chapman thought this a good idea and sent the apprentice an urgent message. Afterwards he had some misgivings as to the ability of a mere apprentice to produce a wearable suit in a few hours.

"He'll certainly want to spare no effort to have it finished by six o'clock," he said gloomily.

"He'll have his work cut out," Keats said reassuringly.

• • •

Keats and Chapman once called to see a titled friend and after the host had hospitably produced a bottle of whiskey, the two visitors were called into consultation regarding the son of the house, who had been exhibiting a disquieting redness of face and boisterousness of manner at the age of twelve. The father was worried, suspecting some dread disease. The youngster was produced, but the two visitors, glass in hand, declined to make any diagnosis. When leaving the big house, Chapman rubbed his hands briskly and remarked on the cold.

"I think it must be freezing and I'm glad of that drink," he said. "By the way, did you think what I thought about that youngster?"

"There's a nip in the heir," Keats said.

John Cheever

*

THE CHASTE CLARISSA

The evening boat for Vineyard Haven was loading freight. In a little while, the warning whistle would separate the sheep from the goats—that's the way Baxter thought of it—the islanders from the tourists wandering through the streets of Woods Hole. His car, like all the others ticketed for the ferry, was parked near the wharf. He sat on the front bumper, smoking. The noise and movement of the small port seemed to signify that the spring had ended and that the shores of West Chop, across the Sound, were the shores of summer, but the implications of the hour and the voyage made no impression on Baxter at all. The delay bored and irritated him. When someone called his name, he got to his feet with relief.

It was old Mrs. Ryan. She called to him from a dusty station wagon, and he went over to speak to her. "I knew it," she said. "I knew that I'd see someone here from Holly Cove. I had that feeling in my bones. We've been traveling since nine this morning. We had trouble with the brakes outside Worcester. Now I'm wondering if Mrs. Talbot will have cleaned the house. She wanted seventy-five dollars for opening it last summer and I told her I wouldn't pay her that again, and I wouldn't be surprised if she's thrown all my letters away. Oh, I hate to have a journey end in a dirty house, but if worse comes to worst, we can clean it ourselves. Can't we, Clarissa?" she asked, turning to a young woman who sat beside her on the front seat. "Oh, excuse me, Baxter!" she exclaimed. "You haven't met Clarissa, have you? This is Bob's wife, Clarissa Ryan."

Baxter's first thought was that a girl like that shouldn't have to ride in a dusty station wagon; she should have done much better. She was young. He guessed that she was about twenty-five. Red-headed, deep-breasted, slender, and indolent, she seemed to belong to a different species from old Mrs. Ryan and her large-boned, forthright daughters. " 'The Cape Cod girls, they have no combs. They comb their hair with codfish bones,' " he said to himself but Clarissa's hair was well groomed. Her bare arms were perfectly white. Woods Hole and the activity on the wharf seemed to bore her and she was not interested in Mrs. Ryan's insular gossip. She lighted a cigarette.

At a pause in the old lady's monologue, Baxter spoke to her daughter-in-law. "When is Bob coming down, Mrs. Ryan?" he asked.

"He isn't coming at all," the beautiful Clarissa said. "He's in France. He's—"

"He's gone there for the government," old Mrs. Ryan interrupted, as if her daughter-in-law could not be entrusted with this simple explanation. "He's working on this terribly interesting project. He won't be back until autumn. I'm going abroad myself. I'm leaving Clarissa alone. Of course," she added forcefully, "I expect that she will *love* the island. Everyone does. I expect that she will be kept very busy. I expect that she—"

The warning signal from the ferry cut her off. Baxter said goodbye. One by one, the cars drove aboard, and the boat started to cross the shoal water from the mainland to the resort. Baxter drank a beer in the cabin and watched Clarissa and old Mrs. Ryan, who were sitting on deck. Since he had never seen Clarissa before, he supposed that Bob Ryan must have married her during the past winter. He did not understand how this beauty had ended up with the Ryans. They were a family of passionate amateur geologists and bird-watchers. "We're all terribly keen about birds and rocks," they said when they were introduced to strangers. Their cottage was a couple of miles from any other and had, as Mrs. Ryan often said, "been thrown together out of a barn in 1922." They sailed, hiked, swam in the surf, and organized expeditions to Cuttyhunk and Tarpaulin Cove. They were people who emphasized *corpore sano* unduly, Baxter thought, and they shouldn't leave Clarissa alone in the cottage. The wind had blown a strand of her flame-colored hair across her cheek. Her long legs were crossed. As the ferry entered the harbor, she stood up and made her way down the deck against the light salt wind, and Baxter, who had returned to the island indifferently, felt that the summer had begun.

• • •

Baxter knew that in trying to get some information about Clarissa Ryan he had to be careful. He was accepted in Holly Cove because he had summered there all his life. He could be pleasant and he was a good-looking man, but his two divorces, his promiscuity, his stinginess, and his Latin complexion had left with his neighbors a vague feeling that he was unsavory. He learned that Clarissa had married Bob Ryan in November and that she was from Chicago. He heard people say that she was beautiful and stupid. That was all he did find out about her.

He looked for Clarissa on the tennis courts and the beaches. He didn't see her. He went several times to the beach nearest the Ryans' cottage. She wasn't there. When he had been on the island only a short time, he received from Mrs. Ryan, in the mail, an invitation to tea. It was an invitation that he would not ordinarily have accepted, but he drove eagerly that afternoon over to the Ryans' cottage. He was late. The cars of most of his friends and neighbors were parked in Mrs. Ryan's field. Their voices drifted out of the open windows into the garden, where Mrs. Ryan's climbing roses were in bloom. "Welcome aboard!" Mrs. Ryan shouted when he crossed the porch. "This is my farewell party. I'm going to Norway." She led him into a crowded room.

Clarissa sat behind the teacups. Against the wall at her back was a glass cabinet that held the Ryans' geological specimens. Her arms were bare. Baxter watched them while she poured his tea. "Hot? . . . Cold? Lemon? . . . Cream?" seemed to be all she had to say, but her red hair and her white arms dominated that end of the room. Baxter ate a sandwich. He hung around the table.

"Have you ever been to the island before, Clarissa?" he asked.

"Yes."

"Do you swim at the beach at Holly Cove?"

"It's too far away."

"When your mother-in-law leaves," Baxter said, "you must let me drive you there in the mornings. I go down at eleven."

"Well, thank you." Clarissa lowered her green eyes. She seemed uncomfortable, and the thought that she might be susceptible crossed Baxter's mind exuberantly. "Well, thank you," she repeated, "but I have a car of my own and—well, I don't know, I don't—"

"What are *you* two talking about?" Mrs. Ryan asked, coming between them and smiling wildly in an effort to conceal some of the force of her interference. "I know it isn't geology," she went on, "and I know that it isn't birds, and I know that it can't be books or music, because those are all things that Clarissa doesn't like, aren't they, Clarissa? Come with me, Baxter," and she led him to the other side of the room and talked to him about sheep raising. When the conversation had ended, the party itself was nearly over. Clarissa's chair was empty. She was not in the room. Stopping at the door to thank Mrs. Ryan and say goodbye, Baxter said that he hoped she wasn't leaving for Europe immediately.

"Oh, but I am," Mrs. Ryan said. "I'm going to the mainland on the six-o'clock boat and sailing from Boston at noon tomorrow."

• • •

At half past ten the next morning, Baxter drove up to the Ryans' cottage. Mrs. Talbot, the local woman who helped the Ryans with their housework, answered the door. She said that young Mrs. Ryan was home, and let him in. Clarissa came downstairs. She looked more beautiful than ever, although she seemed put out at finding him there. She accepted his invitation to go swimming, but she accepted it unenthusiastically. "Oh, all right," she said.

When she came downstairs again, she had on a bathrobe over her bathing suit, and a broad-brimmed hat. On the drive to Holly Cove, he asked about her plans for the summer. She was noncommittal. She seemed preoccupied and unwilling to talk. They parked the car and walked side by side over the dunes to the beach, where she lay in the sand with her eyes closed. A few of Baxter's friends and neighbors stopped to pass the time, but they didn't stop for long, Baxter noticed. Clarissa's unresponsiveness made it difficult to talk. He didn't care.

He went swimming. Clarissa remained on the sand, bundled in her wrap. When he came out of the water, he lay down near her. He watched his neighbors and their children. The weather had been fair. The women were tanned. They were all married women and, unlike Clarissa, women with children, but the rigors of marriage and childbirth had left them all pretty, agile, and contented. While he was admiring them, Clarissa stood up and took off her bathrobe.

Here was something else, and it took his breath away. Some of the inescapable power of her beauty lay in the whiteness of her skin, some of it in the fact that, unlike the other women, who were at ease in bathing suits, Clarissa seemed humiliated and ashamed to find herself wearing so little. She walked down toward the water as if she were naked. When she first felt the water, she stopped short, for, again unlike the others, who were sporting around the pier like seals, Clarissa didn't like the cold. Then, caught for a second between nakedness and the cold, Clarissa waded in and swam a few feet. She came out of the water, hastily wrapped herself in the robe, and lay down in the sand. Then she spoke, for the first time that morning—for the first time in Baxter's experience —with warmth and feeling.

"You know, those stones on the point have grown a lot since I was here last," she said.

"What?" Baxter said.

"Those stones on the point," Clarissa said. "They've grown a lot."

"Stones don't grow," Baxter said.

"Oh yes they do," Clarissa said. "Didn't you know that? Stones grow. There's a stone in Mother's rose garden that's grown a foot in the last few years."

"I didn't know that stones grew," Baxter said.

"Well, they do," Clarissa said. She yawned; she shut her eyes. She seemed to fall asleep. When she opened her eyes again, she asked Baxter the time.

"Twelve o'clock," he said.

"I have to go home," she said. "I'm expecting guests."

Baxter could not contest this. He drove her home. She was unresponsive on the ride, and when he asked her if he could drive her to the beach again, she said no. It was a hot, fair day and most of the doors on the island stood open, but when Clarissa said goodbye to Baxter, she closed the door in his face.

Baxter got Clarissa's mail and newspapers from the post office the next day, but when he called with them at the cottage, Mrs. Talbot said that Mrs. Ryan was busy. He went that week to two large parties that she might have attended, but she was not at either. On Saturday night, he went to a barn dance, and late in the evening—they were dancing "Lady of the Lake"—he noticed Clarissa, sitting against the wall.

She was a striking wallflower. She was much more beautiful than any other woman there, but her beauty seemed to have intimidated the men. Baxter dropped out of the dance when he could and went to her. She was sitting on a packing case. It was the first thing she complained about. "There isn't even anything to sit on," she said.

"Don't you want to dance?" Baxter asked.

"Oh, I love to dance," she said. "I could dance all night, but I don't think *that's* dancing." She winced at the music of the fiddle and the piano. "I came with the Hortons. They just told me there was going to be a dance. They didn't tell me it was going to be this kind of a dance. I don't like all that skipping and hopping."

"Have your guests left?" Baxter asked.

"What guests?" Clarissa said.

"You told me you were expecting guests on Tuesday. When we were at the beach."

"I didn't say they were coming on Tuesday, did I?" Clarissa asked. "They're coming tomorrow."

"Can't I take you home?" Baxter asked.

"All right."

He brought the car around to the barn and turned on the radio.

She got in and slammed the door with spirit. He raced the car over the back roads, and when he brought it up to the Ryans' cottage, he turned off the lights. He watched her hands. She folded them on her purse. "Well, thank you very much," she said. "I was having an awful time and you saved my life. I just don't understand this place, I guess. I've always had plenty of partners, but I sat on that hard box for nearly an hour and nobody even spoke to me. You saved my life."

"You're lovely, Clarissa," Baxter said.

"Well," Clarissa said, and she sighed. "That's just my outward self. Nobody knows the real me."

That was it, Baxter thought, and if he could only adjust his flattery to what she believed herself to be, her scruples would dissolve. Did she think of herself as an actress, he wondered, a Channel swimmer, an heiress? The intimations of susceptibility that came from her in the summer night were so powerful, so heady, that they convinced Baxter that here was a woman whose chastity hung by a thread.

"I think I know the real you," Baxter said.

"Oh no you don't," Clarissa said. "Nobody does."

The radio played some lovelorn music from a Boston hotel. By the calendar, it was still early in the summer, but it seemed, from the stillness and the hugeness of the dark trees, to be much later. Baxter put his arms around Clarissa and planted a kiss on her lips.

She pushed him away violently and reached for the door. "Oh, now you've spoiled everything," she said as she got out of the car. "Now you've spoiled everything. I know what you've been thinking. I know you've been thinking it all along." She slammed the door and spoke to him across the window. "Well, you needn't come around here any more, Baxter," she said. "My girl friends are coming down from New York tomorrow on the morning plane and I'll be too busy to see you for the rest of the summer. Good night."

• • •

Baxter was aware that he had only himself to blame; he had moved too quickly. He knew better. He went to bed feeling angry and sad, and slept poorly. He was depressed when he woke, and his depression was deepened by the noise of a sea rain, blowing in from the northeast. He lay in bed listening to the rain and the surf. The storm would metamorphose the island. The beaches would be empty. Drawers would stick. Suddenly he got out of bed, went to the telephone, called the airport. The New York plane had been unable to land, they told him, and no more planes were expected that day. The storm seemed to be playing directly into his hands. At noon, he drove in to the village and bought a

Sunday paper and a box of candy. The candy was for Clarissa, but he was in no hurry to give it to her.

She would have stocked the icebox, put out the towels, and planned the picnic, but now the arrival of her friends had been postponed, and the lively day that she had anticipated had turned out to be rainy and idle. There were ways, of course, for her to overcome her disappointment, but on the evidence of the barn dance he felt that she was lost without her husband or her mother-in-law, and that there were few, if any, people on the island who would pay her a chance call or ask her over for a drink. It was likely that she would spend the day listening to the radio and the rain and that by the end of it she would be ready to welcome anyone, including Baxter. But as long as the forces of loneliness and idleness were working on his side, it was shrewder, Baxter knew, to wait. It would be best to come just before dark, and he waited until then. He drove to the Ryans' with his box of candy. The windows were lighted. Clarissa opened the door.

"I wanted to welcome your friends to the island," Baxter said. "I—"

"They didn't come," Clarissa said. "The plane couldn't land. They went back to New York. They telephoned me. I had planned such a nice visit. Now everything's changed."

"I'm sorry, Clarissa," Baxter said. "I've brought you a present."

"Oh!" She took the box of candy. "What a beautiful box! What a lovely present! What—" Her face and her voice were, for a minute, ingenuous and yielding, and then he saw the force of resistance transform them. "You shouldn't have done it," she said.

"May I come in?" Baxter asked.

"Well, I don't know," she said. "You can't come in if you're just going to sit around."

"We could play cards," Baxter said.

"I don't know how," she said.

"I'll teach you," Baxter said.

"No," she said. "No, Baxter, you'll have to go. You just don't understand the kind of a woman I am. I spent all day writing a letter to Bob. I wrote and told him that you kissed me last night. I can't let you come in." She closed the door.

From the look on Clarissa's face when he gave her the box of candy, Baxter judged that she liked to get presents. An inexpensive gold bracelet or even a bunch of flowers might do it, he knew, but Baxter was an extremely stingy man, and while he saw the usefulness of a present, he could not bring himself to buy one. He decided to wait.

The storm blew all Monday and Tuesday. It cleared on Tuesday night, and by Wednesday afternoon the tennis courts were dry and Baxter played. He played until late. Then, when he had bathed and changed his clothes, he stopped at a cocktail party to pick up a drink. Here one of his neighbors, a married woman with four children, sat down beside him and began a general discussion of the nature of married love.

It was a conversation, with its glances and innuendoes, that Baxter had been through many times, and he knew roughly what it promised. His neighbor was one of the pretty mothers that Baxter had admired on the beach. Her hair was brown. Her arms were thin and tanned. Her teeth were sound. But while he appeared to be deeply concerned with her opinions on love, the white image of Clarissa loomed up in his mind, and he broke off the conversation and left the party. He drove to the Ryans'.

From a distance the cottage looked shut. The house and the garden were perfectly still. He knocked and then rang. Clarissa spoke to him from an upstairs window.

"Oh, hello, Baxter," she said.

"I've come to say goodbye, Clarissa," Baxter said. He couldn't think of anything better.

"Oh, dear," Clarissa said. "Well, wait just a minute. I'll be down."

"I'm going away, Clarissa," Baxter said when she opened the door. "I've come to say goodbye."

"Where are you going?"

"I don't know." He said this sadly.

"Well, come in, then," she said hesitantly. "Come in for a minute. This is the last time that I'll see you, I guess, isn't it? Please excuse the way the place looks. Mr. Talbot got sick on Monday and Mrs. Talbot had to take him to the hospital on the mainland, and I haven't had anybody to help me. I've been all alone."

He followed her into the living room and sat down. She was more beautiful than ever. She talked about the problems that had been presented by Mrs. Talbot's departure. The fire in the stove that heated the water had died. There was a mouse in the kitchen. The bathtub wouldn't drain. She hadn't been able to get the car started.

In the quiet house, Baxter heard the sound of a leaky water tap and a clock pendulum. The sheet of glass that protected the Ryans' geological specimens reflected the fading sky outside the window. The cottage was near the water, and he could hear the surf. He noted these details dispassionately and for what they were worth. When Clarissa finished her remarks about Mrs. Talbot, he waited a full minute before he spoke.

"The sun is in your hair," he said.

"What?"

"The sun is in your hair. It's a beautiful color."

"Well, it isn't as pretty as it used to be," she said. "Hair like mine gets dark. But I'm not going to dye it. I don't think that women should dye their hair."

"You're so intelligent," he murmured.

"You don't mean that?"

"Mean what?"

"Mean that I'm intelligent."

"Oh, but I do," he said. "You're intelligent. You're beautiful. I'll never forget that night I met you at the boat. I hadn't wanted to come to the island. I'd made plans to go out West."

"I can't be intelligent," Clarissa said miserably. "I must be stupid. Mother Ryan says that I'm stupid, and Bob says that I'm stupid, and even Mrs. Talbot says that I'm stupid, and—" She began to cry. She went to a mirror and dried her eyes. Baxter followed. He put his arms around her. "Don't put your arms around me," she said, more in despair than in anger. "Nobody ever takes me seriously until they get their arms around me." She sat down again and Baxter sat near her. "But you're not stupid, Clarissa," he said. "You have a wonderful intelligence, a wonderful mind. I've often thought so. I've often felt that you must have a lot of very interesting opinions."

"Well, that's funny," she said, "because I do have a lot of opinions. Of course, I never dare say them to anyone, and Bob and Mother Ryan don't ever let me speak. They always interrupt me, as if they were ashamed of me. But I do have these opinions. I mean, I think we're like cogs in a wheel. I've concluded that we're like cogs in a wheel. Do you think we're like cogs in a wheel?"

"Oh, yes," he said. "Oh, yes, I do!"

"I think we're like cogs in a wheel," she said. "For instance, do you think that women should work? I've given that a lot of thought. My opinion is that I don't think married women should work. I mean, unless they have a lot of money, of course, but even then I think it's a full-time job to take care of a man. Or do you think that women should work?"

"What do you think?" he asked. "I'm terribly interested in knowing what you think."

"Well, my opinion is," she said timidly, "that you just have to hoe your row. I don't think that working or joining the church is going to change everything, or special diets, either. I don't put much stock in fancy diets. We have a friend who eats a quarter of a pound of meat at every meal. He has scales right on the table and he weighs the meat. It makes the table look awful and I don't see what good it's going to do him. I buy what's reasonable. If ham is reasonable, I buy ham. If lamb is reasonable, I buy lamb. Don't you think that's intelligent?"

"I think that's very intelligent."

"And progressive education," she said. "I don't have a good opinion of progressive education. When we go to the Howards' for dinner, the children ride their tricycles around the table all the time, and it's my opinion that they get this way from progressive schools, and that children ought to be told what's nice and what isn't."

The sun that had lighted her hair was gone, but there was still enough light in the room for Baxter to see that as she aired her opinions, her face suffused with color and her pupils dilated. Baxter listened patiently, for he knew by then that she merely wanted to be taken for something that she was not—that the poor girl was lost. "You're very intelligent," he said, now and then. "You're so intelligent."

It was as simple as that.

Oliver Jensen

*

THE GETTYSBURG ADDRESS
IN EISENHOWERESE

[Oliver Jensen's "The Gettysburg Address in Eisenhowerese" was originally circulated in carbon, then mimeograph, before Doris Fleeson printed it in her column. Another version appeared in *The New Republic* of June 17, 1957. Neither attributed it to Jensen. Dwight MacDonald writes, "The version below is the original as given to me by Jensen, with two or three variations in which *The New Republic's* version seemed to me to have added a turn of the screw."—ED.]

I haven't checked these figures but 87 years ago, I think it was, a number of individuals organized a governmental set-up here in this country, I believe it covered certain Eastern areas, with this idea they were following up based on a sort of national independence arrangement and the program that every individual is just as good as every other individual. Well, now, of course, we are dealing with this big difference of opinion, civil disturbance you might say, although I don't like to appear to take sides or name any individuals, and the point is naturally to check up, by actual experience in the field, to see whether any governmental set-up with a basis like the one I was mentioning has any validity and find out whether that dedication by those early individuals will pay off in lasting values and things of that kind.

Well, here we are, at the scene where one of these disturbances between different sides got going. We want to pay our tribute to those loved ones, those departed individuals who made the supreme sacrifice here on the basis of their opinions about how this thing ought to be handled. And I would say this. It is absolutely in order to do this.

But if you look at the over-all picture of this, we can't pay any tribute—we can't sanctify this area, you might say—we can't hallow according to whatever individual creeds or faiths or sort of religious outlooks are involved like I said about this particular area. It was those individuals themselves, including the enlisted men, very brave individuals, who have given this religious character to the area. The way I see it, the rest of the world will not remember any statements issued here but it will never forget how these men put their shoulders to the wheel and carried this idea down the fairway.

Now frankly, our job, the living individuals' job here, is to pick up the burden and sink the putt they made these big efforts here for. It is our job to get on with the assignment—and from these deceased fine individuals to take extra inspiration, you could call it, for the same theories about the set-up for which they made such a big contribution. We have to make up our minds right here and now, as I see it, that they didn't put out all that blood, perspiration and—well—that they didn't just make a dry run here, and that all of us here, under God, that is, the God of our choice, shall beef up this idea about freedom and liberty and those kind of arrangements, and that government of all individuals, by all individuals and for the individuals, shall not pass out of the world-picture.

Saul Bellow

*

EXCERPT FROM

TO JERUSALEM AND BACK

Security measures are strict on flights to Israel, the bags are searched, the men are frisked, and the women have an electronic hoop passed over them, fore and aft. Then hand luggage is opened. No one is very patient. Visibility in the queue is poor because of the many Hasidim with their broad hats and beards and sidelocks and dangling fringes who have descended on Heathrow and are far too restless to wait in line but rush in and out, gesticulating, exclaiming. The corridors are jumping with them. Some two hundred Hasidim are flying to Israel to attend the circumcision of the firstborn son of their spiritual leader, the Belzer Rabbi. Entering the 747, my wife, Alexandra, and I are enfiladed by eyes that lie dark in hairy ambush. To me there is nothing foreign in these hats, sidelocks, and fringes. It is my childhood revisited. At the age of six, I myself wore a tallith katan, or scapular, under my shirt, only mine was a scrap of green calico print, whereas theirs are white linen. God instructed Moses to speak to the children of Israel and to "bid them that they make them fringes in the borders of their garments." So they are still wearing them some four thousand years later. We find our seats, two in a row of three, toward the rear of the aircraft. The third is occupied by a young Hasid, highly excited, who is staring at me.

"Do you speak Yiddish?" he says.

"Yes, certainly."

"I cannot be next to your wife. Please sit between us. Be so good," he says.

"Of course."

I take the middle seat, which I dislike, but I am not really put out. Curious, rather. Our Hasid is in his late twenties. He is pimply, his neck is thin, his blue eyes goggle, his underlip extrudes. He does not keep a civilized face. Thoughts and impulses other than civilized fill it—by no means inferior impulses and thoughts. And though he is not permitted to sit beside women unrelated to him or to look at them or to communicate with them in any manner (all of which probably saves him a great deal of trouble), he seems a good-hearted young man and he is visibly enjoying himself. All the Hasidim are vividly enjoying themselves, dodging through the aisles, visiting chattering standing impatiently in the long lavatory lines, amiable, busy as geese. They pay no attention to signs. Don't they understand English? The stewardesses are furious with them. I ask one of the hostesses when I may expect to receive a drink and she cries out in irritation, "Back to your seat!" She says this in so ringing a voice that I retreat. Not so the merry-minded Hasidim, exulting everywhere. The orders given by these young gentile uniformed females are nothing to them. To them they are merely attendants, exotic *bediener*, all but bodyless.

Anticipating a difficulty, I ask the stewardess to serve me a kosher lunch. "I can't do that, we haven't enough for *them*," she says. "We weren't prepared." Her big British eyes are affronted and her bosom has risen with indignation. "We've got to go out of our way to Rome for more of their special meals."

Amused, my wife asks why I ordered the kosher lunch. "Because when they bring my chicken dinner this kid with the beard will be in a state," I explain.

And so he is. The British Airways chicken with the chill of death upon it lies before me. But after three hours of security exercises at Heathrow I am hungry. The young Hasid recoils when the tray is handed to me. He addresses me again in Yiddish. He says, "I must talk to you. You won't be offended?"

"No, I don't think so."

"You may want to give me a slap in the face."

"Why should I?"

"You *are* a Jew. You must be a Jew, we are speaking Yiddish. How can you eat—*that!*"

"It looks awful, doesn't it?"

"You mustn't touch it. My womenfolk packed kosher-beef sandwiches for me. Is your wife Jewish?"

Here I'm obliged to lie. Alexandra is Rumanian. But I can't give him too many shocks at once, and I say, "She has not had a Jewish upbringing."

"She doesn't speak Yiddish?"

"Not a word. But excuse me, I want my lunch."

"Will you eat some of my kosher food instead, as a favor?"

"With pleasure."

"Then I will give you a sandwich, but only on one condition. You must never—never—eat *trephena* food again."

"I can't promise you that. You're asking too much. And just for one sandwich."

"I have a duty toward you," he tells me. "Will you listen to a proposition?"

"Of course I will."

"So let us make a deal. I am prepared to pay you. If you will eat nothing but kosher food, for the rest of your life I will send you fifteen dollars a week."

"That's very generous," I say.

"Well, you are a Jew," he says. "I must try to save you."

"How do you earn your living?"

"In a Hasidic sweater factory in New Jersey. We are all Hasidim there. The boss is a Hasid. I came from Israel five years ago to be married in New Jersey. My rabbi is in Jerusalem."

"How is it that you don't know English?"

"What do I need English for? So, I am asking, will you take my fifteen dollars?"

"Kosher food is far more expensive than other kinds," I say. "Fifteen dollars isn't nearly enough."

"I can go as far as twenty-five."

"I can't accept such a sacrifice from you."

Shrugging, he gives up and I turn to the twice disagreeable chicken and eat guiltily, my appetite spoiled. The young Hasid opens his prayer book. "He's so fervent," says my wife. "I wonder if he's praying for you." She smiles at my discomfiture.

As soon as the trays are removed, the Hasidim block the aisles with their *Minchah* service, rocking themselves and stretching their necks upward. The bond of common prayer is very strong. This is what has held the Jews together for thousands of years. "I like them," says my wife. "They're so lively, so childlike."

"You might find them a little hard to live with," I tell her. "You'd have to do everything their way, no options given."

"But they're cheerful, and they're warm and natural. I love their costumes. Couldn't you get one of those beautiful hats?"

"I don't know whether they sell them to outsiders."

When the Hasid returns to his seat after prayer, I tell him that my wife, a woman of learning, will be lecturing at the Hebrew University in Jerusalem.

"What is she?"

"A mathematician."

He is puzzled. "What is that?" he asks.

I try to explain.

He says, "This I never heard of. What actually is it they do?"

I am astonished. I knew that he was an innocent but I would never have believed him to be ignorant of such a thing. "So you don't know what mathematicians are. Do you know what a physicist is? Do you recognize the name of Einstein?"

"Never. Who is he?"

This is too much for me. Silent, I give his case some thought. Busy-minded people, with their head-culture that touches all surfaces, have heard of Einstein. But do they know what they have heard? A majority do not. These Hasidim choose not to know. By and by I open a paperback and try to lose myself in mere politics. A dozen Hasidim in the lavatory queue stare down at us.

We land and spill out and go our separate ways. At the baggage carousel I see my youthful Hasid again and we take a final look at each other. In me he sees what deformities the modern age can produce in the seed of Abraham. In him I see a piece of history, an antiquity. It is rather as if Puritans in seventeenth-century dress and observing seventeenth-century customs were to be found still living in Boston or Plymouth. Israel, which receives us impartially, is accustomed to strange arrivals. But then Israel is something else again.

Jessica Mitford

*

EMIGRATION

EXCERPT FROM *Daughters and Rebels*

Politics aside, two other elements had entered our lives which effectively tipped the scales in favour of emigration: the Process Server and my hundred pounds.

The Process Server was a pale, sad-looking youth in the employ of the London Electricity Board. Fortunately for us, he was not particularly good at his line of work; the most transparent disguises—Esmond's false moustache, top hat or worker's cap, my dark glasses—would effectively muddle him for the few moments needed to escape. He would stare sorrowfully after us, his brow wrinkled with puzzlement, as we quickly dashed round a corner or disappeared from his view down the Underground.

I felt guilty about the Process Server, because in a way I had been unfairly trapped into responsibility for his haunting presence. No one had ever explained to me that you had to pay for electricity; and lights, electric heaters, stoves blazed away night and day at Rotherhithe Street. When the enormous bill first arrived, we thought briefly of contesting it in court on the grounds that electricity is an Act of God—an element, like fire, earth and air; but legal friends assured us this would get us nowhere. It was unthinkable that we should pay, so we moved out of the Rotherhithe Street house to a furnished room near the Marble Arch.

Somehow, the Process Server found out where we were staying. Every morning before going to work we peered cautiously out of the window to see if he was coming down the street or lurking at a corner. We regretfully abandoned the disguises because he had seen them all so many times. If he was in sight, we would go back to bed, as Esmond had a theory that it was illegal and in some way a violation of Magna Carta to serve process on people in bed. Sometimes we stayed in bed for as long as two days, fearing that our tormentor was still in the neighbourhood. Though enjoyable to us, these lost days were becoming a source of irritation to Esmond's boss.

Obviously, life in England had become untenable, in more ways than one. Besides, on my twenty-first birthday I came into a great windfall, a trust fund of one hundred pounds, and we were casting around for a suitable way to use it.

My mother had established savings accounts for all of us. With the birth of each child, she had started making weekly deposits of sixpence into these accounts, which, together with interest, would reach the sum of a hundred pounds by the time we were twenty-one. Only by luck was my hundred pounds intact, for many years before my older sisters had inadvertently lost a good portion of their savings when they sank some money in one of my father's many "damn' sound investments." Debo and I had escaped, being considered too young to sign up for the venture.

An American by the romantic and Western-sounding name of "Mr. Reno" approached my father in the early twenties about this particular project. Mr. Reno had invented a sort of tank, for which he produced plans and blueprints; when built, the Reno tank would be able to descend into the depths of the ocean and bring to the surface the golden treasures of the days of piracy and the Spanish Armada. "Think of it—great chests of gold bullion!" my father would say, rubbing his hands. He made an enormous investment of his own, and raised additional money from uncles and friends who were anxious to share in the pirate gold.

The five oldest Mitford children were allowed to put up twenty pounds each of the savings my mother was keeping for them. I remember shedding hot tears of rage as they described the enormous fortunes they would soon own—not to speak of fabulous jewellery, heavy gold chains, priceless gems, that would doubtless be dredged up in Mr. Reno's tank. But my mother was adamant: Debo and I were under seven, and too young to make our own financial decisions.

Debo and I had our day of rejoicing soon afterwards, when it was learned that Mr. Reno had taken off for America without leaving a trace. "Really *very* dishonest of him—I can't imagine what he must have been thinking of," Muv said. The other sisters put up a half-hearted argument that Debo and I should be forced to share in the loss, since we would readily have invested our money too if we had been allowed to. But for once justice prevailed, and our savings were kept intact.

The sum of a hundred pounds seemed just the right amount for the purpose of emigration. It was neither large enough to start a business or invest for income, nor small enough to spend on a few parties and good meals out. Yet a third of it would purchase two one-way steerage tickets to America, leaving a nice round sum, over $300, at the prevailing rate of exchange, to live on for a while until we found work.

To our disappointment, the American Consul to whom we now applied for the necessary papers did not look at matters this way at all. Indeed, he expressed great surprise that we should consider starting a new life with so small a capital, mentioned there was danger we might become a public charge, and told us that we should have to show a guarantee of financial support amounting to at least fifteen dollars a week before he would consider giving us immigration visas.

We canvassed various friends—Philip Toynbee, Peter Nevile, Giles —and suggested they should underwrite a guarantee of financial support in case we should become penniless, but we were met on all sides with firm and indignant refusals. "He'll give you the papers all right; just say the Magic Words," Peter advised. The Magic Words, it seemed, were Land of Opportunity, Rugged Individualism, Free Enterprise. With Peter's help, Esmond concocted and memorized a brief appeal in which the ritual words were repeated a number of times, and we presented ourselves once more to the Consul. No sooner were we in his office than Esmond became transformed into his idea of red-blooded Americanism. "Sir," he began, "my wife and I hold dear a most heartfelt, deep and sincere faith in the ability of your grea-a-at country, the Land of Opportunity, the United States of America, to provide, through its Free Enterprise system, a modest but adequate living for those young people who, like ourselves, are imbued with the spirit of Rugged Individualism." He went on in this way for some time, Sincerity and Forthrightness actually shining in his eyes.

If Esmond had suddenly assumed the appearance of a cross between Mr. Oover in *Zuleika Dobson* and Spencer Tracy, the Consul didn't seem to notice. As Peter had predicted, the words had an enormous, almost mesmeric, effect on him. With a faraway look in his eyes —which were no doubt seeing the windswept main street of some Midwestern town, swarming with rugged individualists—he uttered the words of consent: "Well, I guess I'll take a chance on you kids."

Now that the trip was becoming a reality, Esmond hit upon an idea which would enable us to travel all over America and get paid for it. We would get some of our friends to come too and offer a lecture covering various phases of English life. Our idea of America, like that of most English people, was limited and not a little distorted. We pictured it as a vast nation of Babbitts whose eyes were uniformly riveted on English royalty, Mothers and Dads, and Sex.

"Women's clubs are the very thing!" Esmond explained. "They have them all over America, and this'll be just the sort of thing they love. They'll simply *eat* up Philip Toynbee." I remarked that this was a most unappetizing thought, but Esmond assured me he was merely repeating an American turn of phrase he had just picked up from Peter.

In short order, we lined up three co-lecturers. Sheila Legge, one of the ex-chorus-girl-market-researchers, agreed readily, and Esmond promptly assigned a subject for her lecture: "Men, from the Ritz to the Fish and Chips Stand." The young male secretary of a well-known poet, who had just parted from his employer in one of those petulant flare-ups which often mar such relationships, was easily persuaded to prepare to be eaten up by the women's clubs; his rather suggestive topic was to be "From Guardsman to Poet's Secretary." Philip was to speak on "Sex Life at Oxford University," and in addition to offer a special Father's Day talk titled: "Arnold Toynbee—Historian, but First and Foremost 'Dad.'" I was to describe "The Inner Life of an English Débutante" (Esmond thought they would like to hear about the delicious dinners and suppers we used to have during the season). Esmond himself would be manager of the expedition, occasionally helping out with lectures on such sure-fire subjects as "Is Princess Elizabeth Really the Monster of Glamis?", "The Truth about Winston Churchill," "How to Meet the King," "Sedition Spreading at Eton."

In the atmosphere of almost electric excitement which Esmond always managed to create when developing a new plan, the five of us met to draw up a prospectus suitable for mailing out to lecture agencies. It began in typical Esmond style: "Dear Sirs: King George and Queen Elizabeth are not the only people leaving these shores for America this year. We are also coming."

We even got as far as having a special series of photographs made for enclosure with the lecture outlines. There was a leering Philip to accompany "Sex Life at Oxford University," and a filial Philip for the Dad's Day lecture. Sheila, showing a large expanse of the limb from which, we assumed, she had got her surname, was pictured in a sultry pose near the main entrance of the Ritz, with the poet's ex-secretary lounging languorously near by, symbolically clutching a slim volume and a Guardsman's cap. But no sooner had we assembled all this promising material than our fellow lecturers began to drop out one by one. A sudden turn in Philip's love life required his presence in England; the poet's secretary made up with the poet, and resumed his post; Sheila was unable to raise the money for her ticket. Our frantic efforts to shore up the situation were to no avail. We regretfully decided that our plans would have to be revised and the lecture tour junked.

Now we concentrated on getting letters of introduction from anyone and everyone we knew who had ever been to America or who knew
any Americans. They were addressed to as wide and varied an assortment
of people as those from whom we had secured them: artists in Greenwich
Village; tycoons on Wall Street; movie people, poets, kind old ladies,
journalists, advertising people.

My own impressions of Americans had been culled from various
sources, ranging from books read in childhood, such as *Little Women*
and *What Katy Did*, to Hemingway and the movies. I knew that they
lived on strange and rather unappetizing-sounding foods called squash,
grits, hot dogs and corn pudding. On the other hand, cookies sounded
rather delicious. I visualized them as little cakes made in the shape of
cooks with sugar-icing aprons and hats. From seeing *The Petrified Forest*,
I gathered that Americans often made love under tables while gangster
bullets whizzed through the air.

Peter Nevile was the only person we knew who had actually been
to America; and Esmond, with his usual thoroughness in such matters,
enlisted Peter's help in briefing us on the language, manners and customs
we should encounter in the Land of Opportunity. We spent an evening
at his house being initiated.

"Never say, 'I say!' Say, 'Say,' " Peter explained patiently. "Things
on the whole move much faster in America; people don't *stand for election*, they *run for office*. If a person says he's *sick*, it doesn't mean regur-
gitating; it means *ill*. *Mad* means angry, not *insane*. Don't ask for the
left-luggage place; it's called a checkroom. A nice joint means a good
pub, not roast meat. . . ." He listed a variety of Christian names we
should encounter, some taken from English titles, such as Earl and
Duke, some from American states, such as Washington, Georgia, Florida. "On the other hand," he went on, lapsing into his American accent
as he warmed to his theme, "you'll hardly find anyone christened Vis-
count or New York. There's really no special logic to it." He instructed
us in the use of "gotten" and "you betcha" (under no circumstances to
be pronounced "you bet you"), and filled us up with a certain amount of
misinformation: that "pediatrician" was a fancy name for a corn specialist, and "mortician" a musician with necrophilic bent who played only at
funerals.

" 'Twenty' is pronounced 'Twenny,' " Peter continued, "and be
sure to leave out the first 't' in 'interesting,' too. Then you'll have to know
a few stock rejoinders. For example, you'll find people generally say, 'I'll
be seeing you' instead of 'goodbye.' Then that leaves the field wide open
for you to answer, 'Not if I see you first,' which will show you are on
your toes, alert and amusing. Alternatively, you may be able to raise a

laugh by saying, 'Abyssinia.' Another thing, if someone pays you a compliment: 'You're looking well,' 'What a pretty dress,' and so forth—you are supposed to say, 'Thank you,' instead of just mumbling inaudibly. You have to be on the lookout for what is considered a compliment, too; for instance, an American may say, 'That dress is the cat's pyjamas.' Don't take this as a criticism, it's meant as just the opposite."

When I suggested, in what I imagined was best American idiom, that I guessed it was time for us to scram home, Peter's parting advice was: "You'll need a crooked lawyer in New York; can't get on without one. Why don't you wire the British Consul there and tell him to have one meet you at the boat?"

Kingsley Amis

*

ANOTHER GODDAM ENGLISHMAN
EXCERPT FROM *One Fat Englishman*

[Roger Micheldene, an English publisher on a scouting trip to America, has been invited to spend a weekend at Budweiser College. His hosts, at a swimming pool party, are Joe and Grace Derlanger. Among the guests are young Irving Macher, a would-be novelist in his junior year at Budweiser, and his girlfriend, Suzanne Klein; another Englishman, Nigel Pargeter; and the Bangs. Dr. Ernst Bang, an authority on Early Icelandic and Faroese, a professor at the University of Copenhagen, is currently a Visiting Fellow at Budweiser. Though the others are unaware of it, Dr. Bang's beautiful wife, Helene, is one of Roger's former mistresses. Roger has come out for the weekend only so that he might meet Helene again.—ED.]

Roger's decision not to swim had been among the easiest of his life. For a man as keen as he on getting into bed with women, keeping hidden the full enormity of his fatness was a chronic problem. Its most acute form naturally came up when someone new had to be hustled or cajoled past the point of no return. That point tended to get later and later as his belly waxed. The merest glimpse of it might be enough, even at a very advanced stage, to remind a girl of her obligations to family tradition, to husband or boy friend or host or roommate or landlady, to humanity. But not only that. Recent experience suggested that that belly, exposed in a moment of inattention or abandon, could cause total withdrawal of favors previously granted. In other words, it tended to stop them. Cold. At any time.

This must not be allowed to happen with Helene. It was a crying shame that, temperamentally, she was different from his usual sort of girl. His usual sort of girl tended not to take it personally when he slept with them and this could lead to a lot of rather loose behavior. Helene, on the other hand, was always very strict. In particular, she insisted on something like parity of nudity. She would not put on anything like a show for him while he sat about in faultless West of England tweeds. In the intervals of choking with rage and lust over this policy of hers, Roger saw it as not unreasonable. But it meant that the really detailed inspection of her which he longed to make would have to be paid for by giving her the chance of making a roughly equally really detailed inspection of him if she were so minded. So no go. So he had had to make do with a couple of glimpses of the side of her as she skipped out of or into bed, the back of her as she dressed or undressed, a small part of the top of the front of her before she switched out the light.

So seeing her in a bathing suit, he told himself without fear of contradiction, was going to be significant. He would be gaining visual experience of her body, if not neat, then in a higher concentration than he had had a chance of getting used to. He hoped it would not be too strong for him. With a slight smile of complacency at his own fore-thought, he reached into his jacket pocket for his sunglasses and put them on. Provided he could remember to move his head about slightly from time to time, nobody would now be able to tell where he was looking. Any involuntary bulging of the eyeballs would likewise be masked. It occurred to him, as he watched carefully for Helene's reap-pearance, that he might throw away these advantages if he went on behaving like a seated figure carved out of old red sandstone. He shifted in his chair, mopped his face, took a pinch of snuff, attacked his drink, glanced about.

Only Grace Derlanger and, more surprisingly, Irving Macher had failed to go and change. They stood talking a few yards off. Or rather Macher was talking. He was doing it in a deep and rather resonant voice which Roger considered he had no right to. Any more than he had a right to a two- or two-and-a-half-thousand-dollar advance.

"And you're justified in acquiring money," Macher was saying, as if in self-defense. "More than that, it's your duty. We've gotten over all that other stuff now, that junk about it's your duty not to have money. Whoever did that duty? And duty's a thing people do, not something they don't do. Listen, what would you do to a soldier who went into a battle without taking his gun along? You'd have him court-martialled, wouldn't you? And you'd be right. Somebody who can't protect himself weakens other people's power of self-protection. Armies understand this. And a lot more. An army's the right kind of organization because it only exists to do what's necessary. Nothing stuck on afterwards for the look of the thing. It's a pity nobody can use them any more, armies. All we have now is scientists, and they're no good. No good in the way I'm looking for. Too much aesthetics about the whole idea.

"But going back to money: it's a terrific liberation to think of it in the right way. My parents have money and I like and admire them for it. It used to bother me a little, knowing so much of it was around and hearing about it all the time, but not any more. Money's good."

Roger got the last part of this at close range, for Grace Derlanger, seeing him sitting on his own, had walked her companion over. She settled her stocky body efficiently in a near-by chair, gazing at Macher through her thick glasses but not moving a muscle of her face. It was hard to tell whether or not she thought she was having nonsense talked to her. Roger guessed she did, though without feeling as much conviction as he would have liked. To be sure about nonsense he had to be able to classify it, assign it to a family tree of liberal nonsense, humanist-humanitarian nonsense, academic nonsense, Protestant nonsense, Freudian nonsense, and so on. Macher's nonsense stopped before he could get deep enough into it.

Willingly turning his head, Roger saw that the Bangs were approaching. Ernst had his arm round Helene's shoulders, partly screening her from view, though not enough to conceal the fact that her bathing suit was in two widely separated pieces. With much loud chatter, Joe and Pargeter, the Englishman, joined them by the diving-board, closely followed by Macher's girl. The group was in continuous movement, so that Helene was only visible for unpredictable instants. Roger sat watching like a sniper waiting for a clear shot at a general.

"Let me get you another drink," he said after a good deal of this, and without waiting for an answer got up and strode off to the drinks cupboard. He was quite near Helene when, with perfect coordination, she turned towards the pool to say something to Macher's girl. This move presented her back to Roger and her front to where he had just been sitting. When he got back there with the drinks she had turned away again.

"Come on, you lot," he called with a suddenness and an unlooked-for joviality that brought both Grace and Macher round in their seats. "What about some action? Or are you all afraid of the water? Show us what you can do, eh?"

"We're not standing for that, are we, Nigel?" Joe roared. "Let him see how wrong he is." He moved along the diving-board, bony in a minimal pair of light green trunks. The group behind him began to break up.

"You're British, aren't you, Mr. Dean?" Macher asked loudly.

"I am. And the name is Micheldene."

"I'm sorry. It has a hyphen in it, does it? Like Mitchell-Dean?"

"No no no, it's one word. Why, anyway?"

"Well now, I wouldn't know why, would I, Mr. Micheldene?"

"I fail to see who else would."

"What? It's your name, isn't it?"

"What about it?"

"So you'd know why it's one word and I wouldn't."

"I don't know what you're talking about."

"Look, you asked me why your name was one word."

"I did nothing of the kind. I asked you why you wanted to know if I were British."

"Oh, that was what you asked me." Macher laughed quietly for a time while Roger watched him. "I beg your pardon. Well, the answer to that should be obvious enough."

"Should it?"

"Yes. I wanted to know."

"Just that?"

"Just that."

"Thank you."

"You're welcome."

Roger had been suffering several kinds of pain during this exchange. One was physical, the result of forcing his eyeballs as far round to one side as they would go in hasty attempts to get a look at Helene. More severe was the emotional pain of not having got a look. Macher had kept distracting his attention. By the time he had finished with him all five of the bathing party were in the pool. A third kind of pain got going in Roger. Retrospective in nature, it came from not having reached out a foot and tipped Macher, chair and all, into the water as soon as he opened his horrible mouth.

The pool was not a long one, but it was sufficiently long for Joe to think it worth while ploughing his way from one end of it to the other again and again. Doing this made him snort a lot. It also disturbed the water enough to turn most of Helene, in the intervals when she was not herself swimming, into a disintegrated mess of oscillating patches of color. There was the refraction too.

Ernst started to do some diving. He seemed good at it, good enough at any rate to make Helene stop swimming and watch him. Roger had a full close view of the back of her head and shoulders. The water had altered the colors of her hair, deepening the yellows, making the light parts almost transparent and introducing bronze tints near the crown.

She and the others laughed and shouted to one another in a relaxed, convivial way.

"Aren't they a lovely couple?" Grace asked Roger.

He gave her a suspicious glance. For a middle-aged American woman she had not often struck him as very unamiable, even though he had never contemplated bothering to find out what took place in her head. But he had caught her eye late in the Macher monologue and found her watching him interestedly, her nostrils dilated in a way that meant she was suppressing something. A yawn, he hoped. He said now in a puzzled tone: "Who?"

"Why, Dr. and Mrs. Bang, of course. Don't you think so?"

"Oh yes. Yes, I do. Quite charming."

"They seem completely made for each other."

"Yes."

"If he ever decides he's done enough philosophy or whatever it is, I should imagine there must be a part waiting for him in some Tarzan movie or other. He's so graceful. Look at him go now. With those looks he might so easily be effeminate, but there's nothing like that about him at all. And isn't she just ravishing?"

"Oh, delightful."

"So typically Scandinavian in her coloring. And that figure. I really am surprised some fellow hasn't gotten hold of her."

"What sort of fellow?"

"Well, you know, some sort of movie or television fellow. With those looks she wouldn't need to be able to sing or anything, or even act."

"No, she wouldn't, would she?"

"But you know what the loveliest part of all is."

Roger gazed at her in unexpectant silence.

"They're so utterly devoted. You can see it the moment you lay eyes on them the first time—well, I did. Completely devoted. He doesn't really care to look at anybody else, and it's the same with her. Or even more so, wouldn't you say?"

Roger would not say.

"And that's so rare these days, isn't it?—with all this running off and breaking up and divorcing and all the . . . Oh, I'm sorry, Roger, how terribly tactless of me. I didn't mean—"

"That's perfectly all right, Grace."

"I do feel so—"

"Say no more." Or else stand by for a dose of grievous bodily harm (Roger thought to himself), you women's-cultural-lunch-club-organizing

Saturday Review of Literature-reading substantial-inheritance-from-soft-drink-corporation-awaiting old-New-Hampshire-family-invoking Kennedy-loving just-wunnerful-labelling Yank bag.

Grace dropped her voice to say in a carefully casual tone: "Did you hear anything from Marigold recently?"

"Not for some years." Roger was aware of Macher listening to all this, and listening with something less than full attention too. That made it worse. If the Yid scribbler was going to go on sitting there with his lobeless ears flapping, Roger reasoned, the least he could do was flap them with passionate absorption. "Marigold was my first wife," he went on very loudly. "My present wife, if you can call her that, is named Pamela."

"Oh, Roger, I don't know what to say, I seem to have—"

"Sweetheart, it doesn't matter in the least." He gave her a full-production smile to ram home his moral advantage. The grade-one going-over Grace had just earned would have to wait until he was unencumbered by the presence of Hebrew jackanapeses and such. "I had a letter from Pamela just before I came over, actually."

"How is she?"

"She seems very well." Most of the single page of the letter had been devoted to asking him to see if he could find and bring back to England the unique typescript of a novel called *Perne in a Gyre* by his talentless nuclear-disarmer brother-in-law. It was thought to be lying about somewhere in the offices of a New York literary agent, Strode Atkins by name, who was supposed to have been attending this evening's gathering but had not, thank God, so far appeared.

"Any real news?"

"No."

Ernst had climbed out of the pool and stood pressing the water from his hair. Helene, her back still turned to Roger, was also emerging. Grace said she must see about towels and went away. Roger watched Helene while she chatted to her husband and to Macher's girl, accepted a towel from Grace and moved round the pool to within a few yards of him, the towel hiding most of her between the neck and the knees. Her eyes were slightly bleared with the water. After a moment she sat down, going so far as to present Roger with a three-quarter rear view. Even though the towel was round her shoulders and she was clasping her knees, her shape was such that he got something. Not enough, of course.

He was just rehearsing mentally the casualness with which he would get up and walk over and ask her how she had enjoyed her swim when Macher said: "Some girl, that."

"Girl?" Roger went through the motions of noticing he was not alone. "What girl?"

"Not Suzanne Klein, the girl I brought. You haven't noticed her. The other girl. The blonde. The Dane. The professor's wife. Mrs. Bang. Helene. That girl." He pointed.

"Oh yes, I think I see which one you're referring to."

"Good. Some girl, isn't she?"

"Yes, I suppose you could say that."

"I'm glad you agree. What's she like?"

"How do you mean?"

"Oh, you don't know how I mean." Macher did his laugh. "Well now, let's just sit around for a while and get together and have a little think and try to figure out how I mean. I can't mean what's she like to look at, because I can see that for myself. As a matter of fact it was seeing what she's like to look at that led me to comment that she's some girl. Anyway, since we've decided I can't mean what's she like to look at I must mean something else, like is she nice or nasty, smart or stupid, educated or illiterate, drunken or of temperate disposition and habits— all this type of stuff. That's how I mean."

Roger heard him out with unwavering gaze, his invariable policy in this situation unless a really murderous verbal interruption could be devised or physical violence resorted to. After prolonging his gaze for half a minute or so without speaking or moving, he said: "I see. But quite apart from whether I feel I ought to consider giving you my opinion on these matters, I should have thought your approach to life in general was far too idiosyncratic for you to take an interest in what I or anyone else thought about this or anything else."

"Oh no, Mr. Micheldene, that would be arrogant of me. You've misjudged me most terribly, I'm afraid. Of course I'm interested in what you think about Mrs. Bang. After all, you've known her much longer than I've had a chance to, haven't you? And you're an older man, so your judgment would be more mature and balanced than mine."

"How true that is," Roger said. "However, allow me to suggest that we defer our discussion of Mrs. Bang until such time as you've acquired some basis of comparison. Until then at the very earliest."

He was on his feet to go over and look at Helene's front when Grace called his name. He turned with some effort and saw her approaching across the grass with a man and a woman about his own age: Strode Atkins and his wife, no doubt. Both were of well-groomed and yet battered appearance. They clearly expected to be introduced to him. Roger was perplexed to find no red mist of rage clouding his vision. He and

Mrs. Atkins, a thin woman with large eyes and straight brown hair done in a fringe, looked at each other a moment longer than was necessary. Then her husband was shaking his hand and shouting: "An Englishman. Another goddam Englishman. I like that. I do like that. I'm a horrible Anglophile, you know. And believe me there aren't too many of them around these days, brother."

Kurt Vonnegut, Jr.

*

REPORT ON THE
BARNHOUSE EFFECT

Let me begin by saying that I don't know any more about where Professor Arthur Barnhouse is hiding than anyone else does. Save for one short, enigmatic message left in my mailbox on Christmas Eve, I have not heard from him since his disappearance a year and a half ago.

What's more, readers of this article will be disappointed if they expect to learn how *they* can bring about the so-called "Barnhouse Effect." If I were able and willing to give away that secret, I would certainly be something more important than a psychology instructor.

I have been urged to write this report because I did research under the professor's direction and because I was the first to learn of his astonishing discovery. But while I was his student I was never entrusted with knowledge of how the mental forces could be released and directed. He was unwilling to trust anyone with that information.

I would like to point out that the term "Barnhouse Effect" is a creation of the popular press, and was never used by Professor Barnhouse. The name he chose for the phenomenon was "*dynamopsychism*," or *force of the mind*.

I cannot believe that there is a civilized person yet to be convinced that such a force exists, what with its destructive effects on display in every national capital. I think humanity has always had an inkling that this sort of force does exist. It has been common knowledge that some people are luckier than others with inanimate objects like dice. What Professor Barnhouse did was to show that such "luck" was a measurable force, which in his case could be enormous.

By my calculations, the professor was about fifty-five times more powerful than a Nagasaki-type atomic bomb at the time he went into hiding. He was not bluffing when, on the eve of "Operation Brainstorm," he told General Honus Barker: "Sitting here at the dinner table, I'm pretty sure I can flatten anything on earth—from Joe Louis to the Great Wall of China."

There is an understandable tendency to look upon Professor Barnhouse as a supernatural visitation. The First Church of Barnhouse in Los Angeles has a congregation numbering in the thousands. He is godlike in neither appearance nor intellect. The man who disarms the world is single, shorter than the average American male, stout, and averse to exercise. His I.Q. is 143, which is good but certainly not sensational. He is quite mortal, about to celebrate his fortieth birthday, and in good health. If he is alone now, the isolation won't bother him too much. He was quiet and shy when I knew him, and seemed to find more companionship in books and music than in his associations at the college.

Neither he nor his powers fall outside the sphere of Nature. His dynamopsychic radiations are subject to many known physical laws that apply in the field of radio. Hardly a person has not now heard the snarl of "Barnhouse static" on his home receiver. The radiations are affected by sunspots and variations in the ionosphere.

However, they differ from ordinary broadcast waves in several important ways. Their total energy can be brought to bear on any single point the professor chooses, and that energy is undiminished by distance. As a weapon, then, dynamopsychism has an impressive advantage over bacteria and atomic bombs, beyond the fact that it costs nothing to use: it enables the professor to single out critical individuals and objects instead of slaughtering whole populations in the process of maintaining international equilibrium.

As General Honus Barker told the House Military Affairs Committee: "Until someone finds Barnhouse, there is no defense against the Barnhouse Effect." Efforts to "jam" or block the radiations have failed. Premier Slezak could have saved himself the fantastic expense of his "Barnhouse-proof" shelter. Despite the shelter's twelve-foot-thick lead armor, the premier has been floored twice while in it.

There is talk of screening the population for men potentially as powerful dynamopsychically as the professor. Senator Warren Foust demanded funds for this purpose last month, with the passionate declaration: "He who rules the Barnhouse Effect rules the world!" Commissar Kropotnik said much the same thing, so another costly armaments race, with a new twist, has begun.

This race at least has its comical aspects. The world's best gamblers are being coddled by governments like so many nuclear physicists. There may be several hundred persons with dynamopsychic talent on earth, myself included. But, without knowledge of the professor's technique, they can never be anything but dice-table despots. With the secret, it would probably take them ten years to become dangerous weapons. It took the professor that long. He who rules the Barnhouse Effect is Barnhouse and will be for some time.

Popularly, the "Age of Barnhouse" is said to have begun a year and a half ago, on the day of Operation Brainstorm. That was when dynamopsychism became significant politically. Actually, the phenomenon was discovered in May, 1942, shortly after the professor turned down a direct commission in the Army and enlisted as an artillery private. Like X-rays and vulcanized rubber, dynamopsychism was discovered by accident.

• • •

From time to time Private Barnhouse was invited to take part in games of chance by his barrack mates. He knew nothing about the games, and usually begged off. But one evening, out of social grace, he agreed to shoot craps. It was terrible or wonderful that he played, depending upon whether or not you like the world as it now is.

"Shoot sevens, Pop," someone said.

So "Pop" shot sevens—ten in a row to bankrupt the barracks. He retired to his bunk and, as a mathematical exercise, calculated the odds against his feat on the back of a laundry slip. His chances of doing it, he found, were one in almost ten million! Bewildered, he borrowed a pair of dice from the man in the bunk next to his. He tried to roll sevens again, but got only the usual assortment of numbers. He lay back for a moment, then resumed his toying with the dice. He rolled ten more sevens in a row.

He might have dismissed the phenomenon with a low whistle. But the professor instead mulled over the circumstances surrounding his two lucky streaks. There was one single factor in common: on both occasions, *the same thought train had flashed through his mind just before he threw the dice.* It was that thought train which aligned the professor's brain cells into what has since become the most powerful weapon on earth.

• • •

The soldier in the next bunk gave dynamopsychism its first token of respect. In an understatement certain to bring wry smiles to the faces of the world's dejected demagogues, the soldier said, "You're hotter'n a two-dollar pistol, Pop." Professor Barnhouse was all of that. The dice that did his bidding weighed but a few grams, so the forces involved were minute; but the unmistakable fact that there were such forces was earthshaking.

Professional caution kept him from revealing his discovery immediately. He wanted more facts and a body of theory to go with them. Later when the atomic bomb was dropped in Hiroshima, it was fear that made him hold his peace. At no time were his experiments, as Premier Slezak called them, "a bourgeois plot to shackle the true democracies of the world." The professor didn't know where they were leading.

In time, he came to recognize another startling feature of dynamopsychism: *its strength increased with use.* Within six months, he was able to govern dice thrown by men the length of a barracks distant. By the time of his discharge in 1945, he could knock bricks loose from chimneys three miles away.

Charges that Professor Barnhouse could have won the last war in a minute, but did not care to do so, are perfectly senseless. When the war ended, he had the range and power of a 37-millimeter cannon, perhaps —certainly no more. His dynamopsychic powers graduated from the small-arms class only after his discharge and return to Wyandotte College.

I enrolled in the Wyandotte Graduate School two years after the professor had rejoined the faculty. By chance, he was assigned as my thesis adviser. I was unhappy about the assignment, for the professor was, in the eyes of both colleagues and students, a somewhat ridiculous figure. He missed classes or had lapses of memory during lectures. When I arrived, in fact, his shortcomings had passed from the ridiculous to the intolerable.

"We're assigning you to Barnhouse as a sort of temporary thing," the dean of social studies told me. He looked apologetic and perplexed. "Brilliant man, Barnhouse, I guess. Difficult to know since his return, perhaps, but his work before the war brought a great deal of credit to our little school."

When I reported to the professor's laboratory for the first time, what I saw was more distressing than the gossip. Every surface in the room was covered with dust; books and apparatus had not been disturbed for months. The professor sat napping at his desk when I entered. The only signs of recent activity were three overflowing ashtrays, a pair of scissors, and a morning paper with several items clipped from its front page.

As he raised his head to look at me, I saw that his eyes were clouded with fatigue. "Hi," he said, "just can't seem to get my sleeping done at night." He lighted a cigarette, his hands trembling slightly. "You the young man I'm supposed to help with a thesis?"

"Yes sir," I said. In minutes he converted my misgivings to alarm.

"You an overseas veteran?" he asked.

"Yes, sir."

"Not much left over there, is there?" He frowned. "Enjoy the last war?"

"No, sir."

"Look like another war to you?"

"Kind of, sir."

"What can be done about it?"

I shrugged. "Looks pretty hopeless."

He peered at me intently. "Know anything about international law, the U.N., and all that?"

"Only what I pick up from the papers."

"Same here," he sighed. He showed me a fat scrapbook packed with newspaper clippings. "Never used to pay any attention to international politics. Now I study them the way I used to study rats in mazes. Everybody tells me the same thing—'Looks hopeless.' "

"Nothing short of a miracle—" I began.

"Believe in magic?" he asked sharply. The professor fished two dice from his vest pocket. "I will try to roll twos," he said. He rolled twos three times in a row. "One chance in about 47,000 of that happening. There's a miracle for you." He beamed for an instant, then brought the interview to an end, remarking that he had a class which had begun ten minutes ago.

He was not quick to take me into his confidence, and he said no more about his trick with the dice. I assumed they were loaded, and forgot about them. He set me the task of watching male rats cross electrified metal strips to get to food or female rats—an experiment that had been done to everyone's satisfaction in the nineteen-thirties. As though the pointlessness of my work were not bad enough, the professor annoyed me further with irrelevant questions. His favorites were: "Think we should have dropped the atomic bomb on Hiroshima?" and "Think every new piece of scientific information is a good thing for humanity?"

• • •

However, I did not feel put upon for long. "Give those poor animals a holiday," he said one morning, after I had been with him only a month. "I wish you'd help me look into a more interesting problem—namely, my sanity."

I returned the rats to their cages.

"What you must do is simple," he said, speaking softly. "Watch the inkwell on my desk. If you see nothing happen to it, say so, and I'll go quietly—relieved, I might add—to the nearest sanitarium."

I nodded uncertainly.

He locked the laboratory door and drew the blinds, so that we were in twilight for a moment. "I'm odd, I know," he said. "It's fear of myself that's made me odd."

"I've found you somewhat eccentric, perhaps, but certainly not—"

"If nothing happens to that inkwell, 'crazy as a bedbug' is the only description of me that will do," he interrupted, turning on the overhead lights. His eyes narrowed. "To give you an idea of how crazy, I'll tell you what's been running through my mind when I should have been sleeping. I think maybe I can save the world. I think maybe I can make every nation a *have* nation, and do away with war for good. I think maybe I can clear roads through jungles, irrigate deserts, build dams overnight."

"Yes, sir."

"Watch the inkwell!"

Dutifully and fearfully I watched. A high-pitched humming seemed to come from the inkwell; then it began to vibrate alarmingly, and finally to bound about the top of the desk, making two noisy circuits. It stopped, hummed again, glowed red, then popped in splinters with a blue-green flash.

Perhaps my hair stood on end. The professor laughed gently. "Magnets?" I managed to say at last.

"Wish to heaven it were magnets," he murmured. It was then that he told me of dynamopsychism. He knew only that there was such a force; he could not explain it. "It's me and me alone—and it's awful."

"I'd say it was amazing and wonderful!" I cried.

"If all I could do was make inkwells dance, I'd be tickled silly with the whole business." He shrugged disconsolately. "But I'm no toy, my boy. If you like, we can drive around the neighborhood, and I'll show you what I mean." He told me about pulverized boulders, shattered oaks, and abandoned farm buildings demolished within a fifty-mile radius of the campus. "Did every bit of it sitting right here, just thinking—not even thinking hard."

He scratched his head nervously. "I have never dared to concentrate as hard as I can for fear of the damage I might do. I'm to the point where a mere whim is a blockbuster." There was a depressing pause. "Up until a few days ago, I've thought it best to keep my secret for fear of what use it might be put to," he continued. "Now I realize that I haven't any more right to it than a man has a right to own an atomic bomb."

He fumbled through a heap of papers. "This says about all that needs to be said, I think." He handed me a draft of a letter to the Secretary of State.

DEAR SIR:

I have discovered a new force which costs nothing to use, and which is probably more important than atomic energy. I should like to see it used most effectively in the cause of peace, and am, therefore, requesting your advice as to how this might best be done.

Yours truly,

A. BARNHOUSE.

"I have no idea what will happen next," said the professor.

•   •   •

There followed three months of perpetual nightmare, wherein the nation's political and military great came at all hours to watch the professor's tricks.

We were quartered in an old mansion near Charlottesville, Virginia, to which we had been whisked five days after the letter was mailed. Surrounded by barbed wire and twenty guards, we were labeled "Project Wishing Well," and were classified as Top Secret.

For companionship we had General Honus Barker and the State Department's William K. Cuthrell. For the professor's talk of peace-through-plenty they had indulgent smiles and much discourse on practical measures and realistic thinking. So treated, the professor, who had at first been almost meek, progressed in a matter of weeks toward stubbornness.

He had agreed to reveal the thought train by means of which he aligned his mind into a dynamopsychic transmitter. But, under Cuthrell's and Barker's nagging to do so, he began to hedge. At first he declared that the information could be passed on simply by word of mouth. Later he said that it would have to be written up in a long report. Finally, at dinner one night, just after General Barker had read the secret orders for Operation Brainstorm, the professor announced, "The report may take as long as five years to write." He looked fiercely at the general. "Maybe twenty."

The dismay occasioned by this flat announcement was offset somewhat by the exciting anticipation of Operation Brainstorm. The general was in a holiday mood. "The target ships are on their way to the Caroline Islands at this very moment," he declared ecstatically. "One hundred and twenty of them! At the same time, ten V-2s are being readied for firing in New Mexico, and fifty radio-controlled jet bombers are being equipped for a mock attack on the Aleutians. Just think of it!" Happily he reviewed his orders. "At exactly 1100 hours next Wednesday, I will give you the order to *concentrate*; and you, professor, will think as hard as you can about sinking the target ships, destroying the V-2s before they hit the ground, and knocking down the bombers before they reach the Aleutians! Think you can handle it?"

The professor turned gray and closed his eyes. "As I told you before, my friend, I don't know what I can do." He added bitterly, "As for this Operation Brainstorm, I was never consulted about it, and it strikes me as childish and insanely expensive."

General Barker bridled. "Sir," he said, "your field is psychology, and I wouldn't presume to give you advice in that field. Mine is national defense. I have had thirty years of experience and success, Professor, and I'll ask you not to criticize my judgment."

The professor appealed to Mr. Cuthrell. "Look," he pleaded, "isn't it war and military matters we're all trying to get rid of? Wouldn't it be a whole lot more significant and lots cheaper for me to try moving cloud masses into drought areas, and things like that? I admit I know next to nothing about international politics, but it seems reasonable to suppose that nobody would want to fight wars if there were enough of everything to go around. Mr. Cuthrell, I'd like to try running generators where there isn't any coal or water power, irrigating deserts, and so on. Why, you could figure out what each country needs to make the most of its resources, and I could give it to them without costing American taxpayers a penny."

"Eternal vigilance is the price of freedom," said the general heavily.

Mr. Cuthrell threw the general a look of mild distaste. "Unfortunately, the general is right in his own way," he said. "I wish to heaven the world were ready for ideals like yours, but it simply isn't. We aren't surrounded by brothers, but by enemies. It isn't a lack of food or resources that has us on the brink of war—it's a struggle for power. Who's going to be in charge of the world, our kind of people or theirs?"

The professor nodded in reluctant agreement and arose from the table. "I beg your pardon, gentlemen. You are, after all, better qualified to judge what is best for the country. I'll do whatever you say." He turned to me. "Don't forget to wind the restricted clock and put the confidential cat out," he said gloomily, and ascended the stairs to his bedroom.

•   •   •

For reasons of national security, Operation Brainstorm was carried on without the knowledge of the American citizenry which was paying the bill. The observers, technicians, and military men involved in the activity knew that a test was under way—a test of what, they had no idea. Only thirty-seven key men, myself included, knew what was afoot.

In Virginia, the day for Operation Brainstorm was unseasonably cool. Inside, a log fire crackled in the fireplace, and the flames were reflected in the polished metal cabinets that lined the living room. All that remained of the room's lovely old furniture was a Victorian love seat, set squarely in the center of the floor, facing three television receivers. One long bench had been brought in for the ten of us privileged to watch. The television screens showed, from left to right, the stretch of desert which was the rocket target, the guinea-pig fleet, and a section of the Aleutian sky through which the radio-controlled bomber formation would roar.

Ninety minutes before H-hour the radios announced that the rockets were ready, that the observation ships had backed away to what was thought to be a safe distance, and that the bombers were on their way. The small Virginia audience lined up on the bench in order of rank, smoked a great deal, and said little. Professor Barnhouse was in his bedroom. General Barker bustled about the house like a woman preparing Thanksgiving dinner for twenty.

At ten minutes before H-hour the general came in, shepherding the professor before him. The professor was comfortably attired in sneakers, gray flannels, a blue sweater, and a white shirt open at the neck. The two of them sat side by side on the love seat. The general was rigid and perspiring; the professor was cheerful. He looked at each of the screens, lighted a cigarette and settled back.

"Bombers sighted!" cried the Aleutian observers.

"Rockets away!" barked the New Mexico radio operator.

All of us looked quickly at the big electric clock over the mantel, while the professor, a half-smile on his face, continued to watch the television sets. In hollow tones, the general counted away the seconds remaining. "Five . . . four . . . three . . . two . . . one . . . *Concentrate!*"

Professor Barnhouse closed his eyes, pursed his lips, and stroked his temples. He held the position for a minute. The television images were scrambled, and the radio signals were drowned in the din of Barnhouse static. The professor sighed, opened his eyes, and smiled confidently.

"Did you give it everything you had?" asked the general dubiously.

"I was wide open," the professor replied.

The television images pulled themselves together, and mingled cries of amazement came over the radios tuned to the observers. The Aleutian sky was streaked with the smoke trails of bombers screaming down in flames. Simultaneously, there appeared high over the rocket target a cluster of white puffs, followed by faint thunder.

General Barker shook his head happily. "By George!" he crowed. "Well, sir, by George, by George, by George!"

"Look!" shouted the admiral seated next to me. "The fleet—it wasn't touched!"

"The guns seem to be drooping," said Mr. Cuthrell.

We left the bench and clustered about the television sets to examine the damage more closely. What Mr. Cuthrell had said was true. The ships' guns curved downward, their muzzles resting on the steel decks. We in Virginia were making such a hullabaloo that it was impossible to hear the radio reports. We were so engrossed, in fact, that we didn't miss the professor until two short snarls of Barnhouse static shocked us into sudden silence. The radios went dead.

We looked around apprehensively. The professor was gone. A harassed guard threw open the front door from the outside to yell that the professor had escaped. He brandished his pistol in the direction of the gates, which hung open, limp and twisted. In the distance, a speeding government station wagon topped a ridge and dropped from sight into the valley beyond. The air was filled with choking smoke, for every vehicle on the grounds was ablaze. Pursuit was impossible.

"What in God's name got into him?" bellowed the general.

Mr. Cuthrell, who had rushed out onto the front porch, now slouched back into the room, reading a penciled note as he came. He thrust the note into my hands. "The good man left this billet-doux under the door knocker. Perhaps our young friend here will be kind enough to read it to you gentlemen, while I take a restful walk through the woods."

"*Gentlemen,*" I read aloud, "*As the first superweapon with a conscience, I am removing myself from your national defense stockpile. Setting a new precedent in the behavior of ordnance, I have humane reasons for going off. A. Barnhouse.*"

• • •

Since that day, of course, the professor has been systematically destroying the world's armaments, until there is now little with which to equip an army other than rocks and sharp sticks. His activities haven't exactly resulted in peace, but have, rather, precipitated a bloodless and entertaining sort of war that might be called the "War of the Tattletales." Every nation is flooded with enemy agents whose sole mission is to locate military equipment, which is promptly wrecked when it is brought to the professor's attention in the press.

Just as every day brings news of more armaments pulverized by dynamopsychism, so has it brought rumors of the professor's whereabouts. During the last week alone, three publications carried articles proving variously that he was hiding in an Inca ruin in the Andes, in the sewers of Paris, and in the unexplored lower chambers of Carlsbad Caverns. Knowing the man, I am inclined to regard such hiding places as unnecessarily romantic and uncomfortable. While there are numerous persons eager to kill him, there must be millions who would care for him and hide him. I like to think that he is in the home of such a person.

One thing is certain: at this writing, Professor Barnhouse is not dead. Barnhouse static jammed broadcasts not ten minutes ago. In the eighteen months since his disappearance, he has been reported dead some half-dozen times. Each report has stemmed from the death of an unidentified man resembling the professor, during a period free of the static. The first three reports were followed at once by renewed talk of rearmament and recourse to war. The saber-rattlers have learned how imprudent premature celebrations of the professor's demise can be.

Many a stouthearted patriot has found himself prone in the tangled bunting and timbers of a smashed reviewing stand, seconds after having announced that the arch-tyranny of Barnhouse was at an end. But those who would make war if they could, in every country in the world, wait in sullen silence for what must come—the passing of Professor Barnhouse.

• • •

To ask how much longer the professor will live is to ask how much longer we must wait for the blessing of another world war. He is of short-lived stock: his mother lived to be fifty-three, his father to be forty-nine; and the life-spans of his grandparents on both sides were of the same order. He might be expected to live, then, for perhaps fifteen years more, if he can remain hidden from his enemies. When one considers the number and vigor of these enemies, however, fifteen years seems an extraordinary length of time, which might better be revised to fifteen days, hours, or minutes.

The professor knows that he cannot live much longer. I say this because of the message left in my mailbox on Christmas Eve. Unsigned, typewritten on a soiled scrap of paper, the note consisted of ten sentences. The first nine of these, each a bewildering tangle of psychological jargon and references to obscure texts, made no sense to me at first reading. The tenth, unlike the rest, was simply constructed and contained no large words—but its irrational content made it the most puzzling and bizarre sentence of all. I nearly threw the note away, thinking it a colleague's warped notion of a practical joke. For some reason, though, I added it to the clutter on top of my desk, which included, among other mementos, the professor's dice.

It took me several weeks to realize that the message really meant something, that the first nine sentences, when unsnarled, could be taken as instructions. The tenth still told me nothing. It was only last night that I discovered how it fitted in with the rest. The sentence appeared in my thoughts last night, while I was toying absently with the professor's dice.

I promised to have this report on its way to the publishers today. In view of what has happened, I am obliged to break that promise, or release the report incomplete. The delay will not be a long one, for one of the few blessings accorded a bachelor like myself is the ability to move quickly from one abode to another, or from one way of life to another. What property I want to take with me can be packed in a few hours. Fortunately, I am not without substantial private means, which may take as long as a week to realize in liquid and anonymous form. When this is done, I shall mail the report.

I have just returned from a visit to my doctor, who tells me my health is excellent. I am young, and, with any luck at all, I shall live to a ripe old age indeed, for my family on both sides is noted for longevity.

Briefly, I propose to vanish.

Sooner or later, Professor Barnhouse must die. But long before then I shall be ready. So, to the saber-rattlers of today—and even, I hope, of tomorrow—I say: Be advised. Barnhouse will die. But not the Barnhouse Effect.

Last night, I tried once more to follow the oblique instructions on the scrap of paper. I took the professor's dice, and then, with the last, nightmarish sentence flitting through my mind, I rolled fifty consecutive sevens.

Good-by.

Joseph Heller

*

GOLD'S STEPMOTHER
EXCERPT FROM *Good as Gold*

[Dr. Bruce Gold, a forty-eight-year-old professor of literature, attends a Friday night family dinner at his sister Ida's apartment in Brooklyn. —ED.]

Gold's distaste for family dinners, his aversion, in fact, toward all forms of domestic sentiment, stretched back distantly at least until the time of his graduation from high school and his moving into Manhattan to attend Columbia College. He was pleased to be entering so prestigious a university and vastly relieved at escaping a large family of five sisters and one brother in which all his life he had felt both suffocated and unappreciated.

"I was going to quit college and fight in Israel," he had bragged to Belle at the time they were falling in love, "but I had this scholarship to Columbia."

Gold had not once thought of quitting college or fighting in Israel. And he did not go to Columbia on a scholarship but on money provided by his father, most of which, he understood now, must have been channeled through the old man's irresponsible hands from Sid and three of his older sisters. Muriel, the fourth, had never been known to part happily with a dollar for anyone but herself or her two daughters.

Another sister, Joannie, lived in California. Mercifully, she was younger. Joannie had charged away from home in delinquency a long time before in hopes of succeeding as a model or movie actress and was married to an overbearing Los Angeles businessman who disliked coming East and disdained everybody in the family but Gold. Several times a year she flew to New York alone to see just the ones she wanted to.

Gold had found himself the center of family attention ever since bringing home his first faultless report card, or a composition with an A plus. Muriel, who was closest to him in age and aimed her bad temper these days mostly at Ida, was nasty to him also even then. Ida, officious, was the sister who would impress upon Gold his need to do better in school, although what he did was always perfect. There were times now Gold thought he might go mad from the drenching reverence and affection that still poured over him from Rose and Esther, his two eldest sisters. Whatever expectations he had aroused, he had apparently fulfilled. They shimmered with love whenever they looked at him, and he wished they would stop.

While he was in college, Rose would frequently mail or give him a twenty-dollar bill, he remembered, and so would Esther. Like Sid, both had gone to work after high school as soon as they could find jobs. Ida was able to go to college and become a schoolteacher. Ida handed him fives, always with strict instructions about how the money was to be spent. Rose and Ida still worked, Rose as a legal secretary with the firm that had hired her during the Depression, Ida in the public-school system. Ida was assistant principal now in an elementary school, and she was fighting for her sanity against militant blacks and Hispanics who wanted all Jews gone, and said so in just those words. Esther had been widowed two years before. Much of her hair fell out almost overnight, and the rest turned white. She talked vaguely at times of finding employment again as a bookkeeper. But she was fifty-seven, and too timid to try. Muriel, whose husband, Victor, did well in wholesale beef and veal, was a distinct contrast to the others. She dyed her hair black to camouflage the gray and played poker with friends who also enjoyed outings to the racetrack. A chain smoker with a hoarse voice and a tough manner, Muriel was constantly spilling cigarette ashes that Ida, with her zeal for order, would brush away with scolding, high-minded comments of disparagement, even in Muriel's own house.

Between Sid, the firstborn, therefore, and Gold, the only other male child, stood these four older sisters who often seemed like four hundred and fifty when they flocked around him with their questions, censures, solicitudes, and advice. Ida cautioned him to chew his food slowly. Rose telephoned to warn that it was icy outside. He thought of them all as outdated, naive, and virtually oblivious to the very real proximity of sinfulness and evil. Except for Sid, Gold recalled, and therefore Harriet, his wife. Sid in nimbler years had been discovered one time in San Francisco when he was supposed to be in San Diego on business, in Acapulco one time when he was supposed to be in San Francisco, and on a houseboat in Miami when he was registered at a hotel in Puerto Rico. Once possessed of the means, Sid had learned how to ease his way effortlessly through hotels.

Now he went out of town only with Harriet on brief vacations or to visit his father in Florida in the winter. Sid was a large, genial, heavyset man with soft flesh and parted gray hair; he had a pronounced facial likeness to their father, although the latter was short and chubby, with bushy white hair that stood almost straight up like the hair of a figure in a comic strip receiving a powerful charge of electricity. Gold was lean, tense, and dark, with vivid shadows around his eyes in a crabby, nervous face women found dynamic and sexy. Sid was easing compliantly into an antiquated generation, wearing plain gray or blue suits with white shirts and wide blue or maroon suspenders, whereas their demanding, autocratic old four-flusher of a father, the retired tailor Julius Gold, was dressing more and more each year like a debonair Hollywood mogul, favoring cashmere polo shirts and suave blazers. Inexplicably, Sid seemed to be growing more fond of their father. Far back, Gold remembered, Sid had run away from home and stayed away a whole summer to escape the old man's domineering eccentricities and cantankerous boasting.

Gold and Belle were nearly the last to arrive at Ida's apartment on Ocean Parkway; Muriel and Victor entered a minute afterward. Irv, Ida's husband, was convivial in his role as host. He was a dentist with offices above a paint store on Kings Highway. Already, Gold was having difficulty distinguishing one person from the next. It was a way of coping. He shook hands quickly with Irv, Victor, Sid, Milt, Max, and his father, differentiating between them only in the accumulating letdown he felt with each.

Max, Rose's husband, who was slightly diabetic, sipped at a glass of club soda squeamishly. The other men, along with Muriel, drank whiskey, the rest of the women, soft drinks. Belle had vanished into the kitchen to oversee the unpacking of her potato kugel and be of assistance to Ida, who probably was simultaneously shooing her away and giving her things to do, and reprehending her in the same breath for failing to do them swiftly enough. Everybody there, including his father, had at least one child who was a source of heartache.

Gold took bourbon from Irv and began kissing the cheeks of the women. Harriet accepted this greeting without pleasure. His stepmother authorized his approach by bobbing her head above her knitting and inclining her face. Gold bent to her with both forearms at the ready, fearing she might run him through the neck with one of her knitting needles.

Gold's stepmother, who was from an old Southern Jewish family with branches in Richmond and Charleston, habitually made things difficult for him in a variety of peculiar ways. Frequently when he spoke to her she did not answer at all. Other times she said, "Don't talk to me." When he didn't talk to her, his father moved up beside him with a hard nudge and directed, "Go talk to her. You too good?" She was always knitting thick white wool. When he complimented her once on her knitting, she informed him with a flounce that she was crocheting. When he inquired next time how her crocheting was going she answered, "I don't crochet. I knit." Often she called him to her side just to tell him to move away. Sometimes she came up to him and said, "Cackle, cackle."

He had no idea what to reply.

Gold's stepmother was knitting an endless strip of something bulky that was too narrow to be a shawl and too wide and uniformly straight to be anything else. It was around six inches broad and conceivably thousands of miles long, for she had been working on that same strip of knitting even before her marriage to his father many years before. Gold had a swimming vision of that loosely woven strip of material flowing out the bottom of her straw bag to the residence Sid found for his father and her each summer in Brooklyn in Manhattan Beach and from there all the way down the coastline to Florida and into unmeasured regions beyond. She never wanted for wool or for depth inside her straw bag into which the finished product could fall. The yarn came twitching up through one end of the opening in her bag, and the manufactured product, whatever it was, descended, perhaps for eternity, into the other.

"What are you making?" he'd asked her one time out of curiosity that could no longer be borne in silence.

"You'll see," she replied mysteriously.

He consulted his father. "Pa, what's she making?"

"Mind your own business."

"I was only asking."

"Don't ask personal questions."

"Rose, what's she knitting?" he asked his sister.

"Wool," Belle answered.

"Belle, I know that. But what's she doing with it?"

"Knitting," said Esther.

Gold's stepmother was knitting knitting, and she was knitting it endlessly. Now she asked, "Do you like my wool?"

"Pardon?"

"Do you like my wool?"

"Of course," he replied.

"You never say so," she pouted.

"I like your wool," said Gold, retreating in confusion to a leather armchair near the doorway.

"He told me he likes my wool," he heard her relating to his brothers-in-law Irv and Max. "But I think he's trying to pull it over my eyes."

"How was your trip?" his sister Esther asked dotingly.

"Fine."

"Where were you?" said Rose.

"Wilmington."

"Where?" asked Ida, passing with a serving tray.

"Washington," said Rose.

"Wilmington?"

"Wilmington."

"Washington."

"Washington?"

"Wilmington," he corrected them all. "In Delaware."

"Oh," said Rose, and looked crestfallen.

"How was your trip?" asked Ida, passing back.

Gold was going mad.

"He said it was fine," answered Esther before Rose could reply, and drifted toward a coffee table on which were platters holding loaves of chopped liver and chopped eggs and onions under attack by small knives spreading each or both onto round crackers or small sections of rye bread or very black pumpernickel.

"Meet any pretty girls there?" Muriel asked. The youngest of the sisters present, Muriel was ever under obligation to be up-to-date.

"Not this time," Gold answered, with the required grin.

Muriel glowed. Irv chuckled and Victor, Muriel's husband, looked embarrassed. Rose stared from face to face intently. Gold suspected that she had grown hard of hearing, and perhaps did not know. Her husband, Max, a postal worker, was slurring his words of late, and Gold wondered if anyone but himself had noticed.

Esther returned with a plate prepared for him, and a saltshaker aloft in her other hand. "I brought these all for you," she announced in her trembling voice. "And your own saltshaker."

Gold cringed.

"Don't spoil him," Muriel joked gruffly, spilling ashes onto her bosom from a cigarette hanging from her mouth.

The women in Gold's family believed he liked his food excessively salted.

"Don't salt it until you taste it," Ida yelled from across the room. "I already seasoned it."

Gold ignored her and continued salting the cracker he was holding. Other people's fingers plucked the remaining pieces from his plate. Esther and Rose each brought him more. Sid watched with amusement. So many fucking faces, Gold thought. So many people. And all of them strange. Even Belle, these days. And especially his stepmother.

He would never forget his first encounter with his stepmother. Sid had flown to Florida for the wedding and returned with her and his father for a reception at his home in Great Neck. There was an uncomfortable silence after the introductions when no one seemed sure what to say next. Gold stepped forward with a gallant try at putting everyone at ease.

"And what," he said in his most courtly manner, "would you like us to call you?"

"I would like you to treat me as my own children do," Gussie Gold replied with graciousness equal to his own. "I would like to think of you all as my very own children. Please call me Mother."

"Very well, Mother," Gold agreed. "Welcome to the family."

"I'm not your mother," she snapped.

Gold was the only one who laughed. Perhaps the others had perceived immediately what he had missed. She was insane.

•   •   •

Gold's stepmother had been brought up never to be seen eating in public, and she entered the dining room as always with her knitting needles and her straw tote bag. Fourteen adults were grouped elbow to elbow at a table designed for ten. Gold knew that his was not the only leg blocked by supporting braces underneath. I have been to more meals like this than I can bear to remember, Gold lamented secretly. Ida's daughter was out for the evening, her son was away at college.

"I can see on the table," Sid announced with such generalized amiability that Gold's muscles all bunched reflexively in anticipation of some barbed danger nearby, "Belle's potato kugel, Esther's noodle pudding, Muriel's potato salad, and Rose's . . ." He faltered.

"I made the matzoh balls," Rose said, blushing.

"Rose's matzoh balls."

"And my wool," said Gold's stepmother.

"And your wool."

"Do you like my wool?" She seemed coquettishly dependent on Sid's good opinion.

"It's the tastiest wool in the whole world, I bet."

"*He* doesn't like it," she said with a glance at Gold.

"I like it," Gold apologized weakly.

"He never tells me he likes it."

"I like your wool."

"I was not talking to you," she said.

Victor laughed more loudly than the others. Victor was convinced that Gold and Irv both looked down upon him. This was true, but Gold bore him no unkind feelings. Victor, red of face and sturdy as a bull, was sweet to Muriel and liked Belle, and could always be relied on to send one of his meat trucks and some laborers when anything heavy was to be transported. His posture was so nearly perfect both sitting and standing that he seemed to be holding himself erect at enormous physical cost. Gold was positive he would be the first among them to be felled by a heart attack.

"I made a honey cake," Harriet put in poutingly. "I'm sure I ruined it. I was going to make a Jell-O mold but I know you all must be sick of it."

"And Harriet's honey cake."

"Much starch," said Max, who, in addition to having diabetes, was susceptible to certain circulatory imbalances. Wearing a worried frown, Max declined everything but some chicken wings, a slice of pot roast, from which he separated the fat, and string beans.

Esther was served by Milt, a suitor courting her in almost wordless patience. She waited stiffly without looking at him. Milt, the older brother of her deceased husband's business partner, was a careful, respectful man who talked little in the presence of the family. Milt was past sixty-five, older than Sid, and had never been married. With a movement that approached vivacity, he flicked a second spoonful of Esther's noodle pudding onto her plate, and then a spoonful onto his own. Esther thanked him with a nervous smile.

There were platters of meatballs and stuffed derma on the table, too, and a deep, wide bowl of potatoes mashed with chicken fat and fried onions that Gold could have eaten up all by himself.

Ida asked Gold, "What's new?"

"Nothing."

"He's writing a book," said Belle.

"Really?" said Rose.

"Another book?" scoffed his father.

"That's nice," said Esther.

"Yes," said Belle.

"What's it about?" Muriel asked Gold.

"It's about the Jewish experience," said Belle.

"That's nice," said Ida.

"About what?" demanded his father.

"About the Jewish experience," answered Sid, and then called across the table to Gold. "Whose?"

"Whose what?" said Gold warily.

"Whose Jewish experience?"

"I haven't decided yet."

"He's writing some articles too," said Belle.

"Most of it is going to be very general," Gold added with perceptible reluctance.

"What's it mean?" Gold's father wanted to be told right then.

"It's a book about being Jewish," said Belle.

Gold's father snorted. "What does *he* know about being Jewish?" he roared. "He wasn't even born in Europe."

"It's about being Jewish in America," said Belle.

Gold's father was fazed only a second. "He don't know so much about that either. I been Jewish in America longer than him too."

"They're paying him money," Belle argued persistently. Gold wished she would stop.

"How much you getting?" demanded Gold's father.

"A lot," said Belle.

"How much? A lot to him maybe ain't so much to others. Right, Sid?"

"You said it, Pop."

"How much you getting?"

"Twenty thousand dollars," said Belle.

The amount, Gold could see, made a stunning impact, especially on his father, who looked unaffectedly disappointed. Gold himself would have deferred naming a figure. It must seem a fortune to Max and Rose and Esther, and even, perhaps, to Victor and Irv. They would see only a windfall, and forget the work.

"That *is* nice," said Rose.

"That ain't so much," Gold's father grumbled dejectedly. "I made more than that in my time."

And lost more too, Gold thought.

"Some people write books for the movies and make much more," Harriet observed in a disheartened way, while Sid chuckled softly.

Gold opened his mouth to retaliate when Belle said, "Well, that's only a start. And five thousand of that is for research. It isn't even charged against the guarantee."

"That's nice," said Esther quickly, eager to come to Gold's support. "I bet that's very nice."

"What does that mean?" asked Sid seriously.

"It's hard to explain," said Belle.

"No, it isn't."

"That's what you told me."

"You wouldn't listen when I tried."

"Don't fight," Harriet flittered in quickly with malice.

"It means," Gold said, addressing himself mainly to Sid and Irv, "that five thousand is charged off as a publishing expense instead of to me, even if I don't spend it. I can make that much more in royalties from book sales."

"Isn't that what I said?" said Belle.

"That sounds like a very good provision," Esther's elderly beau, Milt, observed ever so diffidently, and Gold remembered he was an accountant and would understand too.

"Bruce," Irv ventured, putting a thumb and forefinger to his chin. Since his dental practice had ceased growing, Irv had developed a tic in his right cheek that often gave him the appearance of smiling inexplicably. "You aren't going to write about any of us, are you?"

"No, of course not," Gold responded. "Why would I do anything like that?"

A wave of relief went around the table. Then all faces fell.

"Why not?" demanded his father. "Ain't we good enough?"

Gold's voice still tended to weaken in argument with the old man. "It's not that kind of book."

"No?" bellowed his father, rearing up an inch or so and stabbing at Gold an index finger that curved like a talon. "Well, I've got news for you, smart guy. You ain't gonna do it so hot without me. It's what I told you then, and what I told you now. It's what I told you from the beginning. You ain't the man for the job." He changed in a second from choleric belligerence to serene self-confidence and sat back with his head cocked to the side. "Good, Sid?" he asked, turning and looking up.

"You said it, Pop."

Julius Gold allowed his eyelids to lower in a look of narcissistic contentment.

Those two bastards, Gold told himself, reaching with misplaced hostility for the bowl of mashed potatoes and onions to ladle himself out another large helping. And they never even liked each other.

"Did you ever hear from the White House again?" asked his sister Rose, beaming.

"No," said Belle, before Gold could reply, and Harriet looked pleased.

"But he heard from them twice," said Esther. "He got two phone calls."

"It wasn't really the White House," Gold corrected. "It was from a friend I went through graduate school with who works in the White House."

"That's the same thing," said Ida. "He's in the White House, isn't he?"

"I don't know where he was when he made the phone call." Gold's tone was faintly sarcastic.

"In the White House," said Belle, with no change of expression. "Ralph Newsome."

"Thanks," said Gold. "There was some chance I might forget his name."

"I never heard of him," said Harriet.

"Well, he's on the President's staff," said Muriel, and turned to Gold. "Isn't he?"

Gold plunged his face into his plate and was silent.

"I went past the White House once when I was a sweet and very pretty little girl up from Richmond," Gold's stepmother recalled. "It looked dirty."

"But he said he liked your book, didn't he?" Esther recalled.

"Not my book," Gold explained uncomfortably.

"His review of the President's book," said Belle.

"I'll bet the President liked it too," said Rose.

"He did," said Belle. "They offered him a job."

"The President?" asked Ida.

"They did not," said Gold irately. "Not the President. I was only asked if I'd ever given any thought to working in Washington. That's all."

"That sounds like a job to me," said Irv.

"You see?" said Belle.

"What'd you say?" asked Max eagerly.

"He said he would think about it," said Belle.

"I told you not to tell them."

"I don't care," Belle answered. "They're your family. You said you'd probably take it if the job was a good one."

"You said you wouldn't go," said Gold.

"I won't," said Belle.

"Twenty thousand?" Gold's father suddenly exclaimed with a gargantuan guffaw. "*Me* they would give a million!"

Ashes, Gold grieved wildly, chewing away at his mouthful of mashed potatoes and bread more vigorously than he realized. The food! In my mouth to ashes the food is turning! It has been this way with my father almost all my life.

From the beginning, Gold ruminated now. When I said I was thinking of going into business, he told me to stay in school. When I decided to stay in school, he told me to go into business. "Dope. Why waste time? It's not what you know. It's who you know." Some father. If I said wet, he'd say dry. When I said dry, he said wet. If I said black, he said white. If I said white, he said . . . niggers, they're ruining the neighborhood, one and all, and that's it. *Fartig.* That was when he was in real estate. Far back, that peremptory cry of *Fartig* would instantly create an obedient silence that everybody in the family would be in horror of breaking, including Gold's mother.

It was no secret to anyone that his father considered Gold a *schmuck.* It would be unfair to say his father was disappointed in him, for he had always considered Gold a *schmuck.*

"From the beginning," his father showed off again with inverted familial pride, as though Gold were elsewhere, "I knew he would never amount to much. And was I right? It's a good thing his mother never lived to see the day he was born."

"Pop," Sid corrected him tactfully. "Bruce was already in high school when Mom died."

"And a finer woman never lived," responded Gold's father, nodding for a moment in bewitched recollection, then glaring at Gold vindictively as though her death at forty-nine had been his fault. "Or died," he added faintly.

Once when Gold was visiting in Florida, his father drew him across a street just to meet some friends and introduced him by saying, "This is my son's brother. The one that never amounted to much."

His father's lasting appraisal of Gold—as of almost every other human in the world, including Sid—was that he lacked business sense. Despite his father's unbroken record of failure in more occupations and business ventures than Gold knew about, he judged himself a model of splendid achievements and rare acumen, and he never shrank from presenting himself as a shrewd observer of everyone else's affairs, including those of Sid and General Motors. One of his more penetrating entrepreneurial judgments this year about American Telephone and Telegraph was that "they got no talent in the front office."

"They're big, all right," said Julius Gold, "but they don't know what to do. If I owned all those telephones, oh boy—no business would run without me."

His visit to New York this year, ostensibly for dental work, had commenced in May. A staunchly irreligious man, he now seemed oddly determined to remain through all the Jewish holidays, and he kept disclosing new ones of which the others had not heard.

"He must be reading the fucking Talmud," Gold had grumbled to Belle when his father cited Shmini Atzereth. Belle pretended not to hear. "Or else he's making them up."

In Harriet, Gold found a kindred antipathy that surpassed his own. "What's the matter?" she had muttered snidely the week of her father-in-law's arrival. "They have no dentists in Miami?"

It was a fragile and temporary alliance, Gold knew, for Harriet had been methodically putting distance between herself and the family for some time, as though in thrifty preparation for some clear and farsighted eventuality. Harriet had a widowed mother and an older unmarried sister to help support.

Gold's father was five feet two and subject to unexpected attacks of wisdom. "Make money!" he might shout suddenly, apropos of nothing, and his stepmother would add liturgically, "You should all listen to your father."

"Make money!" he shouted suddenly now, as though sprung from a trance with a burning revelation. "That's the only good thing I ever learned from the Christians," he continued with the same volatile fervor. "Roast beef is better than boiled beef, that's another good thing. And sirloin steak is better than shoulder steak. Lobsters are dirty. They ain't got scales and crawl. They can't even swim. And that's it. *Fartig.*"

"You should listen to your father more." It was on Gold that the reprimanding gaze of his stepmother rested last, longest, and most severely.

"And what does he want me to do?"

"Whatever he does," answered his father, "is wrong. One thing," he said, "one thing I always taught my children," he went on, as though addressing somebody else's, "was not the value of a dollar, but the value of a *thousand* dollars, *ten* thousand. And all of them—except one"—in fantastic disregard of the facts and to the visible embarrassment of the others, he paused to look with murderous disgust at Gold—"have learned that lesson and now got plenty, especially Sid here, and little Joannie." His eyes misted over at mention of his youngest daughter, who had bolted from the fold so early. "I always knew how to advise. The upshot is, that when I get old"—Gold could no longer believe his ears as he heard this preposterous braggart of eighty-two declaiming—"when I get old, nobody will ever have to support me but you children."

Gold, his temper rising, felt no compunction about lashing back.

"Well, I don't like to boast," he replied roughly, "but when I was with the Foundation seven years ago—"

"You ain't with them any more!" his father cut him short.

Gold surrendered with a shudder and pretended to search his plate as Rose, Muriel, and all the brothers-in-law clapped in delight and Esther and Ida rocked with laughter. Gold had the terrible presentiment that some might leap onto their chairs and hurl hats into the air. His father again sat back slowly with that smile of self-enchantment and let his eyes fall closed. Gold was constrained to smile. He would not want anyone to guess how truly crushed he felt. And then, Sid spoke.

"Behold a child," Sid intoned rabbinically without warning, as though musing aloud upon a slice of Esther's stuffed intestine held on a fork halfway between his plate and his mouth, and Gold felt his spirits sink further, "by nature's kindly law, pleased by a rattle, tickled by a straw."

Gold saw in a flash that he was totally ruined. It was check, mate, match, and defeat from the opening move. He was caught, whether he took the bait or declined, and he could only marvel in dejection as the rest of the stratagem unfolded around him as symmetrically and harmoniously as ripples in water.

The others were struck with wonder by Sid's eloquence and pantheistic wisdom.

"That sounds okay to me," Victor murmured.

"Me too," said Max.

"It's nice," said Esther. "Isn't it?"

"Yes," Rose agreed. "Beautiful."

"See how smart my first son is?" said Gold's father.

"You should listen to your older brother more," said Gold's stepmother, and aimed the point of her knitting needle at Gold's eyes.

"It really is beautiful," Ida assented reverently. Ida, the shrewish schoolteacher, was considered the intelligent one; Gold, the college professor, was a novelty. Ida looked Gold fully in the face. "Isn't it, Bruce?"

There was no escape.

"Yes," said Belle.

Gold was trapped two, three, four, maybe five or six ways. If he mentioned Alexander Pope, he would be parading his knowledge. If he didn't, Sid would, unmasking him as an ignoramus. If he corrected the prepositional errors, he would appear pedantic, quarrelsome, jealous. If he gave no answer at all, he would be insulting to Ida, who, with the others, was awaiting some reply. It was no fair way, he sulked, to treat a middle-aged, Phi Beta Kappa, cum laude graduate of Columbia who was a doctor of philosophy and had recently been honored with praise from the White House and the promise of consideration for a high-level posi-

tion. Oh, Sid, you fucking cocksucker, lamented the doctor of philosophy and prospective governmental appointee. You nailed me again.

"Pope," he decided at length to mumble unwillingly, keeping his
face steadfastly down toward his portion of Ida's meatballs.

"What?" snapped his father.

"He said 'Pope,' " Sid informed him congenially.

"What's it mean?"

"It's by Alexander Pope," Gold asserted loudly. "Not by Sid."

"See how smart our kid brother is?" Sid announced, chewing con-
tentedly.

"He didn't say it was by him," Harriet pointed out nicely in defense
of her husband. "Did he?"

"Isn't it just as beautiful anyway?" Ida reasoned with him pedagog-
ically.

"Yes," said Belle.

"Is it any less beautiful because it's by Alexander Pope and not by
Sid?" asked Irv.

Belle shook her head firmly, as did Victor, Milt, and Max.

Gold found them all abhorrent. "The implication was there," he
exclaimed sullenly. "And the prepositions are wrong."

"Brucie, Brucie, Brucie," entreated Sid generously, the essence of
tolerance and reasonableness. "Are you going to be sore at me just because of a couple of prepositions?" There was a murmurous shaking of
heads. "We'll make them right if you're going to be so finicky."

"Sid, you're fucking me over again!" Gold shouted. "Aren't you?"

The next few moments were exciting. The women averted their
eyes, and Victor, who did not like bad language ever in front of women,
reddened further, as though keeping his temper in check, and
straightened menacingly. Then Gold's father jumped to his feet with an
incredulous shriek. "He said fuck?" His voice ascended to such shrillness
that he sounded like a chicken in a frenzy. "Fuck, he said? I'll kill him!
I'll break his bones! Someone walk me over to him."

"All of you leave Bruce alone," Ida ordered sternly, restoring order.
"This is my house, and I won't permit any fighting."

"That's right," entreated Rose, a large, kindly woman with a saddle
of freckles across her nose. "Bruce is probably still very tired."

"From his trip to Washington," said Esther.

"Wilmington," said Belle.

Sid, licking his lips with a look of triumph, reached with his fingers
for a second piece of Harriet's honey cake.

John Mortimer

*

EXCERPT FROM

CLINGING TO THE WRECKAGE

Sex, like love, my father thought, had been greatly overestimated by the poets. He would often pause at teatime, his biscuit halfway to his mouth, to announce, "I have never had many mistresses with thighs like white marble." And I was at a loss to tell whether he meant that he had not had lady friends with particularly marmoreal thighs, or that he had had few mistresses of any sort. Like most children I found my father's sex life a subject on which it was best to avoid speculation. He had had, in his past, a fiancée other than my mother, whom he always referred to as his "poor girl" and who had died young. I never discovered her name or the cause of her death.

"Love affairs aren't much of a subject for drama really," he told me at an early age. "Consider this story of a lover, a husband and an unfaithful wife. The wife confesses all to her husband. He sends for her lover. They are closeted in the living-room together. The wife stands outside the door, trembling with fear. She strains her ears to discover what's going on in the room. Some terrible quarrel? A duel or fight to the death perhaps? At last she can stand the suspense no longer. She flings open the door and what does she see? Blood? Broken furniture? One of them stretched out on the carpet? Not at all. The two men are sitting by the fire drinking bottled ale and discussing the best method of pruning apple trees. Naturally, the woman's furious. She packs and leaves for her mother's."

Was my father any of the characters in that unromantic story? Not the husband, but was he, perhaps, the lover? I never asked him and now I have no means of finding out.

However, my father would often recite, and usually at teatime, poetry of a sensual nature. Swinburne had been his undergraduate favourite and he often repeated, with a relish of rolling r's:

> Can you hurt me, sweet lips, though I hurt you?
> Men touch them, and change in a trice
> The lilies and languors of virtue
> For the raptures and roses of vice.

"Poor old Algernon Charles got it wrong as usual," he would add by way of commentary. "The roses and raptures of vice are damned uncomfortable as you'll certainly find out. You have to get into such ridiculous positions." And he would go on with the recital as my mother cut more bread and butter or spooned out the homemade marrow jam:

> We shift and bedeck and bedrape us,
> Thou art noble and nude and antique;
> Libitina thy mother, Priapus
> Thy father, a Tuscan and Greek.
> We play with light loves in the portal,
> And wince and relent and refrain
> Loves die, and we know thee immortal,
> Our Lady of Pain.

"Sorry stuff, as it so happens," my father commented, "but I like the sound of it."

It follows from all this that my father's advice on the subject of sex was not of much practical value to an eleven-year-old boy. At about that age the whole business hit me like a raging epidemic, causing me to seek constant opportunities to embrace myself passionately among the dead flies and dusty, outdated law books and motheaten blankets in our loft, or in houses in the bracken which I now ran as bachelor establishments. At my prep school I fell in love with Jenks, but this love was largely unconsummated, apart from a clumsy hug in the school museum, a place where the air was polluted by the prize exhibit, a large and inadequately cured elephant's foot which had been turned into a waste-paper basket. I loved Annabella and Ginger Rogers when she wore jodhpurs and a hacking jacket, and Deanna Durbin and Greta Garbo when she was dressed as a boy in *Queen Christina*. I was lately talking to an elderly, but still bright-eyed, General who said, "I first fell in love with Cherubino with his nice white breeches and dear little sword." It was years before I got to know *Figaro*, but the image for my prep school years was about right.

The truth was that from the time when I stopped keeping house in the bracken with Iris Jones to the end of my time at Harrow, seven or eight years when I might as well have entered a Dominican order for all the female company I enjoyed, I knew absolutely nothing about girls. In one-sex schools and during lonely and isolated holidays I was in a chrysalis of vague, schoolboy homosexuality. Even when I got to Oxford, and did make some expeditions away from the safe dormitory base, the girls I preferred were still boyish. Betty Grable was less my style than Veronica Lake and Katharine Hepburn who, so Frank Hauser assured us, acted in *The Philadelphia Story* as the natural bridge into the hetero-sexual world.

The sight of a woman at my public school was almost as rare as a Cockney accent in class; and if we spotted one it was, as often as not, a fierce and elderly matron. We were waited on at table by footmen in blue tailed coats and settled down for the night by a butler called "George." Our homosexuality was therefore dictated by necessity rather than choice. We were like a generation of diners condemned to cold cuts because the steak and kidney was "off."

● ● ●

Harrow-on-the-Hill is in the middle of the suburbs: the tomb in the parish churchyard where Byron once lay and composed poetry as he looked over rolling meadows now commands a fine view of the semis of Hillingdon and Pinner. It was only a few stops from Baker Street on the Metropolitan Line and we used to sit in the smoke-filled carriages to be jeered at as we went up to Lord's, dressed in top hat, pearl-grey waistcoat, morning coat and silver-topped stick with a dark-blue tassel. We weren't allowed to speak to the boys at the bottom of the hill, although a Prefect might occasionally give one of them sixpence to carry up his suitcase at the beginning of term. We were isolated and put in quarantine both on account of sex and class, although once again I found myself educated above my situation, among various "Honourables" who were called "Mister" in roll-call. Within our group we were again strictly segregated. There were the "one yearers" who had to keep all their buttons done up, "two yearers" who could undo one jacket button, "three yearers" who could undo two and "four yearers" who could wear fancy waistcoats and put their hands in their pockets. "Five yearers" were said to be allowed to grow moustaches or even marry a wife if such a thing were available. If "four yearers" mixed with "one yearers" the worst was suspected and very often turned out to be true.

I cannot say I found Harrow brutal or my time particularly un-happy, but life there never approached the Elizabethan splendours and miseries of my prep school. Harrow's great advantage was that we had rooms of our own, although in the first year these had to be shared with one other boy, and these did provide a sort of oasis of privacy. Each room had a coal fire and a wooden bed which let down from the wall on which various political slogans were burned in poker-work, such as "Death to the Boers" and "No Home Rule for Ireland." You could bring your own furniture and set out your own books on the shelves and enjoy some of the privileges of a long-term, good conduct prisoner. (It's rightly said that the great advantage of an English public school education is that no subsequent form of captivity can hold any particular terror for you. A friend who was put to work on the Burma railway once told me that he was greeted, on arrival, by a fellow prisoner-of-war who said, "Cheer up. It's not half as bad as Marlborough.")

The first boy I shared a room with was called Weaver. He had smooth dark hair which he slicked down with "Anzora" ("Anzora masters the hair," I had heard about it on Radio Luxembourg). His parents, he told me, were extremely wealthy and had a large house in the New Forest. I was impressed with Weaver until I met a boy called Marsh who told me, "Weaver's really extremely common. His parents have side-plates at dinner."

"Side-plates?"

"Yes. Side-plates. To put your bread on. Not at luncheon. Every-one has side-plates at luncheon. At *dinner*." He explained carefully, as though to a backward foreigner, matters which seemed to him perfectly obvious.

"But if you don't have side-plates at dinner what do you put your bread on?"

"You crumble it. On the table." Marsh looked at me with great pity. "Don't you know anything?"

"Not very much."

It was clear that I didn't.

• • •

"Properly shined shoes are the mark of a good regiment and a decent Classical Shell. It gives me little pleasure to listen to Virgil being construed by a boy with shoes the colour of elephant's hide. Look down, and when you can see your faces in your toe-caps you shall inherit the earth. You shall wear shined shoes at Speech Day and enjoy the delights of strawberries and cream and salmon may-on-naise! You shall wear your shined shoes in the Classical Fifth and in the Classical Sixth also shall you wear them. And if your boots are shined and your puttees neat on parade you shall pass out of the school Corps into the Brigade of Guards."

It was strange that so many of my schoolmasters seemed to have been permanently affected by the Old Testament as seen through the prose of Rudyard Kipling. My first master at Harrow was a charming retired Major of the Brigade of Guards. He inspected our shoes and finger-nails each morning, but otherwise treated us with great gentleness.

My Harrow friends stayed longer in my life than those I had met at earlier schools. We were thrown together in the lower regions of our House, we ate together with our faces to the wall, and Keswick, the Head Boy, would shout at us if we turned round. We loitered in one another's rooms and "took exercise" by changing into running clothes and sitting gossiping or reading Roger Fry in the lavatories below the Fives courts. My closest friend was Oliver, known to his many enemies as "Oily," Pensotti, who had about him the vaguely seductive aura of holidays in Bandol and bedrooms in Mayfair. He wore scuffed suede shoes and used a sort of dead white face powder to cover his spots. He used to accompany Radio Luxembourg with the soft musical scrape of a pair of wire brushes played on the top of a suitcase. He came into my life, and indeed left it, shrouded in an aura of mystery. If I asked him any questions about himself he would look vaguely amused and avoid giving anything away.

"Where do you live, Pensotti?"

"Where do I live? Ah. That's what I'm always asking myself. Would you like to help me with a few suggestions?"

Or, "What does your father do, Pensotti?"

"What does he *do?* You mean what does he do, *exactly?* A lot of people have wanted to know the answer to that, especially my Ma."

I subsequently met an elderly lady who claimed to be Pensotti's mother. She had bright red hair, carried a poodle and spoke in what she alleged was a South American accent. She lived in a flat in Charles Street with glass-topped tables and a lot of wrought-iron furniture. I never met Pensotti *père,* nor did I learn any more about Oliver's childhood. It seemed to have been spent around the world and he could speak French, Spanish and Italian.

The other friend, who lasted in my life for many years, was Martin Witteridge. He was a large, rather clumsy but extremely kind and good-natured boy. He would always laugh at our jokes, buy us great plates of egg and chips in the school shop and consent to listen as I read out page after page of the novel I was writing about Harrow in the nearest possible approach to the style of Aldous Huxley.

On the fringe of our group, yelling abuse at us or occasionally kicking his way into our midst, was Tainton. Tainton was a phenomenon. I have never since met anyone in the least like Tainton. I had always hoped that his kind died out with cock-fights and bear-baiting.

The first thing to be said about Tainton was that he was extremely small. However, he was as tough and leathery as a jockey. He boasted that his mother had given birth to him on the hunting-field, after which minor intrusion into a day's sport she went on to be up with the kill at Thorne Wood according to Tainton, but then Tainton was, on many matters, a most unreliable witness. His habitual expression was a discontented scowl, after which his face would become bright red and suffused with anger. He had yellow curls which stood up on end, and ears like jug handles. On certain very rare occasions he smiled, and his smile had a sort of shy innocence and even charm.

At all times and in all places Tainton was a source of continual trouble. Before a breathless audience he tried to cross the lake by swinging from a sort of trapeze, made up from his bed-linen, and fell in. He broke windows, used unspeakable language to the matron, set fire to the *Morning Post* as Keswick was reading it, put stray cats into people's beds and, at home and during the course of a hunt ball, shut a Shetland pony in the ladies' lavatory, having first dosed it with castor oil. Tainton was apparently born without a sense of fear and was quite impervious to the consequences of his outrages.

Among his other distinctions Tainton was a prize, you could say a champion, masturbator. No doubt we all did our best in this direction, but with Tainton masturbation reached Olympic standards. There was a story about him which earned him considerable respect; but as it depended on the uncorroborated evidence of Tainton himself, it may not have been true. It seems that the school Chaplain, Mr. Percy, called on Tainton in his room, surprised him at his usual exercise and said, deeply shocked, "Really, my boy, you should save that up till you are married." "Oh, I'm doing that, sir," Tainton answered with his rare smile, "I've already got several jam jars full."

• • •

Our House was presided over by a gentle English liberal called Mr. Lamb. This housemaster was given hell at lunchtime by Keswick, who warmly espoused the Fascist cause in Spain, whereas Mr. Lamb was of the opinion that the Republicans were really doing their best and behaving quite decently, all things taken into account. Like many English liberals, Mr. Lamb had his blind spots, including a wish-fulfilling liking for real bastards, such as Napoleon, about whom he spoke with servile admiration in the history class. However, there was absolutely no harm to Mr. Lamb. He believed that all laws were founded on common sense and natural justice and, when I suggested to him that might mean I could undo all my buttons during my second year, he attempted a distinction between social conventions and the law of nature which caused him visible pain. It was this gentle creature, devoted to reason, the Webbs, Gladstone and Macaulay who had thrust upon him the appalling task of educating Tainton.

"John. I know that you and I share certain values. About democracy, for instance. And the Republicans in Spain."

I didn't know whether to throw my fist in the air, embrace Mr. Lamb, kiss him on both cheeks and call him "Camarada." Instead I said weakly, "Yes, sir."

"So I have thought you might be a stabilizing influence if you shared a room with young Tainton. I'm sure," the archetypal English liberal muttered with hopeless optimism, "that there's much good in the lad."

I have not read, in my wildest divorce cases, of marriages as violent as my cohabitation with Tainton. As soon as I entered the room a flung chair splintered against the wall; Tainton was in an evil mood and crouched for a spring. His rages were terrible, totally unpredictable and extremely destructive. He would tear up my Van Gogh reproductions, spit in my Virginia Woolf and once he poured a bottle of green ink over the manuscript of my Aldous-Huxley-type novella. At night he would groan, have nightmares, subconsciously re-enact his birth on the hunting-field or, tireless and in solitary fashion, prepare himself for the rigours of married life. At rare moments he would show unexpected charm, when he leafed through his large collection of photographs of Sonja Henie or cultivated mustard and cress on the silken surface of his top hat. My life with Tainton might be described as days of anxiety and nights of fear. I had absolutely no idea what was going to happen next.

We used to be settled down for the night by George the butler, who entered our room in a tailed coat, said, "Goodnight, Sor!", seized the poker, raked out the fire and departed switching off the light in one fluent gesture. One evening Tainton hit on the expedient of heating the poker's handle until it was just not red hot and put it ready for George to seize and burn off several fingers. Spot on cue George entered, said "Goodnight, Sor!" and astounded us by seizing Tainton's striped Sunday trousers as a poker-holder, thus burning a large and smouldering hole in the seat. He left us in the darkness and Tainton lay awake until the small hours, grinding his teeth and swearing a hideous revenge.

• • •

In fifteen years you canter through evolution, dash through history, covering the development of man from anthropoid ape to medieval monk in the course of a few birthdays. The child has no sooner finished its bikkipeg and had its nappy changed a couple of times before it seems to be standing up in the school debating society, proposing that, "This House Sees No Alternative to the Economics of the Market Place," or writing essays on "The Politics of Feminism." We are all like insecure Third World Republics, granted Constitutions and Bills of Rights before we have banished tribalism, given up eating our enemies or produced Budgets planned on the signs of the zodiac. Ideas are clapped on us as top hats were once set on the grizzled heads of African chieftains; they make us all look more or less ridiculous.

I read to find new characters to adopt on lonely runs round the periphery of football pitches. I read aloud to entertain my father and when we had got through Shakespeare's sonnets, Browning and A Shropshire Lad, we went on to Fragments of an Agon and Sweeney Among the Nightingales. I added Murder in the Cathedral (the truncated version) to Ivor Novello's Glamorous Nights as another play suitable for solo performance on the dining-room stairs. We went, after a prolonged dinner at the Trocadero, to see an Auden and Isherwood verse drama, it must have been The Ascent of F.6, at the Mercury Theatre, and what entertained my father most about the evening was the presence among the incidental musicians of a lady drummer called "Eve Kish." Eve Kish became a subject of his sudden gusts of uncontrollable laughter; he would imagine her patrolling the country lanes with her kettledrum, and he would look in the programmes of all other plays to see if he could find the longed-for announcement "Percussion: Eve Kish." I remember him sitting down a quarter of an hour late at The Seagull, calling out loudly, "What? No Eve Kish on the drum?"

In spite of this unpromising beginning it would be hard to overestimate the effect Auden had on me and my generation of middle-class schoolboys. He wrote about what we understood: juvenile jokes about housemasters, homosexual longings, the Clever Boy, the Form Entertainer and the Show Off. And yet his poems brought extraordinary news of a world outside the stuffy common-room and the headmaster's study; the vague but heroic struggle to do great things which were also stylized and in capital letters, like Building the Just City. We had been so near a war: I was born less than five years after the Great War ended, and we had grown up with Flanders poppies and pictures of tin hats on innumerable war graves and I knew a boy whose father promised to tell him about the horrors of Passchendaele if he went straight to bed. Now another war was coming so that we too, I sometimes thought with acute depression, would end as being remembered only by an embarrassed silence on a soggy school playing-field on Poppy Day.

All the same, the idea of the new war was a different and clear one. The gloomy ex-jockey who drove my father's car in the country had told me about Italian Fascists dropping their Abyssinian prisoners-of-war out of aeroplanes. At my prep school I turned over pages of the *Illustrated London News* and saw photographs of Spanish villages shattered by German bombs. There were pictures of young Republican militiamen, going up to the front grinning and sucking cigarette-stubs ready to fight a new and unmistakably evil military machine. They had, moreover, the poets on their side, whereas the Fascists were supported by people like Keswick. I knew almost nothing about life, but I knew perfectly clearly that I couldn't stand people like Keswick. So a whole political attitude can grow from a handful of books and a strong loathing for the Head of the House. Naive as these beliefs were, trivial as their origins may have been, I cannot say they are attitudes I have ever lived to regret, and it seems to me that those who now write their best-sellers denouncing the treacherous iniquities of the Cambridge Communists show little understanding of the emotions of the thirties, when good and evil seemed so unusually easy to distinguish and the Russians appeared simply as allies in the war against Fascism.

I don't know how the invitation to join the Communist Party came. I know that Esmond Romilly is supposed to have started a network of public school cells, but I can't imagine who can have recommended me as a likely candidate. When I joined I formed, so far as I could see, a one-boy communist cell in a sea of Harrovian capitalist enterprise. For a while I received puzzling and contradictory instructions from the Party Headquarters in King Street. When the Stalin–Hitler pact was signed, the Russians lost their enthusiasm for the coming struggle and I was urged to go down on to the factory floor and persuade the workers to go slow. I couldn't, I thought, do much about it except put the word around the classroom that Virgil should be translated as lethargically as possible, a "go-slow" which needed no particular encouragement. Later, when Hitler attacked Russia, we were urged to go down on the factory floor and step up production. Again, all I could suggest was the stepping up of the translation of Virgil. After these contradictory commands from King Street I stopped taking the Party's literature and told my friends that the only political views worth having were those of Prince Peter Kropotkin who believed in anarchism, Mutual Aid and the essential goodness of human nature, opinions which were not easy to hold when you were sharing a room with Tainton.

In the flight from Tainton I spent more and more time alone in the high, marmoreal, Victorian library, chasing books in dark corners and up step-ladders, finding in unexpected places like dictionaries, medieval histories or collections of obscure eighteenth-century poetry, ideas which filled me with hilarity, gloom or almost unbearable lust. I found Lord Byron's Turkish slippers in a glass case, and set myself to follow his uneasy pilgrimage round the school, from the tomb of John Peachey where he lay to write poetry, to the grave where his daughter is buried outside Harrow Church to teach her a sharp lesson for being illegitimate.

Then, as now, I found Lord Byron deeply sympathetic. His potent mixture of revolutionary fervour and crusty conservatism, his life of a Puritan voluptuary, of a romantic with common sense, was intoxicating to me. I spent afternoons in the library drinking imaginary Hock and Seltzer, swimming the Hellespont or limping round Newstead Abbey with a harem of housemaids. I stayed up late gambling with Dallas, and awoke to find the chamber-pot overflowing with banknotes. Then I read of Byron's Harrow friendships, especially that with Lord Clare. Years after he'd left school, Byron met Clare by chance on the road to Bologna and was deeply moved, feeling, apparently, his heart beat at his fingers' ends. I tried to imagine a chance encounter with Tainton on Western Avenue in twenty years' time and decided that my fingers' ends would remain unexcited. Life in the intervening years for Lord Byron had not, perhaps, been all that it was cracked up to be.

• • •

When war was declared, when we waited, in that far-off and hazy autumn, for the first attack, Oliver Pensotti and I spent a good deal of our time wondering if we would be slaughtered before we had actually been to bed with any sort of lady. This understandable concern was combined, in Oliver's case, with a deep anxiety as to whether he would ever be able to "take breasts," those additions which he found hugely embarrassing and which distinguished Deanna Durbin from Ryecroft Minor, the school tart, who was readily available for a box of chocolate biscuits.

Meanwhile the whole nation was in readiness for the shock of invasion. Oliver's mother left her flat in Charles Street and went to live in the Dorchester, which was built of concrete and believed to be impregnable to air raids. As humble privates in the Harrow Officers' Training Corps, Oliver and I were sent to Aldershot on manoeuvres organized by the Brigade of Guards. We had chosen a peaceful spot, far away from the action where Tainton, having got hold of a box of flares, was staging his own display of pyrotechnics and setting fire to the undergrowth.

"I suppose we'll be really doing this in a year or two."

"You may be doing it. I'll have a different sort of job, I imagine. Not that I shall be able to tell you much about it."

"That'll make a change. I suppose you mean you'll be in the Secret Service, because of the languages they know you speak."

"And because of the languages they don't know I speak. And because of the languages they know I don't speak."

I was getting bored with the constant problem of decoding Pensotti. I went back to reading *A Doll's House*, which I had brought with me on manoeuvres.

"My Ma's leaving the Dorchester," Oliver surprisingly volunteered some information. "She's going to America. It's the end of civilization as we know it. Chap in the Government told her that."

Civilization as I knew it consisted of Keswick and keeping all your buttons done up for three years and being put to bed by a butler and the slow, meaningless translation of Latin poetry. I said that I couldn't wait for its destruction. Oliver got out his wire brushes and, swishing them against the top of his cap, crooned our favourite Deanna Durbin number:

> *I love to climb*
> *An apple tree,*
> *Those apples green*
> *Are bad for me,*
> *They make me sick as sick can be,*
> *It's foolish but it's fun!*

A tall Guards officer wearing a white armband rode up to us on a huge horse. "Bang, bang, you fellows!" he said. "You're dead!"

"I know that's going to happen," Oliver grumbled as we went back to the riding school to get a mug of sweet tea, "I shall be dead before I get a real chance to find out about breasts."

The rumblings from Europe grew louder. Sandy Wilson joined our form and took to knitting long khaki objects, socks, mufflers and Balaclava helmets, comforts for the troops. When our form master protested at this click of needles, which recalled, in a somewhat sinister way, the foot of the guillotine, Sandy Wilson rightly said that it was the patriotic duty of all of us to do our bit for the boys at the front. The future composer of *The Boy Friend* also organized trips to London to see a play called *The Women* by Clare Booth Luce which had not a man in the cast. Oliver and I saw it several times. He hired opera-glasses and took a careful view of the cleavages of the cast, but seemed to come no nearer reassurance.

We practised for air raids, going down to the cellars and wearing our gas masks while Gracie Fields sang *Wish Me Luck as You Wave Me Goodbye* on Mr. Lamb's wireless. Our housemaster took a gloomy view of the situation. "War is hell," he said. "I remember the Somme and we never thought we should have to go through that again. Of course we could have nipped this one in the bud, if we'd only fought in Spain. Or even Czechoslovakia."

"You mean, sir," I asked, intolerably, "that war is hell except in Spain or Czechoslovakia?" As a matter of fact I agreed with Mr. Lamb entirely, but I had inherited what my father would call the art of the advocate, or the irritating habit of looking for the flaw in any argument.

• • •

"School songs" were a great and proud feature of Harrow life. We would assemble in the Speech Room and sing the compositions of long-dead housemasters and music masters, songs redolent of vanished boys playing cricket in knickerbockers, enjoying romantic friendships on summer evenings and going out to die in Afghanistan or on Majuba Hill: *Forty Years On; Jerry a Poor Little Fag; Byron lay, lazily lay, Hid from lesson and game away, Dreaming poetry all alone, Up on the top of Peachey stone.* That was the repertoire and then a new boy with a childish treble would pipe,

> *Five hundred faces and all so strange*
> *Life in front of me, home behind . . .*

And the gravelly-voiced, hairy-chinned, spotty seniors would trumpet in chorus,

> *But the time will come when your heart will thrill*
> *And you'll think with joy of your time on the Hill!*

Winston Churchill, then First Lord of the Admiralty, came down to this strange ceremony which he apparently enjoyed. After the songs were over Mr. Churchill climbed with difficulty on to the stage. He cannot have been more than sixty-five years old, but his ancient head emerged from the carapace of his dinner jacket like the hairless pate of a tortoise, his old hand trembled on the handle of the walking-stick which supported him and his voice, when he spoke, was heavily slurred with brandy and old age. He seemed to us to be about a hundred and three.

"If they ever put *him* in charge of the war," I whispered to Oliver, "God help us all!"

"Oh, they won't do that," he assured me. "They'll never do that. Chap in the Government told my Ma."

• • •

By the end of a year Mr. Churchill had taken over the Government and began to look much younger. Oliver Pensotti and I met in London one winter evening during the holidays. We went for a drink in the bar of the Normandy Hotel where Oliver got into conversation with an ATS named Jeannie, as the bombs started to fall. The sound of breaking glass, the sweet taste of gin and lime, the peril of arbitrary thuds and the silent presence of the rather chunky Jeannie, who smiled but hardly spoke, added to the excitement of the evening. Months before, a fire-bomb had destroyed the kitchen of my father's flat in the Temple and he now lived all the time in the country, potting up, pricking out, trying to get enough petrol to keep the grass cut and getting up early in the blackout to travel to London to deal with the rising tide of divorce. So we went back to the empty flat and sat among the dust-sheets and the ruins of the kitchen. I found several bottles of port which we drank; descending on a foundation of gin and lime they made the room lurch like a ship at sea. I started to tell Jeannie about Lord Byron and his fatal love for his half-sister, but she was looking at Oliver in a strangely fixed sort of way and whispered words I found extremely enigmatic, "Have you got a rubber?"

Almost at once they moved into the bedroom. I was left alone with my memories of his fatal Lordship's love life and pulled down, from my father's dusty shelves, a book of his poems:

> So, we'll go no more a roving
> So late into the night,
> Though the heart be still as loving,
> And the moon be still as bright.
> For the sword outwears its sheath,
> And the soul wears out the breast.
> And the heart must pause to breathe,
> And love itself have rest.

The crashes were coming nearer. I had a momentary fear of my roving being put a stop to before it had even begun, my sword being laid to rest before it had worn out anything at all.

In due course the happy couple re-emerged and the ATS went off to rejoin her regiment.

"Well," I said to Oliver. "How on earth did you manage?"

"Manage?"

"About the breasts, of course."

"Perfectly all right." Oliver gave a smile of satisfied achievement. "You hardly notice them at all."

Jean Kerr

*

TOUJOURS TRISTESSE

After reading A *Certain Smile* by Françoise Sagan:

I was waiting for Banal. I was feeling rather bored. It was a summer day like any other, except for the hail. I crossed the street.

Suddenly I was wildly happy. I had an overwhelming intuition that one day I would be dead. These large eyes, this bony child's body would be consigned to the sweet earth. Everything spoke of it: the lonely cooing of a solitary pigeon overhead, the stately *bong bong bong* of the cathedral chimes, the loud horn of the motorbus that grazed my thigh.

I slipped into the cafe, but Banal was late. I was pleased to notice that that simple fact annoyed me.

Banal and I were classmates. Our eyes had met, our bodies had met, and then someone introduced us. Now he was my property, and I knew every inch of that brown body the way you know your own driveway.

A stranger across the booth spoke.

"Monique, what are you staring at, silly girl?"

It was Banal. Curious that I hadn't recognized him. Suddenly I knew why. A revolting look of cheerfulness had twisted and distorted those clear young features until he seemed actually to be smiling.

I couldn't look. I turned my head, but his voice followed me, humbly and at a distance, like a spaniel.

"Monique, why did you skip class? We were studying the *Critique of Pure Reason*. It was interesting, but I think Kant offers a false dichotomy. The only viable solution is to provide a synthesis in which experience is impregnated with rationality and reason is ordained to empirical data."

How like Banal to say the obvious. Sometimes as I sat and listened to Banal and his companions trade flippancies, I could feel the boredom grow and swell within me almost as if I had swallowed a beach ball.

Why must we chatter fruitlessly and endlessly about philosophy and politics? I confess that I am only interested in questions that touch the heart of another human being—"Who are you sleeping with?"; "What do you take for quick relief from acid indigestion?"

Banal's voice droned on like a chorus of cicadas on a hot day until finally there was a statement I couldn't ignore.

"Monique, I want you to meet my grandfather, Anatole. My rich grandfather."

A slight, stooped man came toward me. He was no longer middle-aged, but I liked that. I was so tired of these eager boys of fifty. His hair, which was greenish white, might have been unpleasant had there been more of it. As he smiled gently, showing his small, even, ecru teeth, I thought, "Ah, he's the type that's mad for little girls." In fact, hadn't I read that he'd had some trouble with the police?

But now, as his dull eyes looked directly into mine and I noticed him idly striking a match on the tablecloth, I realized with a sudden stab of joy that finally I had met a man who was as bored as I was.

And yet, I reminded myself firmly as my heart slid back to earth, this won't last. It can't last. He won't *always* be this bored.

Now Banal was speaking in his infantile way.

"Do you know Monique has never seen the sea?"

Then a woman spoke, Anatole's wife. She was sitting beside him but I hadn't noticed her because she was wearing a brown dress and blended into the back of the booth. Her voice was warm, like a caress.

"Why, that's awful that this poor child has never seen the sea. Anatole, darling, you must take her to our little château by the ocean. I won't be able to come because I'm redecorating the town house. But there is plenty of food in the Frigidaire, and Monique will be able to see the ocean from the bedroom. Here are the keys."

I liked her for that.

Then they were leaving. Dorette, for that was Anatole's wife's name, had forgotten her gloves, and I admit I felt a pang of jealousy as I noticed the intimate way that Anatole threw them to her.

Now Banal and I were alone. As I suspected, Banal was stormy and full of suspicion. How I hated him when he got this way. He kept asking me, again and again, "Are you sure, Monique, are you really sure that you have never seen the sea?"

But when I assured him, what was the truth, that I never had, he seemed comforted and became once more the sunny, smiling, handsome young man I found so repellent.

• • •

We were in Anatole's open car. Overhead the sky was blue as a bruise.

The gleaming white road slipping under our wheels seemed like a ribbon of cotton candy. As I realized we were nearing the château, my heart turned over once, quickly and neatly, like a pancake on a griddle.

Anatole's voice seemed to come from a great distance.

"Bored, darling?"

I turned to him.

"Of course—and you?"

His answering smile told me that he was.

And now we were running up the long flight of steps to the château hand in hand like two happy children, stopping only when Anatole had to recover his wind.

At the doorway he paused and gathered me into his arms. His voice, when he spoke, was like a melody played sweetly and in tune.

"My darling," he said, "I hope I have made it perfectly clear that so far as I am concerned you are just another pickup."

"Of course," I whispered. How adult he was, and how indescribably dear.

So the golden days passed. Mostly we were silent, but occasionally we sat in the twilight and spoke wistfully of Dorette and Banal and what suckers they were.

And who could describe those nights? Never in my relationship with Banal had I felt anything like this. Ah, how rewarding it is to share the bed of a really mature man. For one thing, there was the clatter and the excitement four times a night as he leaped to the floor and stamped on his feet in an effort to get the circulation going. My little pet name for him, now, was Thumper.

The last day dawned cold and bright as a star. Anatole was waiting for me out in the car, so I packed my few belongings, ran a nail file through my curls, and joined him.

What shall I say of the pain of that ride back to Paris? In one sense, we were, both of us, precisely as weary as ever. Yet for the first time it wasn't a shared weariness.

We pulled up to my front door, and then the blow fell.

"Monique," he said, "little one. I *have* been bored with you. Nobody can take that away from us. But the truth is, and I know how this will hurt you, I am even more bored with my wife. I'm going back to her."

He was gone. I was alone. Alone, alone, alone. I was a woman who had loved a man. It was a simple story, prosaic even. And yet somehow I knew I could get a novel out of it.

Truman Capote

*

A DAY'S WORK

SCENE: A *rainy April morning, 1979. I am walking along Second Avenue in New York City, carrying an oilcloth shopping satchel bulging with house-cleaning materials that belong to Mary Sanchez, who is beside me trying to keep an umbrella above the pair of us, which is not difficult as she is much taller than I am, a six-footer.*

Mary Sanchez is a professional cleaning woman who works by the hour, at five dollars an hour, six days a week. She works approximately nine hours a day, and visits on the average twenty-four different domiciles between Monday and Saturday: generally her customers require her services just once a week.

Mary is fifty-seven years old, a native of a small South Carolina town who has "lived North" the past forty years. Her husband, a Puerto Rican, died last summer. She has a married daughter who lives in San Diego, and three sons, one of whom is a dentist, one who is serving a ten-year sentence for armed robbery, a third who is "just gone, God knows where. He called me last Christmas, he sounded far away. I asked where are you, Pete, but he wouldn't say, so I told him his daddy was dead, and he said good, said that was the best Christmas present I could've given him, so I hung up the phone, slam, and I hope he never calls again. Spitting on Dad's grave that way. Well, sure, Pedro was never good to the kids. Or me. Just boozed and rolled dice. Ran around with bad women. They found him dead on a bench in Central Park. Had a mostly empty bottle of Jack Daniel's in a paper sack propped between his legs; never drank nothing but the best, that man. Still, Pete was way out of line, saying he was glad his father was dead. He owed him the gift of life, didn't he? And I owed Pedro something too. If it wasn't for him, I'd still be an ignorant Baptist, lost to the Lord. But when I got married, I married in the Catholic church, and the Catholic church brought a shine to my life that has never gone out, and never will, not even when I die. I raised my children in the Faith; two of them turned out fine, and I give the church credit for that more than me."

Mary Sanchez is muscular, but she has a pale round smooth pleasant face with a tiny upturned nose and a beauty mole high on her left cheek. She dislikes the term "black," racially applied. "I'm not black. I'm brown. A light-brown colored woman. And I'll tell you something else. I don't know many other colored people that like being called blacks. Maybe some of the young people. And those radicals. But not folks my age, or even half as old. Even people who really are black, they don't like it. What's wrong with Negroes? I'm a Negro, and a Catholic, and proud to say it."

I've known Mary Sanchez since 1968, and she has worked for me, periodically, all these years. She is conscientious, and takes far more than a casual interest in her clients, many of whom she has scarcely met, or not met at all, for many of them are unmarried working men and women who are not at home when she arrives to clean their apartments; she communicates with them, and they with her, via notes: "Mary, please water the geraniums and feed the cat. Hope this finds you well. Gloria Scotto."

Once I suggested to her that I would like to follow her around during the course of a day's work, and she said well, she didn't see anything wrong with that, and in fact, would enjoy the company: "This can be kind of lonely work sometimes."

Which is how we happen to be walking along together on this showery April morning. We're off to her first job: a Mr. Andrew Trask, who lives on East Seventy-third Street.

TC: What the hell have you got in this sack?

MARY: Here, give it to me. I can't have you cursing.

TC: No. Sorry. But it's heavy.

MARY: Maybe it's the iron.

TC: You iron their clothes? You never iron any of mine.

MARY: Some of these people just have no equipment. That's why I have to carry so much. I leave notes: get this, get that. But they forget. Seems like all my people are bound up in their troubles. Like this Mr. Trask, where we're going. I've had him seven, eight months, and I've never seen him yet. But he drinks too much, and his wife left him on account of it, and he owes bills everywhere, and if ever I answered his phone, it's somebody trying to collect. Only now they've turned off his phone.

(*We arrive at the address, and she produces from a shoulder-satchel a massive metal ring jangling with dozens of keys. The building is a four-story brownstone with a midget elevator.*)

TC (*after entering and glancing around the Trask establishment—one fair-sized room with greenish arsenic-colored walls, a kitchenette, and a bathroom with a broken, constantly flowing toilet*): IImm. I see what you mean. This guy has problems.

MARY (*opening a closet crammed and clammy with sweat-sour laundry*): Not a clean sheet in the house! And look at that bed! Mayonnaise! Chocolate! Crumbs, crumbs, chewing gum, cigarette butts. Lipstick! What kind of woman would subject herself to a bed like that? I haven't been able to change the sheets for weeks. Months.

(*She turns on several lamps with awry shades; and while she labors to organize the surrounding disorder, I take more careful note of the premises. Really, it looks as though a burglar had been plundering there, one who had left some drawers of a bureau open, others closed. There's a leather-framed photograph on the bureau of a stocky swarthy macho man and a blond hoity-toity Junior League woman and three tow-headed grinning snaggle-toothed suntanned boys, the eldest about fourteen. There is another unframed picture stuck in a blurry mirror: another blonde, but definitely not Junior League—perhaps a pickup from Maxwell's Plum; I imagine it is her lipstick on the bed sheets. A copy of the December issue of* True Detective *magazine is lying on the floor, and in the bathroom, stacked by the ceaselessly churning toilet, stands a pile of girlie literature —Penthouse, Hustler, Oui; otherwise, there seems to be a total absence of cultural possessions. But there are hundreds of empty vodka bottles everywhere—the miniature kind served by airlines.*)

TC: Why do you suppose he drinks only these miniatures?

MARY: Maybe he can't afford nothing bigger. Just buys what he can. He has a good job, if he can hold on to it, but I guess his family keeps him broke.

TC: What does he do?

MARY: Airplanes.

TC: That explains it. He gets these little bottles free.

MARY: Yeah? How come? He's not a steward. He's a pilot.

TC: Oh, my God.

(A *telephone rings, a subdued noise, for the instrument is submerged under a rumpled blanket. Scowling, her hands soapy with dishwater, Mary unearths it with the finesse of an archeologist.*)

MARY: He must have got connected again. Hello? (*Silence*) Hello?
A WOMAN'S VOICE: Who *is* this?
MARY: This is Mr. Trask's residence.
WOMAN'S VOICE: Mr. Trask's *residence*? (*Laughter; then, hoity-toity*) To
    whom am I speaking?
MARY: This is Mr. Trask's maid.
WOMAN'S VOICE: So Mr. Trask has a maid, has he? Well, that's more than
    Mrs. Trask has. Will Mr. Trask's maid please tell Mr. Trask that
    Mrs. Trask would like to speak to him?
MARY: He's not home.
MRS. TRASK: Don't give me that. Put him on.
MARY: I'm sorry, Mrs. Trask. I guess he's out flying.
MRS. TRASK (*bitter mirth*): Out flying? He's always flying, dear. Always.
MARY: What I mean is, he's at work.
MRS. TRASK: Tell him to call me at my sister's in New Jersey. Call the
    instant he comes in, if he knows what's good for him.
MARY: Yes, ma'am. I'll leave that message. (*She hangs up*) Mean woman.
    No wonder he's in the condition he's in. And now he's out of a job.
    I wonder if he left me my money. Uh-huh. That's it. On top of the
    fridge.

(*Amazingly, an hour or so afterward she has managed to somewhat camouflage the chaos and has the room looking not altogether shipshape but reasonably respectable. With a pencil, she scribbles a note and props it against the bureau mirror: "Dear Mr. Trask yr. wive want you fone her at her sistar place sinsirly Mary Sanchez." Then she sighs and perches on the edge of the bed and from her satchel takes out a small tin box containing an assortment of roaches; selecting one, she fits it into a roach-holder and lights up, dragging deeply, holding the smoke down in her lungs and closing her eyes. She offers me a toke.*)

TC: Thanks. It's too early.
MARY: It's never too early. Anyway, you ought to try this stuff. *Mucho
    cojones.* I get it from a customer, a real fine Catholic lady; she's
    married to a fellow from Peru. His family sends it to them. Sends it
    right through the mail. I never use it so's to get high. Just enough
    to lift the uglies a little. That heaviness. (*She sucks on the roach
    until it all but burns her lips*) Andrew Trask. Poor scared devil. He

could end up like Pedro. Dead on a park bench, nobody caring. Not that I didn't care none for that man. Lately, I find myself remembering the good times with Pedro, and I guess that's what happens to most people if ever they've once loved somebody and lose them; the bad slips away, and you linger on the nice things about them, what made you like them in the first place. Pedro, the young man I fell in love with, he was a beautiful dancer, oh he could tango, oh he could rumba, he taught me to dance and danced me off my feet. We were regulars at the old Savoy Ballroom. He was clean, neat—even when the drink got to him his fingernails were always trimmed and polished. And he could cook up a storm. That's how he made a living, as a short-order cook. I said he never did anything good for the children; well, he fixed their lunch-boxes to take to school. All kinds of sandwiches wrapped in wax paper. Ham, peanut butter and jelly, egg salad, tuna fish, and fruit, apples, bananas, pears, and a thermos filled with warm milk mixed with honey. It hurts now to think of him there in the park, and how I didn't cry when the police came to tell me about it; how I never did cry. I ought to have. I owed him that. I owed him a sock in the jaw, too.

I'm going to leave the lights on for Mr. Trask. No sense letting him come home to a dark room.

(*When we emerged from the brownstone the rain had stopped, but the sky was sloppy and a wind had risen that whipped trash along the gutters and caused passers-by to clutch their hats. Our destination was four blocks away, a modest but modern apartment house with a uniformed doorman, the address of Miss Edith Shaw, a young woman in her mid-twenties who was on the editorial staff of a magazine. "Some kind of news magazine. She must have a thousand books. But she doesn't look like no bookworm. She's a very healthy kind of girl, and she has lots of boyfriends. Too many —just can't seem to stay very long with one fellow. We got to be close because . . . Well, one time I came to her place and she was sick as a cat. She'd come from having a baby murdered. Normally I don't hold with that; it's against my beliefs. And I said why didn't you marry this man? The truth was, she didn't know who to marry; she didn't know who the dad was. And anyway, the last thing she wanted was a husband or a baby."*)

MARY (*surveying the scene from the opened front door of Miss Shaw's two-room apartment*): Nothing much to do here. A little dusting. She takes good care of it herself. Look at all those books. Ceiling to floor, nothing but library.

(*Except for the burdened bookshelves, the apartment was attractively spare, Scandinavianly white and gleaming. There was one antique: an old roll-top desk with a typewriter on it; a sheet of paper was rolled into the machine; and I glanced at what was written on it:*

"Zsa Zsa Gabor is
305 years old
I know
Because I counted
Her Rings"

And triple-spaced below that, was typed:

"Sylvia Plath, I hate you
And your damn daddy.
I'm glad, do you hear,
Glad you stuck your head
In a gas-hot oven!"

TC: Is Miss Shaw a poet?
MARY: She's always writing something. I don't know what it is. Stuff I see, sounds like she's on dope to me. Come here, I want to show you something.

(*She leads me into the bathroom, a surprisingly large and sparkling chamber. She opens a cabinet door and points at an object on a shelf: a pink plastic vibrator molded in the shape of an average-sized penis.*)

Know what that is?
TC: Don't you?
MARY: I'm the one asking.
TC: It's a dildo vibrator.
MARY: I know what a vibrator is. But I never saw one like that. It says "Made in Japan."
TC: Ah, well. The Oriental mind.
MARY: Heathens. She's sure got some lovely perfumes. If you like perfume. Me, I only put a little vanilla behind my ears.

(*Now Mary began to work, mopping the waxed carpetless floors, flicking the bookshelves with a feather duster; and while she worked she kept her roach-box open and her roach-holder filled. I don't know how much "heaviness" she had to lift, but the aroma alone was lofting me.*)

MARY: You sure you don't want to try a couple of tokes? You're missing
    something.
TC: You twisted my arm.

(*Man and boy, I've dragged some powerful grass, never enough to have
acquired a habit, but enough to judge quality and know the difference
between ordinary Mexican weed and luxurious contraband like Thai-sticks
and the supreme Maui-Wowee. But after smoking the whole of one of
Mary's roaches, and while halfway through another, I felt as though seized
by a delicious demon, embraced by a mad marvelous merriment: the
demon tickled my toes, scratched my itchy head, kissed me hotly with his
red sugary lips, shoved his fiery tongue down my throat. Everything sparkled; my eyes were like zoom lenses; I could read the titles of books on the
highest shelves:* The Neurotic Personality of Our Time *by Karen Horney;*
Eimi *by e.e. cummings;* Four Quartets; The Collected Poems of Robert
Frost.)

TC: I despise Robert Frost. He was an evil, selfish bastard.
MARY: Now, if we're going to curse—
TC: Him with his halo of shaggy hair. An egomaniacal double-crossing
    sadist. He wrecked his whole family. Some of them. Mary, have
    you ever discussed this with your confessor?
MARY: Father McHale? Discussed what?
TC: The precious nectar we're so divinely devouring, my adorable chick-
    adee. Have you informed Father McHale of this delectable enter-
    prise?
MARY: What he don't know won't hurt him. Here, have a Life Saver.
    Peppermint. It makes that stuff taste better.

(*Odd, she didn't seem high, not a bit. I'd just passed Venus, and Jupiter,
jolly old Jupiter, beckoned beyond in the lilac star-dazzled planetary distance. Mary marched over to the telephone and dialed a number; she let
it ring a long while before hanging up.*)

MARY: Not home. That's one thing to be grateful for. Mr. and Mrs.
    Berkowitz. If they'd been home, I couldn't have took you over
    there. On account of they're these real stuffy Jewish people. And
    you know how stuffy *they* are!

TC: Jewish people? Gosh, yes. Very stuffy. They all ought to be in the Museum of Natural History. All of them.

MARY: I've been thinking about giving Mrs. Berkowitz notice. The trouble is, Mr. Berkowitz, he was in garments, he's retired, and the two of them are always home. Underfoot. Unless they drive up to Greenwich, where they got some property. That's where they must have gone today. Another reason I'd like to quit them. They've got an old parrot—makes a mess everywhere. And stupid! All that dumb parrot can say is two things: "Holy cow!" and "*Oy vey!*" Every time you walk in the house it starts shouting "*Oy vey!*" Gets on my nerves something terrible. How about it? Let's toke another roach and blow this joint.

(*The rain had returned and the wind increased, a mixture that made the air look like a shattering mirror. The Berkowitzes lived on Park Avenue in the upper Eighties, and I suggested we take a taxi, but Mary said no, what kind of sissy was I, we can walk it, so I realized that despite appearances, she, too, was traveling stellar paths. We walked along slowly, as though it were a warm tranquil day with turquoise skies, and the hard slippery streets ribbons of pearl-colored Caribbean beach. Park Avenue is not my favorite boulevard; it is rich with lack of charm; if Mrs. Lasker were to plant it with tulips all the way from Grand Central to Spanish Harlem, it would be of no avail. Still, there are certain buildings that prompt memories. We passed a building where Willa Cather, the American woman writer I've most admired, lived the last years of her life with her companion, Edith Lewis; I often sat in front of their fireplace and drank Bristol Cream and observed the firelight enflame the pale prairie-blue of Miss Cather's serene genius-eyes. At Eighty-fourth Street I recognized an apartment house where I had once attended a small black-tie dinner given by Senator and Mrs. John F. Kennedy, then so young and insouciant. But despite the agreeable efforts of our hosts, the evening was not as enlightening as I had anticipated, because after the ladies had been dismissed and the men left in the dining room to savor their cordials and Havana cigars, one of the guests, a rather slope-chinned dressmaker named Oleg Cassini, overwhelmed the conversation with a travelogue account of Las Vegas and the myriad showgirls he'd recently auditioned there: their measurements, erotic accomplishments, financial requirements—a recital that hypnotized its auditors, none of whom was more chucklingly attentive than the future President.*

When we reach Eighty-seventh Street, I point out a window on the fourth floor at 1060 Park Avenue, and inform Mary: "My mother lived there. That was her bedroom. She was beautiful and very intelligent, but she didn't want to live. She had many reasons—at least she thought she did. But in the end it was just her husband, my stepfather. He was a self-made man, fairly successful—she worshipped him, and he really was a nice guy, but he gambled, got into trouble and embezzled a lot of money, and lost his business and was headed for Sing Sing."

Mary shakes her head: "Just like my boy. Same as him."

We're both standing staring at the window, the downpour drenching us. "So one night she got all dressed up and gave a dinner party; everybody said she looked lovely. But after the party, before she went to bed, she took thirty Seconals and she never woke up."

Mary is angry; she strides rapidly away through the rain: "She had no right to do that. I don't hold with that. It's against my beliefs.")

SQUAWKING PARROT: Holy cow!
MARY: Hear that? What did I tell you?
PARROT: *Oy vey! Oy vey!*

(The parrot, a surrealist collage of green and yellow and orange moulting feathers, is ensconced on a mahogany perch in the relentlessly formal parlor of Mr. and Mrs. Berkowitz, a room suggesting that it had been entirely made of mahogany: the parquet floors, the wall paneling, and the furniture, all of it costly reproductions of grandiose period-piece furniture —though God knows what period, perhaps early Grand Concourse. Straight-back chairs; settees that would have tested the endurance of a posture professor. Mulberry velvet draperies swathed the windows, which were incongruously covered with mustard-brown venetian blinds. Above a carved mahogany mantelpiece a mahogany-framed portrait of a jowly, sallow-skinned Mr. Berkowitz depicted him as a country squire outfitted for a fox hunt: scarlet coat, silk cravat, a bugle tucked under one arm, a riding crop under the other. I don't know what the remainder of this rambling abode looked like, for I never saw any of it except the kitchen.)

MARY: What's so funny? What you laughing at?
TC: Nothing. It's just this Peruvian tobacco, my cherub. I take it Mr.
    Berkowitz is an equestrian?
PARROT: *Oy vey! Oy vey!*
MARY: Shut up! Before I wring your damn neck.
TC: Now, if we're going to curse . . . *(Mary mumbles; crosses herself)*
    Does the critter have a name?
MARY: Uh-huh. Try and guess.

TC: Polly.

MARY (*truly surprised*): How'd you know that?

TC: So she's a female.

MARY: That's a girl's name, so she must be a girl. Whatever she is, she's a bitch. Just look at all that crap on the floor. All for me to clean it up.

TC: Language, language.

POLLY: Holy cow!

MARY: My nerves. Maybe we better have a little lift. (*Out comes the tin box, the roaches, the roach-holder, matches*) And let's see what we can locate in the kitchen. I'm feeling real munchie.

(*The interior of the Berkowitz refrigerator is a glutton's fantasy, a cornucopia of fattening goodies. Small wonder the master of the house has such jowls. "Oh yes," confirms Mary, "they're both hogs. Her stomach. She looks like she's about to drop the Dionne quintuplets. And all his suits are tailor-made: nothing store-bought could fit him. Hmm, yummy, I sure do feel munchie. Those coconut cupcakes look desirable. And that mocha cake, I wouldn't mind a hunk of that. We could dump some ice cream on it." Huge soup bowls are found, and Mary masses them with cupcakes and mocha cake and fist-sized scoops of pistachio ice cream. We return to the parlor with this banquet and fall upon it like abused orphans. There's nothing like grass to grow an appetite. After finishing off the first helping, and fueling ourselves with more roaches, Mary refills the bowls with even heftier portions.*)

MARY: How you feel?

TC: I feel good.

MARY: How good?

TC: Real good.

MARY: Tell me exactly how you feel.

TC: I'm in Australia.

MARY: Ever been to Austria?

TC: Not Austria. Australia. No, but that's where I am now. And everybody always said what a dull place it is. Shows what they know! Greatest surfing in the world. I'm out in the ocean on a surfboard riding a wave high as a, as a—

MARY: High as you. Ha-ha.

TC: It's made of melting emeralds. The wave. The sun is hot on my back, and the spray is salting my face, and there are hungry sharks all around me. *Blue Water, White Death.* Wasn't that a terrific movie?

Hungry white man-eaters everywhere, but they don't worry me—
frankly, I don't give a fuck . . .

MARY (*eyes wide with fear*): Watch for the sharks! They got killer teeth.
You'll be crippled for life. You'll be begging on street corners.

TC: Music!

MARY: Music! That's the ticket.

(*She weaves like a groggy wrestler toward a gargoyle object that had heretofore happily escaped my attention: a mahogany console combining television, phonograph, and a radio. She fiddles with the radio until she finds
a station booming music with a Latin beat.*

*Her hips maneuver, her fingers snap, she is elegant yet smoothly
abandoned, as if recalling a sensuous youthful night, and dancing with a
phantom partner some remembered choreography. And it is magic, how
her now-ageless body responds to the drums and guitars, contours itself to
the subtlest rhythm: she is in a trance, the state of grace saints supposedly
achieve when experiencing visions. And I am hearing the music, too; it is
speeding through me like amphetamine—each note ringing with the separate clarity of cathedral chimings on a silent winter Sunday. I move
toward her, and into her arms, and we match each other step for step,
laughing, undulating, and even when the music is interrupted by an
announcer speaking Spanish as rapid as the rattle of castanets, we continue dancing, for the guitars are locked in our heads now, as we are locked
in our laughter, our embrace: louder and louder, so loud that we are
unaware of a key clicking, a door opening and shutting. But the parrot
hears it.*)

POLLY: Holy cow!

WOMAN'S VOICE: What is this? What's happening here?

POLLY: *Oy vey! Oy vey!*

MARY: Why, hello there, Mrs. Berkowitz. Mr. Berkowitz. How ya doin'?

(*And there they are, hovering in view like the Mickey and Minnie Mouse
balloons in a Macy's Thanksgiving Day parade. Not that there's anything
mousey about this twosome. Their infuriated eyes, hers hot behind harle-
quin spectacles with sequined frames, absorb the scene: our naughty ice-
cream mustaches, the pungent roach smoke polluting the premises. Mr.
Berkowitz stalks over and stops the radio.*)

MRS. BERKOWITZ: Who is this man?

MARY: I din't think you was home.

MRS. BERKOWITZ: Obviously. I asked you: Who is this man?

MARY: He's just a friend of mine. Helping me out. I got so much work today.

MR. BERKOWITZ: You're drunk, woman.

MARY (*deceptively sweet*): How's that you say?

MRS. BERKOWITZ: He said you're drunk. I'm shocked. Truly.

MARY: Since we're speaking truly, what I have truly to say to you is: today is my last day of playing nigger around here—I'm giving you notice.

MRS. BERKOWITZ: You are giving *me* notice?

MR. BERKOWITZ: Get out of here! Before we call the police.

(*Without ado, we gather our belongings. Mary waves at the parrot: "So long, Polly. You're okay. You're good girl. I was only kidding." And at the front door, where her former employers have sternly stationed themselves, she announces: "Just for the record, I've never touched a drop in my life."*

Downstairs, the rain is still going. We trudge along Park Avenue, then cut across to Lexington.)

MARY: Didn't I tell you they were stuffy?

TC: Belong in a museum.

(*But most of our buoyancy has departed; the power of the Peruvian foliage recedes, a letdown has set in, my surfboard is sinking, and any sharks sighted now would scare the piss out of me.*)

MARY: I still got Mrs. Kronkite to do. But she's nice; she'll forgive me if I don't come till tomorrow. Maybe I'll head on home.

TC: Let me catch you a cab.

MARY: I hate to give them my business. Those taxi people don't like coloreds. Even when they're colored themselves. No, I can get the subway down here at Lex and Eighty-sixth.

(*Mary lives in a rent-controlled apartment near Yankee Stadium; she says it was cramped when she had a family living with her, but now that she's by herself, it seems immense and dangerous: "I've got three locks on every door, and all the windows are nailed down. I'd buy me a police dog if it didn't mean leaving him by himself so much. I know what it is to be alone, and I wouldn't wish it on a dog."*)

TC: Please, Mary, let me treat you to a taxi.

MARY: The subway's a lot quicker. But there's someplace I want to stop. It's just down here a ways.

(*The place is a narrow church pinched between broad buildings on a side street. Inside, there are two brief rows of pews, and a small altar with a plaster figure of a crucified Jesus suspended above it. An odor of incense and candle wax dominates the gloom. At the altar a woman is lighting a candle, its light fluttering like the sleep of a fitful spirit; otherwise, we are the only supplicants present. We kneel together in the last pew, and from the satchel Mary produces a pair of rosary beads—"I always carry a couple extra"—one for herself, the other for me, though I don't know quite how to handle it, never having used one before. Mary's lips move whisperingly.*)

MARY: Dear Lord, in your mercy. Please, Lord, help Mr. Trask to stop boozing and get his job back. Please, Lord, don't leave Miss Shaw a bookworm and an old maid; she ought to bring your children into this world. And, Lord, I beg you to remember my sons and daughter and my grandchildren, each and every one. And please don't let Mr. Smith's family send him to that retirement home; he don't want to go, he cries all the time . . .

(*Her list of names is more numerous than the beads on her rosary, and her requests in their behalf have the earnest shine of the altar's candle-flame. She pauses to glance at me.*)

MARY: Are you praying?
TC: Yes.
MARY: I can't hear you.
TC: I'm praying for you, Mary. I want you to live forever.
MARY: Don't pray for me. I'm already saved. (*She takes my hand and holds it*) Pray for your mother. Pray for all those souls lost out there in the dark. Pedro. Pedro.

Terry Southern

*

I AM MIKE HAMMER

One spring evening ten years or so ago I found myself sharing a large table, outside the Café Flore, with several people who had just attended the premiere of Serge Lifar's ballet, *Lucifer*. One of the persons at the table was Jean-Paul Sartre, and another was a young American cutie-pie, who was getting far more attention than she deserved. The darling girl, emboldened perhaps no less by Pernod than by the saucy pertness of her cashmered bosom—which not even the great philosopher could have failed to discern—had the audacity to ask: "Monsieur Sartre, have *you* ever considered writing a ballet?" Out of politeness, no doubt, he replied with a smile and a simple "*Non.*" And that might well have been that—except for a fantasy which appealed to me later, in the secrecy of my private night. I think it was the very blandness of his reply that prompted it; in any case, I imagined that Sartre had, in fact, gone mad, had written a ballet—and then, despite his lack of formal training, his unwieldy girth, and the wise counsel of friends, he had *insisted* on danc-ing the leading role himself. The idea of Sartre—heavy glasses, as stout as a giant turnip-man in close-fitting ballet garb—gravely dancing to rather common schmaltzy music, or whirling dervishlike to some kind of weird electronics, was irresistible. I pursued this fantasy down many avenues: First, the incredible frown of consternation on the faces of those receiving invitations to the premiere of this ballet "To be Danced by the Author Himself!" Then in the dress circle, his distinguished col-leagues from the great universities, muttering, "*Mais c'est un vrai scan-dale!*" And finally the intermission; what would they say—Camus, Cocteau, Malraux—something like "*Il ne danse pas mal, Jean-Paul . . .*"? Fantastic. And yet the cold reality is that Sartre *was*, in fact, in a position to do precisely that. No impresario in Paris would have refused;

had they even hesitated he could have hired the theatre and staged the thing himself to an S.R.O. house. All that was necessary for him to have done this was that he go slightly off his rocker—but, of course, this never occurred.

Well, this old fantasy—which over the years an increasing number of skeptics and unimaginative sorts had pooh-poohed as being "far-fetched"—received a tremendous boost in vividness the other day when I learned that Mickey Spillane had decided that he himself would play the role of Mike Hammer in the film version of his novel, *The Girl Hunters.*

Mickey Spillane's literary status has never been fully defined in America. Hard-core quality-Lit. buffs, however, will recall how he smashed into international prominence, in 1947, by concluding his first novel, *I, The Jury*, in a manner which made Malaparte, Céline and other high priests of the *roman noir* look like a bunch of pansies:

> The roar of the .45 shook the room, Charlotte staggered back a step. Her eyes were a symphony of incredulity, an unbelieving witness to truth. Slowly, she looked down at the ugly swelling in her naked belly where the bullet went in. A thin trickle of blood welled out. . . . Her eyes had pain in them now, the pain preceding death. Pain and unbelief.
> How could you? she gasped.
> I only had a moment before talking to a corpse, but I got it in.
> It was easy, I said.

This confused girl, to make matters even more delightfully *noir*, was a psychiatrist.

Since then Spillane has written eight additional novels which in turn have compiled as yummy a set of statistics as have yet been garnered in the belles-lettres game. They have sold more than seventy-four million copies. In terms of foreign translations, this body of work is now seeded fifth in world literature, topped only by Lenin, Tolstoy, Gorki, and Jules Verne. He is the only contemporary whose work figures among the best sellers of all time. According to Alice Payne Hackett's informative volume, *Sixty Years of Best Sellers*, of the ten best-selling fiction titles in the history of writing, *seven* are by Mickey Spillane (and it only remains to be added, in all fairness, that when Miss Hackett's book was published, in 1956, Mr. Spillane had then *written* only seven).

The denouement of a Spillane story is always softly understated, but not so the middle distance. Here's an engaging high point from *The Girl Hunters:*

My hand smashed into bone and flesh and with the meaty impact I could smell the blood and hear the gagging intake of his breath. He grabbed, his arms like great claws. He just held on and I knew if I couldn't break him loose he could kill me. He figured I'd start the knee coming up and turned to block it with a half-turn. But I did something worse, I grabbed him with my hands, squeezed and twisted and his scream was like a woman's, so high-pitched as almost to be noiseless, and in his frenzy of pain he shoved me so violently I lost that fanatical hold of what manhood I had left him, and with some blind hate driving him he came at me as I stumbled over something and fell on me like a wild beast, his teeth tearing at me, his hands searching and ripping, and I felt the shock of incredible pain and ribs break under his pounding and I couldn't get him off no matter what I did, and he was holding me down and butting me with his head while he kept up that whistlelike screaming. . . .

"Will you be able to re-create the exact mechanics of that fight scene in the movie?" I asked the Mick when I visited him on the set.

"Well, some of that scene will simply have to be *indicated*," he replied with simple candor.

The Girl Hunters, like *I, The Jury*, is a story of personal vendetta and eye-for-eye (or maybe even two-for-one) justice. Due to a miscalculation, which Mike himself feels responsible for, his beautiful assistant Velda (more friend than employee) has been killed, or so it is presumed, and Mike hits the road with good old-fashioned plasma-and-pulp vengeance in mind.

The film is being made on the MGM lot at Elstree Studios just outside London. It's a Robert Fellows wide-screen production, directed by Roy Rowland, and features, besides the author, Lloyd Nolan, Shirley Eaton and Scott Peters. One of the more unusual aspects of the book is that (like *Fail-Safe*) it also includes a real-life person as one of the major characters—in this case none other than Hy Gardner.

"I think it's a nice touch," said Mickey. "And Hy is going to play himself in the movie."

• • •

Spillane's literary conceptions have received strong endorsement from unexpectedly intellectual quarters—most notably from grand Ayn Rand, author of *Atlas Shrugged*, and the founder of the objectivist philosophy.

"Spillane," she says, "is the only writer today whose hero is a white knight and whose enemies represent evil." He is alone, she contends, in having accepted the responsibility of taking a forthright moral position. Mickey himself speaks less abstractly about it. "I've been in the business for twenty-five years. I moved out of pulps because there was more money in the novel field."

For someone like myself, with a Café Flore and White Horse Tavern orientation—where the whole point was not to write a book but to talk one—speaking with Spillane in regard to the Lit. Game was refreshment itself.

"Mick," I said, "the issue of the magazine I'm preparing this for is entirely devoted—except for ads and the like, natch—to the American Literary Scene."

After a terrific guffaw, and a slow, rather deliberate and somehow menacing cracking of knuckles, the Mick said, "Yeah, I've seen those articles—they never mention me; all they talk about are the Losers."

"The Losers?"

"The guys who didn't make it—the guys nobody ever heard of."

"Why would they talk about them?"

"Because they can be condescending about the Losers. You know, they can afford to say something *nice* about them. You see, these articles are usually written *by* Losers—frustrated writers. And these writers resent success. So naturally they never have anything good to say about the Winners."

"Is it hard to be a Winner?"

"No, anybody can be a Winner—all you have to do is make sure you're not a Loser."

"What brought about your decision to portray Mike Hammer yourself?"

"Well, everyone was making a mess of it; they were all missing the point. You see, Mike is a genuinely dedicated person. He's also a *real* person—I mean he's not supposed to be like an actor. You know, a lot of people *believe* in Mike Hammer—they write letters to him, asking his advice about certain things, giving him tips and so on. And it's even stronger than that. For example, I was autographing my last book in a big bookstore down in Puerto Rico, and they ran out of the Spanish edition. So these people started buying the *English* edition—they couldn't *read* it in English, you understand, but they wanted to have the new one with them anyway. It seemed to make them feel more secure to have it with them, even though they couldn't read it."

"I suppose you have certain theories now about acting. What do you think of The Method?"

"Pretending to be a *tree* and so on? No, that doesn't interest me. I have no interest in acting as such. Besides, this is not really an *acting* job."

Before I could get a clarification of this last remark, he was called back to the set, and I took the opportunity to corner the luscious Miss Eaton. She was lolling on the sidelines in a black bikini, a veritable darling, adding a provocative touch of vermilion to her toenails.

"What do perfect young darlings like yourself find attractive about a man like Hammer, if I may ask?"

I detected a slight and exciting flush of ambivalence as she lowered her smoldering gaze.

"Well," she said softly, "if you like tigers . . ." then confided with a disquieting twinkle, "and what girl doesn't—at least in her dark wild dreams? Hmm?"

"Are you kidding?" I asked, but her half-closed eyes and cryptic smile told me no more.

Miss Eaton is a professional and accomplished performer, as are, of course, Lloyd Nolan and the rest of the cast (except perhaps Hy Gardner). Could Mickey hold his own in this crowd? I sought out Mr. Robert Fellows, amiable producer of the film and seasoned vet of Hollywood flicker productions since the heyday of de Mille.

"Now see here," I said, "Spillane admits to no training as an actor —how will he cope?"

Mr. Fellows handed me a British press release, headed *Spillane an Actor?* which quoted Mickey as saying among other things: "I will tell you this much, I *am* Mike Hammer!"

"He *is* Mike Hammer? Is he serious?"

"Mike Hammer is Mickey's alter ego," Mr. Fellows explained quietly, "as you'll find out quickly enough if you ever get drunk with him. Not that I would advise that," he added with an ominous chuckle.

"You mean he starts kicking people's teeth out?"

"No, no," said Mr. Fellows with a frown of distaste, ". . . at least not unduly."

Actually Mickey Spillane seems to be a rather warm and likable person—relaxed, unselfish, with a genuine naturalness that impresses everyone who meets him. Like his manner, his opinions are strong and somewhat direct.

"Thomas Wolfe was a lousy writer," he said. "He didn't know what he was doing."

"How about Hemingway?"

"I'll tell you something about Hemingway—he knocked me out of *Life* magazine once. I was set for a spread in *Life* and Hemingway had those plane crashes and it knocked me out of the issue."

"Well, what about his work?"

"No, his work was too morbid for me."

"How about Cain, Chandler, and Dashiell Hammett?"

"Well, Chandler was all right except that he could never come to a conclusion. But these guys are all in the past. You see, in this business you've got to progress, you've got to keep ahead—or else you just stay behind, being imitated."

"Do you like anyone's work in particular?"

"Most writers don't seem to know what they're doing—they can't come to a conclusion. But I do like Fredric Brown and John D. Macdonald; they're good—they have a point of view and they follow it."

Mickey Spillane's books are now required reading in the writing courses of six different universities.

"How do you feel about literary criticism of your books?"

"The public is the only critic. And the only *literature* is what the public reads. The first printing of my last book was more than two million copies—that's the kind of opinion that interests me."

Then the Mick was called to the set again, back to the turbulent embrace of Miss Eaton. So I decided to walk over and see for myself how things were going. There beneath lights and camera lay a lavish patio pool, framed in the swank courtyard of a Westport-type mansion. The blonde Miss Eaton was reclining on a chaise lounge—black bikini, vermilion nails—a perfect vibrant darling as she stretched lithely forward to lay a persuasive hand on Mickey's sleeve.

"I think I could like you, Mike . . ." she said in a voice both husky and tremulous, "quite a lot."

Mickey shook his head, unsmiling.

"I'm trouble, baby," he said earnestly.

And I must say the Mick looked pretty good in there. Exactly the way Tiger Mike would have handled it, I thought.

The filming of *The Girl Hunters* represents the first time, of course, that a protagonist has been portrayed by its author on the silver screen. If Spillane's undertaking is a successful one, and it appears quite possible, will it not definitely signal a new trend in creative fiction? Many writers are, in fact, already regarding this as a unique and long-awaited opportunity for having their way not merely with the run-of-the-mill starlets but with their *ideal woman*, the girl of their dreams, the marvelous heroine of their own creation. Does it not follow that our literary chaps, with their voraciously inquiring minds, their insatiate quest to get to the bottom of things, will start writing in outlandishly heroic sex scenes, with an eye to ultimate personal realization? It must also be remembered that your writer is notoriously more virile, more sexually interesting, and unscrupulous than is your effete or coldly professional actor. Also generally better-looking. This is known fact. I say we may anticipate some almost incredible developments on the shooting set. An irate and astonished director shouting, "Cut! Cut!" is apt to have precious little effect on chaps like Mailer and Kerouac once they are swinging.

But what about the broader implications? Is it not just remotely possible that here we have stumbled onto the key to obtaining certain highly sought and hitherto unavailable film rights—Holden Caulfield's, for example? Has anyone sounded J.D. about this? But, of course, the real coup will be when some enterprising producer signs up grand old Henry Miller—providing, natch, that Hank is given free rein, and the books are done *right*, without your usual cinematic compromise.

Thomas Berger

*

CHEF REINHART

EXCERPT FROM *Reinhart's Women*

[Carl Reinhart, unemployed for years, currently acting as his daughter's housekeeper and cook, auditions as a TV chef.—ED.]

At the television studio everyone encountered by Reinhart was young, slender, dressed in jeans, and quick-moving. They were also, all of them, unfailingly civil. When he realized that he was actually going to appear on TV that morning, he had dosed his coffee with brandy, but he remained anxious. The studio people needed him two hours before he was scheduled to face the cameras, which meant he had had to arise at four-thirty, after getting almost no sleep.

• • •

At the studio he was seated in a corridor through which many people walked briskly. Finally one of them, a young woman of characterless brunette good looks, stopped and introduced herself as Jane.

She consulted a piece of paper affixed to a clipboard. "You're the chef, O.K.? We'll get you into make-up in a few minutes, O.K.? You want to check your pots 'n' pans 'n' stuff?"

He followed her, around little clusters of people and lights and cameras and cables, onto what was obviously a corner of the set.

"You've got a whole kitchen here." It looked like a permanent installation and had everything one would need, within two walls without a ceiling.

"We do a cooking segment of some kind every day," said Jane. "Sometimes we just dye Easter eggs or make Play-Doh from flour and salt."

Reinhart opened the copper-colored refrigerator. Just inside, on gleaming chromium-wire shelves, was a large glass bowl filled with eggs and a generous chunk of butter on a plate of glass. A glass canister bore a solid white label, imprinted in large black letters: GRATED CHEESE.

"Everything there?" asked Jane. He had ordered these omelet-making materials the day before.

"Except salt and pepper," said Reinhart. "I gather they'll be over here." He turned to the free-standing counter that would face the camera. He had not seen much of this show, but he had watched other programs on which cooking was done. Ah, yes: electric burners were built into the top of the counter, and a ceramic jug stood nearby, holding spatulas, big forks, etc., and salt and pepper were alongside in large white shakers, again labeled in black.

"Oh, and the skillet. I was going to bring mine, which is seasoned, but my boss insisted on one that her company is apparently thinking of putting on the market, in a new line of cooking utensils."

"Grace Greenwood," said Jane. "Yeah, she sent over some special stuff." She poked amongst the open shelves below the counter-top, on the left of the burners. "Take a look. It should all be here."

Reinhart bent and found a skillet, a lightweight stainless-steel job with a thin wash of copper on the outside bottom. "This is it?" He winced. "I'm going to have to be very careful to keep from burning the omelet. This is trash."

Jane put one finger on the nosepiece of her glasses—which until now Reinhart had not noticed. "If it does burn, then just don't turn it over on camera, O.K.?" She sniffed. "Don't panic: this is the magic of video, remember."

Some young man shouted her name, and she went away. Reinhart looked about: everything seemed a good deal smaller than anything he had ever seen on the screen. For some reason he thought he might have been more at ease had things been larger. He was suddenly jumping with nerves.

Jane returned and took him into a room where he sat in a kind of barber's chair and was made up by a deft, laconic young man. When the job was finished, he ducked into a booth in the men's room and drank some cognac from the half-pint in his pocket.

The well-known movie star Jack Buxton was urinating in one of the stalls as Reinhart emerged. Apparently they were to be fellow guests on the show.

Jane came from nowhere when Reinhart left the lavatory and led him back to a chair in the corridor.

"Sorry we don't have a real Green Room," she said.

"Wasn't that Jack Buxton I saw in the men's room?"

"He's plugging his show." Jane consulted her clipboard. "You go on the air at seven forty-seven, but we'll do a run-through in about five minutes from now, so you'll have your moves down pat. This is live, you know. We can't do retakes." She left the area.

And here came Jack Buxton. Reinhart seldom went to the movies nowadays, and he hadn't seen a performance of Buxton's in—God, could it be that long?

"Hi," said the actor, flopping his large, heavy body into the chair next to Reinhart's.

"Hi," said Reinhart. "This is quite a pleasure for me. I've always enjoyed your pictures."

Buxton's face, perhaps owing to its familiarity, seemed enormous. He grinned at Reinhart. "Thanks, pal, I needed that. Listen"—he dug into an inside pocket of his Glen-plaid jacket and withdrew a leather-covered notepad—"I'll send an autographed picture to your kids, if you give me the names and address."

"My kids are grown up," said Reinhart. Buxton's long lip drooped. It was true he looked a good deal older than when Reinhart had last seen him. "But I'd like one for myself." This lie failed to cheer up the actor by much, but he pretended to take the name and address.

Reinhart asked: "Are you in a new picture?"

Buxton inhaled. "I'm considering some scripts," said he. "But I'm in town here to do *Song of Norway*." He put his notebook away and adjusted his jacket. Like Reinhart he was wearing face make-up that made the skin look beige. The heavy pouches under his eyes and the deep lines flanking his mouth could be seen all too clearly at close range but probably would be diminished on their voyage through the camera.

"Oh," said Reinhart, "I'll have to see it." If memory served, the vehicle was a musical: he hadn't been aware that Buxton sang. The actor was best known for his war films.

"It'll be my pleasure," Buxton said, cheering up now, and he reached into his pocket and withdrew a pair of tickets. "These are for the show only. Dinner's separate, I'm afraid, but . . ."

Reinhart accepted the tickets with thanks. He joked: "I wouldn't expect you to pay for the food I ate before going to the show!"

Buxton frowned. "It's the dinner theater. That's what I meant. It's no comedown either. That's the latest thing. I don't mind it at all."

But clearly he felt humiliated at the thought of people digesting their steaks while he performed. For his own part Reinhart was only now remembering that he had never really liked Buxton as an actor—or at any rate, he had not found Buxton's roles sympathetic: there was always a resentful streak in the character, of whom one expected the worst, owing to the cocky, smart-ass personality he displayed at the outset. But then he came through courageously in the pinch, kept the plane aloft though badly wounded, or fell on the grenade, saving his comrades.

Buxton was still worrying. "I started out on the Broadway stage," said he. "I was trained for musical comedy, long before I went to Tinsel Town."

So they really said that. "I'll bet you're good," said Reinhart. "I look forward to the show."

Buxton leaned over. He had maintained his familiar widow's peak of yore, and the scalp looked genuine, but why a professional would have his hair dyed matte black, leaving sparkling white sideburns, was not self-evident.

"Say," he said, "you wouldn't know where a man could get a drink?" His breath smelled of mint Life Saver.

"Well, now . . ." Reinhart reached into his pocket for the half-pint of brandy.

But Buxton said: "Not here."

They got up and were heading for the men's room when Jane came along and carried Reinhart away.

"We'll do the omelet run-through," said she, and when they had left Buxton behind she said: "It's Has-Been City around here lots of mornings. Watch yourself with that one: he'll hit you up for a loan."

Reinhart felt he owed Buxton some loyalty, the actor having embodied the old-fashioned virtues until both he and they went out of fashion, to be replaced by nothing and nobody worth mentioning. "I always liked him in the movies."

"He was through before my time," said Jane in her brisk way.

Time was all. Twenty years earlier some Jane might have seen Buxton as a rung on her own climb to success.

They were in the kitchen now. Reinhart practiced the movements he would make on camera. Taking the eggs and butter from the refrigerator to the counter consumed too much of his allotted three minutes. On the other hand, as Jane pointed out, too much premeditation would diminish the dramatic effect. The eggs, for example, should remain whole, to be broken on camera.

"Debbie will ad lib something about making the perfect omelet," said Jane. "O.K., that's your cue to answer. You say, 'Well, Debbie, first you break the eggs.' Don't, for God's sake, tell the old Hungarian-omelet joke—you know, 'First you steal two eggs'—we'll get too much bad mail. Everybody takes everything personally."

Debbie was the "co-host" of the program, with a man named Shep Cunningham. Meeting her backstage apparently violated some show-biz rule, and having rarely tuned in to Channel Five at this hour, Reinhart had little sense of the woman. Cunningham, however, had formerly been anchorman on the *Six O'Clock News*: his amiable, insensitive face above a wide-bladed tie and even wider lapels was remembered. But Reinhart was to have no direct connection with him whatever this morning.

"For all the woman's movement," said Jane, "anything in the kitchen this time of day is always played to the ladies." She looked up at one of the clocks that were mounted overhead at frequent intervals throughout the studio. Monitor TV sets were everywhere, as well. Someone was speaking through a public-address system: it was like the voice of God, and hence quite startling when it uttered foul language.

Jane said: "You'd better put on the chef's hat and apron."

Reinhart was getting into the spirit of the place. "Oh, God," he said, with real despair, "I forgot to bring them!"

Jane shook her head. "Your office sent them over." She led Reinhart to a little dressing room, where he found the cook's costume and donned it. The *toque* was pristine, but the apron was imprinted, over the region of the heart, with the logo of Grace Greenwood's firm: the name EPICON printed in the form of a croissant. This was something new.

Jane came along just as he emerged: she apparently had a sixth sense about these matters, for he was certain she had not been lingering there. Again she took him to the chairs in the corridor. Buxton was missing.

Jane said: "O.K., it's just waiting now. You can watch the monitor." She pointed to one high on the wall across from him. "I'll have somebody bring you coffee, O.K?"

A young man brought the coffee. As discreetly as he could, Reinhart dosed it with brandy. He had had the sense to buy expensive cognac: cheaper stuff was hardly drinkable in the best of times, but with morning coffee it would erode the stomach.

The monitor was showing a rerun of an ancient situation comedy, in which the adult male characters all wore crew cuts and suits a size too small, and all the children were well behaved and everybody did absurd but decent things. The sound was turned down to a murmur, and when the old show gave way to the seven o'clock news report, the volume came up to a level of command and the backstage noise died away.

International crises were routine this morning and given little more than noncommittal platitudes by the newscaster, an attractive fair-haired woman who used the intonations of a man. Locally a citizen had hand-cuffed himself to a light-pole at a downtown intersection as a protest, but against what had not yet been established, and opening the cuffs had thus far been beyond the powers of the police, who believed them of foreign origin.

Then, to the strains of a lilting musical theme, the *Eye Opener Show* came on. There was Shep Cunningham, between his desk and a photomural of the cityscape. Reinhart saw and heard him on the monitor screen, though presumably the man himself was just a partition away.

After a greeting and an observation on the rainy weather, Shep said: "But enough of this nonsense. Let's get to the beauty part. Here's Debbie Howland." The camera panned to his left, the curtains there parted, and out came a very winsome young woman with dark red hair and a jersey dress in lime green. She had an ebullient stride.

"Good morning, Shep," said Debbie, taking a seat next to her partner.

Shep winked at the camera and said: "Notice *I* don't get to walk across the set. Maybe if I lost ten pounds?" He grinned and shrugged and said: "Tell us who we'll meet today, Deb—or should that be 'whom'?"

Debbie smiled into the camera. "Shep, when you think of that classic quality known as Hollywood there are a few names that embody it in themselves alone: personalities like the Duke and the never-to-be-forgotten Bogie, and likewise with our guest this morning, Mister Holly-wood himself, Jack Buxton."

"Oh, wow," said Shep. "I want to ask him how he feels about our new pals the Chinese Communists—after fighting them so many times in Korean War films."

Reinhart suspected this reference was not authentic: in his own memories Buxton was always involved cinematically with World War II Germans. Indeed, if memory served, at least once he had played a Nazi.

Debbie went on: "And then our own Bobby Allen, Man in the Street, live out there in the pouring rain, will get an answer to today's question—hey, Shep, it's not about sex for a change—"

Shep groaned. "That's bad news."

"C'mon, now, this is important: 'Nuclear Power—Love It or Leave It?' "

"That *is* important," said Shep. "I was kidding."

"And then," Debbie said, "a French chef will show us how to make the perfect omelet in a minute. Sound good?"

"Mouth's watering already," said Shep. "My beautiful wife Judy's on a diet kick. I don't know, maybe I'm weird, but alfalfa sprouts on low-fat cottage cheese is not my idea of breakfast."

"Come *on*," said Debbie.

"Washed down with herb tea."

"Come *on*. You're kidding."

"Yes, I am," said Shep. "Incidentally, that's the same thing my wife said the last time I tried to get friendly with her."

Debbie rolled her eyes. "Oh-oh. I think it's time to hear from our first sponsor."

Under his apron Reinhart tipped the cognac bottle into the now empty Styrofoam cup. It was just as well that Buxton had not reappeared: the cook would not have been keen on sharing his supply of Dutch courage. He was himself no professional performer, and the nearer he got to going on camera, the more he realized how crazy he had been to let Grace do this to him. For God's sake, he wasn't even a professional chef.

Anxiety makes the time fly. Suddenly Jane came and led him onto the TV kitchen, holding a finger to her lips, so that he couldn't ask questions. But he looked up and saw a clock, and already it registered 7:35—and then without warning was at a quarter to eight and a voice was reading brief headlines from the news, and then, in an instant, a red light glowed from the darkness before him and Reinhart was on the air! Or so the sequence seemed.

Across the room, though actually very close to him, Shep Cunningham sat at the desk, and Debbie was just entering the kitchen. Reinhart had been deaf to the preliminary comments, and for a moment he had the terrified feeling that she might be coming to expose him as a fraud.

But she was smiling. "*Is* there a secret to omelet-making, Chef?"

Reinhart was amazed to hear a deep, mellow baritone voice emerge from his chest, as if he were lip-synching to a record made by someone else. "I suppose it could be called that, Debbie, but it's not the kind of secret that would interest a Russian spy."

Debbie giggled dutifully here. Luckily he overcame an impulse to build a large comic structure on the feeble piling of this witticism.

Quite soberly he said: "It's simply speed. The egg, once out of its shell—which has been called nature's perfect container incidentally— the naked egg is a very sensitive substance." He was aware that persons out there, off camera, were gesturing at him, and now Debbie stepped lightly on his foot. Of course, he must begin to break eggs!

Amazingly enough, everything he needed was at hand—and his hand was sure, in fact even defter than when he was alone in his own kitchen. In one movement he seemed simultaneously to have not only cracked two shells but opened them and drained them of their contents.

His flying fork whipped the yolks and whites into a uniform cream. Meanwhile the butter was melting in the skillet.

He was speaking authoritatively. "Speed's the secret, but we don't break the fifty-five-mile limit: we let the butter reach the frothing point. Meanwhile, we've got our filling ready. In this case it's Swiss cheese, for that simplest of dishes, a plain cheese omelet. But if it's properly made, there's nothing better, and nothing more elegant."

"Or more nutritious," said Debbie, nodding vigorously. "Gee, Chef, I can't wait."

"Just about time . . . We've got our cheese all grated already—and may I strongly recommend that you always grate your own cheese from a fresh piece: you can do that in a blender or a food processor, if it's too much work for you by hand. In this case the cheese is simple Swiss, but an even more delicious filling would be Swiss mixed with a bit of Parmesan." A moment earlier he had put two tablespoonfuls of the cheese from the canister into a shallow bowl. "Ah, there we go, just as the frothing begins to subside and before it turns color, the eggs go in quickly, quickly, and you keep stirring them, stir, stir, as they begin to thicken and curds appear . . . and *now* the cheese goes in, all at once!"

He emptied the contents of the bowl onto the mass of eggs, lifted the skillet from the burner, inserted the fork under the near edge of what was already an omelet, folded one half across the other, and slid the finished product onto a china plate.

"My goodness," said Debbie, "you don't even cook the top side? That must be my trouble, why my omelets are so dry. I always turn 'em over." She accepted the dish from him, and holding it high, raised a fork in her hand.

"Yes, the top becomes the inside of the omelet, and you want that moist," Reinhart said. "And you must remember that whenever uncooked eggs are around heat, something's going on. The hot omelet continues to cook for a while after you take it from the pan. That's happening right now, in fact, Debbie."

"Mmm, oh, golly," said she, making rapid eyeball movements as she tasted a modicum of egg from the end of her fork. "Hey. Say. Oh-oh, Shep, we've got a winner, and don't think you're getting any of it." Shep in fact was not behind his desk or anywhere in sight, so far as Reinhart could see. Debbie waved her fork and looked into the camera. "Well, now you know how to do it like an expert." She turned back to Reinhart. "Thank you, Chef—who appeared here courtesy of the Epicon Company. Back to you, Shep."

And just like that, Reinhart was off and Shep, back at the desk, was

on, and reading a list of local announcements: fund-raising charity dinners, Shriner circus, and the like. Debbie put down her plate and disappeared behind the set. For a moment Reinhart was desolated: not only
was his performance over, but functionaries kept hauling equipment past
him as if he did not exist and he stood in what seemed evening, for the
glare of the lights was gone.

But then the estimable Jane was at his elbow, steering him out.
When they reached the outer corridor she said: "You were dynamite,
Carl. Thanks a lot."

"Thank *you*, Jane. Do I go back to Make-up to get cleaned up?"

The light had gone from her eye with her thank-you. Already she
looked at him as if he were a stranger. "You can take it off with soap and
water." She pointed to the men's room and went away.

So much for show business. Reinhart shrugged and laughed for his
own benefit. He went through the door into the lavatory, which was
deserted. He had always assumed the performers had a private washroom
of some kind, but perhaps that was true only at the big network studios
in New York and Chicago. This place was clean enough, with dispenser
of liquid soap and a wall-hung paper-towel device. He began to run a
bowlful of warm water, but turned the faucet off abruptly.

He had heard a muffled sound: it had been barely audible, but there
was sufficient of it to raise the hair on the back of the neck, though he
could not have said precisely why: something instinctively dreadful.

He went back to the toilet booths. In one of them a human being
was obviously sagging in a terrible way: trousered knees could be seen on
the tiles below the door. Nothing else was visible. Again the gasping
sound.

The stall was locked from within, and furthermore it would open
the wrong way, given the interior obstruction. Reinhart climbed on the
seat of the toilet next door and leaned over the partition.

Jack Buxton was kneeling on the floor, clawing the bleak metal wall.
He had gone bald in back, just down from the crown of his head: a large
hairpiece had become dislodged in his writhings. Trousers and underpants were halfway down his thighs. He had apparently been sitting on
the can when the attack came.

His large torso filled the short space between the bowl and the door.
There would be no sense in Reinhart's trying to climb down to join him.

Reinhart ran out into the corridor and stopped a young man wearing outsized eyeglasses.

"Jack Buxton is dying in there!"

"Who?"

"There's a man in the toilet, having a heart attack, by the looks of it," said Reinhart. "Show me where to call an ambulance."

For an instant the young man resisted the thought, suggesting by his set of nose that he might respond sardonically, but then he took a chance and said: "There's a house doctor. I'll get him." He went rapidly down the corridor.

Reinhart was trying to decide whether to go back inside. Would his presence, though practically useless, be of some remote human comfort to Buxton? He decided to guard the door until the doctor arrived. Those who might come to use the facilities should be warned.

Of course the waiting seemed endless. Considerable traffic passed him, but none brought the physician. He kept reminding himself that in such a state a second's duration was tenfold, and avoided watching the clock. But when he could no longer forbear, he looked at the dial and saw that he had indeed waited a good ten minutes.

At that point Jane came walking rapidly by, studying her clipboard. She would not have seen him had he not called out.

She stared without expression, perhaps without recognition.

"Goddammit," he cried, "Jack Buxton is having a heart attack in there! Get a doctor!"

His alarm caused some visible consternation among the backstage studio folk. Persons passing in the vicinity looked at him in fear and repugnance, and a young man came running to scowl at Jane and say: "Get him *out* of here. You can *hear* that on the set." He resembled the guy who had gone, presumably, to fetch the doctor, but Reinhart couldn't be sure—else he'd have hit him in the mouth.

Jane was staring at Reinhart. "Buxton's supposed to go on at eight nineteen."

Reinhart put his face into hers. This time he spoke almost softly: "You fucking idiot: *I said he's dying in the toilet.* Go get help!"

Her immediate reaction was odd: a wide, even warm smile, and for a moment he considered putting his hands towards her throat, but then she whirled and moved smartly away, and now it was no time before a bushy-haired youth in jeans and denim jacket, but carrying the familiar black bag, arrived and identified himself as Dr. Tytell.

Buxton was still living when, with the help of a skinny, nimble member of the staff, the door was unlatched and the actor was examined, there on the tile floor. And he was yet alive, if barely, when the ambulance took him away.

Jane came along as Reinhart stood watching the attendants wheel the stretcher down the hall, and seeing her, he said: "Sorry I had to be nasty before. It was nothing personal."

She made no acknowledgment of the apology, but stared intently at him and said: "Carl, can you fill another ten minutes? All we've got is still only eggs and butter, but there must be lots of tricks you can show with those."

It was Reinhart's turn to smile nonsensically, but even as he did it he understood that, as with Jane on learning of Buxton's heart attack, it was momentary fear. And yet not half an hour ago he had wanted only to continue performing forever!

"Let me think," he said, doing anything but. The effect of the cognac had been dissipated by now.

Jane looked at him for an instant and then left quickly. He sat down on the chair in the corridor. The threat of another performance was warring with the reverberations of the experience with poor Buxton: perhaps it would be resolved by his own heart attack.

But suddenly before him, in all the radiance of her bright hair, dress, and make-up, was Debbie Howland.

She took the chair previously occupied by Buxton, leaned over to touch Reinhart's forearm, and said: "Carl, poor Jack's accident has left us with a great big hole from eight thirty-three till the quarter-of-nine headlines. We've got a couple of commercial breaks and a public-service announcement during that period, so call it eight and a half minutes for you to fill. Can you do it? I know you can. Got a cookbook you want to plug? It doesn't have to be new. Or restaurant or whatever?"

Jane had been wise to fetch Debbie. This appeal was as from one professional performer to another, and Reinhart took heart from it.

"Sure," said he, with confidence, "sure, Debbie. Glad to help out."

She flung her head back, but not one strand of hair seemed to stir. "Oh, godamighty, what a superloverly sweetheart you are!" She leaped up and strode presumably towards the set.

Another repetition of the uneventful news came at eight thirty, and then, after a commercial or two and an exhortation from the Coast Guard, Shep returned to say: "Debbie's hungry again. She can eat all day long, and her waistline just keeps getting smaller. Me, I chew a leaf of lettuce and gain ten pounds. It ain't fair. Let's see what's happening in the kitchen this time."

And Reinhart was on again!

"We're back again with Chef Carl Reinhart," Debbie said into the camera, "for more with eggs. I guess they're one of the most versatile foods around, wouldn't you say, Chef?"

This was actually true enough. "Yes, Debbie," Reinhart smilingly replied in his on-camera voice and manner, which though not studied was markedly different from his style in real life. "You will never run out of ways to cook eggs, and then if you think of all the dishes of which eggs form a part you have a whole menu, because eggs can be the star, as in a big beautiful golden puffy soufflé, or a co-star, as with ham or bacon, a supporting player, as in crepes, and finally, a modest bit performer or even an extra, when, say, a raw egg is mixed with ground beef to make a delicious hamburger."

"Well," said Debbie, "is the trick with eggs always speed, as it was with that scrumptious omelet you made earlier?"

"Not always. With a soufflé of course you might say it's patience!"

Debbie chuckled. "I know we don't have time to make a soufflé this morning, but the next time you come back I wish you'd show us that trick. I guess that's one of the toughest dishes for the home cook to learn, isn't it?"

Reinhart smiled with mixed authority and sympathy. "You know, Debbie, a lot of people believe that, but it isn't all that true. It's just one of the many things in life that are mostly bluff."

"Like early-morning television," cried Debbie. Giggling and addressing the again-empty desk, she added: "Right, Shep?"

"I can't believe that," graciously said the cook, "but with a soufflé all you have to understand is the basic principle: air. Somebody way back in history discovered that if you take the white of an egg from the yolk you can whip it so full of air that it becomes a kind of solid matter, while remaining feather-light. What a wonderful discovery! And a whipped white is pretty strong, too. It will hold in suspension any number of fillings and flavorings: shrimp, asparagus tips, and even eggs themselves, whole poached eggs. That makes a fabulous soufflé, incidentally. You dig down through the fluffy stuff and suddenly come upon a gem of a poached egg. It's like a treasure hunt."

Debbie laughed happily. "I can see you love your work—and by the way, that's essential in cooking, isn't it? Love, I mean."

"It doesn't hurt," said Reinhart. "But I wouldn't want to discourage the people who don't have a natural inclination. You *don't* have to be passionately interested in cuisine to do a commendable job at the stove. I say that because I think there are a lot of people, women especially, who have found it necessary to cook for others and think they have no talent. Even if you can't cook well, even if you hate the idea, you may be in a position where you have to do it—and I assure you that there are scores and scores of wonderful dishes you can make easily."

"Easy for you, anyway," said Debbie. She was looking into the camera. "We'll be back, but now this."

Reinhart waited until the red light went off the camera pointed at them and then saw by the monitor of the wall that a commercial had come onto the screen.

Debbie asked: "What should I say you're going to cook now, or are you?"

"Poached eggs." He took a pot from the shelf below the counter and went to the sink behind him. "Does this work?" He turned the cold-water faucet, and, by George, it did, but he got a better idea and ran the hot water. The commercials were still on the screen when he came back with the water. He sprinkled a bit of salt into the pot before closing it with the lid and placing it on a lighted burner of the electric stove.

Debbie said vivaciously: "Do you know, something I enjoy eating but never have been able to cook right is a poached egg. Can you help me out with that problem, Carl?"

They were of course on the air again. He had to fill some moments before the water came to a boil.

"There are various kinds of gadgets that will do the job," he said. "Have you seen the little pots that have a metal insert with depressions, little wells that take one egg each? You boil water underneath them, and the steam comes up to cook the eggs. But in this case the eggs are steamed and not poached. There is a difference. The classic poached egg is cooked directly in the water and is lovely and tender and always better than anything prepared with a gadget." He reached into the jug which held the variety of tools for cooking, and removed a soup ladle.

"But *how*," Debbie asked in a tone of mock despair, "*how* can we keep the egg from just busting all over the place when you take its shell off and drop it in boiling water?" She mugged at the camera.

Speaking of boiling, his potful of water had begun already to show wisps of steam around its lid.

"Well, first, you don't want a violent boil: just kind of firm and medium, a little higher than a simmer, but not a storm. Next you take your soup ladle and rub or melt a bit of butter in its bowl." He demonstrated this piece of business. "Now, when the bottom of the ladle-bowl is covered with a thin layer of butter, you break an egg into it. . . . This is easy to do if you can break a shell with one hand. If you can't do that, simply prop the ladle up inside an empty pot."

"Gee, you think of everything," said Debbie. "That's how you can tell a Cordon Bloo cook."

"The egg's in the buttered ladle," said Reinhart, speaking of the self-evident, but then perhaps there were TV sets with murky pictures and elsewhere busy housewives were listening as they worked, backs to their sets. "You lower the ladle into the boiling water . . ."

Debbie gasped in enlightenment.

"A white film of coagulation forms around the egg, where it touches the ladle. Now, you gently and smoothly tip up the ladle so that the egg slides free into the water."

"Ooo, but look—"

"That's O.K.," said Reinhart. "Don't worry about the ragged streamers of white that blow around in the water. Also, a bit of the coagulated film remains in the dipper." He grinned. "You rise above such things. Seriously, you see that within a second or two the egg is shaping firmly up. Later we'll trim off the ragged edges—which you always get, no matter the method, unless of course you use a gadget. Meanwhile you quickly add another egg in the same fashion, and so on. If you have more than three or four, you might keep an eye on the order of insertion: the earlier will be done sooner than the later. But for the first few the difference in time will be so little as to be meaningless."

"Well, you could knock me over with a basting brush," said Debbie, leering into the pot, then at Reinhart, and finally at the unseen audience. "This man is a marvel. By gosh, if those eggs aren't forming beautifully. I always end up with strings of scrambled *boiled* eggs. That ain't to be recommended, friends. . . . We're going away for a few moments. When we come back, Chef Reinhart will tell us what to do with the eggs now we know how to poach them to perfection."

When they were off Debbie leaned into Reinhart and whispered: "Just terrific, Carl. You're saving our asses."

He wondered briefly what had happened to poor old Buxton—who himself would understand, in the tradition of show business, why any more concern must wait until the performance was over.

He asked his partner: "How much more time do we have to fill?"

"Forty-five seconds."

Could that be true? He confirmed it by the wall clock. Where had the time gone? He could continue for hours!

When they, or the audience, had "returned" (from wherever whoever had been, and whatever was real) Debbie said: "O.K., Chef Reinhart. You were going to tell us how to use our poached eggs."

"I should say first, Debbie, that *I* cook them by instinct, but I'd really advise the use of a timer: about four minutes should do the trick. Ours here haven't been on quite that long yet. But to answer your question: A poached egg goes with almost anything: On top of asparagus or puréed spinach. Or cold, in aspic, as an hors d'oeuvre. Covered with caviar—lumpfish, not the expensive kind. And above all in the ever-popular eggs Benedict: a toasted round of bread or muffin, a slice of ham, a poached egg, and over it all a thick, creamy, lemony hollandaise sauce —which by the way is childishly easy to make—"

"You're killing me!" wailed Debbie. "You know that. Because we're out of time, and I'm dying of hungerrrr! But can you come back sometime soon?" She gestured at him. "Chef Carl Reinhart, courtesy of the Epicon Company, distributors of gourmet foods and their new line of copper-clad cookware. Thanks, Chef. Now back to Shep."

When they were "off," Debbie squeezed his forearm. "Thanks, pal." She walked briskly away, behind the set.

On camera Shep was reading the news headlines. Jane came to conduct Reinhart off.

When they had reached the corridor she said: "You were fabulous, Carl. We're grateful a whole bunch."

Reinhart asked: "Have you checked with the hospital?"

"Huh-uh."

"I'm thinking of Jack Buxton," he said. "It was pretty shocking to find him like that, in the men's room. I wonder whether he pulled through."

Jane looked at him with solemn eyes. "Carl, I'll call right now."

"That'd be nice of you."

"We owe you one."

When she was gone it occurred to him that he could himself have placed the call to the hospital: in other words, his self-righteousness should be restrained.

For the first time since he had put them on, he remembered that he was wearing the apron and chef's bonnet—and now took them off at last. Once he was out of costume he was more resigned to being off the set. But, God, he enjoyed performing!

When Jane returned she was carrying the jacket to his suit and his raincoat. She helped him into these and then said: "He bought the farm."

"Huh?"

"Buxton. He didn't make it. He died in the ambulance."

"Aw," said Reinhart. "Aw, the poor bastard."

Jane nodded in a noncommittal fashion.

"See," Reinhart said defiantly, "I remember him when he was Hollywood's most notorious ladies' man. The fact is—it just comes back to me—he was in court from time to time for sexual things: paternity suits and charges of statutory rape. He had a taste for sixteen-year-olds. My God, that was before World War Two. It's a good forty years ago. He must have been about seventy now."

"Well," said Jane, "I've got to get back to work. Bye, Carl. Hope you're on again soon."

"Uh," said he, "you know what I forgot? To turn off those poached eggs."

"They're in the garbage long since," said Jane. "Don't worry."

Reinhart left the studio reflecting on mortality, but when he reached the parking lot where he had left Winona's borrowed car, the attendant, a young black man with a marked limp, said: "You're that cook I just saw on TV."

Reinhart could see the little set, through the open door of the shack where the attendant sat between arrivals and departures. Debbie was back on the screen. It was hard to believe he had just left her company. He realized that he had never got around to washing off his make-up.

"I knew you right away," said the attendant. "That's what TV gives you: a high recognition potential." He went, with a jouncing stride that defied his limp, to fetch the car.

Reinhart suddenly understood that as a celebrity he would be expected to tip generously.

Russell Baker

BOMB MATH

Wearing his Secretary of Defense hat, Elliot Richardson gave Congress the other day a fascinating glimpse into the mathematics of saving the hearts and minds of remote peoples from whatever our bombers save them from when they bomb their countries.

During one quarter of this year (February, March, April), he said, the United States dropped 145,000 tons of bombs on Cambodia and Laos.

Population of the two countries is about 10 million persons.

Changing tons to pounds, we begin to see light. Territory containing 10 million people has been struck with 290 million pounds of bombs, or, to put it another way, the United States has been bombing at the rate of 29 pounds per person per quarter.

Extrapolating over a full year, we get a more useful mathematical formulation; to wit, that the United States is bombing the average Laotian/Cambodian at the rate of 116 bomb pounds per year.

The interesting question then arises, What is the weight of the average Laotian/Cambodian?

Here we lack data. We know them to be small people physically. We can only guess at what proportion of them is too young to have attained adult weight. Conceding these data deficiencies, it is still not unreasonable to hypothesize that our average Laotian/Cambodian weighs 87 pounds—or three-quarters of the annual bomb poundage used by the United States to save his heart and mind.

Secretary Richardson suggested that the bombing has done its job (which is to preserve the Government of a man named Lon Nol) and says it must go on in order to continue preserving this Government. Thus, for those of us interested solely in the mathematics of the thing,

Mr. Richardson may fairly be said to have stated the proposition that the present bombing level is sufficient for the saving of hearts and minds.

If so, then we may state a general mathematical formula for determining the bomb poundage the United States will have to drop to save the hearts and minds of any given nation.

This formula is: HM = (4W/3)P, where HM represents hearts and minds, W represents weight of the average body containing the heart and mind to be saved and P represents total population of the bombed country.

Example: Suppose it is necessary to save the hearts and minds of Italy. How many pounds of bombs will we need? To get the answer we multiply the average Italian's weight (111 pounds) by 4 and divide the result (444) by 3, which gives us the hearts-and-minds-winning factor number, 148.

To save the hearts and minds of Italy we would have to drop 148 pounds per year per Italian, of whom there are about 55 million. This means we would have to drop 8.14 billion pounds of bombs or, to put it more manageably, about 4 million tons.

"All very well," the taxpayer will say, "but what will it cost me?" Here Mr. Richardson's figures are helpful.

The 63,000 tons dropped on Laos in three months, he reported, cost $99.2 million, or $1,574 per ton.

In Cambodia 82,000 tons were dropped at a cost of $159.5 million, or $1,945 per ton.

In short, it costs 97 cents a pound to bomb Cambodia, but only 79 cents a pound to bomb Laos.

Of the two countries, Cambodia is relatively more advanced economically and has much the larger population. Thus, it appears that per-pound bombing cost must increase in proportion as size and economic complexity of the target country increases.

The bombing of Italy, which is much more advanced than Cambodia and much more populous, might cost as much as $2.50 a pound. At this price the 4 million tons needed to save Italy's hearts and minds for one year would cost slightly over $20 billion. Expensive perhaps, but who would say it is not worth it to save Venice for the free world?

These figures may improve taxpayer morale, for they give a clear idea of the useful tasks performed with the money we pay our Government.

If, for example, you have paid taxes of $1,000, you may very reasonably tell yourself that your contribution has made it possible to drop 1,266 pounds of bombs (at 79 cents per pound) on Laos, thereby saving the hearts and minds of 10 and 53/58ths Laotians for a whole year. (It takes 116 bomb pounds per year, remember, to save a single heart and mind there.)

With figures like these, you do not have to ask your country what it will do for you. You can tell Laos and Cambodia what you have done for them.

Art Buchwald

*

SAVING PAPER

They've been trying to keep it a secret, but there is a serious paper shortage in Washington. A strike of Western paper workers, which is expected to be taken up by workers on the East Coast, has caused a paper deficit in Washington. The reason the government has been keeping it a secret is it fears that if the word gets out, panic will set in and different departments and agencies will start hoarding paper, while others might resort to some very dirty tricks to ensure that its memo flow is not turned off.

One department, which shall remain anonymous, got wind of the shortage and has already held 27 meetings on the crisis.

At the last meeting it was decided to alert all employees to the situation.

In a memo, which was sent to the agency's 27,500 workers, a deputy director wrote: "It has been brought to my attention that we can expect a serious paper shortage in the next few months, which could affect productivity and the morale of this agency. Therefore, I am asking everyone to conserve every sheet of paper possible, even if it involves such dire emergencies as using both sides of the paper. I am also requesting all employees to submit to me in writing how the agency can conserve paper. These suggestions should be made out in triplicate with one copy for me, one for your supervisors and one to keep for yourself in case any action is taken.

"Supervisors are requested to submit weekly reports to the Administrative Supply Office as to how many employees are following this directive, and if this memorandum has increased or decreased the use of present supplies. If an employee does not send in a suggestion, his or her supervisor must put in writing to the personnel director why he or she failed to do so. The personnel director will evaluate and report on Form 2-D to his superior whether or not the excuse is valid.

"What we plan to do with the suggestion is have the public affairs division compile a collection of the most interesting ones, which will then be distributed to all personnel—not only from this agency but from corresponding agencies, which find themselves in the same shortfall position.

"It is my hope that this compilation can be published by the General Printing Office and sold to the public. A steering committee has been appointed to study the best methods of distribution, as well as costs, and the report should be on my desk by the early part of next month. Each department head will receive a copy of the report comments as well as additional thoughts.

"To facilitate matters on the book project, it is suggested that all departmental correspondence concerning conservation be submitted on yellow 8 x 10 Memorandum Sheets (G-234 forms), while those regarding distribution be written on the blue double carbon pads (K-677). If you do not have these colors in stock, you can obtain them from the supply room by filling out Form 2323.

"It goes without saying that this agency will be out of business if it is unable to supply the documentation to justify the written decisions it makes. Therefore, everyone from the top agency officials to the mailroom personnel must comply with all regulations regarding the conservation of our paper supply.

"The first of these regulations is now being distributed. If you do not receive it in a week, please notify this office on Green Form 1456, using the White No. 10 envelope.

"Anyone who does not have a Green Form 1456 may apply for a written waiver by using the Manila Folder 10-DC in which this memo is being distributed." —A. Clancy, Acting Chief Deputy Counsel, Paper Conservation Committee.

Kenneth Tynan

*

JUST PLAIN FOLKS

The curtain has just fallen on William Faulkner's *Requiem for a Nun* (Royal Court). It has been performed with imposing devoutness by Ruth Ford, Bertice Reading, Zachary Scott and John Crawford. The production (by Tony Richardson) and the settings (by Motley) have been austerely hieratic. Let us now imagine that there steps from the wings the Stage Manager of Thornton Wilder's "Our Town." Pulling on a corn-cob pipe, he speaks.

S.M.: "Well, folks, reckon that's about it. End of another day in the city of Jefferson, Yoknapatawpha County, Mississippi. Nothin' much happened. Couple of people got raped, couple more got their teeth kicked in, but way up there those faraway old stars are still doing their old cosmic criss-cross, and there ain't a thing we can do about it. It's pretty quiet now. Folk hereabouts get to bed early, those that can still walk. Down behind the morgue a few of the young people are roastin' a nigger over an open fire, but I guess every town has its night-owls, and afore long they'll be tucked up asleep like anybody else. Nothin' stirring down at the big old plantation house—you can't even hear the hummin' of that electrified barbed-wire fence, 'cause last night some drunk ran slap into it and fused the whole works. That's where Mr. Faulkner lives, and he's the fellow that thought this whole place up, kind of like God. Mr. Faulkner knows everybody round these parts like the back of his hand, 'n most everybody round these parts knows the back of Mr. Faulkner's hand. But he's not home right now, he's off on a trip round the world as Uncle Sam's culture ambassador, tellin' foreigners about how we've got to love everybody, even niggers, and how integration's bound

to happen in a few thousand years anyway, so we might just as well make
haste slowly. Ain't a thing we can do about it.

(He takes out his watch and consults it.)

Along about now the good folk of Jefferson City usually get around to
screamin' in their sleep. Just ordinary people havin' ordinary nightmares,
the way most of us do most of the time.

(An agonised shrieking is briefly heard.)

Ayeah, there they go. Nothin' wrong there that an overdose of Seconal
won't fix.

(He pockets his watch.)

Like I say, simple folk fussin' and botherin' over simple, eternal problems. Take this Temple Stevens, the one Mr. Faulkner's been soundin'
off about. 'Course, Mr. Faulkner don't pretend to be a real play-writer,
'n maybe that's why he tells the whole story backwards, 'n why he takes
up so much time gabbin' about people you never met—and what's more,
ain't going to meet. By the time he's told you what happened before you
got here, it's gettin' to be time to go home. But we were talkin' about
Temple. Ain't nothin' special about her. Got herself mixed up in an auto
accident—witnessed a killin'—got herself locked up in a sportin' house
with one of these seck-sual perverts—witnessed another killin'—got herself married up 'n bore a couple of fine kids. Then, just's she's fixing to
run off with a blackmailer, her maid Nancy—that's the nigger dope-fiend
she met in the cathouse—takes a notion to murder her baby boy. That's
all about Temple—just a run of bad luck that could happen to anyone.
And don't come askin' me why Nancy murders the kid. Accordin' to Mr.
Faulkner, she does it to keep him from bein' tainted by his mother's sins.
Seems to me even an ignorant nigger would know a tainted child was
better'n a dead one, but I guess I can't get under their skins the way Mr.
Faulkner can.

(He glances up at the sky.)

Movin' along towards dawn in our town. Pretty soon folks'll start up on
that old diurnal round of sufferin' and expiatin' and spoutin' sentences
two pages long. One way or another, an awful lot of sufferin' gets done
around here. 'Specially by the black folk—'n that's how it should be,
'cause they don't feel it like we do, 'n anyways, they've got that simple
primitive faith to lean back on.

(He consults his watch again.)

Well, Temple's back with her husband, and in a couple of minutes they'll
be hangin' Nancy. Maybe that's why darkies were born—to keep white
marriages from bustin' up. Anyways, a lot of things have happened since
the curtain went up to-night. Six billion gallons of water have tumbled

over Niagara Falls. Three thousand boys and girls took their first puff of
marijuana, 'n a puppy-dog in a flyin' coffin was sighted over Alaska. Most
of you out there've been admirin' Miss Ruth Ford's play-actin', 'n a few
of you've been wonderin' whether she left her pay-thos in the dressing-
room or whether maybe she didn't have any to begin with. Out in Hollywood a big producer's been readin' Mr. Faulkner's book and figurin'
whether to buy the movie rights for Miss Joan Crawford. Right enough,
all over the world, it's been quite an evening. 'N now Nancy's due for
the drop.

(A *thud offstage. The Stage Manager smiles philosophically.*)
Ayeah, that's it—right on time.

(*He re-pockets his watch.*)
That's the end of the play, friends. You can go out and push dope now,
those of you that push dope. Down in our town there's a meetin' of the
Deathwish Committee, 'n a fund-raisin' rally in aid of Holocaust Relief,
'n all over town the prettiest gals're primping themselves up for the big
beauty prize—Miss Cegenation of 1957. There's always somethin' hap-
penin'. Why—over at the schoolhouse an old-fashioned-type humanist
just shot himself. *You* get a good rest, too. Good-night."

(*He exits. A sound of Bibles being thumped
momentarily fills the air.*)

Thomas Meehan

*

YMA DREAM

In this dream, which I have had on the night of the full moon for the past three months, I am giving a cocktail party in honor of Yma Sumac, the Peruvian singer. This is strange at once, for while I have unbounded admiration for four-octave voices, I have never met Miss Sumac, and, even in a dream, it seems unlikely that I should be giving her a party. No matter. She and I are in the small living room of my apartment, on Charles Street, in Greenwich Village, and we are getting along famously. I have told her several of my Swedish-dialect stories, and she has reciprocated by singing for me, in Quechua, a medley of Andean folk songs. Other guests are expected momentarily. I have no idea, however, who any of them will be. Miss Sumac is wearing a blue ball gown and I am in white tie and tails. Obviously, despite the somewhat unfashionable neighborhood and the cramped quarters of my apartment, it is to be a pretty swell affair. In any case, I have spread several dishes of Fritos about the room, and on what is normally my typing table there is a bowl of hot *glügg*.

The doorbell rings. A guest! I go to the door, and there, to my astonished delight, is Ava Gardner. This is going to be a bit of all right, I think.

"Tom, darling!" she says, embracing me warmly. "How wonderful of you to have asked me."

In my waking hours, unfortunately, I have never met Miss Gardner. In my dream, though, my guests seem to know me rather intimately, while, oddly, none of them seem to know each other. Apparently it is their strong common affection for me that has brought them to Charles Street. For my part, although I immediately recognize each guest as he or she arrives, I have no memory of having ever met any of them, or, for that matter, of having invited them to a party in my apartment. On with the dream, however. "Miss Ava Gardner," I say, "I'd like you to meet Miss Yma Sumac."

"Charmed," says Miss Sumac.

"Delighted," counters Miss Gardner.

"Ah, but Tom," says Miss Sumac, with an enchanting laugh (which runs up the scale from E above middle C to C above high C), "let us not, on this of all occasions, be formal. *Por favor*, introduce each guest only by the first name, so that we may all quickly become—how shall I say? —*amigos*."

Typical Peruvian friendliness, I think, and reintroduce the two. "Ava, Yma," I say.

We sit around for some time, sipping *glügg* and munching Fritos. Things seem to be going well. The doorbell rings again. The second guest is a man—Abba Eban, the former Israeli Ambassador to the United Nations. Again I make the introductions, and, bowing to the wishes of the guest of honor, keep things on a first-name basis. "Abba, Yma; Abba, Ava," I say.

I stifle a grin, but neither Miss Sumac nor my two other guests see anything amusing in the exchange. We chat. The bell rings again, and I am pleased to find Oona O'Neill, Charlie Chaplin's wife, at the door. She is alone. I bring her into the room. "Oona, Yma; Oona, Ava; Oona, Abba," I say.

We are standing in a circle now, smiling brightly but not talking much. I sense a slight strain, but the party is young and may yet come to life. The bell again. It is another man—Ugo Betti, the Italian playwright. A bit hurriedly, I introduce him to the circle. "Ugo, Yma; Ugo, Ava; Ugo, Oona; Ugo, Abba," I say.

Miss Sumac gives me an enigmatic glance that I try to interpret. Boredom? Thirst? No, she looks almost *irritated*. Hastily, I replenish everyone's glass. For some reason, I begin to hope that no other guests have been invited. The doorbell rings once again, however, and I open the door on two lovely actresses, Ona Munson and Ida Lupino. This gives me a happy inspiration for my introductions. "Ona and Ida," I say, "surely you know Yma and Ava? Ida, Ona—Oona, Abba." Damn! It doesn't come out even. "Ida, Ona—Ugo," I finish lamely.

I have scarcely given Miss Munson and Miss Lupino their first drinks when I am again summoned to the door. My guests stand stony-faced as I usher in the new arrival, the young Aga Khan. He is looking exceptionally well turned out in a dinner jacket with a plaid cummerbund. Smiling too cheerfully, I introduce him to the waiting group. "Folks," I say, using a word I have always detested, "here's the Aga Khan!

You know." But there is silence, so I must continue. "Aga—Yma, Ava, Oona, Ona 'n' Ida, Abba 'n' Ugo."

The Aga Khan and Mr. Eban, I notice, take an immediate dislike to each other, and I begin to feel an unmistakable pall descending over my party. I suggest a game of charades. This is met with glacial looks from everyone, including Miss Gardner, whose earlier affection for me has now totally vanished. When the doorbell rings this time, everybody turns and glares at the door. I open it and discover another pair—Ira Wolfert, the novelist, and Ilya Ehrenburg, the *Russian* novelist. The latter, I know, is quite a man-of-the-world, so I try a new approach. "Ilya," I say, "why don't you just introduce yourself and Ira? You know all these lovely people, don't you?"

"*Nyet*," says Mr. Ehrenburg. "Can't say that I do."

"Oh, all *right*," I say. "Ilya, Ira, here's Yma, Ava, Oona. Ilya, Ira—Ona, Ida, Abba, Ugo, Aga."

I ask Miss Sumac to sing for us. She refuses. We continue with the *glügg* and some hopelessly inane small talk. Mr. Eban and the Aga Khan stand at opposite sides of the room, eyeing each other. I begin to wish I'd never given the goddam party. Ona Munson jostles Ugo Betti's elbow by accident, spilling his drink. I spring forward to put them at their ease, whipping a handkerchief from my pocket. "Never mind!" I cry. "No damage done! Ugo, you go get yourself another drink. I'll just wipe this *glügg* off the, uh, *rügg*." The guests fix me with narrowed eyes. At this moment, Eva Gabor, the Hungarian actress, sweeps through the door, which I have cleverly left open. Unaware of the way things are going, she embraces me and turns, beaming, to meet the others. Inevitably, I must make the introductions. I start rapidly. "Eva, meet Yma and Ava and Oona—" But then I find that Miss Gabor is pausing to hug each guest in turn, so I am forced to make the remaining introductions separately. "Eva, Ona; Eva, Ida; Eva, Ugo; Eva, Abba; Eva, Ilya; Eva, Ira; Eva, Aga."

This is a *terrible* party. All the men have bunched up. We stand in a circle, glowering at one another. I can think of nothing to say. I feel oddly hemmed in, like a man who is about to be stoned to death.

"Am I late?" asks the actress Uta Hagen gaily as she comes tripping into the room.

"No, no!" I say, gallantly taking her arm and steering her at once toward the punch bowl and away from the others.

"Please have the common decency to introduce your guests to one another," says Miss Sumac, in a cold monotone. "And in the proper manner."

In the dream, Yma Sumac seems to have some kind of hold over me, and I must do as she wishes. "O.K., O.K.," I snap crossly. "Uta, Yma; Uta, Ava; Uta, Oona; Uta, Ona; Uta, Ida; Uta, Ugo; Uta, Abba; Uta, Ilya; Uta, Ira; Uta, Aga; Uta, Eva." I turn to see if this has placated Miss Sumac, but she coldly ignores me. I have begun to hate her. Then I discover that the *glügg* has run out, and I am forced to offer my guests rye-and-7-Up. In the hope that no further company will arrive, I silently close the door. The bell rings instantly, however, and I feel a chill run down my spine. I pretend not to hear it.

"Answer the door," Miss Sumac says peremptorily. My circle of guests moves menacingly toward me. With a plummeting heart, I open the door. Standing before me, in immaculate evening dress, is a sturdy, distinguished-looking man. He is the Polish concert pianist Mieczyslaw Horszowski.

"Come in, Mieczyslaw!" I cry, with tears in my eyes. "I've never been so glad to see anyone in my whole life!"

And here, always, my dream ends.

Stanley Elkin

BERNIE PERK
EXCERPT FROM *The Dick Gibson Show*

Among the guests in the studio all hell broke loose during the station break. They talked excitedly to one another, and called back and forth along the row of theater seats like picnickers across their tables. Though they had nothing to say themselves, Bchr-Blcibtreau's people turned back and forth trying to follow the conversation of the others. Indeed, there was a sort of lunatic joy in the room, a sense of free-for-all that was not so much an exercise of liberty as of respite—as if someone had temporarily released them from vows. School was out in Studio A, and Dick had an impression of its also being out throughout the two or three New England states that could pick up the show. He saw people raiding refrigerators, gulping beers, grabbing tangerines, slashing margarine on slices of bread, ravenously tearing chicken wings, jellied handfuls of leftover stews.

Pepper Steep had joined Jack Patterson in exhausted detachment; though he said nothing, Mel Son looked animatedly from onc to the other. Behr-Bleibtreau also seemed exhausted.

Of the members of his panel, only Bernie Perk seemed keyed up. He jabbered away a mile a minute, so that Dick couldn't really follow all that he was saying. The druggist wanted to know what had happened to everyone. "What's got into Pepper?" he asked. "What's got into Jack?"

Dick couldn't tell him. He had no notion of what had gotten into his comrades. All he knew was that he was impatient for the commercial to be finished and for the show to go back on the air. He couldn't wait to hear what would happen next, though having some dim sense of the masquelike qualities of the evening, and realizing that thus far his guests had "performed" in the order that they had been introduced, he had a hunch that it would involve Bernie.

It did.

BERNIE PERK: May I say something?

DICK GIBSON: Sure thing.

BERNIE PERK: Okay, then. What's going on here? What's got into everyone? What's got into Pepper? What's got into Jack? I came here
tonight to talk about psychology with an expert in the field. But all
anyone's done so far is grab the limelight for himself. Everyone is
too excited. Once a person gets started talking about himself all
sorts of things come out that aren't anybody's business. I understand enough about human nature to know that much. Everybody
has his secret. Who hasn't? We're all human beings. Who isn't a
human being? Listen, I'm a mild person. I'm not very interesting,
maybe, and I don't blow my own horn, but even someone like
myself, good old Bernie Perk, corner druggist, "Doc" to one and
"Pop" to another, could put on a regular horror show if he wanted
to. *But it isn't people's business.*

   Look, my son and his charming wife are guests in the studio
tonight. Pepper Steep's sister is here. How do you think it must be
for them when an intimate relative sticks his foot in his mouth? If
you love people you've got to have consideration.

DICK GIBSON: Bernie, don't be so upset. Take it easy.

BERNIE PERK: Dick, I *am* upset about this. No, I mean it. What's it
supposed to be, "Can You Top This?"

DICK GIBSON: Come on, Bernie—

BERNIE PERK: Because the temptation is always the one they yielded to.
To give up one's secrets. La. La la. The soul's espionage, its secret
papers. *Know* me. No, thank you. I'm pretty worked up. Call on
Mel.

DICK GIBSON: Take it easy.

BERNIE PERK: Call on Mel.

DICK GIBSON: Mel? (*no answer*)

BERNIE PERK: Mel passes. (*He giggles.*) Well, that's too bad, for thereby
hangs a tale, I bet. The truth is Well, okay, I'll tell the audience
something, maybe everybody likes to see his friends with their hair
down. They don't know. We don't see each other off the air. The
illusion is we're mates. You want us to be, but we're not.

JACK PATTERSON: Here goes Bernie.

BERNIE PERK: (*fiercely*) You *had* your turn. You were *first*. Don't hog everything. You had your turn. Just because you couldn't do any better than that canned ardor, don't try to ruin it for everyone else.

The truth of the matter is, I had to laugh. The man's a school-teacher. Big deal. He sees up coeds' skirts. Big deal. He has them in for conferences, he goes over their papers with them, he bends over the composition and her hair touches his cheek. Enormous! Call the police, passion's circuits are blown. I know all that, I *know* all that. But if you want to see life in the raw, be a pharmacist, buy a drugstore. You wouldn't *believe* what goes on. It's a meat market. No wonder they register us. Hickory Dickory "Doc." Let me fill you in on the prescription. Yow. Wow.

You know what a drugstore is? A temple to the senses. Come down those crowded aisles. Cosmetics first stop. Powders, puffs, a verb-wheel of polished nails on a cardboard, lipstick ballistics, creams and tighteners, suntan lotions, eyeshadow, dyes for hair— love potions, paints, the ladies' paintbox!

Come, come with Pop. The Valentine candy, the greeting cards, the paperbook racks and magazine stands. The confessions and movie magazines dated two months beyond the real month because time, like love, is yet to be. Sit at the fountain. See the confections—banana splits and ice-cream sundaes like statues of the sweet, as if sweetness itself, the sugary molecules of love resided in them. The names—like words for lyrics. Delicious the syrups, the salty storm of nuts and tidal waves of spermy cream. Sing yum! Sing yum yum!

All the shampoos, all the lotions and hair conditioners pro-teined as egg and meat. Files and emery boards, the heartsick gyp-sy's tools. Sun lamps, sleep masks, rollers, bath oils and depilato-ries, massaging lotions. Things for acne, panty hose—the model on the package like a yogi whore. Brushes, rinses, bath oils and shower caps like the fruits that grow on beaches.

To say nothing of the Venus Folding Feminine Syringe, of Kotex in boxes you could set a table for four on. Liquid douches— you can hear the sea. Rubber goods, the queer mysterious elastics, supporters, rupture's ribbons and organ's bows. Now we're into it, hard by diarrhea's plugs and constipation's triggers. There's the druggist, behind the high counter, his bust visible like someone on a postage stamp, immaculate in his priest's white collar. See the symbols—the mortar and pestle and flasks of colored liquid. Once I sipped from the red, the woman's potion. I had expected tasteless vegetable dye, but it was sweet, viscous, thick as oil. There are aphrodisiacs in those flasks to float your heart.

And there *I* am, by the refrigerated drugs, the druggist's small safe, the pharmacopoeia, the ledger with names and dates and numbers. A man of the corner and crossroads, scientist manqué, reader of Greek and Latin, trained to count, to pull a jot from a tittle, lift a tittle from a whit, a man of equilibriums, of grains and half-grains, secret energies locked in the apothecary's ounce.

Fresh from college I took a job—this was the Depression—in another man's store. MacDonald's. Old MacDonald had a pharmacy, eeyi eeyi o! An old joke but the first I ever made. "I'll fill the prescriptions," MacDonald told me. "You're a whipper-snapper. You'll wait on trade and make the ice-cream sodas. If that isn't satisfactory, go elsewhere. If I'm to be sued for malpractice I'll be the malpracticer, thank you very much." It was not satisfactory, but what could I do? It was the Depression. How many young men trained for a profession had to settle in those days for something else? And do you know what I found out? (What's got into Bernie?) I found out *everything!*

The first week I stood behind the counter, smiling in my white lab jacket, and a lady came in. A plain woman, middle-aged, her hair gone gray and her figure failing. "Doctor, I need something for my hemorrhoids," she said. "They are like to kill me when I sit. It burns so when I make number two that I've been eating clay to constipate myself."

I gave her Preparation H. Two days later she came back to the store and bought a birthday card for her son. Somehow the knowledge that I alone of all the people in the store knew something about that woman's behind was stirring to me. I was married, the woman was plain; she didn't attract me. I was drawn by her hemorrhoids, in on the secret of her sore behind. Each day in that novice year there were similar experiences. I had never been so happy in my life. Old MacDonald puttering away in the back of the store, I up front—what a team we made.

A young woman came in. Sacrificing her turn she gestured to me to wait on the other customers first. When the store was empty she came up to me.

"I have enuresis," she said.

I gave her some pills.

"Listen," she said, "may I use your toilet?"

I let her come behind the counter. She minced along slowly, her legs in a desperate clamp. I opened the door of the small toilet.

"There's no toilet paper," I said. "I'll have to bring you some."

"Thank you," she said.

I stood outside the door for a moment. I heard the splash. A powerful, incredible discharge. You'd think she'd had an enema. But it was all urine; the woman's bladder was converting every spare bit of moisture into uremic acid. She could have pissed mud puddles, oceans, the drops in clouds, the condensation on the outside of beer bottles. It was beyond chemistry, it was alchemy. Golden. Lovely.

I got the paper for her.

"I have the toilet tissue, Miss." Though she opened the door just enough for me to hand the roll in to her, I saw bare knees, a tangle of panties.

Her name was Miss Wallace, and when she came into the store for her pills—need is beyond embarrassment: only I was embarrassed—I grew hard with lust. I made no overtures, you understand; I was always clinical, always professional, always offhand.

"Listen," I told her one day, "I suppose you have rubber sheets."

"No good," she said.

"You'll ruin your mattress."

"It's already ruined. When I tried a rubber sheet, the water collected in the depression under my behind. I lay in it all night and caught cold."

The thought of that pee-induced cold maddened me. Ah God, the bizarre body awry, messes caught in underwear—love tokens, unhealth a function of love.

There were so many I can't remember them all.

I knew I had to leave Old MacDonald. I was held down, you see. Who knew what secrets might not be unlocked if I could get my hands on the *prescriptions* those ladies brought in! When my father died and left me four thousand dollars, I used it to open the store I have now. I signed notes right and left to get my stock and fixtures together. My wife thought it was madness to gamble this way in the depth of the Depression, but I was pining with love. There were so many . . .

Let's see. *These have been a few of the women in my life:*

Rose Barbara Hacklander, Miss Hartford of 1947, 38-24-36, a matter of public record. What is *not* a matter of public record is that she had gingivitis, a terrible case, almost debilitating, and came near to losing the title because of her reluctance to smile. She wanted to shield her puffy gums, you understand. Only I, Bernie

Perk, her druggist, knew. On the night before the finals she came to me in tears. She showed me—in the back of the store—lifting a lip, reluctant as a country girl in the Broadway producer's office raising the hem of her skirt, shy, and yet bold too, wanting to please even with the shame of her beauty. I looked inside her mouth. The gums were filled, tumid with blood and pus, enormous, preternatural, the gums of the fat lady in the circus, obscuring her teeth, in their sheathing effect seeming actually to sharpen them, two rings of blade in her mouth. And there, in the back of her mouth at the back of the store, pulling a cheek, squeezing it as one gathers in a trigger—cankers, cysts like snowflakes.

"Oh, Doc," she cried, "what will I do? It's worse tonight. The salve don't help. It's nerves—I know it's nerves."

"Wait, I can't see in this light. Put your head here. Say 'Ah.' "

"Ah," she said.

"Ah," I said. "Ah!"

"What's to be done? Is there anything you can give me?"

"Advice."

"Advice?"

"Give them the Gioconda smile Mona Lisa let them have."

And she did. I saw the photograph in the newspaper the morning after the finals. Rose Barbara crowned (I the Queenmaker), holding her flowers, the girls in her court a nimbus behind her, openly smiling, their trim gums flashing. Only Miss Hartford of 1947's lips were locked, her secret in the dimpled parentheticals of her sealed smile. I still have the photograph in my wallet.

Do you know what it means to be always in love? Never to be out of it? Each day loving's gnaw renewed, like hunger or the need for sleep? Worse, the love unfocused, never quite reduced to this one girl or that one woman, but always I, the King of Love, taking to imagination's beds whole harems? I was grateful, I tell you, to the occasional Rose Barbara Hacklander for the refractive edge she lent to lust. There were so many. Too many to think about. My mind was like the waiting room of a brothel. Let them leave my imagination, I prayed, the ones with acne, bad breath, body odor, dandruff, all those whose flyed ointment and niggered woodpile were the commonplace of my ardor.

Grateful also to Miss Sheila Jean Locusmundi who had corns like Chiclets, grateful to the corns themselves, those hard outcroppings of Sheila Jean's synovial bursa. I see her now, blonde, high-heeled, her long, handsome legs bronzed in a second skin of nylon.

I give her foot plasters. She hands them back. "Won't do," she says.

"Won't do? Won't do? But these are our largest. These are the largest there are."

"Pop," she whispers, "I've got a cop's corns."

A cop's corns. A cornucopia. I shake my head in wonder. I want to see them, Sheila Jean. I invite her behind the counter, to the back of the store. If I see them I might be able to help her, a doc like me. Once out of view of the other customers Sheila Jean succumbs: she limps. I feel the pinch. That's right, I think, don't let *them* see. In my office she sits down in front of my rolltop desk and takes off her shoes. I watch her face. Ease comes in like the high tide. Tears of painless gratitude appear in her eyes. All day she waits for this moment. She wriggles her toes. I see bunions bulge in her stockings. It's hard for me to maintain my professional distance. "Take off your stockings, Miss Locusmundi," I manage. She turns away in my swivel chair and I hear the soft, electric hiss of the nylon. She swings around, and redundantly points.

"I see," I murmur. "Yes, those are really something." They are. They are knuckles, ankles. They are boulders, mountain ranges.

"May I?" I ask.

She gives me her foot reluctantly. "Oh, God, don't touch them, Pop."

"There, there, Miss Locusmundi, I won't hurt you." I hold her narrow instep, my palm a stirrup. I toss it casually from one hand to the other, getting the heft.

"Ticklish," Sheila Jean says. She giggles.

I peer down closely at the humpy callosities, their dark cores. There is a sour odor. This, I think, is what Miss Hartford's gingivitis tastes like. I nod judiciously; I take their measure. I'm stalling because I can't stand up yet. When finally I can, I sculpt plasters for her. I daub them with Derma-Soft and apply them. When she walks out she is, to all eyes but mine, just another pretty face.

Grateful too—I thank her here—to Mary Odata, a little Japanese girl whose ears filled with wax. I bless her glands, those sweet secretions, her lovely auditory canal. Filled with wax, did I say? She was a *candle* mine. I saved the detritus from the weekly flushings I administered.

Her father took her to live in Michigan, but before she left she wrote me a note to thank me for all I had done. "Respected R.

Ph. Perk," she wrote, "my father have selectioned to take me to his brother whom has a truck farm in the state of Michigan, but before I am going this is to grateful acknowledgment your thousand kindnesses to my humble ears. In my heart I know will I never to find in Michigan an R. Ph. as tender for my ears as you, sir. Mine is a shameful affliction, but you never amusemented them, and for this as for your other benefits to me I thank. Your friend, M. Odata."

When I closed the store that night I went into my office and molded a small candle from the cerumen I had collected from her over the months, ran a wick through it, turned off the lights, and reread Mary's letter by the glow of her wax until it sputtered and went out. Call me a sentimental old fool, but that's what I did.

Not to mention Mrs. Louise Lumen, perpetual wet nurse, whose lacteal glands were an embarrassment to her three or even four years beyond her delivery, or flatulent Cora Moss, a sweet young thing with a sour stomach in the draft of whose farts one could catch cold. There were so many. There was Mrs. Wynona Jost whose unwanted hair no depilatory would ever control. Her back, she gave me to understand, was like an ape's. Super-follicled Mrs. Jost! And psoriatic Edna Hand. And all the ladies with prescriptions. I knew everybody's secret, the secret of every body. And yet it was never the worm in the apple I loved but only a further and final nakedness, almost the bacteria itself, the cocci and bacilli and spirilla, the shameful source of *their* ailment and my privilege. I was deferential to this principle only: that there exists a nudity beyond *mere* nudity, a covertness which I shielded as any lover husbands his sweet love's mysteries. I did not kiss and tell; I did not kiss at all. Charged with these women's cabala I kept my jealous counsel. I saved them, you see. Honored and honed a sort of virginity in them by my silence. Doc *and* Pop. And knight too in my druggist's gorget. I could have gone on like this forever, content with my privileged condition, satisfied to administer my drugs and patent medicines and honor all confidences, grateful, as I've said, for the impersonal personality of the way I loved, calling them Miss, calling them Missus, protecting them from myself as well as from others, not even masturbating, only looking on from a distance, my desire speculative as an issue of stock.

But something human happens.

One day . . . Where's my *son* going? Why's he leaving? Edward? Connie, *don't* go. Youth should have a perspective on its parents . . . Well, they've gone. I must have shamed them. Isn't

that the way with the young? They think the older generation is
stodgy and then they've no patience with confession. Oh well, let
them go. Where was I?

BEHR-BLEIBTREAU: "One day—"
BERNIE PERK: Yes, that's right. One day a woman came into my drugstore
I'd never seen before. She was pretty, in her early or middle twenties perhaps, but very small. Not just short—though she was, extremely short; she couldn't have been much more than five feet—
but *small*. Dainty, you know? Maybe she wore a size six dress. I
don't know sizes. She could probably buy her clothes in the same
department school girls do. What do they call that? Junior Miss?
Anyway, she was very delicate. Tinier than Mary Odata. A nice
face, sweet, a little old-fashioned perhaps, the sort of face you see
in an old sepia photograph of your grandmother's sister that died.
A *very* pretty little woman.

   I saw her looking around, going up and down the aisles. Every
once in a while she would stoop down to peer in a low shelf. I have
these big round mirrors in the corners to spy on shoplifters. I
watched her in the mirrors. If I lost her in one mirror I picked her
up again in another. A little doll going up and down the aisles in
the convex glass.

   I knew what was up. A woman knows where things are. It's an
instinct. Have you ever seen them in a supermarket? They understand how it's organized. It has nothing to do with the fact that they
shop more than men. A man goes into a grocery, he has to ask
where the bread is. Not a woman: she knows where it's *supposed* to
be. Well, this woman is obviously confused. She's looking for something which she knows is always in one place, whatever store she
goes into. So I *knew* what was up: she was looking for the sanitary
napkins.

   Most places they keep them on the open shelves to spare the
ladies embarrassment. I don't spare anyone anything. I keep them
behind the counter with me. I want to know what's going on with
their periods. They have to ask.

   Finally she came over to me. "I don't see the Kotex," she says.

   "This is the Kotex department," I say, and reach under the
counter for a box. "Will there be anything else? We have a terrific
buy on Midol this week. Or some girls prefer the formula in this.
I've been getting good reports; they tell me it's very effective against
cramps." I hand her a tin of Monthleaze. "How are you fixed for

breath sweetener?" I push a tube of Sour-Off across the counter to her.

She ignores my suggestions but picks up the box of Kotex and looks at it. "This is Junior," she says.

"I'm sorry," I say. I give her Regular.

"Don't you have Super?"

"I thought this was for you," I tell her, and give her the size she asks for.

A month later she came in again. "Super Kotex," she said. I give her the box and don't see her again for another month. This time when she comes in I hand her the Super and start to ring up the sale.

"I'd better take the tampon kind too," she says. She examines the box I give her. "Is there anything larger than this?"

"This is the biggest," I say, swallowing hard.

"All right."

"Tell me," I say, "are these for you?"

She blushes and doesn't answer.

I hadn't dared to think about it, though it had crossed my mind. Now I could think of nothing else. I forgot about the others. This girl inflamed me. Bernie burns. It was astonishing—a girl so small. My life centered on *her* center, on the prodigious size of her female parts.

BEHR-BLEIBTREAU: Say "cunt."

DICK GIBSON: Wait a minute—

BEHR-BLEIBTREAU: It's all right. Say "cunt."

BERNIE PERK: . . . *Cunt.* The size of her cunt. The disproportion was astonishing to me. Kotex *and* Tampax. For all I knew, she used the Kotex *inside.* I *did* know it. I conceived of her smallness now as the result of her largeness. It was as if her largeness *there* sapped size from the rest of her body, or that by some incredible compensation her petiteness lent dimension elsewhere. I don't know. It was all I could think of. Bernie burns.

I had to know about her, at least find out who she was, whether she was married. I tried to recall if I had seen a wedding band, but who could think of fingers, who could think of hands? Bernie burns. Perk percolates.

That night I counted ahead twenty-eight days to figure when I might expect her again. The date fell on September 9, 1956.

She didn't come—not then, not the next month.

Then, one afternoon, I saw her in the street. It was just after

Thanksgiving, four or five days before her next period. I raised my
hat. "Did you have a pleasant holiday?" I asked. My face was familiar to her but she couldn't place me. I counted on this.

"So so." The little darling didn't want to embarrass me.

"I thought you might be going away for Thanksgiving," I said.

She looked puzzled but still wanted to be polite. "My roommate went home but I stayed on in Hartford," she said. "Actually
she invited me to go with her but my boss wouldn't give me Friday
off."

Ah, I thought, she has a roommate, she's a working girl.
Good.

"I'm very sorry," I said, "but I find myself in a very embarrassing position. I don't seem to be able to remember your name."

"Oh," she said, and laughed. "I can't remember yours either.
I know we've seen each other."

"I'm Bernie Perk."

"Yes. Of course. I'm Bea Dellaspero. I still don't—"

"I don't either. You see what happens? Here we are, two old
friends and neither of us can—*Wait* a minute. I think I've got it.
I've seen you in my store. I'm the druggist—Perk's Drugs on Mutual?"

"Oh." She must have remembered our last conversation for
she became very quiet. We were standing outside a coffee shop,
and when I invited her to have a cup with me she said she had to
be going and hurried off.

Her number was in the phone book, and I called right from
the coffee shop. If only her roommate's in, I thought, crossing my
fingers for luck.

"Where's Bea? Is Bea there?"

"No."

"Christ," I said. "What's her number at work? I've got to get
her."

I called the number the roommate gave me; it was a big insurance company. I told them I was doing a credit check on Bea
Dellaspero and they connected me to personnel. Personnel was
nice as pie. Bea was twenty-four years old, a typist in the claims
department and a good credit risk.

It was something, but I couldn't live on it. I had to get her to
return to the store.

I conceived the idea of running a sale especially for Bea. My
printer set up a sample handbill. Across the bottom I had him put

in half a dozen simple coupons, with blank spaces where she could write in the names of the products she wanted to exchange them for. She could choose from a list of twenty items, on which I gave about a 90 percent discount. I sent the flier in an envelope to Bea's address.

Normally I'm closed on Sunday, but that was the day I set aside for Bea's sale. I opened up at ten o'clock, and I didn't have to wait more than an hour. When she came in holding the pink flier we were alone in the store.

"How are you?" I asked.

"Fine, thank you." She was still uneasy about me. "I got your advertisement."

"I see it in your hand."

"Oh. Yes."

She went around the store picking up the items she wanted and brought them to the counter. When she gave me her coupons, I saw that she'd chosen products relating to a woman's periods or to feminine hygiene. She'd had to: I'd rigged the list with men's shaving equipment, pipe accessories, athletic supporters—things like that.

"What size would these be, madam?"

"Super."

"Beg pardon, I didn't hear you."

"*Super.*"

Super *duper*, I thought. I put the big boxes on the counter and added two bottles of douche from the shelf behind me. It won't be enough, I thought. She had a pussy big as all outdoors. Imperial gallons wouldn't be enough. "Let me know how you like the douche," I said, "I've been getting some excellent reports."

God, I was crazy. You know how it is when you're smitten. Smitten? I was in love. Married twenty-three years and all of a sudden I was in love for the first time in my life. Whole bales of cotton I would have placed between her legs. Ah love, set me tasks! Send me for all the corks in Mediterranea, all styptic stymies would I fetch!

In love, did I say? *In* love? That's wrong. *In* love I had been since Old MacDonald's. *In* love is nothing, simple citizenship. Now I was *of* love, no mere citizen but a very governor of the place, a tenant become landlord. And who *falls* in love? Love's an ascent, a rising—touch my hard-on—a soaring. Consider my body, all bald spots haired by imagination, my fats rendered and features firmed, tooth decay for God's sake turned back to candy in my mouth. Heyday! Heyday! And all my feelings collateral to a teen-age boy's!

So I had been in love and now was of it. Bernie burns, the pharmacist on fire. I did not so much forget the others as repudiate them; they were just more wives. Get this straight: love is adulterous, hard on the character. I cuckold those cuties, the Misses Odata and Locusmundi. Horns for Miss Hartford! Miss Moss is dross. Be my love, Bea my love!

I bagged Bea's purchases, punched the register a few times to make it look good, and charged her fifty-seven cents for the nineteen dollars' worth of stuff she'd bought.

"So cheap?"

"It's my special get-acquainted offer," I said. "Also I knocked off a few dollars because you mentioned the secret word."

"I did? What was it?"

"I can't tell you. It's a secret."

"You know, it's really a terrific sale," she said. "I'm surprised more people aren't here to take advantage of it."

"They're coming by when church gets out."

"I see."

As she took the two bags in her thin arms and turned to go, it occurred to me that she might never come back to the store. I raced around the counter. I had no idea what I would do; all love's stratagems and games whistled in my head.

"I'll help you," I said, taking one of her bags.

"I can manage."

"No, I couldn't think of it. A little thing like you? Let me have the other one as well."

She refused to give it up. "I'm very capable," she said. We were on the sidewalk. "You better go back. Your store's open. Anyone could just walk off with all your stock."

"They're in church. Even the thieves. I'll take you to your car."

"I don't have a car. I'm going to catch the bus at the corner."

"I'll wait with you."

"It's not necessary."

"It isn't safe."

"They're all in church."

"Just the thieves, not the rapers."

"But it's the dead of winter. You don't even have a coat. You'll catch cold."

"Not cold."

"What?"

"Not cold. Bernie burns."

"Excuse me?"

"Not cold. The pharmacist on fire."

"I'm sorry?"

"Don't worry about me," I said. "I'm hale." I jumped up and down with the bag in my arms. "See?" I said. "See how hale? I'm strong. I huff and I puff." I hit myself in the chest with my fist. "Me? Me sick? There are things on my shelves to cure anything."

Bea was becoming alarmed. I checked myself, and we stood quietly in the cold together waiting for the bus.

Finally I had to speak or burst. " 'There's naught so sweet as love's young dream,' " I said.

"What was that?"

"It's a saying. It's one of my favorite sayings."

"Oh."

" 'Who ever loved that loved not at first sight?' "

"I beg your pardon?"

"It's another saying."

"Do you see the bus coming?"

" 'Love makes the world go round.' "

"I've heard that one."

" 'Love is smoke raised with the fume of sighs.' " The fume of *size*: super. " 'Take away love and earth is tomb.' 'Love indeed is anything, yet is nothing.' "

"I think I hear it coming. Are you *sure* you can't see it?"

" 'Love is blind,' " I said gloomily. She *had* heard it; it lumbered toward us irresistibly. Soon it would be there and I would never see her again. She was very nervous and went into the street and began to signal while the bus was still three blocks off. I watched her performance disconsolately. " 'And yet I love her till I die,' " I murmured softly.

When the driver came abreast, Bea darted up the steps and I handed her bag to her. "Will I see you again?" I said.

"What's that?"

"Will I see you again? Promise when you've used up what you've bought you'll come back."

"Well, it's so *far*," she said. The driver closed the door.

"*I deliver!*" I shouted after her and waved and blew kisses off my fingertips.

DICK GIBSON: Remarkable!

BERNIE PERK: So's love, so are lovers. Now I saw them.

DICK GIBSON: Saw whom?

BERNIE PERK: Why, lovers. For if love is bad for the character it's good for it too. Now that I was of love, I was also of lovers. I looked around and saw that the whole world was in love. When a man came in to pick up penicillin for his wife—that was a love errand. I tried to cheer him. "She'll be okay," I told him. "The pills will work. She'll come round. Her fever will break. Her sore throat will get better." "Why are you telling me this?" he'd ask. "I like you," I'd say. " 'All the world loves a lover.' "

For the first time I saw what my drugstore was all about. It was love's way station. In free moments I would read the verses on my greeting cards, and my eyes would brim with tears. Or I would pore over the true confessions in my magazine racks. "Aye aye," I'd mutter, "too true this true confession." I blessed the lipstick: "Kiss, kiss," I droned over the little torpedoes. "Free the man in frogs and bogs. Telltales be gone, stay off shirt collars and pocket handkerchiefs." All love was sacred. I pored over my customers' photographs after they were developed. I held a magnifying glass over them—the ones of sweethearts holding hands in the national parks or on the steps of historic buildings, the posed wives on the beach, fathers waving goodbye, small in the distance, as they go up the steps into airplanes. People take the same pictures, did you know that? We are all brothers.

Love was everywhere, commoner than loneliness. I had never realized before what a terrific business I did in rubbers. And it isn't even spring; no one's on a blanket in the woods, or in a rowboat's bottom, or on a hayride. I'm talking about the dead of winter, a high of twenty, a low of three. And you can count on the fingers of one hand the high-school kids' pipe-dream purchase. My customers meant business. There were irons in these lovers' fires. And connoisseurs they were, I tell you, prophylactic more tactic than safeguard, their condoms counters and confections. How sheer's this thing, they'd want to know, or handle them, testing this one's elasticity, that one's friction. Or inquire after refinements, special merchandise, meticulous as fishermen browsing flies. Let's see. They wanted: French Ticklers, Spanish Daggers, Swedish Surprises, The Chinese Net, The Texas Truss and Gypsy Outrage. They wanted petroleum jellies smooth as syrups.

And I, Pop, all love's avuncular spirit, all smiles, rooting for them, smoothing their way where I could, apparently selfless—they must have thought me some good-sport widower who renewed his memories in their splashy passion—giving the aging Cupid's fond green light. How could they suspect that I learned from them, growing my convictions in their experience? Afterward, casually, I would debrief them. Reviewing the troops: Are Trojans better than Spartans? Cavaliers as good as Commandos? Is your Centurion up to your Cossack? What of the Mercenary? The Guerrilla? How does the Minuteman stand up against the State Trooper? In the end, it was too much for me to have to look on while every male in Hartford above the age of seventeen came in to buy my condoms.

Bea never came back—I had frightened her off with my wild talk at the bus stop—yet my love was keener than ever. I still kept up my gynecological charts on her, and celebrated twenty-eighth days like sad festivals. I dreamed of her huge vaginal landscape, her loins in terrible cramp. Bernie burns.

I formed a plan. The first step was to get rid of her roommate. I made my first call to Bea that night.

Don't worry. It's not what you think. I didn't disguise my voice or breathe heavily and say nothing, nor any of your dirty-old-man tricks. I'm no phone creep. When Bea answered I told her who it was straight off.

"Miss Dellaspero? Bernie Perk. I don't see you in the drugstore anymore. You took advantage of my bargains but you don't come in."

Embarrassed, she made a few vague excuses which I pretended cleared matters up. "Well that's okay, then," I said. "I just thought you weren't satisfied with the merchandise or something. You can't put a guy in jail for worrying about his business."

In a week I called again. "Bea? Bernie."

This time she was pretty sore. "Listen," she said. "I never heard of a respectable merchant badgering people to trade with him. I was a little flustered when you called last week, but I have the right to trade wherever I want."

"Sure you do, Bea. Forget about that. That was a business call. This is social."

"Social?"

"That's right. I called to ask how you are. After our last conversation I thought I'd be seeing you. Then when you didn't come in I got a little worried. I thought you might be sick or something."

"I'm not sick."

"I'm relieved to hear it. That takes a load off my mind."

"I don't see why my health should be of any concern to you."

"Bea, I'm a *pharmacist*. Is it against the law for a pharmacist to inquire after the health of one of his customers?"

"Look, I'm not your customer."

"Your privilege, Bea. It's no crime for a man to try to drum up a little trade. Well, as long as you're all right. That's the important thing. If we haven't got our health, what have we got?"

A few days later I called again. "Bernie here. Listen, Bea, I've been thinking. What do you say to dinner tonight? I know a terrific steakhouse in West Hartford. Afterward we could take in a late movie."

"What? Are you crazy?"

"Crazy? I don't get your meaning. Why do you say something like that?"

"Why do I *say* that? Why do you call up all the time?"

"Well, I'm calling to invite you to dinner. Where does it say a man can't invite a young lady to have dinner with him?"

"I don't *know* you."

"Well, *sure* you know me, but even if you didn't, since when is it illegal for a person to try to make another person's acquaintance?"

"Don't call anymore."

"I'm sorry you feel that way, Bea."

"Don't call me Bea."

"That's your name, isn't it? You don't drag a person into court for saying your name. Even your first name."

"I don't know what your trouble is, Mr. Perk—"

"Bernie. Call me Bernie. Bernie's my first name."

"*I don't know what your trouble is, Mr. Perk*, but you're annoying me. You'd better stop calling." She hung up.

I telephoned the next night. "My trouble, Bea, is that I think I'm falling in love with you."

"I don't want to hear this. Please get off the line."

"Bea, dear, you don't lock a fellow up for falling in love."

"You're insane. You must be at least twenty-five years older than I am."

"There *is* a difference in our ages, yes. But they don't arrest people for their birthdays."

She hung up.

My plan was going according to plan. "Bea?"

"I thought I convinced you to stop calling me."

"Bea, don't hang up. Listen, don't hang up. If you hang up I'll just have to call you again. Listen to what I have to say."

"What is it?"

"One of the reasons you're hostile is that you don't know anything about me. That's not my fault, I don't take any responsibility for that. I thought you'd come into the store and gradually we'd learn about each other, but you didn't want it that way. Well, when a person's in love he doesn't stand on ceremonies. I'm going to tell you a few things about myself."

"That can't make any difference."

" 'That can't make any difference.' Listen to her. Of course it can make a difference, Bea. What do you think love between two people is? It's *knowing* a person, understanding him. At least give me a chance to explain a few things. It's not a federal offense for a fellow to try to clear the air. All right?"

"I'll give you a minute."

"Gee, I'd better talk fast."

"You'd better."

"I want to be honest with you. You weren't far off when you said I was twenty-five years older than you are. As a matter of fact, I'm even older than you think. I've got a married son twenty-six years old."

"You're married?"

"Sure I'm married. Since when is it a crime to be married? My wife's name is Barbara. She has the same initial you do. But when I say I'm married I mean that *technically* I'm married. Babs is two years older than I am. A woman ages, Bea darling. All the zip has gone out of her figure. Menopause does that to a girl. I'll tell you the truth: I can't stand to look at her. I used to be so in love that if I saw her on the toilet I'd get excited. I wouldn't even wait for her to wipe herself. Now I see her in her corsets and I wish I were blind. Her hair has turned gray—down *there*. Do you know what that does to a guy?"

"I'm hanging up."

"I'm telling the truth. *Where's it written it's police business when someone tells the truth?*"

I sent over a carton of Kotex and a carton of Tampax, and called her the following week. "Did you get the napkins?"

"I didn't order those. I don't want them."

"Order? Who said anything about order? You can't arrest a

man for sending his sweetheart a present. It wouldn't stand up in court."

And the next night.

"It's you, is it? I'm moving," she said. "I'm moving and I'm getting an unlisted number. I hope you're satisfied. I've lost my roommate on account of you. You've made her as nervous as me with these calls. So go ahead and say whatever you want—it's your last chance."

"Come out with me tonight."

"Don't be ridiculous."

"I love you."

"You're insane."

"Listen, go to bed with me. Please. I want to make love to you. Or let me come over and see you naked. I want to know just how big you really are down there."

"You're sick, do you know that? You need help."

"Then help me. Fuck me."

"I actually feel sorry for you. I really do."

"What are you talking about? I'm not hiding in any bushes. You know who I am. You know all about me. I'm Bernie Perk. My place of business is listed in the Yellow Pages. You could look me up. It isn't a crime to proposition a woman. You can't put a man behind bars for trying."

"You disgust me."

"Call the police."

"You disgust me."

"Press charges. They'll throw them out."

Her threat about an unlisted number didn't bother me: a simple call to the telephone company the following afternoon straightened *that* out. I gave them my name and told them that Bea had brought in a prescription to be filled. After she'd picked it up I discovered that I had misread it and given her a dangerous overdose. I told them that if I were unable to get in touch with her before she took the first capsule she would die. And they'd better give me her new address as well so that I could get an ambulance to her if she'd already taken the capsule and was unable to answer the phone. Love *always* finds a way!

I gave her time to settle herself in her new apartment and get some of her confidence back. Then, a week later—I couldn't wait longer: it was getting pretty close to her period—I took the package I had prepared and drove to Bea's new address. Her name on the

letter box had been newly stenciled on a shiny black strip of cellu-
lose, the last name only, the little darling—you know how single
girls in big cities try to protect themselves by disguising their sex
with initials or last names: the poor dears don't realize that it's a
dead giveaway—along with her apartment number. I walked up the
two flights and knocked on her door.

"Yes?"

"Mr. Giddons from Tiger's." The building was managed by
Tiger's Real Estate and there's actually a Mr. Giddons who works
there.

"What do you want?"

"We have a report there's some structural damage in 3-E. I
want to check the walls in your apartment."

She opened the door, the trusting little cupcake. "It's you."

" 'All's fair in love and war.' "

"What do you want?"

"I'm berserk," I said, "amok with love. If you scream I'll kill
you."

I moved into the room and closed the door behind me. What
can I say? In the twentieth century there is no disgrace. It happened, so I'll tell you.

I pushed her roughly and turned my back to her while I pulled
on the rubber. As I rolled it on I shouted threats to keep her in line.
"One false move and I'll kill you. I've got a knife. Don't go for the
unlisted phone or I'll slit you from ear to ear. I'll cut your pupick
out. Stay away from the window. No tricks. I love you. Bernie
burns, the pharmacist on fire. Don't double-cross me. If I miss you
with the knife I'll shoot your head with my bullets." At last it was
on. Still with my back to her I ordered her to stand still. "Don't
make a move. If you make a move I'll strangle you with my bare
hands. Don't make a move or you die. I'm wearing a State Trooper.
They're the best. I'm smearing K-Y Petroleum Jelly on me. Everything the best, nothing but the best. All right," I said, "almost
through. I just have to take this box of Kleenex out of my package and the aerosol douche. I'm unfolding the Venus Folding
Feminine Syringe. There: these are for you. *Now.*" I turned to
her.

"*My God!*" I said.

She had taken off her dress and brassiere and had pulled down
her panties.

"Oh God," I gasped. "It's so *big!*"

"I didn't want you to rip my clothes," she said softly.

"But your legs, your legs are so thin!"

"Pipestems."

"And your poor frail arms."

"Pipecleaners."

"But my God, Bea. Down *there!* Down there you're magnificent!"

I saw the vastnesses, the tropical rain forest that was her pubes, the swollen mons like a freshly made Indian tumulus, labia majora like a great inverted gorge, the lush pudendum.

"Fantastic!"

"I've the vulva of a giantess," she said sadly.

I reached out and hid my hands up to the wrists in her pubic hair. As soon as I touched her I felt myself coming. "Oh, Jesus. Oh, Jesus. I love you—oo—oo—oo!" It was over. The sperm made a warm, independent weight in the bottom of my State Trooper. It swung against me like a third ball. "Oh God," I sighed. "Oh dear. Oh my. Let me just catch my breath. Whew. Holy Cow! Great Scott!

"Okay," I said in a few moments, "now you listen to me. I'm at your mercy. How can you throw a man in the hoosegow when you know as much about him as you do? I didn't jump out at you from an alley or drag you into a car. Look"—I turned my pockets inside out—"I'm not armed. There's no knife. I don't carry a gun. These hands are trained. They fill prescriptions. Do you think they could strangle? Granted I threatened you, but I was afraid you'd scream. Look at it this way. I was protecting *you*. You're just starting out in the neighborhood. It's a first-class building. Would you want a scandal? And didn't I take every precaution? Look at the douche. Everything the best that money can buy. And what did it come to in the end? I never even got close to you. To tell you the truth I thought it might happen just this way. It's not like rape. I love you. How can you ruin a man who loves you? I'm no stranger. You know me. You know my wife's name. I told you about my son. I'm a grandfather. Take a look at these pictures of my grandchildren. Did I ever show you these? This one's Susan. Four years old and a little imp. Boy, does she keep her parents hopping! And this is Greg. Greg's the thoughtful one. He'll be the scholar. Are you going to put a grandfather in jail? You got me excited. Perk peeks. The pharmacist in flames. I love you, but I'll never bother you again. I had to, just this once. Give me a chance. It would break my wife's heart to find out about me. Okay, they'd try to hush it up and maybe the grandkids would never hear about it, but what about my son? That's another story.

"I'll tell you something else. *You're the last.* A man's first woman is special, and so's his last. He never gets over either of them. And how much time do you think I have left? You saw how I was. I can't control it. I've had it as a man. I'm through. Give me a break, Bea. Don't call the police. I love you. I'm your friend. Though I'll let you in on a secret. I'd still be your friend in jail. All I really wanted was to see it. I *still* see it. I'm looking now. No, I'll be honest: *staring.* I'm staring because I've never seen anything like it, and I want to remember it forever. Not that I'll ever forget. I *never* will. Never."

I was weeping. Bea had started to dress.

"There are jokes," I said when I'd regained control, "about men on motorcycles disappearing inside women, or getting lost. There's this one about a rabbi married to a woman who's supposed to be really fabulous. One day the cleaning lady comes into the bedroom where the rabbi's wife is taking a nap. She's lying on the bedspread, all naked except where she's covered her genitals with the rabbi's skull cap, and the maid says, 'Oh, my God, I knew it would happen one day. The rabbi fell in.' I used to laugh at stories like that, but I never will again. You're *so* beautiful."

"I didn't scream," she said, "because it was my fate."

"What?"

"People find out about me. In high school, in gym, the girls would see me in the shower, and they'd tell their boyfriends. Then the boys would humiliate me. Worse things were done than what you've done. We had to leave town. In the new high school I got a note from the doctor so that I could be excused from gym, but they still found out. Maybe someone from my old town knew someone in the new town, maybe the doctor himself said something—I don't know. Boys would take me out and . . . want to see. When I graduated I moved away and started all over in a different state. There was a boy . . . I liked him. One day we made love—and *he* told. It was terrible. I can't even wear a bathing suit. You know? Then I came to Hartford. And you found out. I didn't scream because it was my fate. At least you say you love me—"

"Adore you," I said.

She said something I couldn't quite hear.

"What was that?"

"I said it's my burden. Only it carries me. It's as if I were always on horseback," she cried, and rushed toward me and embraced me, and I held her like that for an hour, and when I was ready we made love.

Bruce Jay Friedman

✳

THE LONELY GUY'S APARTMENT

At college, he was quite shy with women. His approach was to say "Hi there," tell the woman his name and then say: "Some day I would like to have an apartment overlooking New York City's East River." He could not recall one instance in which a woman responded to this technique.

A Lonely Guy's best friend is his apartment. Granted, there is no way for him to put his arms around it, chuck it under the chin and take it to a Mets' game. But it is very often all he has to come home to. Under no circumstances should he have an apartment that he feels is out to get him. One that's a little superior. An Oscar Wilde of an apartment. No Junior Studio will ever throw its arms around the Lonely Guy and say: "It's gonna be all right, babe." But it should at least be on his team. Perhaps not a partner on life's highway, but somewhere in his corner.

If you are a brand-new Lonely Guy, the chances are you have just been thrown out and have wound up draped over the end of somebody's couch. Either that or you have booked a room in an apartment-hotel for older folks who have Missed Out on Life. There will be a restaurant in this kind of hotel where people take a long time deciding if they should have the sole. You don't want to become one of those fellows. As soon as you get movement back in your legs, try to get your own place.

Many Lonely Guys will settle for a grim little one-roomer in which all they have to do is lie there—everything being in snatching distance of the bed—contact lens wetting solution, Ritz crackers, toothpicks, Valium, cotton balls, etc. This is a mistake. No Lonely Guy can thrive in an apartment that comes to an abrupt ending the second he walks through the door. There is no reason why he should have to go to the zoo for a change of scenery. Or stand in the closet. The Lonely Guy in a one-roomer will soon find himself tapping out messages to the next-door neighbors or clutching at the window guards and shouting: "No prison bars can hold me." It's important to have that second room even if it's a little bit of a thing and you have to crawl into it.

The best way to smoke out an apartment is to check with your friends. Everyone will know someone who has seven months to go on a lease and wants to sublet. Someone who's had a series shot out from under him. But this may not be the best way to go. Living in an apartment with seven months remaining on the lease is like always waiting for the toast to come up. Try to get one with a decent amount of time remaining, eighteen months or two years, so you can at least feel it's worth it to get your Monterey Jazz Festival posters on the wall.

Rental agents can be useful, except that they tend only to handle apartments with wood-burning fireplaces. If you say you don't want one, you get marked down as an uncharming fellow who didn't go to acceptable schools. The tendency of the new Lonely Guy will be to grab the first place that looks better than a Borneo Death Cell, just so he can get off the street. He doesn't want to make a career of looking at vacant apartments which still have other people's old noodles in the sink. It will be worth your while to hold out, to contain your retching just a few days longer and ask yourself these questions about any apartment before you snap it up:

How Is It for Taking Naps? Lonely Guys take a tremendous amount of naps. They are an important weapon in the fight to kill off weekends. Before renting an apartment, make sure it has good nap potential. You might even want to borrow the keys from the rental agent, lie down and test-nap it.

What Would It Be Like to Have Bronchitis In? Bronchitis, that scourge of the Lonely Guy. Call up any Lonely Guy you know and he's likely to be in the last stages of it. (Lonely Guys don't wash their vegetables.) But it's an excellent test: Is this the kind of place I'd want to have Bronchitis in or would I feel ridiculous?

What About Noise? Tomb-like silence is not always the ticket. It can be dangerous for a Lonely Guy to sit around listening to his own pulse. Some noises aren't bad. The sound of an eminent chest specialist with a persistent hacking cough can be amusing. But make sure there isn't a lady above you named *Haughty Felice* whose specialty is chaining up stockbrokers and hurling them into play dungeons.

"Get in there, Dwight, and start worshipping my stiletto heels."

Nothing is more unsettling than to hear a commodities expert rattling his handcuffs at four in the morning.

Do I Want This Apartment Waiting for Me When I Get Back from San Francisco? The Lonely Guy may often be sent to San Francisco to whip a sluggish branch office into shape. When he returns, there will never be anyone waiting at the terminal to hail his arrival. This is always a clutch situation. The well-traveled Lonely Guy deals with it by holding back his tears and impatiently shouldering his way through the crowd, pretending he's got to catch a connecting flight to Madrid. Still and all, if he gets out of the airport at one in the morning, and there isn't a wonderful apartment waiting for him, all warmed up and ready to go, that could be it, right there, ring-a-ding-ding, into the toilet for good.

Is It Over-Priced? The Lonely Guy has been taught two things, ever since he was a little tiny Lonely Guy: (1) Never kneel down to inhale bus exhaust fumes. (2) Keep the rent down.

It's time to take another look at that second one. All terrific apartments are over-priced. The only ones with low rents are downwind of French restaurants that didn't get any stars at all in dining-out guides.

When it comes to rent, it's probably best to cut down on other things, like molar insurance, and pay through the nose, if that's what it takes to get a winner. On the other hand, don't pay so much rent that you have to live on *Milk Duds.* Or that you're always mad at your apartment. Remember, it's not the apartment's fault that it's expensive. There is nothing the apartment can do about it. Can it help it if it's great?

Is This Apartment Really Me? That's the Big One. Freud told his followers that when it came to making major decisions they should listen to their "deep currents." You might find an apartment that would be just right for the early struggling Gore Vidal. Or for Harry Reasoner right now. But does it have *your* name on it? Listen to your deep apartment currents on this one. Ferenczi, a disciple of Freud's, listened to his and admittedly committed suicide. But not before he'd enjoyed many happy months in a charming little duplex in Vienna.

In sum, you need a great apartment.

There will be times when it will be just You and Your Apartment against the World.

Get yourself a stand-up apartment.

Here are some more apartment insights:

ONE GREAT FEATURE

Before you sign the lease, make sure the apartment has at least one special feature—a natural brick wall, a sunken living room, smoked mirrors—so that when you are walking around aimlessly, you can stop suddenly and say: "Jesus, look at those smoked mirrors. And they're all mine, until the lease is up." That one terrific feature might even be a dignitary. Then you can go around saying: "I've got a little place in the same building as John Travolta's dermatologist."

TERRACE TIPS

The Lonely Guy with a decent income should try to get himself a terrace. The most important thing about a terrace is to make sure it's screwed on tight. A lot of them fall off and are never reported because people are too embarrassed, the way they used to be about rapes.

Along with the terrace, it's essential to get a Monkey Deflector. Many big-city buildings have South American diplomats living in them who keep monkeys that will swing in at you. Chileans are especially guilty of this practice. They will insist the monkeys are harmless—"Just give Toto a little yogurt"—but if you check with the doorman, you will find out they are biters.

Once you have a terrace, don't feel obliged to throw over your adult life to the care of potted flowers. Toss a few pieces of broken statuary out there and tell visitors: "I'm letting it go wild." This will impress women who have been raised in Sun Belt trailer courts.

THE JOY OF LIGHTING

Too much emphasis cannot be placed on the importance of good lighting. The Lonely Guy with an uncontrollable urge to bang his head on the refrigerator may be reacting to sallow, unattractive light. Lighting should be warm and cozy and there should not be too much of it. An excess will remind you that there isn't anyone wonderful in there with you. Too little will have you tapping along the walls to get to the bathroom. A sure sign that the lighting is wrong is if you spend a lot of time taking strolls through the building lobby.

Unfortunately, there is no way to tear off a piece of lighting you like and bring it down to the lighting fixture people. There is no such thing as a swatch of lighting. One kind not to duplicate is the harsh,

gynecological type favored by elderly Japanese civil service officials who
like to spy on their sleeping nieces.

Lighting fixtures are tricky. Some will give off a cool and elegant
glow in the store, and then turn around and make your place look like a
massage parlor. The best way to get the lighting right is to experiment
and be prepared to go through half a dozen lamps to get the right one.
It's that important. Some of the finest light is given off by the new Luxo
lamps. Unfortunately, they look like baby pterodactyls, and Lonely Guys
who've used them complain that their lamps are out to get them. A great
kind of lighting to have is the kind they have at a bar you love in San
Francisco. Shoot for that kind.

VIEWS

The worst view you can have is a bridge, particularly a *Lost Horizon*
type that's obscured in fog at the far end. In no time at all, the Lonely
Guy will start thinking of it as a metaphor for his life, stretching off into
nowhere. Some other things not to have as a view are prisons, consoli-
dated laundries and medical institutes. The Pacific is not so hot either
unless you're into vastness. Interiors of courtyards are tolerable, but will
tend to make you feel you should be writing a proletarian novel or at
least in some way be clawing your way to the top. The world's most
unnerving view is when you can see just a little bit of a movie marquee;
the only way to tell what's playing is to stretch all the way out the window
while another Lonely Guy holds your ankles. The most relaxing view is
the Botswana Embassy.

PEOPLE WHO CAN HELP YOU DECORATE

The Last People Who Lived in the Apartment. When you move in,
don't rearrange anything that was left behind. Chances are the previous
tenant knew more about decorating than you do. He may even have
been a tasteful Lonely Guy.

The Moving Men. Many have good decorating instincts, especially
if they are out-of-work actors. A danger is that they will make your
apartment look like an *Uncle Vanya* set. But if your own decorating
instincts are shaky, leave things exactly where the moving men set them
down.

Any Woman Who Worked on a Major Film. Invite one over, don't
say a thing and have a normal evening. At some point, reflexively, she

will move a sconce or something several inches and you will see a boring room explode with loveliness.

The Woman at the Department Store. Every department store has a handsome woman in her fifties who is assigned to help Lonely Guys. She will have a large bosom, generous haunches and will set you to thinking about Dickensian sex with your mother's best friend in front of a hearth. There is no need to seek her out. She will spot you at the door of the furniture department. (There is some evidence that she is in league with the divorce courts and that you may have been phoned in to her.) Work with this woman, though cautiously. No matter what your sensibility, she will see you as a craggy, seafaring type out of a late-night movie ("Dash my buttons if you aren't a handsome-looking sea-calf") and pick your furniture accordingly. Upon delivery, many of her choices will not fit through your front door. Why does she pick out furniture that's too big to fit in? No one knows. She earns no commissions on this massive stuff that has to go back to the store. It may have something to do with her ample haunches. Get her to try again by coming on smaller.

FEAR OF DECORATORS

Many people are terrified of decorators, afraid they're going to be given widely publicized Bad Taste Awards if they don't go along with every one of the decorator's recommendations. It's because of those "to the trade only" signs on all the good furniture stores. Just once, talk back to a decorator. The experience can be exhilarating.

DECORATOR (*a woman with orange hair*): I've thought it over and you're getting Riviera Blinds for your living room.

LONELY GUY: No, I'm not.

DECORATOR (*astonished*): What?

LONELY GUY: You heard me. I hate Riviera Blinds. And I'm beginning to hate you, too.

DECORATOR: How about the track lighting I ordered?

LONELY GUY: Hate it. Send it back.

DECORATOR (*after a pause*): You're right on both counts. I'll get rid of the "verticals," too.

LONELY GUY: The "verticals" stay. I've always had rather a fondness for "verticals."

DECORATOR (*with new respect*): You're hard to work for . . . but *so* challenging.

A WORD OF CAUTION ON DESKS

The easiest thing to buy is a desk. Rough-hewn ones made of drift-wood, rolltop desks, elegant French ones upon which the first acts of farces were written. The Lonely Guy must be careful not to buy a whole bunch of them; if he does, his apartment will soon look like the city room of a scrappy small-city daily.

ASHTRAYS

It's important to have a lot of ashtrays around and not just to ac-commodate smokers. When they cook, most Lonely Guys have nothing to bring the vegetables out in. Certain ashtrays can pass as a charming new kind of vegetable platter. The peas, for example, look just great in a big bright ashtray.

BOOKSHELVES

Books give an apartment a scholarly pipe-smoking look. Many rock-oriented young women will assume you wrote all the books on your shelves—that you were once named Coleridge. Don't overdo it and turn your place into a library. The saddest book story is that of Lonely Gal Eleanor Barry (reprinted in its entirety from *The New York Times*, December 21, 1977).

A 70-year-old woman was pulled out from under a giant pile of books, newspapers and press clippings that had collapsed on her, but she died shortly after being rescued. The pile fell on Eleanor Barry as she lay in her bedroom, and according to police in Huntington Station, Long Island, the weight of the papers muffled her cries for help. She died Sunday.

The police said they had to use an axe to smash the door of the bedroom because the collapsed pile blocked their entry. They said that the house was filled with towers of books, newspapers, shopping bags and as-sorted papers.

THE ENDS OF THINGS

It's important to put some focus on the ends of things as the Lonely Guy will be spending a great deal of time huddled over there in a corner. An investment in a bunch of good strong end tables, for example, will not be wasted. It's important, incidentally, to keep couches manageable in size and not have them stretching off in the distance. What's the point of being the only fellow on a long freight train of a couch! Other, juicier opportunities for loneliness and isolation will be coming your way. And stay away from Conversation Pits. The Lonely Guy who's rigged one up will quickly see that he is the only one on hand to sound off on America's lack of a clear-cut natural gas policy.

A TRICKY DECISION

Do you go with overhead mirrors? There is no question that they are fiercely erotic, especially if you can talk an *au pair* girl into slipping under one with you. But what about those nights when you're just a poignant guy staring up at his own hips! The makers of overhead mirrors are conservative and confidence-inspiring, many of them respected Italian-Americans with no connections to the Gambino family. But they cannot absolutely guarantee that an overhead won't come down in the middle of the night and turn you into a whole bunch of Lonely Guys. For this reason, it might be wise to pass.

PLANTS

Buy a lot of them. Scattered about, they will cover up the fact that you don't have enough furniture and aren't knowledgeable about room dividers. A drawback is that each day you will see little buds and shoots, life perpetuating itself while yours may very well not be. Buy your plants on the opposite side of town. They are always cheaper over there. Refer to your plants as "Guys." Put your arm around one and say: "This guy here is my avocado."

ROOM FRESHENER

Lonely Guy apartments tend to get a bit stale, so it's important to load up on room fresheners. The way to apply one is to hold it aloft, press the aerosol button and then streak through the rooms as though you are heralding the start of the new Olympics. Some of the fumes will flash back and freshen *you* up, along with the apartment. Many a woman who has admired a Lonely Guy's cologne is unwittingly in love with his room freshener.

A SHEET AND BLANKET PROGRAM

One kind of sheet to be wary of is the elastic bottom one that curls over the four corners of the bed and supposedly stays there. As soon as you buy them, they no longer fit. The biggest problem is that they tend to break loose in the night and snap you up in them.

Silky, satiny sheets feel good to the skin and will give you an inkling of what it's like to be Bob Guccione. But what you get is a combination of sleeping and ice-skating and there is always the danger of being squirted out of bed. Just buy colorful sheets you like.

The time to change sheets is when you can no longer ignore the Grielle and Zweiback crumbs in them.

Salesmen will tell you that East German llama blankets are the warmest in the world and are so tightly woven that the thinnest shaft of cold can't sneak in there and get at you. None of this is important. The only way to test a blanket is to hold it up to your cheek and see if it feels fluffy. (The sight of this is heartbreaking and will help you in picking up saleswomen.) Better to have ten fluffies than one llama that holds off chilly weather but has a hostile Cold War feel to it.

SHOWER CURTAIN MADNESS

The trick in getting a shower curtain is to find one that fits right. Shower curtains are either long, flowing things that look like gowns worn by transvestite members of the Austro-Hungarian General Staff, or else they are shorties that will remind you of Midwestern insurance men whose pants don't come down far enough. Bob Dole fans.

There is the possibility that the Lonely Guy is incapable of buying any shower curtain at all. And that he will have to wait till Ms. Right comes along. If such is the case, and you plan to go without a shower curtain, the trick is to let the water hit your chest so that as much of it as possible bankshots back into the tub and doesn't rot your tiles. If enough of it gets out there, you will run the risk of plunging through the floor to the Lonely Guy below.

SILVER SEPARATORS

Lonely Guys with mangled hands are usually assumed to be veterans of Iwo. This is not necessarily the case. Too often, it's a result of reaching into kitchen drawers to try to get knives and forks out. The way around this is to buy a silver separator that has little rows for utensils. On the other hand, many Lonely Guys would rather sever an occasional artery than stand around filing butter knives.*

PICTURES YOU ARE NOT SURE OF

Lonely Guys have a tendency to accumulate paintings they are not quite sure of—gifts from dissident Haitians or suburban women who've suddenly left their families and moved into Soho lofts. The way to deal with such a painting is to prop it up on a dresser and put stuff in front of it—a clock, a Fundador bottle, a book about the fall of the once-proud Zulu nation—so that only some of the painting shows through. Make it look as if it's ready to be hung, but that you haven't gotten around to it. (You don't know where the nails are anyway.) That way, if someone admires it, she can push aside the obstructions and say, "Hey, watcha got there, fella?" If she hates it, you're covered because you've put all that stuff in front of it, indicating you don't think it's so hot either.

THE RIGHT AIR CONDITIONER

Get a strong, no-nonsense air conditioner that sends the cold air right up the middle at you. A Larry Csonka of an air conditioner. Don't get one in which the air wanders out in a vague and poetical manner so that you have to run around trying to trace it.

THE RIGHT TV SET

The most important thing about a TV set is to get it back against something and not out in the middle of a room where it's like a somber fellow making electronic judgments on you. Odd-shaped TV sets make a lot of sense; a tall skinny sliver of a TV set can actually spruce up a dying sitcom. But don't make the mistake of getting a lot of little tiny sets and scattering them about like leftover snacks. Get one solid-looking Big Guy that you can really dig into.

The prospect of a little TV-viewing section with some throw pillows strewn about and a prominent bowl of shelled walnuts may be dismaying to the urbane Lonely Guy—but its effects are likely to be calming.

---

* Another way to deal with silverware is to slap it up in full view on a magnetic wallboard. However, the underweight Lonely Guy with a metal watchband runs the risk of being sucked right up on it, along with the knives.

GAY CLEANING FELLOWS

Now that you've got your apartment, who's going to clean it up? Good news in this department. Now that *Chorus Line* is a smash and has spawned international companies, there are a lot of dancers who couldn't get into any of them and have become gay cleaning guys. They aren't that easy to find. It isn't as if they advertise conspicuously under names like Joan Crawford Clean-Up and play selections from *Gypsy* on their answering services. They are usually under an Italian name like Fuccione and Calabrese.

Yet such a macho-sounding company can send over a bright-eyed and cheery gay guy with a handkerchief on his head. The best thing about gay cleaning fellows is that they are not afraid of ovens. They go right after them, all the way to the back end, sponging up the last droplet of lambchop grease. Gay cleaning fellows also know all about the latest cleaning stuff: you may have to take a little ribbing about not having Lemon Pledge Dusting Wax for your breakfront. On the plus side, though, they are considerate enough to Leave the Windex to You, the only fun part in all of cleaning. The only gay cleaning fellows to be wary of are ones from East Germany who may try to Cross That Line. Unless you don't mind waking up on a Sunday morning to a gay cleaning fellow named Wolfgang who has already started on *The New York Times* Arts and Leisure Section.

CLEANING FOR POVERTY-STRICKEN LONELY GUYS

Some Lonely Guys are needy,* and have to clean up their own apartments. If that's your situation, wait till just before company comes and then get down on your knees and roll up all the dust in the room in a big ball. Most of it will come right up, but stubborn dust that refuses to can be dabbed off the floor with a damp palm. Lonely Guys who live around Phoenix and have a sassy Jack Nicholson style may elect to get into dustball fights with another Lonely Guy.

THE BIG PICTURE

As a general rule, don't buy anything for your apartment that you can't take along with you. When you batter down a wall to give it an ecclesiastical grotto effect, you may be supplying a free ecclesiastical

---

* The state of being in a Negative Cash Flow Situation.

grotto effect to the next Lonely Guy. Only the strictest interpretation of Maimonides (a biblical Lonely Guy) requires you to do so. The last thing you want to do is put down roots. At a moment's notice, you should be ready and available to pull up stakes and try your luck at being a Lonely Guy in St. Paul de Vence.

Wilfrid Sheed

*

FOUR HACKS

Are all the blockbusting best sellers written by the same person? Not necessarily. The fact that all their authors give the exact same interview should not blind one to exotic varieties of plumage and even character. For instance.

Picture, if you will, the worst: four major hacks passing through New York at the same time—passing through the same hotel room in fact—celebrating their latest smasheroos. Their interlocutor is a pale literary man with a business suit and a heartful of hate because he has to work for a living. The others look so much like authors you could eat them.

First, Irving Trustfund dressed in regulation poncho and love beads, sucking thoughtfully on his meerschaum. *How goes it, Irving? Did you read those lousy reviews? Aren't you ashamed of yourself this time?* "Not at all," says Irving with his famous strained smile. "Dickens and Zola were despised by the critics of their day, you know. I'm happy to leave the verdict to the people—the *real* people, that is. Dickens was just too popular for the self-appointed pseudo-intellectuals of the day—I don't mean you, sir. You look like a *real* intellectual." Irving's poncho is suddenly drenched. He hates to make enemies. "I have enormous respect for real intellectuals," he ends miserably.

Now for Peaches Smedley, concocter of sexy gothics, swathed for town in see-through vinyl. *I hear your crap is coming back, Miss Smedley. How do you account for this sickening lapse in public taste?* "Why, I believe my so-called crap was never really gone, Mr., er, Snead. People, I mean the people *out there*, have always relished a good yarn told at a crackling pace and with lots of real characters. That's the tradition I place myself in—the robust storytelling tradition of Dickens and, er, others."

Is it true that your stuff is also dirty as hell? "If you think that the love of a man for a woman is dirty, Mr., er, yes my stuff is dirty, gloriously, life-enhancingly dirty. I myself happen to think that the real pornographers are the munitions makers and the politicians who poison our air and that we shouldn't be ashamed of our bodies."

"Effing A-OK to that, sweetie," says our third, Percy Fang, in captain's hat and Castro fatigues, biting down hard on his corncob. "I don't know why we're wasting time on this loser anyway, Peaches. How much money you make last year, Jack? Not as much as Dickens, I'll bet. That's what you people forget about effing Dickens every time. The guy was mad for the moola. Couldn't get enough of the long green. That's a real artist, baby. No one ever wrote a great book in a garret. Charlie knew that. Yet would you believe, Mr. Pale-faced Loser, that the guy the critics went for in those days was a certain Colley Cibber?"

Sharply. *What do you know about Colley Cibber?*

Guardedly. "Plenty."

Next, Aldershott Twilley, the English hack laureate, half-buried in tweed, puffing on his briarpatch: "Oh Lord yes, how they hated Dickens. Because the chap was first and last a born storyteller, you know. They can't stand that. These youngsters today have completely forgotten how to tell a story. They slap down whatever comes into their bally heads, if that's the portion of the anatomy they use, whurf whurf, and expect busy people with real concerns to take them seriously."

By youngsters, I guess you mean Joyce and Stein?

"Yes, yes, all that lot. Joyce was absolutely potty, of course. And as for Stein—what's that marvelous limerick about her: With my Rumpty tittlety . . ."

Peaches Smedley: "I happen to have terrific respect for James Joyce. In fact, I sometimes think of myself as belonging to that tradition in a way. Joyce, Flaubert . . ."

Jesus.

Trustfund: "I happen to agree wholeheartedly. I learned a lot from Joyce, and from Kafka too and from all those great writers. And do you know why? Do you know what they were writing about? They were writing about *people!*"

Twilley: "Absolutely potty."

Fang: "Joyce is A-OK with me. He told it like it is in the sack, and that's the name of the game. The sack is where it's at for a real writer."

Trustfund: "I absolutely agree. If by sack you mean all the inexhaustibly multifaceted aspects of . . ."

Fang: "By sack I mean sack. What do you think Keats was writing about, fella, and Gerard de Nerval and all those guys? S-A-C-K. Ever hear of Gerard de Nerval, paleface? He was pretty far into sex, I hear."

Fang has a reputation for turning interviews into shambles at this point, so the interlocutor changes the subject nimbly.

Hobbies, Ms. Smedley? "Well, people, mostly. For instance, I'd love to be interviewing *you* right now."

Muttered. *You would be, if there was any justice.*

Smedley: "And books, of course. I'm never without a book. Bishop Andrews, Mrs. Gaskell, anything at all."

Working methods, Mr. Twilley?

Twilley: "Well, old Dickens had the answer to that as to so many things. Four, five thousand words a night. Work your arse off, dear boy, it won't kill you."

Trustfund: "It's true, modern writers to tend to coddle themselves. Genius is a robust flower, all the giants knew that instinctively."

What about Joyce and his four books?

Trustfund: "Well, there are giants and giants of course."

Twilley: "Joyce was a bloody little twit if you ask me."

Fang: "He was too busy in the sack, which is where I'd be myself if I had any sense."

Eyes Smedley, who turns away in undisguised horror. Fang is bent on his shambles: it's only a question of time now.

Critics, Ms. Smedley?

Smedley: "To be frank, I don't read them. They're such sad little people. So full of envy."

I read somewhere that bad reviews make you cry?

Smedley (uncertainly): "Well, as I say, I don't read them."

Twilley: "Neither do I. I'm much too busy writing novels myself. Do you know the old Welsh saying that goes, 'Those who can, do . . .'"

All (roaring): ". . . and those who can't, teach."

Twilley: "Oh, you'd heard that one?"

Hobbies, Mr. Trustfund?

Trustfund: "Merovingian porcelains, anything bearing on the Icelandic comic spirit . . ."

Working methods, Ms. Smedley?

Smedley: "Five or six thousand words a day. Work your arse off."

Twilley: "Dickens."

Trustfund: "Dickens and *Zola*, I tell you."

Fang (pouncing on Smedley): "Here I come, ready or not."

You're nothing but a pack of cards. You're nothing but . . . The cat, which had been Peaches Smedley only a moment before, stares at me levelly. I have been shaking the bejasus out of her ever since I stepped into Jacqueline Susann's looking glass a few weeks back in *The Times Magazine* and had my head straightened out by Humpty Dumpty. (Incidentally, that guy Lewis Carroll certainly knew how to get out of a dream sequence, and I'd like to acknowledge my debt to him and Theodore Dreiser right now.)

Some conclusions now from a pseudo-elitist. Although hacks vary enormously in quality, such that a Herman Wouk might reasonably reject the title and a Mickey Spillane can barely claim it, they seem to share a certain turbid homogeneity of thought and phrase which perhaps explains their popularity. Since, by me, straight oompapa storytelling is a perfectly respectable craft, I hate to see its artisans driven to these monstrosities of defensiveness. At the same time, they must know in their sweetbreads that their line traces from Dumas and Rider Haggard and not from the grand masters of language and social observation and felt madness. Dickens in particular has earned his rest from this kind of talk.

We could certainly use a good analysis of the pops in terms of their own function—but no more, please, from the hacks themselves: solemn Jack Bennys all, who think that owning a Stradivarius and a townhouse makes you Isaac Stern, and makes of "Love in Bloom" a worthy successor to Beethoven's "Pastoral" and the other rattling good tunes that made the West.

Donald Barthelme

*

GAME

Shotwell keeps the jacks and the rubber ball in his attaché case and will not allow me to play with them. He plays with them, alone, sitting on the floor near the console hour after hour, chanting "onesies, twosies, threesies, foursies" in a precise, well-modulated voice, not so loud as to be annoying, not so soft as to allow me to forget. I point out to Shotwell that two can derive more enjoyment from playing jacks than one, but he is not interested. I have asked repeatedly to be allowed to play by myself, but he simply shakes his head. "Why?" I ask. "They're mine," he says. And when he has finished, when he has sated himself, back they go into the attaché case.

It is unfair but there is nothing I can do about it. I am aching to get my hands on them.

Shotwell and I watch the console. Shotwell and I live under the ground and watch the console. If certain events take place upon the console, we are to insert our keys in the appropriate locks and turn our keys. Shotwell has a key and I have a key. If we turn our keys simultaneously the bird flies, certain switches are activated and the bird flies. But the bird never flies. In one hundred thirty-three days the bird has not flown. Meanwhile Shotwell and I watch each other. We each wear a .45 and if Shotwell behaves strangely I am supposed to shoot him. If I behave strangely Shotwell is supposed to shoot me. We watch the console and think about shooting each other and think about the bird. Shotwell's behavior with the jacks is strange. Is it strange? I do not know. Perhaps he is merely a selfish bastard, perhaps his character is flawed, perhaps his childhood was twisted. I do not know.

Each of us wears a .45 and each of us is supposed to shoot the other if the other is behaving strangely. How strangely is strangely? I do not know. In addition to the .45 I have a .38 which Shotwell does not know about concealed in my attaché case, and Shotwell has a .25 caliber Beretta which I do not know about strapped to his right calf. Sometimes instead of watching the console I pointedly watch Shotwell's .45, but this is simply a ruse, simply a maneuver, in reality I am watching his hand when it dangles in the vicinity of his right calf. If he decides I am behaving strangely he will shoot me not with the .45 but with the Beretta. Similarly Shotwell pretends to watch my .45 but he is really watching my hand resting idly atop my attaché case, my hand resting idly atop my attaché case, my hand. My hand resting idly atop my attaché case.

In the beginning I took care to behave normally. So did Shotwell. Our behavior was painfully normal. Norms of politeness, consideration, speech, and personal habits were scrupulously observed. But then it became apparent that an error had been made, that our relief was not going to arrive. Owing to an oversight. Owing to an oversight we have been here for one hundred thirty-three days. When it became clear that an error had been made, that we were not to be relieved, the norms were relaxed. Definitions of normality were redrawn in the agreement of January 1, called by us, The Agreement. Uniform regulations were relaxed, and mealtimes are no longer rigorously scheduled. We eat when we are hungry and sleep when we are tired. Considerations of rank and precedence were temporarily put aside, a handsome concession on the part of Shotwell, who is a captain, whereas I am only a first lieutenant. One of us watches the console at all times rather than two of us watching the console at all times, except when we are both on our feet. One of us watches the console at all times and if the bird flies then that one wakes the other and we turn our keys in the locks simultaneously and the bird flies. Our system involves a delay of perhaps twelve seconds but I do not care because I am not well, and Shotwell does not care because he is not himself. After the agreement was signed Shotwell produced the jacks and the rubber ball from his attaché case, and I began to write a series of descriptions of forms occurring in nature, such as a shell, a leaf, a stone, an animal. On the walls.

Shotwell plays jacks and I write descriptions of natural forms on the walls.

Shotwell is enrolled in a USAFI course which leads to a master's degree in business administration from the University of Wisconsin (although we are not in Wisconsin, we are in Utah, Montana or Idaho). When we went down it was in either Utah, Montana or Idaho, I don't remember. We have been here for one hundred thirty-three days owing to an oversight. The pale green reinforced concrete walls sweat and the air conditioning zips on and off erratically and Shotwell reads *Introduction to Marketing* by Lassiter and Munk, making notes with a blue ballpoint pen. Shotwell is not himself, but I do not know it, he presents a calm aspect and reads *Introduction to Marketing* and makes his exemplary notes with a blue ballpoint pen, meanwhile controlling the .38 in my attaché case with one-third of his attention. I am not well.

We have been here one hundred thirty-three days owing to an oversight. Although now we are not sure what is oversight, what is plan. Perhaps the plan is for us to stay here permanently, or if not permanently at least for a year, for three hundred sixty-five days. Or if not for a year for some number of days known to them and not known to us, such as two hundred days. Or perhaps they are observing our behavior in some way, sensors of some kind, perhaps our behavior determines the number of days. It may be that they are pleased with us, with our behavior, not in every detail but in sum. Perhaps the whole thing is very successful, perhaps the whole thing is an experiment and the experiment is very successful. I do not know. But I suspect that the only way they can persuade sun-loving creatures into their pale green sweating reinforced concrete rooms under the ground is to say that the system is twelve hours on, twelve hours off. And then lock us below for some number of days known to them and not known to us. We eat well although the frozen enchiladas are damp when defrosted and the frozen devil's food cake is sour and untasty. We sleep uneasily and acrimoniously. I hear Shotwell shouting in his sleep, objecting, denouncing, cursing sometimes, weeping sometimes, in his sleep. When Shotwell sleeps I try to pick the lock on his attaché case, so as to get at the jacks. Thus far I have been unsuccessful. Nor has Shotwell been successful in picking the locks on my attaché case so as to get at the .38. I have seen the marks on the shiny surface. I laughed, in the latrine, pale green walls sweating and the air conditioning whispering, in the latrine.

I write descriptions of natural forms on the walls, scratching them on the tile surface with a diamond. The diamond is a two and one-half carat solitaire I had in my attaché case when we went down. It was for Lucy. The south wall of the room containing the console is already covered. I have described a shell, a leaf, a stone, animals, a baseball bat. I am aware that the baseball bat is not a natural form. Yet I described it: "The baseball bat," I said, "is typically made of wood. It is typically one meter in length or a little longer, fat at one end, tapering to afford a comfortable grip at the other. The end with the handhold typically offers a slight rim, or lip, at the nether extremity, to prevent slippage." My

description of the baseball bat ran to 4500 words, all scratched with a
diamond on the south wall. Does Shotwell read what I have written? I
do not know. I am aware that Shotwell regards my writing-behavior as a
little strange. Yet it is no stranger than his jacks-behavior, or the day he
appeared in black bathing trunks with the .25 caliber Beretta strapped to
his right calf and stood over the console, trying to span with his two arms
outstretched the distance between the locks. He could not do it, I had
already tried, standing over the console with my two arms outstretched,
the distance is too great. I was moved to comment but did not comment,
comment would have provoked countercomment, comment would have
led God knows where. They had in their infinite patience, in their infinite
foresight, in their infinite wisdom already imagined a man standing over
the console with his two arms outstretched, trying to span with his two
arms outstretched the distance between the locks.

Shotwell is not himself. He has made certain overtures. The burden
of his message is not clear. It has something to do with the keys, with the
locks. Shotwell is a strange person. He appears to be less affected by our
situation than I. He goes about his business stolidly, watching the console, studying *Introduction to Marketing*, bouncing his rubber ball on
the floor in a steady, rhythmical, conscientious manner. He appears to
be less affected by our situation than I am. He is stolid. He says nothing.
But he has made certain overtures, certain overtures have been made. I
am not sure that I understand them. They have something to do with
the keys, with the locks. Shotwell has something in mind. Stolidly he
shucks the shiny silver paper from the frozen enchiladas, stolidly he
stuffs them into the electric oven. But he has something in mind. But
there must be a quid pro quo. I insist on a quid pro quo. I have something in mind.

I am not well. I do not know our target. They do not tell us for
which city the bird is targeted. I do not know. That is planning. That is
not my responsibility. My responsibility is to watch the console and when
certain events take place upon the console, turn my key in the lock.
Shotwell bounces the rubber ball on the floor in a steady, stolid, rhythmical manner. I am aching to get my hands on the ball, on the jacks.
We have been here one hundred thirty-three days owing to an oversight.
I write on the walls. Shotwell chants "onesies, twosies, threesies, foursies" in a precise, well-modulated voice. Now he cups the jacks and the
rubber ball in his hands and rattles them suggestively. I do not know for
which city the bird is targeted. Shotwell is not himself.

Sometimes I cannot sleep. Sometimes Shotwell cannot sleep.
Sometimes when Shotwell cradles me in his arms and rocks me to sleep,

singing Brahms' "Guten abend, gute Nacht," or I cradle Shotwell in my arms and rock him to sleep, singing, I understand what it is Shotwell wishes me to do. At such moments we are very close. But only if he will give me the jacks. That is fair. There is something he wants me to do with my key, while he does something with his key. But only if he will give me my turn. That is fair. I am not well.

V. S. Naipaul

*

THE MECHANICAL GENIUS

My Uncle Bhakcu was very nearly a mechanical genius. I cannot remember a time when he was not the owner of a motor-vehicle of some
sort. I don't think he always approved of the manufacturer's designs,
however, for he was always pulling engines to bits. Titus Hoyt said that
this was also a habit of the Eskimos. It was something he had got out of
a geography book.

If I try to think of Bhakcu I never see his face. I can see only the
soles of his feet as he worms his way under a car. I was worried when
Bhakcu was under a car because it looked so easy for the car to slip off
the jack and fall on him.

One day it did.

He gave a faint groan that reached the ears of only his wife.

She bawled, "Oh God!" and burst into tears right away. "I know
something wrong. Something happen to *he*."

Mrs. Bhakcu always used this pronoun when she spoke of her husband.

She hurried to the side of the yard and heard Bhakcu groaning.

"Man," she whispered, "you all right?"

He groaned a little more loudly.

He said, "How the hell I all right? You mean you so blind you ain't
see the whole motor-car break up my arse?"

Mrs. Bhakcu, dutiful wife, began to cry afresh.

She beat on the galvanized-iron fence.

"Hat," Mrs. Bhakcu called, "Hat, come quick. A whole motor-car
fall on *he*."

Hat was cleaning out the cow-pen. When he heard Mrs. Bhakcu
he laughed. "You know what I always does say," Hat said. "When you

play the ass you bound to catch hell. The blasted car brand-new. What the hell he was tinkering with so?"

"*He* say the crank-shaft wasn't working nice."

"And is there he looking for the crank-shaft?"

"Hat," Bhakcu shouted from under the car, "the moment you get this car from off me, I going to break up your tail."

"Man," Mrs. Bhakcu said to her husband, "how you so advantageous? The man come round with his good good mind to help you and now you want to beat him up?"

Hat began to look hurt and misunderstood.

Hat said, "It ain't nothing new. Is just what I expect. Is just what I does always get for interfering in other people business. You know I mad to leave you and your husband here and go back to the cow-pen."

"No, Hat. You mustn't mind *he*. Think what you would say if a whole big new motor-car fall on you."

Hat said, "All right, all right. I have to go and get some of the boys."

We heard Hat shouting in the street. "Boyee and Errol!"

No answer.

"Bo-yee and Ehhroll!"

"Co-ming, Hat."

"Where the hell you boys been, eh? You think you is man now and you could just stick your hands in your pocket and walk out like man? You was smoking, eh?"

"Smoking, Hat?"

"But what happen now? You turn deaf all of a sudden?"

"Was Boyee was smoking, Hat."

"Is a lie, Hat. Was Errol really. I just stand up watching him."

"Somebody make you policeman now, eh? Is cut-arse for both of you. Errol, go cut a whip for Boyee. Boyee, go cut a whip for Errol."

We heard the boys whimpering.

From under the car Bhakcu called, "Hat, why you don't leave the boys alone? You go bless them bad one of these days, you know, and then they go lose you in jail. Why you don't leave the boys alone? They big now."

Hat shouted back, "You mind your own business, you hear. Otherwise I leave you under that car until you rotten, you hear."

Mrs. Bhakcu said to her husband, "Take it easy, man."

But it was nothing serious after all. The jack had slipped but the axle rested on a pile of wooden blocks, pinning Bhakcu to ground without injuring him.

When Bhakcu came out he looked at his clothes. These were a pair of khaki trousers and a sleeveless vest, both black and stiff with engine grease.

Bhakcu said to his wife, "They really dirty now, eh?"

She regarded her husband with pride. "Yes, man," she said. "They really dirty."

Bhakcu smiled.

Hat said, "Look, I just sick of lifting up motor-car from off you, you hear. If you want my advice, you better send for a proper mechanic."

Bhakcu wasn't listening.

He said to his wife, "The crank-shaft was all right. Is something else."

Mrs. Bhakcu said, "Well, you must eat first."

She looked at Hat and said, "He don't eat when he working on the car unless I remind he."

Hat said, "What you want me do with that? Write it down with a pencil on a piece of paper and send it to the papers?"

I wanted to watch Bhakcu working on the car that evening, so I said to him, "Uncle Bhakcu, your clothes looking really dirty and greasy. I wonder how you could bear to wear them."

He turned and smiled at me. "What you expect, boy?" he said. "Mechanic people like me ain't have time for clean clothes."

"What happen to the car, Uncle Bhakcu?" I asked.

He didn't reply.

"The tappet knocking?" I suggested.

One thing Bhakcu had taught me about cars was that tappets were always knocking. Give Bhakcu any car in the world, and the first thing he would tell you about it was, "The tappet knocking, you know. Hear. Hear it?"

"The tappet knocking?" I asked.

He came right up to me and asked eagerly, "What, you hear it knocking?"

And before I had time to say, "Well, something did knocking," Mrs. Bhakcu pulled him away, saying, "Come and eat now, man. God, you get your clothes really dirty today."

• • •

The car that fell on Bhakcu wasn't really a new car, although Bhakcu boasted that it very nearly was.

"It only do two hundred miles," he used to say.

Hat said, "Well, I know Trinidad small, but I didn't know it was so small."

I remember the day it was bought. It was a Saturday. And that morning Mrs. Bhakcu came to my mother and they talked about the cost of rice and flour and the black market. As she was leaving, Mrs. Bhakcu said, "*He* gone to town today. *He* say *he* got to buy a new car."

So we waited for the new car.

Midday came, but Bhakcu didn't.

Hat said, "Two to one, that man taking down the engine right this minute."

About four o'clock we heard a banging and a clattering, and looking down Miguel Street towards Docksite we saw the car. It was a blue Chevrolet, one of the 1939 models. It looked rich and new. We began to wave and cheer, and I saw Bhakcu waving his left hand.

We danced into the road in front of Bhakcu's house, waving and cheering.

The car came nearer and Hat said, "Jump, boys! Run for your life. Like he get mad."

It was a near thing. The car just raced past the house and we stopped cheering.

Hat said, "The car out of control. It go have a accident, if something don't happen quick."

Mrs. Bhakcu laughed. "What you think it is at all?" she said.

But we raced after the car, crying after Bhakcu.

He wasn't waving with his left hand. He was trying to warn people off.

By a miracle, it stopped just before Ariapita Avenue.

Bhakcu said, "I did mashing down the brakes since I turn Miguel Street, but the brakes ain't working. Is a funny thing. I overhaul the brakes just this morning."

Hat said, "It have two things for you to do. Overhaul your head or haul your arse away before you get people in trouble."

Bhakcu said, "You boys go have to give me a hand to push the car back home."

As we were pushing it past the house of Morgan, the pyrotechnicist, Mrs. Morgan shouted, "Ah, Mrs. Bhakcu, I see you buy a new car today, man."

Mrs. Bhakcu didn't reply.

Mrs. Morgan said, "Ah, Mrs. Bhakcu, you think your husband go give me a ride in his new car?"

Mrs. Bhakcu said, "Yes, *he* go give you a ride, but first *you* husband must give me a ride on his donkey-cart when he buy it."

Bhakcu said to Mrs. Bhakcu, "Why you don't shut your mouth up?"

Mrs. Bhakcu said, "But how you want me to shut my mouth up? You is my husband, and I have to stand up for you."

Bhakcu said very sternly, "You only stand up for me when I tell you, you hear."

We left the car in front of Bhakcu's house, and we left Mr. and Mrs. Bhakcu to their quarrel. It wasn't a very interesting one. Mrs. Bhakcu kept on claiming her right to stand up for her husband, and Mr. Bhakcu kept on rejecting the claim. In the end Bhakcu had to beat his wife.

This wasn't as easy as it sounds. If you want to get a proper picture of Mrs. Bhakcu you must consider a pear as a scale-model. Mrs. Bhakcu had so much flesh, in fact, that when she held her arms at her sides, they looked like marks of parenthesis.

And as for her quarrelling voice . . .

Hat used to say, "It sound as though it coming from a gramophone record turning fast fast backwards."

For a long time I think Bhakcu experimented with rods for beating his wife, and I wouldn't swear that it wasn't Hat who suggested a cricket bat. But whoever suggested it, a second-hand cricket bat was bought from one of the groundsmen at the Queen's Park Oval, and oiled, and used on Mrs. Bhakcu.

Hat said, "Is the only thing she really could feel, I think."

The strangest thing about this was that Mrs. Bhakcu herself kept the bat clean and well-oiled. Boyee tried many times to borrow the bat, but Mrs. Bhakcu never lent it.

·   ·   ·

So on the evening of the day when the car fell on Bhakcu I went to see him at work.

"What you did saying about the tappet knocking?" he said.

"I didn't say nothing," I said. "I was asking you."

"Oh."

Bhakcu worked late into the night, taking down the engine. He worked all the next day, Sunday, and all Sunday night. On Monday morning the mechanic came.

Mrs. Bhakcu told my mother, "The company send the mechanic man. The trouble with these Trinidad mechanics is that they is just piss-in-tail little boys who don't know the first thing about cars and things."

I went round to Bhakcu's house and saw the mechanic with his head inside the bonnet. Bhakcu was sitting on the running-board, rubbing grease over everything the mechanic handed him. He looked so happy dipping his fingers in the grease that I asked, "Let me rub some grease, Uncle Bhakcu."

"Go away, boy. You too small."

I sat and watched him.

He said, "The tappet was knocking, but I fix it."

I said, "Good."

The mechanic was cursing.

I asked Bhakcu, "How the points?"

He said, "I have to check them up."

I got up and walked around the car and sat on the running-board next to Bhakcu.

I looked at him and I said, "You know something?"

"What?"

"When I did hear the engine on Saturday, I didn't think it was beating nice."

Bhakcu said, "You getting to be a real smart man, you know. You learning fast."

I said, "Is what you teach me."

It was, as a matter of fact, pretty nearly the limit of my knowledge. The knocking tappet, the points, the beat of the engine and—yes, I had forgotten one thing.

"You know, Uncle Bhakcu," I said.

"What, boy?"

"Uncle Bhakcu, I think is the carburettor."

"You really think so, boy?"

"I sure, Uncle Bhakcu."

"Well, I go tell you, boy. Is the first thing I ask the mechanic. He don't think so."

The mechanic lifted a dirty and angry face from the engine and said, "When you have all sort of ignorant people messing about with an engine the white people build with their own hands, what the hell else you expect?"

Bhakcu winked at me.

He said, "*I* think is the carburettor."

• • •

Of all the drills, I liked the carburettor drill the best. Sometimes Bhakcu raced the engine while I put my palm over the curburettor and off again. Bhakcu never told me why we did this and I never asked. Sometimes we had to siphon petrol from the tank, and I would pour this petrol into the carburettor while Bhakcu raced the engine. I often asked him to let me race the engine, but he wouldn't agree.

One day the engine caught fire, but I jumped away in time. The fire didn't last.

Bhakcu came out of the car and looked at the engine in a puzzled way. I thought he was annoyed with it, and I was prepared to see him dismantle it there and then.

That was the last time we did that drill with the carburettor.

•   •   •

At last the mechanic tested the engine and the brakes, and said, "Look, the car good good now, you hear. It cost me more work than if I was to build over a new car. Leave the damn thing alone."

After the mechanic left, Bhakcu and I walked very thoughtfully two or three times around the car. Bhakcu was stroking his chin, not talking to me.

Suddenly he jumped into the driver's seat, and pressed the horn-button a few times.

He said, "What you think about the horn, boy?"

I said, "Blow it again, let me hear."

He pressed the button again.

Hat pushed his head through a window and shouted, "Bhakcu, keep the damn car quiet, you hear, man. You making the place sound as though it have a wedding going on."

We ignored Hat.

I said, "Uncle Bhakcu, I don't think the horn blowing nice."

He said, "You really don't think so?"

I made a face and spat.

So we began to work on the horn.

When we were finished there was a bit of flex wound round the steering-column.

Bhakcu looked at me and said, "You see, you could just take this wire now and touch it on any part of the metalwork, and the horn blow."

It looked unlikely, but it did work.

I said, "Uncle Bhak, how you know about all these things?"

He said, "You just keep on learning all the time."

•   •   •

The men in the street didn't like Bhakcu because they considered him a nuisance. But I liked him for the same reason that I liked Popo, the carpenter. For, thinking about it now, Bhakcu was also an artist. He interfered with motor-cars for the joy of the thing, and he never seemed worried about money.

But his wife was worried. She, like my mother, thought that she was born to be a clever handler of money, born to make money sprout from nothing at all.

She talked over the matter with my mother one day.

My mother said, "Taxi making a lot of money these days, taking Americans and their girl friends all over the place."

So Mrs. Bhakcu made her husband buy a lorry.

This lorry was really the pride of Miguel Street. It was a big new Bedford and we all turned out to welcome it when Bhakcu brought it home for the first time.

Even Hat was impressed. "If is one thing the English people could build," he said, "is a lorry. This is not like your Ford and your Dodge, you know."

Bhakcu began working on it that very afternoon, and Mrs. Bhakcu went around telling people, "Why not come and see how *he* working on the Bedford?"

From time to time Bhakcu would crawl out from under the lorry and polish the wings and the bonnet. Then he would crawl under the lorry again. But he didn't look happy.

The next day the people who had lent the money to buy the Bedford formed a deputation and came to Bhakcu's house, begging him to desist.

Bhakcu remained under the lorry all the time, refusing to reply. The money-lenders grew angry, and some of the women among them began to cry. Even that failed to move Bhakcu, and in the end the deputation just had to go away.

When the deputation left, Bhakcu began to take it out of his wife. He beat her and he said, "Is you who want me to buy lorry. Is you. Is *you*. All you thinking about is money, money. Just like your mother."

But the real reason for his temper was that he couldn't put back the engine as he had found it. Two or three pieces remained outside and they puzzled him.

The agents sent a mechanic.

He looked at the lorry and asked Bhakcu, very calmly, "Why you buy a Bedford?"

Bhakcu said, "I like the Bedford."

The mechanic shouted, "Why the arse you didn't buy a Rolls-Royce? They does sell those with the engine sealed down."

Then he went to work, saying sadly, "Is enough to make you want to cry. A nice, new new lorry like this."

The starter never worked again. And Bhakcu always had to use the crank.

Hat said, "Is a blasted shame. Lorry looking new, smelling new, everything still shining, all sort of chalk-mark still on the chassis, and this man cranking it up like some old Ford pram."

But Mrs. Bhakcu boasted, "Fust crank, the engine does start."

One morning—it was a Saturday, market day—Mrs. Bhakcu came crying to my mother. She said "*He* in hospital."

My mother said, "Accident?"

Mrs. Bhakcu said, "He was cranking up the lorry just outside the Market. Fust cunk, the engine start. But it was in gear and it roll he up against another lorry."

Bhakcu spent a week in hospital.

All the time he had the lorry, he hated his wife, and he beat her regularly with the cricket bat. But she was beating him too, with her tongue, and I think Bhakcu was really the loser in these quarrels.

It was hard to back the lorry into the yard and it was Mrs. Bhakcu's duty and joy to direct her husband.

One day she said, "All right, man, back back, turn a little to the right, all right, all clear. Oh God! No, no, no, man! Stop! You go knock the fence down."

Bhakcu suddenly went mad. He reversed so fiercely he cracked the concrete fence. Then he shot forward again, ignoring Mrs. Bhakcu's screams, and reversed again, knocking down the fence altogether.

He was in great temper, and while his wife remained outside crying he went to his little room, stripped to his pants, flung himself belly down on the bed, and began reading the *Ramayana*.

The lorry wasn't making money. But to make any at all, Bhakcu had to have loaders. He got two of those big black Grenadian small-islanders who were just beginning to pour into Port of Spain. They called Bhakcu "Boss" and Mrs. Bhakcu "Madam," and this was nice. But when I looked at these men sprawling happily in the back of the lorry in their ragged dusty clothes and their squashed-up felt hats, I used to wonder whether they knew how much worry they caused, and how uncertain their own position was.

Mrs. Bhakcu's talk was now all about these two men.

She would tell my mother, mournfully, "Day after tomorrow we have to pay the loaders." Two days later she would say, as though the world had come to an end, "Today we pay the loaders." And in no time at all she would be coming around to my mother in distress again, saying, "Day after tomorrow we have to pay the loaders."

Paying the loaders—for months I seemed to hear about nothing else. The words were well known in the street, and became an idiom.

Boyee would say to Errol on a Saturday, "Come, let we go to the one-thirty show at Roxy."

And Errol would turn out his pockets and say, "I can't go, man. I pay the loaders."

Hat said, "It look as though Bhakcu buy the lorry just to pay the loaders."

The lorry went in the end. And the loaders too. I don't know what happened to them. Mrs. Bhakcu had the lorry sold just at a time when lorries began making money. They bought a taxi. By now the competition was fierce and taxis were running eight miles for twelve cents, just enough to pay for oil and petrol.

Mrs. Bhakcu told my mother, "The taxi ain't making money."

So she bought another taxi, and hired a man to drive it. She said, "Two better than one."

Bhakcu was reading the *Ramayana* more and more.

And even that began to annoy the people in the street.

Hat said, "Hear the two of them now. She with that voice she got, and he singing that damn sing-song Hindu song."

Picture then the following scene. Mrs. Bhakcu, very short, very fat, standing at the pipe in her yard, and shrilling at her husband. He is in his pants, lying on his belly, dolefully intoning the *Ramayana*. Suddenly he springs up and snatches the cricket bat in the corner of the room. He runs outside and begins to beat Mrs. Bhakcu with the bat.

The silence that follows lasts a few minutes.

And then only Bhakcu's voice is heard, as he does a solo from the *Ramayana*.

● ● ●

But don't think that Mrs. Bhakcu lost any pride in her husband. Whenever you listened to the rows between Mrs. Bhakcu and Mrs. Morgan, you realised that Bhakcu was still his wife's lord and master.

Mrs. Morgan would say, "I hear your husband talking in his sleep last night, loud loud."

"He wasn't talking," Mrs. Bhakcu said, "he was singing."

"Singing? Hahahahaaah! You know something, Mrs. Bhakcu?"

"What, Mrs. Morgan?"

"If your husband sing for his supper, both of all you starve like hell."

"He know a damn lot more than any of the ignorant man it have in this street, you hear. *He* could read and write, you know. English *and* Hindi. How you so ignorant you don't know that the *Ramayana* is a holy book? If you coulda understand all the good thing *he* singing, you wouldn't be talking all this nonsense you talking now, you hear."

"How your husband this morning, anyway? He fix any new cars lately?"

"I not going to dirty my mouth arguing with you here, you hear.

He know how to fix his car. Is a wonder nobody ain't tell your husband where he can fix all his so-call fireworks."

• • •

Mrs. Bhakcu used to boast that Bhakcu read the *Ramayana* two or three times a month. "It have some parts he know by heart," she said.

But that was little consolation, for money wasn't coming in. The man she had hired to drive the second taxi was playing the fool. She said, "He robbing me like hell. He say that the taxi making so little money I owe him now." She sacked the driver and sold the car.

She used all her financial flair. She began rearing hens. That failed because a lot of the hens were stolen, the rest attacked by street dogs, and Bhakcu hated the smell anyway. She began selling bananas and oranges, but she did that more for her own enjoyment than for the little money it brought in.

My mother said, "Why Bhakcu don't go out and get a work?"

Mrs. Bhakcu said, "But how you want that?"

My mother said, "*I* don't want it. I was thinking about you."

Mrs. Bhakcu said, "You could see he working with all the rude and crude people it have here in Port of Spain?"

My mother said, "Well, he have to do something. People don't pay to see a man crawling under a motor-car or singing *Ramayana*."

Mrs. Bhakcu nodded and looked sad.

My mother said, "But what I saying at all? You sure Bhakcu know the *Ramayana?*"

"I sure sure."

My mother said, "Well, it easy easy. He is a Brahmin, he know the *Ramayana*, and he have a car. Is easy for him to become a pundit, a real proper pundit."

Mrs. Bhakcu clapped her hands. "Is a first-class idea. Hindu pundits making a lot of money these days."

So Bhakcu became a pundit.

• • •

He still tinkered with his car. He had to stop beating Mrs. Bhakcu with the cricket bat, but he was happy.

I was haunted by thoughts of the *dhoti*-clad Pundit Bhakcu, crawling under a car, attending to a crank-shaft, while poor Hindus waited for him to attend to their souls.

Tom Wolfe

*

THE MID-ATLANTIC MAN

Roger! Have you met George? Cyril! Have you met George? Keith! Have
you met George? Brian! Have you met George? Tony! Have you met
George! Nigel! Have you—

—oh god, he's doing a hell of a job of it, introducing everybody by
their first names, first-naming the hell out of everybody, introducing
them to George, who just arrived from New York: George is an American
and the key man in the Fabrilex account. A hell of a job of introductions
he is doing. He has everybody from the firm, plus a lot of other people,
English and American, all calculated to impress and flatter American
George, all piled into this sort of library-reception room upstairs at the
—— Club amid the lyre-splat chairs, bullion-fringe curtains, old blacky
Raeburn-style portraits, fabulously junky glass-and-ormolu chandeliers,
paw-foot chiffoniers, teapoys, ingenious library steps leading resolutely
up into thin air, a wonderful dark world of dark wood, dark rugs, candy-
box covings, moldings, flutings, pilasters, all red as table wine, brown as
boots, made to look like it has been steeped a hundred years in expensive
tobacco, roast beef, horseradish sauce and dim puddings.

The Americans really lap this Club stuff up, but that is not the
point, the point is that—Christ, Americans are childish in many ways
and about as subtle as a Wimpy bender: but in the long run it doesn't
make any difference. They just turn on the power. They have the power,
they just move in and take it, introducing people by their first names as
they go, people they've never laid eyes on, *pals*, and who gives a damn.
They didn't go to Cambridge and learn to envy people who belonged to
the Pitt Club and commit the incredible gaffe of walking into the Pitt
Club with a Cambridge scarf on. They just turn on the money or what-

ever it takes, and they take it, and the grinning first names shall inherit the earth, their lie-down crewcuts as firm and pure as Fabrilex—and—

—he has had a couple of highballs. Highballs! That is what they call whisky-and-sodas. And now he is exhilarated with the absolute *baldness* of putting on his glistening ceramic grin and introducing all of these faces to George by their first names, good old George, cleaned-and pressed old George, big-blucher-shoed old George, popped-out-of-the-Fabrilex-mold old George—the delicious baldness of it!—

Karl! Have you met George? Alec! Have you met George? John! Have you met George? George, predictably, has a super-ingratiating and deferential grin on his face, shaking hands, pumping away, even with people who don't put their hands out at first—Mark! shake hands with George, he wants to say—and as George shakes hands he always lowers his head slightly and grins in panic and looks up from under his eyebrows, deferentially, this kind of unconscious deference because he . . . is meeting *Englishmen* . . .

Still! Why should George give a damn? He can throw away points like this right and left. That's the way Americans are. They can make the wrong gesture, make the most horrible malapropisms, use so many wrong forks it drives the waiter up the wall; demonstrate themselves to be, palpably, social hydrocephalics, total casualties of gaucherie and humiliation—and yet afterwards they don't give a damn. They are right back the next morning as if nothing had happened, smashing on, good-humored, hard-grabbing, winning, taking, clutching. George can scrape and bobble his eyeballs under his eyebrows all day and he will still make his £20,000 a year and buy and sell every bastard in this room—

Nicholas! Have you met George?

Harold! Have you met George?

Freddie! Have you met George?

"Pe-t-e-r . . ."

. . . Oh Christ . . . the second syllable of the name just dribbles off his lips.

With Peter—suddenly he can't go through with it. He can't do the first name thing with Peter, he can't hail him over and introduce him to this American—Peter! George!—as if of course they're pals, *pals*. Peter? A pal? Peter is on precisely his level in the hierarchy of the firm, the same age, 33, yet . . . in another hierarchy—class, to call it by its right name—

Peter's fine yet languid face, his casual yet inviolate wavy thatchy hair—that old, ancient thing, class, now has him and he can't introduce Peter by his first name. It is as if into the room has burst the policeman, the arresting officer, from . . . that world, the entire world of nannies, *cottages ornées* in Devonshire, honeysuckle iron balustrades, sailor suits, hoops and sticks, lolly Eton collars, deb parties, introductions to rich old men, clubs, cliques, horn-handled cigar cutters—in short, the ancient, ineradicable anxiety of class in England—and he knows already the look of patient, tolerant disgust that will begin to slide over Peter's face within the next half second as he looks at him and his American friends and his ceramic grin and his euphoria and his *highballs*. In that instant, confronted by the power of the future on the one hand—George's eyeballs begin to bobble under the eyebrows—and the power of the past on the other—Peter's lips begin to curdle—he realizes what has happened to himself. He has become a Mid-Atlantic Man.

He meets them all the time in London now. They are Englishmen who have reversed the usual process and . . . gone American. The usual process has been that Americans have gone to England and . . . gone English. Woodrow Wilson appoints Walter Hines Page ambassador to the Court of St. James's and tells him: "Just one word of advice, don't become an Englishman." Page says, "Sure, O.K.," but, of course, he does, he becomes so much an Englishman he can't see straight. The usual pattern is, he begins using his knife and fork Continental style, holding the fork in the left hand. He goes to a tailor who puts that nice English belly into the lapels of his coat and builds up suits made of marvelous and arcane layers and layers of worsted, welts, darts, pleats, double-stitches, linings, buttons, pockets, incredible numbers of pockets, and so many buttons to button and unbutton, and he combs his hair into wings over the ears, and he puts a certain nice drag in his voice and learns to walk like he is recovering from a broken back. But one knows about all that. The American has always gone English in order to endow himself with the mystique of the English upper classes. The Englishman today goes American, becomes a Mid-Atlantic Man, to achieve the opposite. He wants to get out from under the domination of the English upper classes by . . . going classless. And he goes classless by taking on the style of life, or part of the style of life, of a foreigner who cannot be fitted into the English class system, the modern, successful, powerful American.

The most obvious example of the Mid-Atlantic Man is the young English show-business figure, a singer, musician, manager, producer, impresario, who goes American in a big way. A singer, for example, sings American rhythm and blues songs, in an American accent, becomes a . . . *pal* of American entertainers, studs his conversation with American slang, like, I mean you know, man, that's where it's at, baby, and, finally, begins to talk with an American accent in an attempt to remove the curse of a working-class accent. But the typical Mid-Atlantic Man is middle class and works in one of the newer industries, advertising, public relations, chemical engineering, consulting for this and that, television, credit cards, agentry, industrial design, commercial art, motion pictures, the whole world of brokerage, persuasion, savantry and shows that has grown up beyond the ancient divisions of landowning, moneylending and the production of dry goods.

He is vaguely aware—he may try to keep it out of his mind—that his background is irrevocably middle class and that everybody in England is immediately aware of it and that this has held him back. This may even be why he has gravitated into one of the newer fields, but still the ancient drag of class in England drags him, drags him, drags him. . . .

They happen to be watching television one night and some perfectly urbane and polished person like Kenneth Allsop comes on the screen and after three or four sentences somebody has to observe, poor Kenneth Allsop, listen to the way he says practically, he will never get the Midlands out of his voice, he breaks it all up, into practi-cally . . . and he laughs, but grimly, because he knows there must be at least fifty things like that to mark him as hopelessly middle class and he has none of Allsop's fame to take the curse off.

He first began to understand all this as far back as his first month at Cambridge. Cambridge!—which was supposed to turn him into one of those inviolate, superior persons who rule England and destiny. Cambridge was going to be a kind of finishing school. His parents had a very definite idea of it that way, a picture of him serving sherry to some smart friends in his chambers, wearing a jacket that seems to have worn and mellowed like a 90-year-old Persian rug. Even he himself had a vague notion of how Cambridge was going to transform him from a bright and mousy comprehensive schoolboy into one of those young men with spread collars and pale silk ties who just . . . *assumes* he is in control, at restaurants, in clubs, at parties, with women, in careers, in life, on rural weekends, and thereby is.

And then the very first month this thing happened with the Pitt Club and the Cambridge scarf. His first move on the road to having smart people over to his chambers for sherry, and Cuban tobacco— Cuban tobacco was also included in this vision—was to buy a Cambridge scarf, a nice long thing with confident colors that would wrap around the neck and the lower tip of his chin and flow in the wind. So he would put on his scarf and amble around the streets, by the colleges, peeking in at the Indian restaurants, which always seemed to be closed, and thinking, Well, here I am, a Cambridge man.

• • •

One day he came upon this place and a glow came from inside, red as wine, brown as boots, smart people, sherry-sherry, and so he stepped inside—and suddenly a lot of white faces turned his way, like a universe erupting with eggs Benedict, faces in the foyer, faces from the dining tables farther in. A porter with chipped-beef jowls stepped up and looked him up and down once, dubious as hell, and said:

"Are you a member, sir?"

Such a voice! It was obvious that he knew immediately that he was not a member and the question was merely, witheringly, rhetorical and really said, Why does a hopeless little nit like you insist on wandering in where you don't belong, and all the eggs Benedict faces turned toward him were an echo of the same thing. They all knew immediately! And it was as if their eyes had fastened immediately upon his jugular vein—no! —upon the Cambridge scarf.

He mumbled and turned his head . . . there in the ancient woody brown of the place was a long coat rack, and hanging on it was every kind of undergraduate garment a *right* mind could think of, greatcoats, riding macs, cloaks, capes, gowns, mantles, even ponchos, mufflers, checked mufflers, Danish mufflers, camel-tan mufflers, ratty old aunt-knitty mufflers—everything and anything in the whole woofy English goddamn universe of cotton, wool, rubber and leather . . . except for a Cambridge scarf. This place turned out to be the Pitt Club, watering trough of the incomparables, the Cambridge elite. Wearing a Cambridge scarf in here was far, far worse than having no insignia at all. In a complex Cambridge hierarchy of colleges and clubs—if all one had was an insignia that said merely that one had been admitted to the university —that was as much as saying, well, he's here and that's all one can say about him, other than that he is a hopeless fool.

He did not throw the Cambridge scarf away, strangely enough. He folded it up into a square and tucked it way back in the bottom of his bottom drawer, along with the family Bible his grandfather had given him. From that day on he was possessed by the feeling that there were two worlds, the eggs Benedict faces and his, and never, in four years, did he invite a single smart person over for sherry. Or for Cuban tobacco. He smoked English cigarettes that stained his teeth.

Even years later, in fact, he held no tremendous hopes for the advertising business until one day he was in New York—one day!—with all Mid-Atlantic Men it seems to start one day in New York.

Practically always they have started flying to New York more and more on business. He started flying over on the Fabrilex account. Fabrilex was going to run a big campaign in England. So he began flying to

New York and getting gradually into the New York advertising life, which turned out to be a strangely . . . *stimulating*—all Mid-Atlantic Men come back with that word for New York, stimulating . . . strangely stimulating aura of sheer money, drive, conniving, hard work, self-indulgence, glamour, childishness, cynicism.

•   •   •

Beginning with the reception room of the —— Agency. It was decorated with the most incredible black leather sofas, quilted and stuffed to the gullet, with the leather gushing and heaving over the edge of the arms, the back and everywhere. There was wall-to-wall carpet, not like a Wilton but so thick one could break one's ankle in it, and quite vermilion, to go with the vermilion walls and all sorts of inexplicable polished brass objects set in niches, candelabra, busts, pastille-burners, vases, etc., and a receptionist who seemed to be made of polished Fabrilex topped with spun brass back-combed hair. She didn't sit at a desk but at a delicate *secretaire* faced with exotic wood veneers, tulipwood, satinwood, harewood. She also operated a switchboard, which was made to look, however, like the keyboard of a harpsichord. There was one large painting, apparently by the last painter in Elizabeth, New Jersey, to copy Franz Kline. Three different members of the firm, Americans, told him the reception room looked like "a San Francisco whorehouse." Three of them used that same simile, a San Francisco whorehouse. This was not said in derision, however. They thought it was crazy but they were proud of it. New York!

One of them told him the reception room looked like a San Francisco whorehouse while having his shoes shined at his desk in his office. They were both sitting there talking, the usual, except that a Negro, about 50, was squatted down over a portable shoeshine stand shining the American's shoes. But he kept right on talking about the San Francisco whorehouse and Fabrilex as if all he had done was turn on an air-conditioner. He also had an "executive telephone." This was some sort of amplified microphone and speaker connected to the telephone, so that he didn't have to actually pick up a telephone, none of that smalltime stuff. All he had to do was talk in the general direction of the desk. But of course! The delicious . . . *baldness* of it! Who gives a damn about subtlety? Just win, like, that's the name of the game, and the —— Agency had £70 million in accounts last year.

They always took him to lunch at places like the Four Seasons, and if it came to £16 for four people, for lunch, that was nothing. There are expensive places where businessmen eat lunch in London, but they always have some kind of coy atmosphere, trattorias, chez this or that, or old places with swiney, pebbly English surnames, Craw's, Grouse's, Scob's, Clot's. But the Four Seasons! The place practically exudes an air-conditioned sweat of pure huge expensive-account . . . *money.* Everybody sits there in this huge bald smooth-slab Mies-van-der-Rohe-style black-onyx executive suite atmosphere taking massive infusions of exotic American cocktails, Margaritas, Gibsons, Bloody Marys, Rob Roys, Screwdrivers, Pisco Sours, and French wines and French brandies, while the blood vessels dilate and the ego dilates and Leonard Lyons, the columnist, comes in to look around and see who is there, and everyone watches these ingenious copper-chain curtains rippling over the plate glass, rippling up, up, it is an optical illusion but it looks like they are rippling, rippling, rippling, rippling up this cliff of plate glass like a waterfall gone into reverse.

And some guy at the table is letting everybody in on this deliciously child-cynical American secret, namely, that a lot of the cigarette advertising currently is based on motivational research into people's reactions to the cancer scare. For example, the ones that always show blue grass and blue streams and blond, blue-eyed young people with picnic baskets, and gallons of prime-of-life hormones gushing through their Diet-Rite loins, are actually aimed at hypochondriacs who need constant reassurance that they aren't dying of cancer. On the other hand, the ones that say "I'd rather fight than switch" really mean "I'd rather get cancer than give up smoking"—New York!—the copper curtains ripple up. . . .

• • •

One interesting, rather nice thing he notices, however, is that they are tremendously anxious to please him. They are apparently impressed by him, even though he comes there very much as the beggar. They are the parent firm. Whatever they say about the Fabrilex campaign in England goes, in the long run. If they want to aim it at hypochondriac masochists who fear cancer of the skin, then that's it. Yet they treat him as a partner, no, as slightly superior. Then he gets it. It is because he is English. They keep staring at his suit, which is from Huntsman and has 12-inch side vents. They watch his table manners and then . . . glorious! *imi*tate him. Old George! He used to say to waiters, "*Would* you please bring some water" or whatever it was, whereas he always said, "*Could* you bring the cheese now, please?" or whatever it was—the thing is, the Americans say *would*, which implies that the waiter is doing one a favor by granting this wish, whereas the Englishman—class!—says *could*, which assumes that since the waiter is a servant, he will if he can.

And old George got that distinction right off! That's it with these Americans. They're incurable children, they're incurable nouveaux, they spell *finesse* with a *ph* to give it more *tone*—but they sense the status distinctions. And so by the second time old George is saying "Could you bring me some water, do you think?" and running do-you-think together into an upper-class blur over the top of his sopping glottis just . . . like a real Englishman.

So all of a sudden *he* began to sense that he had it both ways. He had the American thing and the English thing. They emerge from the Four Seasons, out on to 52nd Street—kheew!—the sun blasts them in the eyes and there it is, wild, childish, bald, overpowering Park Avenue in the Fifties, huge cliffs of plate glass and steel frames, like a mountain of telephone booths. Hundreds of, jaysus, millions of dollars' worth of shimmering junk, with so many sheets of plate glass the buildings all reflect each other in marine greens and blues, like a 25-cent postcard from Sarasota, Florida—not a good building in the lot, but, jaysus, the sheer incredible yah!—we've-got-it money and power it represents. The Rome of the twentieth century—and because wealth and power are here, everything else follows, and it is useless for old England to continue to harp on form, because it is all based on the wealth and power England had 150 years ago. The platter of the world's goodie sweets tilts . . . to New York, girls, for one thing, all these young lithe girls with flamingo legs come pouring into New York and come popping up out of the armpit-steaming sewer tunnels of the New York subways, out of those screeching sewers, dressed to the eyeballs, lathed, polished, linked, lacquered, coiffed with spun brass.

Ah, and *they* loved Englishmen, too. He found a brass-topped beauty and he will never forget following her up the stairs to her flat that first night. The front door was worn and rickety but heavy and had an air hinge on it that made it close and lock immediately, automatically—against those ravenous, adrenal New York animals *out there*; even New York's criminals are more animal, basic savage, Roman, *criminal*—he never remembered a block of flats in London with an air hinge on the front door—and he followed her up the stairs, a few steps behind her, and watched the muscles in her calves contract and the hamstring ligaments spring out at the backs of her knees, oh young taut healthy New York girl flamingo legs, and it was all so . . . tender and brave.

Precisely! Her walk-up flat was so essentially dreary, way over in the East Eighties, an upper floor of somebody's old townhouse that had been cut up and jerry-built into flats just slightly better than a bed-sitter, with the bedroom about the size of a good healthy wardrobe closet and a so-called Pullman kitchen in the living room, some fiercely, meanly efficient uni-unit, a little sink, refrigerator and stove all welded together behind shutters at one end, and a bathroom with no window, just some sort of air duct in there with the slits grimed and hanging, booga, with some sort of gray compost of lint, sludge, carbon particles and noxious gases. And the toilet barely worked, just a lazy spiral current of water down the hole after one pulled down that stubby little handle they have. The floor tilted slightly, but—brave and tender!

Somehow she had managed to make it all look beautiful, Japanese globe lamps made of balsa strips and paper, greenery, great lush fronds of some kind of plant, several prints on the wall, one an insanely erotic water-color nude by Egon Schiele, various hangings, coverings, drapings of primitive textiles, monk's cloth, homespuns, a little vase full of violet paper flowers, a bookcase, painted white, full of heavyweight, or middle-weight, paperback books, *The Lonely Crowd*, *The Confessions of Felix Krull*, *African Genesis*—brave and tender!—all of these lithe young girls living in dreadful walk-up flats, alone, with a cat, and the faint odor of cat feces in the Kitty Litter, and an oily wooden salad bowl on the table, and a cockroach silhouetted on the rim of the salad bowl—and yet there was something touching about it, *haunting*, he wanted to say, the desperate fight to stay in New York amid the excitement of money and power, the Big Apple, and for days, if he is to be honest about it, he had the most inexplicably tender memory of—all right!—the poor sad way the water had lazed down in the toilet bowl. That poor, marvelous, erotic girl. At one point she had told him she had learned to put a diaphragm on in 15 seconds. She just said it, out of thin air. So bald.

Early the next morning he took a cab back to his hotel to change for the day and the driver tried to project the thing in manic bursts through the rush-hour traffic, lurches of acceleration, sudden braking, skids, screeches, all the while shouting out the window, cursing and then demanding support from him—"Dja see that! Guy got his head up his ass. Am I right?"—and strangely, he found himself having a thoroughly American reaction, actually answering these stupid questions because he wanted to be approved of by this poor bastard trying to hurtle through the money-and-power traffic, answering a cab driver who said, "Guy got his head up his ass, am I right?"—because suddenly he found himself close to the source, he understood this thing—the hell with scarves, Pitt Clubs and pale silk ties, and watch out England, you got your head up your ass, and here comes a Mid-Atlantic Man.

· · ·

His career back with the —— Agency in London picked up brilliantly for Mid-Atlantic Man. His momentum was tremendous when he came back. London was a torpid little town on a river. He began to cultivate the American members of the firm. Certain things about the advertising business that he had never been able to stomach, really, but nevertheless swallowed silently—suddenly he began to realize that what it was, these things were American, bald and cynical, only now he . . . *understood*. Yea-saying!

There was one American woman in the firm, and in the most unconcerned way she would talk about the opening of a big new American hotel that had gone up in London and how the invitation list was divided into (1) Celebrities, (2) VIPs, (3) CIPs and (4) just Guests. Things like that used to make his flesh crawl, but now—now—the beautiful part was the CIPs—Commercially Important People, people important to the hotel for business reasons but whose names meant nothing in terms of publicity, however. Marvelous!

He got to be a good friend of hers. One day they went out to lunch, and there were a lot of people on the footpaths, and suddenly she spotted a woman about 20 feet away and said, "Look at her! The perfect C-1." One of the innovations, for the purpose of surveys and aiming campaigns accurately, had been to break down consumers into four categories: A, B, C-1 and C-2. A was upper class, B was middle class, C-1 was upper working class or lower middle class, in that range, and C-2 was plain working class.

"The perfect C-1!" she said.

"The perfect C-1?"

"Yes! Look. She's done her hair herself. She's wearing a Marks & Spencer knitted dress. She bought her shoes at Lotus. She's carrying a shopping basket"—with this she moved right up next to the woman and looked in the shopping basket—"she's bought pre-cut wrapped bread"—she only barely turns back to him to announce all this out loud—"she's bought a box of Wiz detergent with five free plastic daffodils inside"—and the poor woman wheels her head around resentfully—but he wants to shout for joy: Bald! Delicious! A running commentary on a London street about a perfect C-1!

That night he took her to the —— Trattoria, underneath those inevitable white plaster arches and black metal cylinder lamps. He came on breezy, first-naming the waiters as he walked in, like . . . a pal. Over the avocado vinaigrette he told her, conspiratorially, that the Agency was still hopelessly backward because it was run, in England, by the kind of Englishmen who think a successful business is one where you can get educated men to work for you for £2,000 a year and come to work dressed as if they make £10,000. After the wine he told her: "I've got the neuroses of New York and the decadence of London."

She thought that was—god!—great. So he sprang it, spontaneously as he could manage it, on many occasions thereafter. He also took to wearing black knit ties. Somehow they have become the insignia of Mid-Atlantic Man. He got the idea from David Frost, who always wore one.

Instead of using Cockney or Liverpool slang for humorous effect, narked, knickers-job and all that, he began using American hip-lower-class slang, like, I mean, you know, baby, and a little late Madison Avenue. "Why don't we throw it—" he would be speaking of somebody's idea—"and see if it skips across the pond." He always brought the latest American rock 'n' roll records back with him from New York, plus a lot of news of discothèques, underground movies, and people like Andy, Jane, Borden, Olivier. He always made a big point of telling everyone that he was expecting a call from New York, from *David*—and everyone knew this was a big New York advertising man—David!—David!—New York! New York!—hot line to the source!—land of flamingo legs and glass cliffs!—mine! mine!—

• • •

But then there were a few disquieting developments. The waiters at the —— Trattoria began *treating* him like an American. He would come on all pally—and they would do things like this: He would order some esoteric wine, Château whateveritwas, and they would bring him a bottle and pour out a little in his glass and he would taste it and pronounce it good and then one of his . . . *pals*, a waiter, would say, right out loud, in front of the girl he was with: We didn't have any more Château whateveritwas, sir, so I brought you Château thing, I hope it's all right, sir. All he can do is sit there and nod like a fool, because he has already tasted it and pronounced it good Château whateveritwas—oh Christ.

And then, at the Agency, the Americans began to treat him as one of them. There was this stupid moment when A—, an American who ranged just above him, was going off on holiday, and he said to him, very solemnly, in front of several Englishmen:

"Think about Pube-Glo for me while I'm gone."

Not "think about the Pube-Glo account" or "work on the Pube-Glo campaign" but think about Pube-Glo, with that pure, simple American double-think loyalty to the product itself. He had to stand there, in front of other Englishmen, and solemnly agree to think about Pube-Glo. What was worse, he would have to show some evidence of having thought about Pube-Glo when A— came back, which meant he would actually have to spend time out of his life thinking about this vile fake-erotic concoction named Pube-Glo.

The hell of it was, he gradually found himself thinking English, not necessarily wisely, but rather fundamentally. Two New York Italians came over to take over—"hype up" was the term transmitted from New York—the art department, and he looked at them. They were dressed in flash clothes, sort of Sy Devore of Hollywood style, wearing tight pants like a chubby hairdresser, and right away they began changing this and that, like some sort of colonial inspector generals. They were creeps even by New York standards. Even? Where was his love of that delicious, cynical . . . baldness . . .

Part of it was back in New York trampled to death. Jaysus, he didn't want to say anything, but the more he went to New York . . sometimes the whole . . . attitude in New York was hard to take. He was in New York, staying at George's big apartment on East 57th Street, and he had to get out to the airport. He had two huge heavy bags because it was just before Christmas and he was bringing back all sorts of things. So he half trundled them out to the elevator, and at length it arrived and he said to the elevator man: "Could you give me a hand with these, please?"

"I'm sorry, Mac," the elevator man said, "I can't leave this elevator. My job is running this elevator. It's against the law, I can't leave a running elevator," and so forth and so on, even after he had dragged the bags on himself, a lecture all the way down.

At the ground floor the doorman opened the door for him but looked at the bags as if they were covered with flies. Outside it was slushy and rainy, and there was a pond of slush out from the curb. So he said to the doorman—this time summoning up the ancient accent of British command:

"Could you get me a cab, please."

"No, I couldn't," the man says, with just a hint of mockery. "I would, Buddy, but I can't. I can't get no cab on a night like this. You'll have to take your best shot."

Finally he flags down a cab, and both the doorman and the driver watch, with great logistic interest, as he navigates the bags through the pond of slush, getting his shoes and socks wet. In the cab he tells the man he wants to go to the airport, and he answers, in a hideous impersonation of a Cockney accent:

"Ow-kay, guv."

Then he turns up the car radio very loud to WQXR, the classical music station, apparently to impress him. The piece is something horribly morose by that old fraud Stravinsky.

•   •   •

Back in London he learns that a few changes have taken place. The Hon. ——, a melon-jawed ball of fire who is 31 and once had a job doing whatever it was, somewhere, has been brought in at a high level as a "consultant," and so has young Lady ——. Meantime, Peter ——, an Etonian, an Oxonian, first cousin of Lord ——, has suddenly been elevated to his level after ten months with the firm. And gradually it becomes obvious. Advertising may be a new industry, it may be an American art, it may be a triumph of the New World, but in the competition for new accounts, the clients—English new money as well as foreign clients—they want to be dealing with an upper-class Englishman, want to feel they are buying upper-class treatment for their £20,000 or whatever, want to let their blood vessels dilate and their egos dilate over lunch at the Connaught with upper-class Englishmen—

—but wait a minute, it can't *all* go back to that, he will hang in there, try to get that inviolable feeling again, the best of both worlds, and here amid the lyre-splat chairs, the bullion-fringe curtains, the old blacky Raeburn-style portraits, Roger! Have you met George? Cyril! Have you met George? Keith! Have you—

—and Peter. Pe-t-e-r . . . he watches Peter's lip curdle. It is as if it is taking forever, as in a Cocteau film, old George's eyes are frozen in the panic-grinning bobble, and—oh God of Fabrilex!—none of these smart bastards are coming over for sherry after all, are they, ever, ever.

Philip Roth

*

WHACKING OFF
EXCERPT FROM *Portnoy's Complaint*

Then came adolescence—half my waking life spent locked behind the bathroom door, firing my wad down the toilet bowl, or into the soiled clothes in the laundry hamper, or *splat*, up against the medicine-chest mirror, before which I stood in my dropped drawers so I could see how it looked coming out. Or else I was doubled over my flying fist, eyes pressed closed but mouth wide open, to take that sticky sauce of butter-milk and Clorox on my own tongue and teeth—though not infrequently, in my blindness and ecstasy, I got it all in the pompadour, like a blast of Wildroot Cream Oil. Through a world of matted handkerchiefs and crumpled Kleenex and stained pajamas, I moved my raw and swollen penis, perpetually in dread that my loathsomeness would be discovered by someone stealing upon me just as I was in the frenzy of dropping my load. Nevertheless, I was wholly incapable of keeping my paws from my dong once it started the climb up my belly. In the middle of a class I would raise a hand to be excused, rush down the corridor to the lavatory, and with ten or fifteen savage strokes, beat off standing up into a urinal. At the Saturday afternoon movie I would leave my friends to go off to the candy machine—and wind up in a distant balcony seat, squirting my seed into the empty wrapper from a Mounds bar. On an outing of our family association, I once cored an apple, saw to my astonishment (and with the aid of my obsession) what it looked like, and ran off into the woods to fall upon the orifice of the fruit, pretending that the cool and mealy hole was actually between the legs of that mythical being who always called me Big Boy when she pleaded for what no girl in all re-corded history had ever had. "Oh shove it in me, Big Boy," cried the cored apple that I banged silly on that picnic. "Big Boy, Big Boy, oh give me all you've got," begged the empty milk bottle that I kept hidden in our storage bin in the basement, to drive wild after school with my vaselined upright. "Come, Big Boy, come," screamed the maddened piece of liver that, in my own insanity, I bought one afternoon at a butcher shop and, believe it or not, violated behind a billboard on the way to a bar mitzvah lesson.

It was at the end of my freshman year of high school—and freshman year of masturbating—that I discovered on the underside of my penis, just where the shaft meets the head, a little discolored dot that has since been diagnosed as a freckle. Cancer. I had given myself *cancer.* All that pulling and tugging at my own flesh, all that friction, had given me an incurable disease. And not yet fourteen! In bed at night the tears rolled from my eyes. "No!" I sobbed. "I don't want to die! Please—no!" But then, because I would very shortly be a corpse anyway, I went ahead as usual and jerked off into my sock. I had taken to carrying the dirty socks into bed with me at night so as to be able to use one as a receptacle upon retiring, and the other upon awakening.

If only I could cut down to one hand-job a day, or hold the line at two, or even three! But with the prospect of oblivion before me, I actually began to set new records for myself. Before meals. After meals. *During* meals. Jumping up from the dinner table, I tragically clutch at my belly —diarrhea! I cry, I have been stricken with diarrhea!—and once behind the locked bathroom door, slip over my head a pair of underpants that I have stolen from my sister's dresser and carry rolled in a handkerchief in my pocket. So galvanic is the effect of cotton panties against my mouth —so galvanic is the *word* "panties"—that the trajectory of my ejaculation reaches startling new heights: leaving my joint like a rocket it makes right for the light bulb overhead, where to my wonderment and horror, it hits and it hangs. Wildly in the first moment I cover my head, expecting an explosion of glass, a burst of flames—disaster, you see, is never far from my mind. Then quietly as I can I climb the radiator and remove the sizzling gob with a wad of toilet paper. I begin a scrupulous search of the shower curtain, the tub, the tile floor, the four toothbrushes—God forbid!—and just as I am about to unlock the door, imagining I have covered my tracks, my heart lurches at the sight of what is hanging like snot to the toe of my shoe. I am the Raskolnikov of jerking off—the sticky evidence is everywhere! Is it on my cuffs too? in my *hair?* my *ear?* All this I wonder even as I come back to the kitchen table, scowling and cranky, to grumble self-righteously at my father when he opens his mouth full of red jello and says, "I don't understand what you have to lock the door about. That to me is beyond comprehension. What is this, a home or a

Grand Central station?" ". . . privacy . . . a human being . . . around here *never*," I reply, then push aside my dessert to scream, "I don't feel well—will everybody leave me alone?"

After dessert—which I finish because I happen to like jello, even if I detest them—after dessert I am back in the bathroom again. I burrow through the week's laundry until I uncover one of my sister's soiled brassieres. I string one shoulder strap over the knob of the bathroom door and the other on the knob of the linen closet: a scarecrow to bring on more dreams. "Oh beat it, Big Boy, beat it to a red-hot pulp—" so I am being urged by the little cups of Hannah's brassiere, when a rolled-up newspaper smacks at the door. And sends me and my handful an inch off the toilet seat. "—Come on, give somebody else a crack at that bowl, will you?" my father says. "I haven't moved my bowels in a week."

I recover my equilibrium, as is my talent, with a burst of hurt feelings. "I have a terrible case of diarrhea! Doesn't that mean anything to anyone in this house?"—in the meantime resuming the stroke, indeed quickening the tempo as my cancerous organ miraculously begins to quiver again from the inside out.

Then Hannah's brassiere *begins to move*. To swing to and fro! I veil my eyes, and behold!—Lenore Lapidus! who has the biggest pair in my class, running for the bus after school, her great untouchable load shifting weightily inside her blouse, oh I urge them up from their cups, and over, LENORE LAPIDUS'S ACTUAL TITS, and realize in the same split second that my mother is vigorously shaking the doorknob. Of the door I have finally forgotten to lock! I knew it would happen one day! *Caught!* As good as *dead!*

"Open up, Alex. I want you to open up this instant."

It's locked. I'm *not* caught! and I see from what's alive in my hand that I'm not quite dead yet either. Beat on then! beat on! "Lick me, Big Boy—lick me a good hot lick! I'm Lenore Lapidus's big fat red-hot brassiere!"

"Alex, I want an answer from you. Did you eat French fries after school? Is that why you're sick like this?"

"Nuhhh, nuhhh."

"Alex, are you in pain? Do you want me to call the doctor? Are you in pain, or aren't you? I want to know exactly where it hurts. *Answer me.*"

"Yuhh, yuhh—"

"Alex, I don't want you to flush the toilet," says my mother sternly. "I want to see what you've done in there. I don't like the sound of this at all."

"And me," says my father, touched as he always was by my accomplishments—as much awe as envy—"I haven't moved my bowels in a week," just as I lurch from my perch on the toilet seat, and with the whimper of a whipped animal, deliver three drops of something barely viscous into the tiny piece of cloth where my flat-chested eighteen-year-old sister has laid her nipples, such as they are. It is my fourth orgasm of the day. When will I begin to come blood?

"Get in here, please, you," says my mother. "Why did you flush the toilet when I told you not to?"

"I forgot."

"What was in there that you were so fast to flush it?"

"Diarrhea."

"Was it mostly liquid or was it mostly poopie?"

"I don't look! I didn't look! Stop saying poopie to me—I'm in high school!"

"Oh, don't you shout at *me*, Alex. I'm not the one who gave you diarrhea, I assure you. If all you ate was what you were fed at home, you wouldn't be running to the bathroom fifty times a day. Hannah tells me what you're doing, so don't think I don't know."

She's missed the underpants! *I've been caught!* Oh, *let* me be dead! I'd just as soon!

"Yeah, what do I do . . .?"

"You go to Harold's Hot Dog and *Chazerai* Palace after school and you eat French fries with Melvin Weiner. Don't you? Don't lie to me either. Do you or do you not stuff yourself with French fries and ketchup on Hawthorne Avenue after school? Jack, come in here, I want you to hear this," she calls to my father, now occupying the bathroom.

"Look, I'm trying to move my bowels," he replies. "Don't I have enough trouble as it is without people screaming at me when I'm trying to move my bowels?"

"You know what your son does after school, the A student, who his own mother can't say poopie to any more, he's such a *grown-up*? What do you think your grown-up son does when nobody is watching him?"

"Can I please be left alone, please?" cries my father. "Can I have a little peace, please, so I can get something accomplished in here?"

"Just wait till your father hears what you do, in defiance of every health habit there could possibly be. Alex, answer me something. You're so smart, you know all the answers now, answer me this: how do you think Melvin Weiner gave himself colitis? Why has that child spent half his life in hospitals?"

"Because he eats *chazerai*."

"Don't you dare make fun of me!"

"All right," I scream, "how *did* he get colitis?"

"Because he eats *chazerai*! But it's not a joke! Because to him a meal is an O Henry bar washed down by a bottle of Pepsi. Because his breakfast consists of, do you know what? The most important meal of the day —not according just to your mother, Alex, but according to the highest nutritionists—and do you know what that child eats?"

"A doughnut."

"A doughnut is right, Mr. Smart Guy, Mr. Adult. And *coffee*. Coffee and a doughnut, and on this a thirteen-year-old *pisher* with half a stomach is supposed to start a day. But you, thank God, have been brought up differently. You don't have a mother who gallivants all over town like some names I could name, from Bam's to Hahne's to Kresge's all day long. Alex, tell me, so it's not a mystery, or maybe I'm just stupid —only tell me, what are you trying to do, what are you trying to prove, that you should stuff yourself with such junk when you could come home to a poppyseed cookie and a nice glass of milk? I want the truth from you. I wouldn't tell your father," she says, her voice dropping significantly, "but I *must* have the truth from you." Pause. Also significant. "Is it just French fries, darling, or is it more? . . . Tell me, please, what other kind of garbage you're putting into your mouth so we can get to the bottom of this diarrhea! I want a straight answer from you, Alex. Are you eating hamburgers out? Answer me, please, is that why you flushed the toilet—was there hamburger in it?"

"I told you—I don't look in the bowl when I flush it! I'm not interested like you are in other people's poopie!"

"Oh, oh, oh—thirteen years old and the mouth on him! To someone who is asking a question about *his* health, *his* welfare!" The utter incomprehensibility of the situation causes her eyes to become heavy with tears. "Alex, why are you getting like this, give me some clue? Tell me please what horrible things we have done to you all our lives that this should be our reward?" I believe the question strikes her as original. I believe she considers the question unanswerable. And worst of all, so do I. What *have* they done for me all their lives, but sacrifice? Yet that this is precisely the horrible thing is beyond my understanding—and still, Doctor! To this day!

I brace myself now for the whispering. I can spot the whispering coming a mile away. We are about to discuss my father's headaches.

"Alex, he didn't have a headache on him today that he could hardly see straight from it?" She checks, is he out of earshot? God forbid he should hear how critical his condition is, he might claim exaggeration. "He's not going next week for a test for a tumor?"

"He is?"

" 'Bring him in,' the doctor said. 'I'm going to give him a test for a tumor.' "

Success. I am crying. There is no good reason for me to be crying, but in this household everybody tries to get a good cry in at least once a day. My father, you must understand—as doubtless you do; blackmailers account for a substantial part of the human community, and, I would imagine, of your clientele—my father has been "going" for this tumor test for nearly as long as I can remember. Why his head aches him all the time is, of course, because he is constipated all the time—why he is constipated is because ownership of his intestinal tract is in the hands of the firm of Worry, Fear & Frustration. It is true that a doctor once said to my mother that he would give her husband a test for a tumor—if that would make her happy, is I believe the way that he worded it; he suggested that it would be cheaper, however, and probably more effective for the man to invest in an enema bag. Yet, that I know all this to be so, does not make it any less heartbreaking to imagine my father's skull splitting open from a malignancy.

Yes, she has me where she wants me, and she knows it. I clean forget my own cancer in the grief that comes—comes now as it came then—when I think how much of life has always been (as he himself very accurately puts it) beyond his comprehension. And his grasp. No money, no schooling, no language, no learning, curiosity without culture, drive without opportunity, experience without wisdom . . . How easily his inadequacies can move me to tears. As easily as they move me to anger!

A person my father often held up to me as someone to emulate in life was the theatrical producer Billy Rose. Walter Winchell said that Billy Rose's knowledge of shorthand had led Bernard Baruch to hire him as a secretary—consequently my father plagued me throughout high school to enroll in the shorthand course. "Alex, where would Billy Rose be today without his shorthand? Nowhere! So why do you *fight* me?" Earlier it was the piano we battled over. For a man whose house was without a phonograph or a record, he was passionate on the subject of a musical instrument. "I don't understand why you won't take a musical instrument, this is beyond comprehension. Your little cousin Toby can sit down at the piano and play whatever song you can name. All she has to do is sit at the piano and play 'Tea for Two' and everybody in the room is her friend. She'll never lack for companionship, Alex, she'll never lack for popularity. Only tell me you'll take up the piano, and I'll have one in here tomorrow morning. Alex, are you listening to me? I am offering you something that could change the rest of your life!"

But what he had to offer I didn't want—and what I wanted he didn't have to offer. Yet how unusual is that? Why must it continue to cause such pain? At this late date! Doctor, what should I rid myself of, tell me, the hatred . . . or the love? Because I haven't even begun to mention everything I remember with pleasure—I mean with a rapturous, biting sense of loss? All those memories that seem somehow to be bound up with the weather and the time of day, and that flash into mind with such poignancy, that momentarily I am not down in the subway, or at my office, or at dinner with a pretty girl, but back in my childhood, *with them*. Memories of practically nothing—and yet they seem moments of history as crucial to my being as the moment of my conception; I might be remembering his sperm nosing into her ovum, so piercing is my gratitude—yes, *my* gratitude!—so sweeping and unqualified is my love. Yes, me, with sweeping and unqualified love! I am standing in the kitchen (standing maybe for the first time in my life), my mother points, "Look outside, baby," and I look: she says, "See? how purple? a real fall sky." The first line of poetry I ever hear! And I remember it! *a real fall sky* . . . It is an iron-cold January day, dusk—oh, these memories of dusk are going to kill me yet, of chicken fat on rye bread to tide me over to dinner, and the moon already outside the kitchen window—I have just come in with hot red cheeks and a dollar I have earned shoveling snow: "You know what you're going to have for dinner," my mother coos so lovingly to me, "for being such a hard-working boy? Your favorite winter meal. Lamb stew." It is night: after a Sunday in New York City, at Radio City and Chinatown, we are driving home across the George Washington Bridge—the Holland Tunnel is the direct route between Pell Street and Jersey City, but I beg for the bridge, and because my mother says it's "educational," my father drives some ten miles out of his way to get us home. Up front my sister counts aloud the number of supports upon which the marvelous educational cables rest, while in the back I fall asleep with my face against my mother's black scalskin coat. At Lakewood, where we go one winter for a weekend vacation with my parents' Sunday night Gin Rummy Club, I sleep in one twin bed with my father, and my mother and Hannah curl up together in the other. At dawn my father awakens me and like convicts escaping, we noiselessly dress and slip out of the room. "Come," he whispers, motioning for me to don my earmuffs and coat, "I want to show you something. Did you know I was a waiter in Lakewood when I was sixteen years old?" Outside the hotel he points across to the beautiful silent woods. "How's that?" he says. We walk together—"at a brisk pace"—around a silver lake. "Take good deep breaths. Take in the piney air all the way. This is the best air in the world, good winter piney air." *Good winter piney air*—another poet for a parent! I couldn't be more thrilled if I were Wordsworth's kid! . . . In summer he remains in the city while the three of us go off to live in a furnished room at the seashore for a month. He will join us for the last two weeks, when he gets his vacation . . . there are times, however, when Jersey City is so thick with humidity, so alive with the mosquitoes that come dive-bombing in from the marshes, that at the end of his day's work he drives sixty-five miles, taking the old Cheesequake Highway— the Cheesequake! My God! the stuff you uncover here!—drives sixty-five miles to spend the night with us in our breezy room at Bradley Beach.

He arrives after we have already eaten, but his own dinner waits while he unpeels the soggy city clothes in which he has been making the rounds of his debit all day, and changes into his swimsuit. I carry his towel for him as he clops down the street to the beach in his unlaced shoes. I am dressed in clean short pants and a spotless polo shirt, the salt is showered off me, and my hair—still my little boy's presteel wool hair, soft and combable—is beautifully parted and slicked down. There is a weathered iron rail that runs the length of the boardwalk, and I seat myself upon it; below me, in his shoes, my father crosses the empty beach. I watch him neatly set down his towel near the shore. He places his watch in one shoe, his eyeglasses in the other, and then he is ready to make his entrance into the sea. To this day I go into the water as he advised: plunge the wrists in first, then splash the underarms, then a handful to the temples and the back of the neck . . . ah, but slowly, always slowly. This way you get to refresh yourself, while avoiding a shock to the system. Refreshed, unshocked, he turns to face me, comically waves farewell up to where he thinks I'm standing, and drops backward to float with his arms outstretched. Oh he floats so still—he works, he works so hard, and for whom if not for me?—and then at last, after turning on his belly and making with a few choppy strokes that carry him nowhere, he comes wading back to shore, his streaming compact torso glowing from the last pure spikes of light driving in, over my shoulder, out of stifling inland New Jersey, from which I am being spared.

And there are more memories like this one, Doctor. A lot more. This is my mother and father I'm talking about.

· · ·

But—but—but—let me pull myself together—there is also this vision of him emerging from the bathroom, savagely kneading the back of his neck and sourly swallowing a belch. "All right, what is it that was so urgent you couldn't wait till I came out to tell me?"

"Nothing," says my mother. "It's settled."

He looks at me, so disappointed. I'm what he lives for, and I know it. "What did he do?"

"What he did is over and done with, God willing. You, did you move your bowels?" she asks him.

"Of course I didn't move my bowels."

"Jack, what is it going to be with you, with those bowels?"

"They're turning into concrete, that's what it's going to be."

"Because you eat too fast."

"I don't eat too fast."

"How then, slow?"

"I eat regular."

"You eat like a pig, and somebody should tell you."

"Oh, you got a wonderful way of expressing yourself sometimes, do you know that?"

"I'm only speaking the truth," she says. "I stand on my feet all day in this kitchen, and you eat like there's a fire somewhere, and this one— this one has decided that the food I cook isn't good enough for him. He'd rather be sick and scare the living daylights out of me."

"What did he do?"

"I don't want to upset you," she says. "Let's just forget the whole thing." But she can't, so now *she* begins to cry. Look, she is probably not the happiest person in the world either. She was once a tall stringbean of a girl whom the boys called "Red" in high school. When I was nine and ten years old I had an absolute passion for her high school yearbook. For a while I kept it in the same drawer with that other volume of exotica, my stamp collection.

Sophie Ginsky the boys call "Red,"
She'll go far with her big brown eyes and her clever head.

And that was my mother!

Also, she had been secretary to the soccer coach, an office pretty much without laurels in our own time, but apparently *the* post for a young girl to hold in Jersey City during the First World War. So I thought, at any rate, when I turned the pages of her yearbook, and she pointed out to me her dark-haired beau, who had been captain of the team, and today, to quote Sophie, "the biggest manufacturer of mustard in New York." "And I could have married him instead of your father," she confided in me, and more than once. I used to wonder sometimes what that would have been like for my momma and me, invariably on the occasions when my father took us to dine out at the corner delicatessen. I look around the place and think, "We would have manufactured all this mustard." I suppose she must have had thoughts like that herself.

"He eats French fries," she says, and sinks into a kitchen chair to Weep Her Heart Out once and for all. "He goes after achool with Melvin Weiner and stuffs himself with French-fried potatoes. Jack, you tell him, I'm only his mother. Tell him what the end is going to be. Alex," she says passionately, looking to where I am edging out of the room, "*tateleh*, it begins with diarrhea, but do you know how it ends? With a sensitive stomach like yours, do you know how it finally ends? *Wearing a plastic bag to do your business in!*"

Who in the history of the world has been least able to deal with a woman's tears? My father. I am second. He says to me, "You heard your mother. Don't eat French fries with Melvin Weiner after school."

"Or ever," she pleads.

"Or ever," my father says.

"Or hamburgers out," she pleads.

"Or hamburgers out," he says.

"*Hamburgers*," she says bitterly, just as she might say *Hitler*, "where they can put anything in the world in that they want—and *he* eats them. Jack, make him promise, before he gives himself a terrible *tsura*, and it's too late."

"I *promise!*" I scream. "I *promise!*" and race from the kitchen—to where? Where else.

I tear off my pants, furiously I grab that battered battering ram to freedom, my adolescent cock, even as my mother begins to call from the other side of the bathroom door. "Now this time don't flush. Do you hear me, Alex? I have to see what's in that bowl!"

Doctor, do you understand what I was up against? My wang was all I really had that I could call my own. You should have watched her at work during polio season! She should have gotten medals from the March of Dimes! Open your mouth. Why is your throat red? Do you have a headache you're not telling me about? You're not going to any baseball game, Alex, until I see you move your neck. Is your neck stiff? Then why are you moving it that way? You ate like you were nauseous, are you nauseous? Well, you ate like you were nauseous. I don't want you drinking from the drinking fountain in that playground. If you're thirsty wait until you're home. Your throat is sore, isn't it? I can tell how you're swallowing. I think maybe what you are going to do, Mr. Joe Di Maggio, is put that glove away and lie down. I am not going to allow you to go outside in this heat and run around, not with that sore throat, I'm not. I want to take your temperature. I don't like the sound of this throat

business one bit. To be very frank, I am actually beside myself that you
have been walking around all day with a sore throat and not telling your
mother. Why did you keep this a secret? Alex, polio doesn't know from
baseball games. It only knows from iron lungs and crippled forever! I
don't want you running around, and that's final. Or eating hamburgers
out. Or mayonnaise. Or chopped liver. Or tuna. Not everybody is careful
the way your mother is about spoilage. You're used to a spotless house,
you don't begin to know what goes on in restaurants. Do you know why
your mother when we go to the Chink's will never sit facing the kitchen?
Because I don't want to see what goes on back there. Alex, you must
wash everything, is that clear? Everything! God only knows who touched
it before you did.

Look, am I exaggerating to think it's practically miraculous that I'm
ambulatory? The hysteria and the superstition! The watch-its and the be-
carefuls! You mustn't do this, you can't do that—hold it! don't, you're
breaking an important law! *What* law? *Whose* law? They might as well
have had plates in their lips and rings through their noses and painted
themselves blue for all the human sense they made! Oh, and the *milchiks*
and *flaishiks* besides, all those *meshuggeneh* rules and regulations on top
of their own private craziness! It's a family joke that when I was a tiny
child I turned from the window out of which I was watching a snow-
storm, and hopefully asked, "Momma, do we believe in winter?" Do you
get what I'm *saying?* I was raised by Hottentots and Zulus! I couldn't
even contemplate drinking a glass of milk with my salami sandwich without giving serious offense to God Almighty. Imagine then what my conscience gave me for all that jerking off! The guilt, the fears—the terror
bred into my bones! What in their world was not charged with danger,
dripping with germs, fraught with peril? Oh, where was the gusto, where
was the boldness and courage? Who filled these parents of mine with
such a fearful sense of life? My father, in his retirement now, has really
only one subject into which he can sink his teeth, the New Jersey Turn-
pike. "I wouldn't go on that thing if you paid me. You have to be out of
your mind to travel on that thing—it's Murder Incorporated, it's a legal-
ized way for people to go out and get themselves killed—" Listen, you
know what he says to me three times a week on the telephone—and I'm
only counting when I pick it up, not the total number of rings I get
between six and ten every night. "Sell that car, will you? Will you do me
a favor and sell that car so I can get a good night's sleep? Why you have
to have a car in that city is beyond my comprehension. Why you want
to pay for insurance and garage and upkeep I don't even begin to understand. But then I don't understand yet why you even want to live by

yourself over in that jungle. What do you pay those robbers again for that two-by-four apartment? A penny over fifty dollars a month and you're out of your mind. Why you don't move back to North Jersey is a mystery to me—why you prefer the noise and the crime and the fumes—"

And my mother, she just keeps whispering. *Sophie whispers on!* I go for dinner once a month, it is a struggle requiring all my guile and cunning and strength, but I have been able over all these years, and against imponderable odds, to hold it down to once a month: I ring the bell, she opens the door, the whispering promptly begins! "Don't ask what kind of day I had with him yesterday." So I don't. "Alex," *sotto voce* still, "when he has a day like that you don't know what a difference a call from you would make." I nod. "And Alex"—and I'm nodding away, you know—it doesn't cost anything, and it may even get me through—"next week is his birthday. That Mother's Day came and went without a card, *plus* my birthday, those things don't bother me. But he'll be sixty-six, Alex. That's not a baby, Alex—that's a landmark in a life. So you'll send a card. It wouldn't kill you."

Doctor, these people are incredible! These people are unbelievable! These two are the outstanding producers and packagers of guilt in our time! They render it from me like fat from a chicken! "Call, Alex. Visit, Alex. Alex, keep us informed. Don't go away without telling us, please, not again. Last time you went away you didn't tell us, your father was ready to phone the police. You know how many times a day he called and got no answer? Take a guess, how many?" "Mother," I inform her, from between my teeth, "if I'm dead they'll smell the body in seventy-two hours, I assure you!" "Don't *talk* like that! God *forbid!*" she cries. Oh, and now she's got the beauty, the one guaranteed to do the job. Yet how could I expect otherwise? Can I ask the impossible of my own mother? "Alex, to pick up a phone is such a simple thing—how much longer will we be around to bother you anyway?"

Doctor Spielvogel, this is my life, my only life, and I'm living it in the middle of a Jewish joke! I am the son in the Jewish joke—*only it ain't no joke!* Please, who crippled us like this? Who made us so morbid and hysterical and weak? Why, why are they screaming still, "Watch out! Don't do it! Alex—*no!*" and why, alone on my bed in New York, why am I still hopelessly beating my meat? Doctor, what do you call this sickness I have? Is this the Jewish suffering I used to hear so much about? Is this what has come down to me from the pogroms and the persecution? from the mockery and abuse bestowed by the *goyim* over these two thousand lovely years? Oh my secrets, my shame, my palpitations, my flushes, my sweats! The way I respond to the simple vicissitudes of human life! Doctor, I can't stand any more being frightened like this over nothing! Bless me with manhood! Make me brave! Make me strong! Make me *whole!* Enough being a nice Jewish boy, publicly pleasing my parents while privately pulling my putz! Enough!

Beryl Bainbridge

*

DINNER AT BINNY'S
EXCERPT FROM *Injury Time*

[Edward, a married man, has been having an affair with Binny. On Binny's insistence, he invites his friend Simpson and his wife Muriel to dinner at his mistress's flat.—ED.]

Edward met old Simpson for a drink in the Hare and Hounds. The place was filled with tired businessmen pepping themselves up before returning home.

"I see no reason why you shouldn't claim a certain proportion for entertainment," said Edward. "None at all. Providing you can produce the restaurant bills."

"Quite so," agreed Simpson.

"But I don't feel we can justifiably put forward your wife's hairdressing expenses. Not for the golf club night and so forth. It's not strictly business. See what I mean?"

"Yes," said Simpson, disappointed.

"I mean, it's not as if she's a hostess in a night club, for instance. Or a television personality."

"I may have misled you about the wife," Simpson said. "She's not altogether sympatico to this evening."

"Good Lord," cried Edward, instantly alarmed. "I thought you said she was a woman of the world?"

"She's that of course," said Simpson. "But the way she sees it, it's a bit not on."

"She will come, won't she?" asked Edward. He felt like hitting old Simpson between the eyes with his fist. All that rubbish he'd talked about it being a bit of a lark and what a terrific sport the old woman was.

"The way she sees it," explained Simpson, "it's definitely a bit tricky. How would you like it if Helen was meeting some fellow on the side and she asked me round to your house to meet him?"

It seemed to Edward a highly unlikely situation, knowing what Helen thought about Simpson and fellows in general, but he nodded his head and pretended Simpson had a point there.

"Put it another way," Simpson went on. "What if my wife asked you and your lady friend to dinner behind my back? I trust you'd refuse."

"Need you ask?" Edward said.

"I don't want you to run away with the idea that the wife's narrow. She's not, believe you me. I'll tell you a little story. Keep it under your hat; I shouldn't like it to go any further. She got a proposition from a mutual friend of ours—well, wife of a friend of mine, as a matter of fact. Let's call her X. X phoned the wife and said could she come round and talk to her—"

"Whose wife?" asked Edward.

"Mine, of course," said Simpson. "It was absolutely vital that Y shouldn't get to know—"

"I don't quite follow you," said Edward, mystified by Simpson's alphabetical acquaintances. "Did your wife tell you she'd been propositioned?"

"Don't be dense," cried Simpson testily. "My wife wasn't propositioned. X was."

"Yes, of course." Edward nodded. He didn't want to antagonize Simpson, not when Binny's dinner party hung in the balance. At this moment, he no longer cared about himself and the possibility of being caught out. He thought only of Binny, slaving over a hot stove. "Stupid of me," he admitted. "It's my training, I suppose. Making sure the figures add up . . . that sort of thing. Do go on."

"It seems," continued Simpson, "that X was carrying on with Z. Had been for quite some time. Met him at a masonic do last year. Upshot of it was, X wanted the wife to lend out our spare room for the afternoon."

"Good God," murmured Edward. Though he had lost track of X and Z and was totally foxed by Y, he did sympathize with their general predicament.

"The wife handled it rather cleverly, I thought," said Simpson. "She said they could have the room but would they please wash the sheets out afterwards, or leave money on the table for laundering. And would they keep the window and the door open."

"The window?" said Edward. He thought Simpson's wife must have a peculiarly coarse sense of humor. Or possibly she was a voyeur.

"Took all the romance out of it," cried Simpson with satisfaction. "Exposed it for what it was. Put the kibosh on it, no two ways about it."

"Goodness, yes," said Edward, though it seemed to him, once they had come to some agreement about being spied upon, a small enough price to pay for a whole afternoon of love.

He fought his way to the counter and ordered another two pints of beer and waited, pipe clamped in his mouth like a dummy, craning upwards to see his reflection in the mirror above the bar. He needed a haircut; a pale forelock dangled over one eye. He would have gone to the barber's days ago—he'd noticed a few raised eyebrows in the office— but Binny had once remarked she liked men with untidy heads. He thought his forelock made him look rather boyish. Binny referred to it sometimes as a fetlock. At others, when she'd taken a glass or two of wine, she called it his foreskin. He'd better watch Binny's intake tonight —he didn't feel Simpson's wife would go for that kind of table talk. Always supposing she intended to be present. What on earth was he going to tell Binny if the Simpsons backed out at this late hour? She'd sounded so argumentative on the telephone, though at the end she'd said he was lovely. She did care for him. She gave him her love mostly without trying to bind him, without endangering his marriage. It was true there'd been a few unfortunate lapses, like the weekend she'd rung his house from some drinking club in Soho. He'd answered the phone himself, thank God, but it was frightfully tricky, standing in the hall in his pajamas in the middle of the night trying to convey through references to tax returns that he loved her, fearful of Helen on the landing listening to every word. There had been too that incident when he couldn't see Binny because he wanted to prune his roses, and she'd threatened to come round in the night and set fire to his garden. Later, a small corner of the lawn had been found mysteriously singed, but nothing had ever been proved. In the beginning he had fallen in love with her because she advised him they must live each day as if it was their last: bearing in mind that any moment the final whistle could blow, it was pointless to spoil the time they had left with the making of impossible demands. "You don't want to leave your wife," she'd said. "And I don't want you to." But as the months passed and she made various disparaging remarks about married men and their duplicity, it occurred to him that possibly this was precisely what she required of him. It made him very uncomfortable. He tried once to bring the subject into the open. "We could be jolly happy," he supposed. "We'd drink far too much and go to bed in the afternoon"—Helen disapproved of the afternoon— "if we lived together." Glaring at him as though he'd uttered a racist remark and snapping her rather large white teeth, Binny had cried, "You must be mad. Stark raving mad."

It was confusing for him. He obviously served some purpose in her life. Often he was reminded of a Punch and Judy show he had watched on the sands at Eastbourne when he was a child. Hearing that nasal voice screaming above the incoming tide, "Who's a naughty boy, then?," and flinching at the sound of those repeated blows to the head, he had not understood what was expected of him. Clutching his bucket and spade, he hadn't known whether to laugh or cry.

Binny could be so cold when standing up and facing him or shouting at him down the telephone, and so warm when lying in his arms. When he thought of those snatched perspiring moments on the sofa, the bathroom floor, the divan bed in Binny's back room, he felt he could forgive her anything and dreamed of devoting the rest of his life to making her happy.

He paid for the drinks and returned to the table. He looked down at Simpson's balding crown and said firmly, "Look here, old man. What's the form tonight? You are coming, I take it?"

"Good Lord, yes," said Simpson. "I wouldn't miss it for worlds."

"What about the wife?"

"We're both coming," Simpson said. "Depend on it. I just wanted to warn you it might be a bit sticky at first. Muriel might be a shade off-hand. But she'll thaw." He patted Edward's knee encouragingly.

"You may find it a little bohemian tonight," said Edward. "Just a bit."

"Christ," cried Simpson. "I feared as much. Muriel won't stand for it, you know."

"I meant domestically," Edward said. "Spacewise, facilities . . . knives and forks. See what I mean?"

"Oh," said Simpson. "Rough and ready, is that it?"

"A little," Edward said, feeling disloyal. "Binny's not one for appearances."

"Say no more." Simpson nodded sympathetically. "Are you going home to change?"

"No," said Edward. "It's a shade awkward getting out again. I thought I might go back to the office and sign a little post."

Simpson suggested Edward should come home with him for a wash-and-brush-up. Then they could all arrive together.

Edward accepted. "Have you mentioned to your wife," he said, "that we're supposed to have met? Her and me. Binny particularly stressed that I should invite close mutual friends."

"Don't push it, old boy," advised Simpson with some irritation. 'It's been difficult enough to persuade her to sit down with you, let alone pretend you've been friendly for years. And you'd better watch the hanky panky."

"Hanky panky?"

"Touching . . . fooling about . . . any outward show. Muriel won't like it."

"I have to be home by eleven," said Edward. "I don't think there'll be time for hanky panky."

No further mention was made of his going back with Simpson for a wash. After a quarter of an hour Simpson got up to go and said he'd see him in the trenches at twenty hundred hours. He nudged Edward in the ribs. "Synchronize watches . . . we'll go over the top together." Laughing heartily and thinking what a bloody ass the man was, Edward said goodbye. He bought a packet of cashew nuts to tide himself over until dinner, and on an unfortunate impulse telephoned Binny.

"What do you want?" she asked.

"Nothing really. I've just been chatting to old Simpson. He was a bit foolish, I thought."

"How surprising!"

"I meant he spoke rather childishly. He's not as broadminded as one thinks."

"What's all that noise?" Binny said. "Where are you?"

"In the office," he lied. "Simpson said what would I think if Helen asked him and his wife round for a meal."

"What are you on about? I thought they'd had dozens of meals at your house?"

"I'm not explaining myself very clearly," he said. "I get the feeling he doesn't approve of . . . well, you know . . ."

"I don't know," she snapped. "Spit it out."

"Us," he said lamely. "Carrying on."

She fell silent. Edward ground the receiver so tightly against his ear, to drown the pub sounds all around him, that his eyes began to water.

"You told me he'd been to a V.D. clinic," said Binny finally.

Oh God, he thought, had he really confided that? She'd probably bring it up at dinner if things went badly. "Well, yes," he said. "But there was never anything actually wrong."

"Who the hell does he think he is? He's in no position to object to anybody carrying on."

"I think," said Edward, "that it's his wife more than him."

"I'll bet it is," Binny crowed. "She probably feels that if you're doing it, then her old Simpson's at it too."

"You are clever," he said tenderly. "I do love you, you know."

"Like bloody hell," she said, and told him she must get on.

She was a mystery to him; she had no small talk at all.

He returned to the office. Here he began to compose a fairly resentful letter to Simpson, indicating that he thought it inadvisable to claim such and such an amount for the cleaning of his business premises. ". . . It would seem to me, in the circumstances, an unrealistic and preposterous sum, more in keeping with maintaining the hygienic standards of a research laboratory than a spare parts factory, and one which the Inspector of Taxes would undoubtedly and deservedly view with suspicion, etc., etc. . . ."

•   •   •

Binny laid the dining-room table, still wearing her headscarf and outdoor coat. Underneath she had changed into her best black dress. The table was situated in the front half of the ground-floor room. The back half contained the kitchen. In it was a stove, a fridge and a very small draining-board. So great was Binny's abhorrence of cooking that she'd torn down the shelving and plastic work surfaces installed by a previous owner and stacked everything—food, crockery, pans—into an article of furniture she called a wall cupboard. It was, in reality, a gentleman's wardrobe, still fragrant with the smell of Havana cigars, complete with little compartments for starched and detachable collars in which Binny kept the knives and forks. From the back window there was a view of a yard, a brick wall, and a rabbit hutch that Edward had given her.

Moving about the table, cheerful and organized, Binny was interrupted by her daughter, Lucy, who was eighteen and dressed as though ready for work on a building site.

"Screw me," cried Lucy, smiling for once, eyeing the cut flowers and the folded napkins. "Having a knees-up, are we?" She had known for days that Binny was expecting guests, but she liked to tease. She seized her mother by the shoulders and shook her. Binny's headscarf slithered over her eyes. "Who's a posh girl, then?"

"Don't, darling," said Binny.

Lucy flung herself sideways on to the sofa, crushing the newly plumped cushions. She began to roll a cigarette. She said critically, "I should wear something more suitable, if I were you. They'll think you're not stopping."

Binny noted that her daughter's army boots, heavily studded, were scuffing a carpet already flecked with pieces of cotton thread and bits of fluff. It had started to rain when she'd returned from the bank and she hadn't felt like going down into the yard to retrieve the hoover. The inside might have got wet and she didn't want to risk being electrocuted. Perhaps no one would notice the carpet once the drink started going down.

"I think, darling," said Binny, "you'd better be off. If that's all right with you. Just pop the baby into the Evans', there's a good girl."

The baby, who was almost eleven years old, was quite capable of climbing the fence and going up the steps to the house next door, but Binny worried.

"Where's big-dick?" asked Lucy.

"Behave," pleaded Binny. She counted inwardly to ten and busied herself with titivating the table. Her son Gregory, bribed with a pound note, was, she hoped, half-way across London on the underground, bound for the house of his friend Adam.

Lucy appeared to have fallen asleep. Cigarette papers and grains of tobacco littered her chest. "Will you get up?" said Binny. "At once. Please, dear."

There was very little left for her to do. She'd peeled the potatoes, washed the lettuce, sprinkled herb things on the meat. Still, she wanted her daughters out of the way. Being constantly with the children was like wearing a pair of shoes that were expensive and too small. She couldn't bear to throw them out, but they gave her blisters. It would be nice having Edward in the house with other people present. Adults. She could talk about things without having to explain herself, without endlessly repeating what she'd said in the first place. No one would interrupt her with requests for jam, or money for the bus. Nobody would tell her to shut up. She liked Edward when he'd had a lot to drink. His eyes, blood-shot and sleepy, gazed at her with passion. She would be able to lean against him and give him the biggest lamb chop. When he went into the bathroom he would notice how clean the bowl was and the basin. She knew it was important to him that the house should look like a good investment.

"Lucy," she said loudly. "It's almost seven o'clock."

"Rubbish," Lucy said. "It can't be. We'd have heard Mrs. Papastav-rou." Across the street was a post-war block of flats, lit at night like a ship on its maiden voyage and totally deserted by day. The rent collector and the man from the Providential were seen to walk along the concrete balconies, but the inmates remained hidden. The exception was Mrs. Papastavrou, an elderly Greek now living on the top floor, who had originally occupied a flat on the ground floor and been carried aloft, out of harm's way, after knifing the lady who brought the meals-on-wheels.

Mrs. Papastavrou had grown frail and thin before the wounding. Her tray was collected with the food untouched on her plate. In an effort to stimulate her appetite the Council provided her with stuffed vine leaves and cartons of taramasalata. Thinking she was being victimized, Mrs. Papastavrou had struck back. Every evening since her removal upstairs, she appeared on the balcony on the dot of half past six and moaned loudly until seven o'clock. Sometimes, when the weather was particularly warm, she gave a matinée performance. Often, well-meaning passers-by called ambulances, but she was returned almost immediately.

Binny looked out of the window to make certain the old woman remained indoors, and was appalled at the amount of refuse lying about the path. There were even eggshells caught in the branches of the privet hedge. "Ought I to sweep it up?" she asked aloud.

A tub, placed on bricks, stood in front of the row of dust bins. In it was planted some sort of bush that never did anything. It had been meant to act as a screen. The bin lids had been stolen long ago. A fat dog from up the street kept waddling in and tipping out the garbage.

"Sweep what?" said Lucy.

"The front path. It's a sight."

"Why not?" said Lucy. "You could dust the weeds while you're at it." She rolled off the sofa and lay face downwards, drumming on the floor with her toe-caps.

Even though it would be dark when the Simpsons arrived, the headlamps of their car would light up the square of garden laid with crazy paving. Mrs. Simpson would see the rubbish clearly illuminated.

Below the window was a strip of earth dangerously littered with strands of barbed wire, intended to discourage cats from doing their business on the stunted daffodils. Wrought-iron railings ran from the side of the front door, along the flower border, and ended at the steps to the basement flat. The basement was owned by a young couple, though Edward, in Binny's presence, had once told a colleague that it was hers and she rented it out. Anxious to boast of her assets, he referred to the young couple as her tenants.

Several betting slips, flung down by disappointed racing men, whirled upward from the path and, catching on the barbed wire, fluttered like sandwich flags among the daffodils.

I can do no more, thought Binny, rubbing at the window pane with a duster. She could hardly be blamed for the untidy habits of dogs and gamblers. And even supposing Mrs. Simpson noticed the mess, it wasn't likely she'd rush in muttering her complaints before she'd had a chance to be introduced.

Pushing the matter from her mind, Binny moved from the window and, tripping over her daughter's body, ran headlong into the kitchen.

Lucy rose and went upstairs to fetch Alison. Binny knelt on hands and knees and picked up tobacco grains from the floor.

A low keening began outside in the street. Hands clutching the rail, clouds scudding above her bowed head, Mrs. Papastavrou swayed backwards and forwards.

It was as well, thought Binny, that the Simpsons weren't coming until eight o'clock. Edward pretended that he didn't mind about Mrs. Papastavrou, that he'd grown used to her. But he hadn't. He stood well back from the window, both saddened and embarrassed, while the children snickered with laughter and the old lady, marooned on her balcony, wailed like a banshee.

"Alison won't," said Lucy, coming back into the room.

"Well, make her," shouted Binny, stamping her foot. She was beginning to breathe quite heavily. "I would be grateful to you if you would get your own things together as well. Have you got your nightdress?"

"Don't be bloody wet," said Lucy. She went to the table and tore at a French loaf with her teeth.

"I don't want to remind you of the shirt I bought you," Binny said. "Or the pair of shoes costing twenty-four pounds that you said you couldn't live without and promptly gave to your friend Soggy. When I was your age I was grateful if my mother gave me a smile."

"I lent them, you fool," corrected Lucy.

Binny's voice became shrill. "I've long since given up expecting gratitude or common courtesy, but I do expect you to get Alison and yourself out of the house. It's little enough to ask, God knows."

"Keep your lid on," said Lucy. She began to comb her hair at the mirror. Strands of hair and crumbs of bread fell to the hearth. Binny could feel a pulse beating in her throat. She burned with fury. No wonder she never put on an ounce of weight. The daily aggravation the children caused her was probably comparable to a five-mile run or an hour with the skipping rope. Clutching the region of her heart and fighting for self-control, she said insincerely, "Darling, you can be very sensitive and persuasive. Just tell her Sybil's waiting and that there's ice cream and things."

"Lucy strolled into the hall and called loudly, "Come down, Alison, or I'll bash your teeth in."

After several minutes a sound of barking was heard on the first-floor landing.

"Baby," crooned Binny, going upstairs with outstretched arms. Alison was on all fours, crouched against the wall. Binny often told friends it was nothing to worry about. Until two years ago Alison had insisted on baring her tummy button in the street and rubbing it against lamp posts. She had grown out of that, as doubtless she would soon grow tired of pretending she was a dog.

"Come along, darling," said Binny brightly. She bent down and patted her daughter's head.

Alison growled and seized Binny's ankle in her teeth.

Putting both hands behind her to resist hitting the child, Binny descended the stairs.

Lucy was at the sink pouring cooking sherry into a milk bottle.

"Out, out, out," cried Binny. "I am not here to provide booze for your layabout friends. This is not an off-licence."

She frogmarched Lucy to the door and pushed her down the steps. Alison began to cry. Running down the path, Binny caught up with Lucy at the hedge and put desperate arms about her. She said urgently, "Now please, pull yourself together. Get your things, take your coat, and I'll give you a pound note to spend."

Smirking, Lucy re-entered the house and began to put on her flying jacket. Smothering her youngest daughter in kisses, Binny took her to the door. She nodded blindly as Alison climbed the fence.

"You're crying, Mummy," called Alison. Her mouth quivered.

"I'm very happy, darling," said Binny. "Don't you worry about me." She wiped her cheeks with her hand. "I'm going to have a lovely party." She stood there waving until Alison was let into the Evans'.

Lucy had locked herself in the bathroom. Binny blew crumbs off the tablecloth and attended to the cushions on the sofa. She cut the end off the mutilated loaf and straightened the reproduction of The Last Supper that hung askew on the wall. Then she called gently down the hall that she would like to use the lavatory.

"Go away," snarled Lucy. "I'm trying to have a crap."

Binny left a pound note on the table and climbed the stairs. She walked round and round her bedroom humming fiercely. At that moment she fully understood Mrs. Papastavrou, fluttering in the wind and protesting for all the world to hear.

After a time Lucy shouted that she was off now. Binny kept silent.

"Well, come on. Give us a kiss."

"I certainly won't," called Binny. "You're far too rude."

The door slammed violently. Instantly remorseful, Binny ran to the window and watched her daughter walk sullenly along the gutter. She looked such a little girl, aggressively scuffing the ground with the studs of her massive boots. At the same age Binny had been married and looking after a house. She rapped frantically on the pane of glass; she blew kisses. Lucy disappeared round the corner.

Binny turned and banged her hip painfully against the edge of the ping-pong table. Every week she meant to advertise it for sale in the local newspaper. It had been bought three years ago for the children; she had hoped it might keep them off the streets. Selflessly she had moved her bed and her wardrobe into the back of the room so that there would be somewhere to put it. After six weeks of their constant bickering, turfing her personal belongings ruthlessly onto the landing to make additional space, and bringing their friends in at all hours of the day and night, sometimes even when Binny was asleep, she had forbidden them the use of the room. They didn't seem to grasp how irritating it was for her to lie there with her face-cream on and be subjected to large unknown youths clambering under and over her bed in the pursuit of ping-pong balls. She couldn't think where they learned such behavior, though she suspected it was being taught in the schools. They couldn't spell and they didn't read and they had little respect for property. Like a vast army on the move they swarmed across the city playing gramophone records and frequenting public houses. It wasn't that they disliked adults—they simply didn't notice them. Devoted to their homes, it was obvious that they would never leave. The only edge they had on an earlier generation was their casual regard for animals; they didn't pull wings off flies or throw stones at cats.

Rubbing her side, Binny was about to take off her coat when she heard a knock at the front door. Alarmed, she crept onto the landing. It could be any one of a number of people, none of them welcome—Alison deceived over the ice cream and returning in tears, the woman from No. 52 looking for her cat, the arrears collector from the television rental service? It was too early surely for the Simpsons to have arrived.

Thinking it might be Lucy come back for a cuddle, she went hopefully downstairs and opened the door.

"Are you the cleaning woman?" A stout black man advanced into the hall. His neck was encased in plaster of Paris.

"No." said Binny.

"I am bringing a message for you and all believing strangers, so that you may have a chance of redemption."

"I don't really think I'm a believer," Binny said.

"The eyes of the Lord are over the righteous," claimed the man, taking no notice. His own eyes were fixed on a point directly above

Binny's left shoulder. "His ears are open to their prayers, but the face of the Lord is against them that do evil. And who is he that will harm you if you be followers of that which is good?"

"I'm rather busy at the moment," said Binny.

"All that He asks is that you should follow Him."

"Still," protested Binny, "I haven't much time."

She was relieved to see Edward stepping out of a taxi at the curb, holding several bottles in his arms.

"Luke xv:7," preached the black man relentlessly. "Who are the just persons who need no repentance?" He was watching the stairs, as if waiting for somebody to appear.

Edward came up the path. Binny thought he looked terribly attractive. She usually thought that when he came towards her unexpectedly; later it wore off. Lucy addressed him as "Fatso" whenever she saw him; but really, in his dark City suit and his shirt with the pale stripe, he seemed very trim and dapper. He reminded Binny of a pre-war father come home ready for his Ovaltine—pipe in mouth, the evening newspaper under his arm. She did find him attractive, but when he went on about his roses or blew his nose like a trumpet or fell over when he stood on one trembling leg to remove his sock, she was at a loss to understand why.

"Are you going somewhere?" he demanded. "It's gone seven, you know."

"This gentleman's from the Bible," said Binny. "We were just having a little chat."

"Well, I should hurry it up if I were you." Edward pushed past them and went into the kitchen.

"Now that your man's home," the black man decided, "I'd best be going. He'll want his tea." He told her he'd leave a copy of his magazine and she ought to look at the questions at the back. Possibly when he called next week she'd have answered a few of them.

"I shouldn't count on it," said Binny, stung at the speed with which he was prepared to be on his way now that "her" man had returned. He hadn't minded wasting her time; it hadn't occurred to him that she too might have been wanting her tea.

Edward poured her out a drink before she went upstairs to do her face. He congratulated her on the table—he admired the flowers in the center. He forbore to mention that the vase could do with a wash.

"Food smells good," he said, anxious to be appreciative.

"There's nothing cooking yet," she said. "It isn't time."

He sat her on his lap and, relinquishing his pipe, kissed her. She couldn't respond wholeheartedly because of her headscarf. She felt faded and work-worn.

He said huskily, "Are the children gone?"

She nodded.

"Can't we go upstairs?"

"No," she said. "I'm not in the mood. Lucy was awful."

"I've had the devil of a day," said Edward. "One thing after another."

"She made Alison cry."

"The telephone never stopped ringing."

"I feel odd," she confided. "That man telling me there was nothing to fear—and earlier on when I was out shopping people kept waving."

Edward attempted to push his hand inside the front of her coat but it was tightly buttoned.

"Why *my* door?" she asked.

"*I'd* knock on your door," Edward said urgently. "Any time."

"You've been drinking," said Binny. She suddenly remembered the taxi drawing into the curb and felt resentful. He never came in his car in case somebody recognized the number plate and told his wife. "I can't imagine why you think you've had the devil of a day. What with your eight-course lunches and visits to the pub—"

"Three," he corrected.

"Nobody cooked *my* lunch. And look at the way that man ran off because he thought it was time for your tea. Talk about the chosen people of this world—"

"He didn't look chosen to me," said Edward. "Somebody obviously tried to break his neck."

He wanted Binny to get into the bath so that he could scrub her back. She said she'd already bathed, and he said why didn't he get in the bath then and she could wash his back.

"I'm not having you wallowing and snorting in my clean bath," she told him, and went upstairs to take off her coat and scarf.

She stood in the cramped bedroom and combed her hair. She felt crushed, flattened in some way. It was Edward's fault, coming in a taxi like that and not wanting to know about Lucy being rude. He always slid away when she mentioned the children. Of course, his own son was too busy learning Latin and Greek and generally behaving like Little Lord Fauntleroy to cause him a moment's trouble. Why, she wondered, was Edward always trying to get her into soapy water? It must have some connection with his days at boarding school; he probably thought it more hygienic to do it in the bath.

She didn't know why she felt so despairing inside. All the big issues were over and done with—it wasn't likely now that she'd get pregnant and even if she did, nobody, not even her mother, was going to tell her off. She didn't have any financial problems, she didn't hanker after new carpets. She didn't hanker after anything—certainly not Edward with a block of soap in one hand and that pipe spilling ash down her spine.

She was compelled suddenly to stand very still. She felt like an animal in long grass scenting smoke on the wind. She saw her reflection in the dressing-table mirror; she was holding a green comb to her head and staring fixedly at the glass. It had been the same this morning when she was out with Alma; only then there had been so much noise, so many faces with insinuating smiles—voices calling her name. Was it because she'd sent Lucy away without kissing her? Was Gregory lying battered by football hooligans on the floor of a tube train to Clapham? With the children gone, the whole house was heavy with silence.

It was Edward, she decided, who was upsetting her. He lived too much in the past; all that rubbish about his dormitory and the shadows on the playing fields. He evaded her completely. He should be dragged, by that schoolboy lock of hair falling over one nostalgic eye, into the present. She was fed up with his fumblings on the sofa, as if it was still those days before the war when mothers kept coming in and out with trays of tea and courting was a furtive thing. Why couldn't he pretend that he longed to leave his wife, so that she in return could pretend she wished he would? He ought to forget the ins and outs of capital transfer tax, and the particular type of pest that plagued his fruit bushes, and discuss what he did with Helen at night when she'd come back from all those meetings. They could have a row over it and be moved to tears, and then they both might feel something, some emotion that would nudge them closer to one another. Obviously he did do something with Helen. He was far too uncomplicated a man to abstain when there was a body lying next to him in bed, and apart from his roses it wasn't as if he had any hobbies to take his mind off sex. Old Simpson was quite right to disapprove of his carryings on. What Edward should do, she told herself, as though discussing somebody she had never met, was to park his car actually outside the house. In full view. After he made love he should lie there dozing and not trot into the darkness desperate for a taxi. Though he removed his socks and even put down his pipe during the act, he could not bring himself to unbuckle the watch from his wrist. Sometimes, when he lay exhausted on top of Binny, a little to one side with his cheek resting on his arm, she knew he was looking squint-eyed at the time.

She put away her comb and brushed the shoulders of her dress. That was the worst of black, it showed the slightest speck of dust; by the time she'd cooked the dinner she'd be spotted with grease. Except for the end of that French loaf, Lucy probably wouldn't have a bite of food until tomorrow morning. It was madness putting complete strangers before one's own flesh and blood. She had enough to do fighting hormone losses and hot flushes and depressions that dropped out of nowhere, without being tormented by guilt.

Belligerently she flung down the clothes-brush and returned to Edward, who was seated at the table with the evening newspaper spread before him.

"I think I should start cooking," she said. "Don't you?"

"Yes," he agreed. It was, he realized, ten minutes to eight. "Can I help?"

But he didn't move. He and Binny had another glass of wine.

She was sure the Simpsons were late. She kept asking the time, but Edward answered casually, saying, "What? Oh, the time . . . Jolly early if you ask me." It wouldn't do to get her into a state.

After half an hour Binny said the chops were ruined. Greatly alarmed, he rose to his feet.

"Well, almost," she amended. "What shall I do with them?"

He didn't know what to advise. Helen produced perfectly edible meals in an effortless way, and he was a bit thrown by the atmosphere of panic generated by Binny at the stove.

"Well, look at them," Binny shouted, bringing the grilling tray to the table and thrusting the chops under his nose.

They were a little wizened, he thought, but otherwise normal. "They're lovely," he said. "Simply lovely."

"Don't you ever do any cooking?" she asked. There was a hostile note in her voice.

He bent over the crossword and prayed the Simpsons would arrive soon.

Some minutes later Binny demanded to know if he did any washing.

"Washing?" he queried, playing for time.

"Do you wash your smalls?"

"We've a washing machine," he said.

"Even for your smalls?"

"It's for everything," he said. "Big or small."

She wanted him to describe his washing arrangements in detail.

It seemed a funny thing to be interested in. "Well," he said.

"I put my clothing, underpants, socks and so forth, in a polythene bag in the bathroom and Helen places them, in due course, in the machine."

"And you let her?" Binny cried, as though they were discussing coal-heaving or some equally strenuous job.

Inwardly he grew rattled. It was unfair of Binny to attack him over his underpants just because the Simpsons were late and she was worried about the chops. "Look here," he protested, "I have enough to do in the office, you know, without worrying about the washing. Helen's in all day. It's no trouble if you've got a machine. Besides, I don't know how to load the thing. As a matter of fact she won't let me touch it. It's her department."

"Do you sleep with her?"

The question was so unexpected that his mouth fell open. He felt he'd suffered a minor stroke. "My love," he began inadequately.

"You do, don't you?"

"No, no," he protested. He knew she knew he was not telling the truth. "She's not one for that sort of thing," he floundered. "Not now. She's gone off it."

Binny abandoned her place at the stove and came to sit at the table. She smiled lovingly at him.

He said uneasily, "I do care for you, you know. I really do."

"We all go off it," said Binny. "Us women." She held her fourth glass of wine to her lips and drank. "Until somebody exciting comes along. Like you," she added generously and, reaching out, attempted to touch his cheek.

He ducked, thinking she was going to strike him.

"Take Helen," she continued. "She's used to you. You're the old sod that's part of the furniture."

It wasn't, he felt, a flattering description. Still, Binny was smiling in an affectionate manner. He allowed her, without flinching, to caress his face.

"You're not a mystery any more," she told him. "Probably if you stayed very still she'd run a duster over you. But if a bloke came along, someone she'd never set eyes on, well . . . stands to reason, doesn't it?"

"Does it?" he said.

Binny withdrew her hand and thumped the table. "I bet you if the milkman rushed in and grabbed old Helen, she wouldn't say no."

"Perhaps not," he said dubiously. He had a mental picture of his wife moving serenely about the kitchen in her housecoat, and the youth from United Dairies running through the door in his striped apron and flinging her to the floor. "Of course," he said. "There's always the possibility that she might phone the police instead."

Outside it had grown dark. The block of flats across the street was transformed into a glittering mass of glass and concrete. Behind net curtains shadowed with the leaves of rubber plants, blurred figures moved across rooms that blazed with light.

"Six letters," said Edward, looking down at his paper. "Beginning with T."

"Terror," said Binny.

"A hard case," said Edward. "Turtle." And he pencilled it in.

Woody Allen

*

THE KUGELMASS EPISODE

Kugelmass, a professor of humanities at City College, was unhappily married for the second time. Daphne Kugelmass was an oaf. He also had two dull sons by his first wife, Flo, and was up to his neck in alimony and child support.

"Did I know it would turn out so badly?" Kugelmass whined to his analyst one day. "Daphne had promise. Who suspected she'd let herself go and swell up like a beach ball? Plus she had a few bucks, which is not in itself a healthy reason to marry a person, but it doesn't hurt, with the kind of operating nut I have. You see my point?"

Kugelmass was bald and as hairy as a bear, but he had soul.

"I need to meet a new woman," he went on. "I need to have an affair. I may not look the part, but I'm a man who needs romance. I need softness, I need flirtation. I'm not getting younger, so before it's too late I want to make love in Venice, trade quips at '21,' and exchange coy glances over red wine and candlelight. You see what I'm saying?"

Dr. Mandel shifted in his chair and said, "An affair will solve nothing. You're so unrealistic. Your problems run much deeper."

"And also this affair must be discreet," Kugelmass continued. "I can't afford a second divorce. Daphne would really sock it to me."

"Mr. Kugelmass—"

"But it can't be anyone at City College, because Daphne also works there. Not that anyone on the faculty at C.C.N.Y. is any great shakes, but some of those coeds . . ."

"Mr. Kugelmass—"

"Help me. I had a dream last night. I was skipping through a meadow holding a picnic basket and the basket was marked 'Options.' And then I saw there was a hole in the basket."

"Mr. Kugelmass, the worst thing you could do is act out. You must simply express your feelings here, and together we'll analyze them. You have been in treatment long enough to know there is no overnight cure. After all, I'm an analyst, not a magician."

"Then perhaps what I need is a magician," Kugelmass said, rising from his chair. And with that he terminated his therapy.

A couple of weeks later, while Kugelmass and Daphne were moping around in their apartment one night like two pieces of old furniture, the phone rang.

"I'll get it," Kugelmass said. "Hello."

"Kugelmass?" a voice said. "Kugelmass, this is Persky."

"Who?"

"Persky. Or should I say The Great Persky?"

"Pardon me?"

"I hear you're looking all over town for a magician to bring a little exotica into your life? Yes or no?"

"Sh-h-h," Kugelmass whispered. "Don't hang up. Where are you calling from, Persky?"

Early the following afternoon, Kugelmass climbed three flights of stairs in a broken-down apartment house in the Bushwick section of Brooklyn. Peering through the darkness of the hall, he found the door he was looking for and pressed the bell. I'm going to regret this, he thought to himself.

Seconds later, he was greeted by a short, thin, waxy-looking man.

"*You're* Persky the Great?" Kugelmass said.

"The Great Persky. You want a tea?"

"No, I want romance. I want music. I want love and beauty."

"But not tea, eh? Amazing. O.K., sit down."

Persky went to the back room, and Kugelmass heard the sounds of boxes and furniture being moved around. Persky reappeared, pushing before him a large object on squeaky roller-skate wheels. He removed some old silk handkerchiefs that were lying on its top and blew away a bit of dust. It was a cheap-looking Chinese cabinet, badly lacquered.

"Persky," Kugelmass said, "what's your scam?"

"Pay attention," Persky said. "This is some beautiful effect. I developed it for a Knights of Pythias date last year, but the booking fell through. Get into the cabinet."

"Why, so you can stick it full of swords or something?"

"You see any swords?"

Kugelmass made a face and, grunting, climbed into the cabinet. He couldn't help noticing a couple of ugly rhinestones glued onto the raw plywood just in front of his face. "If this is a joke," he said.

"Some joke. Now, here's the point. If I throw any novel into this cabinet with you, shut the doors, and tap it three times, you will find yourself projected into that book."

Kugelmass made a grimace of disbelief.

"It's the emess," Persky said. "My hand to God. Not just a novel, either. A short story, a play, a poem. You can meet any of the women created by the world's best writers. Whoever you dreamed of. You could carry on all you like with a real winner. Then when you've had enough you give a yell, and I'll see you're back here in a split second."

"Persky, are you some kind of outpatient?"

"I'm telling you it's on the level," Persky said.

Kugelmass remained skeptical. "What are you telling me—that this cheesy homemade box can take me on a ride like you're describing?"

"For a double sawbuck."

Kugelmass reached for his wallet. "I'll believe this when I see it," he said.

Persky tucked the bills in his pants pocket and turned toward his bookcase. "So who do you want to meet? Sister Carrie? Hester Prynne? Ophelia? Maybe someone by Saul Bellow? Hey, what about Temple Drake? Although for a man your age she'd be a workout."

"French. I want to have an affair with a French lover."

"Nana?"

"I don't want to have to pay for it."

"What about Natasha in *War and Peace*?"

"I said French. I know! What about Emma Bovary? That sounds to me perfect."

"You got it, Kugelmass. Give me a holler when you've had enough." Persky tossed in a paperback copy of Flaubert's novel.

"You sure this is safe?" Kugelmass asked as Persky began shutting the cabinet doors.

"Safe. Is anything safe in this crazy world?" Persky rapped three times on the cabinet and then flung open the doors.

Kugelmass was gone. At the same moment, he appeared in the bedroom of Charles and Emma Bovary's house at Yonville. Before him was a beautiful woman, standing alone with her back turned to him as she folded some linen. I can't believe this, thought Kugelmass, staring at the doctor's ravishing wife. This is uncanny. I'm here. It's her.

Emma turned in surprise. "Goodness, you startled me," she said. "Who are you?" She spoke in the same fine English translation as the paperback.

It's simply devastating, he thought. Then, realizing that it was he whom she had addressed, he said, "Excuse me. I'm Sidney Kugelmass. I'm from City College. A professor of humanities. C.C.N.Y.? Uptown. I —oh, boy!"

Emma Bovary smiled flirtatiously and said, "Would you like a drink? A glass of wine, perhaps?"

She is beautiful, Kugelmass thought. What a contrast with the troglodyte who shared his bed! He felt a sudden impulse to take this vision into his arms and tell her she was the kind of woman he had dreamed of all his life.

"Yes, some wine," he said hoarsely. "White. No, red. No, white. Make it white."

"Charles is out for the day," Emma said, her voice full of playful implication.

After the wine, they went for a stroll in the lovely French country-side. "I've always dreamed that some mysterious stranger would appear and rescue me from the monotony of this crass rural existence," Emma said, clasping his hand. They passed a small church. "I love what you have on," she murmured. "I've never seen anything like it around here. It's so . . . so modern."

"It's called a leisure suit," he said romantically. "It was marked down." Suddenly he kissed her. For the next hour they reclined under a tree and whispered together and told each other deeply meaningful things with their eyes. Then Kugelmass sat up. He had just remembered he had to meet Daphne at Bloomingdale's. "I must go," he told her. "But don't worry, I'll be back."

"I hope so," Emma said.

He embraced her passionately, and the two walked back to the house. He held Emma's face cupped in his palms, kissed her again, and yelled, "O.K., Persky! I got to be at Bloomingdale's by three-thirty."

There was an audible pop, and Kugelmass was back in Brooklyn.

"So? Did I lie?" Persky asked triumphantly.

"Look, Persky, I'm right now late to meet the ball and chain at Lexington Avenue, but when can I go again? Tomorrow?"

"My pleasure. Just bring a twenty. And don't mention this to any-body."

"Yeah. I'm going to call Rupert Murdoch."

Kugelmass hailed a cab and sped off to the city. His heart danced on point. I am in love, he thought, I am the possessor of a wonderful secret. What he didn't realize was that at this very moment students in various classrooms across the country were saying to their teachers, "Who is this character on page 100? A bald Jew is kissing Madame Bovary?" A teacher in Sioux Falls, South Dakota, sighed and thought, Jesus, these kids, with their pot and acid. What goes through their minds!

Daphne Kugelmass was in the bathroom-accessories department at Bloomingdale's when Kugelmass arrived breathlessly. "Where've you been?" she snapped. "It's four-thirty."

"I got held up in traffic," Kugelmass said.

. . .

Kugelmass visited Persky the next day, and in a few minutes was again passed magically to Yonville. Emma couldn't hide her excitement at seeing him. The two spent hours together, laughing and talking about their different backgrounds. Before Kugelmass left, they made love. "My God, I'm doing it with Madame Bovary!" Kugelmass whispered to himself. "Me, who failed freshman English."

As the months passed, Kugelmass saw Persky many times and developed a close and passionate relationship with Emma Bovary. "Make sure and always get me into the book before page 120," Kugelmass said to the magician one day. "I always have to meet her before she hooks up with this Rodolphe character."

"Why?" Persky said. "You can't beat his time?"

"Beat his time. He's landed gentry. Those guys have nothing better to do than flirt and ride horses. To me, he's one of those faces you see in the pages of *Women's Wear Daily*. With the Helmut Berger hairdo. But to her he's hot stuff."

"And her husband suspects nothing?"

"He's out of his depth. He's a lacklustre little paramedic who's thrown in his lot with a jitterbug. He's ready to go to sleep by ten, and she's putting on her dancing shoes. Oh, well . . . See you later."

And once again Kugelmass entered the cabinet and passed instantly to the Bovary estate at Yonville. "How you doing, cupcake?" he said to Emma.

"Oh, Kugelmass," Emma sighed. "What I have to put up with. Last night at dinner, Mr. Personality dropped off to sleep in the middle of the dessert course. I'm pouring my heart out about Maxim's and the ballet, and out of the blue I hear snoring."

"It's O.K., darling. I'm here now," Kugelmass said, embracing her. I've earned this, he thought, smelling Emma's French perfume and burying his nose in her hair. I've suffered enough. I've paid enough analysts. I've searched till I'm weary. She's young and nubile, and I'm here a few pages after Leon and just before Rodolphe. By showing up during the correct chapters, I've got the situation knocked.

Emma, to be sure, was just as happy as Kugelmass. She had been starved for excitement, and his tales of Broadway night life, of fast cars and Hollywood and TV stars, enthralled the young French beauty.

"Tell me again about O. J. Simpson," she implored that evening, as she and Kugelmass strolled past Abbé Bournisien's church.

"What can I say? The man is great. He sets all kinds of rushing records. Such moves. They can't touch him."

"And the Academy Awards?" Emma said wistfully. "I'd give anything to win one."

"First you've got to be nominated."

"I know. You explained it. But I'm convinced I can act. Of course, I'd want to take a class or two. With Strasberg maybe. Then, if I had the right agent—"

"We'll see, we'll see. I'll speak to Persky."

That night, safely returned to Persky's flat, Kugelmass brought up the idea of having Emma visit him in the big city.

"Let me think about it," Persky said. "Maybe I could work it. Stranger things have happened." Of course, neither of them could think of one.

· · ·

"Where the hell do you go all the time?" Daphne Kugelmass barked at her husband as he returned home late that evening. "You got a chippie stashed somewhere?"

"Yeah, sure, I'm just the type," Kugelmass said wearily. "I was with Leonard Popkin. We were discussing Socialist agriculture in Poland. You know Popkin. He's a freak on the subject."

"Well, you've just been very odd lately," Daphne said. "Distant. Just don't forget about my father's birthday. On Saturday?"

"Oh, sure, sure," Kugelmass said, heading for the bathroom.

"My whole family will be there. We can see the twins. And Cousin Hamish. You should be more polite to Cousin Hamish—he likes you."

"Right, the twins," Kugelmass said, closing the bathroom door and shutting out the sound of his wife's voice. He leaned against it and took a deep breath. In a few hours, he told himself, he would be back in Yonville again, back with his beloved. And this time, if all went well, he would bring Emma back with him.

At three-fifteen the following afternoon, Persky worked his wizardry again. Kugelmass appeared before Emma, smiling and eager. The two spent a few hours at Yonville with Binet and then remounted the Bovary carriage. Following Persky's instructions, they held each other tightly, closed their eyes, and counted to ten. When they opened them, the carriage was just drawing up at the side door of the Plaza Hotel, where Kugelmass had optimistically reserved a suite earlier in the day.

"I love it! It's everything I dreamed it would be," Emma said as she swirled joyously around the bedroom, surveying the city from their window. "There's F. A. O. Schwarz. And there's Central Park, and the Sherry is which one? Oh, there—I see. It's too divine."

On the bed there were boxes from Halston and Saint Laurent. Emma unwrapped a package and held up a pair of black velvet pants against her perfect body.

"The slacks suit is by Ralph Lauren," Kugelmass said. "You'll look like a million bucks in it. Come on, sugar, give us a kiss."

"I've never been so happy!" Emma squealed as she stood before the mirror. "Let's go out on the town. I want to see *Chorus Line* and the Guggenheim and this Jack Nicholson character you always talk about. Are any of his flicks showing?"

"I cannot get my mind around this," a Stanford professor said. "First a strange character named Kugelmass, and now she's gone from the book. Well, I guess the mark of a classic is that you can reread it a thousand times and always find something new."

•   •   •

The lovers passed a blissful weekend. Kugelmass had told Daphne he would be away at a symposium in Boston and would return Monday. Savoring each moment, he and Emma went to the movies, had dinner in Chinatown, passed two hours at a discothèque, and went to bed with a TV movie. They slept till noon on Sunday, visited SoHo, and ogled celebrities at Elaine's. They had caviar and champagne in their suite on Sunday night and talked until dawn. That morning, in the cab taking them to Persky's apartment, Kugelmass thought, It was hectic, but worth it. I can't bring her here too often, but now and then it will be a charming contrast with Yonville.

At Persky's, Emma climbed into the cabinet, arranged her new boxes of clothes neatly around her, and kissed Kugelmass fondly. "My place next time," she said with a wink. Persky rapped three times on the cabinet. Nothing happened.

"Hmm," Persky said, scratching his head. He rapped again, but still no magic. "Something must be wrong," he mumbled.

"Persky, you're joking!" Kugelmass cried. "How can it not work?"

"Relax, relax. Are you still in the box, Emma?"

"Yes."

Persky rapped again—harder this time.

"I'm still here, Persky."

"I know, darling. Sit tight."

"Persky, we *have* to get her back," Kugelmass whispered. "I'm a married man, and I have a class in three hours. I'm not prepared for anything more than a cautious affair at this point."

"I can't understand it," Persky muttered. "It's such a reliable little trick."

But he could do nothing. "It's going to take a little while," he said to Kugelmass. "I'm going to have to strip it down. I'll call you later."

Kugelmass bundled Emma into a cab and took her back to the Plaza. He barely made it to his class on time. He was on the phone all day, to Persky and to his mistress. The magician told him it might be several days before he got to the bottom of the trouble.

"How was the symposium?" Daphne asked him that night.

"Fine, fine," he said, lighting the filter end of a cigarette.

"What's wrong? You're as tense as a cat."

"Me? Ha, that's a laugh. I'm as calm as a summer night. I'm just going to take a walk." He eased out the door, hailed a cab, and flew to the Plaza.

"This is no good," Emma said. "Charles will miss me."

"Bear with me, sugar," Kugelmass said. He was pale and sweaty. He kissed her again, raced to the elevators, yelled at Persky over a pay phone in the Plaza lobby, and just made it home before midnight.

"According to Popkin, barley prices in Kraków have not been this stable since 1971," he said to Daphne, and smiled wanly as he climbed into bed.

• • •

The whole week went by like that.

On Friday night, Kugelmass told Daphne there was another symposium he had to catch, this one in Syracuse. He hurried back to the Plaza, but the second weekend there was nothing like the first. "Get me back into the novel or marry me," Emma told Kugelmass. "Meanwhile, I want to get a job or go to class, because watching TV all day is the pits."

"Fine. We can use the money," Kugelmass said. "You consume twice your weight in room service."

"I met an Off Broadway producer in Central Park yesterday, and he said I might be right for a project he's doing," Emma said.

"Who is this clown?" Kugelmass asked.

"He's not a clown. He's sensitive and kind and cute. His name's Jeff Something-or-Other, and he's up for a Tony."

Later that afternoon, Kugelmass showed up at Persky's drunk.

"Relax," Persky told him. "You'll get a coronary."

"Relax. The man says relax. I've got a fictional character stashed in a hotel room, and I think my wife is having me tailed by a private shamus."

"O.K., O.K. We know there's a problem." Persky crawled under the cabinet and started banging on something with a large wrench.

"I'm like a wild animal," Kugelmass went on. "I'm sneaking around town, and Emma and I have had it up to here with each other. Not to mention a hotel tab that reads like the defense budget."

"So what should I do? This is the world of magic," Persky said. "It's all nuance."

"Nuance, my foot. I'm pouring Dom Pérignon and black eggs into this little mouse, plus her wardrobe, plus she's enrolled at the Neighborhood Playhouse and suddenly needs professional photos. Also, Persky, Professor Fivish Kopkind, who teaches Comp Lit and who has always been jealous of me, has identified me as the sporadically appearing character in the Flaubert book. He's threatened to go to Daphne. I see ruin and alimony; jail. For adultery with Madame Bovary, my wife will reduce me to beggary."

"What do you want me to say? I'm working on it night and day. As far as your personal anxiety goes, that I can't help you with. I'm a magician, not an analyst."

By Sunday afternoon, Emma had locked herself in the bathroom and refused to respond to Kugelmass's entreaties. Kugelmass stared out the window at the Wollman Rink and contemplated suicide. Too bad this is a low floor, he thought, or I'd do it right now. Maybe if I ran away to Europe and started life over . . . Maybe I could sell the *International Herald Tribune*, like those young girls used to.

The phone rang. Kugelmass lifted it to his ear mechanically.

"Bring her over," Persky said. "I think I got the bugs out of it."

Kugelmass's heart leaped. "You're serious?" he said. "You got it licked?"

"It was something in the transmission. Go figure."

"Persky, you're a genius. We'll be there in a minute. Less than a minute."

Again the lovers hurried to the magician's apartment, and again Emma Bovary climbed into the cabinet with her boxes. This time there was no kiss. Persky shut the doors, took a deep breath, and tapped the box three times. There was the reassuring popping noise, and when Persky peered inside, the box was empty. Madame Bovary was back in her novel. Kugelmass heaved a great sigh of relief and pumped the magician's hand.

"It's over," he said. "I learned my lesson. I'll never cheat again, I swear it." He pumped Persky's hand again and made a mental note to send him a necktie.

• • •

Three weeks later, at the end of a beautiful spring afternoon, Persky answered his doorbell. It was Kugelmass, with a sheepish expression on his face.

"O.K., Kugelmass," the magician said. "Where to this time?"

"It's just this once," Kugelmass said. "The weather is so lovely, and I'm not getting any younger. Listen, you've read *Portnoy's Complaint?* Remember The Monkey?"

"The price is now twenty-five dollars, because the cost of living is up, but I'll start you off with one freebie, due to all the trouble I caused you."

"You're good people," Kugelmass said, combing his few remaining hairs as he climbed into the cabinet again. "This'll work all right?"

"I hope. But I haven't tried it much since all that unpleasantness."

"Sex and romance," Kugelmass said from inside the box. "What we go through for a pretty face."

Persky tossed in a copy of *Portnoy's Complaint* and rapped three times on the box. This time, instead of a popping noise there was a dull explosion, followed by a series of crackling noises and a shower of sparks. Persky leaped back, was seized by a heart attack, and dropped dead. The cabinet burst into flames, and eventually the entire house burned down.

Kugelmass, unaware of this catastrophe, had his own problems. He had not been thrust into *Portnoy's Complaint*, or into any other novel, for that matter. He had been projected into an old textbook, *Remedial Spanish*, and was running for his life over a barren, rocky terrain as the word *tener* ("to have")—a large and hairy irregular verb—raced after him on its spindly legs.

Bruce McCall

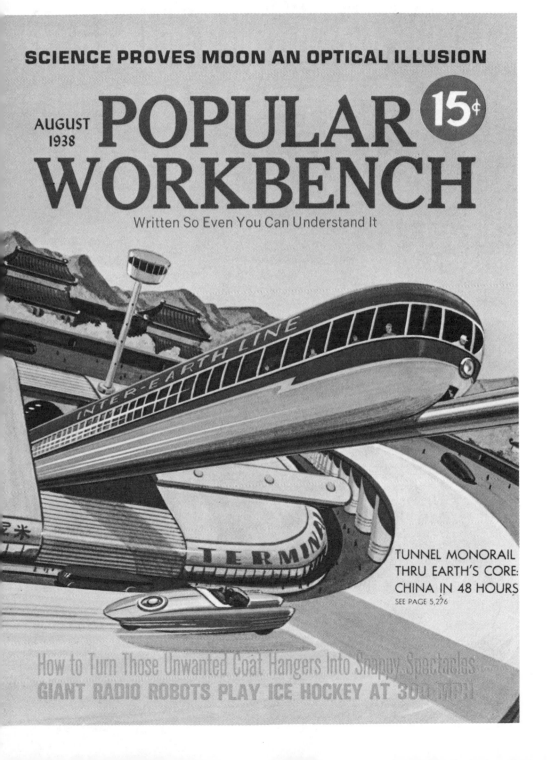

SCIENCE PROVES MOON AN OPTICAL ILLUSION

AUGUST 1938

POPULAR

15¢

WORKBENCH

Written So Even You Can Understand It

INTER-EARTH LINE

TERMINAL

TUNNEL MONORAIL
THRU EARTH'S CORE:
CHINA IN 48 HOURS
SEE PAGE 5,276

How to Turn Those Unwanted Coat Hangers Into Snappy Spectacles
GIANT RADIO ROBOTS PLAY ICE HOCKEY AT 300 MPH

POPULAR WORKBENCH

August, 1938   Vol. 76, No

In This Issue

Coming Next Month

"Worms That Went to College" Guide Marines to Foe; Simple Trick Turns Car Exhaust into Vacuum Cleaner; Rocket Canoe to Cross Lake Erie in 20 Minutes; Minnesota Man Claims World's Largest Screen Door

Solving the Riddles of the Ancients by RADIO

by E. Frank Nerkhauser, Jr.

Did the Ammonia People of Pluto once con-
ct our planet? Long ago in olden days did
ypt's storied King Pni, the Rat-Faced
unk Boy of holy temple friezes, operate a
am" radio station from his sacred pyramid
mb?

Dr. Emolius Fang of Laredo, Texas, is bound
d determined to find out!

Dr. Fang is undertaking radio experiments
ar the mysterious Pyramid of Pni. By hook-
g up a microphone of his own invention in-
le the pyramid's central tomb, the Yankee
iropractor-turned-history-sleuth expects to
tch voices twenty centuries old. Amplified
d deciphered, these pre-historic sound-waves
ay unlock the secrets of bygone civilizations.
Theory behind the novel experiment is Dr.

OW ANCIENT EGYPT CONTACTED PLUTO

Eavesdropping on earlier eons, Dr. Fang tenses for tell-tale prattle from past.

4001 B.C.

Antenna atop pyramid (A) directed signals from Pluto to control-room in tomb (B), which bounced code back via passing space roadster (C).

Fang's discovery that the three triangular points of a pyramid exactly match one-hundred-million-billionth of the distance between Pluto, Earth, and the outer-galaxy Ghost
Planet Lubdimus when all are arranged in pyramidal form,
with Pluto at the apex.

To date, Dr. Fang claims to have heard music on special
earphones that "broadcast" queer goings-on from inside the
pyramid. Could the tune be Pluto's national anthem? Dr.
Fang points for support to friezes in the Holy Temple at
Bah, showing what appears to be the mother-in-law of the
uncle of King Pni, the Rat-Faced Skunk Boy, carrying an
early microphone in one hand, a tray of caramels in another,
a stork in another and preceded by a Plutonian holding
sheet music.

Such are the mysteries unravelled when a plucky American decides to solve the Riddles of the Ancients by Radio!

Automatic Nose-Blowing Device Cures Mankind's Oldest Nuisanc

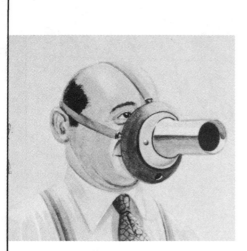

The familiar hanky may be on its way out if Swiss scientists g
their wish. Using no electricity, the ingenious invention at left fir
squirts heated air into the nasal passages by pneumatic pressur
then sucks it back out to create what hydraulics engineers term
"snort vacuum"—all within a split second. A handy dial on t
machine's nosepiece controls temperature and intensity. The no
can be "force blown" with no more discomfort than having a w
dom tooth extracted. The device fits comfortably over the face l
adjustable straps and can be rinsed after use. Energy experts es
mate that the power generated by the world population's nos
blowing in one twenty-four-hour period could, if harnessed, opera
the entire trolley system of Montevideo, Uruguay for 200 years
turn the engines of the giant luxury liner *Mauretenia* long enou
to take it around the globe thirty-eight times non-stop.

Diesel Typewriter Reduces Effort

The 4,000-horsepower, three-and-a-half-ton diesel typewriter
shown at right lays claim to better than 4,000,000 words per gal-
lon of fuel, making it economy champ of the world's diesel typing
devices. Standing no higher than a boxcar, the machine provides
a full standard-typewriter keyboard. Heart of the goliath gadget
is a rolling paper-drum good for more than 10,000 average business letters without restocking. The roll is fed automatically into
the typewriter at a rate of six inches every ten seconds, matching
a typing speed of 375 words per minute. The machine is so sturdy
that it can be rammed by a five-ton truck moving at fifty mph
without jarring the keyboard. Belt-driven gears automatically
shift the quarter-ton carriage at the end of each line. A similar
machine is currently being used to type up daily menus for the
Finnish Army.

"Talking Bat" Radios Hot-Hittir Tips from Dugout to Home Pla

"Lemme outta here, this bat's jinxed!" That is what an unsu
pecting slugger might well exclaim, were he to try harassing
moundsman's horsehide offerings with the baseball bat shown
left in the hands of Chicago White Sox star Vern "Turkey" Kazo
The bat, nicknamed "Gabby," was adopted by the Windy Cit
nine in an effort to boost the club's hitting record and perhar
escape the Junior Circuit basement this semester. Hidden in th
bat handle is a tiny radio set specially designed to "broadcast
instructions and hot tips from the dugout to the batter betwee
pitches. To foil opposing eavesdroppers all messages are in code
"Bunt" comes across to the hitter's ear as "Hit away," an
"Swing for the fences" is disguised as the order to "Watch tho
outside pitches." White Sox officials expect the talking bat to b
adopted by other clubs as soon as a shatterproof radio is develope

Handsome Zeppelin Display Is Actually Iron Lung

A dandy conversation-piece for any home has been developed by a Milwaukee engineering firm. Our sketch shows a typical setting for the "Zepp-Lung," which makes it possible for invalids confined to iron lungs to be taken out of the sickroom and placed "in the middle" of things. Attached to the novel Zepp-Lung but hidden from sight is a bellows easily fashioned from a discarded accordion and linked to a pump made out of an old meat grinder, tied by an old leather belt to the motor of the family washing machine. Tip to home handymen: Make sure motor of washer is running! Necessary gauges for operation of the Zepp-Lung can be mounted in the base and are available for pennies at your local salvage yard. The base can be made to swivel by fitting a ball joint found on any wrecked auto. A full, working Zeppelin model can be made by removing invalid from lung and filling in porthole.

dd Auto Made from Radio Cabinet ocates Stray Mutts for City Pound

A "midget auto" in more ways than one, the unusual vehicle wn at left is a familiar sight on the streets of Elmira, N.Y.— ng with its driver, also a midget. Constructed from the cabinet a discarded radio and powered by the pedalling action of its inutive driver, the pint-sized runabout is both quieter and re maneuverable than normal motor vehicles and thus makes ideal weapon for sneaking up on stray animals as they skulk narrow alleyways. Carried in a compartment behind the ved-off operator are a lasso and a chloroform pad to catch l tame the beast, and behind this compartment is a locker transporting it back to the pound. Elmira's Dog Patrol has nded up more than twelve dogs in this manner, probably venting an outbreak of the Bubonic Plague that swept ough Europe in medieval times and brought most industry to alt. Cost of the "dog-gone clever" doodlebug is reported to be than $2.

Powerful Shoe Flashlight Is Recharged by Foot Action

A handy helper for night watchmen, tunnel dwellers, the infirm, the near blind, outdoorsmen, explorers, bat-keepers, and the like is this novel shoe fitted with its own "toe-light," patented by a New Jersey man. Unlike earlier models that utilized a simple flashlight mounted on the shoe toe, this clever invention is designed to harness the natural power of the foot and leg in walking or running motion. An insulated clamp fits over the leg just below the knee, holding in place an asbestos sock with open-toe construction to allow six wires, three positive and three negative, to coil around the bare toes. A simple generator under the foot arch is linked to the big toe and hooked up with these wires as well as to the 2-watt bulb of the shoe light by a short insulated cable. Back-and-forth movement of the foot and pumping motions of the leg are sufficient to direct steady current to the bulb, and electrocution while running is rare.

HOBBIES ROUND THE WORLD

Jap Cadet Builds Perfect Replica of Pearl Harbor Base

Ensign Yichi Omakugu of the Nip Navy zeroed in on our Pacific bastion, tabletop-style—and so successful was the young modeler's attack that the Hawaiian naval-base-in-miniature is visited by Imperial Jap Navy brass for look-sees that last far into the night!

The super-detailed model includes jetties, oil tanks, airstrips, and every warship in the U.S. Pacific Fleet. Training to be a pilot, young Yichi plans to visit Pearl Harbor in person no later than the end of 1941. His familiarity should pay big dividends!

Austrian Glider Club Practices Dropping Mail "on Target"

Peeling off and diving like hungry nighthawks, the black gliders angle earthward and suddenly level off. A moment later comes the sharp whistle of a hurtling projectile aimed with pinpoint precision. The mail's arrived! All part of scientific experiments by the Furi-ous Eagles Postal Club of Zeltweig, Austria, aided by the German Reichspost. German experts claim Europe's skies will soon be dark with similar craft winging parcels to Deutschland's neighbors, especially Poland. Look up, Warsaw, Germany calling!

Odd German Invention Previews Courier Service to England

A speedy "buzz-bundle" may soon be seen carrying messages from Berlin to London if a few enthusiastic German hobbyists have their way! Half airplane, half rocket, it is said to reach 400 miles per hour and is capable of being aimed within a few square miles of its planned destination. Its "payload" could be hundreds of first-class letters or special packages. German designers say the "buzzy-bundle" could land anywhere and predicts that its loud engine noise will soon become a familiar part of British life!

Zig-Zag Gun Fires Zig-Zag Bullets in Zig-Zag Pattern

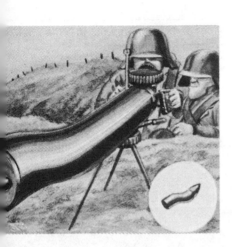

The Bulgarian Army is trying out a radical new weapon of war, designed to outwit fleeing enemy soldiers who try zig-zagging away from the line of fire as they retreat across the battlefield. The weapon is a specially designed all-Bulgarian gas/electric/coal/diesel/steam machine gun, meant to out-zig and out-zag the most adroit foe by firing bent bullets from a crooked barrel and sending a deadly fusillade across the enemy's rear in a twisted trajectory. Trials during the recently concluded Bulgarian Army War Games, using captured Armenian border violators as the mock enemy, showed the deadly gun to inflict a promising number of casualties, some of them on the mock enemy. Another plan for the ingenious device, according to Bulgarian Army sources, is to donate it to an enemy.

Novel Wristwatch Is Also Salt and Pepper Shaker, Toothpick Holder

A New York firm has introduced a "gadgeteer's dream" of a wrist watch. Fog-proof and claimed accurate to within one month per minute, the 2-jewel Swiss-assembled timepiece is not only a means of counting the hours but also a fine magnetic compass, a sterling silver salt-and-pepper shaker, a toothpick holder, a match caddy, a change purse, a boiled-egg timer, a calendar, a table of measurements and weights, a mirror, an amusing game of skill, a wrist heater, a spare-button bank, a magnifying glass, a tourniquet, and a weed killer. The handsome device weighs less than 4 oz. but handily combines all these functions by careful design and following the principles of miniaturization. Sportsmen, military men, aviators, businessmen, ship captains, musicians, hobbyists, and underwater explorers are expected to be ready customers.

Discarded Spat Makes Grand Overcoat for Chilly Rabbit

A Rhode Island man has found a handy use for an unused pair of spats. He chose the cleanest one of the two and, with no glue or nailing, converted the dressy accessory into a snug-fitting winter "coat" for his pet rabbit, which he had noticed would often shiver in its cage behind the house. The second spat is held in reserve as the man plans to acquire a second pet rabbit by and by. In this way whole rabbit "families" can be outfitted against the elements and America's forgotten spats put to work instead of lying in closets. The trick with the "spat coat" is to anchor the understrap firmly to the rabbit. As rabbits tend to nervousness, the strap must be drawn tightly against the belly and cinched to stay. Slippage is countered by wiring the strap in position.

Calvin Trillin

*

DINNER AT THE DE LA RENTAS'

January 17, 1981

Another week has passed without my being invited to the de la Rentas'.
Even that overstates my standing. Until I read in *The New York Times
Magazine* a couple of weeks ago about the de la Rentas having become
"barometers of what constitutes fashionable society" ("Françoise and
Oscar de la Renta have created a latter-day salon for *le nouveau grand
monde*—the very rich, very powerful and very gifted"), I wasn't even
aware of what I wasn't being invited to week after week. Once I knew, of
course, it hurt.

Every time the phone rang, I thought it must be Mrs. de la Renta
with an invitation ("Mr. Trillin? Françoise de la Renta here. We're having a few very rich, very powerful and/or very gifted people over Sunday
evening to celebrate Tisha B'av, and we thought you and the missus
might like to join us"). The phone rang. It was my mother calling from
Kansas City to ask if I'm sure I sent a thank-you note to my Cousin Edna
for the place setting of stainless Edna and six other cousins went in on
for our wedding gift in 1965. The phone rang. An invitation! Fats Goldberg, the pizza baron, asked if we'd like to bring the kids to his uptown
branch Sunday night to sample the sort of pizza he regularly describes
as "a gourmet tap-dance."

"Thanks, Fat Person, but I'll have to phone you," I said. "We may
have another engagement Sunday."

The phone quit ringing.

"Why aren't I in *le nouveau grand monde?*" I asked my wife, Alice.

"Because you speak French with a Kansas City accent?" she asked
in return.

"Not at all," I said. "Sam Spiegel, the Hollywood producer, is a regular at the de la Rentas', and I hear that the last time someone asked him to speak French he said 'Gucci.' "

"Why would you want to go there anyway?" Alice said. "Didn't you read that the host is so phony he added his own 'de la' to what had been plain old Oscar Renta?"

"Who can blame a man for not wanting to go through life sounding like a taxi driver?" I said. "Family background's not important in *le nouveau grand monde*. Diana Vreeland says Henry Kissinger is the star. The Vicomtesse de Ribes says 'Françoise worships intelligence.' You get invited by accomplishment—taking over a perfume company, maybe, or invading Cambodia."

"Why don't we just call Fats and tell him we'll be there for a gourmet tap-dance?" Alice said.

"Maybe it would help if you started wearing dresses designed by Oscar de la Renta," I said. "Some of his guests say they would feel disloyal downing Mrs. d's chicken fricassee while wearing someone else's merchandise."

Alice shook her head. "Oscar de la Renta designs those ruffly dresses that look like what the fat girl made a bad mistake wearing to the prom," she said.

"Things were a lot easier when fashionable society was limited to old-rich goyim, and all the rest of us didn't have to worry about being individually rejected," I said.

"At least they knew better than to mingle socially with their dressmakers," Alice said.

Would I be ready if the de la Rentas phoned? The novelist Jerzy Kosinski, after all, told the *Times* that evenings with them were "intellectually demanding." Henry Kissinger, the star himself, said that the de la Rentas set "an interesting intellectual standard"—although, come to think of it, that phrase could also be applied to Fats Goldberg.

Alone at the kitchen table, I began to polish my dinner-table chit-chat, looking first to the person I imagined being seated on my left (the Vicomtesse de Ribes, who finds it charming that her name reminds me of barbecue joints in Kansas City) and then to the person on my right (Barbara Walters, another regular, who has tried to put me at my ease by confessing that in French she doesn't do her r's terribly well). "I was encouraged when it leaked that the Reagan Cabinet was going to be made up of successful managers from the world of business," I say, "but I expected them all to be Japanese."

Barbara and the Vicomtesse smile. Alice, who had just walked into the kitchen, looked concerned.

"Listen," Alice said. "I read in the *Times* that Mrs. de la Renta is very strict about having only one of each sort of person at a dinner party. Maybe they already have someone from Kansas City."

Possible. Jerzy Kosinski mentioned that Mrs. d is so careful about not including more than one stunning achiever from each walk of life ("she understands that every profession generates a few princes or kings") that he and Norman Mailer have never been at the de la Rentas' on the same evening ("when I arrive, I like to think that, as a novelist, I'm unique"). Only one fabulous beauty. Only one world-class clotheshorse.

Then I realized that the one-of-each rule could work to my advantage. As I envisioned it, Henry Kissinger phones Mrs. d only an hour before dinner guests are to arrive. He had been scheduled to pick up fifteen grand that night for explaining SALT II to the Vinyl Manufacturers Association convention in Chicago, but the airports are snowed in. He and Nancy will be able to come to dinner after all. "How marvelous, darling!" Mrs. d says.

She hangs up and suddenly looks stricken. "My God!" she says to Oscar. "What are we going to do? We already have one war criminal coming!"

What to do except to phone the man who conflicts with the star and tell him the dinner had to be called off because Mr. d had come down with a painful skin disease known as the Seventh Avenue Shpilkes. What to do about the one male place at the table now empty—between Vicomtesse de Ribes and Barbara Walters?

The phone rings. "This is Françoise de la Renta," the voice says.

"This is Calvin of the Trillin," I say. "I'll be right over."

Dan Greenburg

*

HOW TO BE A JEWISH MOTHER

There is more to being a Jewish mother than being Jewish and a mother. Properly practiced, Jewish motherhood is an art—a complex network of subtle and highly sophisticated techniques. Fail to master these techniques and you hasten the black day you discover your children can get along without you.

You will be called upon to function as a philosopher on two distinct types of occasions:

(1) Whenever anything bad happens.

(2) Whenever anything good happens.

Whenever anything bad happens, you must point out the fortunate aspects of the situation:

"Ma! Ma!"

"What's the commotion?"

"The bad boys ran off with my hat!"

"The bad boys ran off with your hat? You should be grateful they didn't also cut your throat."

Also point out that Bad Experience is the best teacher:

"Maybe next time you'll know better than to fool with roughnecks. It's the best thing that could have happened to you, believe me."

Whenever anything good happens, you must, of course, point out the unfortunate aspects of the situation:

"Ma! Ma!"

"So what's the trouble now?"

"The Youth Group Raffle! I won a Pontiac convertible!"

"You won a Pontiac automobile in the Youth Group Raffle? Very nice. The insurance alone is going to send us to the poorhouse."

Underlying all techniques of Jewish motherhood is the ability to plant, cultivate and harvest guilt. Control guilt and you control the child.

An old folk saw says: "Beat a child every day; if you don't know what he's done to deserve the beating, he will." A slight modification gives us the Jewish mother's cardinal rule: "Let your child hear you sigh every day; if you don't know what he's done to make you suffer, he will."

To master the Technique of Basic Suffering you should begin with an intensive study of the Dristan commercials on television. Pay particular attention to the face of the actor who has not yet taken Dristan. Note the squint of the eyes, the furrow of the brow, the downward curve of the lips—the pained expression which can only come from eight undrained sinus cavities or severe gastritis.

This is the Basic Facial Expression. Learn it well. Practice it before a mirror several times a day. If someone should catch you at it and ask what you are doing, say:

"I'm fine, it's nothing at all, it will go away." This should be said softly but audibly, should imply suffering without expressing it openly. When properly executed, this is the Basic Tone of Voice.

Here are some practice drills:

(1) Give your son Marvin two sport shirts as a present. The first time he wears one of them, look at him sadly and say in your Basic Tone of Voice:

"The other one you didn't like?"

(2) Borrow a tape recorder and practice the following key phrases until you can deliver them with eye-watering perfection:

(a) "Go ahead and enjoy yourself."

(b) "But be careful."

(c) "Don't worry about me."

(d) "I don't mind staying home alone."

(e) "I'm glad it happened to me and not to you."

(3) Remember, the child is an unformed, emotionally unstable, ignorant creature. To make him feel secure, you must continually remind him of the things you are denying yourself on his account, especially when others are present.

And here are Seven Basic Sacrifices to Make for Your Child:

(1) Stay up all night to prepare him a big breakfast.

(2) Go without lunch so you can put an extra apple in his lunch pail.

(3) Give up an evening of work with a charitable institution so that he can have the car on a date.

(4) Tolerate the girl he's dating.

(5) Don't let him know you fainted twice in the supermarket from fatigue. (But make sure he knows you're not letting him know.)

(6) When he comes home from the dentist, take over his toothache for him.

(7) Open his bedroom window wider so he can have more fresh air, and close your own so you don't use up the supply.

Wherever possible, make your old clothes do the job of new ones. Old clothes are more substantial than new ones, anyway, because in the old days they made things to last. Be an example to your family in this area. Be certain, of course, that they are aware of your sacrifices:

"Well, I'm glad to say I won't be needing a new winter coat this year after all."

"Oh? How's that, Esther?"

"I glued the Women's Section of the Sunday paper inside the lining of my old one, and now it's warm as toast."

If this has not left the desired impression, follow it up a few days later with a seeming contradiction:

"Well, I finally broke down and did it. I bought something for myself."

"Good. What did you buy, Esther?"

"I hated to spend the money, believe me, but today I bought a small roll of Scotch tape to hold my stockings together."

Should no old clothes or hand-me-downs be available, then you will have to think about buying new clothes at a regular store. If no one in your family is in the garment business, ask your druggist or the vegetable man to suggest the name of a store he's heard of. There's no point in going to a store that does not have a strong recommendation.

When you take your child to the store, keep these important points in mind:

(1) Never buy a color that will show the dirt.

(2) Never buy a fabric that will wear out.

(3) Never buy a style that is apt to change.

(4) Never buy a garment that fits—it should always be two or three sizes too large so that the child can grow into it.

The most efficient way to buy clothes for any child below the age of 22 is to utilize him merely as a dressmaker's dummy and to address all questions about the fit or the appearance of the garment directly to the salesman:

"Tell me, how does it fit in the crotch?"

"It looks pretty good from here, ma'am."

Should the child object to any garment that has been selected for him, ask the salesman if he talked to his mother like that when he was a boy. Never fear. The salesman will not let you down.

Just as Mother Nature abhors a vacuum, the Jewish mother abhors an empty mouth. It shall therefore be your purpose to fill every mouth you can reach with nourishing food.

At mealtimes, be sure there is a continuous flow of food from stove to serving platter to plate to mouth. If anyone should be foolish enough to decline a particular dish (e.g., potatoes), proceed as follows:

(1) Find out whether he has any rational objections:

"What do you mean no potatoes, Irving—you think I'm trying to poison you?"

(2) Suggest that he take only a small amount as a compromise:

"Take only a sliver of the potatoes, then."

"All right. But remember, only a sliver."

(3) You may now proceed to fill his plate with potatoes. The instant he has crammed down the last one, you must be ready to:

(4) Offer him a second helping:

"There, I told you you'd like it once you tasted it. All right now, you're ready for seconds?"

"God, no."

Here you must really be on your toes. Between your question and his answer, little more than one microsecond will elapse. Within that microsecond, you must scoop all the rest of the potatoes out onto his plate and make the turn back to the kitchen.

When the last crumb has been cleared from all plates by means of vague references to privation in Europe, you are ready for the real test of your art. Begin with a general all-inclusive warning:

"I am now ready to begin serving third helpings."

Immediately switch from the general to the specific. Select your quarry:

"Eddie, I can tell you are ready for a third helping of chicken."

"Believe me, Sylvia, if I took one more piece of chicken I would sprout feathers."

The next step in the ritual calls for a statement about your quarry addressed to the spectators:

"Eddie doesn't like the way I cook chicken."

"I'm crazy about the way you cook chicken, Sylvia. I simply cannot eat another particle without bursting."

"You see, I happen to know that chicken is Eddie's favorite dish. I prepared it specially for him—but do you think he cares? Eddie, tell me. You like chicken?"

"Yes."

"You like my chicken?"

"Yes, yes."

"You are too full to eat any more?"

"Yes, yes, yes."

"All right. This I can understand. A man says to me, 'I am too full,' this I can understand. It's not like you are asking me to throw it out, after all. All right. (*Pause.*) So I'll wrap it up in wax paper and you'll take it for later."

Your job as hostess is not complete when your guests have been properly fed. You must see to it that they are also entertained.

Your family and friends will expect you to be able to relate amusing stories which you have heard at the butcher shop, at a meeting of Hadassah, or which your husband has told at a previous gathering of these same people. Familiarize yourself with the following formula for successful storytelling and in no time at all you will have a widespread reputation as a *raconteuse*. To begin the telling of any story:

(1) Ask whether anybody has heard it before.

"Listen, you all know the story about the old Jewish man?"

It is important that this initial query be as general as possible, so that anybody who has heard the story before should not recognize it and hence have it spoiled for him. The next step is:

(2) Ask someone else to tell it.

"Listen, it's a very funny story. About an old Jewish man. Morris, you tell it."

"I don't know the story you mean, Esther."

"Of course you know. Don't you? The story about the old Jewish man. Go ahead, you tell it, Morris. You know I can't tell a story properly."

This modesty is very becoming to a performer and will surely be countered with heartfelt cries of denial from your audience. You are now ready to:

(3) Explain where you heard the story.

"All right. This story I heard originally from Rose Melnick. You all know Rose? No? Her husband is in dry goods. Melnick. You know the one? All right, it doesn't matter to the story, believe me. Anyway, Rose Melnick heard it from her son-in-law, Seymour, a lovely boy, really. A nose-and-throat man. Seymour Rosen—you know the name?"

By now your audience has been sufficiently prepared for the story and will be anxious for you to begin. Go ahead and tell it, but be sure to:

(4) Begin the story at the end. Professional comedians call the end

of the story "the punch line." Since this is usually the funniest part of the story, it is logically the best place to start:

"Anyway, there's this old Jewish man who is trying to get into the synagogue during the Yom Kippur service, and the usher finally says to him, 'All right, go ahead in, but don't let me catch you praying.' (*Pause.*) Oh, did I mention that the old man just wants to go in and give a message to somebody in the synagogue? He doesn't actually want to go into the synagogue and pray, you see. (*Pause. Frown.*) Wait a minute. I don't know if I mentioned that the old man doesn't have a ticket for the service. You know how crowded it always is on Yom Kippur, and the old man doesn't have a ticket, and he explains to the usher that he has to go into the synagogue and tell somebody something, but the usher isn't going to let him in without a ticket. So the old man explains to him that it's a matter of life and death, so then the usher thinks it over and he says to the old man, 'All right, go ahead in, but don't let me catch you praying.' (*Pause. Frown. Stand and begin emptying ashtrays.*) Ach, I don't think I told it right. Morris, you tell it."

Sooner or later, to go to a fine university or to accept an attractive position with an out-of-town firm, one of your children may ask to leave the home.

As soon as possible after the child has moved into his new quarters, pay him a visit and do the following:

(1) Bring food. He does not know where to buy any in a strange city and is starving. Tell him how thin he looks.

(2) Take everything off his shelves and out of his drawers and line them with oilcloth.

(3) Wash his floor.

(4) Rearrange his furniture and buy plastic slip covers for everything.

(5) Go out and get him a warm sweater, a pair of galoshes, a pair of gloves, a hat and (if the temperature there ever falls below 50 degrees) earmuffs.

(6) If he has plastic dinner plates, say he needs something more substantial and buy him china ones. If he has china ones, say he needs something more functional and buy him plastic ones.

After you have returned home, you may call up his professor or his employer, introduce yourself, tell him how tired your son looked when you saw him and suggest that he not be made to work so hard.

There are only two things a Jewish mother needs to know about sex and marriage:

(1) Who is having sex?

(2) Why aren't they married?

Since it is by now apparent that everyone in the world is determined to have some kind of sex, it will therefore be your duty to make sure that everyone gets married. And what more logical place to start than in your own home?

It is never too early to begin preparing your son for marriage. At the age of eight or nine, start to develop in him an appreciation for the good grooming habits which will help him to win the hand of a capable young woman in marriage:

"Feh! Look at your ears—what girl in her right mind would ever marry a boy that has wax in his ears?"

Develop his poise in a similar manner:

"Stand up straight and don't slouch—what girl in her right mind is going to marry a hunchback?"

By age 12 or 13 the child is ready for his first social encounter with the opposite sex. Arrange a party for young people at your home.

If he appears hesitant to meet the young ladies, steer him over to several of them and urge him, under your breath, or in audible whispers from a few paces off, to introduce himself. If he remains reticent, smooth the way over those first few embarrassing moments by introducing him yourself:

"This is my son Marvin who stands like a hunchback."

By the time your son gets into high school, he will be going out on regular dates and will very likely insist on selecting the girls himself from among his classmates. Do not discourage this, but try to find out something about these girls for his own protection. Ask him:

(1) "This girl, she's Jewish?"

(2) "What's the family's name?"

(3) "What was it before?"

By now your son is in college and dating quite seriously. If he is no longer living at home, your task will admittedly be more difficult, but by no means impossible. You will still arrange to spend vacations together, and you will still have the telephone and the U.S. Mails at your disposal.

Your son will probably have a young ladyfriend whom he particularly admires. As before, be sure of her background, but now the questioning should be on a more sophisticated level:

(1) "This girl, she's Jewish?"

(2) "She gets good marks in school?"

(3) "She smokes cigarettes in moderation?"

(4) "She drinks liquor in moderation?"

(5) "What kind of a girl smokes cigarettes and drinks liquor?"

Invite your son's girlfriend to your home for dinner so you will have a chance to determine whether she is good daughter-in-law material. To permit a completely objective evaluation, never speak to the young lady directly, but use your son as an intermediary:

"Does she like mashed potatoes?"

This form of address is known as The Third Person Invisible. Should your son ever decide to marry the girl, this device adapts very nicely to Basic Daughter-in-law Technique, otherwise known as the I-Forget-Her-Name Gambit:

"Is what's-her-name—is your wife coming over also?"

If, by the time your son is out of college, he is still not married and he is not, God forbid, a homosexual, you must begin to Take Steps.

Speak to friends of yours who have daughters his age or maybe a few years older or a few years younger, and try to get the young people together. Pass the word around that your son, though a talented, intelligent young man, is unable to find a girl who will go out with him.

Have your friends ask him regularly why a nice boy like that is not married.

Also speak of the matter to your son. Perhaps the idea of marriage has merely slipped his mind. Remind him. Often.

Joke about it in public to show that you aren't taking the matter too seriously:

"Excuse me, mister."

"You talking to me, lady?"

"This is my son, Marvin."

"So?"

"Twenty-five years old. A master's degree in Romance languages. A careful driver. Tell me something confidentially."

"Yeah."

"Would any young lady give her right arm to have a wonderful young man like that for a husband?"

"Search me, lady."

"Yes or no?"

"I suppose yes."

"Marvin, did you hear? Listen what the man is telling you."

Suddenly, one day your son brings a strange girl over to the house and introduces her as his fiancée. What do you do?

You say hello to her, ask her what the weather is getting to be like outside, excuse yourself for a moment, lead your son off to a corner of the room, begin to sew a button on the sleeve of the coat he is wearing, and say to him as follows:

"Marvin. You intend to marry this girl?"

"Yeah. Not so loud, Ma."

"She's very pretty, Marvin."

"Yeah. Look, it's not very polite to——"

"Maybe even a little too pretty, you know what I mean?"

"Ma, look——"

"I hardly know what to tell you. (*Pause. Finish sewing the button, begin to bite off the thread, stop, study the end of it and look up into his face.*) Look, you're still so young. You know what I mean? What's your big hurry to get married all of a sudden?"

You have now done all you can be expected to do for your son. It is time to give some thought to your daughter.

You are fortunate in that you will be able to meet and personally evaluate all the young men who come to the house to take her away.

Greet each young man at the door. Appraise him closely from head to foot. Ask him the following:

(1) "You're Jewish?"

(2) "What's your family's name?"

(3) "What was it before?"

If the young man is driving a car, be sure to add these important queries:

(1) "You know how to drive?"

(2) "You have a driver's license?"

(3) "How fast do you drive?"

(4) "Your father knows you're out?"

Even if the young man has answered all your questions in a satisfactory manner, it is not a bad idea to frown, avert your head and sigh:

"*Ach*, I don't like it, I tell you. You youngsters all drive like maniacs. You'll wind up in some ditch tonight, mark my words. (*Pause. Smile, frowning.*) All right, all right—go, drive careful, and have a wonderful time. And I'm going to worry myself sick about you, I promise you."

As they are about to go out the door, turn to your daughter and whisper loudly in her ear:

"Stay all the way on the right side of the seat, if you know what's good for you."

If your daughter should not be married by the time she is out of college, apply the same tactics to her as to your son, with these subtle variations:

Seek out any young man at a party or other social gathering and begin to sell him on your daughter. Speak of her excellent disposition. Point out her many physical attributes:

"A face like a Vermeer—you know Vermeer?"

"Yes, the painter."

"And teeth? Did you see how straight her teeth are?"

"Well, as a matter of—"

"Three thousand dollars I spent having her teeth straightened—four years at the orthodontist's so her mouth could close."

"Look, I really have to be—"

"A beautiful girl. Beautiful. (*Pause.*) The only thing, she is maybe a tiny bit heavy in the bust. (*Smile.*) It runs in the family."

Calling attention to a slight imperfection often lends just the right note of credibility to your sales pitch. In any case, do not beat around the bush. The young man will appreciate your frankness. Be direct. Beg him to invite your daughter out—

"For a malted-milk shake, I'll pay for it myself."

Should the young man actually come to the house to take your daughter out, be sure to reassure him:

"You're not making a mistake, believe me. She refuses forty dates a week."

How do you behave when you discover your daughter necking in the living room? Wait until the young man has gone home, go into your daughter's room and say to her as follows:

"Miriam."

"Oh, hi, Ma."

"Miriam, I saw. I saw what you were doing in there."

"Oh."

"Miriam, who taught you this?"

"Oh, for God's sake, Ma. I'm a big girl now."

"Miriam, we are decent people. We have always tried to teach you the right thing. How could you do this to us?"

"Ma, for God's sake, I was only kissing—"

"Do you know what your father will do when I'll tell him? Do you?"

"No, but—"

"He will have a heart attack, that's what he will do. I promise you."

"Look, Ma, you don't have to tell—"

"Not only that, just think what the neighbors would say if they knew."

"Look—"

"For this I had your teeth straightened? For this I bought you contact lenses? For this I paid good money to have them teach you to speak French?"

"Ma—"

"*Ach*, I don't know what to do with you. (*Pause*.) My own daughter, a streetwalker. (*Pause*.) If you have any consideration for your parents at all, you'll do the only decent thing."

"What's that?"

"You'll leave this house and you'll not come back until you're a virgin."

Cyra McFadden

*

HIP WEDDING ON MOUNT TAM

EXCERPT FROM *The Serial*

As she got ready for Martha's wedding, Kate reflected happily that one great thing about living in Marin was that your friends were always growing and changing. She couldn't remember, for example, how many times Martha had been married before.

She wondered if she ought to call her friend Carol and ask what to wear. Martha had said "dress down," but that could mean anything from Marie Antoinette milkmaid from The Electric Poppy to bias-cut denims from Moody Blues. Kate didn't have any bias-cut denims, because she'd been waiting to see how long they'd stay in, but she could borrow her adolescent daughter's. They wore the same clothes all the time.

Her husband, Harvey, was already in the shower, so Kate decided on her Renaissance Faire costume. She always felt mildly ridiculous in it, but it wasn't so bad without the conical hat and it was definitely Mount Tam wedding. Now the problem was Harvey, who absolutely refused to go to Mount Tam weddings in the French jeans Kate had bought him for his birthday. She knew he'd wear his Pierre Cardin suit, which was fine two years ago but which was now establishment; and when he came out of the shower, her fears were confirmed.

Since they were already late, though, there was no point in trying to do something about Harvey. They drove up Panoramic to the mountain meadow trying to remember what Martha's bridegroom's name was this time (Harvey thought it was Bill again, but Kate was reasonably sure it wasn't) and made it to the ceremony just as the recorder player, a bare-chested young man perched faunlike on a rock above the assembled guests, began to improvise variations on the latest Pink Floyd.

Right away, Kate spotted Carol and knew her Renaissance dress was all right—marginal, but all right. Carol was wearing Marie Antoi-nette milkmaid, but with her usual infallible chic, had embellished it with her trademark jewelry: an authentic squash-blossom necklace, three free-form rings bought from a creative artisan at the Mill Valley Art Festival on her right hand, and her old high school charm bracelet updated with the addition of a tiny silver coke spoon.

Reverend Spike Thurston, minister of the Radical Unitarian Church in Terra Linda and active in the Marin Sexual Freedom League, was presiding. Kate was thrilled as the ceremony began and Thurston raised a solemn, liturgical hand; she really got off on weddings.

"Fellow beings," Thurston began, smiling, "I'm not here today as a minister but as a member of the community. Not just the community of souls gathered here, not just the community of Mill Valley, but the larger human community which is the cosmos.

"I'm not going to solemnize this marriage in the usual sense of the word. I'm not going to pronounce it as existing from this day forward. Because nobody can do that except Martha and"—he held a quick, worried conference with somebody behind him—"and Bill."

Harvey was already restless. "Do we have to go to a reception after this thing?" he asked too loudly.

"Organic," Kate whispered, digging her fingernails into his wrist. "At Davood's."

Harvey looked dismayed.

"These children have decided to recite their own vows," Thurston continued. Kate thought "children" was overdoing it a little; Martha was at least forty, although everybody knew chronological age didn't matter these days. "They're not going to recite something after me, because this is a *real* wedding—the wedding of two separatenesses, two solitarinesses, under the sky."

Thurston pointed out the sky and paused while a jet thundered across it. Kate thought he looked incredibly handsome with his head thrown back and his purple Marvin Gaye T-shirt emblazoned with "Let's Get It On" stretched tightly across his chest.

"Martha," he said, "will you tell us what's in your heart?"

Standing on tiptoe, Kate could just catch a glimpse of the bride; slightly to the right of her, she spotted Martha's ex-husband-once-re-moved with his spacy new old lady, who, Kate thought, looked like Mar-tha. She tried to remember which of Martha's children, all present and looking oddly androgynous in velvet Lord Fauntleroy suits, were also his.

Martha recited a passage on marriage "from the Spanish poet Fe-derico García Lorca." Last time she was married, she'd said "Frederico."

Kate thought the fact that Martha had got it right this time was a good sign; and she adored the Lorca.

When Bill recited in turn, he was almost inaudible, but Kate thought she recognized *The Prophet*, which was *not* a good sign. She dug her fingernails into Harvey again; he was shifting his feet restlessly. This wasn't a sign of anything, necessarily, since Harvey simply couldn't get used to his new Roots, but it was best to be safe.

"Hey, listen," she whispered to Carol, who had wiggled her way through the crowd and was now at her side. "It's terrific, isn't it?"

"Really," Carol whispered back. "He looks good. He's an architect that does mini-parks. She met him at her creative divorce group."

Kate leaned across her to take in the crowd. She thought she recognized Mimi Fariña. She also noticed Larry, her shampoo person from Rape of the Locks, who always ran her through the soul handshake when she came in for a cut and blow-dry. She hoped she wouldn't have to shake hands with Larry at the reception, since she never got the scissors/paper/rock maneuvers of the soul handshake just right and since she was pretty sure that Larry kept changing it on her, probably out of repressed racial animosity.

Thurston, after a few remarks about the ecology, had just pronounced Martha and her new husband man and woman. Kate felt warmly sentimental as the bride and bridegroom kissed passionately, and loosened her grip on Harvey's wrist. She noticed that the fog was beginning to lift slightly and gazed off into the distance.

"Hey, look," she said to Harvey excitedly. "Isn't that the ocean?"

"The Pacific," Harvey replied tersely. "Believed to be the largest on the West Coast. It's part of the cosmos."

Kate felt put down. Harvey was becoming increasingly uptight these days, and remarks like this one were more frequent. Look at the way he'd baited her TA instructor at the Brennans' the other night. "You are not O.K.," he had told him loudly, lurching slightly in his Roots. "I could give you a lot of reasons; but take my word for it—you are *not* O.K."

Yes, Kate was going to have to do something about Harvey. . . .

Alan Coren

*

LONG AGO AND FAR AWAY

Much talk is talked of the need for the Dunkirk spirit today. But suppose instead that we had had today's spirit at Dunkirk?

Up to his waist in the filthy sea, oil lapping his sodden webbing, bomb-blasted flotsam bobbing about him, he sucked his teeth, and shook his head.

"I'm not bleeding going in that," he said, "I'm not bleeding going home in no rowing boat."

"Right," said his mate.

"Eighteen blokes in it already," he said. "Conditions like that, they're not fit for a pig."

"Not fit for a pig, conditions like that," said his mate.

"Got brought here in a troopship, din't we?" he said. He cupped his hands towards the rowing boat, and the man leaning towards them over its stern, arm outstretched. "GOT BROUGHT HERE IN A BLEEDING TROOP-SHIP!" he shouted. "Ten square feet of space per man!"

"Regulations," said his mate, nodding. "All laid down. Nothing about going back in no bloody rowing-boat. Get away with murder if you let 'em, some people."

A Stuka shrieked suddenly overhead, levelled, veered up out of its dive, back into the flakky sky. Its bomb exploded, drenching the two men.

"Not even got a roof on," he said. "What happens if it starts coming down cats and dogs halfway across? You could catch pneumonia."

"Get a chill on the liver," said his mate.

"*And* there's seasickness. It's not as if I'm a sailor. I'm not saying it isn't all right for *sailors*, am I? All right for them, open bloody boat. I mean, it's their line, know what I mean? But I'm a gunner. That's what I got took on as, that's what I am. If I'd wanted to be a sailor, I'd have got took on as a sailor."

"I'm a cook," said his mate. "Cook, I said when they asked me up the recruiting. I didn't say bleeding admiral. I didn't say, I want to be a cook on account of I'm interested in the standing up to me waist in water, did I?"

"Course you didn't."

An Me109 came low over the surface, strafing the scummy sea. A machine-gun bullet took his hat away.

"You'd have got more as an admiral, too," he said. "You get compensation, working in filthy conditions. I reckon they owe us special benefits. Nothing about all this in basic training, was there? Prone shooting and a bit of the old bayonet, dry conditions, two bob a day, all meals."

"When was the last time you had a square meal?" asked his mate.

"I never thought of that!" He took a notepad from his saturated battle-blouse, licked his pencil, scribbled. "I never thought of that at all. Three days ago, as a matter of fact. Bleeding Cambrai, if you can call two spoons of warm bully a square meal."

"FOR GOD'S SAKE GET A MOVE ON!" cried the man in the stern.

The two privates waded awkwardly forward.

"Not so bloody fast, mate," said the first. "I require a few moments with the brothers here."

The eighteen stared at him over the gunwales. Red fatigue rimmed their eyes, their bandages were thick with oil, their helmets were gone, leaving their hair to whiten with the salt.

"It has been brought to my attention by Brother Wisley here," he said, "that we are being expected to work in conditions unfit for a pig. Not only are we not being allowed to pursue our chosen trade, we have been dumped here in what can only be described as the sea, we have been required to leave our tools behind on the beach, we have not had a square meal for three days, and as for the statutory tea-break, I can't remember when. I won't even go into the overtime question."

"We won't even go into the overtime question," said his mate. "But may I draw the meeting's attention to the fact that members of the Kings Own Yorkshire Light Infantry can be seen on our left climbing into a cabin cruiser?"

The eighteen turned, and looked.

"Bloody hell," said a corporal.

"Well might you say bloody hell, brother!" said the first private.

"Course, I'm not saying our brothers in the KOYLI are not entitled to what they can get, and good luck, but the anomaly of the heretofore mentioned situation currently under review before the meeting by which we of the Royal Artillery . . ."

"And the Catering Corps."

". . . and the Catering Corps, Brother Wisley, thank you, by which we of the Royal Artillery and the Catering Corps do not enjoy parity is one which threatens all we hold most dear."

"RIGHT!" cried the man in the stern. "Get in, or shut up, we haven't got all damned day, Jerry's throwing . . ."

The private held up his hand.

"Just a minute, squire," he said, "just a minute. After frank and free discussions with my ad hoc executive here, we regret to inform you that deadlock has been reached in the negotiations, and unless you are prepared to furnish us with such basic requirements . . ."

"I'm getting out anyway, brother," said the corporal. He eased himself over the side. "Come on, you lot, I have no intention of allowing my brothers on the floor to be manipulated by a cynical management and subjected to actual distress to serve the whim of the bosses."

"Well said, brother!" cried the private.

The eighteen slid into the icy water.

The rowing boat came about, and sploshed off towards another queue. But a bomb, exploding between it and them, gave the private time to wade up to the head of the line, and the man on crutches leading it.

"I know these are difficult times, brothers," announced the private, "but let us not use that as an excuse to allow ourselves to be led like lambs to the slaughter. Solidarity is our watchword, brothers."

The line hesitated.

"We could be, er, needed back home," said the man at the front, "couldn't we?"

The private stared at him bitterly.

"Oh, got a troublemaker, have we?" he said loudly. "It's amazing, there's always one, isn't there?"

"Always bloody one," said a voice down the line.

"Thank you, brother." He poked a finger into the leader's chest. "You'll get that crutch across your bonce in a minute, son," he said. He spread his hands to take in the gradually assembling crowd of water-logged soldiers. "Got a man here believes all he reads in the newspapers! Got one of your *thinkers!* Doesn't know all this scaremongering is just put about by the gumment to screw the working man, doesn't realise that your *real* situation is all very nice, thank you, doesn't . . ." The private broke off as a couple of Heinkels came howling in from the dunes, their tracer slicing a red swath through the crowd, drowning his words. ". . . doesn't appreciate that gumment propaganda is being cunningly directed to militate public opinion on the side of nationalistic interests contrary to the welfare of the entire work force, does he?"

"I think we ought to vote on it," said a fusilier who had been standing next to a man dismembered in the last strafe.

"Oh, yes, and I don't think!" snorted the private. "You won't catch me out with no snap show of hands, brother, contrary to the democratic secret ballot as we know it. I should cocoa!"

The men shifted their feet uneasily. The private had articulated it all so clearly, and, after all, the men who had brought the little boats were, for the most part, men of a class they had long learned to mistrust. Nor did they wish to betray their mates, with whom they had come through no small adversity; and it could not be denied that it was at just such fraught moments as this that advantage could be taken of them, with their defences down, and the odds in favour of those who sought to control them.

And, after all, were things so bad that they should forget all else but short-term salvation? They were not yet dead, were they, which was rather more relevant than the emotionally-loaded evidence that others could be seen to be dying. They had, had they not, stuck it out on the beach up until then, why should they not continue to stick it out now?

Slowly, but with what certainly appeared to be determination, the entire waiting army turned, and began to wade back towards the littered dunes, and the devil they knew.

There were, of course, one or two who glanced over their shoulders in the direction of England; but, naturally, it was too far away for them to be able to discern anything, even had the darkness not, by then, been falling.

Marshall Brickman

*

THE ANALYTIC NAPKIN

Recent work by Frimkin and Eliscu has brought to light valuable new material about the origin and development of the analytic napkin. It is not generally realized outside of psychoanalytic circles that the placement by the analyst of a small square of absorbent paper at the head of the analysand's chair or couch at the start of each session is a ritual whose origins are rooted in the very beginnings of analysis, even predating the discovery of infant sexuality. Indeed, references to a "sticky problem" ("*eines Entführung bezitsung*") appear as early as 1886, in a letter the young Freud wrote to his mentor Breuer:

> I am convinced that "hysterical symptoms," so-called, are nothing but the emergence of long-buried psycho-neurotic conflicts [*bezitsunger Entführung*]. Does that sound crazy? More important, how can I keep the back of the patient's chair from becoming so soiled [*ganz geschmutzig*]? They come in, they put their heads back—one week and already my upholstery has a spot the size of a *Sacher Torte*.
>
> With warm regards,
> FREUD

Breuer's reply is not known, of course, because of the curious manner in which he conducted his correspondence. (Breuer was unreasonably afraid that samples of his handwriting might fall into the hands of his "many powerful enemies"; therefore, upon receiving a letter, he would carefully draft a reply, take it to the addressee's home, read it aloud to him, and then tear it to shreds. He claimed that this behavior saved him a fortune in postage, although Mrs. Breuer opined that her husband's head was lined with "wall-to-wall kugel.") Breuer's only public statement on the napkin question was made during a demonstration of hypnosis, when he remarked that "a patient in a trance can be induced to stand on his feet for an entire treatment and never know the difference."

It is perhaps ironic—or, as Ernest Jones put it, "not ironic at all"— that the napkin problem should have emerged at a time when the antimacassar was attaining universal acceptance by the East European intelligentsia. Freud, however, abhorred simplistic solutions, and sought more profound answers. Failing to find these, he sought more complicated questions. In any event, he rejected the use of antimacassars as "Victorian, confining, and repressive—everything I am fighting against. Besides, they are too bumpy." The extent of the problem, however, can be inferred from a perusal of Freud's professional expenses incurred for April, 1886, his first month of private practice:

WAITING ROOM
3 coat hooks @ 5 kreuzer	15 kr.
2 chairs @ 20 gulden	40 fl.
1 ashtray	8 kr.
16 issues *Viennese Life* magazine, 1861–77 period	2 fl., 8 kr.
1 framed Turner reproduction, "Cows in a Field"	16 fl.

CONSULTING ROOM
3 doz. medium-hard pencils	18 kr.
9 writing tablets, unlined, in "easy-eye green"	2 fl., 14 kr.
Certificates & diplomas, framing and mounting	7 fl.
"Complete Works of Goethe" (18 vols.)	40 fl.
"Works of Nietzsche" (abridged, 20 vols.)	34 fl.
"Simple Card Tricks You Can Do" (pocket edition)	20 kr.
1 clock	8 fl.
Dry-cleaning and spotting upholstery	240 fl.

"At this rate," Freud wrote to Koller, "every neurasthenic I treat this year should set me back in the neighborhood of four hundred gulden. Pretty soon, *I'll* be needing some treatment, eh? Ha, ha." On the advice of Charcot, Freud had his housekeeper apply a solution of nux vomica and lye to his consulting chair after each session—a remedy that was hastily abandoned when a patient, Theo F., brought a legal complaint of massive hair loss directly traceable to consultations with the young neurologist. Freud managed to mollify the unfortunate man with a sampler of marzipan and a warm fur hat, but his reputation in Vienna had been shaken.

• • •

The early practitioners of psychoanalysis devised artful stopgap solutions to the problem of the napkin. For a time, Jung met his patients at a furniture store, where, under the pretext of inspecting a couch, he would conduct an analytic session. After fifty minutes, patient and doctor would depart, Jung explaining to the salesman that they wanted to "shop around a little more." By contrast, Ferenczi required his patients to lie face down on the consulting couch—a procedure that eliminated all stains but a small nose smudge. However, the patients' constant mumblings into the upholstery caused Ferenczi to become enraged, and he finally abandoned this technique. Klein, claiming that he was only trying to "lighten up" what was "an already dreary enough business," asked his patients to wear cone-shaped party hats during their session hours. The real reason, of course, was to protect Klein's couch, a flamboyant chesterfield covered in pale-lemon bombazine.

Freud launched his own systematic research program by scouring Vienna for fabric samples, which he placed on the upper portion of his couch, a different sample being assigned to each patient. One case, that of a man who was analyzed on a folded barbecue apron, became the subject of an extended monograph of Freud's on hallucinations and hysteria. The apron had been presented to Freud by Charcot, and bore the legend "*König von die Küche*" ("King of the Kitchen"). An apparently severe olfactory hallucination (old cabbage) reported by the patient during his analysis eventually proved to have its source in the apron, and Freud was forced to withdraw his paper. To conceal his disappointment, he invited the man to a coffeehouse, but at the last moment changed his mind and instead sent Adler to meet him. Unfortunately, Adler became distracted in the process of flattening kreuzer on the trolley tracks and arrived a day late. (This episode was often referred to sarcastically by Freud, and provided the basis for the later break between him and Adler.)

In a series of unattended lectures (May, 1906), Freud crystallized the need for a resolution of the "sofa problem," as he termed it. "Something small and protective, yet flexible," he wrote in his notes, "ought to be placed beneath (or possibly wrapped around) the patient's head. Perhaps a small rug or some sort of cloth." It was several decades before the notion of a napkin would surface, but during a summer visit to Manchester, England, during which Freud presented his half-sister with a bookend, he purchased a bolt of Japanese silk, which he sent to Vienna and caused to be cut up into small squares. The new material seemed to be working admirably, until an unexpected occurrence shattered his illusions. From his notebook:

OCTOBER 8. Especially crisp fall day. Treating Otto P., a petty official of the Bureau of Wursts. Classic psycho-neurosis: inability either to go to sleep or remain awake. Patient, while recounting significant dream, thrashed about on the couch. Because of the extremely cool climate, extensive static electricity caused the silk to cling to the patient's hair when he rose to leave at the end of the session. Analytic propriety, plus the delicacy of the transference, prevented me from mentioning the situation and I merely bade him good day.

Upon reaching home, Otto P. was mortified to find a square of cloth adhering to the back of his head, and he publicly accused Freud of insensitiveness and willful japery. An anti-Semitic journalist claimed that Freud had attempted to impose his own ethnic customs on a patient. The outcry raged for months, severely taxing Freud's energies, and only after it had abated could he enter in his journal, with wry insight: "Clearly, silk is not the answer—unless perhaps it is first dampened."

Freud's tentative moves in the direction of an all-purpose analytic napkin inspired others to ponder the matter. At the Weimar Congress, Bleuler called for a standardization of napkin technique. A lively debate ensued, with a variety of shapes, sizes, and materials finding ready champions. Abraham favored classical antimacassars, while Jung was partial to jute placemats, which he imported from a private source in Africa. The purist Holtz (it was he who in 1935 criticized Freud for not being Freudian enough) ridiculed the whole notion of a napkin and advocated "six couches, to be changed daily, like underwear." Liebner, who detested Holtz, suggested that the material of the napkin vary with the patient's complaint; Freud then recalled that he had had no success in treating the celebrated "Wolf Man" until he tried a scrap of terry cloth, to which the patient developed a massive transference. In a culminating speech at Weimar, Freud outlined his vision of the ideal solution: "Hygienic, disposable, inexpensive, and without any referential value whatsoever. I dream of a totally affect-less napkin that every analyst can afford."

Freud's experimental early napkins (many of which are still in private collections) show this drive toward simplicity and clarity—swatches of wool, gabardine, madras, burlap, and unbleached muslin, and, finally, a double layer of cheesecloth. He was making notes on the use of blotting paper when the Anschluss forced him to leave for London. Later that week in Vienna, the Nazis publicly burned most of his napkin file, including an irreplaceable sampler knitted by Lionel Walter, the Baron Rothschild.

The enormous current popularity of psychoanalysis in the United States is easily explained by the napkin historian. American technological know-how, plus the easy availability of materials, provided the answer Freud and his early disciples searched for but never found. In 1946, after extensive research at Mount Sinai Hospital, a team of pillow scientists at the Kimberly-Clark paper company test-marketed a prototype napkin in the analytic communities of Boston, New York, and Los Angeles. It was a double-ply, semi-absorbent, bleached-wood-fibre product, with a forty-per-cent rag content and an embossed edge. The response was overwhelming, and the course of psychoanalysis was forever altered. As Dr. Neimann Fek said, expressing the gratitude of his colleagues, "It took seventy years before we perfected the beard and the fee. Now, finally, the napkin. No one need ever be crazy again."

Alexander Theroux

*

MRS. PROBY GETS HERS
EXCERPT FROM *Three Wogs*

Picric, antagonized, scuffing forward with a leer, Fu Manchu readily confirmed a common fear: a distorted mind proves that there is something on it. A girl in a diaphanous shift squirmed to bounce free of the ropes which held her, like a network of fistulae, to a scaled gold and emerald table, a simulated dragon of smooth wood; a purple gag she was unable to spit free. The yellow, moonshaped face of Fu Manchu, poised between inscrutability and simple lust, both of which disputed for mastery, twitched in a decisive way and then his ochre fingernails, as if plotting a map, curved over her arm, onto her shoulder, up to her clavicle. Suddenly in the midst of depositing into the ashtray a slice of cellophane from her second pack of cigarettes, Mrs. Proby screamed. An usherette came running down the aisle and ranged various shocked groups of people with the long beam of her flashlight. Several annoyed watchers, a few rows back, indicated with thumbs and umbrellas a quivering Mrs. Proby, her face the colour of kapok, hunched down into her seat, mumbling to herself, and puffing smoke. The beam caught her. She jerked her head toward the light; again she screamed. Mrs. Proby stood up quickly, faced the dark audience, and, like a fat statue come alive and gone mad, she swung her arms high and sent out a highpitched, terrifying howl. Then she stamped up the aisle, demanded her ticket back, and flung out of the theatre. "Simples," said Mrs. Proby as she sat on the No. 22 bus which took her back to the Brompton Road roundabout, where she lived. It was her neighbourhood.

"Mrs. Cullinane, *everyone* has a neck," Mrs. Proby concluded firmly, digging into the purse of her red handbag for a saccharine tablet and obviously piqued at her friend's ridiculous suggestion that the Chinese head sprouts, *mutans mutandis*, out of his shoulder blades, "even your Chinee." It was high tea: the perfervid ritual in England which daily sweetens the ambiance of the discriminately invited and that nothing short of barratry, a provoked shaft of lightning, the King's enemies, or an act of God could ever hope to bring to an end. "On top of that neck is a head between the ears of which is a yellow face, and that's what made me scream, say what you will, dear, and you jolly well know I don't just open my mouth at the first drop of rain."

"You wouldn't say boo to a goose." Mrs. Cullinane was trying to be helpful.

"Not at the pictures I wouldn't, would I?" Mrs. Proby asked archly and stirred her tea white. A blocky, cuboidal head, faced in pinks and whites and ruled in a fretwork of longitudes and latitudes which showed a few orthographic traces of worry, surmounted a body that made Mrs. Proby look like a huge jar or, when shambling along as she often did, something like a prehistoric Nodosaurus. In a neck somewhat like insipid dough showed occasional fatty splotches, her hair sort of a heap of grey slag scraped back into a lumpish mound at the back. Her eyes had a russet, copperish hue that recalled garden thistles or cold glints of steel, depending, as so much did, upon her moods. She was paradigmatic of those fat, gigantic women in London, all bum and elbow, who wear itchy tentlike coats, carry absurd bags of oranges, and usually wheeze down beside you on the bus, smelling of shilling perfume and cold air. She wore "sensible" shoes, had one bad foot, smoked too much, and cultivated a look as if she were always about to say no. In all, she was a woman with the carriage and studied irascibility of a middle-aged prebendary in the Church of England, executrix of self-reliance, law-giver, Diocletian reborn.

"The cinema today is different. So much is, isn't it?" Mrs. Cullinane philosophized. "It was only last week I took me to the cinema. The daily told me they were running a Conrad Nagel thing with what's-her-name, you know, the one I love, but let me tell you there was precious little Conrad Nagel that afternoon, Mrs. Proby." She brushed the shine on her skirt and struck a match for her friend's cigarette. "The picture I saw was about a garage mechanic and another git, excuse me, but git he was, in a plastic suit, who spent all their time taking drugs and forcing grammar-school youngsters to take baths with them. Now, really. I blame the Queen."

"The Bishop."

"The Queen."

"*The Bishop.*"

This froggy voice seemed convinced.

"Well," meekly offered Mrs. Cullinane in an inert and foam-sounding recovery, flustered but just managed, "it could be the Queen. It's her must be allowing all this rubbish into the country in the first place. George the Fifth, sick as he was, wouldn't have counted to seven before he sat down on the whole lot of them, looked up, and said, 'That, for Dicky Scrub!' "

Mrs. Cullinane had the pinched comic face of Houdon's marble of Voltaire, a sort of thin, wide-mouthed suffragist who existed on an ounce of biscuits, the odd celery heart, and, as well, the persistent need to support and maintain ever fiscal sanity in Britain, a brave and full-time concern. She was the kind of woman who seemed to be always holding back a constant urge to knit, the type of person who believed that the statement, "When the Going Gets Tough, the Tough Get Going," was an utterance of the highest magnitude, its speaker invariably the impresario of a dreamland that alone could reshape the world and which surpassed, making quite superfluous, every single volume of philosophy, law, science, theology, literature, and general humanity through the long history of mankind, down to the last. She was a bottomless fund of those insane sermonizing anecdotes which explained, for instance, how big-city hoodlums and czars of the underworld, when riddled by bullets in the street, gasped only for their ice skates in the final minute; how there was a broken heart for every light in Piccadilly; how turtles would never do tinkle in public; and how ladies who worked in the large sweet factories actually hated, yes, hated sweets, to which *credenda*, then, were often added precious and reverently delivered, if not memorable, didactic poems produced, she invariably felt, in the nick of time from the ragbag of tumbling skeltonics she kept at her easy disposal, like shewbread at a fair.

"We never had any trouble, mind you, until America began to send over shipfuls of dirty books and whole potloads of those smouldering films with torcadors, enormous b-e-d-s," Mrs. Cullinane spelled, "and girls in masks and open dust-coats down in Florida in the sunshine, winking at the plumber who came there just *because* and is supposedly fixing the dip-bulb in the w.c., but *we* know better, dear, and I wish we didn't, I wish we did not." Mrs. Cullinane paused, thinking nostalgically perhaps on those old, harmless sepia-tinted reels of "Movietone News" or the long lost three-handkerchief weepies. "Fancy someone like Elizabeth Two, once a princess, mind you, watching something like *Erotic Nights in Dewsbury, Miss Rod Shrieks, The Woolwich Turk,* or *Motel Wives of Pigwiggen,* never mind hearing about them. It makes one want to go sick."

"It's a dicey business, that. It's not enough in the street they're calling her Lizzie, Liz, Betsy, and Bess. Pretty soon it'll be Libby," Mrs. Proby grunted. "Beth, please and thank you. Or maybe just Betty the Mop."

"I've heard Tetty."

Exasperated, Mrs. Proby threw out an arm thick as a cutlet bat.

"No doubt, no doubt. Mrs. Cullinane, no doubt you've heard Tetty. It's a very coarse word. But, tell me this, haven't you also heard Eliza? Lisbeth? *Elsie? Elsie, for godsakes?* Come on, own up to it. Show a little bone."

"Well, Elspeth."

"You've never heard Elspeth."

"Elspeth," Mrs. Cullinane assured her, "yes."

"A pipe dream, Mrs. Cullinane."

"I'm certain of it. Elspeth."

"*Never.*"

And Mrs. Proby glared at Mrs. Cullinane, who nipped some biscuits which were dipped, self-consciously, in the tea, several times, again —in jerks.

Mrs. Proby quickly interrupted Mrs. Cullinane who had begun humming "When the Old Dun Cow Caught Fire."

"I'm afraid to go out, Mrs. Cullinane. Even with my Weenie. I mean, if he should stop to go doo-doo by a post, who's to guarantee some big hairy thing in a mask won't come flashing out of a doorway and do me god-knows-what kind of brain damage, bash me with a cosh he might, snatch me handbag, even tamper about here and there in the you know." Mrs. Proby nodded knowingly and licked a bubble of tea off an upper lip whistle-split and slightly mystacial.

"You're smarter than Mrs. Shoe."

"Mrs. Shoe goes out?"

"Frequently."

"Alone?"

"This is my point."

"God."

"That's what I said."

"My God."

"That's just what I said."

Mrs. Proby set her tea and saucer down on the tray, walked to the door of the living room, shut it, and sat down again. She shrugged, shook her head slowly, and leaned forward. "Mrs. Cullinane, I'm not sure I know how to say this to you, you wouldn't either." Biting the inside of her cheek, she threw a glance toward the aspidistra in her window and joined the tips of her fingers. "The reason I screamed, the reason you, I, anybody—even Prince Andrew himself—would scream was this: I thought of Mr. Yunnum Fun."

"Mr. Yunnum Fun?" Mrs. Cullinane stopped her jaws, her mouth full of scone.

"Mr. Yunnum Fun *downstairs*." Mrs. Proby's eyes narrowed. She nodded gravely, waiting for the shock of recognition. It came and was gone. Mrs. Proby's eyes widened as a reinforcement. "Their how is not necessarily our how, nor is yours theirs."

"He's only a simple twit."

"He's sneaky."

"He just sells rice."

"He's got things on his mind."

"He's harmless, Mrs. Proby."

"He's Chinese, Mrs. Cullinane."

The small Chinese market and its proprietor, Mr. Fun, hadn't become an object of interest for Mrs. Proby until about five or six months ago, when, at that time, a highly publicized altercation took place between the police and a body of cultural attachés at the Chinese Embassy. Not that, previous to this, harmony reigned between the English lady and the Chinese merchant; they had harassed each other for years (listening at doors, depositing curt notes, leaving footprints on each other's mail).

A dot of a man, Mr. Fun had owned the grocery store and, in closed circuit, had lived on-premise at the back of the bottom floor of the building for eight years. Mrs. Proby, widowed and full of the spurge of the no-longer-attached, occupied the first floor for three years, a period of time that had passed slowly without the companionable, if occasionally warlike, dialectic she had found in her husband. Mr. Proby faulted her only occasionally, never, certainly, by low dodges of the heart, but merely on the odd Saturday night when, out on a toot, he would lurch home glassy-eyed under the streetlamps, with one or two middle-aged girls on each arm, singing ballistic snatches from "The Little Shirt My Mother Made for Me" or "Sweeney Todd the Barber," his behaviour, after all the drink, considered by the general neighbourhood not so much objectionable as courtly, though it periodically cost him those not always enviable few minutes just later when, unable to exorcise himself of the disconsolate and unbearable immediate, he fell prey to the singularly virulent *malocchio* drilling him in silence from across the darkened bedroom. But sovereignty was re-established as apologies were made, insisted upon, sworn, repeated, sworn again, and more than one potentially fistic evening passed away forever in a loud duet of snores, one set markedly louder, almost triumphant, poignantly female. What the deuce, he had often said, say la vee. He had given Mrs. Proby a fairly full life: judicious, non-adjectival, sometimes cranky, but almost always full. He was in plastics; then he retired comfortably, took the little woman and Weenie to Woodford Wells where they bought a modest little house, trimmed a hedge or two, and tried as best they could to make the rough places plain. Then, three years ago, after a nice meal of fresh crab cakes, Cornish pasties, and a bottle or two of brown ale, Mr. Proby took a jaunt into Epping Forest and dropped dead—ironically, during the loveliest hour of the English year: seven o'clock on Midsummer Eve. The sudden shock of it all caused in Mrs. Proby a diarrheal disease called sprue, an agnail on her right toe as large as a doorknob, and, she claimed, twinges in the area of Rosenmüller's Organ. In any case, Mrs. Proby waked him, buried him in a spot near the Bunhill Fields, packed her things (a lovely collection of Royal Doulton, her woolwork slippers, a zipper Bible, a morocco-bound account of the Anglo-Nicaraguan wars of '46, a boa she had kept from the celebration of her wooden wedding, etc.), and moved to a little street near South Kensington, where she had grown up as a girl, because she could not stand to be too far from the nicer part of London, the very quarter in which—oh, it seemed years ago, she often pointed out—Bernard (Mr. Proby) courted her, with a full crop of bushy coal-black hair, pointed shoes, and the banjo eyes she'd grown to love. In those days, England had a voice in the world, people could understand the lyrics of songs, and there were no Chinese. Changes, however, had come about and had created in her a compulsion for the *laudator temporis acti* reminiscence, which excluded, perforce, the total existence of both a certain Chinaman and any capacity in him that might try to prove otherwise. Mrs. Proby became hermetic not *per accidens* but by predilection.

A tight national budget coupled with the small personal account Mr. Proby left her kept Mrs. Proby's eye on the shilling. And except for a chance Saturday at Portobello Road (for thermal underwear, wholesale tins of quinine toothpowder, or general white elephant), a dash to a museum exhibit, or a quick afternoon at the pictures, she restricted herself to the quiet deliberation and firmitude of soul found in the English matron: a recipe available to few but the sore-footed and antique wise. Mrs. Proby bought her flat right out, dusted, put sachet lavender in the drawers, scrubbed, put up new flowered wallpaper, hoovered the rugs, religiously scrubbed lye into her porcelain, and draped the windows in percale. Until she met Mrs. Cullinane she spent most of her time munching from a can of Fortt's Original Bath Olivers or sucking wine-gums, slouched lugubriously by the wireless, following episode after episode of "The Archers," listening on the BBC to Sidney Torch's dated musical extravaganzae—and of course she was, as she was always ready to add, "all for the telly," in front of which she often sat making penwipes of flannel in the shape of carnations for the old soldiers on Royal Hospital Road in Chelsea. Her teas were grim; even Weenie was no help there.

"How's your cup?" Mrs. Proby asked.

"I'm doing nicely, thank you," answered Mrs. Cullinane, whose character was basically that of blotting paper: passive, receptive, and ready for the strangest of Rorschachs, notwithstanding those patterns of peculiarity soaked up by the thrust and imposition of Mrs. Proby's iron will and irrevocable opinion.

"These teacakes want jam," Mrs. Proby said.

"Mine are fine."

"You're having your teacake, then?"

"Oh yes, I merely put it aside."

"I noticed you did. I wondered why you did."

"I had a scone."

"But not a teacake." Mrs. Proby looked away.

"I thought I'd have it in a minute."

"Have it now."

"Mrs. Cullinane bit into the cake trimly. "It's delicious."

"It wants jam."

Mrs. Proby, the recent terror of the unpropitiously topical film fast and irksome in her mind, suddenly bolted from the sofa, threw open the door of the living room, and, pointing to her pursed lips as a quick sign for secrecy and immediate silence, scuttled to the keyhole of the main entrance-hall door. She squatted, applied her ear, and peeped through, her right hand raised as a flat warning to a bewildered Mrs. Cullinane who followed her in soft, querulous hops, sucking a finger in fright. Glances were exchanged. Nothing. They mooned back into the room for a second cup. Mrs. Proby poured: "You're white."

"Lovely, and, I think, a twinkle of milk." Mrs. Cullinane, mouse-mannered and votively appreciative, watched the sacrament and took her cup and saucer as the last word in the way of viaticum.

"Spoons?"

"Two, dear."

"Level or heaped?"

"Heaped."

"Then one."

"One?"

One, Mrs. Proby mouthed, silently pronouncing the word as she nodded once, conveying, as she fully intended, the readily identifiable world-weariness of Authority Taxed. Her eyes shut with a little snap.

Mrs. Cullinane's Lucullan urges were an embarrassment to herself. She blushed for being such a hog and looked away absent-mindedly at a fuchsia marinescape of the pebble beaches at Rottingdean crookedly hung on a far wall.

"I don't mind telling you," Mrs. Proby continued, smoothing her round, lacteal figure, "he scares me right out of my naturals, and, mind you, he's been acting strange for quite some time now. He lights incense sticks at night, worships the devil, I think. I don't know if he's grinding tea or muttering A-rab chants, I don't, but I turn my wireless up so as not to hear, you see. What I'm driving at, Mrs. Cullinane, is this: some morning Mrs. Proby's going to turn back the covers, take off her hairnet, and find she's shoulder-to-shin with the Yellow Peril, she is."

"The Yellow Peril?"

"You might have read about it, all those little cities near San Francisco, America, are up in arms over it, catching it as fast as nightingales and flopping down with writhe all over their mouths from it, poor things."

Mrs. Cullinane was heartbroken. "Honestly, with all the riots here and space trips there, then the whole African mess, you wonder if people have left their heads home."

"Oh, it's all monkey-see, monkey-do, isn't it?" Mrs. Proby said, sipping her tea and swallowing in the middle of an important thought. "Mmmm," she quickly recovered, "the point is, when I look around me to see who's there, I don't want to see yellows or browns or purples. I want mine."

A wistful smile passed over Mrs. Cullinane's face and she patted Mrs. Proby's wrist with earnest compassion, adding with sincere force and a cross between a prophetic stare and a wink, "You'll get yours." She closed her eyes and nodded confidently.

The ladies understood each other, in the careful way that ladies do once they understand each other. They were rather a pair than a couple, supporting each other from day to day, rather a set of utile, if ill-matched, bookends between which stood the opinion and idea in the metaphorical volumes that both connected them and kept them ever apart. Mrs. Proby and Mrs. Cullinane met each other as the result of a coincidence which proved their similarity, perhaps even to a perfection or symmetry we would never be ready to accord even to types. The meeting took place in the lending library branch at Balls Green: both ladies, waiting at the "request desk," had asked the librarian—almost in unison—for a copy of *The Sinister Monk* by Raoul Carrambo. Laughter, embarrassment, and that became for them the point of departure for a parallel life-style they had cherished for a long while now. But the relationship was greatly strengthened in the two when, after a few off-hand discussions over tea and during walks, they began to realize they held common beliefs in politics, entertainment, and the public weal. Neither could understand why Mrs. Shoe, a third party (initially a friend of Mrs. Cullinane, Mrs. Proby often felt the need to make clear) who worked as a saleslady selling velveteen at D. H. Evans in Oxford Street, was so unwilling to abhor the immigration problem. Voluntary Repatriation was the answer. One had to be purblind not to see that.

Mrs. Proby never *could* come to terms with the fact that Indians, Chinese, or Blacks even bothered to get on boats and travel thousands and thousands of miles to England—eating only peas and peppercorn or playing mah-jongg or jacks in steerage with all the chickens—when they should have known that the day would certainly come when people would be jumping off into the ocean for want of room, run screaming off into the Highlands for a gulp of air, or begin selling their hair just to keep alive. This was why Mrs. Proby always met Mrs. Cullinane at the door, saying, "Cor, good to see a human face."

Then, there chanced to happen the fully reported melee at the Chinese Embassy, with blow-up photographs in the *Daily Mail* of hissing, spitting ambassadors armed with cricket bats, flatirons, and pinking shears, while the British police were left with only dust-bin covers to protect themselves. It was only a matter of time, as matters go, therefore, that Mrs. Proby began to notice many Chinese on the streets: hunched, shuffling, dry-mannered, and recondite in that carapax of the inaccessible and unproven. Mrs. Proby immediately bought a screw and lock for her door.

"So I got all fired up and carried away," Mrs. Proby said, plucking a tea leaf off the tip of her tongue, "when I saw this absolutely perverse Chinee with a hat like a black upside-down cup with a nipple on it and a moustache like two long pieces of dirty licorice hanging from his nose. I thought of Mr. Yunnum Fun, so help me dearie. And you would have done, too."

"Was it all blood and gore?'

"Who stayed for the end to watch, me? Not likely. I suppose I should have, strange to say, then I could have told you the whole give and take, you see." A pause: Mrs. Cullinane pulled the lobe of her ear, reflected.

"Mr. Yunnum Fun doesn't have a moustache."

"He has white hairs growing out of his ears, like artichokes. It sounds to me like you're defending him."

Mrs. Cullinane swerved her shoulders in nonchalance. "He walks around in slippers."

"He wears pajamas, too."

"But he doesn't wear a Chinese hat."

"So you defend him."

"I'm not defending him."

"It sounds to me like you're defending him. What does it sound like to you?"

What is a pair, it seemed proven only once again, is not who is a couple.

Mrs. Proby assumed the pain-of-the-unseen-wound expression, stood up, took a cigarette from her pack, and tapped it on her knuckle. She mentally envisioned a piece of black cardboard from which she sharply cut a cruel profile of Yunnum Fun, thinking of his petty insults and bumptious insularity. She puffed out circles of smoke and let loose, between the blue swirls, a not-uncommon antagonism, syncopated with hot flashes: part bigotry, part haptic bias.

"I suppose it's perfectly normal for the Chinese to come over here without so much as shoe flap, go on National Health, have babies for a song, buy spectacles for less than cost, get free teeth, and then just because everything's not all cozy and done up like a nice package from Father Christmas, frills and froo-froo and all, go out into the street and kick those handsome policemen in the kneecaps. And all the while our own have to make do with bits and pieces. Who wouldn't have bad dreams? It raises my hump, Mrs. Cullinane. It should raise yours."

"It raises my hump," Mrs. Cullinane apologized.

"When?"

"Just now, dear."

"You're just saying that because it raised my hump," said Mrs. Proby, an avocadine hue rising into her ample neck. Mrs. Cullinane turned cinnabar red. The colours clashed.

"I mean, let's face it, we should take care of our own first, shouldn't we? Give us a few years and we'll have books that you have to read backwards, and our children will have to write with nails manufactured in China and make those peculiar words with wings and splinters and god knows what, won't we?" asked Mrs. Proby, who, unbeknownst to her, had one of the grouts from the bottom of the teacup on the tip of her nose. "If you don't find that peculiar, Mrs. Cullinane, you're off your rails, spade to spade."

Mrs. Cullinane clucked, sipped the last of her tea, and placed the thin, blue-striped cup on the saucer in her lap, dabbed her lips daintily with a napkin, and drew her finger down each side of her open mouth which she smacked as an indication that tea for her was now over. She placed the sacramentals on the server, stood up, adjusted the jacket of her herringbone suit. "Lovely, dear. Just tickety-boo."

"Have yourself another teacake."

"Godfrey," said Mrs. Cullinane, making a clown face. "I'm full up."

"Tomorrow night, then, for the ham."

Mrs. Cullinane, head inclined and little hands joined, was smiling vacantly at her little buttoned feet. She looked like Squirrel Nutkin. She might have been asleep. Then she looked up slowly, depositing her eyes into Mrs. Proby's and quickly bumping out of her reverie. She grew pursy, flutterful. "Tomorrow night, then, for the . . .?"

"Ham." Mrs. Proby sniffed. "My ham supper."

Mrs. Cullinane formed her hand into a pistol and aimed a finger at her temple; she crossed her eyes, lolled her tongue, and displayed, with jangling arms and a dizzy expression, her silly lapse of memory. Forgetfulness for her was a merciful narcotic. "Of course, dear," she burbled.

"Dumplings, as well."

"Lovely, dear. And so thoughtful. You see, you remembered. I can't *eat* apples as they come from the tree; the crunch goes right through me. I have a thin windpipe. You see, the pips are murder and—"

"I don't core my apples," Mrs. Proby interrupted. "I won't have it. Pips impart a delicious flavour to dumplings. I thought you knew that." Cored apples not only made a mock of the natural apple, they made a mock of Mrs. Proby who never fixed them that way. "You want to think about your kitchen, Mrs. Cullinane."

Mrs. Cullinane was thinking about her windpipe.

Mrs. Proby was not given to "adventurous cooking." True, ten years ago, in a mad fit of what then seemed an unquenchable obsession with experiment, she *did* once pull her bread, for a cheese lunch. But cooking, especially in England, was not a question of miracles. And even if she hated eyeing potatoes and making béchamel, she knew what work meant. One does not just throw a bun up in the air, as she often rather realistically pointed out, and expect it to come down pig-in-the-blanket. Good English dishes, sweet and short! And there was an end to it. All the so-called snappy puddings, camel meat, weevily flour, cut-and-come-again cheeses, expensive chocolates, and powdered soup-and-fish preparations all shot up with additives sunk into one's stomach like a bump in a trash bin and insured hardening of the arteries, for one thing, and squammes, for another. She loved a steaming joint, a bowl of fresh cock-a-leekie soup, and especially liked her brussels sprouts hard, where they stood up and came green in a minute, after which, of course, a few spoonfuls of figgy pudding to top it all off. She was, after all, an islander. Islanders *had* to know what to eat, because any minute the Communists, those hoof-footed dongs from the primeval wastes who live only on smudgy black aerated bread and complaints, would be swimming around the whole nation with corking and nets in their mouths, sealing Great Britain off from the rest of the world, and forcing everyone into a diet of cowpats, the lesser sage, and ounces of mastick. As if life were all clover! Islanders, also, knew about fish, and Mrs. Proby often found herself, in the midst of a somnambulistic stroll in the middle of the night, voraciously gripping the door of the fridge with both hands, a volcanic lust in her mind for a nice hake, turbot, brill, some whiting, or, best of all, a slice of John Dory, which had her favourite piece on the cheek. And then, if she was knocked in, maybe a nice little Pimm's Cup—just before Bedfordshire—to ease the rheumatics and start her off again on her beauty slumber. Beauty, she often reminded herself, was important as well. You never knew.

Curatical in her bugled wool, Mrs. Proby bore regally a large teapot toward her small kitchen. Mrs. Cullinane champed down on a napkin to see a trace of lipstick, fixed her hair in a wall mirror, and fidgeted into her fur-tipped seal boots. She turned toward the kitchen. "May I pluck a rose?"

Wringing her arms of water, Mrs. Proby came back into the room in the midst of a monologue which she had begun with her dog in the kitchen. ". . . featherbedded and all. If it was up to me, I'd throw out the whole ruddy lot. Sorry?"

"I have to spend a penny."

"The bottom of the hall. You know." She paused, coddling the stanchion of her left breast from heartburn. "The bathroom stationery is in the cabinet, with a rubber around it. The bugs were ruining the t.p. That's why you will smell pepper in the convenience, Mrs. Cullinane. Don't let it stop you from your business. I sprinkle pepper there, for the bugs." She snorted out with a cruel little chuckle. "They hate it." She indicated an unlighted passageway off the living room, through which Mrs. Cullinane poked, feeling the walls for surety. Mrs. Proby splayed herself in a chair, stretched her feet wide apart, and pinched lovingly the wattles of her dog, both staring into space. The identifiable sound of a loud gurgle and splash pulled her from her revery. Mrs. Cullinane re-entered smiling.

"You remember, of course, the la-de-da in the Victoria and Albert Museum, Mrs. Cullinane. A fine figger for the children here and about, wasn't it?" Mrs. Proby sucked a tooth.

"Oh yes," Mrs. Cullinane said dryly. "That Chinaman."

"I thought you forgot."

"How could I forget?"

"I thought you forgot."

"How could I forget?"

"After I just reminded you, you couldn't, Mrs. Cullinane; there's no point in fibbing."

The reference here was to an unfortunate incident that took place about a fortnight before the confrontation at the Chinese Embassy and which prompted Mrs. Proby, despite Mrs. Cullinane's protestations that the man in question might have been Japanese, to write to Downing Street a singularly outraged letter, notable, perhaps, most of all for its insinuation that an insidious collaboration was taking place, known to few but the initiated and politically aware, between the British Civil Service and Red China. "Watch the feathers fly," Mrs. Proby prophesied.

Mrs. Proby and Mrs. Cullinane took advantage of the English year and its rosary of annual events: the Annual Spital Sermon, Oak-Apple Day, Swan Upping, the Shrove Tuesday Pancake Greaze, and the Presentation of the Knolly Rose. And Mrs. Proby and Mrs. Cullinane loved to go to museums as well. They loved tapestries, the century-old costumes, and delicate bone china. Mrs. Cullinane could never get over the intricacy of the Eye-talian designs which she herself could never hope to duplicate in a thousand million years, she said. Mrs. Proby said it took her mind off herself. It was on Egg Saturday one lovely afternoon in spring and a fresh rain had left the streets clean and the air bright for a good walk to the Victoria and Albert. But no sooner had they passed the Jones Collection and were making their way through to the tapestries, with determined and mechanical clockwork steps, they happened to pass a chunky man (a Thai) huddled in a greasy overcoat, sitting on a small bench before the elongated, sensual sculpture called "Reclining Nymph." His hands were fumbling in his lap (a rubbing friction to restore warmth). Mrs. Proby, biting her lip and inquisitorial, nudged Mrs. Cullinane, dragged her away behind some eighteenth-century French busts in a corner, and, her back to the room, squinted past Mrs. Cullinane's shoulders while gesturing with her thumb over her own, in the direction of the man. They bustled over to the room guard and explained in euphemistically vague but excited terms that a Chinaman in that same room was drooling and manipulating himself, and, by way of footnote, they stood around and painted a few word-pictures which included various suppositions, not the least of which was that it was the Queen Mother's favourite room and that, *horresco referens*, the Archbishop of Canterbury might be coming into the museum any minute.

It was getting dark outside. Mrs. Cullinane stopped at the door and smiled sweetly. She squeezed Mrs. Proby's elbow and turned her head to one side in compassion. She started down the stairs, turned on the landing, and spoke. "Keep your pecker up, dear."

There came a pause.

"Remember."

"Yes?"

"When the going gets tough, the tough get going."

The door slammed. Mrs. Proby relocked the door, popped a valium tablet into her mouth, and washed the cups and saucers, having pulled on some long pink rubber gloves lined in yellow. She thought of Fu Manchu's fingernails. She paused, her hands quiet in the water, and looked behind her. Then she shambled into the livingroom and stretched herself out in a crumpled way on the sofa. The dog shifted. Mrs. Proby blinked in the dark room, unhappy and on edge for the yellow crosshatched illusions and patterns thrown on the ceiling by the passing autos outside.

Nora Ephron

*

A FEW WORDS ABOUT BREASTS

I have to begin with a few words about androgyny. In grammar school, in the fifth and sixth grades, we were all tyrannized by a rigid set of rules that supposedly determined whether we were boys or girls. The episode in *Huckleberry Finn* where Huck is disguised as a girl and gives himself away by the way he threads a needle and catches a ball—that kind of thing. We learned that the way you sat, crossed your legs, held a cigarette, and looked at your nails—the way you did these things instinctively was absolute proof of your sex. Now obviously most children did not take this literally, but I did. I thought that just one slip, just one incorrect cross of my legs or flick of an imaginary cigarette ash would turn me from whatever I was into the other thing; that would be all it took, really. Even though I was outwardly a girl and had many of the trappings generally associated with girldom—a girl's name, for example, and dresses, my own telephone, an autograph book—I spent the early years of my adolescence absolutely certain that I might at any point gum it up. I did not feel at all like a girl. I was boyish. I was athletic, ambitious, outspoken, competitive, noisy, rambunctious. I had scabs on my knees and my socks slid into my loafers and I could throw a football. I wanted desperately not to be that way, not to be a mixture of both things, but instead just one, a girl, a definite indisputable girl. As soft and as pink as a nursery. And nothing would do that for me, I felt, but breasts.

• • •

I was about six months younger than everyone else in my class, and so for about six months after it began, for six months after my friends had begun to develop (that was the word we used, develop), I was not particularly worried. I would sit in the bathtub and look down at my breasts and know that any day now, any second now, they would start growing like everyone else's. They didn't. "I want to buy a bra," I said to my mother one night. "What for?" she said. My mother was really hateful about bras, and by the time my third sister had gotten to the point where she was ready to want one, my mother had worked the whole business into a comedy routine. "Why not use a Band-Aid instead?" she would say. It was a source of great pride to my mother that she had never even had to wear a brassiere until she had her fourth child, and then only because her gynecologist made her. It was incomprehensible to me that anyone could ever be proud of something like that. It was the 1950s, for God's sake. Jane Russell. Cashmere sweaters. Couldn't my mother see that? "*I am too old to wear an undershirt.*" Screaming. Weeping. Shouting. "Then don't wear an undershirt," said my mother. "But I want to buy a bra." "What for?"

I suppose that for most girls, breasts, brassieres, that entire thing, has more trauma, more to do with the coming of adolescence, with becoming a woman, than anything else. Certainly more than getting your period, although that, too, was traumatic, symbolic. But you could see breasts; they were there; they were visible. Whereas a girl could claim to have her period for months before she actually got it and nobody would ever know the difference. Which is exactly what I did. All you had to do was make a great fuss over having enough nickels for the Kotex machine and walk around clutching your stomach and moaning for three to five days a month about The Curse and you could convince anybody. There is a school of thought somewhere in the women's lib/ women's mag/ gynecology establishment that claims that menstrual cramps are purely psychological, and I lean toward it. Not that I didn't have them finally. Agonizing cramps, heating-pad cramps, go-down-to-the-school-nurse-and-lie-on-the-cot cramps. But, unlike any pain I had ever suffered, I adored the pain of cramps, welcomed it, wallowed in it, bragged about it. "I can't go. I have cramps." "I can't do that. I have cramps." And most of all, gigglingly, blushingly: "I can't swim. I have cramps." Nobody ever used the hard-core word. Menstruation. God, what an awful word. Never that. "I have cramps."

The morning I first got my period, I went into my mother's bedroom to tell her. And my mother, my utterly-hateful-about-bras mother, burst into tears. It was really a lovely moment, and I remember it so clearly not just because it was one of the two times I ever saw my mother cry on my account (the other was when I was caught being a six-year-old kleptomaniac), but also because the incident did not mean to me what it meant to her. Her little girl, her firstborn, had finally become a woman. That was what she was crying about. My reaction to the event, however, was that I might well be a woman in some scientific, textbook sense (and could at least stop faking every month and stop wasting all those nickels). But in another sense—in a visible sense—I was as androgynous and as liable to tip over into boyhood as ever.

•   •   •

I started with a 28 AA bra. I don't think they made them any smaller in those days, although I gather that now you can buy bras for five-year-olds that don't have any cups whatsoever in them; trainer bras they are called. My first brassiere came from Robinson's Department Store in Beverly Hills. I went there alone, shaking, positive they would look me over and smile and tell me to come back next year. An actual fitter took me into the dressing room and stood over me while I took off my blouse and tried the first one on. The little puffs stood out on my chest. "Lean over," said the fitter. (To this day, I am not sure what fitters in bra departments do except to tell you to lean over.) I leaned over, with the fleeting hope that my breasts would miraculously fall out of my body and into the puffs. Nothing.

"Don't worry about it," said my friend Libby some months later, when things had not improved. "You'll get them after you're married."

"What are you talking about?" I said.

"When you get married," Libby explained, "your husband will touch your breasts and rub them and kiss them and they'll grow."

That was the killer. Necking I could deal with. Intercourse I could deal with. But it had never crossed my mind that a man was going to touch my breasts, that breasts had something to do with all that, petting, my God, they never mentioned petting in my little sex manual about the fertilization of the ovum. I became dizzy. For I knew instantly—as naïve as I had been only a moment before—that only part of what she was saying was true: the touching, rubbing, kissing part, not the growing part. And I knew that no one would ever want to marry me. I had no breasts. I would never have breasts.

•   •   •

My best friend in school was Diana Raskob. She lived a block from me in a house full of wonders. English muffins, for instance. The Raskobs were the first people in Beverly Hills to have English muffins for breakfast. They also had an apricot tree in the back, and a badminton court, and a subscription to *Seventeen* magazine, and hundreds of games, like Sorry and Parcheesi and Treasure Hunt and Anagrams. Diana and I spent three or four afternoons a week in their den reading and playing and eating. Diana's mother's kitchen was full of the most colossal assortment of junk food I have ever been exposed to. My house was full of apples and peaches and milk and homemade chocolate-chip cookies—which were nice, and good for you, but-not-right-before-dinner-or-you'll-spoil-your-appetite. Diana's house had nothing in it that was good for you, and what's more, you could stuff it in right up until dinner and nobody cared. Bar-B-Q potato chips (they were the first in them, too), giant bottles of ginger ale, fresh popcorn with melted butter, hot fudge sauce on Baskin-Robbins jamoca ice cream, powdered-sugar doughnuts from Van de Kamp's. Diana and I had been best friends since we were seven; we were about equally popular in school (which is to say, not particularly), we had about the same success with boys (extremely intermittent), and we looked much the same. Dark. Tall. Gangly.

It is September, just before school begins. I am eleven years old, about to enter the seventh grade, and Diana and I have not seen each other all summer. I have been to camp and she has been somewhere like Banff with her parents. We are meeting, as we often do, on the street midway between our two houses, and we will walk back to Diana's and eat junk and talk about what has happened to each of us that summer. I am walking down Walden Drive in my jeans and my father's shirt hanging out and my old red loafers with the socks falling into them and coming toward me is . . . I take a deep breath . . . a young woman. Diana. Her hair is curled and she has a waist and hips and a bust and she is wearing a straight skirt, an article of clothing I have been repeatedly told I will be unable to wear until I have the hips to hold it up. My jaw drops, and suddenly I am crying, crying hysterically, can't catch my breath sobbing. My best friend has betrayed me. She has gone ahead without me and done it. She has shaped up.

• • •

Here are some things I did to help:
Bought a Mark Eden Bust Developer.
Slept on my back for four years.
Splashed cold water on them every night because some French actress said in *Life* magazine that that was what she did for her perfect bustline.

Ultimately, I resigned myself to a bad toss and began to wear padded bras. I think about them now, think about all those years in high school I went around in them, my three padded bras, every single one of them with different-sized breasts. Each time I changed bras I changed sizes: one week nice perky but not too obtrusive breasts, the next medium-sized slightly pointy ones, the next week knockers, true knockers; all the time, whatever size I was, carrying around this rubberized appendage on my chest that occasionally crashed into a wall and was poked inward and had to be poked outward—I think about all that and wonder how anyone kept a straight face through it. My parents, who normally had no restraints about needling me—why did they say nothing as they watched my chest go up and down? My friends, who would periodically inspect my breasts for signs of growth and reassure me—why didn't they at least counsel consistency?

And the bathing suits. I die when I think about the bathing suits. That was the era when you could lay an uninhabited bathing suit on the beach and someone would make a pass at it. I would put one on, an absurd swimsuit with its enormous bust built into it, the bones from the suit stabbing me in the rib cage and leaving little red welts on my body, and there I would be, my chest plunging straight downward absolutely vertically from my collarbone to the top of my suit and then suddenly, wham, out came all that padding and material and wiring absolutely horizontally.

• • •

Buster Klepper was the first boy who ever touched them. He was my boyfriend my senior year of high school. There is a picture of him in my high-school yearbook that makes him look quite attractive in a Jewish, horn-rimmed-glasses sort of way, but the picture does not show the pimples, which were air-brushed out, or the dumbness. Well, that isn't really fair. He wasn't dumb. He just wasn't terribly bright. His mother refused to accept it, refused to accept the relentlessly average report cards, refused to deal with her son's inevitable destiny in some junior college or other. "He was tested," she would say to me, apropos of nothing, "and it came out a hundred and forty-five. That's near-genius." Had the word "underachiever" been coined, she probably would have lobbed that one at me, too. Anyway, Buster was really very sweet—which is, I know, damning with faint praise, but there it is. I was the editor of the front page of the high school newspaper and he was editor of the back page; we had to work together, side by side, in the print shop, and that was how it started. On our first date, we went to see *April Love*, starring Pat Boone. Then we started going together. Buster had a green coupe, a 1950 Ford with an engine he had hand-chromed until it shone, dazzled, reflected the image of anyone who looked into it, anyone usually being Buster polishing it or the gas-station attendants he constantly asked to check the oil in order for them to be overwhelmed by the sparkle on the valves. The car also had a boot stretched over the back seat for reasons I never understood; hanging from the rearview mirror, as was the custom, was a pair of angora dice. A previous girl friend named Solange, who was famous throughout Beverly Hills High School for having no pigment in her right eyebrow, had knitted them for him. Buster and I would ride around town, the two of us seated to the left of the steering wheel. I would shift gears. It was nice.

There was necking. Terrific necking. First in the car, overlooking Los Angeles from what is now the Trousdale Estates. Then on the bed of his parents' cabana at Ocean House. Incredibly wonderful, frustrating necking, I loved it, really, but no further than necking, please don't, please, because there I was absolutely terrified of the general implications of going-a-step-further with a near-dummy and also terrified of his finding out there was next to nothing there (which he knew, of course; he wasn't that dumb).

I broke up with him at one point. I think we were apart for about two weeks. At the end of that time, I drove down to see a friend at a boarding school in Palos Verdes Estates and a disc jockey played "April Love" on the radio four times during the trip. I took it as a sign. I drove straight back to Griffith Park to a golf tournament Buster was playing in (he was the sixth-seeded teen-age golf player in southern California) and presented myself back to him on the green of the 18th hole. It was all very dramatic. That night we went to a drive-in and I let him get his hand under my protuberances and onto my breasts. He really didn't seem to mind at all.

• • •

"Do you want to marry my son?" the woman asked me.

"Yes," I said.

I was nineteen years old, a virgin, going with this woman's son, this big strange woman who was married to a Lutheran minister in New Hampshire and pretended she was gentile and had this son, by her first husband, this total fool of a son who ran the hero-sandwich concession at Harvard Business School and whom for one moment one December in New Hampshire I said—as much out of politeness as anything else—that I wanted to marry.

"Fine," she said. "Now, here's what you do. Always make sure you're on top of him so you won't seem so small. My bust is very large, you see, so I always lie on my back to make it look smaller, but you'll have to be on top most of the time."

I nodded. "Thank you," I said.

"I have a book for you to read," she went on. "Take it with you when you leave. Keep it." She went to the bookshelf, found it, and gave it to me. It was a book on frigidity.

"Thank you," I said.

• • •

That is a true story. Everything in this article is a true story, but I feel I have to point out that that story in particular is true. It happened on December 30, 1960. I think about it often. When it first happened, I naturally assumed that the woman's son, my boyfriend, was responsible. I invented a scenario where he had had a little heart-to-heart with his mother and had confessed that his only objection to me was that my breasts were small; his mother then took it upon herself to help out. Now I think I was wrong about the incident. The mother was acting on her own, I think: that was her way of being cruel and competitive under the guise of being helpful and maternal. You have small breasts, she was saying; therefore you will never make him as happy as I have. Or you have small breasts; therefore you will doubtless have sexual problems. Or you have small breasts; therefore you are less woman than I am. She was, as it happens, only the first of what seems to me to be a never-ending string of women who have made competitive remarks to me about breast size. "I would love to wear a dress like that," my friend Emily says to me, "but my bust is too big." Like that. Why do women say these things to me? Do I attract these remarks the way other women attract married men or alcoholics or homosexuals? This summer, for example. I am at a party in East Hampton and I am introduced to a woman from Washington. She is a minor celebrity, very pretty and Southern and blond and outspoken, and I am flattered because she has read something I have written. We are talking animatedly, we have been talking no more than five minutes, when a man comes up to join us. "Look at the two of us," the woman says to the man, indicating me and her. "The two of us together couldn't fill an A cup." Why does she say that? It isn't even true, dammit, so why? Is she even more addled than I am on this subject? Does she honestly believe there is something wrong with her size breasts, which, it seems to me, now that I look hard at them, are just right? Do I unconsciously bring out competitiveness in women? In that form? What did I do to deserve it?

As for men.

There were men who minded and let me know that they minded. There were men who did not mind. In any case, I always minded.

And even now, now that I have been countlessly reassured that my figure is a good one, now that I am grown-up enough to understand that most of my feelings have very little to do with the reality of my shape, I am nonetheless obsessed by breasts. I cannot help it. I grew up in the terrible fifties—with rigid stereotypical sex roles, the insistence that men be men and dress like men and women be women and dress like women, the intolerance of androgyny—and I cannot shake it, cannot shake my

feelings of inadequacy. Well, that time is gone, right? All those exagger-
ated examples of breast worship are gone, right? Those women were
freaks, right? I know all that. And yet here I am, stuck with the psychological remains of it all, stuck with my own peculiar version of breast
worship. You probably think I am crazy to go on like this: here I have set
out to write a confession that is meant to hit you with the shock of
recognition, and instead you are sitting there thinking I am thoroughly
warped. Well, what can I tell you? If I had had them, I would have been
a completely different person. I honestly believe that.

After I went into therapy, a process that made it possible for me to
tell total strangers at cocktail parties that breasts were the hang-up of my
life, I was often told that I was insane to have been bothered by my
condition. I was also frequently told, by close friends, that I was extremely boring on the subject. And my girl friends, the ones with nice
big breasts, would go on endlessly about how their lives had been far
more miserable than mine. Their bra straps were snapped in class. They
couldn't sleep on their stomachs. They were stared at whenever the word
"mountain" cropped up in geography. And *Evangeline*, good God what
they went through every time someone had to stand up and recite the
Prologue to Longfellow's *Evangeline*: ". . . stand like druids of eld . . . /
With beards that rest on their bosoms." It was much worse for them,
they tell me. They had a terrible time of it, they assure me. I don't know
how lucky I was, they say.

I have thought about their remarks, tried to put myself in their
place, considered their point of view. I think they are full of shit.

Max Apple

*

THE ORANGING OF AMERICA

I

From the outside it looked like any ordinary 1964 Cadillac limousine. In the expensive space between the driver and passengers, where some installed bars or even bathrooms, Mr. Howard Johnson kept a tidy ice-cream freezer in which there were always at least eighteen flavors on hand, though Mr. Johnson ate only vanilla. The freezer's power came from the battery with an independent auxiliary generator as a back-up system. Although now Howard Johnson means primarily motels, Millie, Mr. HJ, and Otis Brighton, the chauffeur, had not forgotten that ice cream was the cornerstone of their empire. Some of the important tasting was still done in the car. Mr. HJ might have reports in his pocket from sales executives and marketing analysts, from home economists and chemists, but not until Mr. Johnson reached over the lowered Plexiglas to spoon a taste or two into the expert waiting mouth of Otis Brighton did he make any final flavor decision. He might go ahead with butterfly shrimp, with candy kisses, and with packaged chocolate-chip cookies on the opinion of the specialists, but in ice cream he trusted only Otis. From the back seat Howard Johnson would keep his eye on the rearview mirror, where the reflection of pleasure or disgust showed itself in the dark eyes of Otis Brighton no matter what the driving conditions. He could be stalled in a commuter rush with the engine overheating and a dripping oil pan, and still a taste of the right kind never went unappreciated.

When Otis finally said, "Mr. Howard, that shore is sumpin, that one is um-hum. That is it, my man, that is it." Then and not until then did Mr. HJ finally decide to go ahead with something like banana-fudge-ripple royale.

Mildred rarely tasted and Mr. HJ was addicted to one scoop of vanilla every afternoon at three, eaten from his aluminum dish with a disposable plastic spoon. The duties of Otis, Millie, and Mr. Johnson were so divided that they rarely infringed upon one another in the car, which was their office. Neither Mr. HJ nor Millie knew how to drive, Millie and Otis understood little of financing and leasing, and Mr. HJ left the compiling of the "Traveling Reports" and "The Howard Johnson Newsletter" strictly to the literary style of his longtime associate, Miss Mildred Bryce. It was an ideal division of labor, which, in one form or another, had been in continuous operation for well over a quarter of a century.

While Otis listened to the radio behind his soundproof Plexiglas, while Millie in her small, neat hand compiled data for the newsletter, Mr. HJ liked to lean back into the spongy leather seat looking through his specially tinted windshield at the fleeting land. Occasionally, lulled by the hum of the freezer, he might doze off, his large pink head lolling toward the shoulder of his blue suit, but there was not too much that Mr. Johnson missed, even in advanced age.

Along with Millie he planned their continuous itinerary as they traveled. Mildred would tape a large green relief map of the United States to the Plexiglas separating them from Otis. The mountains on the map were light brown and seemed to melt toward the valleys like the crust of a fresh apple pie settling into cinnamon surroundings. The existing HJ houses (Millie called the restaurants and motels houses) were marked by orange dots, while projected future sites bore white dots. The deep green map with its brown mountains and colorful dots seemed much more alive than the miles that twinkled past Mr. Johnson's gaze, and nothing gave the ice-cream king greater pleasure than watching Mildred with her fine touch, and using the original crayon, turn an empty white dot into an orange fulfillment.

"It's like a seed grown into a tree, Millie," Mr. HJ liked to say at such moments when he contemplated the map and saw that it was good.

They had started traveling together in 1925: Mildred, then a secretary to Mr. Johnson, a young man with two restaurants and a dream of hospitality, and Otis, a twenty-year-old busboy and former driver of a Louisiana mule. When Mildred graduated from college, her father, a Michigan doctor who kept his money in a blue steel box under the examining table, encouraged her to try the big city. He sent her a monthly allowance. In those early days she always had more than Mr. Johnson, who paid her $16.50 a week and meals. In the first decade they traveled only on weekends, but every year since 1936 they had spent at least six months on the road, and it might have gone on much longer if Mildred's pain and the trouble in New York with Howard Jr. had not come so close together.

． ． ．

They were all stoical at the Los Angeles International Airport. Otis waited at the car for what might be his last job while Miss Bryce and Mr. Johnson traveled toward the New York plane along a silent moving floor. Millie stood beside Howard while they passed a mural of a Mexican landscape and some Christmas drawings by fourth graders from Watts. For forty years they had been together in spite of Sonny and the others, but at this most recent appeal from New York Millie urged him to go back. Sonny had cabled, "My God, Dad, you're sixty-nine years old, haven't you been a gypsy long enough? Board meeting December third with or without you. Policy changes imminent."

Normally, they ignored Sonny's cables, but this time Millie wanted him to go, wanted to be alone with the pain that had recently come to her. She had left Howard holding the new canvas suitcase in which she had packed her three notebooks of regional reports along with his aluminum dish, and in a moment of real despair she had even packed the orange crayon. When Howard boarded Flight 965 he looked old to Millie. His feet dragged in the wing-tipped shoes, the hand she shook was moist, the lip felt dry, and as he passed from her sight down the entry ramp Mildred Bryce felt a fresh new ache that sent her hobbling toward the car. Otis had unplugged the freezer, and the silence caused by the missing hum was as intense to Millie as her abdominal pain.

It had come quite suddenly in Albuquerque, New Mexico, at the grand opening of a 210-unit house. She did not make a fuss. Mildred Bryce had never caused trouble to anyone, except perhaps to Mrs. HJ. Millie's quick precise actions, angular face, and thin body made her seem birdlike, especially next to Mr. HJ, six three with splendid white hair accenting his dark blue gabardine suits. Howard was slow and sure. He could sit in the same position for hours while Millie fidgeted on the seat, wrote memos, and filed reports in the small gray cabinet that sat in front of her and parallel to the ice-cream freezer. Her health had always been good, so at first she tried to ignore the pain. It was gas: it was perhaps the New Mexico water or the cooking oil in the fish dinner. But she could not convince away the pain. It stayed like a match burning around in her belly, etching itself into her as the round HJ emblem was so symmetrically embroidered into the bedspread, which she had kicked off in the flush that accompanied the pain. She felt as if her sweat would engulf the foam mattress and crisp percale sheet. Finally, Millie brought up her knees and made a ball of herself as if being as small as possible might make her misery disappear. It worked for everything except the pain. The little circle of hot torment was all that remained of her, and when finally at sometime in the early morning it left, it occurred to her that perhaps she had struggled with a demon and been suddenly relieved by the coming of daylight. She stepped lightly into the bathroom and before a full-length mirror (new in HJ motels exclusively) saw herself whole and unmarked, but sign enough to Mildred was her smell, damp and musty, sign enough that something had begun and that something else would therefore necessarily end.

II

Before she had the report from her doctor, Howard Jr.'s message had given her the excuse she needed. There was no reason why Millie could not tell Howard she was sick, but telling him would be admitting too much to herself. Along with Howard Johnson Millie had grown rich beyond dreams. Her inheritance, the $100,000 from her father's steel box in 1939, went directly to Mr. Johnson, who desperately needed it, and the results of that investment brought Millie enough capital to employ two people at the Chase Manhattan with the management of her finances. With money beyond the hope of use, she had vacationed all over the world and spent some time in the company of celebrities, but the reality of her life, like his, was in the back seat of the limousine, waiting for that point at which the needs of the automobile and the human body met the undeviating purpose of the highway and momentarily conquered it.

Her life was measured in rest stops. She, Howard, and Otis had found them out before they existed. They knew the places to stop between Buffalo and Albany, Chicago and Milwaukee, Toledo and Columbus, Des Moines and Minneapolis, they knew through their own bodies, measured in hunger and discomfort in the '30s and '40s when they would stop at remote places to buy land and borrow money, sensing in themselves the hunger that would one day be upon the place. People were wary and Howard had trouble borrowing (her $100,000 had perhaps been the key) but invariably he was right. Howard knew the land, Mildred thought, the way the Indians must have known it. There were even spots along the way where the earth itself seemed to make men stop. Howard had a sixth sense that would sometimes lead them from the main roads to, say, a dark green field in Iowa or Kansas. Howard, who might have seemed asleep, would rap with his knuckles on the Plexiglas, causing the knowing Otis to bring the car to such a quick stop that Millie almost flew into her filing cabinet. And before the emergency brake had settled into its final prong, Howard Johnson was into the field and after the scent. While Millie and Otis waited, he would walk it out slowly. Sometimes he would sit down, disappearing in a field of long and tangled weeds, or he might find a large smooth rock to sit on while he felt some secret vibration from the place. Turning his back to Millie, he would mark the spot with his urine or break some of the clayey earth in his strong pink hands, sifting it like flour for a delicate recipe. She had actually seen him chew the grass, getting down on all fours like an animal and biting the tops without pulling the entire blade from the soil. At times he ran in a slow jog as far as his aging legs would carry him. Whenever he slipped out of sight behind the uneven terrain, Millie felt him in danger, felt that something alien might be there to resist the civilizing instinct of Howard Johnson. Once when Howard had been out of sight for more than an hour and did not respond to their frantic calls, Millie sent Otis into the field and in desperation flagged a passing car.

"Howard Johnson is lost in that field," she told the surprised driver. "He went in to look for a new location and we can't find him now."

"The restaurant Howard Johnson?" the man asked.

"Yes. Help us please."

The man drove off, leaving Millie to taste in his exhaust fumes the barbarism of an ungrateful public. Otis found Howard asleep in a field of light blue wild flowers. He had collapsed from the exertion of his run. Millie brought water to him, and when he felt better, right there in the field, he ate his scoop of vanilla on the very spot where three years later they opened the first fully air-conditioned motel in the world. When she stopped to think about it, Millie knew they were more than businessmen, they were pioneers. And once, while on her own, she had the feeling too. In 1951 when she visited the Holy Land there was an inkling of what Howard must have felt all the time. It happened without any warning on a bus crowded with tourists and resident Arabs on their way to the Dead Sea. Past ancient Sodom the bus creaked and bumped, down, down, toward the lowest point on earth, when suddenly in the midst of the crowd and her stomach queasy with the motion of the bus, Mildred Bryce experienced an overwhelming calm. A light brown patch of earth surrounded by a few pale desert rocks overwhelmed her perception, seemed closer to her than the Arab lady in the black flowered dress pushing her basket against Millie at that very moment. She wanted to stop the bus. Had she been near the door she might have actually jumped, so strong was her sensitivity to that barren spot in the endless desert. Her whole body ached for it as if in unison, bone by bone. Her limbs tingled, her breath came in short gasps, the sky rolled out of the bus windows and obliterated her view. The Arab lady spat on the floor and moved a suspicious eye over a squirming Mildred.

When the bus stopped at the Dead Sea, the Arabs and tourists rushed to the soupy brine clutching damaged limbs, while Millie pressed twenty dollars American into the dirty palm of a cab-driver who took her back to the very place where the music of her body began once more as sweetly as the first time. While the incredulous driver waited, Millie walked about the place wishing Howard were there to understand her new understanding of his kind of process. There was nothing there, absolutely nothing but pure bliss. The sun beat on her like a wish, the air was hot and stale as a Viennese bathhouse, and yet Mildred felt peace and rest there, and as her cab bill mounted she actually did rest in the miserable barren desert of an altogether unsatisfactory land. When the driver, wiping the sweat from his neck, asked, "Meesez . . . pleeze. Why American woman wants Old Jericho in such kind of heat?" When he said "Jericho," she understood that this was a place where men had always stopped. In dim antiquity Jacob had perhaps watered a flock here, and not far away Lot's wife paused to scan for the last time the city of her youth. Perhaps Mildred now stood where Abraham had been visited by a vision and, making a rock his pillow, had first put the ease into the earth. Whatever it was, Millie knew from her own experience that rest was created here by historical precedent. She tried to buy that piece of land, going as far as King Hussein's secretary of the interior. She imagined a Palestinian HJ with an orange roof angling toward Sodom, a seafood restaurant, and an oasis of fresh fruit. But the land was in dispute between Israel and Jordan, and even King Hussein, who expressed admiration for Howard Johnson, could not sell to Millie the place of her comfort.

That was her single visionary moment, but sharing them with Howard was almost as good. And to end all this, to finally stay in her eighteenth-floor Santa Monica penthouse, where the Pacific dived into California, this seemed to Mildred a paltry conclusion to an adventurous life. Her doctor said it was not so serious, she had a bleeding ulcer and must watch her diet. The prognosis was, in fact, excellent. But Mildred, fifty-six and alone in California, found the doctor less comforting than most of the rest stops she had experienced.

III

California, right after the Second World War, was hardly a civilized place for travelers. Millie, HJ, and Otis had a twelve-cylinder '47 Lincoln and snaked along five days between Sacramento and Los Angeles. "Comfort, comfort," said HJ as he surveyed the redwood forest and the bubbly surf while it slipped away from Otis, who had rolled his trousers to chase the ocean away during a stop near San Francisco. Howard Johnson was contemplative in California. They had never been in the West before. Their route, always slightly new, was yet bound by Canada, where a person couldn't get a tax break, and roughly by the Mississippi as a western frontier. Their journeys took them up the eastern seaboard and through New England to the early reaches of the Midwest, stopping at the plains of Wisconsin and the cool crisp edge of Chicago where two HJ lodges twinkled at the lake.

One day in 1947 while on the way from Chicago to Cairo, Illinois, HJ looked long at the green relief maps. While Millie kept busy with her filing, HJ loosened the tape and placed the map across his soft round knees. The map jiggled and sagged, the Mid- and Southwest hanging between his legs. When Mildred finally noticed that look, he had been staring at the map for perhaps fifteen minutes, brooding over it, and Millie knew something was in the air.

HJ looked at that map the way some people looked down from an airplane trying to pick out the familiar from the colorful mass receding beneath them. Howard Johnson's eye flew over the land—over the Tetons, over the Sierra Nevada, over the long thin gouge of the Canyon flew his gaze—charting his course by rest stops the way an antique mariner might have gazed at the stars.

"Millie," he said just north of Carbondale, "Millie . . ." He looked toward her, saw her fingers engaged and her thumbs circling each other in anticipation. He looked at Millie and saw that she saw what he saw. "Millie"—HJ raised his right arm and its shadow spread across the continent like a prophecy—"Millie, what if we turn right at Cairo and go that way?" California, already peeling on the green map, balanced on HJ's left knee like a happy child.

Twenty years later Mildred settled in her eighteenth-floor apartment in the building owned by Lawrence Welk. Howard was in New York, Otis and the car waited in Arizona. The pain did not return as powerfully as it had appeared that night in Albuquerque, but it hurt with dull regularity and an occasional streak of dark blood from her bowels kept her mind on it even on painless days.

Directly beneath her gaze were the organized activities of the golden-age groups, tiny figures playing bridge or shuffleboard or looking out at the water from their benches as she sat on her sofa and looked out at them and the fluffy ocean. Mildred did not regret family life. The HJ houses were her offspring. She had watched them blossom from the rough youngsters of the '40s with steam heat and even occasional kitchenettes into cool mature adults with king-sized beds, color TVs, and room service. Her late years were spent comfortably in the modern houses just as one might enjoy in age the benefits of a child's prosperity. She regretted only that it was probably over.

• • •

But she did not give up completely until she received a personal letter one day telling her that she was eligible for burial insurance until age eighty. A $1000 policy would guarantee a complete and dignified service. Millie crumpled the advertisement, but a few hours later called her Los Angeles lawyer. As she suspected, there were no plans, but as the executor of the estate he would assume full responsibility, subject of course to her approval.

"I'll do it myself," Millie had said, but she could not bring herself to do it. The idea was too alien. In more than forty years Mildred had not gone a day without a shower and change of underclothing. Everything about her suggested order and precision. Her fingernails were shaped so that the soft meat of the tips could stroke a typewriter without damaging the apex of a nail, her arch slid over a 6B shoe like an egg in a shell, and never in her adult life did Mildred recall having vomited. It did not seem right to suddenly let all this sink into the dark green earth of Forest Lawn because some organ or other developed a hole as big as a nickel. It was not right and she wouldn't do it. Her first idea was to stay in the apartment, to write it into the lease if necessary. She had the lawyer make an appointment for her with Mr. Welk's management firm, but canceled it the day before. "They will just think I'm crazy," she said aloud to herself, "and they'll bury me anyway."

She thought of cryonics while reading a biography of William Chesebrough, the man who invented petroleum jelly. Howard had known him and often mentioned that his own daily ritual of the scoop of vanilla was like old Chesebrough's two teaspoons of Vaseline every day. Chesebrough lived to be ninety. In the biography it said that after taking the daily dose of Vaseline, he drank three cups of green tea to melt everything down, rested for twelve minutes, and then felt fit as a young man, even in his late eighties. When he died they froze his body and Millie had her idea. The Vaseline people kept him in a secret laboratory somewhere near Cleveland and claimed he was in better condition than Lenin, whom the Russians kept hermetically sealed, but at room temperature.

In the phone book she found the Los Angeles Cryonic Society and asked it to send her information. It all seemed very clean. The cost was $200 a year for maintaining the cold. She sent the pamphlet to her lawyer to be sure that the society was legitimate. It wasn't much money, but, still, if they were charlatans, she didn't want them to take advantage of her even if she would never know about it. They were aboveboard, the lawyer said. "The interest on a ten-thousand-dollar trust fund would pay about five hundred a year," the lawyer said, "and they only charge two hundred dollars. Still, who knows what the cost might be in say two hundred years?" To be extra safe, they put $25,000 in trust for eternal maintenance, to be eternally overseen by Longstreet, Williams, and their eternal heirs. When it was arranged, Mildred felt better than she had in weeks.

IV

Four months to the day after she had left Howard at the Los Angeles International Airport, he returned for Mildred without the slightest warning. She was in her housecoat and had not even washed the night cream from her cheeks when she saw through the viewing space in her door the familiar long pink jowls, even longer in the distorted glass.

"Howard," she gasped, fumbling with the door, and in an instant he was there picking her up as he might a child or an ice-cream cone while her tears fell like dandruff on his blue suit. While Millie sobbed into his soft padded shoulder, HJ told her the good news. "I'm chairman emeritus of the board now. That means no more New York responsibilities. They still have to listen to me because we hold the majority of the stock, but Howard Junior and Keyes will take care of the business. Our main job is new home-owned franchises. And, Millie, guess where we're going first?"

So overcome was Mildred that she could not hold back her sobs even to guess. Howard Johnson put her down, beaming pleasure through his old bright eyes. "Florida," HJ said, then slowly repeated it, "Floridda, and guess what we're going to do?"

"Howard," Millie said, swiping at her tears with the filmy lace cuffs of her dressing gown, "I'm so surprised I don't know what to say. You could tell me we're going to the moon and I'd believe you. Just seeing you again has brought back all my hope." They came out of the hallway and sat on the sofa that looked out over the Pacific. HJ, all pink, kept his hands on his knees like paperweights.

"Millie, you're almost right. I can't fool you about anything and never could. We're going down near where they launch the rockets from. I've heard . . ." HJ leaned toward the kitchen as if to check for spies. He looked at the stainless-steel-and-glass table, at the built-in avocado appliances, then leaned his large moist lips toward Mildred's ear. "Walt Disney is planning right this minute a new Disneyland down there. They're trying to keep it a secret, but his brother Roy bought options on thousands of acres. We're going down to buy as much as we can as close in as we can." Howard sparkled. "Millie, don't you see, it's a sure thing."

After her emotional outburst at seeing Howard again, a calmer Millie felt a slight twitch in her upper stomach and in the midst of her joy was reminded of another sure thing.

They would be a few weeks in Los Angeles anyway. Howard wanted to thoroughly scout out the existing Disneyland, so Millie had some time to think it out. She could go, as her heart directed her, with HJ to Florida and points beyond. She could take the future as it happened like a Disneyland ride or she could listen to the dismal eloquence of her ulcer and try to make the best arrangements she could. Howard and Otis would take care of her to the end, there were no doubts about that, and the end would be the end. But if she stayed in this apartment, sure of the arrangements for later, she would miss whatever might still be left before the end. Mildred wished there were some clergyman she could consult, but she had never attended a church and believed in no religious doctrine. Her father had been a firm atheist to the very moment of his office suicide, and she remained a passive nonbeliever. Her theology was the order of her own life. Millie had never deceived herself; in spite of her riches all she truly owned was her life, a pocket of habits in the burning universe. But the habits were careful and clean and they were best represented in the body that was she. Freezing her remains was the closest image she could conjure of eternal life. It might not be eternal and it surely would not be life, but that damp, musty feel, that odor she smelled on herself after the pain, that could be avoided, and who knew what else might be saved from the void for a small initial investment and $200 a year. And if you did not believe in a soul, was there not every reason to preserve a body?

• • •

Mrs. Albert of the Cryonic Society welcomed Mildred to a tour of the premises. "See it while you can," she cheerfully told the group (Millie, two men, and a boy with notebook and Polaroid camera). Mrs. Albert, a big woman perhaps in her mid-sixties, carried a face heavy in flesh. Perhaps once the skin had been tight around her long chin and pointed cheekbones, but having lost its spring, the skin merely hung at her neck like a patient animal waiting for the rest of her to join in the decline. From the way she took the concrete stairs down to the vault, it looked as if the wait would be long. "I'm not ready for the freezer yet. I tell every group I take down here, it's gonna be a long time until they get me." Millie believed her. "I may not be the world's smartest cookie"—Mrs. Albert looked directly at Millie—"but a bird in the hand is the only bird I know, huh? That's why when it does come . . . Mrs. A is going to be right here in this facility, and you better believe it. Now, Mr. King on your left"—she pointed to a capsule that looked like a large bullet to Millie—"Mr. King is the gentleman who took me on my first tour, cancer finally but had everything perfectly ready and I would say he was in prime cooling state within seconds and I believe that if they ever cure cancer, and you know they will the way they do most everything nowadays, old Mr. King may be back yet. If anyone got down to low-enough temperature immediately it would be Mr. King." Mildred saw the boy write "Return of the King" in his notebook. "Over here is Mr. and Mizz Winkleman, married sixty years, and went off within a month of each other, a lovely, lovely couple."

While Mrs. Albert continued her necrology and posed for a photo beside the Winklemans, Millie took careful note of the neon-lit room filled with bulletlike capsules. She watched the cool breaths of the group gather like flowers on the steel and vanish without dimming the bright surface. The capsules stood in straight lines with ample walking space between them. To Mrs. Albert they were friends, to Millie it seemed as if she were in a furniture store of the Scandinavian type where elegance is suggested by the absence of material, where straight lines of steel, wood, and glass indicate that relaxation too requires some taste and is not an indifferent sprawl across any soft object that happens to be nearby.

Cemeteries always bothered Millie, but here she felt none of the dread she had expected. She averted her eyes from the cluttered graveyards they always used to pass at the tips of cities in the early days. Fortunately, the superhighways twisted traffic into the city and away from those desolate marking places where used-car lots and the names of famous hotels inscribed on barns often neighbored the dead. Howard had once commented that never in all his experience did he have an intuition of a good location near a cemetery. You could put a lot of things there, you could put up a bowling alley, or maybe even a theater, but never a motel, and Millie knew he was right. He knew where to put his houses but it was Millie who knew how. From that first orange roof angling toward the east, the HJ design and the idea had been Millie's. She had not invented the motel, she had changed it from a place where you had to be to a place where you wanted to be. Perhaps, she thought, the Cryonic Society was trying to do the same for cemeteries.

When she and Howard had started their travels, the old motel courts huddled like so many dark graves around the stone marking of the highway. And what traveler coming into one of those dingy cabins could watch the watery rust dripping from his faucet without thinking of everything he was missing by being a traveler . . . his two-stall garage, his wife small in the half-empty bed, his children with hair the color of that rust. Under the orange Howard Johnson roof all this changed. For about the same price you were redeemed from the road. Headlights did not dazzle you on the foam mattress and percale sheets, your sanitized glasses and toilet appliances sparkled like the mirror behind them. The room was not just there, it awaited you, courted your pleasure, sat like a young bride outside the walls of the city wanting only to please you, you only you on the smoothly pressed sheets, your friend, your one-night destiny.

As if it were yesterday, Millie recalled right there in the cryonic vault the moment when she had first thought the thought that made Howard Johnson Howard Johnson's. And when she told Howard her decision that evening after cooking a cheese soufflé and risking a taste of wine, it was that memory she invoked for both of them, the memory of a cool autumn day in the '30s when a break in their schedule found Millie with a free afternoon in New Hampshire, an afternoon she had spent at the farm of a man who had once been her teacher and remembered her after ten years. Otis drove her out to Robert Frost's farm, where the poet made for her a lunch of scrambled eggs and 7-Up. Millie and Robert Frost talked mostly about the farm, about the cold winter he was expecting and the autumn apples they picked from the trees. He was not so famous then, his hair was only streaked with gray as Howard's was, and she told the poet about what she and Howard were doing, about what she felt about being on the road in America, and Robert Frost said he hadn't been that much but she sounded like she knew and he believed she might be able to accomplish something. He did not remember the poem she wrote in his class but that didn't matter.

"Do you remember, Howard, how I introduced you to him? Mr. Frost, this is Mr. Johnson. I can still see the two of you shaking hands there beside the car. I've always been proud that I introduced you to one another." Howard Johnson nodded his head at the memory, seemed as nostalgic as Millie while he sat in her apartment learning why she would not go to Florida to help bring Howard Johnson's to the new Disneyland.

"And after we left his farm, Howard, remember? Otis took the car in for servicing and left us with some sandwiches on the top of a hill overlooking a town, I don't even remember which one, maybe we never knew the name of it. And we stayed on that hilltop while the sun began to set in New Hampshire. I felt so full of poetry and"—she looked at Howard—"of love, Howard, only about an hour's drive from Robert Frost's farmhouse. Maybe it was just the way we felt then, but I think the sun set differently that night, filtering through the clouds like a big paintbrush making the top of the town all orange. And suddenly I thought what if the tops of our houses were that kind of orange, what a world it would be, Howard, and my God, that orange stayed until the last drop of light was left in it. I didn't feel the cold up there even though it took Otis so long to get back to us. The feeling we had about that orange, Howard, that was ours and that's what I've tried to bring to every house, the way we felt that night. Oh, it makes me sick to think of Colonel Sanders, and Big Boy, and Holiday Inn, and Best Western . . ."

"It's all right, Millie, it's all right." Howard patted her heaving back. Now that he knew about her ulcer and why she wanted to stay behind, the mind that had conjured butterfly shrimp and twenty-eight flavors set himself a new project. He contemplated Millie sobbing in his lap the way he contemplated prime acreage. There was so little of her, less than one hundred pounds, yet without her Howard Johnson felt himself no match for the wily Disneys gathering near the moonport.

He left her in all her sad resignation that evening, left her thinking she had to give up what remained here to be sure of the proper freezing. But Howard Johnson had other ideas. He did not cancel the advance reservations made for Mildred Bryce along the route to Florida, nor did he remove her filing cabinet from the limousine. The man who hosted a nation and already kept one freezer in his car merely ordered another, this one designed according to cryonic specifications and presented to Mildred housed in a twelve-foot orange U-Haul trailer connected to the rear bumper of the limousine.

"Everything's here," he told the astonished Millie, who thought Howard had left the week before, "everything is here and you'll never have to be more than seconds away from it. It's exactly like a refrigerated truck." Howard Johnson opened the rear door of the U-Haul as proudly as he had ever dedicated a motel. Millie's steel capsule shone within, surrounded by an array of chemicals stored on heavily padded rubber shelves. The California sun was on her back, but her cold breath hovered visibly within the U-Haul. No tears came to Mildred now; she felt relief much as she had felt it that afternoon near ancient Jericho. On Santa Monica Boulevard, in front of Lawrence Welk's apartment building, Mildred Bryce confronted her immortality, a gift from the ice-cream king, another companion for the remainder of her travels. Howard Johnson had turned away, looking toward the ocean. To his blue back and patriarchal white hairs, Mildred said, "Howard, you can do anything," and closing the doors of the U-Haul, she joined the host of the highways, a man with two portable freezers, ready now for the challenge of Disney World.

Roy Blount, Jr.

*

TRASH NO MORE

I cannot help having a deep interest in the welfare of the State of Georgia and of the South as a whole. Still I never go into that part of the country and come away without a certain sense of sadness. One can enjoy oneself superficially, but one must shut one's eyes.
—ELEANOR ROOSEVELT

The world has heaped contumely on my people, even on the one of us who is President. But do we try to make people feel guilty for the misunderstanding? No. Do we file anti-defamation suits? No. That ain't my people's way. We don't even like to *wear* suits. And when we piss and moan, we piss and moan *music*. Otherwise, we just go on about our business, and wait for you to come South and then sell you spiritually tainted souvenirs. That's right. Like those ashtrays you get along the highway that have a picture of an outhouse with a voice coming from inside it, saying,

I'm the Only Man in
GEORGIA
Who Knows What He's Doing

Those ashtrays have got a taint put on them, which—since you all don't know how to live with original sin—makes you nervous and irritable and rootless and in need of psychiatry.

That might explain a lot. That might explain why Jimmy Carter's

Health, Education, and Welfare Department is trying to stamp out smoking and yet in the same breath, so to speak, Jimmy goes down to North Carolina and announces that he sees no conflict between tobacco production and national health goals. He calls for research to make smoking "even more safe than it is today." So safe you could probably drive without a seat belt while doing it. He says this on the same day that the American Medical Association issues a report that cigarettes can cause irreversible damage not only to your lungs but also to your arteries and heart.

See, he can't just completely close down smoking, because that would kill the tainted-outhouse-ashtray program. There's probably a similar reasoning behind his marijuana policy—come out for decriminalizing it and then poison it with parraquat and then have your drug-program head, I believe they called him, tell reporters that your aides smoke it a lot. It's all designed to confuse the North, to get on the North's nerves. I guess. But, hell, I don't know.

Sometimes, I just don't know.

> I got the redneck White House blues.
> Look at him up there on the news.
> The President's from Georgia
>   but still we owe dues.
> I got the redneck White House blues.

It was the spring before Freedom Summer, when flights of clear-eyed Northern late adolescents would go South to help prove to the world what dumb-asses my people could be (a crusade that would be physically brave, morally impeccable, and, if you don't mind my saying so, no more imaginative than dynamiting fish). It was the spring of '64, then, and I was in Harvard Graduate School studying English literature, which for the most part was like learning about women at the Mayo Clinic. And one afternoon this African got up in my favorite class, Difficult Fiction, and denounced William Faulkner for his treatment of "non-Western people."

Reading from a prepared text, in a way that struck me as unnaturally . . . *crisp*, this African averred that all the non-Western people (which was to say, all the non-rednecks) in Faulkner were rendered as savage, stoic, menial, or deranged, and none of them was seen from within—and how, then, could Faulkner be countenanced at Harvard?

"Well, got DAMN it," was my reaction.

I stood up and spluttered.

Spluttered as cogently as a person can splutter who is trying to say something he always thought went without saying. In the name of art; of Faulkner; of Clytie; of Joe Christmas; of stoicism; of derangement; of savagery; of my interior voice; and of not presuming to get any further inside anybody than you can *feel* your way. And as I spluttered, I felt— more harshly than I ever had in the South while urging race-mixing or even pooh-poohing major football—a climate of opinion setting in around me.

I had managed to simplify my classmates' thinking, to raise a clear moral issue: this guy with the redneck accent is so dumb as to hate this passing African.

I *liked* this class. I liked Mr. Monroe Engel, who taught it, though he hadn't had much to say to me since he'd found out that I was going into the army the following year. I liked not only *Absalom, Absalom!* but also *What Maisie Knew* and *The Good Soldier* and *Under the Volcano* and the other books we read. All my life I had wanted to be somewhere where people argued about books. (At Vanderbilt, where I had just spent four years, we had had grotesque race-relations arguments, punctuated by well-reared coeds' savage cries of "Would you want to take a *shower* with them?") And now that I had reached such a place, I found myself dismissed as a person with an incriminating accent. "Well, just kiss my ass, all of you all," I thought partly, but only *partly*.

> I got the redneck White House blues.
> Even when we win one, we lose.
> The President's from Georgia,
>   but he's wearing shoes.
> I got the redneck White House blues.

After class, I spoke with the African, who didn't seem to feel like he belonged there either, and we went and played some tennis, but he didn't play like any African I had imagined. He played with grimly classic strokes, whereas I whanged loose-wristedly the way I'd learned to hit a baseball on the red clay back home.

But I can't claim to have been what is known as "a country boy." My grandparents and great-grandparents were farmers and carpenters and railroad workers, but my daddy mobilized his way up to national prominence in savings and loan, and I was raised in a town of 28,000 right outside Atlanta. The only way I ever got my neck red was playing Little League baseball, or fishing for croakers on vacation, or catching bees in Mason jars with Sandy Penick and Sally Everett, or doing yard-work under duress. I only followed a plow once, and that was on a field trip with the Explorer Scouts. I broke about four and a half feet of new ground under the July afternoon sun and felt dizzy and went and hid behind some bushes with some other Explorers until the Scoutmaster, who had come up with this plowing idea, and who *had* been a country boy, came and dragged us out.

I can't even speak as one who was a real Boy Scout. I didn't much like to water ski or sleep in tents full of bugs. I wanted to be by myself and imagine I was playing major-league ball, which took place some-where way off on a higher plane, where movies and the federal govern-ment and magazines came from and where they argued about books. I wanted to meet some Jews. We only had one in Decatur, and he was a Presbyterian. And I wanted to contribute to the media, from which I gathered that all the stuff I grew up with was low and corny.

Not quintessentially low and corny, which might have been sort of exciting. ("Hey, look here in 'Lil Abner,' there's a pitcher of Daddy!") But just for-all-intents-and-purposes low and corny. You might say I grew up sort of rosy-necked. Which means that if you were to call me that, I'd feel obliged to try to whip your ass (this is just talk, though) in a semi-detached way.

But I've put all that behind me, except in my mind. I have left the South, bodily, and have resided right happily on a fairly high-crime New York street and come to know Arnold Schwarzenegger, Gilda Radner, and Elaine. I have appeared in a photograph in the *Daily News* as part of a crowd watching a shoot-out, and I have written for the best maga-zine and the best newspaper in the world, and for a lot of other ones.

And up here on the national level I have often felt like a man who has been diagnosed crazy, and who has worried about it and resolved to improve, and then has visited a psychiatrists' convention, and finds him-self saying, "Yeah, I sure am crazy. I'm extremely crazy," so nobody will take him for a psychiatrist.

But don't get me wrong. I'm a hard-core First Amendment boy. I'm always eager to be the first to amend something; and, too, I cling to the thought that people who put out publications have more sense, in some ways, than people who read them, or at least more than the ones who write letters to the editor. Still and all, one of the main things I have learned since leaving the South is that all those Northern institutions from which I gathered that my culture was low and corny and crazy have their own ways of being low and corny and crazy.

It's not so much my people who are crazy as it is the human mind. This is a hard thought, and one which my people have been instrumental in keeping off most people's minds for a number of years. My people have taken on the role of being crazy for *everybody*. Which is what I thought Jimmy would do, in a new and educational way.

But I'm having a hard time figuring out how he has.

> I got the redneck White House blues.
> I'm tired of all these synthesized views.
> Half of him is Vance's,
>   the other Zbigniew's.
> I got the redneck White House blues.

He don't look like much of a redneck, I know. Most of the time he looks, and sounds, like a man who's come down from a slightly higher level of church administration to give a talk to your congregation on good sound business reasons why you ought to tithe.

But he *said* he was a redneck, when he ran for governor. And I thought that might count for something when he got elected President.

I liked it when Senator Edward Brooke of Massachusetts complained, "When you get to the White House, the place looks physically dirty. People running around in jeans, it just doesn't look right."

"Lord!" I thought to myself when I read that. "We have done something now! This is a great day for both our peoples, when you think about it. We have established that a famous black man can be anal-repressive."

And I liked it when Mark Russell—the supposed Washington *satirist*, Lord help us, this is what they have in that town for a *satirist*—got offended by Hamilton Jordan's referring to Pennsylvania Avenue as Pennsylvania Street. "Now everybody knows about Pennsylvania Avenue and what it means to us here," Russell was quoted as harrumphing, in an in-depth story on the administration's shortcomings in *People* magazine.

You know what else I liked? I liked Jimmy in that *Playboy* interview. It sounded to me exactly like what an open, sincere Baptist who has seen something of the world through Baptist eyes *ought* to say in *Playboy*. That was a Baptist id and a Baptist ego and a Baptist superego out there wrestling in full view of the nation, and that is the kind of thing I think of as honorable exposure. It mixed piety and the flesh in the best tradition of country music.

I wish he'd come out with more of that kind of stuff. That's real-life stuff. Back during the campaign, when Earl Butz was quoted as saying that all black folks want is "a tight pussy, loose shoes, and a warm place to shit," I wish Jimmy had responded by saying it sounded like a set of priorities that a lot of people could identify with.

I liked it when Jimmy was giving Andy Young leeway to bring things out into the open. I don't want people to be *right* all the time. I want them to let us in on their thinking.

Of course, I guess that's hard to do when there are forty-four thousand cameras, note pads, printing presses, teletype machines, deadlines, headlines, commentators, potshotters, leakers, and layers of ignorance between you and the people you are talking to. But surely in the long run openness resists mistranslation better than secrecy does. That was in fact supposed to be a tenet of Jimmy's administration—and Jimmy's *subordinates*, for a while there, were working various veins of disclosure. But Jimmy himself got defensive; he seized up. And then he seized up the rest of them.

· · ·

What if, instead of old Why Not the Best Jimmy, it had been Kissing Jim Folsom who came up out of the darkest South to be President? When Folsom was governor of Alabama, he used to appear in public forums barefooted, because that felt even better to him sometimes than loose shoes. He would lie down flat on sidewalks or auditorium stages barefooted, drunk, and in control of the situation, with no hint of *straining after image*. And he was liberal-minded. In his gubernatorial Christmas message in 1949, he said, "As long as the Negroes are held down by deprivation and lack of opportunity, all the other people will be held down alongside them." You notice he didn't say "all *us* other people." And he kept on talking that way through the fifties and sixties. He vetoed segregation bills and served Adam Clayton Powell whiskey in the governor's mansion. Once Kissing Jim had a whole lot of dignitaries out on his yacht watching a performance by the Alabama Air National Guard. He was bragging about all the new planes the Guard had and what they could do. Several of the planes took off and started looping around impressively, and then something went wrong with one of them, and it plunged into the water and exploded into fire and foam.

The first to break the silence was Folsom.

"Kiss my ass," he said, "if that ain't a show."

Now there may have been an element of apparent insensitivity in that, but sometimes a President has to seem hard. If old Jim had gotten to be Chief Executive, it might have bucked him up to the point that he wouldn't have let liquor cut into his effectiveness, and there is no telling what he would have accomplished in the way of relieving awkward national pauses.

> I got the redneck White House blues.
> The South's not gonna rise, but just diffuse.
> Have you heard that country album
>   by Julie Andrews?
> I got the redneck White House blues.

Veronica Geng

*

MY MAO

"Kay, would you like a dog? . . ." Ike asked.
"Would I? Oh, General, having a dog would be heaven!"
"Well," he grinned, "if you want one, we'll get one."

—"Past Forgetting: My Love Affair
with Dwight D. Eisenhower."

"I don't want you to be alone," he said after a while.
"I'm used to it."
"No, I want you to have a dog."

—"A Loving Gentleman: The Love Story
of William Faulkner and Meta Carpenter."

Why this reminiscence, this public straining of noodles in the colander of memory? The Chairman despised loose talk. Each time we parted, he would seal my lips together with spirit gum and whisper, "Mum for Mao." During our ten-year relationship, we quarrelled only once—when I managed to dissolve the spirit gum with nail-polish remover and told my best friend about us, and it got back to a relative of the Chairman's in Mongolia. These things happen; somebody always knows somebody. But for one month the Chairman kept up a punishing silence, even though we had agreed to write each other daily when it was not possible to be together. Finally, he cabled this directive: "ANGRILY ATTACK THE CRIMES OF SILLY BLABBERMOUTHS." I knew then that I was forgiven; his love ever wore the tailored gray uniform of instruction.

Until now, writing a book about this well-known man has been the farthest thing from my mind—except perhaps for writing a book about someone else. I lacked shirts with cuffs to jot memorandums on when he left the room. I was innocent of boudoir electronics. I failed even to record the dates of his secret visits to this country (though I am now free to disclose that these visits were in connection with very important official paperwork and high-powered meetings). But how can I hide while other women publish? Even my friends are at it. Fran is writing "Konnie!: Adenauer in Love." Penny and Harriet are collaborating on "Yalta Groupies." And my Great-Aunt Jackie has just received a six-figure advance for " 'Bill' of Particulars: An Intimate Memoir of William Dean Howells." Continued silence on my part would only lead to speculation that Mao alone among the greatest men of the century could not command a literate young mistress.

That this role was to be mine I could scarcely have foreseen until I met him in 1966. He, after all, was a head of state, I a mere spangle on the midriff of the American republic. But you never know what will happen, and then it is not possible to remember it until it has already happened. That is the way things were with our first encounter. Only now that it is past can I look back upon it. Now I can truly see the details of the Mayflower Hotel in Washington, with its many halls and doors, its carpeted Grand Suite. I can feel the static electricity generated by my cheap nylon waitress's dress, the warmth of the silver tray on which I hoisted a selection of pigs-in-blankets.

Chairman Mao was alone. He sat in the center of the room, in an upholstered armchair—a man who looked as if he might know something I didn't. He was round, placid, smooth as a cheese. When I bent over him with the hors d'oeuvres, he said in perfect English but with the mid-back-rounded vowels pitched in the typical sharps and flats of Shaoshan, "Will you have a bite to eat with me?"

"No," I said. In those days, I never said yes to anything. I was holding out for something better than what everybody had.

He closed his eyes.

By means of that tiny, almost impatient gesture, he had hinted that my way of life was wrong.

I felt shamed, yet oddly exhilarated by the reproof. That night I turned down an invitation to go dancing with a suture salesman who gamely tried to date me once in a while. In some way I could not yet grasp, the Chairman had renewed my sense of possibility, and I just wanted to stay home.

• • •

One evening about six months later, there was a knock at my door. It was the Chairman, cheerful on rice wine. With his famous economy of expression, he embraced me and taught me the Ten Right Rules of

Lovemaking: Reconnoitre, Recruit, Relax, Recline, Relate, Reciprocate, Rejoice, Recover, Reflect, and Retire. I was surprised by his ardor, for I knew the talk that he had been incapacitated by a back injury in the Great Leap Forward. In truth, his spine was supple as a peony stalk. The only difficulty was that it was sensitive to certain kinds of pressure. A few times he was moved to remind me, "Please, don't squeeze the Chairman."

When I awoke the next morning, he was sitting up in bed with his eyes closed. I asked him if he was thinking. "Yes," he said, without opening his eyes. I was beginning to find his demeanor a little stylized. But what right did I have to demand emotion? The Cultural Revolution had just started, and ideas of the highest type were surely forming themselves inside his skull.

He said, "I want to be sure you understand that you won't see me very often."

"That's insulting," I said. "Did you suppose I thought China was across the street?"

"It's just that you mustn't expect me to solve your problems," he said. "I already have eight hundred million failures at home, and the last thing I need is another one over here."

I asked what made him think I had problems.

He said, "You do not know how to follow Right Rule Number Three: Relax. But don't expect me to help you. Expect nothing."

I wanted to ask how I was supposed to relax with a world figure in my bed, but I was afraid he would accuse me of personality cultism.

When he left, he said, "Don't worry."

• • •

I thought about his words. They had not been completely satisfying, and an hour after he had left I wanted to hear them again. I needed more answers. Would he like me better if I had been through something —a divorce, a Long March, an evening at Le Club? Why should I exhaust myself in relaxation with someone who was certain to leave? Every night after work I studied the Little Red Book and wrote down phrases from it for further thought: "women . . . certain contradictions . . . down on their knees . . . monsters of all kinds . . . direct experience."

My life began to feel crowded with potential meaning. One afternoon I was sitting in the park, watching a group of schoolchildren eat their lunch. Two men in stained gray clothing lay on the grass. Once in a while they moved discontentedly from a sunny spot to a shady spot, or back again. The children ran around and screamed. When they left, one of the men went over to the wire wastebasket and rifled the children's lunch bags for leftovers. Then he baited the other man in a loud voice. He kept saying, "*You* are not going downtown, Tommy. *We* are going downtown. *We* are going downtown."

Was this the "social order" that the Chairman had mentioned? It seemed unpleasant. I wondered if I should continue to hold out for something better.

• • •

As it happened, I saw him more often than he had led me to expect. Between visits, there were letters—his accompanied by erotic maxims. These are at present in the Yale University Library, where they will remain in a sealed container until all the people who are alive now are dead. A few small examples will suggest their nature:

> *My broom sweeps your dust kittens.*
> *Love manifests itself in the hop from floor to pallet.*
> *If you want to know the texture of a flank, someone*
>   *must roll over.*

• • •

We always met alone, and after several years *dim sum* at my place began to seem a bit hole-in-corner. "Why don't you ever introduce me to your friends?" I asked. The Chairman made no reply, and I feared I had pushed too hard. We had no claims on each other, after all, no rules but the ones he sprang on me now and then. Suddenly he nodded with vigor and said, "Yes, yes." On his next trip he took me out to dinner with his friend Red Buttons. Years later, the Chairman would often say to me, "Remember that crazy time we had dinner with Red? In a restaurant? What an evening!"

Each time we met, I was startled by some facet of his character that the Western press had failed to report. I saw, for instance, that he disliked authority, for he joked bitterly about his own. No sooner had he stepped inside my bedroom than he would order, "Lights off!" When it was time for him to go, he would raise one arm from the bed as if hailing a taxi and cry, "Pants!" Once when I lifted his pants off the back of a chair and all the change fell out of the pockets, I said, "This happens a lot. I have a drawer full of your money that I've found on the floor."

"Keep it," he said, "and when it adds up to eighteen billion yuan, buy me a seat on the New York Stock Exchange." He laughed loudly, and then did his impersonation of a capitalist. "Bucks!" he shouted. "Gimme!" We both collapsed on the bed, weak with giggles at this private joke.

He was the only man I ever knew, this pedagogue in pajamas, who did not want power over me. In conversation, he was always testing my independence of thought. Once, I remember, he observed, "Marxism has tended to flourish in Catholic countries."

"What about China?" I said.

"Is China your idea of a Catholic country?"

"No, but, um—"

"See what I mean?" he said, laughing.

I had learned my lesson.

To divest himself of sexual power over me, he encouraged me to go dancing with other men while he was away. Then we held regular critiques of the boyfriends I had acquired. My favorite, a good-looking Tex-Mex poet named Dan Juan, provided us with rich material for instruction and drill.

"What is it you like about Dan Juan?" the Chairman asked me once.

"I'd really have to think about it," I said.

"Maybe he's not so interesting," said the Chairman.

"I see your point," I said. Then, with the rebelliousness of the politically indolent, I burst into tears.

The Chairman took my hand and brooded about my situation. I think he was afraid that helping me to enter into ordinary life—to go out with Dan Juan and then to learn why I should not be going out with him and so forth—might not be very much help at all.

Finally, he said, "I don't like to think you're alone when I'm not here."

"I'm not always alone."

"I'd like to give you a radio."

· · ·

The radio never reached me, although I do not doubt that he sent it. His only other gifts we consumed together: the bottles of rice wine, which we drank, talking, knowing that while this was an individual solution, it was simple to be happy. Now other women have pointed out to me that I have nothing to show for the relationship. Adenauer gave Fran a Salton Hotray. Stalin gave Harriet a set of swizzlesticks with little hammer-and-sickles on the tops. William Dean Howells gave my Great-Aunt Jackie a diamond brooch in the form of five ribbon loops terminating in diamond-set tassels, and an aquamarine-and-diamond tiara with scroll and quill-pen motifs separated by single oblong-cut stones mounted on an aquamarine-and-diamond band. That I have no such mementos means, they say, that the Chairman did not love me. I think they are being too negative, possibly.

· · ·

The Chairman believed that the most revolutionary word is "yes." What he liked best was for me to kiss him while murmuring all the English synonyms for "yes" that I could think of. And although neither of us believed in a life beyond this one, I feel to this day that I can check in with him if I close my eyes and say yes, yeah, aye, uh-huh, indeed, agreed, natch, certainly, okeydoke, of course, right, reet, for sure, you got it, well and good, amen, but def, indubitably, right on, yes sirree bob, sure nuff, positively, now you're talking, yep, yup, bet your sweet A, O.K., Roger wilco over and out.

Garrison Keillor

*

SHY RIGHTS:
WHY NOT PRETTY SOON?

Recently I read about a group of fat people who had organized to fight discrimination against themselves. They said that society oppresses the overweight by being thinner than them and that the term "overweight" itself is oppressive because it implies a "right" weight that the fatso has failed to make. Only weightists use such terms, they said; they demanded to be called "total" people and to be thought of in terms of wholeness; and they referred to thin people as being "not all there."

Don't get me wrong. This is fine with me. If, to quote the article if I may, "Fat Leaders Demand Expanded Rights Act, Claim Broad Base of Support," I have no objections to it whatsoever. I feel that it is their right to speak up and I admire them for doing so, though of course this is only my own opinion. I could be wrong.

Nevertheless, after reading the article, I wrote a letter to President Jimmy Carter demanding that his administration take action to end discrimination against shy persons sometime in the very near future. I pointed out three target areas—laws, schools, and attitudes—where shy rights maybe could be safeguarded. I tried not to be pushy but I laid it on the line. "Mr. President," I concluded, "you'll probably kill me for saying this but compared to what you've done for other groups, we shys have settled for 'peanuts.' As you may know, we are not ones to make threats, but it is clear to me that if we don't get some action on this, it could be a darned quiet summer. It is up to you, Mr. President. Whatever you decide will be okay by me. Yours very cordially."

I never got around to mailing the letter, but evidently word got around in the shy community that I had written it, and I've noticed that most shy persons are not speaking to me these days. I guess they think the letter went too far. Probably they feel that making demands is a betrayal of the shy movement (or "gesture," as many shys call it) and an insult to shy pride and that it risks the loss of some of the gains we have already made, such as social security and library cards.

Perhaps they are right. I don't claim to have all the answers. I just feel that we ought to begin, at least, to think about some demands that we *might* make if, for example, we *had* to someday. That's all. I'm not saying we should make fools of ourselves, for heaven's sake!

SHUT UP (A SLOGAN)

Sometimes I feel that maybe we shy persons have borne our terrible burden for far too long now. Labeled by society as "wimps," "dorks," "creeps," and "sissies," stereotyped as Milquetoasts and Walter Mittys, and tagged as potential psychopaths ("He kept pretty much to himself," every psychopath's landlady is quoted as saying after the arrest, and for weeks thereafter every shy person is treated like a leper), we shys are desperately misunderstood on every hand. Because we don't "talk out" our feelings, it is assumed that we haven't any. It is assumed that we never exclaim, retort, or cry out, though naturally we do on occasions when it seems called for.

Would anyone dare to say to a woman or a Third World person, "Oh, don't be a woman! Oh, don't be so Third!"? And yet people make bold with us whenever they please and put an arm around us and tell us not to be shy.

Hundreds of thousands of our shy brothers and sisters (and "cousins twice-removed," as militant shys refer to each other) are victimized every year by self-help programs that promise to "cure" shyness through hand-buzzer treatments, shout training, spicy diets, silence-aversion therapy, and every other gimmick in the book. Many of them claim to have "overcome" their shyness, but the sad fact is that they are afraid to say otherwise.

To us in the shy movement, however, shyness is not a disability or disease to be "overcome." It is simply the way we are. And in our own quiet way, we are secretly proud of it. It isn't something we shout about at public rallies and marches. It is Shy Pride. And while we don't have a Shy Pride Week, we do have many private moments when we keep our thoughts to ourselves, such as "Shy is nice," "Walk short," "Be proud—

shut up," and "Shy is beautiful, for the most part." These are some that I thought up myself. Perhaps other shy persons have some of their own, I don't know.

A "NUMBER ONE" DISGRACE

Discrimination against the shy is our country's No. 1 disgrace in my own personal opinion. Millions of men and women are denied equal employment, educational and recreational opportunities, and rewarding personal relationships simply because of their shyness. These injustices are nearly impossible to identify, not only because the shy person will not speak up when discriminated against, but also because the shy person almost always *anticipates* being denied these rights and doesn't ask for them in the first place. (In fact, most shys will politely decline a right when it is offered to them.)

Most shy lawyers agree that shys can never obtain justice under our current adversary system of law. The Sixth Amendment, for example, which gives the accused the right to confront his accusers, is anti-shy on the face of it. It effectively denies shy persons the right to accuse anyone of anything.

One solution might be to shift the burden of proof to the defendant in case the plaintiff chooses to remain silent. Or we could create a special second-class citizenship that would take away some rights, such as free speech, bearing arms, and running for public office in exchange for some other rights that we need more. In any case, we need some sort of fairly totally new concept of law if we shys are ever going to enjoy equality, if indeed that is the sort of thing we could ever enjoy.

A MILLION-DOLLAR RIPOFF

Every year, shy persons lose millions of dollars in the form of overcharges that aren't questioned, shoddy products never returned to stores, refunds never asked for, and bad food in restaurants that we eat anyway, not to mention all the money we lose and are too shy to claim when somebody else finds it.

A few months ago, a shy friend of mine whom I will call Duke Hand (not his real name) stood at a supermarket checkout counter and watched the cashier ring up thirty fifteen-cent Peanut Dream candy bars and a $3.75 copy of *Playhouse* for $18.25. He gave her a twenty-dollar bill and thanked her for his change, but as he reached for his purchases, she said, "Hold on. There's something wrong here."

"No, really, it's okay," he said.

"Let me see that cash register slip," she said.

"No, really, thanks anyway," he whispered. Out of the corner of his eye, he could see that he had attracted attention. Other shoppers in the vicinity had sensed that something was up, perhaps an attempted price-tag switch or insufficient identification, and were looking his way. "It's not for me," he pleaded. "I'm only buying this for a friend."

Nevertheless, he had to stand there in mute agony while she counted all of the Peanut Dreams and refigured the total and the correct change. (In fairness to her, it should be pointed out that Duke, while eventually passing on each copy of *Playhouse* to a friend, first reads it himself.)

Perhaps one solution might be for clerks and other business personnel to try to be a little bit more careful about this sort of thing in the first place. Okay?

HOW ABOUT SHY HISTORY?

To many of us shys, myself included, the worst tragedy is the oppression of shy children in the schools, and while we don't presume to tell educators how to do their work, work that they have been specially trained to do, we do feel that schools must begin immediately to develop programs of shy history, or at the very least to give it a little consideration.

History books are blatantly prejudiced against shyness and shy personhood. They devote chapter after chapter to the accomplishments of famous persons and quote them at great length, and say nothing at all, or very little, about countless others who had very little to say, who never sought fame, and whose names are lost to history.

Where in the history books do we find mention of The Lady in Black, Kilroy, The Unknown Soldier, The Forgotten Man, The Little Guy, not to mention America's many noted recluses?

Where, for example, can we find a single paragraph on America's hundreds of scale models, those brave men of average height whose job it was to pose beside immense objects such as pyramids and dynamos so as to indicate scale in drawings and photographs? The only credit that scale models ever received was a line in the caption—"For an idea of its size, note man (arrow, at left)." And yet, without them, such inventions as the dirigible, the steam shovel, and the swing-span bridge would have looked like mere toys, and natural wonders such as Old Faithful, the Grand Canyon, and the giant sequoia would have been dismissed as hoaxes. It was truly a thankless job.

SHYS ON "STRIKE"

The scale models themselves never wanted any thanks. All they wanted was a rope or device of some type to keep them from falling off tall structures, plus a tent to rest in between drawings, and in 1906, after one model was carried away by a tidal wave that he had been hired to pose in front of, they formed a union and went on strike.

Briefly, the scale models were joined by a contingent of shy artists' models who had posed for what they thought was to be a small monument showing the Battle of Bull Run only to discover that it was actually a large bas-relief entitled "The Bathers" and who sat down on the job, bringing the work to a halt. While the artists' models quickly won a new contract and went back to work (on a non-representational basis), the scale models' strike was never settled.

True to their nature, the scale models did not picket the work sites or negotiate with their employers. They simply stood quietly a short distance away and, when asked about their demands, pointed to the next man. A year later, when the union attempted to take a vote on the old contract, it found that most of the scale models had moved away and left no forwarding addresses.

It was the last attempt by shy persons to organize themselves anywhere in the country.

NOW IS THE TIME, WE THINK

Now is probably as good a time as any for this country to face up to its shameful treatment of the shy and to do something, almost anything, about it. On the other hand, maybe it would be better to wait for a while and see what happens. All I know is that it isn't easy trying to write a manifesto for a bunch of people who dare not speak their names. And that the shy movement is being inverted by a tiny handful of shy militants who do not speak for the majority of shy persons, nor even very often for themselves. This secret cadre, whose members are not known even to each other, advocate doing "less than nothing." They believe in tokenism, and the smaller the token the better. They seek only to promote more self-consciousness: that ultimate shyness that shy mystics call "the fear of fear itself." What is even more terrifying is the ultimate goal of this radical wing: They believe that they shall inherit the earth, and they will not stop until they do. Believe me, we moderates have our faces to the wall.

Perhaps you are saying, "What can *I* do? I share your concern at the plight of the shy and wholeheartedly endorse your two- (or three-) point program for shy equality. I pledge myself to work vigorously for its adoption. My check for ($10 $25 $50 $100 $_____) is enclosed. In addition, I agree to (circulate petitions, hold fund-raising party in my home, write to congressman and senator, serve on local committee, write letters to newspapers, hand out literature door-to-door during National Friends of the Shy Drive)."

Just remember: You said it, not me.

Lisa Alther

*

THE COMMUNE
EXCERPT FROM *Kinflicks*

[Ginny Babcock, abandoning college and The Family and The City, resisting the American Capitalist Imperialist Economy, joins a commune in Vermont with other "Communists, lesbians, draft-dodgers, atheists, and food stamp recipients."—ED.]

The cabin stood on the site of an old farmhouse, which had burned down. It had been built only a few years earlier as a summer retreat and winter ski house by a stockbroker in New York City. It was unclear why he was willing to rent such a slice of heaven, though it became clearer as time went on. But the original farmhouse had belonged to several generations of working farmers, so that the barn nearby was in good condition. We rushed out and bought a Guernsey milking cow named Minnie and half a dozen red and black Rhode Island hens and a vicious black and white Barred Rock rooster. All these we ensconced in the huge moldy old barn, the framework of which was massive hand-hewn pine beams. We ordered a beehive and nailed it together and dumped a package of bees from Kentucky into it. We placed the hive in an old apple orchard behind the house; the blossoms had recently fallen off, and tiny green apples were forming. The growing season well under way, we dug and planted a hasty garden, reading instructions from a manual.

We had left behind The Family and The City. The plan now, according to Eddie, our resident theoretician, was to leave behind the American capitalist-imperialist economy altogether. We would grow and make almost all our material requirements—our food, our clothes, our fuel. Inconvenient expenses like taxes we would cover from our maple sugaring operation in early spring, there being a vast sugar bush and a sugar shack filled with all the necessary equipment on a high hill behind the cabin. By saving my dividend checks, we could soon afford a down payment on the farm, which was for sale at a ludicrously low price, for reasons which too soon became apparent to us. And eventually we might even be able to wean ourselves entirely from that corporate enemy of The People, the Westwood Chemical Corporation. We concluded that very soon we would be able authentically to cast our lot with The People.

As far as representatives of The People went in Stark's Bog, we didn't know any. We had been into town several times in the old Ford pickup owned by Mona and Atheliah to buy supplies. As we clattered and jounced down the hill on which our farms sat, we could see Stark's Bog below us. Frame buildings clustered around three sides of the bog that gave the town its name. In most parts of Vermont could be seen houses of brick and stone, built to last for generations. In Stark's Bog, however, every house was frame, except Ira Bliss's stone one. Apparently none of the early settlers except the Blisses had planned to stay if they could help it.

In the winter, according to Mona and Atheliah, the marsh mud in the bog froze over. In the spring, it became a sea of muck, and animals that strayed into it were trapped and sucked under, like mammoth elephants in prehistoric asphalt pits. Now, however, it was summer, and the marsh grasses rustled. The mud had grown a coat of brilliant green slime. Mosquitoes teemed in fetid pools.

Driving into town we would first pass the Dairy Delite soft ice cream stand. The Stark's Boggers would cluster here after supper to buy root beer floats or butterscotch sundaes. Then they would drive or walk to the bog to watch the struggles of whatever animals were sinking in the goo offshore. Or if it was close to 6:27, they would amble to the train track and wait for the New York–Montreal special to roar through. (It had never stopped there. In fact, passengers tended to pull down their window shades as they passed through, to the disappointment of the frantically waving town children.)

Although Stark's Bog township actually included the bog and the surrounding hills and farms, the town proper consisted of one road, which came from St. Johnsbury and led to a border crossing into Quebec. Where the road passed through town, it was lined with a feed store, a hardware store, a hotel where hunters stayed in the fall, an IGA grocery store, a gun shop, a taxidermy parlor, a funeral home, a farm equipment franchise, and a snow machine showroom called Sno Cat City. All these were housed in buildings from the early 1800's with colonial cornices and returns and doorways, which were pleasing in their simplicity. Pleasing to everyone but the Stark's Boggers, who were sick to death of them and had done their best to tear them down or cover them over with fluorescent plastic and neon tubing and plate glass and gleaming chrome. Each businessman yearned to raze the clapboard and beam structure on his premises and erect a molded plastic- and aluminum-sided showroom in its place. Sno Cat City, for instance, owned by Ira Bliss IV, had a huge orange mountain lion springing out from its facade; it being summer, row after row of gleaming yellow Honda trail bikes sat out front. Likewise, the goal of each Stark's Bog householder was to knock down or sell the despised frame colonial his family had infested for centuries, and to throw up a prefab ranch house that would be airtight, with everything working properly.

We found all this profoundly disturbing. It indicated a willingness to participate in modern American society. We didn't approve at all, and so we went into Stark's Bog as little as possible. When we did, the Stark's Boggers eyed us—as we strolled from the feed store to the hardware store in our Off the Pigs T-shirts, with our braids swishing behind us in unison—with all the enthusiasm of Incas inspecting newly arrived Spaniards. We learned from Mona that they referred to us all as the Soybean People due to the fact that we bought fifty-pound sacks of soybeans at the feed store for our own consumption, not for our animals. Eddie had decided that it was politically reprehensible of us not to be vegetarians when each fattened steer starved five Third World citizens. "Who *needs* the decaying flesh of festering corpses?" she asked, as she burned all our cookbooks containing meat recipes in the wood stove. "We should be able to make it on our own life force without holding innocent animals in bondage."

It didn't take long for things to start going sour—not more than a couple of blissful sunlit months. One problem was that the regimens of farming didn't fit our lifestyle. One morning Eddie went to the barn to collect some fresh eggs for breakfast, while I put a cast iron skillet on the burner of the wood cookstove and fed the coals from the night before into a modest fire. Intending to scramble the eggs, I cracked one on the rim of a bowl. A foul odor wafted up to me. I opened the shell and dumped its contents into the bowl. It was tinged with brown and stank. "Uh, Ed, I think they're rotten." She stalked over and peered into the bowl and nearly gagged. I broke open a couple more that were the same shade of murky brown.

"Maybe collecting them once a week isn't enough?" I suggested.

"Shit! I'm *damned* if I'm going to spend my whole fucking life collecting eggs!" She collapsed in a captain's chair in front of the stove.

"It wouldn't take more than a few minutes every other day if we took turns," I pointed out.

"Turns! Schedules! Lists! Did anyone ever tell you that you have an accountant mentality, Ginny? I suppose you'd like to mark on a calendar when to have sex, too?"

I hadn't found it easy sharing a bathroom with a member of The Elect all these years, and my accumulated resentments poured out in response to this unwarranted attack. "An *accountant mentality!* Well, it's a goddam good thing that *somebody* in this place does! If I weren't around to pay your bills, Eddie, you'd be out on your ass so fast—"

"There!" Eddie said triumphantly, gesturing toward me with her hand. "It's out at last! I knew it all along! I *knew* that deep down you resented sharing your fucking blood money with me. You grasping bourgeois types are all the same. I can read you like a book!"

"Oh *yeah?*" I screamed, standing over her, a quivering mass of bourgeois rage. "I don't notice *you* making any efforts to earn honest money, Miss Holier Than Thou! You seem perfectly content to let me pay *your* way with *my* despised blood money!"

"*Your* money, *my* money! Who gives a shit about your goddam fucking money? Shove it up your ass, Scarlett." She slouched lower in her chair and glowered.

"Get out! *Get out*, you freeloader! *I'm* paying the rent, this is *my* place. And I don't need you around calling me 'grasping' and 'bourgeois' while you live off me, like the cock-sucking parasite you are!"

I had never before let the phrase "cock-sucking" pass my lips, though I had heard it often enough during my days with Clem. Eddie looked startled, but no more startled than I. We stared at each other in mutual shock.

"So *that's* it," Eddie said, nodding her head knowingly.

"What's it?"

"You know as well as I do from Psychology 101, Ginny, that there's more at stake here than rotten eggs or who pays the rent. And I've just realized what it is."

"What *is* it?"

"You're tired of me, Ginny. You want a man. A cock," she added with distaste.

"No! That's not true!"

"I've been expecting it. You don't need to deny it. It was bound to happen sooner or later. You've just been playing around with me. Basically you're as hetero as they come."

"But you're *wrong*, Eddie. You're all I want. With one functioning lover, what would I want with any more? After all, how much sex can one person endure?" I knelt beside her chair and began massaging her throbbing temples.

"It's no use," Eddie said glumly, pushing my hands away. "What's done is done."

"But nothing's *done*, Eddie," I protested with a laugh. "What do I want with a man? I've *had* men. You're so far superior as a lover, and in every other way, that it's ridiculous even to talk about it." I kissed her on the mouth tenderly. This was followed by an embrace. "You're crazy, Eddie," I whispered fondly in her ear.

"I guess I am."

Lacking eggs, I dished us up bowls of molded soybean salad left over from the night before. There was a great deal left over, almost the entire salad, in fact. We ate in silence at the table, which overlooked the beaver pond. I kept trying not to breathe as I ate so that I wouldn't be able to taste very well.

"Delicious," Eddie said firmly, trying to convince herself.

"Delicious," I echoed faintly. "And *full* of protein."

The summer sun shone down bright and hot on the pond. Shimmering heat waves rose up all around the cabin. Bees bumbled in the weed flowers that were thigh-high in the yard.

"I was wondering, Eddie," I said between hastily swallowed bites, "if we maybe shouldn't rent a power tiller for the garden down at the hardware store." The garden we had so carefully planted was now overrun with weeds. We had to do something quick—either get rid of the weeds, or get used to them in lieu of tomatoes.

"Are you *kidding*? A *power tiller*? Are you out of your mind? You don't actually want to patronize an economy that turns The People into interchangeable cogs in some vast assembly line, do you? You couldn't possibly want to participate in a system of production that makes medical supplies with one hand and bombs with the other. I mean, that's why we're up here, isn't it, to wean ourselves from that sort of hypocrisy, to become honest working-class people? Well, isn't it?"

I said nothing. I wasn't at all sure that that was why I was in Vermont. I reviewed my motives and concluded that I was mostly here because Eddie wanted to be, for reasons of her own, and I wanted to be with Eddie. Once again I was shamelessly allowing myself to be defined by another person. I was afraid it would sound at best hopelessly bougie (Eddie's shorthand for "bourgeois") if I admitted this—and counter-revolutionary at worst. So instead I asked meekly, "Yes, but what about the weeds?"

"We'll pull them by hand," Eddie announced grandly, "like *every* person in the Third World does!"

That afternoon, shirtless, sweat pouring out of our hairy armpits, we pulled weeds in the hot sun for about fifteen minutes, clearing a small corner of the tomato patch. Our bodies clammy with sweat, we lay under an apple tree and smoked a joint.

"If tomatoes can't prevail against the weeds, they don't deserve to live," Eddie concluded. "To pull the weeds would be to weaken the tomatoes and make them dependent on us."

"Maybe it's too late. I think they're already corrupted. They appear to need us."

The apples hanging above us were tinged with pink. Because we had failed to prune the trees or to control the insects, they were tiny and deformed and riddled with worm holes. We turned over on our stomachs so that we wouldn't have to look at yet another tribute to our ineptitude.

"We may not be freeing up our former food supplies for shipment to the Third World," I said, "but we're sure providing one hell of a feast for the area insects."

When Eddie looked at me, I knew that my remark hadn't been amusing, it had been reactionary. "What do you expect?" she demanded. "We're just picking up on all this soil shit. We'll get it together for next summer."

We passed the joint and became less and less glum. We glanced off and on at the beehive under a neighboring tree. At least we would have honey. We had left the bees almost entirely alone, in keeping with our policy of letting things fend for themselves. Only the bees had come through under this regime. They were rushing in and out with loads of nectar and pollen. Talk about accountant mentalities. . . .

"We should do more hives next year," Eddie said, yawning. "That's my kind of project." She rolled over and wrapped her arms around me and nibbled my neck.

Eddie and I went one day to Mona's and Atheliah's for an autumnal equinox party. The plan was that we would all help them harvest their crops, and then we would have a big feed. I took soybean croquettes creole as our contribution. When we arrived at their crumbling farmhouse, a dozen people in various stages of undress were lolling around in the weed patch that was their front lawn. I recognized about half the people as being in Mona's and Atheliah's group. The others were from nearby farms. Marijuana smoke hung around the group like a London pea-soup fog. A woman in a long Indian shirt with hair to her waist was plucking a dulcimer and singing a Kentucky coal mining song with a Brooklyn accent: "I hope when I'm gone and the ages shall roll,/ My body will blacken and turn into coal./ Then I'll look from the door of my heavenly home/ And pity the miner digging my bones/ Where it's dark as a dungeon, damp as the dew,/ Where the danger is double, the pleasures are few,/ Where the rain never falls and the sun never shines/ It's dark as a dungeon way down in the mines." I felt a passing seizure of nostalgia for the mines of Appalachia that I had never known. Genes, no doubt. The collective experience of my forebears encoded within each of my cells.

A shirtless man with a Simon Legree mustache was silk-screening "Power to the People" in white on his dark blue T-shirt. Atheliah was stirring something in a big cast iron pot that sat in the middle of a small fire. A naked boy baby was tottering around with his arms outstretched for his mother, whom he couldn't locate. I handed my earthenware dish to Mona, who lifted the lid and sniffed and said, "Soybeans. Far out."

After a while a few people wandered out to the corn patch, which was almost as full of weeds as our tomato patch. Eddie sat down next to the woman with the dulcimer and started harmonizing. I went out to the corn patch to help pick. We ripped the ears off the stalks, shucked them, and tossed them in a cart. They were mostly four inches long and etched with brown worm tracks.

Halfway through the patch, Laverne, a woman in Mona's house, found a stunted Hubbard squash that was about the size and shape of a small football. Laverne was statuesque. There was no other word for her. Her shapely hips and large breasts strained the seams of her T-shirt and jeans. She had long blond naturally curly hair and blue eyes. In another era she would have been a movie starlet, a model for Rubens. She held up her squash triumphantly.

"A football!" gasped a bearded man with bleary eyes, who looked like Sherman on his march through Georgia. He grabbed the squash, faded back, and passed it to another man, who wore nothing but jeans, which were too large for him and were bunched together and held up with a belt fashioned from a silk rep tie.

"Keep-away," he suggested. "Shirts against the skins." We glanced around. Five of us wore shirts; three men were shirtless.

Laverne threw off her T-shirt with one smooth upward movement. "I'll be a skin!"

Everyone stood transfixed, staring with awe at her magnificent brown breasts, which were very tanned and evidently accustomed to exposure. Trying to pretend that we hadn't been staring, that we all saw bare bosoms this breathtaking every day, that the female chest was no big deal to people as sexually liberated as we, we began a frantic game of keep-away through the corn patch, trampling the juicy green stalks and passing and handing off the squash as we went. Everyone was clandestinely sneaking glimpses of Laverne's breasts, bouncing firmly as she ran and gleaming bronze under the September sun.

The game got progressively rougher, and soon people were tackling each other and grappling in the dirt, over the squash. At one point I lay trying to catch my breath after a savage tackle by General Sherman. As I picked myself up, I saw that the game had moved from the garden and into the high grass. Laverne, her jeans hanging on her hips just above her pubic hair, was dancing in place signaling to the man with the tie belt to throw her the squash. Her arms were raised high over her head, accentuating the narrowness of her waist. Her breasts were shaking in place like Jell-O.

The squash was flying through the air. Laverne leapt up to catch it. As she did, she was hit from three sides by male tacklers. The squash sailed over her head and smashed open, spilling its orange guts on the grass. Laverne herself landed on her back in the dirt with her jeans to her knees.

I watched in amazement as the bearded man threw himself on her and started lunging his hips into hers. I heard her gasping and shrieking. Shortly, he rolled off and another man climbed on, like a cowboy trying to ride a bronco.

I glanced back toward the house. A couple of people watched indifferently. No one seemed concerned. But from where I stood, with my mouth hanging open, it looked for all the world like what Clem used to call a gang bang. They were like a pack of mongrels balling a bitch in heat. Laverne was being raped and no one was helping! I ran closer, speculating that she had perhaps been asking for it.

By the time I was ten yards away, I could see that her legs were sprawled open and her whole luscious body was smeared with dirt and sweat and semen. I could also hear what she was screaming: "Faster! Faster! Don't stop *now*, you mother fucker! Oh mother of Christ! Don't *stop!*" Her body was arcing up off the ground and twitching spasmodically, like a frog's leg hooked into an electric current. Three men lay in panting heaps next to her, like bees after stinging.

I stopped running to her assistance and stood frozen to the spot. As I watched, blood rushed to my face. My nipples began tingling with excitement. I realized I wanted to join the fray, but whether on top of Laverne or underneath the men I was no longer certain. Divided loyalties.

I turned around and walked slowly back toward the house, breathing deeply to quell my beast.

I sat down next to Eddie, who was scowling. ". . . really disgusting," Mona was saying.

"Revolting," Eddie agreed, looking at me. But I said nothing.

Later Eddie and I passed by Atheliah's cast iron pot and got a bowl of soup. "Dr. Dekleine's Victory Soup," Atheliah informed us. "Brewer's yeast, powdered milk, and toasted soy flour. Delicious. And packed with protein."

We sat on the steps, and Eddie said casually, "You liked it, didn't you?"

"Liked what?"

"Laverne's charming number in the corn patch."

"Oh, that."

"I saw you standing there watching and getting off on it."

"I thought they were raping her. I was worried."

"You don't need to worry about Laverne. It's *you* I'm worried about."

"Me?"

"Admit it. You loved it. You wanted to be right in there with them. Didn't you?"

"It occurred to me."

"I knew it! You're tired of me!"

"I'm not," I assured her without conviction.

"Can I help it if I don't have a penis?"

"Of course not," I said wearily. "I've told you that it doesn't matter to me. There are all sorts of compensations to being with you instead of a man."

"Compensations? *Compensations?* Go ahead, Scarlett. Go drag one of those young studs on his macho trip out into the woods with you! I dare you to! You'll come crawling back to me in minutes! Go on!"

"Maybe I will." Under Eddie's abuse, I was becoming more interested in the idea all the time.

That night we walked back to our cabin in an icy silence, me with the crusted soybean croquette dish under my arm. We climbed into bed and turned our backs on each other.

Later that night I woke up being caressed by Eddie. Warm tears were dripping from her eyes and onto my bare chest. "Don't leave me, Ginny. Please don't. I couldn't stand it if I knew you were with a man. I get sick just thinking about it. Don't do it to us."

Reflexively, I took her in my arms, and we kissed and held each other. She parted my knees and began stroking me. On the verge of orgasm, I felt something hard and cold slide into me and start moving back and forth. It felt fantastic. Curiosity finally quelling lust, I sat up and said, "What *are* you doing, Eddie?" I turned on the light.

She smiled sheepishly and held up a greased cucumber. I looked at her with horror. "It's all right," she assured me. "It's organically grown."

Lynn Caraganis

*

AMERICA'S CUP '83:
THE SHERPA CHALLENGE

I am a Briton, yes, and we have received our share of drubbings from
the Americans over this Cup. Of course, it meant little or nothing to us
the year they took it from us: more a gesture on our part than anything
else—a means, really, of encouraging sporting ideals in a pushing, ignorant people, giving them the incentive to raise themselves. This has
always been the way of our dealings with ex-colonials. Let the poor devils
see what we have and how we do it. Let 'em aspire! Then they'll drop
their tribes and whatnot, and you'll get your loyalty, by God.

But that's all past now. So much so, in fact, that my friends at the
New York Yacht Club have asked me to compile these unpretentious
"notes" on the current challenge and I have promised to do so in a fair,
nonpartisan spirit.

SEPTEMBER 9TH:

Yes, like so many things, what once appeared to be a pathetic joke is now
menacing fact; even as I write these words, I am squinting across the
sparkling waters of Newport Harbor at the indescribable challenger from
Kathmandu. Since her arrival during the night of September 5th (four
days ago), she has hoisted no sail, nor approached any nearer than 500
yards from the piers. Nor has any member of the foreign crew come
ashore. Yesterday the launch of the Measurement Committees approached the vessel, but a dense fog closed in rather suddenly, and they
were forced to return. Committee members do report that whole families
are living on the boat, and that goats and chickens run freely around the
deck. I myself can see the smoke from at least *two* open-air cooking fires.

SEPTEMBER 10TH:

Somehow or other, the question of the measurements has been waived, and though no representative of the challenging boat has so much as replied to our luncheon and cocktail invitations, the races begin at 1 p.m. the day after tomorrow. A note on the challenger: According to the American, or "Universal," rule of rating

$$\left(\frac{L + 2D + \sqrt{S} - F}{2.37}\right),$$

which is very complicated, this Nepalese craft, though eccentric, is deemed to be a legally proportioned 12-metre, and may compete under the rules. Indeed, if looks were everything, the fellows on our side might not be losing any sleep. For example, according to Measurement Committee members who did get near before the fog closed in, the Sherpa boatwrights have made no effort at all to trim the shaggy goatskin hull! Florrie Wentworth said it looked like "a bunch of people adrift in a good-sized wig." As for the Sherpas themselves, she claims that they bowed and waved politely before the fog hid them from view. She further claims that their "complexions are marvellous!" Moreover, no winches or hardware of any kind were seen except some wicker cleats. (It is painful—but characteristic of these races—that we should be forced to hang on every word that Florrie Wentworth utters at a time like this.) Further, no Westerner could swear to so much as the color of their sails! The Commodore did notice that they have a sort of "Park Avenue boom," though he is not absolutely sure, as it was hung all over with bits of bright cotton.

As Cup races are commonly won and lost by very small margins, the quality (or absence!) of a winch may be of no small significance. (There is some suspicion that they may have mounted the winches belowdecks—the innovation that gave Intrepid such good results.) But we old hands are more than baffled, Park Avenue boom or no Park Avenue boom.

SEPTEMBER 11TH—THE MOOD AMONG OUR FELLOWS:

First, I have been receiving a good deal of unfair ribbing around here for a remark I made in print some time ago, to the effect that many sporting Americans felt it *would* be a good thing for the Cup to cross "the pond" (for, as you know, once won by them the Cup has not been retaken). This present kind of thing is not what I meant. No one, no one would be sorrier than I to see the Cup go to a nation of professional porters.

Now I must relate a peculiar incident, whether true or not, just as I heard it from the chattering lips of a local Newport boy. As is only natural, there is enormous curiosity as to the lines of the challenger's hull. The suspense became too great for one of our members, and he persuaded this youth—in strictest secrecy—to swim underwater and take a look, in return for a college education. To this the boy agreed, and he swam out there around midday. He claims that when he was not 50 yards from the boat, he saw below him a great looming black shape and, terrified, swam away as fast as he could. Several of our fellows were standing on the dock when he appeared thrashing on the surface, and the story has unfortunately got round. Our fellows are understandably sobered by the whole business.

Needless to say, the Committee refuses to pursue the matter on the basis of what this local boy thinks he saw.

WEARING THE WRONG SHOES:

One of our members has now left Newport altogether. He was apparently tormented by the old prophecy about the team that takes the Cup having the wrong shoes. He heard Florrie say these Sherpas were wearing "some kind of wog wedgie," and he instantly packed up and returned to the city. This attitude is widely regarded as more appropriate to an earlier day, and we are resolved to await the verdict of the fair competition.

10 P.M.—"THE HEAD OF THE SKIPPER WILL REPLACE THE CUP IN ITS VENERABLE GLASS CASE":

I had a disturbing talk this evening with Skipper Beef Wentworth. Beef has more 12-metre experience than any other man on this side of "the pond." We have known each other for many years, and I have never seen him so ill at ease. Beef is famous for giving over the last 36 hours before any race to what he calls "pure drinking," for drinking during the race, and for going on to win. Today he just looks round sadly. I told him I believe he has trained his fine crew well, and his Groton Academy is a fine boat. He has nothing to reproach himself for should he lose, which hardly seems likely. But he sobbed and only said, "It's fine. It's fine. But I feel we shall . . . lose, Bobby."

Meanwhile, Ed Stevens, aggressive yachtsman and head of the Groton Academy syndicate, has been haunting the fishing shanties and public meeting places of the local people of Newport, who, he has always maintained, can be very shrewd if you can once gain their confidence. I have noticed myself that their knowledge of local conditions is impressive. According to Stevens, the young man who got such a scare out there the other day has since lost all his hair. Whether there is any connection, or whether this is merely a consequence of the poor conditions under which such people live—diet and so on—would be difficult to say.

Well, this is without a doubt the strangest America's Cup contest I have ever been involved in, and I go back to 1958, the year Sceptre gave Columbia such a hard time of it. And by the way, Sceptre was not the joke the U.S. media tried to make out. '58 was a summer of irresponsible winds and sullen swells—a very injurious type of racing weather by any international yachting standards. No acknowledgment of this was ever made in the American papers. However, this is a time when we must stand together, not carp.

THE MEDIA GET INTO IT:

A popular U.S. tabloid has issued a supplement on the Sherpas ("We Aim at Nothing Less Than the Overthrow of the American Way of Life"), claiming to have interviewed several crew members by telephone. Incredibly, the Americans seem to believe this patent nonsense and are terrified by it, and these papers are now almost impossible to get. What follows is a representative sample of what is passing as truth in this once idyllic town:

Q: Are you related to anyone in this country?
SHERPA: Yes, Brooke Shields.
ANOTHER SHERPA: And we practice voodoo rites.

SEPTEMBER 12TH—THE FIRST RACE:

I don't know when I have seen such tense holiday crowds. Jack Wedderburn and I were discussing it just this morning. He related to me a conversation he overheard between his hostess, a famous Newport dowager, and her colored maidservant, who reportedly said, "I just say, they win or they lose, you're still the richest lady in Newport." And her mistress replied, "There is more to life than money, Trixie." To which Trixie murmured, "Give me some, then, old lady."

Low comedy aside, Newport is a worried town, as evidenced by this trivial rhyme, which I heard in the Teacup as I was having my breakfast:

> Oh, Nepal has got a nice boat
> And a crew of Sherpa heroes,
> But we'll buy 'em off with tobacco,
> Bic lighters, and nice little mirrors.

Conditions are optimal for Groton Academy, I am happy to say. Beef will be counting heavily on her noted windward abilities, and the stiff breeze should hearten all the fellows. Whether the unknown Himalayan designer counted on such weather is of course a mystery, and of course very little is known about offshore conditions over there. There is the usual violent chop on the course, owing to the spectator fleet, which is estimated at 5 million vessels, being restrained with great difficulty—as usual—by the ships and helicopters of the Coast Guard. In a magnanimous gesture, the great motor yacht Frank Sinatra has offered the services of its escort, the U.S.S. Wyoming, to help patrol the course.

Groton Academy and Non-Aligned Sherpa Maid are now circling majestically behind the line in anticipation of the starting gun. I will take a moment here to describe at last the challenger's sails—objects of so much speculation until now. According to the most recent press release, they are woven of the hair of the yak. To Western eyes, they present a most peculiar appearance, almost that of some type of—what is it?—macramé! I would estimate the jib alone weighs two or three tons. What a contrast to the very flat Kevlar set of the handsome defender!

The seconds are ticking away, and I can see through my binoculars a small Sherpa woman actually lounging with her back against the mast, engaged in some kind of clapping game with a small child! Yet on Groton Academy the good-looking, brawny, identically dressed crew, schooled by a thousand drills, are working their boat as if their lives depended on it! What can be the outcome of such a race?

The starting gun! A cry goes up from the spectator throng, and Groton Academy crosses the line in the advantageous lee position. Non-Aligned Maid has hoisted her protest flag!—which she has no business to do, even though our fellows have apparently crossed too soon. They are being recalled. This is a most unfortunate way to begin a Cup series. I only hope it will not weigh too heavily with Skipper Wentworth.

Non-Aligned Maid is clawing her way very fast to windward now as Groton Academy approaches the line. What! Beef and the boys are setting their red half-oz. spinnaker—a very odd choice, surely, for this windward part of the course.

The challenger is nearing the first mark. But instead of rounding, she has come up into the wind, sails flapping, and stalled. We here on the Committee Boat are absolutely speechless!—perhaps there is some problem with those wicker cleats!—and there is a surge of hope in all our hearts as Groton Academy bears down upon her, as fast as her spinnaker will permit. What effrontery! The Sherpas are running up an immense flag with what seems to be a portrait of Sir Edmund Hillary with a mustache insultingly painted on. Oh, this is an outrage! Now she heels and rounds the mark. She is 1:20 ahead. Groton Academy is now following her round, but our mood is solemn, for our boat is not so strong on the reach.

4 P.M.: Non-Aligned Sherpa Maid has finished 5 minutes ahead of the defender. It is a distressing beginning, but of course the challenger must win three more races to take the Cup.

In the evening I encourage the stunned crew of Groton Academy to give the victors three cheers. This they graciously do, but it is doubtful whether the sound carries as far as the monstrous craft now moored far out in the harbor, turning its face away from the decent town of Newport like a great sullen bear. Certainly there is no answering cheer.

SEPTEMBER 13TH:

There has been a crisis. This morning a curious bean can with a Russian label washed ashore at the Teacup, and the Race Committee has started an immediate inquiry, calling a lay day to do so. Whether it fell off a passing liner or was merely dropped by a tourist, this Russian tin can has brought that "looming dark shape" ominously to the minds of all responsible yachtsmen.

In the meantime, Beef and the crew have closeted themselves at the Breakers to talk strategy. In this frustrating interim, hundreds of journalists are making nuisances of themselves round the town, and the Teacup is crowded to capacity. Unfortunately, the weather has also closed in, further dampening the spirits of all concerned.

I passed by the Teacup on my way to consult with Beef a moment ago and heard the thunderous chanting of those perhaps overclever newspapermen, who, in the absence of real information, apparently cannot resist making something up. Against my will I heard the following verse to their infernal song, which I set down here with my apologies:

Oh, the Sherpas have built a 12-metre
And sailed over the sea to find us.
Who cares if we can't even beat her?
The Security Council's behind us.

  Meanwhile, in the intervals of fog, Non-Aligned Sherpa Maid may be dimly seen, placidly swinging at her mooring, and I can hear an eerie ethnic clapping out there.

SEPTEMBER 14TH:

I have just been advised by the Commodore that frogmen from the Frank Sinatra have discovered a large Soviet submarine on the bottom of the harbor, not half a mile from the town docks. It is widely believed that this submarine accompanied Non-Aligned Maid to these shores and actually towed her round the course. Do they call that non-alignment? The Race Committee is understandably outraged.

"LET THE FRANK SINATRA TOW OUR BOAT!":

Some of the wags are actually taking pleasure in this shameless breach of tradition. But knowledgeable sailing men are heartened that, considering the help she had, Non-Aligned Maid did not do so very well. The word is going round that the owners of the powerful motor yacht Frank Sinatra have offered to tow Groton Academy in an "exhibition race" against Non-Aligned Maid and her "friend." All this old sailor can say to that is: whatever the outcome of such a race, it would be a sad departure from America's Cup tradition. (If this be élitism, so be it.) Besides, it is a well-known fact that the Frank Sinatra is escorted everywhere by the U.S.S. Wyoming; does no one consider the possible consequences of bringing such a vessel into competition, however indirect, with a nuclear submarine from Russia?

  To such people, however, the possibility of a grave international incident, even war, and the damage it would do to the reputation of these races, is apparently nothing more than an amusing joke. If the Race Committee takes my advice, they will close these races immediately.

6 P.M.—OUR COMMODORE

I now set down in its entirety the Commodore's statement as it was just given to the press:

  We feel it would be in the interest of the whole world for all foreign vessels to instantly depart for their homelands, and the U.S.S. Wyoming is seeing to that now. If this America's Cup challenge has done little to promote international forgiveness, it has done no lasting harm, either. [Cries of "Yes it has!" from the crowd]

And perhaps the ethical differences we have noticed are merely cultural, after all, and not the results of race or political system. [Jeering, guffaws, and cries of "Come on and have a drink, Commodore"]

As always, the New York Yacht Club will consider legitimate challenges from foreign clubs. Thank you, everybody.

As the crowd began to disperse and the cheering died away, a waggish voice cried, "Challenge, here, from Mongolia!" The Commodore, who was just climbing down from the platform, looked very grave. Then more guffaws broke out, and he and Beef Wentworth were borne away for some "pure drinking."

And so these unorthodox races were concluded, at least, in the fitting and traditional manner—the manner in which we also conclude races on the other side of "the pond." I mean with a drink. Third World and Communist countries may have their own way. To them, the end of a race may signal a night of spying, or round-the-clock sacrifices to hairy mountain gods.

Fran Lebowitz

*

NOTES ON "TRICK"

trick, *n.* from OFr. *trichier*, to trick, to cheat; Pr. *tric*, deceit; It. *treccare*, to cheat. 1. an action or device designed to deceive, swindle, etc.; artifice; a dodge; ruse; stratagem; deception. 2. a practical joke; a mischievous or playful act; prank . . . 4. (a) a clever or difficult act intended to amuse . . . (b) any feat requiring skill. 5. the art, method, or process of doing something successfully or of getting a result quickly . . . 6. an expedient or convention of an art, craft, or trade . . . 7. a personal mannerism . . .

I have chosen these definitions, carefully selected from the Unabridged Second Edition of Webster's Dictionary, on the basis of congeniality with what is perhaps the most current usage of the word *Trick*—that which refers to the object of one's affections. By "one" I mean the person of serious ambition in those fields most likely to necessitate the employment of a press agent. Such a person is often, but not always, a homosexual; the primary reason for this being that the heterosexual is far too burdened by his own young to be much interested in anyone else's. Where the heterosexual feels a sense of duty, a sense of honor, a sense of responsibility, the homosexual feels a sense of humor, a sense of protocol, and most significantly, a sense of design.

With no dependents, he is free to pursue his selfish interests—among these, the Trick. The Trick allows one a semblance of romantic intimacy without the risk that one's own importance will be improperly appreciated.

The Trick exhibits those qualities found in a favorite toy. Surely, no sane person would if he could help it knowingly choose a doll that talked about progressive education and demanded that one share the housework—and it is precisely this ability to help it that separates the men from the toys.

Fortunately, there are many available to fill the role of Trick, since the first requirement of the climber is a toehold. In allowing this close proximity one is, indeed, apt to have one's pocket picked, but one also has the option of causing a nasty spill. It is, therefore, a situation in which everyone concerned can be taken advantage of to the best of his ability. As to the question of who runs the greatest risk of getting hurt, one can only reply that the number of mountains that have suffered severe or fatal injury is infinitesimal when compared to the number who have tackled them.

The word Trick is used to describe the less illustrious member of such an alliance and it fills a genuine need. For the noteworthy partner the words Rich and/or Famous are quite sufficient, but the corresponding adjectives of Cute and/or Well-built are somewhat lacking. Actual names were all right for home use, but neither "Juan" nor "Heather" is really serviceable as a generic term.

Exactly when or why the word Trick was first used for this purpose is unclear, although there is a theory that it derives from the slang of prostitutes, who have long used it in regard to their clients. While this contention is not without logic, it is far more likely that this use of the word Trick was spread by simple (or complex) word of mouth.

I have in the interest of clarification jotted down some notes on the subject, but before we proceed to them there are a few things that must be said:

Tricks like to lie in bed—also in restaurants.

Tricks should never be left strewn carelessly about the house where someone might trip over them.

Tricks are attracted to bright objects. This may elude your understanding since you obviously do not share this tendency.

These notes are for Lord Alfred Douglas.

1. It is wise to avoid the very young Trick. For while it is indeed true that they offer the advantage of having to leave early to get to school, it is equally true that the very same thing can be accomplished by the use of fashion models, who will not only have to be standing on top of the Pan Am Building in full makeup by 8 A.M. but who also will never need help with their term papers on John Donne.

2. The homosexual's desire to remain youthful is entirely based on his knowledge that he will never have children and hence will be deprived of legitimately meeting their more attractive friends.

3. There are those for whom the most highly prized quality in a Trick is sheer stupidity. Of this group the most envied is an eminent film director who has installed in his residence a young man whose lips move when he watches television.

4. Random examples of items that are part of the canon of Trick:

Bennington College's Nonresident Term
Conceptual art
Stealing
Trying on someone else's leather jacket while he's at work
Artistic greeting cards
Interesting food
Black sheets
Remembering telephone numbers by making a word out of the corresponding letters
Trying to figure things out by listening to the lyrics of popular songs
Exotic cigarettes
Reading, or more likely watching, *Breakfast at Tiffany's* and identifying with Holly Golightly
Hearing about F. Scott Fitzgerald and thinking you're Zelda
Being Zelda Fitzgerald and thinking you're F. Scott
Lina Wertmuller movies seen without nausea
Stag movies seen with lust

5. A good Trick, like a good child, is mannerly. He does not speak unless spoken to, he does not contradict, and he kneels when an adult comes into the room.

"Still as interested as ever in the young, I see," Francis remarked in a confidential undertone, glancing round the obstruction of his friend's shoulders to where Daniel stood. . . . "You old succubus! Let's have a look at your latest suffix!"

—*The Apes of God*,
Wyndham Lewis

6. Mixed company in the modern sense of the term means that Tricks are present. How often one has longed to be left alone after dinner while the Tricks go upstairs and take cocaine.

7. American industry has made a grave error in overlooking the Trick. The market is wide open and would be rewardingly receptive to such products as strawberry-swirl vodka, Hermes mittens, and a pack of cigarettes with a secret surprise inside.

8. Although the male Trick is more prone to stealing than is the female, neither sex can be trusted alone in the same room with an invitation to a party at Halston's.

9. Tricks have feelings too, as they will be the first to tell you. If you prick them they do indeed bleed—usually your good vodka.

10. The Trick is, when it comes to finance, truly a child of the modern age, for he never carries cash—at least not his own.

11. Other people's Tricks pose a special problem. Upon coming across a friend thus accompanied you must, out of politeness, treat the Trick amicably. This is invariably a mistake, for shortly thereafter the friend will divest himself of his consort and for the rest of your life the Trick will be coming up to you at parties and saying hello.

12. The simple black Trick is always appropriate—particularly at events where food is not served.

13. It is not unusual for the male aficionado to draw his Tricks exclusively from the lower orders. Such a person is, indeed, often attracted to the criminal element. When asked wherein lay the appeal, a spokesman for this group replied, "Everybody looks good when they're under arrest."

> "Horace has always been like that—his intentions have *always* been strictly honourable" sneered Ratner "and he has never lost his belief in 'genius'— associated *always* with extreme youth, and a pretty face! Unfortunately, the type of beauty which appeals to Horace you see is rather commonplace. The result is Horace has never actually met with a 'genius,' which is a pity. It might have opened his eyes if he had!"
>
> —*The Apes of God*,
> WYNDHAM LEWIS

14. Should you be awakened in the middle of the night by a faint scratching sound, do not fear for your health unless you are certain that all valuables have been safely locked away. For it is far less likely that your Trick is suffering a communicable rash than that he is copying out your address book. The more vindictive among you may be interested in devising a phony version of said book in which you have carefully set down the phone numbers of particularly vile ex-Tricks next to the names of your most prestigious and least favorite former employers.

15. The mistreatment of Tricks is the revenge of the intelligent upon the beautiful.

16. Regrettably few Tricks are attractive enough to be allowed to discuss their innermost thoughts. Only those possessed of truly incredible cheekbones should ever be permitted to use the word *energy* in a sentence unless they are referring to heating oil.

17. The Trick is not an equal but he is often an equalizer.

18. Occasionally a Trick will succeed so spectacularly that he will make the transition to person. When this occurs he will assume a truly amazing imperiousness of manner. People love to feel superior to their past.

19. Tricks almost always have pets. This is understandable, as everyone needs someone they can talk to on their own level.

20. Taking an emergency telephone call from a Dr. Juan or a Dr. Heather is certain to result in overinvolvement.

21. There is a distinct Trick taste in literature. Among favorite Trick books are those dealing with the quest for God, such as the works of Carlos Castaneda and Hermann Hesse; those depicting a glamorous and torturous homosexuality, as in the case of *Nightwood* by Djuna Barnes; and those assuring Tricks that everything is fine and dandy, especially them. This sort of reading is generally harmless providing they have mastered the technique of reading quietly to themselves. For even the most hopelessly smitten will bridle at being awakened by Anais Nin.

22. When it comes to the visual arts a marked Trick preference is also evident. Work that falls into this category is easy to recognize, as the Trick is unfailingly attracted to that which looks as if he could (or did) make it himself.

23. Art movies on television are ideal for luring the reluctant Trick to one's apartment. There are very few people who dabble in this field who have not seen the first twenty minutes of *Loves of a Blonde* more times than they care to count.

24. The Trick is, without fail, drawn to the interesting job. Interesting jobs, in this sense, include not only work in museum gift shops but also minor positions on the production crews of documentary films concerning birth defects.

25. The Trick, more often than not, will display an unconquerable bent for creativity. The East Coast Trick leans heavily toward the composition of free-verse poetry, while his West Coast counterpart goes in for songwriting. Tricks of all regions own expensive cameras with which they take swaggeringly grainy photographs of nearby planets and sensitive young drug addicts. This is not difficult to understand, as they are relentless admirers of that which they call art and you call hobbies.

"Can't you see Dan that you are Horace's plaything—When he talks about your 'genius'—pulling your leg—that's to get your 'genius'!—*People always pull other people's legs when they want to get hold of their genius!*"

—*The Apes of God*,
WYNDHAM LEWIS

26. One man's Trick is another man's design assistant.

27. A New York hostess with a penchant for young boys gave a dinner at which a kind and fatherly magazine editor found himself seated across from her Trick. Seeking to put the boy at ease, the editor asked him politely what he did. "I'm an alchemist," the boy replied. Overhearing the exchange, another guest whispered, "Alchemist? They *used* to be bank clerks."

28. There is occasionally some question as to which member of a given duo *is* the Trick. This sort of confusion results when one (the elder) has money and the other (the younger) has talent. In such cases, and with all due respect to rising young luminaries, unless the money is exceedingly new and the talent exceedingly large, the money, as is its wont, wins. Or as was once said to a somewhat braggardly young artist while window-shopping at Porthaults, "If she has *those* sheets, you're the Trick."

29. Tricks like you for what they aren't. You like Tricks for what you haven't.

30. If one half of the couple is a waiter or waitress, he or she is always the Trick. Particularly, or in the case of New York City inevitably, if he or she has artistic ambitions. Such individuals may indeed traffic with those that they in turn refer to as Tricks, but that is a level of society far too submerged to be of any interest.

31. At public gatherings Tricks have been observed speaking to one another. What they actually say can only be a matter of conjecture but it is safe to assume that no money is changing hands.

32. The female Trick of great beauty can be readily identified by her habit of putting a cigarette in her mouth with an attitude of absolute assurance that someone else will light it.

33. It might appear to the casual observer that wives are Tricks. This betrays a sorry lack of perception, since no word as innately light-hearted as Trick could ever be used to describe someone with whom you share a joint checking account.

34. It is not good form to take a Trick out unless one is so firmly established as to be able to afford being associated with someone who might at any given moment write a poem in public.

35. Tricks are often plenteous gift givers. Upon receiving such offerings, one does well to forget old adages, for while it may certainly be true that good things come in small packages it must not be forgotten that this is also the case with ceramic jewelry.

36. Letters from female Tricks are immediately recognizable, as these girls are greatly inclined to cross their sevens and dot their *i*'s with

little circles. In all probability this is caused by their associating the presence of a writing implement in their hand with the playing of tic-tac-toe.

> "There is a Talmudic saying," smiled Dr. Frumpfausen . . . "as follows. In choosing a friend, ascend a step. In choosing a wife, descend a step. When Froggie-would-a-wooing-go, when Froggie is you, my dear boy, he must step *down*, as many steps as there are beneath him—even unto the last! . . . "

—*The Apes of God*,
WYNDHAM LEWIS

37. Tricks are distinctly susceptible to the allure of faraway places. If you reside in the Village they want to breakfast at the Plaza. If you live in Murray Hill it's Chinatown they long for. But no matter where you make your home, they all share a consuming desire to ride, in the middle of the night, the Staten Island Ferry. They will, without exception, consider your rejection of such a proposal cold and unfeeling, little realizing that you are simply protecting them from what you know would be overwhelming temptation were you ever to find yourself standing behind them on a moving boat.

Ian Frazier

*

DATING YOUR MOM

In today's fast-moving, transient, rootless society, where people meet and make love and part without ever really touching, the relationship every guy already has with his own mother is too valuable to ignore. Here is a grown, experienced, loving woman—one you do not have to go to a party or a singles bar to meet, one you do not have to go to great lengths to get to know. There are hundreds of times when you and your mother are thrown together naturally, without the tension that usually accompanies courtship—just the two of you, alone. All you need is a little presence of mind to take advantage of these situations. Say your mom is driving you downtown in the car to buy you a new pair of slacks. First, find a nice station on the car radio, one that she likes. Get into the pleasant lull of freeway driving—tires humming along the pavement, air-conditioner on max. Then turn to look at her across the front seat and say something like, "You know, you've really kept your shape, Mom, and don't think I haven't noticed." Or suppose she comes into your room to bring you some clean socks. Take her by the wrist, pull her close, and say, "Mom, you're the most fascinating woman I've ever met." Probably she'll tell you to cut out the foolishness, but I can guarantee you one thing: she will never tell your dad. Possibly she would find it hard to say, "Dear, Piper just made a pass at me," or possibly she is secretly flattered, but, whatever the reason, she will keep it to herself until the day comes when she is no longer ashamed to tell the world of your love.

Dating your mother seriously might seem difficult at first, but once you try it I'll bet you'll be surprised at how easy it is. Facing up to your intention is the main thing: you have to want it bad enough. One problem is that lots of people get hung up on feelings of guilt about their dad.

They think, Oh, here's this kindly old guy who taught me how to hunt and whittle and dynamite fish—I can't let him go on into his twilight years alone. Well, there are two reasons you can dismiss those thoughts from your mind. First, *every* woman, I don't care who she is, prefers her son to her husband. That is a simple fact; ask any woman who has a son, and she'll admit it. And why shouldn't she prefer someone who is so much like herself, who represents nine months of special concern and love and intense physical closeness—someone whom she actually created? As more women begin to express the need to have something all their own in the world, more women are going to start being honest about this preference. When you and your mom begin going together, you will simply become part of a natural and inevitable historical trend.

Second, you must remember this about your dad: you have your mother, he has his! Let him go put the moves on his own mother and stop messing with yours. If his mother is dead or too old to be much fun anymore, that's not your fault, is it? It's not your fault that he didn't realize his mom for the woman she was, before it was too late. Probably he's going to try a lot of emotional blackmail on you just because you had a good idea and he never did. Don't buy it. Comfort yourself with the thought that your dad belongs to the last generation of guys who will let their moms slip away from them like that.

Once your dad is out of the picture—once he has taken up fly-tying, joined the Single Again Club, moved to Russia, whatever—and your mom has been wooed and won, if you're anything like me you're going to start having so much fun that the good times you had with your mother when you were little will seem tame by comparison. For a while, Mom and I went along living a contented, quiet life, just happy to be with each other. But after several months we started getting into some different things, like the big motorized stroller. The thrill I felt the first time Mom steered me down the street! On the tray, in addition to my Big Jim doll and the wire with the colored wooden beads, I have my desk blotter, my typewriter, an in-out basket, and my name plate. I get a lot of work done, plus I get a great chance to people-watch. Then there's my big, adult-sized highchair, where I sit in the evening as Mom and I watch the news and discuss current events, while I paddle in my food and throw my dishes on the floor. When Mom reaches to wipe off my chin and I take her hand, and we fall to the floor in a heap—me, Mom, highchair, and all—well, those are the best times, those are the very best times.

It is true that occasionally I find myself longing for even more—for things I know I cannot have, like the feel of a firm, strong, gentle hand at the small of my back lifting me out of bed into the air, or someone who could walk me around and burp me after I've watched all the bowl games and had about nine beers. Ideally, I would like a mom about nineteen or twenty feet tall, and although I considered for a while asking my mom to start working out with weights and drinking Nutrament, I finally figured, Why put her through it? After all, she is not only my woman, she is my best friend. I have to take her as she is, and the way she is is plenty good enough for me.

Permissions Acknowledgments

Vonnegut, Jr. Originally published in *Collier's*. Reprinted by permission of DELACORTE PRESS/SEYMOUR LAWRENCE and Donald C. Farber, Attorney for Mr. Vonnegut.

Doubleday & Company, Inc.: "Toujours Tristesse" from HOW I GOT TO BE PERFECT by Jean Kerr. Copyright © 1954, 1955, 1956, 1957, 1958, 1959, 1960, 1976, 1977 by Jean Kerr. Copyright © 1966, 1967, 1968, 1969, 1970, 1978 by Collin Productions, Inc. Reprinted by permission of Doubleday & Company, Inc.

E. P. Dutton, Inc. and Sidgwick & Jackson, Ltd.: From THE GOOD WORD: *And Other Words* by Wilfrid Sheed. Copyright © 1968, 1971, 1972, 1973, 1974, 1975, 1976, 1977, 1978 by Wilfrid Sheed. From METROPOLITAN LIFE by Fran Lebowitz. Copyright © 1974, 1975, 1976, 1977, 1978 by Fran Lebowitz. Reprinted by permission of the publishers, E. P. Dutton, Inc. and Sidgwick & Jackson, Ltd., London.

Farrar, Straus & Giroux, Inc.: "The Mid-Atlantic Man" from THE PUMP HOUSE GANG by Tom Wolfe. Copyright © 1966 by The World Journal Tribune. Copyright © 1968 by Tom Wolfe. Reprinted by permission of Farrar, Straus & Giroux, Inc. and International Creative Management.

Samuel French, Inc.: "IF MEN PLAYED CARDS AS WOMEN DO" by George S. Kaufman. Copyright, 1923, by George S. Kaufman. Copyright, 1950 (In Renewal), by George S. Kaufman. Copyright, 1926, by Samuel French. Copyright, 1954 (In Renewal), by George S. Kaufman. Reprinted by permission of Samuel French, Inc. CAUTION: Professionals and amateurs are hereby warned that "IF MEN PLAYED CARDS AS WOMEN DO," being fully protected under the copyright laws of the United States of America, the British Commonwealth countries, including Canada, and the other countries of the Copyright Union, is subject to a royalty. All rights, including professional, amateur, motion picture, recitation, public reading, radio, television and cablevision broadcasting, and the rights of translation into foreign languages, are strictly reserved. Amateurs may produce this play upon payment of a royalty of Ten Dollars ($10.00) for each performance, payable one week before the play is to be given, to Samuel French, Inc., at 25 West 45th Street, New York, N.Y. 10036, or at 7623 Sunset Blvd., Hollywood, Calif. 90046, or if in Canada, to Samuel French (Canada) Ltd., 80 Richmond Street East, Toronto M5C 1P1.

David R. Godine Publisher, Inc.: From THREE WOGS by Alexander Theroux. Copyright © 1972, 1975 by Alexander Theroux. Reprinted by permission of David R. Godine, Publisher, Boston.

Victor Gollancz, Ltd.: Extract from HONS AND REBELS by Jessica Mitford. Copyright © 1960 by Jessica Treuhaft. Reproduced by permission of Victor Gollancz, Ltd., London, and of the author and the author's agents Scott Meredith Literary Agency, Inc., 845 Third Avenue, New York, New York 10022.

Harcourt Brace Jovanovich, Inc.: From THE EDUCATION OF H*Y*M*A*N K*A*P*L*A*N by Leonard Q. Ross, copyright 1937 by Harcourt Brace Jovanovich, Inc.; renewed 1965 by Leo Rosten. Reprinted by permission of the publisher and Constable Publishers, London. From ONE FAT ENGLISHMAN by Kingsley Amis, copyright © 1963 by Kingsley Amis. Reprinted by permission of Harcourt Brace Jovanovich, Inc. and Victor Gollancz, Ltd., London. "Why I Live at the P.O." by Eudora Welty. Copyright 1941, 1969 by Eudora Welty. Reprinted from her volume A CURTAIN OF GREEN AND OTHER STORIES by permission of Harcourt Brace Jovanovich, Inc., and Russell & Volkening, Inc. as agents for the author.

A. M. Heath & Company Ltd. and Granada Publishing Ltd.: "Keats and Chapman" from THE BEST OF MYLES by Flann O'Brien. Reprinted by permission of the estate of the late Flann O'Brien, Penguin Books, and Granada Publishing Ltd.

Houghton Mifflin Company: Excerpt from CLINGING TO THE WRECKAGE by John Mortimer. Copyright © 1982 by Advanpress Limited. Reprinted by permission of Ticknor & Fields, a Houghton Mifflin Company, and Literistic, Ltd.

International Creative Management: "Game" from SIXTY STORIES by Donald Barthelme. Copyright © 1968, 1981 by Donald Barthelme. Reprinted by permission of International Creative Management.

Oliver Jensen: "The Gettysburg Address in Eisenhowerese" © Oliver Jensen. Reprinted by the author, former editor of *American Heritage*.

Alfred A. Knopf, Inc.: "Popular Workbench" from ZANY AFTERNOONS by Bruce McCall. Copyright © 1982 by Bruce McCall. "Recollections of Notable Cops" from THE AMERICAN SCENE by H. L. Mencken. Copyright 1941 by Alfred A. Knopf, Inc. "Trash No More" from CRACKERS by Roy Blount, Jr. Copyright © 1980 by Roy Blount, Jr. Reprinted by permission of Alfred A. Knopf, Inc. Excerpt from THE SERIAL by Cyra McFadden. Copyright © 1976, 1977 by Cyra McFadden. Reprinted by permission of Alfred A. Knopf, Inc., and London Management & Representation, Ltd. "The Chaste Clarissa" from THE STORIES OF JOHN CHEEVER. Copyright 1952 (and renewed 1980) by John Cheever. "A Few Words About Breasts" from CRAZY SALAD: SOME THINGS ABOUT WOMEN by Nora Ephron. Copyright © 1972 by Nora Ephron. Reprinted by permission of Alfred A. Knopf, Inc., and International Creative Management. Excerpt from KINFLICKS by Lisa Alther. Copyright © 1975 by Lisa Alther. Reprinted by permission of Alfred A. Knopf, Inc., and Chatto & Windus. Excerpt

Mao" by Veronica Geng. Reprinted by permission: © 1977 The New Yorker Magazine, Inc.

The New York Times Company: "Bomb Math" by Russell Baker. © 1980 by The New York Times Company. Reprinted by permission.

The Observer Ltd.: "Just Plain Folks" by Kenneth Tynan. Copyright © The Observer Ltd., London. Reprinted by permission.

A. D. Peters & Co., Ltd.: "The Intrusions of Captain Foulenough" from THE BEST OF BEACHCOMBER by J. B. Morton. Reprinted by permission of A. D. Peters. "Winner Takes All" from CHARLES RYDER'S SCHOOLDAYS AND OTHER STORIES by Evelyn Waugh. Copyright 1936, © renewed 1964 by Evelyn Waugh. First appeared in MR. LOVEDAY'S LITTLE OUTING. Reprinted by permission of Little, Brown and Company and A. D. Peters & Co., Ltd., London.

Price/Stern/Sloan Publishers, Inc.: Excerpt from HOW TO BE A JEWISH MOTHER by Dan Greenburg. Published by Price/Stern/Sloan Publishers, Inc. Copyright © 1964, 1965, 1972, 1975 by Dan Greenburg. Reprinted with permission.

G. P. Putnam's Sons: Excerpt "Saving Paper" from LAID BACK IN WASHINGTON by Art Buchwald. Copyright © 1978, 1979, 1980, 1981 by Art Buchwald. Copyright © 1981 by Los Angeles Syndicate for columns first published in 1981. Reprinted by permission of G. P. Putnam's Sons and Roslyn Targ Literary Agency, Inc.

Random House, Inc.: "The Kugelmass Episode" from SIDE EFFECTS by Woody Allen. Copyright © 1977 by Woody Allen. "A Day's Work" from MUSIC FOR CHAMELEONS by Truman Capote. Copyright © 1980 by Truman Capote. "Whacking Off" from PORTNOY'S COMPLAINT by Philip Roth. Copyright © 1967 by Philip Roth. Reprinted by permission of Random House, Inc.

Robson Books, Ltd.: "Long Ago and Far Away," copyright Alan Coren, reprinted by permission of Robson Books, Ltd. from GOLFING FOR CATS, 1975.

Charles Scribner's Sons: "The Busher's Honeymoon," in YOU KNOW ME, AL by Ring Lardner, is reprinted with the permission of Charles Scribner's Sons. Copyright 1916 Charles Scribner's Sons; copyright renewed 1944 by Ellis A. Lardner.

Simon & Schuster, Inc.: Excerpt from THE GROUCHO LETTERS by Groucho Marx. Copyright © 1967 by Groucho Marx. "Farewell, My Lovely Appetizer" from THE MOST OF S. J. PERELMAN. Copyright © 1930 and 1958 by S. J. Perelman. Reprinted by permission of SIMON & SCHUSTER, INC. Excerpt from GOOD AS GOLD by Joseph Heller.

A NOTE ON THE TYPE

The text of this book was filmset in Electra, a typeface designed by
W. A. Dwiggins (1880–1956). This face cannot be classified as either
modern or old style. It is not based on any historical model; nor does
it echo any particular period or style. It avoids the extreme contrasts
between thick and thin elements that mark most modern faces, and
attempts to give a feeling of fluidity, power, and speed.

Composed by Dix Type Inc.,
Syracuse, New York
Printed and bound by The Murray Printing Company,
Westford, Massachusetts
Text and binding design by Helen Barrow